U0890779

全国英语等级考试 第三级

PETS-3

融媒体高分教程

主编 黄雅丹 丁娓娓 纪 燕 张 钰

编辑委员会

主 任
莫纪平

副主任
季 兵 陆雨林

成 员
张东萍 刘彬霞 邵应清 常 玲

江苏大学出版社
JIANGSU UNIVERSITY PRESS
镇 江

图书在版编目(CIP)数据

PETS—3融媒体高分教程 ：英文 / 黄雅丹等主编. —
镇江 ：江苏大学出版社，2021.1（2021.3重印）
ISBN 978-7-5684-1494-4

Ⅰ. ①P… Ⅱ. ①黄… Ⅲ. ①全国公共英语等级考试
—教材 Ⅳ. ①H310.42

中国版本图书馆CIP数据核字(2021)第021903号

PETS-3 融媒体高分教程
PETS-3 Rongmeiti Gaofen Jiaocheng

主　　编/黄雅丹　丁娓娓　纪　燕　张　钰
责任编辑/柳　艳
出版发行/江苏大学出版社
地　　址/江苏省镇江市梦溪园巷30号(邮编：212003)
电　　话/0511-84446464(传真)
网　　址/http://press.ujs.edu.cn
排　　版/镇江市江东印刷有限责任公司
印　　刷/句容市排印厂
开　　本/787 mm×1 092 mm　1/16
印　　张/22.5
字　　数/680千字
版　　次/2021年1月第1版
印　　次/2021年3月第2次印刷
书　　号/ISBN 978-7-5684-1494-4
定　　价/58.00元

如有印装质量问题请与本社营销部联系(电话:0511-84440882)

前　言

本教程为参加全国英语等级考试第三级（PETS－3）的考生量身定制，旨在帮助广大考生尤其是在职考生在有限的时间内高效了解考试、掌握考试技能并最终顺利通过考试。

本教程以高等教育出版社出版的《全国英语等级考试考试大纲（2015 版）》为编写依据，以历年真题为素材，按模块详细剖析各题型考点，总结应试技巧，以典型示例对技巧加以运用。教程主要囊括了“大纲解析”“高分指南”“真题及解析”“实战演练”“必备词汇”等内容，布局科学合理，目标明确。既能让考生全面而又充分地了解考试及各题型的解题技巧，又能够通过实战演练检验考生的学习效果，帮助考生切实把握考试要点并熟练掌握考试技巧。需要说明的是，“必备词汇”部分编者仅保留 PETS－3 等级要求的释义，在减轻考生负担的同时，可帮助考生更有针对性地积累词汇。此外，本教程每节都配有相关课程的视频讲座，考生扫描二维码即可观看。

本教程由一线 PETS－3 教师执笔编写而成，由于水平有限，在编写的过程中难免有疏漏之处，诚望广大读者不吝赐教。

愿所有考生顺利通过考试，提升英语综合运用能力！

编　者

目　录

一、PETS-3 的形式、内容与结构

概　述

PETS－3 的形式、
内容与结构

1. 关于考试的组成

PETS 第三级考试由笔试和口试两项独立考试组成。

2. 关于考试指导语和题目用语

PETS 第三级考试中，笔试、口试的指导语均为英文。口试所提供的引导性材料中可能会涉及少量的中文。

3. 关于笔试答题卡和口试登分卡的使用

PETS 第三级笔试使用一张答题卡，考生在卡上填涂和书写。

PETS 第三级口试使用一张口试成绩登分卡。口试开始前考生在卡上填好自己的考号等有关信息，口试结束后口试教师在卡上填上考生的口试成绩。

4. 关于考试的时间、题量和原始赋分

PETS 第三级笔试包括听力、阅读和写作三部分，各部分及总体的答题时间、题量和原始赋分（除特殊情况外，每题 1 分），如表 1 所示：

表 1　考试时间、题量和原始赋分

部分	时间（分钟）	题量	原始赋分	备注
听力	25	25	25	
阅读	50	30	25	D 节每题 0.5 分。
写作	45	2	30	A 节满分为 10 分。 B 节满分为 20 分。
笔试总计	120	55＋2	80	

PETS 第三级口试包括三节，考试时间共计 10 分钟。

5. 关于笔试分数权重

为处理好考试中题目数量、赋分与各种技能的考查关系，PETS 第三级笔试采用了分数加权的办法，即对各部分题目的原始赋分分别给予不同的权重，使之能够平衡各种技能的考查关系。

PETS 第三级笔试中各部分所占分数权重如表 2 所示：

表 2　笔试各部分权重

部分	权重（%）
听力	30
阅读	40
写作	30
合计	100

各部分赋分加权的总和为 100 分。考生得到的考试成绩是其各部分原始得分经过加权处理后的分数总和。

例如，某考生听力部分原始得分为 20 分，经加权处理后的分数应为 24 分（$20 \div 25 \times 30 = 24$ 分）；其阅读部分原始得分为 20 分，经加权处理后的分数应为 32 分（$20 \div 25 \times 40 = 32$ 分）；其写作部分原始得分为 16 分，经加权处理后的分数应为 16 分（$16 \div 30 \times 30 = 16$ 分）。该考生未经过加权的原始总分为 56 分，各部分经加权后的总分应为 72 分。

6. 关于合格成绩

PETS 第三级笔试成绩是笔试各部分原始得分加权后的总和，满分 100 分，60 分以上（含 60 分）为合格。

PETS 第三级口试成绩是两名口试教师所给分数加权后的总和，满分 5 分，3 分以上（含 3 分）为合格。

笔试内容和结构

PETS 第三级笔试的全部试题在一份试卷中，包括听力、阅读和写作三个部分。考试时间为 120 分钟。

第一部分　听力

该部分由 A、B 两节组成，考查考生理解英语口语的能力。

A 节（10 题）：考查考生理解简短对话的具体信息、主旨要义、进行推理和引申等能力。要求考生根据所听到的 10 段简短对话（总长约 400 词），从每题所给的 4 个选择项中选出最佳选项。每段录音材料只播放一遍。

B 节（15 题）：考查考生理解对话和独白的具体信息、主旨要义、进行推理和引申等能力。要求考生根据所听到的 4 段对话或独白（每段平均约 200 词，总长约 800 词），从每题所给的 4 个选择项中选出最佳选项。每段录音材料只播放一遍。

问题不在录音中播放，仅在试卷上印出。

每段录音材料播放前、后都有适当停顿，用作读题和答题时间。

听力考试进行时，考生将答案标在试卷上；听力部分结束前，考生有 3 分钟的时间将答案转涂到答题卡上。

该部分所需时间约为 25 分钟（含转涂时间）。

第二部分　阅读

该部分由 A、B、C、D 四节组成，考查考生理解书面英语的能力。

A 节（10 题）：考查考生理解文章的具体信息、主旨要义、进行推理和引申等能力。要求考生根据所提供的 2 篇文章的内容（每篇平均约 350 词），从每题所给的 4 个选择项中选出最佳选项。

B 节（5 题）：考查考生理解段落主旨要义的能力。要求考生从 7 个选择项中排除 2 个干扰项，将正确的概括选项与 5 段文字（总长约 350 词）逐一搭配成对。

C 节（5 题）：考查考生理解文章结构及单句之间、段落之间的关系的能力。在一篇约 350 词的文章中留出 5 处空白，要求考生从文后所给的 7 句话中选出分别能放进文章中空白处的 5 句，使补足后的文章意思通顺、前后连贯。

D 节（10 题）：考查考生对话篇中词汇意义与用法的掌握情况以及对语篇连贯的理解。在一篇 200 ~ 250 词的文章中留出 10 处空白，要求考生从文后所给的 15 个单词中选出分别能放进文章中空白处的 10 个，使补足后的文章意思通顺、前后连贯。

该部分所需时间约为 50 分钟。

第三部分　写作

该部分由 A、B 两节组成，考查考生的书面表达能力。

A 节：考生根据所给情景和任务要求写出约 100 词（标点符号不计算在内）的通知、申请或信函等。

B 节：考生阅读一篇英语文章（200 ~ 250 词），写出一篇约 120 词（标点符号不计算在内）的短文，要求概括所给文章大意，并予以适当评论。

该部分所需时间约为 45 分钟。

PETS 第三级笔试结构表如表 3 所示：

表 3　PETS 第三级笔试结构表

部分	节	考试信息	考察要点	题型	题量	时间
第一部分 听力	A	10 段短对话（共约 400 词）放一遍	理解主旨要义；获取事实性的具体信息；进行有关的判断、推理和引申；理解说话者的意图；理解说话者的态度和语气	单项选择（四选一）	10	25
	B	4 段长对话或独白（共约 800 词）放一遍			15	
第二部分 阅读	A	2 篇文章（每篇约 350 词）	理解主旨要义；理解文中具体信息；进行有关的判断、推理和引申；理解作者的写作意图；理解作者的态度和语气；根据上下文推测生词词义；理解文章的结构及单句之间、段落之间的关系；区分文章的要点和细节信息	单项选择（四选一）	10	50
	B	5 段文字（共约 350 词）	理解主旨要义	选择搭配（七选五）	5	
	C	1 篇文章（约 350 词）	理解文章结构及单句之间、段落之间的关系	补全文章（七选五）	5	

续表

部分	节	考试信息	考察要点	题型	题量	时间
第二部分 阅读	D	1 篇文章 (200~250 词)	词汇意义与用法；语篇连贯	选词填空 (十五选十)	10	50
第三部分 写作	A	情景和任务要求	写通知、申请、信函等	应用文写作 (约 100 词)	1	45
	B	1 篇文章 (200~250 词)	概括文章大意并评论	综合写作 (约 120 词)	1	

口试内容和结构

口试分为三节，考查考生用英语进行口头交际的能力，口试结构表如表 4 所示。考试时间约 10 分钟。

口试采取两名口试教师和两名考生的形式。一名口试教师不参与交谈，专事评分；另一名口试教师主持口试，随时与考生交谈并评分。专事评分的教师所给分数的权重占考生口试成绩的三分之二，主持口试的教师所给分数的权重占考生口试成绩的三分之一。

A 节：考查考生回答询问、提供信息的能力。

要求考生回答口试教师提出的关于学生日常生活、工作、学习等方面的问题。

该节约需 2 分钟时间。

B 节：考查考生与他人交流、表达观点的能力。

要求考生就所给图片和话题进行交流和讨论。

该节约需 3 分钟时间。

C 节：考查考生进行连续表达的能力。

要求考生描述所给图片内容，并阐述自己的观点。

该节约需 5 分钟时间。

表 4　PETS 第三级口试结构表

节	时间 (分钟)	形式	为考生提供的考试信息	考生需完成的任务	分数
A	2	考生回答问题	口试教师提出的问题	提供个人信息；谈论过去及现在的经历；谈论将来的打算	5
B	3	考生相互交流	图片和话题	询问和提供具体信息；交流看法	
C	5	考生连续表达	图片	描述一般性现象；阐述个人观点	

考试结构图

PETS 第三级考试结构如图 1 所示：

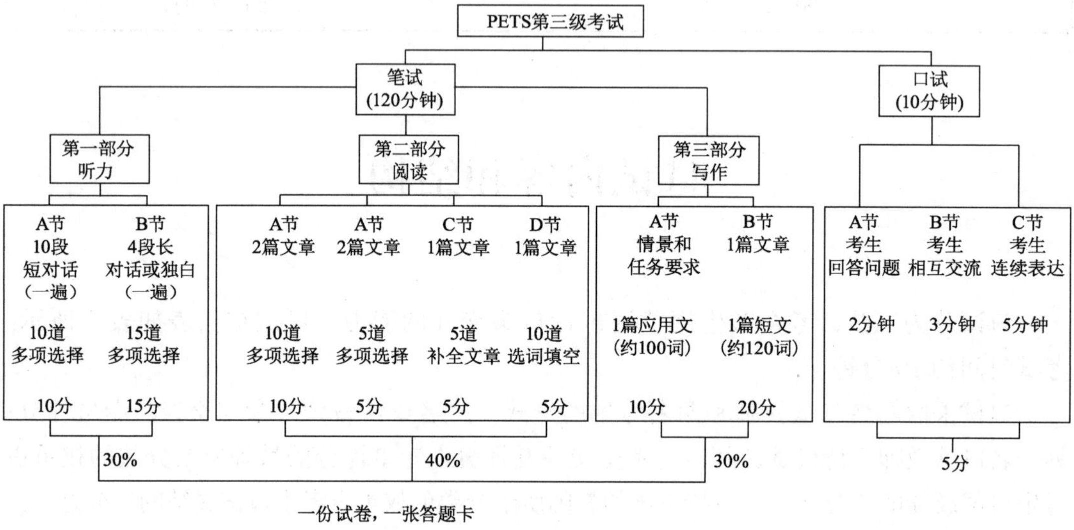

图 1　PETS 第三级考试结构图

二、PETS-3 高分指南

听力 A 节　短对话

短对话

听力 A 节考查考生理解简短对话的具体信息、主旨要义、进行推理和引申等能力。共 10 题，总长约 400 词，每段录音材料只播放一遍，每题有约 15 秒的答题时间。要求考生根据所听到的 10 段简短对话，从每题所给的 4 个选项中选出最佳选项。

一、命题剖析

PETS 第三级考试听力 A 节短对话部分主要考查以下内容：职业身份题、人物关系题、请求建议题、行动计划题、场所地点题、时间数字题、因果关系题、观点态度题和分析推理题。

二、应试技巧

（一）职业身份题和人物关系题

职业身份题和人物关系题常见的提问方式有："Who is the man/woman?" "What's the man's/ woman's occupation?" "What's the probable relationship between the speakers?" "Who do you think the man is talking to?" 等。

常被考察的人物之间的关系有：driver-policeman，teacher-student，salesperson-customer，husband-wife，receptionist-tourist，lawyer-client，doctor-patient，waiter/waitress-customer，secretary-boss，shop assistant-customer，colleague-officer，friend-enemy 等。

考生有时需要根据说话者的不同语气和口吻来推测其身份或关系。例如，留意说话者之间是否使用敬语，从而推测其关系是否是上司和下属的关系。

例题： 2. Who is Mr. Johnson according to the speakers?（2018 年 3 月真题）

[A] Their former colleague.　　[B] Their former neighbor.

[C] Their former teacher.　　[D] Their former client.

【听力原文】

W：Guess who I met at the grocery store this morning?

M：Well，I can't imagine.

W：Do you remember Mr. Johnson? He used to live in the building next to ours.

M：Oh，yes，now I remember. He had dark hair and wore glasses.

【解析】 答案为 B。本题为人物关系题。问题：根据两位说话者，谁是 Mr.

Johnson？根据画线部分可以得知 Mr. Johnson 曾经住在他们的隔壁楼里，所以 Mr. Johnson 是他们以前的邻居，本题正确答案为 B 选项。

（二）请求建议题和行动计划题

请求建议题和行动计划题一般是说话者正在做某事、建议做某事、决定做某事或让某人做某事等等。这些题型常见的提向方式有："What does the woman suggest the man do?" "What is the man going to do?" "What does the woman ask the man to do?" 及 "What is the woman doing at the moment?" 等。

例题 1：1. What is the woman doing at the moment?（2016 年 3 月真题）

[A] Having a break. [B] Having a coffee.

[C] Writing a report. [D] Visiting the man.

【听力原文】

M：Got a time have a coffee with me now?

W：You call me at a bad time. <u>I'm writing a report and is due in an hour.</u>

M：You really like leaving things to the last minute.

W：I know. It's a terrible habit.

【解析】答案为 C。本题为行动题。问题：女士目前正在干什么？男士邀请女士喝咖啡，女士表示这不是一个好时机。根据画线部分可以得知女士正在写报告，报告一小时后就要到期了，故该题正确答案为 C 选项。

例题 2：2. What does the woman ask the man to do?（2016 年 3 月真题）

[A] Repair her windows. [B] Take care of her house.

[C] Take a rest for a few days. [D] Go to the seaside with her.

【听力原文】

W：Oh, we are going away to the seaside for a few days.

<u>Can you keep an eye on my home while I'm away?</u>

M：Certainly, Jackie. Make sure you lock the doors and shut all the windows.

W：Thanks. It's very kind of you.

【解析】答案为 B。本题为建议题。问题：女士让男士干什么？女士要去海边几天，画线部分的意思为："当我不在的时候，你能帮我照看我的家吗？"选项 B 中的短语 take care of 是原文中 keep an eye on 的同义转述，故正确答案为 B 选项。

（三）场所地点题

场所地点题一般有以下三种情况：一是要求考生根据对话中出现的显示特定场所的词，猜测说话人在什么地方交谈；二是根据对话中涉及的几个地点提问；三是某一说话者问路或准备去哪儿。

该类题型常见的提问方式有："Where does the conversation most probably take place?" "Where are the speakers?" 等。

例题： 8. Where is the man's house located?（2016 年 3 月真题）

[A] Near a park.

[B] By a restaurant.

[C] Close to a highway.

[D] In a Chinese neighborhood.

【听力原文】

M：I've just moved to my new house.

W：Really? How about the neighborhood?

M：It's nice. And there is a forest park nearby.

W：Are there any restaurants around? I mean if you want to eat out.

M：A great Chinese restaurant is just five minutes' drive away.

【解析】 答案为 A。本题为场所地点题。问题：男士的房子在哪里？男士刚搬了新家，根据画线部分可以得知在房子的附近有一个森林公园，故正确答案为 A 选项。对话的最后提及该房子距离一家很棒的中式餐馆只有 5 分钟车程，但并不意味这房子位于华人社区，所以选项 D 为干扰项，且具有一定的迷惑性。

考生应掌握一些与特定场所或地点相关的高频词汇，以便能够迅速判断相关场所或地点，正确回答这类问题。

词汇拓展

【学校场景】

optional course　选修课

required course　必修课

final exam　期终考试

mid-term/middle exam　期中考试

makeup　补考

oral test　口试

quiz　课堂测验

public school　公立学校

private school　私立学校

semester/term　学期

attend/have a lecture　上课

cut/skip a class　逃课

miss a class　错过了课

major in　主修

scholarship　奖学金

president　校长

dean　院长

professor　教授

lecturer　讲师

coordinator　班主任

doctor　博士

master　硕士

bachelor　学士

freshman　大一新生

sophomore　大二学生

junior　大三学生

senior　大四学生

teaching assistant　助教

research assistant　助研

【图书馆场景】

lend/borrow　借书

reference book　参考书

renew　续借

overdue　过期

return 还书

fine 罚金

【机场场景】

book 订票

timetable 时间表

destination 目的地

one-way ticket 单程票

round-trip ticket 来回票

non-stop/direct flight 直航

first-class cabin 头等舱

business cabin 商务舱

economy cabin 经济舱

confirm the flight 确认航班

check in 登记

boarding card 登机牌

security check 安检

see off 送行

keep in touch 保持联系

safe landing 安全着陆

board 登机

take off 起飞

departure 离港

land 着陆

arrival 进港

pick up 接机

transfer/lay over/stop over 转机

【医院场景】

see a doctor 去医院看医生

send for a doctor 让医生出诊

health center/clinic 门诊

physician 内科医生

surgeon 外科医生

dentist 牙医

make an appointment 预约

emergency 急诊

check up/exam 检查

cold 感冒

flu 流感

sore throat 嗓子痛

headache 头痛

fever 发烧

toothache 牙疼

stomachache 胃疼

injection 注射

operation 手术

prescribe 开药方

pill/tablet 药片

liquid 药水

medical result 诊断结果

【宾馆场景】

make a reservation 预订房间

confirm a reservation 确认预订

cancel a reservation 取消预订

fully booked/full up 客满

porter 行李员

tip 小费

reception 前台

check in 登记入住

check out 退房

single room 单人房

double room/twin room 双人房

suite 套房

room service 客房服务

lobby 大堂

bathroom/toilet/closet restroom 厕所

【饭店场景】

eat out 出去吃

take away 外带

fast food 快餐

book a table 订位子

waiter/waitress 服务员

menu 菜单

order 点菜

appetizer 开胃菜

main course 主食

dessert 餐后甜点

bill 账单

service charge 服务费

change 找零

tip 小费

（四）时间数字题

时间数字题都涉及数字，做题时必须快速反应，可以在选项旁白的空白处做笔记。该类题型提问方式一般为："When... ?""What time... ?""How old... ?""How much... ?"及"How many... ?"等。所涉及的数字主要包括：时间、日期、年代、年龄、价格、数量、速度、距离、房号及电话号码等。就数字种类来说，主要有基数词、序数词、百分数和分数等。

考生需要注意辨清近音数字，如后缀-ty 和-teen 的区别，同时不要轻易选择与原文中时间读音完全相同或者部分相同的选项，因为这类选项是干扰选项的可能性比较大。此外，考生还需注意时间先后顺序，抓住表示时间先后顺序的介词 before，after，until 等。

例题：2. When will the bank open on Sundays?（2015 年 9 月真题）

[A] From 8：30 a. m. to 8：30p. m.

[B] From 9：30 a. m. to 6：30 p. m.

[C] From 8：30 a. m. to 6：30p. m.

[D] From 9：30 a. m. to 3：30 p. m.

【听力原文】

M：When will the bank open?

W：It opens from 8：30 a. m. to 6：30 p. m. from Monday to Friday，and it opens from 9：30a. m. to 3：30 p. m. on Saturday and Sunday.

【解析】答案为 D。本题为时间数字题。问题：银行在周日什么时间营业？根据画线部分可以得知银行在周六和周日的营业时间为 9：30 a. m. –3：30 p. m.，故正确答案为 D 选项。女士同事也说了从周一到周五的营业时间为 8：30 a. m. to 6：30 p. m.，具有一定的迷惑性，故 C 选项为干扰选项。

（五）因果关系题

对于因果关系题，考生只要理清事情的因果关系就能选出正确答案，题目通常针对原因来提问。

该题型常见提问形式有："Why does the woman/man... ?""What's the reason for... ?"等。考生需要熟悉表示因果关系的单词或短语，如：because，since，for，so，as，cause，because of，now that，due to，thanks to，owing to，as a result of，that's why...， give rise to, be responsible for, result in, result from, so that... , such... that... , as a consequence 等。

例题 1：6. Why is the woman angry with her son?（2016 年 3 月真题）

[A] He ignored traffic signals. [B] He failed to repair her car.

[C] He didn't attend his class. [D] He didn't take her advice.

【听力原文】

M：You look furious, Mary. How come?

W：My son had an accident. He wasn't hurt, but my car was damaged.

M：But it wasn't too bad.

W：Sure. But he is still taking driving lessons. He just ignored my warning.

M：He should have known better.

【解析】答案为 D。本题为因果关系题。问题：为什么女士对她的儿子生气？男士说女士看起来很生气，为什么？How come 是 why 的近义表达。女士回答说她的儿子出了事故，没有受伤，但是车被毁了。画线部分的意思是："事情不算太糟，但是他还在驾校学习，他无视我的警告。"选项 D 说他没有听取她的意见，是画线部分的同义转述，故正确答案为选项 D。同时，考生一定要注意转折词 but 后面常常是考点。

例题 2：7. Why does the man feel sorry?（2016 年 3 月真题）

[A] He forgot his Dad's birthday.

[B] He didn't buy a birthday present.

[C] He didn't put the cake in the fridge.

[D] He arrived late for his dad's birthday.

【听力原文】

W：Do you know this is the first time we have been all together for dad's birthday since his retirement?

M：Yes, I do. I am sorry about that. I was working.

W：All right. We saved you a piece of cake in the fridge.

【解析】答案为 D。本题为因果关系题。问题：男士为什么感到抱歉？女士说："你知道这是我们第一次在爸爸退休后聚到一起为他过生日吗？"女士的语气中有责怪男士的意思。从画线部分可以得知，男士当时正在工作，他的家人给他留了一块蛋糕。我们可以推测男士因为工作迟到了，没能按时赶到父亲的生日聚会，故正确答案为 D 选项。

（六）观点态度题

观点态度题主要涉及对话双方对所交谈的话题表示出的态度。该类题型常见提问形式有："What does the woman/man think of... ?""How does the man feel about... ?"等。

例题：9. What does the woman say about the data in the article?（2016 年 3 月真题）

[A] It is original. [B] It is reliable.

[C] It is questionable. [D] It is authoritative.

【听力原文】

M: Do you believe it, Mary? Accessible use of mobile-phones over many years could increase the risk of cancer.

W: Well, I read that article too. But I doubt it. There are huge question marks over the reliability of the data.

【解析】答案为 C。本题为观点态度题。问题：关于文章里的数据，女士是怎么说的？男士引出话题说常年使用手机可能会增加癌症的风险。女士表示她也看了那篇文章，转折词 but 后面的内容是考点。画线部分的意思是："但是我持质疑的态度。数据的可靠性有大大的问号。"选项 C 中的 questionable 是"怀疑的"，故正确答案为 C。

本题对词汇量有一定的要求。对话中的 accessible 是"可使用的；可到达的；可接近的；可进入的；可见到的"。干扰项中 original 是"原创的"，reliable 是"可靠的"，authoritative 是"权威的"。

考生听录音时首先要注意对话双方的态度是否相同，因为这类问题往往问的是其中一人的态度或看法，所以要分清各自的态度。注意有时说话人的态度比较含蓄，甚至是通过语气、语调的变化来体现的。考生在听的过程中要注意辨别语调，把握说话者的态度，比如降调一般表示肯定的语气，而升调则通常表示疑问或否定。另外，陈述句用升调同样可以用来表示怀疑、否定或不解。考生也要注意虚拟语气的使用，因为虚拟语气所承载的内容往往与事实相反。因此听的时候须用心思考，然后迅速做出判断。

词汇拓展

表态度观点的高频词汇：

表示赞成：approve, agree, share, prefer, wise, reasonable, favorable, absolutely

表示反对：disapprove, disagree, unwise, ridiculous, foolish, childish

表示喜欢：love, enjoy, wonderful, fascinating, be fond of, be keen on

表示厌烦：dislike, bored/ boring, be tired of

表示关心：concerned, careful, care about

表示怨恨或生气：hate, angry, anger

表示害怕或担心：fearful, frightened, worried, nervous

表示批评或讽刺：critical, criticize, ironic, find fault with

表示失望或灰心：disappointed, discouraged

表示后悔或遗憾：regret, regretful, pity, shame

表示漠然或热情：indifferent, careless, enthusiastic

表示积极或消极：active, positive, negative

表示自信或自负：confident, arrogant, proud

表示乐观或悲观：optimistic，pessimistic

表示糟糕的语气：

It's too bad/tough.

Tough luck!

What a pity!

Oh! No!

表示惊讶的语气：

Boy!

My God/Goodness!

Oh，boy!

WOW!

表示赞美的语气：

Wonderful!

My favourite!

Terrific!

Cool! / Super cool!

表示否定的语气：

Nope!

Are you serious?

But...

No kidding/joking.

Are you kidding?

Who told you that?

（七）分析推理题

分析推理题主要考查考生在听懂听力原文的基础上进行引申推理的能力，要求考生能听懂说话人的言外之意、弦外之音，从而做出合理的判断。其在历年听力理解中占据比重较大，是最具难度的一类短对话题型。

由于这种题型往往会隐藏说话人的观点和看法，多为一个说话人提出自己的观点，另一人不作正面回答，所以答案无法从材料中直接获得，因此也是考生比较容易失分的一个题型。该题型常见提问形式有："What do we learn from the conversation?" "What does the woman/man mean/imply?"

例题 1：3. What do we learn about the woman from the dialogue?（2016 年 3 月真题）

[A] She bought a suitable skirt.

[B] She wanted to purchase a skirt.

[C] She returned a skirt to the shop.

[D] She complained about the service.

【听力原文】

W：<u>These skirts are just what I have been looking for.</u> Have you got the medium sizes of them?

M：I'm afraid not, Madam. They appeared to be temporarily out of stock.

W：Oh, how disappointing. When will you have some mediums in?

M：We should be getting in some until next Monday.

【解析】答案为 B。本题为分析推理题。问题：从这个对话中我们可以得知什么？根据画线部分可以得知这些裙子正是女士一直寻找的，下文两人在讨论裙子的尺寸及有没有货，男士最后说下周一就会有中号，由此可以推测女士想买一条裙子，而目前还没有买到，故正确答案为 B 选项。Out of stock 的意思是"缺货"。衣服尺码 Sizes：S = small 小码；M = medium 中码；L = large 大码；XL = extra large 特大码。

例题 2：4. What does the man say to the woman?（2016 年 3 月真题）

[A] He envies her a lot. [B] He enjoys cooking.

[C] He usually eats out. [D] He runs a restaurant.

【听力原文】

W：How often do you eat out，James?

M：Well，very often，almost five times a week.

W：Wow. I really envy you.

M：Don't envy me. It's for business. In fact，I'm tired of restaurant food.

Sometimes I really miss our home-cooked meal.

【解析】答案为 C。本题为分析推理题。问题：男士对女士说了什么？问题对男士部分提问，所以考生要特别注意男士说的话。从画线部分可以得知，男士因为工作经常在外面吃饭，几乎是一周五次，实际上已经厌烦了餐馆的饭菜，选项 C 中的 usually 符合在外吃饭的频率，故正确答案为 C 选项。

例题 3：5. What are the speakers talking about?（2016 年 3 月真题）

[A] Gardening. [B] Air quality.

[C] Hot weather. [D] Lack of rain.

【听力原文】

W：Well，the dry conditions are really severe.

M：But it's not surprising actually. Because we have had much rain this year.

W：Well，if it could rain even a drop，my flowers in the garden will come back in a heartbeat.

【解析】答案为 D。本题为分析推理题。问题：两位说话者在谈论什么？女士引出话题，说干旱的情况真的非常严重。男士表示这不令人感到意外，因为今年已经有了许多雨水。画线部分为虚拟语气，女士的意思是：如果下一滴雨，我花园里的花就会活过来，我们推测真实的情况是一滴雨都没有下，故正确答案 D 选项。

例题 4：10. What does the man tell the woman?（2016 年 3 月真题）

[A] The best time for job interviews. [B] The strategies for job interviews.

[C] His comments on her recent work. [D] His congratulations on her good luck.

【听力原文】

M：Mary，a recent study on job interviews says the best meeting time is between 9 and 11 in the morning，and the worst is after 3 in the afternoon.

W：Good news indeed. Mine is at 10 a. m.

M：Oh，you are lucky.

【解析】答案为 A。本题为分析推理题。问题：男士告诉女士什么？问题对男士部分提问，所以考生要特别关注男士的话。根据画线部分可以得知，男士告诉女士的是面试的最佳和最糟时间段，故正确答案为 A 选项。B 选项指的是面试的策略，具有一定的迷惑性，是干扰项。

三、注意事项

（一）树立信心，沉着冷静

某些考生在听力考试中带有恐惧心理，由于心情紧张使精神不能集中，甚至使原来很熟悉的表达都变得陌生，从而影响正常水平的发挥。因此考生务必在考试前调整好心态，使自己充满信心，保持沉着冷静，排除一切心理负担，积极主动地迎接考试。建议考生在进入考场前听几套 PETS-3 听力真题，使自己提前进入听力考试状态。

（二）浏览题目，预见内容

考生在拿到试卷后，要利用正式放音前的一段时间和录音间的停顿，迅速浏览问题和选项。首先应扫视问题并在大脑中记住这个问题的关键，这样在听录音时就可以有的放矢地捕捉所需要的信息，紧接着速读 4 个选项。4 个选项中多次重复的词，通常是原对话中的关键词，可以帮助还原对话内容，考生也可根据选项的内容做一个合理的联想与猜测。选项之间的差异往往是考察的重点，是解题的关键。

（三）当机立断，勇敢选择

听力考试中录音只播放一次，答题时间很短，答案转瞬即逝，这就需要考生迅速做出判断，选择答案。如果在某一题上答题失误，考生要果断放弃，不要纠结，以免影响后面的听力答题。考生要明白有舍才有得的道理。

（四）排除干扰项

答案的 4 个选择项中 3 个为干扰项。在遇到难题无法抉择时，利用排除干扰项法来选择不失为一个好的解题技巧。干扰项通常具备以下特征之一：与原文读音相似或字形相似的选择项；不合情理、不合逻辑的选项；与主题无关的选项；与原文一模一样。

（五）重视转折词的使用

转折词后往往是考点所在，如 but，however，while，although，yet，actually，well，really，as a matter of fact，in fact，to tell you the truth 等。

听力是一个复杂的思维过程。掌握准确的语音、丰富的词汇和正确的语法知识是做好听力理解题的基础。同时，考生还必须掌握丰富的英语国家文化背景知识，这对于做出正确的预见和推理十分重要。考生在备考的过程中也要有意识地补充这方面的文化知识，积累一些常用的俚语俗语。在此基础上，个别词句的遗漏或费解对听力理解不会造成太大的障碍，考生不必纠结。在听录音的过程中一定要心态平和，不急不躁，集中注意力，这是做好听力理解的前提。

听力 B 节　长对话

长对话

听力 B 节考查考生理解对话和独白的具体信息、主旨要义、进行推理和引申等能力。此节共 15 题，有四段对话或独白，每段平均约 200 词，总长约 800 词。每段录音材料只播放一遍，问题不在录音中播放，仅在试卷上印出。考生从每题所给的 4 个选项中选出最佳选项。

一、命题剖析

（一）听力长对话环节更加注重考生在听录音的过程中对篇章的理解能力

在长对话中，问答形式的对话是考官青睐的考点，而且考试的重点往往落在答语上。长对话的开头部分是常见出题点，可通过起始句中的核心词汇判断话题与场景。在长对话中，第一个发言的人第一句话通常是寒暄，第二句话引出话题；而第二个人的第一句话通常就转入对话题的讨论。因此，听清起始句中的核心词汇非常重要，这样就能判断场景和话题，并可据此回答主旨题，以及与主题相关的推断题。长对话的另一个出题规律就是在结尾处，针对将要做什么，或者提出什么建议进行提问。答题的关键就在于锁定结尾处的核心词。

（二）独白（通常是讲座/讲话）注重考生对细节的关注

与对话差不多，独白类型的听力理解大部分题目都是细节题或推断题，应特别留意文章中表示时间、地点、年代、数字、事物特征、事物优缺点、原因、结果、目的等内容。

二、应试技巧

（一）在长对话环节，要跟上说话者的节奏，抓有承上启下作用的信息句

1. 表示层次与顺序的句子，一般由 first，second，in the end，in addition，furthermore，finally 等引导。

2. 表示意义转折的句子，一般由 but，however，on the contrary，instead，unfortunately，however，yet，although，nevertheless 等引导。

3. 表示因果关系的句子，一般由 because，since，for，thus，as a result 等引导。

（二）要留意特殊词

1. 注意比较级、最高级：first，earliest，most，the most important reason，the chief，

the simplest

2. 注意异同：differ，different，alike，similar，resemble，same，have something in common

（三）要留意数字时间

1. 数字时间定位包括年代定位和过去现在对比定位两种形式。

2. 当数字时间和比较级、最高级组合在一起的时候，或是数字时间出现在文章开始和结束时，答案肯定在附近。

（四）留意独白的开头和结尾

考生要特别留意独白的开头和结尾，核心词往往出现在这些位置。

三、典型示例

（一）对话类

例题 1. *Questions* 18 – 21 *are based on the following dialogue.*（2015 年 3 月真题）

18. What is probably the man's position?

[A] Dean of Students.

[B] Lecturer in Speech Communication.

[C] Professor of Business Administration.

[D] Chairman of the Journalism Department.

【听力原文】

W：Dr. Steven，I am thinking about **changing my major** before the end of the **freshman year**.

M：What are you **studying** now?

W：I am taking three **general requirements** and American history and American literature this **semester**. Last semester I took four requirements and freshman French.

M：I believe it's not too late to change your major because you've mainly taken general requirements which all freshmen have to take. Also we have twelve **electives** so the two lit courses will be included in them，so you can change your major without losing any **credits**.

W：I am very happy to know I am still able to **change my major**. I am interested in writing newspaper articles，and after finishing my degree I would like to work for some newspaper firm.

M：Oh，I think you will be a good writer.

【解析】答案为 D。本题需要通过话题词汇识别场景并推测人物身份/关系。从 changing my major，freshman year，semester，credits 等词汇可得知是学习场景对话。女生想要转专业，在对话开头她称男士为 Dr. Steven，可知是师生间的对话。男士问女生现在学哪些课程，女生进行了详细的回答。男士对课程设置十分了解，认为该女生可以在不损失学分的情况下转专业。女生提到她对新闻写作感兴趣，综合以上信息，可推断男士应是新闻专业的负责人，故选 D。

19. What does she have to take before she begins practical training?

[A] English sociology. [B] Journalism 121.

[C] Freshman French. [D] Journalism 112.

【听力原文】

W：Dr. Steven, when do students **start practical training**?

M：They **don't** begin practical training in reporting **until** the **sophomore year**. Journalism 121 normally is taken in the **freshman year** as a general background course.

【解析】答案为 B。本题需要理解原文中定位词和表示大学年级的词汇，并对数字表达进行辨析。首先 start practical training 是问题中 begins practical training 的同义转述，通过这个定位。男士的回答中有一个 not... until... 句型，本句中考生还需要识别 sophomore year（大二）这个词汇，由本句得知 practical training（实习）是大二才开始。接下来听到 freshman year（大一）的通识教育课程是 Journalism 121，此处需要辨析干扰项 D 中的数字表达。最后得出 B 是正确的。

20. How many courses did she take last semester?

[A] 3. [B] 4. [C] 5. [D] 6.

【听力原文】

M：What are you studying now?

W：**I am taking** three general requirements and American history and American literature this semester. **Last semester** I **took** four requirements and freshman French.

【解析】答案为 C。本题需要考生能够识别不同时态的表达，以及处理数字的简单加减计算。首先通过题目中的时态及 last semester 判断需要找出过去已学课程的数量。女生回答的第一句话用了现在进行时，因此可以很快确定这句话里的数字是干扰项。第二句话提到定位词 last semester，使用的时态是一般过去式，因此 four requirements（4 门必修课）加新生法语课（freshman French）一共 5 门，选 C。

21. What year is the woman going to be in?

[A] The junior year. [B] The freshman year.

[C] The senior year. [D] The sophomore year.

【听力原文】

W：I see. I will take the course **next semester**. Thank you very much for your help.

M：You're welcome. I look forward to seeing you in my department.

【解析】答案为 D。本题是词汇考点，考查考生对大学四个年级的词汇表达是否熟悉。此外，和上题一样，时态的表达可以很快帮助排除干扰项。题目中 going to be in 表示该生即将升入哪个年级。从女生的话 I will take the course next semester. 从上下文中（第 19 题）可得知她下学期将选的是 practical training 这门课程，因此女生即将上大二，选 D。

【点评】

本题为学习相关类对话，此类场景涉及的方面有学期计划、课程介绍、选课、讨论课程的难易程度或对课程的偏好等。如果是师生间就某一话题进行讨论，则有可能涉及论文题目、研究方向、资料查找等。

词汇拓展

【学生】

freshman 大一学生
sophomore 大二学生
junior student 大三学生
senior student 大四学生
undergraduate 本科生
graduate student 硕士生
doctor student 博士生
boarder 住宿生
auditor/guest student 旁听生
bachelor's degree 学士学位

【教师】

president 大学校长
principal 中学校长
lecturer 讲师
assistant 助教
adviser 顾问
coordinator 班主任
associate professor 副教授
full professor 教授

【选课】

credit 学分
credit course 有学分的课程
advanced course 高级课程
introduction course 初级课程
course sheet 选课单
assistantship 助学金
commencement 毕业典礼
elective 选修课
compulsory 必修的
curriculum 课程
register for 注册，登记
economics 经济学
accounting 会计学

【考试】

review 复习
make up an exam 补考
quiz 测验
test anxiety 考试焦虑症
fail in exam 考试不及格

例题 2. *Questions* 18 – 21 *are based on the following interview with John Smith, chairman of National Weight and Health Association* (*NWHA*). (2018 年 3 月真题)

18. What did the NWHA survey aim to explore?

[A] The incidences of obesity.
[B] Popular views on obesity.
[C] Ways to fight obesity.
[D] The causes of obesity.

【听力原文】

W：Good evening. Welcome back to *Miss Know It All*. For today's **program**, Mr. John Smith, chairman of National Weight and Health Association, has come with **findings** from our recent NWHA **survey** on **obesity**. Now, Mr. Smith, what is the **purpose** of your survey?

M：We wanted to explore how people around the world **view** obesity or being **overweight**. Actually, obesity has gone global.

【解析】答案为B。本题考查同义替换。通过女士的前两句发言，可推断这是一个访谈节目的对话，主题是一个关于肥胖症的调查研究。女士的第一个问题提到purpose，是题目中aim的同义转述。男士回答他们调查的目的是找出全世界人们是如何看待肥胖这一问题的，view是动词，意为“看待”，而B选项popular views（view做名词），是原句的同义转述，故选B。

19. How many people in the world are rated as being overweight?

[A] 16 million. [B] 18 million.

[C] 1.6 billion. [D] 1.8 billion.

【听力原文】

W：How did you do it?

M：We interviewed 16,000 people in 16 countries.

W：**How large is the overweight population** of the world according to your estimates?

M：1.6 **billion** including 18 **million** children under age 5.

【解析】答案为C。本题考查数字表达的辨析。在对话中多次出现数字，通过How large即为题目中的How many可定位答案在这个问题的答语中。主持人问：“根据你的估计，全世界有多少超重人口？”男士回答：“16亿，包括1800万5岁以下儿童。”因为问的是肥胖症总人口数，故18 million是干扰项，选C。

20. In which country do people feel the most pressure to be thin?

[A] Brazil. [B] India.

[C] France. [D] America.

【听力原文】

W：Really surprising, isn't it? And what are your findings about **people's attitudes** regarding obesity?

M：Our survey found that people in **Brazil feel the most pressure** to be thin, 83% of **Brazilians** think **there is too much emphasis placed on** weight. French are most likely to blame Americans. They use American's fast food as an excuse for their overweight problem.

【解析】答案为A。本题考查考生对细节的辨认能力。女士在这一轮的问题是people's attitudes，是题目中do people feel的同义转述，可定位答案在接下来的回答中。问题中用了最高级the most pressure，而男士说：“我们的调查发现，觉得减肥压力最大的是巴西人。”这个句子中同时具备关键词pressure，最高级的表达the most，以及进一步的解释 there is too much emphasis placed on，因此符合题意，选 A。

21. Who are most likely to blame their parents for obesity?

[A] The French. [B] The Swiss.

[C] Germans. [D] Russians.

【听力原文】

Russians are **most likely to** blame their parents for obesity. They are followed by Germans and Indians. When asked who encouraged them to try to lose weight, the Swiss tend to exclude their doctor.

W: Stay tuned for more about the NWHA survey, we will be back soon after the break.

【解析】答案为 D。本题和上题相同，考查考生对细节的辨认能力。男士说："俄罗斯人最有可能把肥胖归咎于父母。"注意表述中使用了最高级 be most likely to。因此 D 为正确选项。其他选项虽然在文中提及，但语义不符，为干扰项。

【点评】

本题是采访座谈类对话。对话涉及的方面可能包括采访目的、人物身份、成功的原因、被访者做某事的动机、今后的计划等。

（二）独白类

例题： *Questions* 11 – 13 *are based on the following passage about the transportation in the future.*（2016 年 9 月真题）

11. What will be used to power cars in the next few decades?

[A] Gas [B] Electricity

[C] Solar energy [D] Alcohol

【听力原文】

In the next few decades, people are going to travel very differently from the way they do today. Everyone **is going to drive electrically-powered cars**, so in the few years, people won't worry about running out of gas.

【解析】答案为 B。本题考查定位以及时态，独白短文在开头第一句话出题的频率是很高的。开头第一句 in the next few decades 与题目中提法相同，可以定位。题目中问未来的汽车能源，而文章第二句用了将来时，人们开 electrically-powered cars，因此能源类型是电能，选 B。

12. What will future news reports focus on when talking about transportation?

[A] Road conditions. [B] Highway traffic.

[C] Air traffic conditions. [D] New traffic rules.

【听力原文】

Transportation in the future won't be limited to the ground; many people predict that the traffic will quickly move to the sky. **In the coming years**, **instead of** radio reports about road conditions and highway traffic, **news reports will talk about traffic jams in the sky**. But the sky isn't the limit.

【解析】 答案为 C。本题考查考生识别同义替换及细节辨认的能力。In the coming years 与题目中的 future 相一致。instead of 在这里表示“不是……而是……”，traffic jams 属于交通状况 traffic conditions，而 sky 与 air 对应，因此选 C。

13. What will passengers be asked to do when they travel to the moon?

[A] Carry little luggage. [B] Go through a health check.

[C] Arrive 10 minutes earlier for boarding. [D] Undergo security check.

【听力原文】

In the future, you will probably even be able to take a trip to the moon. **Instead of listening to** regular airplane announcements, **you will hear someone say**: the spacecraft to the moon leaves in 10 minutes. Please check your equipment. And remember no more than 10 ounces of carry-on baggage are allowed.

【解析】 答案为 A。本题考查考生语义理解和细节辨认的能力。在最后一句中，考试将听到广播内容的列举：“去月球的宇宙飞船 10 分钟后离开。请检查一下你的设备。记住随身携带的行李不能超过 10 盎司。”与选项比对后，B、C、D 均与原文不一致，而 10 盎司对于行李而言是非常轻的重量，因此只有 A 符合。

实战演练及解析

(2017 年 9 月听力 Part B)

2017. 9 Part B

Directions:

You will hear four dialogues or monologues. Before listening to each one, you will have 5 seconds to read each of the questions which accompany it. While listening, answer each question by choosing A, B, C or D. After listening, you will have 10 seconds to check your answer to each question. You will hear the recording ***only once****.*

Questions 11 – 13 are based on the following dialogue about buying cars.

11. What kind of car does the woman plan to buy?

[A] A wagon. [B] A sports car.

[C] An estate car. [D] An energy-saving jeep.

12. Why did the man buy a jeep?

[A] He got a special price for it.

[B] He found its style attractive.

[C] It has bigger room than an estate car.

[D] It suits long trips better than an estate car.

13. Whom does the man introduce to the woman for buying a car?

[A] A reporter. [B] A car specialist.

[C] His friend. [D] His colleague.

Questions 14 – 17 *are based on the following dialogue between a man and a woman.*

14. How long has the man been working here?

[A] One day. [B] Two weeks.

[C] One month. [D] Two years.

15. What kind of job does the woman have now?

[A] A training job. [B] A seasonal job.

[C] A permanent job. [D] A management job.

16. What is the man's wish for the future?

[A] To have a business of his own.

[B] To have a career in fashion design.

[C] To become a computer expert.

[D] To become a company manager.

17. When does the conversation take place?

[A] During lunchtime. [B] During a work break.

[C] Before a day's work. [D] Before a job interview.

Questions 18 – 21 *are based on the following dialogue between a reporter and a health expert.*

18. Who are the research subjects of Dr. Stone's study?

[A] Elderly patients. [B] Seriously ill patients.

[C] People who never get sick. [D] People who have just recovered.

19. What does Professor Smith do every day?

[A] He goes swimming. [B] He takes a long nap.

[C] He does weight-lifting. [D] He takes a cold shower.

20. What do we learn about Mary?

[A] She is a former nurse. [B] She works in a hospital.

[C] She works for Dr. Stone. [D] She is a former professor.

21. What does Mary credit her health to?

[A] Balanced diet. [B] Social network.

[C] Regular exercise. [D] Memory training.

Questions 22 – 25 *are based on the following interview with an actor.*

22. What did the man receive for his role in the movie?

[A] A lot of fans. [B] A lot of money.

[C] Many awards. [D] Many comments.

23. What does the movie tell us?

[A] It is never too late to learn. [B] It is hard for the old to lean.

[C] Education is beyond the poor. [D] Education leads to a better life.

24. Why did the character miss his education when he was young?

[A] His country was at war. [B] He had to join the army.

[C] Education was too costly. [D] There were few schools then.

25. Why does the man say the role is challenging for him?

[A] It covers a long time span. [B] It is hard to play an old man.

[C] He has to act in rough situations. [D] He has limited freedom in acting.

You now have 3 minutes to transfer all your answers from your test booklet to your ANSWER SHEET.

That is the end of listening section.

【答案】

11. C　12. A　13. C　14. C　15. B　16. A　17. B　18. C

19. D　20. A　21. B　22. C　23. A　24. C　25. A

【听力原文及解析】

Questions 11 – 13

W: What kind of car should I buy, Larry? I like to get something we can use for a long trip as well as taking the children around town.

M: Well, we have a jeep. We like it when we travel.

W: We thought about a jeep, but I understand they are not very fuel-efficient.

M: Our Jeep is better than the most of the jeeps on the market. *Consumer Report* said it's the most fuel-efficient of any of the jeeps.

W: Did *Consumer Report* compare jeeps with estate cars? We thought about an estate car.

M: I don't remember the exact number, but I do remember that the jeep was less efficient than estate cars. (12) We decided to against estate car because we got a better price on the jeep. The dealer was running a special sale.

W: (11) Well, I like the style of the estate cars better than the jeeps and it has room for all the equipment for the children. We need a larger car.

M: (13) My friend works at the dealer's shop north of the town. He was telling me about the sale they are going to start next month. You might be able to get an estate car cheaper if you wait till then. Here is his card.

W: Thanks, that sounds like a good idea. I'll go and see what he has.

11. 问题：女士打算买什么样的车？

【解析】答案为 C。此题为观点判断题。对话的开头，女士提到她想买一辆既可以用来长途旅行，也可以带孩子们在城里开的车。经过一番讨论后，女士明确表态说："比起吉普车，我更喜欢旅行车的风格，它的空间可以容纳孩子们的装备。我们需要空间大一点的车。"故 C 选项旅行车为正确答案。

12. 问题：男士为什么买吉普车？

【解析】答案为 A。此题为细节辨认题。本题考查对因果关系的理解，男士提到他们决定不买旅行车的原因是吉普车的价格更优惠。这家经销商当时正在进行特价销售。故应选 A“他以特价买到了车。”B 意为：“他觉得它的风格很吸引人。”C 意为：“它的空间比旅行车大。”D 意为：“它比旅行车更适合长途旅行。”

13. 问题：男士给想买车的女士推荐了谁？

【解析】答案为 C。此题为细节辨认题。对话的末尾男士说：“我朋友在城北的一家经销店工作。他曾告诉我他们下个月有打折活动。如果你等到那时候买旅行车，也许价格能便宜些。这是他的名片。”因此 C 选项符合题意。A、B、D 选项均未提及。

必背词汇

wagon *n.* 四轮运货马车；轿车

sports car *n.* 跑车

estate car *n.* 旅行轿车

jeep *n.* 吉普车

energy-saving *n.* 节能的

dealer *n.* 经销商

specialist *n.* 专家

Questions 14 – 17

W：Hello, I'm Jennifer. I'm new here.

M：Nice to meet you, Jennifer. I'm David. (14) I just had my first month here. (15) Are you a seasonal helper too?

W：Yes, but I hope I can stay on after the holidays.

M：Me too. It depends on us in part. We have to do a god job and go the extra mile.

W：I agree. Hard work will finally pay off.

M：Right. You know, the manager of the shoe department started just two years ago as a temporary worker. He's about our age. I bet you will be the manager of the company someday.

W：I'd like a career in fashion design. There are a lot of opportunities for advancement.

M：(16) I want to owe my own store one day, so I want to learn all I can.

W：I'm taking designing classes in college. There's a lot to learn.

M：It's a hard work, but it has rewards. I find satisfaction in doing a job well.

W：If you enjoy doing something, it's easier. I just finished watching the orientation videos. Now I'm training on the computers. It's fun so far.

M：Yes, it is. Oh! (17) It looks like my break is almost over. I need to work now. It's been nice talking to you.

14. 问题：这男士在这里工作多久了？

[C]**【解析】**细节辨认题。对话的开头，女士说自己是新来的；男士说自己刚在这里工作了一个月。故 C 选项为正确答案。

15. 问题：这位女士现在做什么工作？

【解析】答案为 B。此题为身份/场景推断题。对话开头男士问女士："你也是季节性帮工吗？"女士答："是的，但我希望假期后我能留下来。"A. 培训工作 B. 季节性工作 C. 固定的工作 D. 管理工作，故 B 选项为正确答案。

16. 问题：这位男士对未来有什么期望？

【解析】答案为 A。此题为细节辨认题。男士说："我希望有一天能拥有自己的店，所以我想学习所有能学的东西。"这与选项 A "拥有自己的生意"相符合，故 A 选项为正确答案。B 选项"从事时装设计工作"是这位女士的愿望。C 选项"成为计算机专家"和 D 选项"成为公司经理"是干扰项。

17. 问题：对话发生在什么时候？

【解析】答案为 B。此题为细节推断题。从上下文可推断两人是同事关系，对话结束时男士说："我的休息时间好像快结束了。我要开始工作了。"因此 B 为正确选项。

必背词汇

seasonal helper 季节性帮工
temporary worker 临时工
fashion design 时装设计
advancement *n.* 晋升
orientation *n.* 上岗前的培训

*Questions*18 – 21

W：(18) Dr. Stone, you have studied 25 people who never get sick. Could you give us some easy-to-follow tips on how they've successfully stayed away from illness in their whole lives?

M：Our study shows that some habits will help you to stay well and live longer. Such as cold shower, napping, weightlifting and swimming.

W：(19) Do you mean that taking a cold shower is good for our health?

M：(19) Yes. Professor Smith is 82 years old now. He has taken a cold shower every day for most of his adult life, and never suffers from colds.

W：That sounds great. Maybe I can try it myself. What else can we do to keep us against illness?

M：Besides exercise, friends are also very important. You might not think having a social network would count as much as diet and exercise when it comes to good health. But studies have found that good friends can protect against everything from memory-lost to heart attacks, to infectious diseases. (20) Mary is a former nurse. She can't remember being ill in all her 75 years, (21) and she credits this to the fact that she is constantly seeking out new friends. Sociability increases self-respect which in turn supports the immune system.

18. 问题：斯通博士的研究对象是谁？

【解析】答案为 C。此题为细节辨认题。在学术研究中，subject 表示接受试验者；研究对象。从对话开头女士提到："斯通博士，您研究了 25 个从不生病的人。"得出 C

选项为正确答案。D 选项中的 recover 表示“康复”。

19. 问题：史密斯教授每天都做些什么？

【解析】答案为 D。此题为细节辨认题。在说明洗冷水澡有益健康的时候，博士引用了史密斯教授的例子：“史密斯教授现在 82 岁了。在成人时期的大部分时间里，他每天都洗冷水澡，而且从不感冒。”因此，D 是正确选项。“A. 游泳；B. 中午睡个长觉；C. 练习举重”都是干扰项，其中游泳、午睡、举重是和洗冷水澡一起作为长寿的生活方式在对话中被提及的，但与本题意思不符。

20. 问题：我们可以得知哪些有关玛丽的信息？

【解析】答案为 A。此题为语义理解题。former“前任的；先前的”。提到 Mary 这个案例的时候，提到她曾是一名护士。故选择 A。

21. 问题：玛丽把她的健康归功于什么？

【解析】答案为 B。此题为语义理解题。credit to 认为是……的功劳；把……归于。全文最后一句提到：“她把这归功于她不断地寻找新朋友。社交增加自尊，而自尊反过来又支撑了免疫系统。”A. 均衡饮食；B. 社会交往；C. 定期锻炼；D. 记忆训练。故 B 与原文符合，是正确选项。

必背词汇

subject *n.* 接受试验者；研究对象

napping *n.* （日间的）小睡，打盹

infectious *adj.* 传染的；有传染性的

credit to 认为是……的功劳；把……归于

balanced diet 均衡饮食

Questions 22 – 25

W：Congratulations on all the success you have received from your role in *The First Greater*. （22）<u>Have you taken it all in yet? You have so many awards for it.</u>

M：Yes, I've taken it all in. It's very exciting. I hope it can leave a better thing for me and for other people.

W：Why do you think this role is so touching?

M：（23）<u>I think it's a role that enhances the idea that education is important. It is also a role that inspires people, particularly those have missed out on going to school, realizing that an old man at the age of 84, can still want to go to school and learn to read and write.</u>

W：Were there aspects of him that were challenging for you? Having to play an elderly man?

M：（25）<u>Yes, the character is challenging in many ways. He's many characters in one.</u> （24）<u>He is a young man who missed education because it was expensive,</u> and then he joins the struggle for independence. When the country finally gets its freedom, he has become an old man. (25) You have a young man, you have an old man. I had to devise ways of portraying those characteristics in those situations.

22. 问题：这个人通过扮演电影中的角色得到了什么？

【解析】答案为 C。此题为语义推断题。第一句女士祝贺了对方在塑造了电影 *The First Greater* 的角色时获得了很多成就。接着问他："你是不是已经接受了所有奖项？这个角色为你赢得了这么多奖项。" award 在这个语境中表示"奖；奖项"，因此答案是 C。

23. 问题：这部电影告诉我们什么？

【解析】答案为 A。此题为语义理解题。女士问："你觉得这个角色为什么这么感人？"男士说："我认为这部电影强调了教育的重要性。这个角色也激励了人们，尤其是那些错过了上学机会的人，他让人们意识到一个 84 岁的老人仍然可以渴望上学，并学习如何读写。" A. 学习永远不嫌晚；B. 老年人学习很困难；C. 穷人没有接受教育的机会；D. 教育使生活更美好。A 选项符合题意。

24. 问题：为什么这个人物年轻时错过了接受教育的机会？

【解析】答案为 C。此题为细节辨认题。在描述这个电影人物的细节中，寻找一个有因果关系的句子。"他是个因为学费昂贵而错过了接受教育的年轻人。" 选项 C 中的 costly 是原文中 expensive 的同义转述，C 为正确选项。

25. 问题：为什么男士说这个角色对他来说很有挑战性？

【解析】答案为 A。此题为语义理解题。答案是对最后一段话的理解，男士说这个角色在很多方面都很有挑战性。"他是许多角色的集合体……要同时饰演一个年轻人和一个老人。我必须找出在这些情况下刻画人物不同特征的方法。" 所以角色的挑战性来自于对青年和老年两个不同时期的人物塑造。选项 A 表示"它包含了很长的时间跨度"符合题意，是正确选项；而 B 表示"扮演一个老人很难"是对原文片面的理解；C 表示"他得在困难的环境中进行表演"是对原文 those situations 的误解；D 表示"他在表演的时候自由发挥的空间有限"原文未提及。

必背词汇

award *n.* 奖；奖品

enhance *v.* 提高，增强

inspire *v.* 激励；启发

portray *v.* 扮演（角色）；描述；描绘

characteristics *n.* 特性，特征

阅读 A 节　多项选择

多项选择

阅读部分由 A、B、C 三节组成，考查考生理解书面英语的能力。全国英语等级考试三级大纲对本部分的测试内容、考查要点、题型、题量、分值及答题时间等都做出了具体的要求。全面了解这些具体要求，能帮助考生更清楚地把握复习的方向。

阅读理解部分全面介绍了大纲规定的阅读能力的构成和培养，包括理解主旨要义；理解文中具体信息；根据上下文推测生词的词义；进行有关的判断、推理和引申；理解文中的概念性含义；理解文章的结构及单词之间、段落之间的关系；快速阅读较长的文字材料，获取有关信息；理解作者的意图、观点或态度。针对考查每一种能力的题型，我们应认真分析真题当中考查过的同类题型，从中学习一些具体的应试技巧，每部分之后还应做一些专项阅读训练。考试前还应了解和适应和大纲样题形式完全一致的阅读理解模拟训练题。

A 节（10 题）：考查考生理解书面英语的能力，包括理解文章的具体信息、主旨要义、进行推理和引申等能力。要求考生根据所提供的 2 篇文章的内容（每篇平均约 350 词），从每题所给的 4 个选择项中选出最佳选项。

一、命题剖析

综合近几年全国英语等级考试的真题，Part A 的试题题型主要分为四大类，即细节题、推断题、主旨大意题、词义推断题。这部分所考查的内容一般不会是从文章能直接找到答案的，而需要考生运用自己的语言知识、逻辑知识等进行推敲和理解。虽然提供 4 个答案供考生进行选择，但干扰项大多具有迷惑性，这就要求考生对所读文章内容达到真正的理解。

二、应试技巧

（一）阅读理解解题步骤

1. 读问题，划出标志词或关键词

快速浏览题目，对 5 个题目有大概印象以便阅读时有侧重点。一般来说，对于本身已经明确其考查内容的题目，标志词和关键词是比较容易找到的，只看一下题干即可，而对于那些并没有出现标志词和关键词的题目，如：The author suggests that，可以在解答试题时浏览选项作出解答。

2. 略读文章

在略读中，首先阅读第一段，因为第一段通常会告诉我们作者将要讨论的话题。然后阅读下面各段的第一句话，以对每个段落的内容有大概的了解，然后再阅读最后一段，以帮助我们对文章内容进行概括，或了解作者的评价、态度等。

3. 解答试题

根据试题中的标志词和关键词，找到试题在文章中对应的句子，并对其进行仔细阅读，然后对比四个选项，选出正确答案。

（二）解题技巧

1. 细节题

细节题即客观事实题，在考试中占有较大的比重，每篇阅读理解都有至少两道细节题，目的是考查学生对重要事实和细节的辨认与记忆能力，以及通过对语句的理解与分析来考查考生的语言理解能力和运用能力。事实或细节是文章中用来论证或说明主题的依据，这类试题主要考查考生是否掌握了作者用来阐述主题的有关事实和细节，对文章的理解是否全面，是否透彻。这类问题不掺杂主观内容而是针对文章的某个具体细节如时间、地点、人物、原因、结果、条件、现象等的提问。PETS 三级考试中所出现的细节题一般包括两种类型，即直接理解题和是非判断题。

细节题常见的提问方式有以下几种：

The new system will mostly benefit those who ________.（考查人物）

Emotional intelligence is important because ________.（考查原因）

According to the passage, the author intended to tell Maria how to ________.（考查方式）

For a newly-established business, burn rate refers to ________.（考查事实）

The best solution to the female brain drain in universities is to ________.（考查目的）

The author states all of the items, except ________.（是非判断）

细节题属于“直接解答型”题，答案往往可以从原文中找到。做题原则如下：

找定位词。仔细阅读题干，根据题干中的关键词或词组，回文章中定位，迅速锁定文章相关段落和语句，常见的定位词：时间、地点、人名、专有名词、特有信息等。需要注意的是有时候选项中有好几项出现在原文中，这时要结合题干来筛选。

定位顺序。一般出题顺序都会按照文章的行文顺序。

替换同义词。两相对照，最终确定答案。通常细节题的答案在文章中都会找到，但是答案的表述和原文会有所差别，常常不是文章中的原话，而是词语或句子的同义表达。例如：difficult = complicated，manager = managerial，同义词往往是答案所在。

正确选项有如下特点：

关键词直接复现，原文中的关键词转换成意义相同或相近的词，或称同义替换，此为正确选项。

选项中符合一般常识，意义富有哲理，属于普遍现象的往往是正确答案。

选项中含有绝对语气词的一般不是答案，如：must，always，never，only，completely。

词性或语态的转换。选项把原文中的一些词变换词性，或者改变原文句子的语态，使之成为正确选项。

同义转换类需对原文信息进行准确理解并简单推理，观察词义、词性及语态的变化。复习时应掌握英语的多种表达法。

干扰选项有如下特点：

“偷梁换柱”选项。即部分正确，部分错误。在选项的前半句或前大半句中用原文的结构和词汇，只是在最后换了几个词，而使考生出错。所以在判断选项时，一定要非常仔细，尤其要注意选项中出现的定语和状语是否与文章中的一致，是否被命题人偷偷换掉了定语、状语。

“张冠李戴”选项。即是原文信息，但不是题目要求内容。虽然观点和所说的话在文章中出现过，并且是正确的，但是却用错了位置，以达到混淆视听的目的。

“无中生有”的选项。即符合常识，但不是文章内容。在做题目、看选项时，一定要读原文，一定要根据文章中说到的内容去做判断。

“所答非所问”的选项。即选项文不对题，选项不能回答问题。命题人把文章中出现过的一些单词和句子，放在选项中，虽然选项单独看是正确的，但是却不能回答题目中的问题，这样的选项有很大的迷惑性。

错误选项就是命题人用以干扰考生思维的陷阱。即使基本读懂文章，也不能轻松做对全部题目。有些干扰项不仅语言复杂，而且欺骗性强。为了提高辨别错误或干扰信息的能力，有必要了解干扰项的种种特征，使我们在种种命题人设置的陷阱面前，做到胸有成竹。

例题分析

例题 1

【原文】Today, given the job losses of the past year, fewer unhappy couples will risk starting separate households. Furthermore, the housing market meltdown will make it more difficult for them to finance their separations by selling their homes.

【题目】In addition to job losses, what stands in the way of unhappy couples getting a divorce?

[A] A sense of insecurity. [B] Mounting family debts.

[C] Difficulty in getting a loan. [D] Falling housing prices.

【参考译文】现今，鉴于过去一年的失业情况，更少不幸福的夫妻会去承担分居的风险。而且，房地产市场的崩溃将使他们更加难以通过出售房屋来负担分开的费用。

【解析】答案为 D。首先，根据题干的 job losses 定位到原文的这几句。本题询问除了失业外，还有什么阻碍了不幸福的夫妻离婚。本段提到两个原因，第一个原因是 job losses，对应题干。第二句开头的 furthermore（而且）提示了本题的答案，即房地产市场的崩溃（meltdown）让不幸福的夫妻更加难通过卖房来负担分开的费用。故答案为 D“下跌的房价”。

解答本题的关键是准确定位及正确理解 meltdown 的意思。meltdown 的英文解释为 a situation in which prices fall by a very large amount，即“价格的大幅下跌”。A 意为“不安全感”，其中的 insecurity 利用上一段中的 insecure jobs 设置干扰，与本题没有关系；B“不断增加的家庭债务”和 C“很难获得贷款”在原文中没有提到。

例题 2

【原文】 We tend to think of the Depression as a time when families pulled together to survive huge job losses. By 1932, when nearly one-quarter of the workforce was unemployed, the divorce rate had declined by around 25% from 1929. But this doesn't mean people were suddenly happier with their marriages. Rather, with incomes decreasing and insecure jobs, unhappy couples often couldn't afford to divorce. They feared neither spouse could manage alone.

【题目】 In the Great Depression many unhappy couples chose to stick together because ________.

[A] starting a new family would be hard

[B] they wanted to better protect their kids

[C] living separately would be too costly

[D] they expected things would turn better

【参考译文】 想到大萧条，我们往往觉得那个时候一家人齐心协力，共度大规模的失业潮。到 1932 年为止，已有将近四分之一的工人失业，而相比 1929 年，离婚率下降了 25% 左右。但是，这并不意味着人们突然间就对婚姻更满意了。相反，随着收入的下降和工作变得不稳定，不幸福的夫妻常常是离不起婚。他们担心任何一方都没法独自应对困境。

【解析】 答案为 C。根据题干中的“unhappy couples”和“stick together”定位至本段最后两句。本题询问为什么大萧条时期许多不幸福的夫妻选择在一起。本段指出在大萧条时期，离婚率在下降，最后两句指出离婚率下降的原因：不幸福的夫妻离不起婚，他们担心任何一方都没法独自应对困境。C“分开生活的成本太高”中的 too costly 是对 couldn't afford 的同义替换，故为答案。A“组织一个新的家庭会很难”不如 C 具体，因为“难”并不一定就指经济因素，所以不准确。B“他们想要更好地保护自己的孩子”和 D“他们期待事情会好转”都没有在原文中提及。

例题 3

【原文】 The privacy issue has already landed Facebook in hot water in Washington. In April, Senator Charles Schumer called on Facebook to change its privacy policy. He also urged the Federal Trade Commission to set guidelines for social-networking sites. “I think the senator rightly communicated that we had not been clear about what the new products were and how people could choose to use them or not to use them," Schrage admits.

【题目】 What does Senator Charles Schumer advocate?

[A] Setting guidelines for advertising on websites.

[B] Formulating regulations for social-networking sites.

[C] Banning the sharing of users' personal information.

[D] Removing ads from all social-networking sites.

【参考译文】 隐私问题使 Facebook 在华盛顿陷入困境。四月，参议员查尔斯舒默呼吁 Facebook 改变其隐私政策。他还敦促联邦贸易委员会为社交网站制定指导方针。施拉格承认："我觉得参议员准确传达了这一信息：我们不清楚新产品是什么，人们可以选择使用或不使用这些产品。"

【解析】 答案为 B。根据题干中的人名 Senator Charles Schumer 定位至本段。该段第二句出现这个人名，原文中的 call on 对应题目中的 advocate，提到他呼吁 Facebook 修改隐私政策，接下来说他还敦促联邦贸易委员会为社交网站制定指导方针。B 中的 Formulating regulations 与原文 set guidelines 语义一致，故正确。A 选项偷梁换柱，将原文的"为社交网站制定方针"换成了"为网络广告制定方针"；C"禁止分享用户个人信息"和 D"移除所有的社交网站广告"都不能在这段找到依据。

2. 主旨题

主旨即文章的中心思想，是对文章内容的概括。任何一段文章都会围绕一个中心进行讨论、说明或描述。段落的构成有其内在的规律，其中心思想往往是通过段落中的主题句来体现的。做好主旨题的关键在于能快速准确地找出篇章或段落的主题句，或抓住文章或段落的中心思想。主题句具有如下特点：有明显的概括性；句子结构简单；段落中其他句子均用来解释支持或扩充主题句所表达的主题思想。

如何在阅读中找到主题句来确定中心思想呢？一般来说，一篇文章的主题句通常位于首段或尾段，有时也出现在文章的中间段落。段落的主题句通常位于段首或段尾，有时也在段落的中间。

主题句在段首，作者开门见山提出主题，然后用细节来对主题句所表达的思想进行解释说明，主题句在段落中起着"先声夺人"的作用。

主题句在段尾，作者在结尾归纳文章的中心思想，主题句在段落中起着"画龙点睛"的作用。

主题句在段中，作者先陈述细节以支撑观点，然后在段落中间表达中心思想，主题句在段落中起着"承上启下"的作用。

还有一种主题句的位置，在段落中看不到，需要考生根据段落的上下文来总结。

如有主题句，就能很容易确定文章或段落的主题。如果没有明显的主题句，就带着问题细读文章的首段和尾段找出其中心，抓住每个段落的主题句，明确文章的中心思想。

注意：如果文章主旨题出现在第一题，先不要做这道题，把后面的题做完后再回头做第一题，这样可以节省很多时间。

主旨题分为两类，一类是考查作者的态度和写作目的，另一类是根据文章内容为文章确定标题。这类题考查对短文整体的概括和理解能力，所选择的答案也应该是能够概括全篇文章的主旨和内容，而不是文章中某个具体段落的小结，更不是某些句子意思的重现。因此做此类题型时，考生一定要有“篇章观念”。

通常的提问形式有以下几种：

What's the main idea of this passage?

What does this passage discuss?

Which of the following sentences best summarize the author's points?

Which of the following states the theme of this passage?

The author's purpose in writing this passage?

What's the best title of this passage?

正确选项一般有如下特点：

为文章确定标题时，抓住关键词。越是反复出现的名词或动词短语，越与文章主旨有关。

判断作者写作目的的题，除了抓住文章主旨大意外，还要注意文中一些表达观点态度的动词和短语。

注意一些判断性的、发表议论和观点的句子。

干扰选项一般有如下特点：

局部信息，某一段大意或某一句未展开的话。

外延过大，所含内容超出篇章范围。

无关信息，即未提及或找不到依据的信息。

以文中事实、细节代替抽象概括的主题大意。

例题分析

例题 1

【原文】 When we talk about Americans barely into adulthood who are saddled with unbearable levels of debt, the conversation is almost always about student loan debt. But there's a growing body of evidence suggesting that today's young adults are also drowning in credit-card debt-and that many of them will take this debt to their graves.

【题目】 What is the main idea of the first paragraph?

[A] Many young Americans will never be able to pay off their debts.

[B] Credit cards play an increasingly important role in college life.

[C] Credit cards are doing more harm than student loans.

[D] The American credit card system is under criticism.

【参考译文】当我们谈论那些刚刚步入成年而又负债累累的美国人的时候，我们谈话的内容几乎全部是学生贷款债务。但是，越来越多的证据显示，今天的年轻人也陷入了信用卡债务的泥潭之中——很多人将会把这一债务带进坟墓。

【解析】答案为 A。由题干中的 the first paragraph 定位到第一段。第一段通过学生贷款引出年轻人的信用卡债务。最后一句中"今天的年轻人也陷入了信用卡债务的泥潭之中——很多人将会把这一债务带进坟墓"点明了文章主题。由此可见，很多年轻人永远都偿还不完他们的债务，故答案为 A。

例题 2

【原文】In recent years, a growing body of research has shown that our appetite and food intake are influenced by a large number of factors besides our biological need for energy, including our eating environment and our perception of the food in front of us.

Studies have shown, for instance, that eating in front of the TV (or a similar distraction) can increase both hunger and the amount of food consumed. Even simple visual cues, like plate size and lighting, have been shown to affect portion size and consumption.

A new study suggested that our short-term memory also may play a role in appetite. Several hours after a meal, people's hunger levels were predicted not by how much they'd eaten but rather by how much food they'd seen in front of them-in other words, how much they remembered eating.

This disparity (差异) suggests the memory of our previous meal may have a bigger influence on our appetite than the actual size of the meal, says Jeffrey M. Brunstrom, a professor of experimental psychology at the University of Bristol.

"Hunger isn't controlled solely by the physical characteristics of a recent meal. We have identified an independent role for memory for that meal," Brunstrom says. "This shows that the relationship between hunger and food intake is more complex than we thought."

These findings echo earlier research that suggests our perception of food can sometimes trick our body's response to the food itself. In a 2011 study, for instance, people who drank the same 380-calorie (卡路里) milkshake on two separate occasions produced different levels of hunger-related hormones (荷尔蒙), depending on whether the shake's label said it contained 620 or 140 calories. Moreover, the participants reported feeling more full when they thought they'd consumed a higher-calorie shake.

What does this mean for our eating habits? Although it hardly seems practical to trick ourselves into eating less, the new findings do highlight the benefits of focusing on our food and avoiding TV and multitasking while eating.

The so-called mindful-eating strategies can fight distractions and help us control our appetite, Brunstrom says.

【题目】 1. What is the main idea of the passage?

[A] Eating distractions often affect our food digestion.

[B] Psychological factors influence our hunger levels.

[C] Our food intake is determined by our biological needs.

[D] Good eating habits will contribute to our health.

【参考译文】

近年来，越来越多的研究表明：除了对能量的生理需要外，人们的食欲和食物摄取受到诸多因素的影响，包括人们的饮食环境和对面前食物的认知。

研究表明，例如，在电视机（或者类似的消遣）前饮食能够同时增加饥饿感和食物的摄取量。即使是简单的视觉信号，比如餐盘的尺寸和灯光，也被证实会对食物分量和摄取量造成影响。

新的研究显示人们的短期记忆同样对食欲起作用。饭后几小时，决定人们饥饿程度的不是他们已食用的食物量，而是他们吃饭时面前所见到的食物量，换言之，是他们所记得的食物量。

布里斯托大学实验心理学教授 Jeffrey M. Brunstrom 认为：这种差异表明人们之前的饮食记忆对食欲造成的影响可能超过食物的真实数量对食欲造成的影响。

“饥饿程度不仅仅与最近所食食物的特征有关。我们已经确认了最近饮食在记忆中的独立作用。”Brunstrom 说，“这表明饥饿程度和食物摄取之间的关系要比我们想象的复杂得多。”

这些发现印证了早期的研究。早期研究表明，人们对食物的认知有时会欺骗身体对食物做出反应。例如：在 2011 年的一项研究中，参与者在两个不同场合食用了同样含有 380 卡路里的奶昔，但是，根据奶昔标签上标注的是 620 卡路里还是 140 卡路里，参与者分泌出了不同水平的与饥饿相关的荷尔蒙。而且，根据报告，当参与者认为自己食用了高卡路里的奶昔时，他们感觉更饱。

这对于人们的饮食习惯意味着什么呢？尽管新发现在让人减少饮食方面显得不切实际，但是确实能使人们认识到专注于食物、避免饮食时看电视或同时进行多项活动的益处。

【解析】 答案为 B。由题干中的 main idea 定位全文，首先找到各部分的主题句，主要在首段、末段及各段首句。通读全文，我们可以将文章分为三个部分：第一部分提出论点——人们的食欲和食物摄取量受到环境和对面前食物的认知等诸多因素的影响。第二部分引用相关科学研究论证这些影响因素，特别指出饮食环境、对食物的记忆、食物包装上的标签对人产生的心理暗示作用等会影响饮食。最后一部分指出研究对人们饮食习惯的意义，并提出通过“用心饮食”来控制食欲的建议。对食物及饮食环境的认知，对食物的记忆，食物标签产生的心理暗示等都属于心理因素。统观全文，作者一直围绕心理因素对食欲的影响展开论述，故答案为 B。

3. 推理题

与细节题相似，推理题也是对文章具体内容的判断。但推理不但要求掌握文章所表达的字面含义，还要从表面推出更深层含义，这类问题主要考查考生对文章中的一个观点或立场的理解程度，而这种观点或立场是作者在文章中强烈暗示但并没有明确表明的。这部分往往难度大，出错也最多。推理题包括：针对文章中的某个细节进行推断；根据文章推测作者的观点、目的、态度和思路；推断文章中没出现的前一段或下一段的内容。

因此，推理题要求考生在通篇理解文章的基础上，抓住文章的主题和细节，分析文章结构；或根据上下文的内在联系，来挖掘文章的深层含义，从而做出推断。

推理题的正确答案，往往不是原文某句话的照搬与照抄，而是原文某句话的同义改写或某几句话的总结与归纳，需要考生揣摩作者未在该句明确表达的含义。

通常的提问形式有：

From the passage we can draw the conclusion that ________.

It is implied/indicated/suggested that ________.

What's implied but not stated by the author is that ________.

Paragraph... indicates that ________.

It can be inferred/concluded from the passage that ________.

The report/study/research seems to suggest that ________.

We can learn/conclude from the passage that ________.

Which of the following can be inferred ________.

What can you infer from this passage?

What does this passage imply?

由以上提问方式可以看出，推理题大致可以分为归纳推理题和细节推理题。

归纳推理题要求归纳文章的主题和思想，或对某个部分或细节进行归纳，或归纳事情的原因和目的。对于归纳推理题，如果选项内容都正确，选择概括文章内容最全面的选项。

细节推理题需要就细节进行一定的总结概括。对于细节推理题，首先要明确题干所指内容所在的段落，然后从关键词的上下文寻找突破口，进行适当的归纳、总结和推断。

因此，推理题要求我们从总体上和逻辑上来理解文章，而不是只停留在语言层面和进行逐字逐句的分析。

干扰选项的特点：

是对原文内容的简单重复，不是推理得出的结论，没有读懂文章的“弦外之音”。

与原文相反的内容，或不合常理不合逻辑的结论。

文章没有涉及，纯属主观推断得出的结论，即用自己的观点代替作者的本意。

例题分析

例题

【原文】 Today's economic crisis could well generate a similar number of couples whose relationships have been irreparably（无法弥补地） ruined. So it's only when the economy is healthy again that we'll begin to see just how many broken families have been created.

【题目】 What can be inferred from the last paragraph?

[A] A stable family is the best protection against poverty.

[B] Money is the foundation of many a happy marriage.

[C] Few couples can stand the test of economic hardships.

[D] The economic recovery will see a higher divorce rate.

【参考译文】 如今的经济危机可能造成了同样多关系已经破灭、感情无可挽回的夫妻。因此，只有当经济再次回暖，我们才能看到已经产生了多少个破碎的家庭。

【解析】 答案为 D。根据题干直接定位至最后一段。最后一句是 "So it's only when the economy is healthy again that we'll begin to see just how many broken families have been created." 这是一个强调句型，强调的是只有当经济再次回暖，我们才会知道产生了多少个破碎的家庭。结合前文所提到的："经济危机之初，不幸福的夫妻因为离不起婚，勉强生活在一起。但一旦经济好转，他们就会离婚。" 因此 D "经济恢复最终会让离婚率上升" 是作者的观点，故选 D。回答有关 infer 提问的推断题，往往要结合文章观点来选择答案。A "一个稳定的家庭是防止贫困最好保护"、B "金钱是许多幸福婚姻的基础" 和 C "几乎没有夫妻能经受经济困难的考验" 都不是这篇文章要表达的观点。

4. 词义推断题

词汇题一般会明确地告诉阅读者出题点在哪里，不需要阅读者查找所考查内容。该题型是阅读测试中较难的题型，考查方式为该词在句子中是什么意思，一个词组是什么意思，或者考一个句子的弦外之音。一般来说，答案不会是单词最基本的意思，而应该是引申的意思或用法，这就需要考生注意语义和语境，并且注意篇章结构及逻辑关系。

常用的猜测词义的方法：

定义法：利用文中的定语、同位语、定义等进行推测。

上下文法：利用上下文之间的结构和逻辑关系进行推测。

符号法：利用一些表示并列关系的标点符号，进行同义词推测。如冒号、分号、破折号等进行推测。

关联词法：如并列关联词或转折词，通过同义词或反义词进行猜测。

构词法：根据单词的前缀、词根、后缀等结构。

排除法：如果直接从文章推断词义比较困难，可以从选项着手，采取排除法。

（1）通过因果关系猜词通过因果关系猜词

首先是找出生词与上下文之间的逻辑关系，然后才能猜词。有时文章借助关联词（如 because，as，since，for，so，thus，as a result，of course，therefore 等）表示前因后果。

例如：You shouldn't have blamed him for that，for it wasn't his fault. 通过 for 引出的句子所表示的原因（那不是他的错），可猜出 blame 的词义是“责备”。

（2）通过同义词和反义词的关系猜词

通过同义词猜词，一是要看由 and 或 or 连接的同义词词组，如 happy and gay，即使我们不认识 gay 这个词，也可以知道它是愉快的意思；二是看在进一步解释的过程中使用的同义词，如 Man has known something about the planets Venus，Mars，and Jupiter with the help of spaceships. 此句中的 Venus（金星）、Mars（火星）、Jupiter（木星）均为生词，但只要知道 planets 就可猜出这几个词都属于“行星”这一义域。

通过反义词猜词，一是看表转折关系的连词或副词，如 but，while，however 等；二是看与 not 搭配的或表示否定意义的词语，如：He is so homely，not at all as handsome as his brother. 根据 not at all... handsome 我们不难推测出 homely 的意思，即不英俊、不漂亮的意思。

（3）通过构词法猜词

根据前缀、后缀、复合、派生等构词知识判断生词词义。如：She is unlikely to have stolen the money.（“un”含否定意义，故为“不太可能”之意。）

（4）通过定义或释义关系来推测词义

例如：But sometimes，no rain falls for a long，long time. Then there is a dry period，or drought. 从 drought 所在句子的上文我们得知很久不下雨，于是便有一段干旱的时期，即 drought，由此可见 drought 意思为“久旱”“旱灾”。而 a dry period 和 drought 是同义语。这种同义或释义关系常由 is，or，that is，in other words，be called 或破折号等来表示。

（5）通过句法功能来推测词义

例如：Bananas，oranges，pineapples，coconuts and some other kind of fruit grow in warm areas. 假如 pineapples 和 coconuts 是生词，我们可以从这两个词在句中所处的位置来判断它们大致的意思。从句中不难看出 pineapples，coconuts 和 bananas，oranges 是同类关系，同属 fruit 类，因此它们是两样水果，准确地说，是菠萝和椰子。

（6）通过描述猜词

描述即作者对该人或该物做出的外在相貌或内在特征的描写。例如：The penguin is a kind of sea bird living in the South Pole. It is fat and walks in a funny way. Although it cannot fly，it can swim in the icy water to catch the fish. 从例句的描述中可以得知 penguin 是一种生活在南极的鸟类。后面更详尽地描述了该鸟类的生活习性。

（7）根据常识猜词

如：The door was so low that he hit his head on the lintel.（lintel“过梁”）

Afraid of waking the baby up, she tiptoed out of the room.（tiptoed“踮着脚走，蹑手蹑脚”）

综上，词义推断题可采用以下做题步骤：

首先根据题目在原文中找出该词汇出现的地方；词汇题的正确答案经常蕴藏在原文该词汇出现的附近，因此要注意单词所在的上下文，尤其是上下句，结合各种猜词技巧理解该单词的含义；如果该词汇是简单词汇，则其字面意思必然不是正确答案，要根据上下文得出其在特定场合更深刻的意思；猜词义时要注意特殊标点、定语从句、构词的前后缀等，例如，冒号前的词汇的意思可以由冒号后的部分归纳，破折号之后词汇的意思可以由破折号之前的部分推测等；如果考察的词语较难，感觉很难有分析的线索时，尝试将确定的答案代入原文，看上下文逻辑是否通顺，如果通顺就是正确答案；如果考句子的含义而导致分析完全没有思路时，不妨结合文章问题来分析，可以体现主题，或与主题的逻辑一致，一般就是答案。

干扰项特点：与所考词汇形似；如果考的是熟词，含有常规词义的往往是错误选项。

例题分析

例题 1

【原文】“Getting the cold shoulder” means that some one is actually in a way that makes you feel unwanted. The very words create a picture: You can imagine a friend turning away so that, instead of a warm greeting, you receive only his shoulder-a “cold” shoulder.

【题目】The expression “getting the cold shoulder” means ________.

[A] being treated rudely by paying no attention to you

[B] greeting you friendly

[C] greeting you by rubbing shoulders with you

[D] feeding you cold meat

【解析】本题考查的是短语“Getting the cold shoulder”的意思，通过信号词 means 可知，后面的内容都是对这一短语的解释，“……意思是有人让你感觉不被需要。这几个词语产生这样一幅画面：你可以想象一个朋友转身离去，而不是热情问候，你接收到的只有他的肩膀，一个‘冰冷’的肩膀”，故选 A“被粗鲁地对待，没有被重视”。

例题 2

【原文】This is the Shadowland of hope, and anyone with a dream must learn to live there.

【题目】“Shadowland” in the last sentence refers to ________.

[A] the wonderland one often dreams about

[B] the bright future that one is looking forward to

[C] the state of uncertainty before one's final goal is reached

[D] a world that exists only in one's imagination

【解析】此题可以利用并列关系来猜测词义。首先，and 后面的句子告诉我们“任何有梦想的人必须要学会在那里生活”，这暗含了“那里”不好的环境。再从 and 可知，两个分句的逻辑是一致的，据此 Shadowland 也应该是不利的环境，故选择 C 项。

5. 态度题

阅读理解中作者的观点、态度题就是指针对作者的写作意图、观点态度和对事件的评价设问的阅读理解题目。在文章中，作者不仅要客观地进行叙述和说明，往往还会明确某种态度，如对某一观点或赞同或反对，或肯定或批评。因此这类题主要考查学生对作者的观点、感情、态度、写作目的和意图的理解能力。常见提问方式有：

What is the tone (mood) of the passage?

The author's attitude towards... might be summarized as (seems to be) ________.

The author is most critical of ________.

What is the opinion of the writer in this passage?

What's the author's attitude towards... ?

What does the author mean by saying "... "?

How does the author feel about... ?

态度题要求能对暗含在文章中人物的行为动机、事件的前因后果及作者未言明的倾向、意图、态度和观点等进行合乎逻辑的分析、判断和推理。题目中常出现以下单词：may, infer, imply, can be learned that, suggest, conclude 等。态度类的问题要从篇章的体裁入手，一般来说，在说明文中作者的态度是客观的（objective）或中立的（neutral），而在议论文中，作者的观点才会显得多种多样。推测态度时，要注意文章中表达态度的褒义词、中性词、贬义词。

褒义词：admiring 令人羡慕的，concerned 关切的，enthusiastic 热情的，humorous 幽默的，interesting 有趣的，optimistic 乐观的，pleasant 愉快的，polite 礼貌的，positive 赞成的，praising 赞扬的，supporting 支持的。

中性词：indifferent 冷漠的，informative 提供信息的，impartial 不偏袒的，impersonal 不带个人感情的，objective 客观的，subjective 主观的。

贬义词：sarcastic 讽刺的，biased 有偏见的，cynical 悲观的，挖苦的，depressed 沮丧的，disappointed 失望的，ironic 讽刺的，negative 否定的，反对的，pessimistic 悲观的，sensitive 敏感的，worried 担忧的。

注意：不要把自己的态度揉入其中，还要注意区分考查是作者的态度还是作者引用别人的态度；当作者的态度没有明确提出时，要学会根据作者在文章中所运用的具有褒贬含义的语言去判断作者的态度，如，wonderfully, successfully, unfortunately, doubtfully 等；某一事物是好是坏，作者对它是支持是反对，态度一般都很明确，而带中立色彩的词最不可能是正确答案。当作者对某事物的态度时，表示“客观”的词多为正确选项，如 objective，impartial，unbiased 等；问作者对文中提到的人物或他们的观点态度时，答案多是肯定或否定，支持或反对。如，critical，approval，opposed，supporting 等；既然作者写了文章，他的态度就不可能是漠不关心的，因此见到 indifferent，uninterested 可以首先排除。

例题分析

例题 1

【原文】 While reformulating recipes（配方）is one way to improve public health，it should be part of a multi-sided approach. The key is to remember that there is not just one solution. To deal with obesity，a mixture of approaches-including reformulation，taxation and adjusting portion sizes-will be needed. There is no silver bullet.

【题目】 What does the author mean by saying，at the end of the passage，“There is no silver bullet”（Line 4，Para 7）?

[A] There is no single easy quick solution to the problem

[B] There is no hope of success without public cooperation

[C] There is on hurry in finding ways to solve the obesity problem

[D] There is no effective way to reduce people's sugar consumption

【参考译文】 尽管重新设计配方是改善公共健康的一种方式，但它应该成为一个多方面举措的一部分。关键是牢记并不是只有一种解决方案。为了应对肥胖，需要一个混合的解决方案，包括重新设计配方、征税和调整各成分含量。万能药是不存在的。

【解析】 由题干中“There is no silver bullet”定位至本段最后一句：To deal with obesity，a mixture of approaches-including reformulation，taxation and adjusting portion sizes-will be needed. There is no silver bullet. 作者在本段提出了改善公共健康需要多方面措施，包括重新设计配方、征税和调整各成分含量等。“There is no silver bullet.”是对第三局的总结和进一步说明，A“该问题没有唯一的轻松快速解决的方案”是对该句最好的解释，故本题答案为 A。B“公众不合作就没有成功的希望”、C“无需着急解决肥胖问题”、D“减少人们对糖的消费没有有效的方式”在原文中均未涉及，故排除。

例题 2

【原文】 Whenever I see anyone buying a National Lottery ticket I want to stop them and ask if they know just where their money is going.

The lottery money is supposed to go to charity-but it makes me angry to see some of the so-called “good causes” it's being used to support. Also，Camelon，the organizers，have made a profit of £ 10. 8 million in five months. We hear now that a lot of that money is boosting the pay packets of the company's bosses.

For the past 10 years I've been helping to raise funds for a cancer research charity called

Tenovus. My husband, Sandy, died from cancer 11 years ago-he was only 51. There's been a long line of deaths in our family through cancer and it's been devastating. I've also lost two sisters-in-law, my brother, Michael, my father-in-law and my father. That's apart from several close friends.

So who really are the winners in the National Lottery When I think of all that money people could be donating to cancer research, I could weep. It's time people realized how charities across the country are suffering because of the National Lottery. It's disheartening and so infuriating.

【题目】 From the text we can conclude that ________.

[A] the writer is enthusiastically supporting the National Lottery.

[B] the writer has objections to the National Lottery.

[C] the writer believes that the Lottery money should be used for cancer research.

[D] the writer is just expressing her feelings about collecting money for charity.

【解析】 通读全文，会找到一些明确表明作者态度的表达，如第一段中的"I want to stop them"，第二段第一句"it makes me angry"，最后一段最后一句"It's disheartening and so infuriating"。

很明显作者的观点是反对国家彩票的，所以A项是错误的；B项是正确的；作者说"彩票收入本应用于慈善事业"，并没有说用于癌症研究。所以C不正确；D项的表述不能概括作者对彩票业与慈善事业关系的看法。故选B。

通过以上对阅读部分的讲解，考生应该熟练运用考试大纲中所列阅读技能，如略读、扫读、跳读等技巧，在平时的阅读训练中要注意各种题型的做题策略。在近年的考试中，阅读理解题型不断变化，较难的主旨类和推理类比重加大。尽管所选材料题材广泛，包罗万象，但其体裁选用和题型设置相对稳定，提问方式大同小异，因而考生可通过熟悉各种题型及其应试策略，提高阅读理解部分的做题正确率。

阅读 B 节　选择搭配

选择搭配

一、命题剖析

PETS 第三级阅读 Part B 是选择搭配题，一般选自报纸、杂志或访谈节目。该题型的设置为五个人就一个相同的话题发表各自的看法，分为五个小段落，一般共 350 词左右。文章后面给出题目，分两部分内容，左边是五个发言人的名字，右边给出七条表述，其中有五条分别概括文章中五个人的观点，另有两条是干扰项。考生要能够从七条表述中选出五条并和相应的人名进行搭配。

从选文题材上看，主要分为两类内容。一类是关于自己在生活中某一方面的经历体验，如“母女关系”“网络购物”等。这类话题贴近生活，文章多带有记叙性质，句式相对较为简单，口语化表达也相对较多。另一类是关于对某事物或现象的看法，如对“成功”“财富”的不同理解。这类话题相对更加正式，用词也相对比较正式。

二、答题指南

根据该题型的特点及近年来的真题分析，选择搭配题出题方式多为主旨题，考察考生对每个段落主旨大意的理解。但也有相当数量的细节题和少量的推理题，打破考生思维惯性，考察其对重要细节的把握。在解题时如果对某主旨题把握不大，考生可以先解答其他相对简单的细节题，而后利用排除法，在剩余选项里再选择主旨题的正确答案。

（一）主旨题

主旨题主要对考生的阅读速度和理解能力做出考察。在做该类题时，考生应采取略读的策略，快速地找到段落的主题句，再将主题句与包含相同关键词的某一条或几条表述进行比较，确定正确答案。主旨题的正确答案通常不包含细节内容，不出现过分肯定或绝对化的词语。

通常来说，主题句会位于段落中如下四个位置：

段落开头。开门见山，在段首给出主题句是英文文章常用的段落结构。在段首给出主题句后，作者将展开细节对主题句所表达思想进行说明论证。

段落结尾。作者首先给出论证说明的细节，然后在段落结尾处给出归纳总结，采用了分总的写作结构。

段落中间。作者段落开头先提出某问题或观点，在对此进行细节性的解释或论证后，提出段落主题，而后进行进一步的解释论证。

段落首尾呼应。作者在段落开头给出主题句，通过细节性解释论证后，在结尾再次点名主题，与开头主题句对应，往往做出进一步引申。

（二）细节题

细节题主要是针对文章具体叙述本身提问，比如事情的时间、地点、过程、原因等。该题型几乎都可以在原文中找到与答案直接相关的信息，或者是其转写。在解答细节题时，考生应该采用略读的方式首先在原文中定位到与某条表述相关的信息，再仔细阅读进行比较，确定是否为正确选项。细节题的正确选项通常会出现对原文的转写，常见方法如下：

1. 同义替换

利用同义词改写原文中的一些关键词，选项包含越多与原文相关的同义词，越可能是正确选项。如：

原文：Something you do effortlessly might pose a great difficulty for a handicapped person.

题目：The efforts of the disabled people deserve greater admiration.

原文中的 handicapped 在题目中被替换成 disabled，两者词义皆为“残疾的”。此外 person 和 people 之间也做了同义词替换。

同义替换不仅仅局限于单词和单词的替换，有时也可能是词组间的替换。如：

原文：In fact, it's the balance of praise along with constructive criticism...

题目：Praise combined with criticism is helpful.

原文中的 along with（随着）在题目中被替换为 combined with（结合），同时题目还省略了原文 constructive（建设性的，积极的）一词，考生要能够识别替换加省略的组合改写方式。

2. 上下义词替换

上义词是对事物的概括性、抽象性说明；下义词是事物的具体表现形式或更为具体的说明。如“水果”一词是较为抽象的概括，“苹果”是更加具体化的一种水果。“水果”是“苹果”的上义词，“苹果”是“水果”的下义词。这种替换方式在阅读考题中也很常见，且通常都是文章中是更加具体的下义词，题目中概括为其上义词。如：

原文：...I would break down my goals, problems and obstacles into little pieces.

题目：I would break down the task to achieve the goal I am passionate about.

原文中的 goals（目标），problems（问题）and obstacles（障碍）在题目中被概括成 task（工作，任务）。

3. 否定/反义词替换

通过具有否定含义的单词或反义词实现原文和题目之间的转写，如：

原文：No longer do the writers spend a fortune...

题目：The writer can save the money of sending copies to...

原文有 spend a fortune（花一大笔钱），题目有 save the money（省钱），这两个词组虽然互为反义，但考生应注意到两个词组同属一个话题词汇，都是关于“钱”，很有可能是反义加否定的改写方式。同时，原文中还包含具有否定含义的词组 no longer（不再），整句话意思为“作者不再花钱”，与题目“作者省钱”是同样含义。

4. 解释替换

用更加具体化的描述对某概念或某行为做出解释。通常来说，文章里多为具体化的解释，题目里是较为概括的表述，如：

原文：You may think it is not important whether your body can bend easily or not, but it is. Stretching your muscles regularly will help you to move effectively.

题目：Regular stretching improves body's flexibility.

原文中 your body can bend easily，move effectively 解释了题目中 body's flexibility 的含义。

此外，原文和题目还可能会做出词性转换（常见有名词、动词、形容词之间的相互转换）、语态转换（主动语态与被动语态）等方式的改写。

（三）推理题

在 Part B 选择搭配中，少数情况下会考查推理，该题型主要考查对原文信息的推理引申。在解答推理题时，考生应结合段落的主题思想和细节信息，综合性地做出推断。推理题的正确选项通常直接表明文章信息，往往以相对间接的方式进行表述。

三、应试技巧

第一步：看。在阅读文章及题目前，考生应先“看一看”题目要求（directions）。题目要求会明确给出考生即将阅读的 5 段文章所涉及的话题。在了解讨论话题后，考生能够调动与此相关联的背景知识，以达到更快更准理解文章和题目表述的目的。

第二步：画。看完 directions 后，考生应跳过文章，看到试题的 7 条表述（statements），“画一画”每条表述的关键词，利用关键词确定文章中相对应的段落。但是考生应注意，题目中的关键词和文章中使用的词汇有极大的可能被进行各种形式的转写。

关键词可以分成两类，第一类是比较容易被找到的数字、时间、人名、地名、特殊符号等。但是考生应注意，数字和时间的写法可能会出现阿拉伯数字和英文单词表述之间的替换；特殊符号也可能和英语单词相替换，比如百分号% 可能被替换成 percent，英镑符号 ¥ 可能被替换成 pound。如果题目表述中没有出现第一类比较容易定位的关键词，则需要用到第二类关键词：表达了句子最重要含义的实义词（不包括主题中心词），或者最具有独特含义、容易被找到的词。通常来说，优先选择名词，因为名词被转写的可能性相对最小。其次是动词和形容词。此外，一些不常用词汇、比较长的单词因使用频率低，不易被替换，也可以成为关键词。

每条表述下给 1－2 个关键词或词组画线即可，不宜过多。在开始阅读文章前先快速记忆划关键词，在阅读过程中如有遗忘，应翻回到题目再次记忆。

第三步：读。“读一读”5 段文章。考生应采用略读的方式，快速浏览一段文章，注意把握文章的主题句和题目表述的关键词，如果找到主题句或关键词相关信息，则可以停下阅读，进入一下步骤。在阅读过程中，对题目所划关键词可能出现的转写，要尤其关注。

第四步：比。在文章中找到题目表述里的关键词信息后，“比一比”题目表示的整体意思与文章是否相符。在这一步骤，考生需重点关注未画线部分的意思在文章中是否出现。如果未画线部分在文章中提及，此选项为正确答案；如未提及，此选项为该段落干扰选项或其他段落答案。如考生能够确定其为干扰项，可直接排除此选项，因为一个干扰项往往只对应一个段落，不会对其他段落再进行干扰。

如果“比一比”之后，考生发现文章中虽然出现了题目某句的关键词，但该句中其他部分的内容未在文章中出现，则应回到文章，继续阅读剩余部分直至再次发现其他关键词信息。

第五步：标。对于已经比对过的选项，考生可在其字母标号上做出三种不同的标记，以利用排除法解答剩余题目。对于十分确定为正确答案的选项，将其标号划去。若某选项为“陷阱”，在其选项标号上划×；在解答其他题目时，标有上述两种记号的选项都可以被排除，这样便缩小了选择范围，降低了题目难度。但如果解题过程中有段落无法找到答案，还是应该再比对一下标有排除符号的选项。如果觉得某选项可能是某段答案，却又不十分确定，可先行进行选择，但在其选项标号上额外加注“?”。在阅读其他段落找不到与之相匹配的正确表述时，可对带有“?”的选项再次进行考量。

Part B 选择搭配题 5 个段落之间既有相关性，又相互独立。考生应阅读完一个段落做出选择后，再阅读下一个段落，逐段解题，不应把文章 5 个段落一起读完再做题。如果阅读完某个段落之后无法确定其正确的选项，可以将这个段落放一放，先阅读后面段落，待其他段落都找出答案后，利用排除法在剩余选项里再进行选择。

四、典型示例：2017 年 3 月真题

Part B Directions:

Read the texts from a magazine article in which five women wrote a response to an article on mother-daughter relationship. For questions 36－40, match the name of each person to one of the statements (A－G) given below. Mark your answers on ANSWER SHEET.

Lucy

As the mother of two girls, I was moved to tears by your article, because it echoed so many of my own feelings. I don't think I should feel ashamed or that I am failing my child in any way because I feel like this. I think it's really normal and I love the way you have put into words what so many mums feel at this stage in their lives.

Anna

My husband and I both read this article and we think it is moving, thoughtful, and the ending is wonderful. People cannot deny that jealousy is a natural emotion between children and parents. It is wonderful to see someone emotionally mature enough to be so aware of their own feelings, and celebrate them. You have written what I am sure most mothers feel, but are too scared to admit.

Beth

There is some form of jealousy between mother and daughter. I remember suspecting that my mother was jealous of me but kept it under wraps. I understood that my mother was not happy with my father and the good relationship between myself and him. The strange thing is years later, my own daughter and her father have a good relationship with each other and I can feel jealousy creeping in.

Clare

When I realized my daughter had become a young woman, I was not jealous. At first I felt sad that I had lost my little girl, then I accepted this and rejoiced in her loveliness. I feel protective towards her because it is too natural for young girls to meet men. Offer your child advice on things like wearing fancy clothes which men do see as charming, and hope that she enjoys her life.

Ruth

I think that a mature person judges herself based on her own qualities. A loving mother does not compare herself to her children and advertise her unhealthy thoughts to the world in a newspaper. I am surrounded all day at work by hot, smart young undergraduates, many of whom are hotter and smarter than I was at their age. When they succeed socially and academically, I feel happy for them.

Now match the name of each person (36 – 40) to the appropriate statement.

Note: there are two extra statements.

Statements

36. Lucy
37. Anna
38. Beth
39. Clare
40. Ruth

[A] You have spoken out the true feelings of mothers like me.
[B] It is helpful for mothers to reveal their hidden feelings.
[C] Emotionally mature mothers understand their daughters.
[D] I understand my mother now, being a mother myself.
[E] You have expressed what most mothers feel but dare not say.
[F] Do your duty as a mother and hope for the best for your daughter.
[G] A mother should not envy her children and make public her improper feelings.

【解析】

解答该题时，可以按照“看、画、读、比、标”的步骤进行。首先，看一看题目要求（Direction）：Read the texts from a magazine article in which five women wrote a response to an article on mother-daughter relationship。由此，考生可以得知文章来源是杂志（a magazine article），5 个人讨论的话题是关于母女关系（mother-daughter relationship）。基于这个信息，考生可以调动与母女关系、家庭关系等相关的储备知识。

然后，考生应该跳过 5 段文章，看到题目区域。左侧的 5 个人名跳过不看以节省时间，看到右侧 7 条表述，画取关键词（词组）。画取的时候注意避免文章的主题词，即和母女关系相关的词语，因为这些词语作为文章的中心可能会多次多处出现，不利于考生进行匹配。

[A] You have spoken out the true feelings of mothers like me. 此条表述没有人名、地名、时间、数字等比较容易寻找的第一类关键词（分类见上文），那么考生只能关注第二类关键词，即表达句子最实质、最中心的含义的词语，词性选择顺序依次为名词、动词、形容词。根据句意：你说出了像我这样的母亲们的真实感受，可画取 true feelings 作为关键词。

[B] It is helpful for mothers to reveal their hidden feelings. 选取关键词标准和依据同上，后文不再重复阐述。根据句意：这有助于母亲们透露出她们隐藏着的感受，可画取 reveal their hidden feelings 作为关键词。

[C] Emotionally mature mothers understand their daughters. 根据句意：情感成熟的母亲们能够理解她们的女儿，可画取 emotionally mature 作为关键词。为了减少关键词数量，方便考生短时间记忆，understand their daughters 在这一步时可不画为关键词，待文章中发现 emotionally mature 相关表述时，再在周围寻找这一词组。

[D] I understand my mother now, being a mother myself. 根据句意：自己做了母亲后，我现在能够理解我的母亲了，understand my mother 和 being a mother myself 都可以作为关键词。但是 understand my mother 表达意思相对没有那么具体，初步判断在文章中比较难定位，因此选择 being a mother myself 作为关键词。

[E] You have expressed what most mothers feel but dare not say. 根据句意：你表达了大多数母亲不敢说出口的感受，画取 dare not say 作为关键词。

[F] Do your duty as a mother and hope for the best for your daughter. 根据句意：承担作为母亲的责任，希望能够为女儿做到最好，画取 duty as a mother，hope for the best 作为关键词。

[G] A mother should not envy her children and make public her improper feelings. 根据句意：一个母亲不应该嫉妒自己的女儿，不应该把她不适感受公之于众，画取 not envy her children，make public her improper feelings 作为关键词。

关键词画取完毕后，考生应快速记忆关键词，然后开始读文章。读完一段或者一部分，可以再回到题目再次进行记忆，如此反复。在阅读时，考生不需要逐字逐句仔细地阅读、理解，重点应抓取段落主旨句及题目关键词。

第 36 题 Lucy（第一段）：

主旨题。该段第一句为主旨句，其中 feelings 可提示考生选项 A 、B、E、G，几个选项都包含 feelings（E 选项中动词 feel 也视为 feelings）。经过进一步比对，发现选项 A 中，feelings of mothers like me 对应文章 my own feelings ，spoken out（说出）对应 echoed（回应）。选项 A 的主要信息在这段文章中基本找到了相对应的部分，因此 36 题答案为 A。

第 37 题 Anna（第二段）：

主旨题。按照从前往后的阅读顺序，考生可能会先注意到该段中 emotionally mature（情感成熟）在选项 C 中出现。但仔细寻找后发现选项 C 的后半部分 understand their daughters（理解她们的女儿），该段文章中相对应的内容为 aware of their own feelings（察觉到自己的感受），两处内容不符，因此可以排除选项 C，并画上排除符号。但如果解题过程中有段落无法找到答案，还是应该再比对一下标有排除符号的选项。

最后一句为该段主旨句，其中 what I am sure most mothers feel 对应选项 E 中 what most mothers feel，文章中 but are too scared to admit 对应选项 E 中 but dare not say，两处的转折都用了转折词 but，并未改写。句间关系词考生应加以注意，即使是经过转写，句子之间的逻辑关系也不会改变，可以成为一个重要的提示点。因此 37 题答案为 E。

第 38 题 Beth（第三段）：

主旨题。第一句是主旨句，表明母女之间有某种形式的嫉妒。后文进一步具体讲述了 Beth 作为女儿和作为母亲对父女关系亲密的不同感受。选项 G 有 jealousy 同义词 envy（嫉妒），但 envy 前有否定词 not，且后半句 make public her improper feelings 与该段主题不符，因此可以暂时排除选项 G。其余选项里暂时没有找到与该段主旨相符的内容，可以先搁置该段，最后用排除法解答。

此题考点在该段的最后一句，文章中 my own daughter 对应选项 D 中 being a mother myself ，文章中 I can feel jealousy creeping in（悄悄混进）对应该选项 I understand my mother now（我现在能够理解我妈妈当年对我和爸爸关系亲密的嫉妒）。因此 38 题答案为 D。

第 39 题 Clare（第四段）：

细节题。该段第一句是主旨句，提出母亲因女儿年轻而嫉妒。第二句中 at first，then 等词是常见的细节展开词汇，考生在阅读时应一带而过。最后一句提出解决办法：给孩子一些建议，希望女儿能够享受生活。这是一个十分标准的论证段落，先提出观点或问题，然后进行分析论证，最后提出解决办法。

考生在解题时根据第一句 jealous 一词会关注到选项 G，但是该选项并未表述本段主旨或细节，具体原因在 38 题已经分析，此处不再重复。本题的考点比较隐蔽，考生可以将该段暂时搁置，最后用排除法解题。

选项 F 对应本段最后一句，do your duty as a mother（承担起做母亲的职责）对应文章 offer your child advice（给你的孩子提出建议），hope for the best for your daughter（希望你的女儿能得到最好的）对应文章 hope that she enjoys her life（希望她能享受人生）。因此本题答案为 F。

第 40 题 Ruth（第五段）：

主旨题。文章第一句是主旨句，提出一个成熟的人应该根据自身素质对自己做出评判。第二句对其做了进一步解释，一个有爱的母亲不会拿自己和孩子做比较，也不会把孩子不健康的想法公之于众，对应选项 G，一个母亲不应该嫉妒自己的女儿，不应该把她不适感受公之于众。文章中 A loving mother does not compare herself to her children 对应选项 G. A mother should not envy her children，文章 advertise her unhealthy thoughts to the world 对应该选项 make public her improper feelings。本题虽然能够在文章里找到完整相对应的句子，但转写程度较高，难以识别，具有一定难度。因此本题答案为 G。

阅读 C 节　补全文章

补全文章

一、命题剖析

笔试的第三部分是补全短文，在一篇约 350 词的文章中留出 5 处空白，要求考生从文后所给的 7 句话中选出 5 个符合语法知识、逻辑结构和前后内容衔接的选项，补充到原文画线的填充处，使原文成为一篇意思通顺、前后连贯的短文，“七选五”其实跟传统题型完形填空有相似之处，完形填空空出的是词，而七选五空出的是句子或段落，但是它们的考察方式都是一样的，只要考生选择的答案能够使行文连贯，符合英文的语法及习惯表达就行，因此，这两类题型在做题方法上有共通之处。

这类题本意是要考查较高的阅读能力、基础知识（语法、词汇等）和综合逻辑思维推理能力，以及理解文章结构和单句之间、段落之间的关系的能力，难度较大，各选项环环相扣，选错了一个至少错两个甚至更多，因此是最令人头痛的题型。

空白处在文中的位置有 3 种，即段首、段中和段尾。根据英语短文的特点，主题句一般在句首和句尾，因而空白处在句首出现时，考查考生对掌握和概括短落大意的能力；空白处出现在句中时，考查考生把握上下文之间意义联系的能力；空白处出现在段尾时，考查考生掌握和概括段落大意的能力，或是根据已读材料进行推理和判断的能力。另外，补全短文的文章体裁多样，有记叙文也有说明文。从历年考题来看，空白处几乎都设置于段中或段尾，可见主要是考查考生把握上下文之间意义联系的能力，或是根据已读材料进行推理和判断的能力，因此考生要学会利用上下文寻找解题的线索。

二、应试技巧

（一）做题思路

从分析题型知道，这类题其实是前两类考题即第一部分阅读理解和第二部分概括大意连线搭配题的综合，它考查的是找出各选项在原文的出处，并且这个出处已经确定了 5 个填充处给予选择。所以，做前两类题的步骤和技巧，特别是思路和逻辑推理方法，在这类题中运用更合适、更能体现和更能发挥得淋漓尽致。

另外，从该题型给出的选项中我们可以发现一些特点：该题型选项大致可分为主旨概括句段（文章整体内容）、过渡性句段（文章结构）和注释性句段（上下文逻辑意义、举例子）三类。另外两个多余的干扰项也可以通过这三个特点来排除，例如主旨概括句段要么过于宽泛要么以偏概全或偏离主题，过渡性句段不能反映文章的行文结构，注释性句段与上文脱节等。

针对这类题的要求和特点：是要在 7 个选项句子中分别选出 5 个符合语法知识、逻辑结构和前后内容意思衔接的选项，补充到原文画线的填充处（是在某段落之前、之后或两句子之中），使原文成为一篇意思完整、前后连贯的短文。根据其要求与特点，有的放矢，我们运用综合分析排除法来选出正确的答案：一是不“符合语法知识”的排除，二是不“符合逻辑结构”的排除，三是不能使填充处“前后内容衔接、意思连贯”的排除。

要正确运用这些方法，当然能通读并读懂原文最好，但对部分考生来说很难做到，我们的思路总是要化复杂为简单、化难为易、化大为小来做题，所以，我们要把短文化为句子、句子化为单词来做，这样就简单得多了。因此，做这类题的重点，一是选项句子，而选项句子重点是它的中心词，包括名词、代词和连接词，这三种词是我们必须重视的，也是我们了解该选项句子意思运用上述三种方法的前提；二是填充处的前后段或前后句子，弄清楚这个填充处所在位置的意义及其前后段或前后句子的逻辑关系和内容意思，也是运用上述方法的前提。

（二）做题方法

1. 分析选项句子

首先快速浏览全文，了解全文主旨大意。然后分析选项，找出各选项句子的中心词，包括名词、代词和连接词，这三种词是我们了解该选项句子意思关键点。根据各选项句子的大概意思，初步设想一下它们最有可能的位置和彼此顺序。另外，通过阅读选项，有可能找出跟其他选项表达完全不同意思的句子或段落，这样的话我们就可以直接将该选项排除。

2. 重点看填充处的前后段或前后句子

按顺序了解填充处前后段或前后句子的逻辑关系和大概内容意思。这也是类似于找中心句子与中心词的方法，找出前后段最接近填充处的句子的中心词（名词、代词和连接词），或者找出填充处前后句子的中心词，了解其大概意思和相互间的逻辑关系。弄清楚这个填充处所在位置的意义以及其前后段或前后句子的逻辑关系和内容意思，再化复杂为简单、化难为易、化大为小来做题。由于“七选五”空出的是整个句子或段落，而这些句段之间，必然有一种联系，因此我们可以通过选项中某个名词或动词跟空前或空后的一致性或者逻辑相关性来确定这两个句段之间有一种关联性，从而选择正确的答案。

3. 直接分析排除

把选项句子中心词及其大意与填充处前后段或前后句子的逻辑关系及大意进行对照，综合分析排除，一是不“符合语法知识”的排除，二是不“符合逻辑结构”的排除，三是不能使填充处“前后内容衔接、意思连贯”的排除。最后理顺并最终确定最有可能的选项或直接确定答案，并把确定了的答案把它划去和把最有可能的选项写到填充处，无论能否确定答案，都要接着往下做下一个填空处，以此类推。因为这类题是7选5，基本上是一个萝卜一个坑，每个选项最多只能用一次，并且基本上都必须用上，所以，不能确定最后唯一答案时，基本上可以通过做其他的填充处，甚至到最后把所有的填充处综合起来推敲，也可以确定各填充处的答案，因此，不要急于求成，困死在某一个填充处上。

4. 通读整句或整段来检查是否选定的答案与原文在语法和语义上都相一致

综上所述，这部分题目的解答既要注意所填部分与原句在语义上的匹配，同时还要注意所填部分与原句前后在语法上的匹配。

5. 注意代词或定冠词

在做这类题目的时候，一定要注意文中出现的人称代词或者指示代词，因为我们知道，代词是指代一个名词或者一个句子的，然后通过代词在句子中所做的成分我们可以推断出它指代的内容，我们要做的就是从选项中找出含有相应内容的句段。

6. 注意特殊疑问词

如果选项中或空前出现特殊疑问词，一定要把这句话仔细读几遍，因为对于不同特殊疑问词的回答方式是不一样的，比如对 why 的回答，后面要有 because 等表原因的词；对 when 的回答，后面要有表时间的状语；对 where 的回答，后面要有表地点的名词；对 how 的回答，后面要有方式状语等。

7. 注意关系连词

一些表示转折的连词如 but，however，yet，though，nevertheless 等，另外还有一些表示并列关系的连词如 and，also，as well as，neither... nor，either... or，not only... but also，on one hand... ，on the other hand 等。通过不同的连词我们可以推知句段与句段之间不同的逻辑关系，从而找出在最符合行文逻辑的正确选项。

（三）常见的段落内部及段落之间的逻辑关系

常见的段落内部及段落之间的逻辑关系分为以下几种：顺承关系、转折关系、比较或对照关系、列举或举例关系。

顺承关系是指前后两个句子在意思上是相承或并列的。后句延续前一句的内容或是对其进行补充或进一步阐述。标志词：besides，further，moreover，in addition，furthermore，also，not only... but also，and then 等。

因果关系即前面叙述内容是引起后面内容的原因，即前因后果，或前果后因。标志词：so，because，as，thus，since，for，due to，therefore，so that，hence，in that，accordingly，consequently，as a result，as a consequence，result from，result in 等。

转折关系即前后两种观点或事实意思相反。标志词有：but，however，yet，although，though，nevertheless，despite 等。

比较、对照关系即比较强调意义上的相似性，对照侧重前后两方面意义上的不同或相反。标志词有 likewise，at the same time，in the same way，in comparison，in contrast， instead, unlike, just as, rather than, on the contrary, on the other hand, whereas 等。

列举、举例关系主要通过列举事实或论据论证某一观点。标志词有 for example, for instance, for one thing, for another 等。

了解选项的特点，更有利于我们选对答案，判断方法；在标记了原文与选项的关键词以后，可以按照下列原则判断原文的空与选项是否匹配：

词汇衔接：正确选项中的关键词一般重复前一句的关键词，也与下一句的关键词相呼应；

逻辑衔接：正确选项与原文空之前的句子在逻辑上是连贯的，例如，前一句使用 although，那么正确选项的内容应该与之相反；

代词衔接：正确选项中代词之后的关键词一定在原文的前一句谈论过，例如，如果选项中说 this reward，而且这一选项是正确答案，那么原文中的空之前的句中一定出现过 reward 这个词或它的同义词。

另外，正确选项有如下特点：复现，包括同义反复、反义反复、上下义反复；错误选项有如下特点：以偏概全，扩大范围，偏离主题。

三、典型示例

例题 1

On the north bank of the Ohio river sits Evansville, Ind., home of David Williams, 52, and of a riverboat casino (a place where gambling games are played). During several years of gambling in that casino, Williams a state auditor earning $ 35, 000 a year, lost approximately $ 175, 000. He had never gambled before the casino sent him a coupon for $ 20 worth of gambling.

He visited the casino, lost the $ 20 and left. On his second visit he lost $ 800. The casino issued to him, as a good customer, a "Fun Card", which when used in the casino earns points for meals and drinks, and enables the casino to track the user's gambling activities. For Williams, these activities become what he calls "electronic heroin".

(1) ________________. In 1997 he lost $ 21, 000 to one slot machine in two days. In March 1997 he lost $ 72, 186. He sometimes played two slot machines at a time, all night, until the boat locked at 5 a. m, then went back aboard when the casino opened at 9 a. m. Now he is suing the casino, charging that it should have refused his patronage because it knew he was addicted. It did know he had a problem.

In March 1998, a friend of Williams's got him involuntarily confined to a treatment center for addictions, and wrote to inform the casino of Williams's gambling problem. The casino included a photo of Williams among those of banned gamblers, and wrote to him a "cease admissions" letter. Noting the "medical/psychological" nature of problem gambling behaviors, the letter said that before being readmitted to the casino he would have to present medical/psychological information demonstrating that patronizing the casino would pose no threat to his safety or well-being.

(2) ________________. The Wall Street Journal reports that the casino has 20 signs warning, "Enjoy the fun and always bet with your head, not over it." Every entrance ticket lists a toll-free number for counseling from the Indiana Department of Mental Health. Nevertheless, Williams's suit charges that the casino, knowing he was "helplessly addicted to gambling," intentionally worked to "lure" him to "engage in conduct against his will." Well.

(3) ________________. The fourth edition of the Diagnostic and Statistical Manual of Mental Disorders says "pathological gambling" involves president, recurring and uncontrollable pursuit less of money than of the thrill of taking risks in quest of a windfall.

(4) ________________. Pushed by science, or what claims to be science, society is reclassifying what once were considered character flaws or moral failings as personality disorders skin to physical disabilities.

(5) ________________. Forty-four states have lotteries, 29 have casinos, and most of these states are to varying degrees dependent on - you might say addicted to - revenues from wagering. And since the first Internet gambling site was created in 1995, competition for gambler's dollars has become intense. The Oct. 28 issue of Newsweek reported that 2 million gamblers patronize 1, 800 virtual cosines every week, with $ 3. 5 billion being lost on Internet wagers this year, gambling has , passed pornography as the webs' most profitable business.

[A] Although no such evidence was preserved, the casino's marketing department continued to pepper him with mailings. And he entered the casino ad used his Fun Card without being detected.

[B] It is unclear what luring was required, given his compulsive behavior. And in what sense was his will operative?

[C] By the time he had lost $ 5, 000, he said to himself that if he could get back to even, he would quit, one night he won $ 5, 500, but he did not quit.

[D] Gambling has been a common feature of American life forever, but for a long time it was broadly considered a sin, or a social disease. Now it is a social policy, the most important and aggressive promoter of gambling in America is the government.

[E] David Williams suit should trouble this gambling nation. But don't bet on it.

[F] It is worrisome that society is medicalizing more and more behavioral problems, often defining as addiction what earlier, sterner generations explained as weakness of will.

[G] The anonymous, lonely, undistracted nature of online gambling is especially conductive to compulsive behavior. But even if the government knew how to more against

Internet gambling, what would be its grounds for doing so?

【解析】

做题步骤：

首先，标记空前、后句中的关键词。

本文以 Williams 为例，讨论赌博的危害性。各个空前后句的关键词标记如下：

空前：名词词组 electronic morphine（电子吗啡，意思是上瘾），数字 20、800；空后：数字 21，000 等。说明空中要填入的选项可能包含数字，并且描述了赌博上瘾的情况。

名词 letter 等。说明空中要填入的选项可能包含 letter 或其同义词。

引号中的关键词：lure，conduct against his will.

关键词：diagnostic，mental disorder，pathological 说明空中要填入的选项可能涉及与医学有关的行为。

空后句中的关键词：forty-five states 说明空中要填入的选项可能涉及政府行为。而且 forty-five states 是具体说明，那么它前面的空应该是总论政府的行为。

其次，标记选项中的关键词。

[A]"such evidence""mailings""Such evidence"说明空的前一句可能提到过一种 evidence（证据），选项中的 continued to pepper him with mailings 说明空的前一句提到过 mailings（写信）一类的东西。

[B] luring，will. What luring 说明 luring 或其同义词在前一句出现过。His will 说明 will 或其同义词在前一句出现过。

[C] 数字 5，000；赌博上瘾（did not quit）。说明前一句可能提到数字，而且涉及赌博上瘾的说明。

[D] common feature；social policy；government.

[E] David Williams's suit；this gambling nation.

[F] medicalizing more and more behavioral problems. more and more 说明空前已经以医疗方式（medicalizing）处理过类似问题。

[G] online gambling.

再次，比较两类关键词。

将 7 个选项的关键词与 5 个空的前后句中的关键词进行比较，发现匹配的是：1 与 C、2 与 A、3 与 B、4 与 F、5 与 D。

最后，代入原文。

将确定的选项代入原文，发现意义上与逻辑上都通顺，因此为正确答案。

具体分析如下：

1. C　文章前三段讲述威廉姆斯染上毒瘾的全过程。前两段描述了他的赌博经历，其中第二段提到他分别输掉了 20 美元的优惠券及 800 美元，第三段空格后又提到他分别输掉了 2.1 万美元和 72186 美元，这些数字越来越大，从侧面表明他的毒瘾越来越大。空格前后都与威廉姆斯赌博的具体例证有关，前后文信息中出现了大量的数字，由此可推断需填入的部分与他输赢的数目有关。选项中只有 C 项出现数字 5000、5500 美元，恰好介于前后数字 800 美元和 21000 美元之间，内容与上下文衔接合理，故为答案。

2. A　空格前一段是针对第三段末提到的“It did know he had a problem”“赌场早就知道威廉姆斯有问题”而提出的证据。该段末提到如果威廉姆斯要再次进入赌场，就必须出示生理和心理状况的相关信息（present... information），以证明光顾赌场不会对他的安全和健康带来任何威胁。浏览选项，可发现 A 项与第四段末的句子存在词义复现，如 present 和 evidence 等；且 A 项开头的 such evidence 与空格前的 medical/psychological information 形成合理的指代关系。故答案为 A。

3. B　第六段提到赌场虽然有张贴劝人理性赌博的启示，但威廉姆斯控告赌场暗地里却鼓励他这个已经无法自拔的人继续赌博；第八段则从医学的角度来分析“病态赌博行为”，故推测第七段的内容应与强制性行为和病态赌博有关。空格前一句提到了威廉姆斯对赌船的指控，即明知他赌博成瘾，但仍“引诱”（lure）他继续从事违反他意愿（will）的行为。B 选项中有出现 lure，his will 等词，且内容上也衔接合理，故为答案。F 项也出现了相关词汇 will，但该项中的“将行为问题医疗化”在上下文找不到所指，故排除。G 项出现相关词 compulsive behavior “强迫性行为”，看似与上文对应，但该项论述的重点是“网络赌博”，在上下文也找不出所指。

4. F　上一段提到了“病态赌博行为”，而空格后则提到社会现在把从前是性格或道德的缺陷说成是类似于生理缺陷的人格障碍。因此空格处应该是对赌博行为的分析。空格前一段提到了 pathological gambling 的定义；空格后一句讲：社会正把从前被视为性格或道德的缺陷重新定义（society is reclassifying... as...）。F 项的结构与这一句惊人的一致：（society is medicalizing... often defining as...）。词汇上也有诸多同义复现，如：behavioral problems 对应 personality disorders，而 earlier 与 once 对应，weakness of will 与 character flaws or moral failings 对应。由此可确定答案为 F。

5. 空格前说到社会正重新定义一些现象；空格后提到各州都不同程度地依赖来自彩票和赌场的收益。前后都是关于 society “社会”和 states “州政府”的行为，空格处的内容应与此有关。D 项、F 项和 G 项都是政府行为，分别有 government 和 society 的关键词复现，可视为备选项。D 项首句提到 Gambling has been a common feature；后一句提到美国政府是赌博的最大推动者，内容上能承前启后，故 D 为答案。

F 项在内容上能承前，却不能启后。而 G 项与 Internet gambling 有关，最后一段第二句出现 since the first Internet gambling 这些字眼，这表明 G 项应该在最后一段之后出现，故可排除。

【参考译文】

52 岁的大卫·威廉姆斯居住在印第安纳州的埃文斯威乐城，该城坐落在俄亥俄河的北岸，河上有一条赌船。就在这条赌船上，威廉姆斯这位年薪 35,000 美元的州审计员几年下来在赌场中输掉了近175,000美元。而在赌场送给他一张20美元赌资的优惠券之前他从未沾染过赌博。

他去了赌场，输掉了这20美元，然后离开了。第二次去赌场，他输掉了800美元。作为优质顾客，他得到一张赌场发给他的"游乐卡"。这种卡在赌场使用时可积分换食物和饮料，使赌场可以跟踪记录使用者的赌博活动。威廉姆斯把赌博行为称之为"电子海洛因"。

(1)［C］输到5,000美元时，他对自己说，如果能够赢回来，他就不赌了。一天晚上他赢了5,500美元，但是却没有停下来。1997年，他曾经有一次在两天之内在同一台老虎机上输掉了21,000美元。1997年3月份他输掉了72,186美元。他有时候同时玩两台老虎机，通宵不归，直到早晨5点赌船关门，然后等赌场9点开放时再回来。现在他正在起诉赌场，指责其既然知道他上瘾却没有拒绝他的光顾。赌场确实知道他有问题。

1998年3月，一个朋友将威廉姆斯强制送进了戒瘾治疗中心接受治疗，并书面告知赌场威廉姆斯的赌博问题。赌场当即将威廉姆斯的照片列入被禁赌人员之中，并给他写了一封"禁止进入赌场"的信。在说明赌博行为本质上对人生理和心理所造成的危害的同时，信中还指出，如果要再次进入赌场，他必须出示生理和心理状况的相关信息，证明光顾赌场不会对他的安全和健康造成任何威胁。

(2)［A］尽管他没有提交此类相关证明，赌场的营销部仍然不断给他寄送大量的宣传材料，他又上了赌船，并且使用了"游乐卡"，可是谁也没有抓住他。根据《华尔街日报》报道，赌场有20个警示标志："享受乐趣……赌博时要理智，不能失控"，每张门票上都有来自印第安纳州心理健康部门的免费咨询电话。然而威廉姆斯案起诉赌场明明知道他"不可救药地沉迷于赌博"，仍然故意"引诱"他"做出违背自己意愿的行为"。说得好。

(3)［B］考虑到他做出的这种强迫性冲动行为，我们不清楚到底是什么样的诱惑。在何种意识下他的意志力才起作用？《心理障碍诊断统计手册》第四版指出，"病理性赌博"指持续反复且无法自控地追求与其说是钱，倒不如说是刺激的行为，即甘冒风险以少量金钱去博取一笔横财的刺激的行为。

(4)［F］令人不安的是，社会正在用医学方法处理越来越多的行为问题，而过去更为严厉的前辈们将其解释为意志力薄弱，此问题现在常常被定义为"沉溺症"。在科学或者所谓"科学"的推动下，社会将曾经我们所认为的性格缺陷，道德过失重新归类为类似于生理障碍的"性格疾病"。

(5)［D］赌博一直是美国人生活的普遍特征，但是长期以来，它被普遍认为是一种罪过或者一种社会疾病。现在赌博却成为一种社会政策：在美国，对赌博最重要、最积极的推动者就是政府。44个州发行彩票，有29个州开赌场，而且这些州中大多数不同程度地依赖（可能你会说是"沉迷于"）赌博收入。自1995年第一个在线赌博网站建立以来，争夺赌徒们的钱的竞争变得越来越激烈。据《新闻周刊》10月28日报道，每周有 200 万个赌徒光顾 1,800 个虚拟赌场。今年赌徒们在网络赌博中输掉 35 亿美元，赌博成为网络上超过色情的最有利可图的行业。

例题 2

The time for sharpening pencils, arranging your desk, and doing almost anything else instead of writing has ended. The first draft will appear on the page only if you stop avoiding the inevitable and sit, stand up, or lie down to write. (1) ________________

Be flexible. Your outline should smoothly conduct you from one point to the next, but do not permit it to railroad you. If a relevant and important idea occurs to you now, work it into the draft. (2) ________________ Grammar, punctuation, and spelling can wait until you revise. Concentrate on what you are saying. Good writing most often occurs when you are in hot pursuit of an idea rather than in a nervous search for errors.

(3) ________________ Your pages will be easier to keep track of that way, and, if you have to clip a paragraph to place it elsewhere, you will not lose any writing on the other side. If you are working on a word processor, you can take advantage of its capacity to make additions and deletions as well as move entire paragraph by making just a few simple keyboard commands. Some software programs can also check spelling and certain grammatical elements in your writing. (4) ________________ These printouts are also easier to read than the screen when you work on revision.

Once you have a first draft on paper, you can delete material that is unrelated to your thesis and add material necessary to illustrate your points and make your paper convincing. The student who wrote The A&P as a State of Mind wisely dropped a paragraph that questioned whether Sammy displays chauvinistic attitudes toward women. (5) ________________

Remember that your initial draft is only that. You should go through the paper many times-and then again-working to substantiate and clarify your ideas. You may even end up with several entire versions of the paper. Rewrite. The sentences within each paragraph should be related to a single topic. Transitions should connect one paragraph to the next so that there are no abrupt or confusing shifts. Awkward or wordy phrasing or unclear sentences and paragraphs should be mercilessly poked and prodded into shape.

[A] To make revising easier, leave wide margins and extra space between lines so that you can easily add words, sentences, and corrections. Write on only one side of the paper.

[B] After you have clearly and adequately developed the body of your paper, pay particular attention to the introductory and concluding paragraphs. It's probably best to write the introduction last, after you know precisely what you are introducing. Concluding paragraphs demand equal attention because they leave the reader with a final impression.

[C] It's worth remembering, however, that though a clean copy fresh off a printer may look terrific, it will read only as well as the thinking and writing that have gone into it. Many writers prudently store their data on disks and print their pages each time they finish a draft to avoid losing any material because of power failures or other problems.

[D] It makes no difference how you write, just so you do. Now that you have developed a topic into a tentative thesis, you can assemble your notes and begin to flesh out whatever outline you have made.

[E] Although this is an interesting issue, it has nothing to do with the thesis, which explains how the setting influences Sammy's decision to quit his job. Instead of including that paragraph, she added one that described Lengel's crabbed response to the girls so that she could lead up to the A&P policy he enforces.

[F] In the final paragraph about the significance of the setting in A&P, the student brings together the reasons Sammy quit his job by referring to his refusal to accept Lengel's store policies.

[G] By using the first draft as a means of thinking about what you want to say, you will very likely discover more than your notes originally suggested. Plenty of good writers don't use outlines at all but discover ordering principles as they write. Do not attempt to compose a perfectly correct draft the first time around.

【解析】

1. D　空格前面的句子“The first draft will appear on the page only if you stop avoiding the inevitable and sit, stand up, or lie down to write”告诉读者如果写文章时只要作者不再试图避免一些事情，不管你是站着、坐着还是躺着写作，第一稿就会跃然纸上。空格后面的句子“Be flexible. Your outline should smoothly conduct you from one point to the next, but do not permit it to railroad you”中出现了新的信息：outline（提纲），因此从前后文的语义关系来看，下文中可能会出现和 outline 相关的内容。对比选项，D 选项提到用什么方式来写作不重要，重要的是定下一个题目，然后可以通过整理笔记来填充你的 outline（提纲），在语义上，此选项和空格前面提到的坐着写、站着写、躺着呼应，同时词汇 outline 在试题中复现，因此可以确定是正确答案。

2. G　空格前面的句子“If a relevant and important idea occurs to you now, work it into the draft”主要叙述了如何把 idea（思想）转化为 draft（草稿），语义主要集中在 idea 和 draft 上面。空格后面的句子“Grammar, punctuation, and spelling can wait until you revise. Concentrate on what you are saying. Good writing most often occurs when you are in hot pursuit of an idea rather than in a nervous search for errors”强调的内容同样是写作中思想的重要性：when you are in hot pursuit of an idea rather than in a nervous search for errors（找到一个好的想法，而不是去纠正其中的错误）。因此，要填入的内容或表达的重点应当是 idea 或者是文中出现的 what you are saying。对比选项可以发现，选项 G 的首句话“By using the first draft as a means of thinking about what you want to say”复现了前文中的 draft，同时又复现了后文中的“Concentrate on what you are saying”，因此 G 选项是

正确答案。

3. A　空格后面的句子“Your pages will be easier to keep track of that way, and, if you have to clip a paragraph to place it elsewhere, you will not lose any writing on the other side.”中出现了 that way，所以上文中会说到具体的哪种方式，同时本句话的后半部分叙述的是文章的修改问题。因为这句话是并列结构，因此句中的 that way 指代的内容应当是这句话后半部分表达的“对文章的修改”。同时，that way 所指代的内容要体现在试题中。对比选项，选项 A“To make revising easier, leave wide margins and extra space between lines so that you can easily add words, sentences, and corrections. Write on only one side of the paper.”中提到了对文章修改的信息，和下文叙述的内容一致，文章的语义连贯，是正确答案。

4. C　空格后面提到“These printouts are also easier to read than the screen when you work on revision”（修改的时候，看打印出来的材料比看电脑屏幕容易）。限定词 these 修饰的单词 printouts（打印出来的东西）一定会出现在试题中。对比选项，C 选项中很明显地有同现词 copy 还有 printer，它们对应下文中所提及的打印出来的材料，因此是正确答案。

5. E　前文提到 Sammy 这个人，这是一个线索词，选项中 E 和 F 中都包含这个词，但是此段的主题句提到“you can delete material that is unrelated to your thesis”在写作中要删去与主题不相关的素材，E 选项中的“instead of including that paragraph,”也就意味着删去了这段，和主题句对应。而 F 选项只是在说最后一段的具体内容，和本段的主题句不相关，故不符合题意。

【参考译文】

削铅笔，整理桌子，你做这做那就是不动笔写，可是到头来还得写。坐也好，站也罢，躺也行，只有停止徒劳的拖延，开始动笔写，初稿才会呈现在纸上。（1）［D］<u>其实怎么写并不重要，关键是你要付诸笔端。既然已经把主题扩展为一个初步的命题，下面要做的就是整理笔记，不管你的现有提纲是怎样的，开始着手充实它吧。</u>

要灵活变通。列提纲应该是指导你从一个观点顺利过渡到另一个观点，但不是让你不越雷池半步。如果脑子里突然闪现出一个重要的相关观点，那就把它写进文稿中去。（2）［G］<u>把初稿当作思考的媒介，看看你究竟想要表达什么内容，这样你很可能会发现一些最初做笔记时未想到的东西。有很多优秀的作家根本不用提纲，而是边写边组织。别指望第一稿就写出完美无瑕的佳作。</u>语法、标点符号和拼写问题可以等到修改阶段来处理。专注于你想表达的内容；通常的情况是，当你热衷于探究某个观点，而不是紧张地寻找错误时，方可产生佳作。

（3）［A］<u>为了修改方便，页边空白和行距应留得大一些，以便添加词语、句子，或进行修改。稿纸只写一面。</u>这样更方便检索页码。如果你得剪掉某一段粘贴到别处去，稿纸背面的内容也不会因此丢失。如果你用文字处理软件来写作，你可以发挥其功能，只需几个简单的键盘指令，就可以添加或删减内容，甚至移动整个段落。有些软件还能帮你检查写作中出现的拼写错误和语法错误。(4) [C] 但是，应该记住，刚从打印机上打出的文本虽然外表整洁好看，但是文章读上去好不好，还在于文本所包含的思想和所写下的内容。许多作家都很谨慎，会把他们的资料存在盘里，每写好一稿就把它打印出来，以免万一因断电或其他什么问题导致材料遗失。此外，修改时，看打印稿比看屏幕更方便。

一旦有了纸质版的初稿，就可以删减与论题无关的材料，并添加一些必要的素材来阐明观点，使你的文章更具说服力。写“The A & P as a State of Mind”一文的学生很明智地删除了讨论萨米对女性的态度是否带有沙文主义那个段落。(5) [E] 这个话题虽然有趣，但和主题无关，因为论文的主题是要说明环境如何影响萨米并使他做出辞职的决定。删去这一段后，她添加了一段话，描述兰格尔如何乖戾恶劣地对待那几个女孩，这样作者就可进一步讨论兰格尔所施行的 A&P“政策”。

切记，初稿仅仅是初稿。你仍然需要一而再、再而三地把文章颠过来倒过去地看，并进行多次修改，使得观点更具说服力，条理更清晰。甚至到最后，你可能会写出几个完全不同的版本。要重写每个段落。就一个主题，段落中的句子必须与其关联。段与段之间应有衔接，这样才不会让人感到突兀或不知所云。凡拗口、冗长或含混的句子、段落都得无情地被百般打磨、万般锤炼，使之最终成型。

总结：综合以上分析，补全短文题关键在于弄清楚空格所在句与上下文的逻辑关系，分析已知信息，把握主旨大意。通读选项，标记关键词。分析空格处上下文内容，比对选项，从逻辑关系和内容两方面进行判断选择。

step 1：通读全文，确定文章主题。(重点阅读文章的首尾段、段首句)

step 2：阅读并分析各选项内容，寻找线索。

step 3：仔细分析文章空白处的上下文内容。(根据结构的一致性、语篇的连贯性与逻辑性，还有各种衔接技巧比对选项，锁定答案)

step 4：代入选项，检查答案是否合理。

阅读 D 节　选词填空

选词填空

一、命题剖析

阅读 Part D 选词填空部分重点考查的单词词性：名词、动词、形容词、副词，偶尔也有考查介词的情况。

在历年的 PETS 第三级考试阅读 Part D 中，对动词和名词的考查所占的比例最大，其次是形容词和副词，偶尔也有考查介词的情况。

二、应试技巧

（一）浏览全文，明确大意，抓住中心

由于选词填空考查的重点是单词在一定语境下的运用能力，因此考生能否把握文章的总体结构，理解诸如一致性、连贯性、逻辑性等语段、语篇的整体特征也是非常重要的。考生应站在全篇的角度，从整体出发，弄清文章的总体结构。解题时，考生首先应该浏览整篇文章，确定文章的中心或主要说明的话题。选词填空文章大概在200～250 词，建议用约 1 分钟时间完成略读。通过对文章的分析，结合每段的首句和末句，把握文章的结构，把握文章的主题和背景。选词填空短文的第一句对全文的内容有概括提示作用，所以一定要认真读懂第一句，通常短文的第一句不设置空格。通晓了解全文结构和大意，有助于考生在做题的过程中如鱼得水，信手拈来。选词填空的 15 个选项的词义大多互不关联，词性也各不相同，其中有 5 个干扰项，一定要先了解文章大意，带着文章脉络去找正确选项，避免解题时的盲目性。

（二）阅读选项，按词性分类

选词填空选项中的 15 个单词是考查的关键，本题重点考查的词类对象主要为实义词（notional words）中的四种，按照词性归类为动词、名词、形容词和副词。我们应该仔细阅读 15 个选项，判断词性，根据词性将每个单词进行分类归纳，如：动词（v.）、名词（n.）、形容词（adj.）、副词（adv.）等。熟悉的单词快速标明词性和词义，不熟悉的单词或者不认识的单词只需标明词性，然后根据名词、动词、形容词、副词四大类按规律在试卷上排列。将单词分类之后，就大大降低了此题的难度。因为原来 15 选 1 的形式，变成了 4 选 1，3 选 1，甚至 2 选 1 的情况了。缩小了选择范围，也就减少了做题的工作量，提高了选择的效率和正确率。考生在充分熟练该步骤之后，也不一

定要在卷面上标注词义，甚至词性，解题时灵活机动，在大脑中完成该步骤即可。

词性判断及分类是做选词填空题的重要一步，有利于缩小选择范围，节省答题时间，提高正确率。篇章中空格所需词性的判断，有以下规律可循：

1. *确定空格为名词*

若空格处前面为冠词、形容词或者及物动词，空格处应填入名词；若空格处后面是动词，空格处应填入名词，作为该动词的主语；若空格处前面是介词，空格处充当介词宾语，应填入一个名词或动名词。

2. *确定空格为动词*

若空格处前面已经有名词/代词作主语，后面又有名词/代词作为动词的宾语，空格处应为及物动词；若空格处前面是名词/代词，后面没有宾语，空格处就应填不及物动词；若空格处前面是名词/代词，空格处后面是副词/介词，空格处就应填不及物动词，与副词/介词构成固定搭配；若空格处前面是名词/代词，后面是形容词，空格处就应填 be 动词或系动词。其中 be 动词一般不会被考查，此处应填入系动词；若空格处前有不定式标志 to，空格处就应填入动词原形；若 to 是介词，后面就应填动名词。

3. *确定空格为形容词*

若空格处前面或者后面为名词，空格处可能填入形容词；若空格处前面是副词，空格处可能填入形容词；若空格处前面是系动词或 be 动词，空格处可能填入形容词作表语。

4. *确定空格为副词*

若空格处前面或者后面为动词，空格处可能填入副词；若空格处后面是形容词，空格处可能填入副词；当一句话完整的时候，句首句尾应填入副词。

（三）瞻前顾后，巧妙选择

在选择时，考生利用语法知识，根据原文中空格前后的单词或者前后语句来初步确定每个空格应填词汇的词性，缩小选择范围。然后，根据上下文的内在逻辑结构，从分类好的单词组中选择出词性、意思、语法都符合要求的最佳选项。选中的选项需在词性、单复数、时态和意义方面均符合上下文的要求。所以考生要特别注意“瞻前顾后”，保持文章前后通顺、流畅。考生在做题过程中一定要利用排除法逐渐减少备选词汇，即选择一个划掉一个。这样操作，有利于考生节省时间和精力，提高准确率。若是在解题过程中碰到难度高的空格，考生一时无法选择，建议暂时跳过，先做其他有把握的空格，最后再来解决难题。

（四）复读全文，检查核对

填空完成后，再次复读全文，查漏补缺，核实答案。要检查上下文是否通顺，内在逻辑关系是否连贯，单词的形式是否正确。

三、典型示例

例题 1：2017 年 9 月真题

Do you give your children money when they perform well at school?

According to a study, such an action could be __46__ to their development, and cause them to be more materialistic as adults. The study suggests that those who were rewarded and spoiled were more likely to think possessions define who they are. "Using material possessions to express love or reward children for their __47__ can have bad effect," wrote the authors of the study. "It can __48__ materialism in them."

The authors surveyed 701 adults to measure the long-term __49__ of material parenting. They were asked to describe their current life situation and values, and also reported on a __50__ of childhood circumstances, their relationship with their parents, and the rewards and punishments they received.

Results showed adults who had received more material rewards and punishments as children were more likely than others to use possessions to define who they are. And they were likely to continue rewarding themselves with material __51__.

Parents should, therefore, be cautious about using material possessions to express their love and reward their children for good behavior, __52__ the authors. They say __53__ emphasis on material possessions during childhood can have significant effects. It can __54__ "the way for their children to grow up to be more likely than others to __55__ people with expensive possessions and judge success by the kinds of things people own," the authors conclude.

[A] achievements	[B] admire	[C] blame
[D] careful	[E] develop	[F] excessive
[G] goods	[H] harmful	[I] impact
[J] level	[K] motivate	[L] pave
[M] responsibilities	[N] variety	[O] warn

解题思路：

考生可以参考如下方法把选项进行词性标注并分类：

[A] achievements *n-s*	[B] admire *v.*	[C] blame *v.*
[D] careful *adj.*	[E] develop *v.*	[F] excessive *adj.*
[G] goods *n-s*	[H] harmful *adj.*	[I] impact *n.*
[J] level *n.*	[K] motivate *v.*	[L] pave *v.*
[M] responsibilities *n-s*	[N] variety *n.*	[O] warn *v.*

标注并分类后结果如下：6 个名词，其中 3 个单数形式（I；J；N），3 个复数形式（A；G；M）。6 个动词，全部为动词原形（B；C；E；K；L；O）。3 个形容词（D；F；H）.

【解析】

46. 答案为 H。根据空格前的 be 判断，这里缺少一个形容词。前文提到用金钱作为对孩子的奖励，后文提到“并会使他们像成人一样崇尚物质主义”，所以这里应该是研究表明这种做法是不妥的，纵观3 个形容词选项，只有 H 项 harmful “有害的” 符合句意，故选 H。

47. 答案为 A。根据空格前后判断，这里缺少一个名词。这里应该是家长对孩子取得好成绩时进行奖励会产生坏影响，纵观 6 个名词选项，achievements “成绩，成就” 符合句意，故选 A。

48. 答案为 E。根据空格前后判断，这里缺少一个动词。由于空前是情态动词 can，这里必须是动词原形。这里的意思大概是它会使孩子产生物质主义，纵观 6 个动词选项，develop “产生，发展” 符合句意，故选 E。

49. 答案为 I。根据空前的形容词 long-term 判断，这里缺少一个名词。这里应该是作者对 701 名成年人进行调查，研究父母对孩子长期物质奖励的影响，纵观剩余的名词选项，impact 可作名词，意为“影响”，符合句意，故选 I。

50. 答案为 N。根据空格前的冠词 a 判断，这里缺少一个单数名词。此名词和前后词组成一个固定搭配，a variety of 意为“各种各样的”，符合句意，故选 N。

51. 答案为 G。根据空格前后判断，这里缺少一个名词。空格前的 material 是用来修饰空格处的名词。这里应该是从小得到物质奖励的孩子长大后也很可能继续用物质来奖励自己，纵观剩余的名词选项，goods “商品，物品” 符合句意，故选 G。

52. 答案为 O。根据空格前后判断，这里缺少一个动词，其主语是空格后的 the authors。这里应该是家长应当对这种做法提高警惕，这是作者对家长的警告，纵观剩余的动词选项，warn “警告” 符合句意，故选 O。

53. 答案为 F。根据空格前后判断，这里缺少一个形容词。这里应该是在孩子童年时期过分地强调物质的重要性会对孩子产生很大的影响，纵观剩余的形容词选项，excessive “过分的，过度的” 符合句意，故选 F。

54. 答案为 L。根据空格前后判断，这里缺少一个动词原形，且与后面的 the way 搭配，此处是为孩子铺设这样的一条道路，纵观剩余的动词选项，pave “铺设” 符合句意，故选 L。

55. 答案为 B。根据空格前后判断，这里缺少一个动词，该动词与后面的动词 judge 是并列关系。这里应该是孩子在成长的过程中比别的孩子更容易去仰慕那些有贵重财物的人，纵观剩余的动词选项，admire “钦佩，仰慕” 符合句意，故选 B。

针对干扰项的解析：

[C] blame，动词，意为“责怪，指责”。

[D] careful，形容词，意为“小心的，仔细的”。

[J] level，名词，意为“水平”。

[K] motivate，动词，意为“使有动机，促动，激发”。

[M] responsibilities，复数名词，意为“责任”。

【参考译文】

当你的孩子在学校表现好的时候你会给他钱吗?

根据一项研究,这种行为可能会(46)［H］不利于他们的成长,并会使他们像成人一样崇尚物质主义。研究表明那些被奖励和宠坏的孩子更可能用物质定义自己。研究的作者写道:"用物质来表达爱或者奖励孩子的(47)［A］好成绩,会产生不好的影响。这会使他们(48)［E］产生物质主义思想。"

作者调查了701名成年人,研究父母物质奖励的长期(49)［I］影响。他们被要求描述自己目前的生活状态和价值观,并描述(50)［N］各种童年环境、他们与父母的关系和他们所受到的奖励和惩罚。

研究结果表明在童年受到物质奖励和惩罚的成年人更倾向于用物质定义和表达他们自己,并很可能继续用(51)［G］物质来奖励自己。

作者(52)［O］告诫父母,要谨慎使用物质来表达对孩子的爱和奖励。他们认为在童年时期(53)［F］过分强调物质会产生重要的影响。作者总结,它会给孩子(54)［L］铺设这样的一条道路:"孩子在成长的过程中比别的孩子更倾向于去(55)［B］仰慕那些有贵重财物的人,并通过拥有的东西来判断一个人的成功。"

例题2:2017年3月真题

Some of the greatest successes you can think of began with failure. What a big __46__ a little continued effort and determination can make.

Workplace expert Nan Russell, author of "The Titleless Leader: How to Get Things Done When You're Not in Charge" offers a number of __47__ of people who were deemed failures-and then turned successful.

Albert Einstein was __48__ to be mentally challenged as a child and told he would never amount to anything. Need we say how that one turned out?

Walt Disney was fired from the *Kansas City Star* because the editor thought he lacked __49__ .

Chester Carlson's early Xerox machines were __50__ by 20 companies before he finally found a business partner.

Thomas Edison failed thousands of times before inventing the light bulb. There are many quotes from the great inventor that are worth __51__ to memory. Here's just one: "Many of life's failures are people who did not realize how __52__ they were to success when they gave up."

So, while failure may not feel good, it's often an essential part of success, the trial-and-error that can lead to greater things. If you spend all your time __53__ about past mistakes, you might not notice when real opportunity arrives, so by all __54__, learn from your mistakes then put them behind you, roll up your sleeves and get back to work.

Here's one more quote from Edison for us to think about: "If we all did the things we are __55__ of, we would astound ourselves."

[A] capable	[B] close	[C] combination
[D] committing	[E] contributing	[F] creativity
[G] difference	[H] encouraged	[I] examples
[J] judged	[K] means	[L] rejected
[M] typical	[N] ways	[O] worrying

【解析】

考生可以参考如下方法把选项进行词性标注并分类：

[A] capable *adj.*	[B] close *adj.*	[C] combination *n.*
[D] committing *v-ing*	[E] contributing *v-ing*	[F] creativity *n.*
[G] difference *n.*	[H] encouraged *v-ed*	[I] examples *n-s*
[J] judged *v-ed*	[K] means *n.*	[L] rejected *v-ed*
[M] typical *adj.*	[N] ways *n-s*	[O] worrying *v-ing*

标注并分类后结果如下：6 个名词，其中 4 个单数（C；F；G；K），2 个复数（I；N）。6 个动词，其中 3 个动词-ing 形式（D；E；O），3 个位动词-ed 形式（H；J；L）。3 个形容词（A；B；M）。当然，B 选项 close 有时也用做动词，K 选项 means 也有可能是动词的三单形式，考生要具体情况具体分析，做到灵活机动。

【解析】

46. 答案为 G。根据空格前后判断，这里缺少一个单数名词。后面的动词是 make，所以这个名词需要和 make 进行搭配。文章第一句说了成功和失败的关系，成功很有可能是由失败开始的。持续的努力和决心能带来不同的结果，纵观 4 个单数名词选项，make a difference 是唯一的选择，意为"有所不同"，故选 G。

47. 答案为 I。根据空格前的 a number of 判断，这里缺少一个复数名词。纵观 2 个复数名词选项，examples 符合句意，意为"例证"，故选 I。

48. 答案为 J。根据空格前后判断，这里缺少一个动词被动语态。纵观所有动词-ed 选项，judged 符合句意，意为"被判断"，故选 J。

49. 答案为 F。根据空格前后判断，这里缺少一个名词做动词 lack 的宾语。纵观剩余的名词选项，creativity 符合句意，意为"创造力"，故选 F。

50. 答案为 L。根据空格前后判断，这里缺少一个动词被动语态。纵观所有剩余的动词-ed 选项，这里应是"被拒绝"的意思，故选 L。

51. 答案为 E。根据空格前的 worth 判断，这里考查的结构是 be worth doing，所以这里缺少一个现在分词。纵观所有动词-ing 选项，contributing 符合句意，且可以和介词 to 进行搭配，意为"对……有贡献"，故选 E。

52. 答案为 B。根据空格前后判断，这里缺少一个形容词。纵观形容词选项，close 符合句意，意为"接近的，靠近的"，故选 B。

53. 答案为 O。根据空格前后判断，这里缺少一个现在分词，此处考查的是 spend ... doing... 。纵观剩余的动词-ing 选项，worrying 符合句意，意为"担心"，故选 O。

54. 答案为 K。此处 by all means 是一个固定搭配，意为“一定，务必”，故选 K。

55. 答案为 A。根据空格前后判断，这里缺少一个可以和介词 of 搭配的形容词。纵观剩余的形容词选项，capable 符合句意，意为“有能力的”，故选 A。

针对干扰项的解析：

[C] combination，名词，意为“结合，联合体”。

[D] committing，动词-ing 形式，commit to 意为“对……作出承诺，承担义务”。

[H] encouraged，动词-ed 形式，意为“鼓励”。

[M] typical，形容词，意为“典型的”。

[N] ways，名词复数形式，意为“道路，方法”。

很明显，[D] committing 是针对 [E] contributing 所设置的干扰项，[N] ways 是针对 [K] means 所设置的干扰项。

【参考译文】

你能想到的一些最伟大的成功都是从失败开始的。一点点持续的努力和决心能带来非常大的(46) [G] 不同。

职场专家南·罗素（Nan Russell）是《无头衔领导者：在你不在主管职位上时如何把事情做好》一书的作者，他提供了许多被认为是失败的人，然后成功的(47) [I] 例子。

阿尔伯特·爱因斯坦小时候曾被(48) [J] 判定智力有问题，并且说他永远都做不成任何事情。还需要再提他后来的成就吗？

沃尔特·迪士尼曾经被《堪萨斯星报》解雇，因为主编认为他缺少(49) [F] 创造力。

在最终找到生意合伙人之前，查斯特·卡尔逊最初设计的施乐复印机被 20 家公司(50) [L] 拒绝。

托马斯·爱迪生在发明灯泡前失败了上千次。这位伟大的发明家有很多话(51) [E] 值得我们记住。比如这一句：“生活中的许多失败是因为人们在放弃的时候没有认识到他们距离成功有多(52) [B] 近。”

所以，虽然失败并不好受，但它往往是成功必不可少的一部分，不断地试错可以引我们向着更伟大的成果前进。如果你把所有的时间都花在(53) [O] 担忧过去的错误上，你也许不会注意到真正的机会已经来了，所以请(54) [K] 一定要从你的错误中学习——然后把它们留在身后，卷起袖子重新开始工作。

这里还有一句爱迪生说的值得我们思考的话：“如果把我们(55) [A] 能做到的都做了，最终连我们自己都会被吓到。”

四、应试注意事项

要确保动词的形式正确，选择合适的时态和语态；要确保主从句时态一致；名词要注意单复数；辨析近义词，两个近义词中有一个是干扰项；注意句子间的逻辑关系：转折、对比、因果、递进、并列；先易后难，利用排除法，缩小选择范围。

写作 A 节　应用文写作

应用文写作

一、命题剖析

写作 Part A 是应用文写作，题目给出一个情景或任务，要求考生写篇应用文对此作出回应。不要照抄题目中的单词，而要用自己的语言。考生必须陈述所有提及的要点，并确保观点有逻辑地组织在一起。写完后，检查拼写以及是否达到 100 词。PETS 三级考试写作 A、B 两个部分的答题时间共 45 分钟。写作原始赋分为 30 分，Part A 满分为 10 分。建议考生在 20 分钟内完成 Part A，以留出足够时间给写作 Part B。

应用文与生活、社会的联系紧密，实用性强，格式方面有约定俗成的要求。无论题目中给出的情景是通知、申请或信函，都必须按照规范化的格式来写，不能随意改变格式。写信时，语域（即正式、一般、非正式的话语）也很重要。

二、评分方法与评分标准解读

（一）评分原则（同时适用于 Part A 和 Part B）

1. 评分过程

评分时，先根据文章的内容和语言初步确定其所属档次，然后以该档次的要求来衡量，确定或调整档次，最后给分。

2. 文章长度

Part A 文章字数要求为 100 词左右。文章过短（70 词以下）或过长（130 词以上），从得分中减去 1 分。

3. 拼写与标点符号

拼写与标点符号是语言准确性的一个方面，应视其对交际的影响程度予以评分。英、美式拼写及词汇用法均可接受。

4. 书写

如书写较差，以致影响交际，将分数降低一个档次。

（二）Part A 一般评分标准

评分侧重点在于：

（1）信息点的覆盖；

（2）内容的组织；

（3）语言的准确性；

（4）格式和语域的恰当；

（5）对语法结构和词汇多样性的要求将根据具体试题作调整；

（6）允许使用提示语中出现过的关键词，但使用提示语中的词组或句子将被扣分。

档次	描述
第五档 （9 ~ 10 分）	很好地完成了试题规定的任务： · 包含并有效阐述所有内容要点； · 使用了丰富的语法结构和词汇； · 语法结构和词汇准确，错误极少； · 有效地使用了多种衔接手法，内容连贯、流畅，层次清晰； · 格式与语域恰当贴切； · 对目标读者完全产生了预期的效果。
第四档 （7 ~ 8 分）	较好地完成了试题规定的任务： · 包含所有内容要点，少数要点未能有效阐述； · 使用了较丰富的语法结构和词汇； · 语言基本准确，只有在试图使用较复杂结构或较高级词汇时才有个别错误； · 比较有效地使用了一些衔接手法，内容较连贯，层次较清晰； · 格式与语域较恰当； · 对目标读者产生了预期的效果。
第三档 （5 ~ 6 分）	基本完成了试题规定的任务： · 虽漏掉一些内容，但包含多数内容要点； · 语法结构和词汇基本满足任务的需求； · 有一些语法结构和词汇错误，但不影响理解； · 使用了简单的衔接手法，内容基本连贯，层次基本清晰； · 格式与语域基本合理； · 对目标读者基本产生了预期的效果。
第二档 （3 ~ 4 分）	未能按要求完成试题规定的任务： · 漏掉一些内容要点，写了一些无关内容； · 语法结构单调、词汇项目有限； · 有较多语法结构和词汇错误，影响了对写作内容的理解； · 未使用必要的衔接手法，内容缺少连贯性； · 格式与语域不恰当； · 未能清楚地传达信息给读者。
第一档 （1 ~ 2 分）	未完成试题规定的任务： · 明显遗漏主要内容，且有许多不相关的内容： · 语法结构和词汇很单调，使用了较多题目中的词组或句子； · 语言错误多，有碍读者对内容的理解，语言运用能力差； · 缺乏衔接手法，内容不连贯，缺少组织、分段： · 无格式与语域概念； · 未能传达信息给读者。
0 分	· 所传达的信息或所用语言太少，无法评价；内容与要求无关或无法辨认。

（三）Part A 具体评分细则（对三档及三档以上作文的具体要求）及样题

具体评分细则：

内容：这是一封写给志愿者组织的求职商务电子邮件，回应其招聘广告。按题目要求须包括：先向对方表示愿意参加该组织的一项或多项工作，然后说明自己具备相关的工作能力和英语水平，以及可以从事志愿者工作的时间，最后希望对方及时答复。

准确性：文章语句完整，表达准确，用词和语法结构正确，单词拼写和标点使用没有错误。

多样性：语言规范，词汇丰富，句式多样。

连贯性：采用恰当的衔接手法，行文自然流畅；内容连贯，合乎逻辑。

格式与语域：符合求职商务邮件的书写要求。

目标读者：通过此邮件，收信人能够明白写信人愿意从事哪些志愿者工作，其相关工作能力和英语水平如何，以及能够从事志愿者工作的时间，并知晓写信人希望及时答复。

样题：

You have read the following advertisement about a volunteer program for an international sports event. You want to get in touch with the organizer.

Volunteers Wanted
Tasks: interpreting, guiding, reception work, medical aid, driving, etc.
Good level of English required.
Contact us at volunteerswanted@ gmail. com

Writing an email to the organizer, telling about:

(1) your interest in the program;

(2) your qualifications for the task (s);

(3) your time available for the task (s).

You should write about 100 words. Do not sign your own name at the end of your email. Use "Wang Lin" instead.

（四）各档范文评分（第三档及以上）

以下是三位考生（考生 A、考生 B、考生 C）的文章、点评及评分档。

1. 考生 A

Dear organizer,

I'm glad to write to you. I have read the Volunteer Wanted, which is about a volunteer program for an international sports event. And I have a big interest in it. It's a good way to develop my communicate skill.

And I'm always warm-hearted at volunteers work and have been a volunteer at a local school for a long time. So I think I could do a good job: interpreting, guiding, reception work and so on. It's better for me if I work for the medical aid. Besides, I have gotten the good level of English that required. And my time is suitable for all the time.

Hope for your reply.

Wang Lin

评语：

内容：基本包括了题目要求的内容，但个别要点写得较简略。

准确性：有一些表达错误，如："develop my communicate skill" "I'm always warm-hearted at volunteers work" 等。

多样性：对不同语法结构与词汇的使用基本达到要求。

连贯性：合理使用一些衔接手法，但也有一些多余，如："And"。格式与语域结尾处应有 "Sincerely" 或 "Yours" 等。

目标读者：读者可对作者的意愿、能力、工作时间等有一定了解。

档次：第三档

2. 考生 B

Dear organizer,

I have read the advertisement and know that you need volunteers badly. I like sports events and I always want to try my best to do something for the event. Here comes the opportunity. I'm confident that I can do the guiding work well, because I'm familiar with the traffic situation around, and I'm patient and polite. Besides, I can help the medical aid work, too. I major in medicine in my university. I know the medicine a lot and can do aid measure in the emergency.

I have spare time this weekend. I'm looking forward to hearing from you soon.

Wang Lin

评语：

内容：包含所有内容要点。

准确性：语言基本准确，有一些表达不当，如 ... can do aid measure in the emergency" 等。

多样性：使用了较丰富的语法结构和词汇，如 ... you need volunteers badly" "I'm confident that... " 等。

连贯性：层次较清晰，语义较连贯。

格式与语域：基本恰当，结尾处应有 "Sincerely" 或 "Yours" 等。

目标读者：读者能较清楚地了解作者的意愿、能力和工作时间。

档次：第四档

3. 考生 C

Dear sir or madam,

I'm writing to you in the hope that you could accept me as one of the volunteers in your program as the ad says. I'm very interested in doing the interpretation and guiding work for the international sports event.

I'm fluent in English for I have studied in the US for five years. Besides, I used to guide foreign visitors to go around my hometown, and I liked that job very much.

I'm not very busy at my work these days and I can spend three hours working for the event every day. Of course, if you could give me that chance.

Looking forward to your reply.

Sincerely,

Wang Lin

评语：

内容：包含所有内容要点。

准确性：语言准确，基本没有错误或不当之处。

多样性：使用了丰富的表达方式，如“in the hope that”“spend three hours working for”等。

连贯性：内容连贯流畅，有效地使用了多种衔接手法。

格式与语域：格式与语域恰当。

目标读者：读者能全面了解作者的意愿、能力和工作时间。

档次：第五档

总的来说，综合写作的评分重点包括：内容的完整性、语言的准确性、多样性、连贯性，格式和语域是否恰当，以及目标读者即语言接收对象是否能了解作者表达的主要内容。

完整性指文章应包含题目中的所有要点。准确性指考生在写作中是否能够在正确的语境下使用词汇、短语等，是否正确地使用了句式结构、语法结构等。同时，准确性也包括对拼写、标点等方面的要求。多样性指语言表达方式丰富，使用了多样化的词汇、句式、语法结构等，不得照抄提示语中的词组或句子。连贯性指段落内部的句子应按照一定的关系凝聚在一起使段落结构严谨，条理清晰，衔接自然流畅。连贯性往往通过代词和连接词来实现，它们就是一个段落的纽带，贯穿始终。

三、重点解读

英文书信一般说来由六部分组成，信头、信内地址、称呼、正文、结束语和签名。在 PETS 三级考试中，只要求写出称呼、正文、结束语和签名。根据应用的场景，分为正式信函（formal）、一般信函（semi-formal）和非正式信函（informal）。

（一）语域

语域（register）即在适当的上下文背景下使用适当的词语。在正式文章中，必须使用正式语域，即不应该使用非正式语言，例如非正式单词 kids, ok，而应该用较为正式的等同词来替代：children, all right 或 acceptable。写信时，语域很重要。要确保书信正式，考生所使用的语言不要过于非正式，或者写信给你熟识的人时，不要过于正式。

（二）称呼

对收信人的称谓，应与左边线对齐，在称呼后常用逗号。正式信函（formal），如公务信件，不知对方的名字和性别，可以用 Dear Sir or Madam，或 Dear 加收信人头衔（如："Dear Editor,"）；如知道收信人的姓名和性别，一般使用 Dear Mr. /Mrs. /Miss/ Ms. Surname（如："Dear Mr. Green,"）。一般信函（semi-formal），则通常使用 Dear First name（如："Dear John,"）。非正式信函（informal）通常是写给家人或关系亲密的朋友，可用"Hi Mum"，等开头。考试中提供的场景大多属于正式或一般信函。

2016—2019 年考试的英文书信场景如下：

2019 年 9 月　咨询信（formal）

2019 年 3 月　申请书（formal）

2018 年 9 月　道歉信（formal）

2018 年 3 月　私人信件（semi-formal）

2017 年 9 月　请假信（formal）

2017 年 3 月　投诉信（formal）

2016 年 9 月　求职信（formal）

2016 年 3 月　在论坛发帖（semi-formal）

（三）正文

正文是书信的主体。英文书信的正文开头是直接说明写信人的身份及写信的目的，然后提出具体的情况、想法或者要求，并加以必要的解释或说明。英文书信语言应层次清楚，言简意赅。以下为一些常见的书信词汇或套话：

申请书/求职信：interview, applicant, be considered

典型句型：I would like to be considered for the position advertised.

I am available to attend an interview at any time.

道歉信：sorry, excuse, forgive, apologize

典型句型：I am writing to apologize for my behavior last night.

I hope that you will forgive me for behaving in this way.

投诉信：dissatisfied, complain, unhappy

典型句型：I would like to complain about the treatment I received at your hotel.

咨询信：wonder, ask, help

典型句型：I would like to enquire about renting a car.

感谢信：grateful, appreciate

典型句型：I am very grateful for the amount of time you have given up to help me.

接受/回绝邀请的回信：would be delighted, attend, invitation, confirm

典型句型：Unfortunately, I will not be able to attend the party.

（四）结束语

常用的表示感谢的结束语有：

I would (very much) appreciate it/be (most) grateful if you could...

Thank you (very much) for your...

Your... would be (very much) appreciated.

常用的表示盼望回复的结束语有：

I look/Looking forward to your early reply/hearing from you soon.

I would appreciate your early reply/ response.

Your early reply/response will be appreciated.

注意短语动词 to look forward to 接 do + ing：

I am looking forward to seeing you soon. 我盼望着早日见到你。

在正式书信里，经常用一般现在时而不是现在进行时

I look forward to hearing from you in the near future. 我盼望着很快能收到你的来信。

(五) 签名

通常包含结尾词和签名。结尾词在签名的上一行，首字母大写，加逗号。根据应用场合，如果是正式书信，通常可用“Yours sincerely”，介于正式与非正式之间，可用“Best wishes”，写给熟悉的朋友或家人的非正式信件，可用“Lots of love”等。根据题目要求，结尾签名通常用“Wang Lin”或其他题目中要求使用的姓名。

四、范文点评

(一) 咨询信

You are preparing for an English test and are in need of some reference books. Write a letter to the sales department of a bookstore to ask for:

(1) detailed information about the books you want;

(2) methods of payment;

(3) time and way of delivery.

You should write about 100 words. Do not sign your own name at the end of your letter. Use “Wang Lin” instead. (2019 年 9 月真题)

【真题解析】

本文的收信人是书店的销售部，不知收信人的具体名字和性别，称呼用 Dear Sir or Madam，语言应简洁、正式。正文一定要覆盖题目中所列出的三项要点，即自己所需书籍的详细信息、付款方式、送货时间和方式。注意最后的写信人名字要写“Wang Lin”。正文推荐结构如下：开头——自我介绍，表明写作目的；主体——提出咨询内容；结尾——表示感谢，期待回复。

【参考范文】

Dear Sir or Madam,

As I am planning to take College English Test Band 4 (CET-4), I have decided to place an order of some reference books. Therefore, I would be grateful if you could supply me with the following information.

Firstly, could you please send me a booklist with detailed information, including authors, publishing houses and prices? Secondly, I would like to know methods of payment. Do you accept online orders via Ali Pay? Thirdly, how many days will it take to get the books? I would like to know if you could deliver them by post to 118 Fuxing Road, Shanghai.

I would appreciate your early response.

Yours sincerely,

Wang Lin

(114 words)

【写作模板】

Dear Sir or Madam,

________________. (交代写信的情景) Therefore, I would be grateful if you could supply me with the following information. (表明写作意图)

First of all, ________________? (咨询问题一) Secondly, ________________? (咨询问题二) Thirdly, ________________? (咨询问题三)

I would appreciate your early response. (表示急需信息的迫切心情和谢意)

Yours sincerely,

Wang Lin

【语言拓展】

说明写作目的:

I would be grateful if you could supply/provide me with the following information.

I am anxious to obtain/urgently in need of information about...

Could you please supply/provide me with some information about... ?

I am writing to inquire about (the details of) ...

提出咨询问题:

I would like to know/ask/inquire if...

I need to know/wonder if...

I need to have more information about...

I would be interested to know if...

(二) 申请书/求职信

Suppose you are a major in Art of Central Academy of Fine Arts. After graduation you decide to pursue your study in the graduate school in Yale University. Write a letter of application for admission, which should include the following points:

(1) make an application;

(2) provide your personal information and academic documents;

(3) express your hope for a reply.

You should write about 100 words. Do not sign your own name at the end of your letter. Use "Wang Lin" instead. (2019 年 3 月真题)

【真题解析】

首先，在正文开头交代写信的目的，即申请入学。

其次，介绍个人的基本情况，包括学历、专业、工作或实习经验，进行的研究情况及在校成绩等。可说明自己的经济资助情况，是否准备申请奖学金等。内容要实事求是，言简意赅。

最后，结尾可提出自己的需求，希望获得更多入学信息等，并对对方可能给予的帮助表示感谢，并期望得到对方回复，并附上自己的联系方式。

【参考范文】

Dear Sir or Madam,

I am writing to apply for admission to your program for postgraduate studies.

Currently, I am a senior in Art at Central Academy of Fine Arts, China. I have completed all the required undergraduate courses with satisfactory scores. My diligence and love for challenges have earned me several awards for excellent students in our university. Official copies of my transcript and of my TOEFL scores are being sent from the offices concerned. I would also like to know about the possibility of receiving financial support, for example, a scholarship, from your university.

Please contact me by e-mail at wanglin@ sina. com. Thank you very much in advance for your attention to these matters. I look forward to hearing from you soon.

Yours sincerely,

Wang Lin

(128 words)

【写作模板】

Dear Sir or Madam,

I am writing to apply for ________________. (表明写作意图) Enclosed with this letter are ________________. (提供个人详细资料)

Currently, I am ________________. (目前身份) For the past three years, my ________________. (资历一) Last year, my ________________. (资历二) ________________. (资历三) In addition, I have ________________. (资历四)

I would appreciate it if you could take my application into serious consideration. (对收信人的考虑表示感谢) Please contact me at your earliest convenience. (期待答复)

Yours sincerely,

Wang Lin

【语言拓展】

说明申请/求职意图：

I am writing to apply for admission to your college/university/program/institute...

I am writing to express my interest in the position/opening/post/vacancy that you recently advertised.

I am writing in reply to your advertisement in... for someone to...

I have recently learned from... that you have openings/ are seeking a person to fill the vacancy.

提供更详细个人信息：

I have enclosed... for your convenience.

Enclosed is my resume, which details my qualifications and work experience.

I will be available for an interview anytime.

If further information is needed, please (do not hesitate to) let me know.

表示自信：

My qualifications and work experience make me the right person for the position.

My personality is well suited to working as a...

I believe I can be of significance/value to your institute/company/corporation.

I am confident that I am qualified for...

（三）道歉信

You have made an appointment with Prof. Wang, but failed to keep it. Write a letter to

(1) apologize for your failure to keep the appointment

(2) explain your reason to your teacher

(3) express your wish to make another appointment

You should write about 100 words. Do not sign your name at the end of your letter. Use "Li Ming" instead. You do not need to write the address. （2018 年 9 月真题 ）

【真题解析】

道歉信在正文开头应直接交代写信的目的，诚恳地向对方表示歉意。第二段应具体解释未能赴约的原因，内容应简洁明了，语气要诚恳。最后再次表示歉意，恳切邀请老师重新预约见面时间，并期待对方答复。

此外，要注意书信格式，注意信件后面的写信人名字要写"Li Ming"。

【参考范文】

Dear Prof. Wang,

I am writing to apologize for not being able to keep our appointment. It was inconsiderate of me not to tell you earlier that I could not make it.

I remembered very well that Tuesday morning was the regular time for our appointment. Unfortunately, I had a bad cold and fainted on the bus and was sent to the hospital at once. I should have called to inform you when I recovered. But I found that my mobile phone was lost in the chaos.

Please accept my sincere apology for any inconvenience I have caused. I would be grateful if you could make another appointment with me later this week. I am looking forward to hearing from you.

Yours sincerely,

Li Ming

(124 words)

【写作模板】

Dear ________,

I am writing to apologize for ________________. (表明写信意图) It was terribly rude of me not to ________________. (表明道歉的原因)

I remembered very well that ________________. Unfortunately, ________________. (失约原因) I should have ________________, but ________________. (未提前通知的原因)

Again, I am terribly sorry for my rudeness. (再次表示歉意) To make up for my rudeness, I want to ________________. (补救办法) So please let me know your decision. (表示希望得到答复)

Yours sincerely,

Li Ming

【语言拓展】

表示歉意:

I am sorry/regret to tell/inform you that

I am writing to apologize/make an apology for...

It was terribly/awfully/ careless of me to...

Again, I apologize/am sorry for having caused you so much trouble/ inconvenience.

I hope that this has not caused you too much trouble/inconvenience.

(四) 请假信

You work for a foreign company. Now you want to ask for a short period of leave. Write an email to your boss Mr. Smith to tell him:

(1) why you want to ask for leave;

(2) how long you want to be away;

(3) what you plan to do about your current work.

You should write about 100 words. Do not sign your own name at the end of your email. Use "Wang Lin" instead. (2017 年 9 月真题)

【真题解析】

根据题目要求，本文开头称呼应为“Dear Mr. Smith,”正文的开头通常用简洁的陈述性文字表明写信的目的。信件主体部分要紧扣题目中列出的写作任务（通常有三个要求），不能遗漏。另外，文章布局尽量合理，可一一回应题目中要求写出的要点。最后注意落款及全文字数是否足够。

【参考范文】

Dear Mr. Smith,

I am writing to ask for a short period of leave next month.

My grandmother is planning to celebrate her 90th birthday on April 10th with the whole family. Since my grandparents live in another city, to participate in this special occasion, I would need to be away from work for three days, from April 9th to April 11th. I've sorted out every possible work in advance. Besides, my colleague Joe would be able to help if there's any urgent work.

I would be very grateful if you could allow me this time. These three days are very important to my grandmother and the whole family.

Best wishes,

Wang Lin

(113 words)

【写作模板】

Dear ________,

I am writing to ask for ________________. （表明写信意图）

________________. （交代请假原因）Since ________________, I would need to be away from work ________________. （说明请假时间）I've sorted out ________________ in advance. Besides, ________________. （交代工作安排）

I would be very grateful if you could ________________. （表达感谢）

Best wishes,

Wang Lin

【语言拓展】

I would (very much) appreciate it/be (most) grateful if you could...

Thank you (very much) for your...

Do you think that it would be possible for me to...?

（五）投诉信

You found some problem with the book you bought from a US online bookstore. Write the bookstore an email to let it know:

(1) when you bought the book;

(2) what problem you found with the book;

(3) what solution you expect.

You should write about 100 words. Do not sign your own name at the end of your email. Use "Wang Lin" instead. (2017 年 3 月真题)

【真题解析】

此信应反映自己所买书籍出现的问题，并提出解决诉求。写信时应注意：反映的问题要明确，叙述所反映的问题给自己带来的不便，并提出期待的解决方案。语气坚决，但措辞要礼貌。

【参考范文】

Dear Sir or Madam,

March 13, 2020, I purchased a set of *National Geographic Explorer Collection* from your online bookstore. Unfortunately, I have had problems with both the books. Specifically, I have the following complaints.

First, instead of a collection of 10 books you claimed on the website, I only received 8 books. Moreover, the quality of the books are not well accepted. They look so old and dirty. In addition, I ordered a hardback version, but you sent me the paperback.

I am requesting a refund, or you could mail me a new set of books. May I get your reply before April 10th.

Yours sincerely,

Wang Lin

(109 words)

【写作模板】

Dear Sir or Madam,

________________, I purchased ________________. (简介情况) Unfortunately, I have had problems with ________________. Specifically, I have the following complaints. (表明写信意图)

First, ________________. (投诉原因一) Moreover, ________________. (投诉原因二) In addition, ________________. (投诉原因三)

I am requesting ________________. (解决办法). May I get your reply before ________________. (表明态度)

Yours sincerely,

Wang Lin

【语言拓展】

说明投诉的目的：

I have had problems with...

I am writing to complain about/make a complaint about...

I am very dissatisfied /unhappy with...

I regret to say that... has/have seriously affected...

I find it dishonest and unacceptable that your company/store...

提出解决办法：

I would appreciate any measures you could take to...

We expect to be compensated for...

We claim a refund of... because... was not up to the promised standard.

（六）私人信件

Write a letter to Andy and tell her about your situation. The letter must include：

（1）your family；

（2）your school or work；

（3）your hobby.

You should write about 100 words. Do not sign your own name at the end of the letter. Use "Wang Lin" instead.（2018 年 3 月真题）

【真题解析】

根据题目要求，本文开头称呼应为"Dear Andy，" 正文的开头通常用简洁的陈述性文字表明写作背景。信件主体部分要紧扣题目中列出的写作任务，分别是介绍家庭近况、学校或工作近况、业余爱好，三点不能遗漏。最后注意落款及全文字数是否足够。本文介于正式与非正式之间，结束问候语可用"Best wishes"。

【参考范文】

Dear Andy，

I hope this finds you and your family well. I'm writing now to let you know about my recent situation.

My grandparents came to live with us last month. It's a great fun to live with them. I really admire the relationship between my mother and my grandmother. Besides，I applied for a job at a new company. Although the competition was fierce，I was admitted as a senior manager！The pay is better and the workplace is within 10 minutes' walk from home！On weekends，I would enjoy some leisure time. I'm quite keen on swimming and watching movies.

How are you getting on these days？Expect to hear from you！

With love，

Wang Lin

（118 words）

（七）邀请函

You want to invite John Smith，your former English teacher，to attend a reunion party of your class. Write an email to him，

（1）telling him the purpose of the party，time and place of the party，etc.；

（2）expressing your wish for his accepting the invitation.

You should write approximately 100 words. Do not use your own name at the end of your email. Use "Wang Lin" instead. （2014 年 3 月真题）

【真题解析】

邀请函一定要将邀请的时间、地点、场合写清楚。邀请函不论长短，一般都包括以下内容：向对方表示简短的寒暄或问候；说明邀请对方参加什么活动及邀请的原因；说明活动安排的细节；如果有必要，请对方确认能否应邀。

【参考范文】

Dear John Smith,

I am writing to invite you to attend the 10th anniversary reunion party of our class, which will be held on Saturday, the 18th of September at 6：30 p. m. at Rose Hotel, No. 118, Binjiang Road.

We have graduated for 10 years and we all missed the beautiful atmosphere of the campus. That is why we hold this party trying to recollect our early memories. You, our tutor, are the first person we wish to invite. If you accept our sincere invitation, please inform us at your earliest convenience, enabling us to make the necessary preparations.

Yours Sincerely,

Wang Lin

（102words）

写作 B 节　综合写作

命题剖析及评分标准

一、命题剖析

写作 Part B 是材料作文，材料内容通常包含较为深刻的、与我们生活密切相关的社会现象或问题，既考查考生的综合写作能力，也要求考生作文表达内容具有一定的深度，主要考查学生的综合写作能力。《全国英语等级考试大纲》（2015 版）将 Part B 材料由原来漫画、图表等形式，改为阅读一篇 200 ~ 250 词的英语文章。材料文章体裁多样，包括记叙文、说明文、采访、书信等，话题范围涉及与我们生活息息相关的社会现象和问题，如教育、职业道德、身体健康、家庭关系、环境保护、人口增长、文化交流等。与之前相对直观，简单的漫画、图表作文相比，综合写作的难度有所提升。但是，由于其材料的开放性、灵活性，考生有了更多的发挥空间。

考生在阅读材料文章后，应写出一篇约 120 词（标点符号不计算在内）的短文，要求概括文章大意，并予以适当评论。考生要能够把握文章的中心内容，并且围绕中心内容，进行有深度、有根据的论证。

PETS 三级考试写作 A、B 两个部分的答题时间共 45 分钟。建议考生留 25 ~ 30 分钟完成 Part B。该题原始赋分为 30 分，Part B 满分为 20 分。

二、评分方法与评分标准

（一）评分原则

1. 评分过程

评分时，先根据文章的内容和语言初步确定其所属档次，然后以该档次的要求来衡量，确定或调整档次，最后给分。

2. 文章长度

文章过短（80 词以下）或过长（160 词以上），从得分中减去 2 分。

3. 拼写与标点符号

拼写与标点符号是语言准确性的一个方面，应视其对交际的影响程度予以评分，英、美式拼写及词汇用法均可接受。

4. 书写

如书写较差，以致影响交际，将分数降低一个档次。

（二）Part B 部分一般评分标准

Part B 部分评分时，主要从以下四个方面考虑：

（1）对原文要点的理解和呈现情况，分析和评论的合理性；

（2）语法结构和词汇丰富性，是否抄写原文词组或句子；

（3）语法结构和词汇的准确性；

（4）文章的组织结构，上下文的衔接与连贯。

分析和评论的内容不作限制，具有较大的弹性，只要言之成理，均可得分。

档次	描述
第五档 （17～20 分）	很好地完成了试题规定的任务： 原文理解完全准确，包含所有要点，评论合理； 语言丰富、得当，完全没有抄写； 语法结构和词汇准确，错误极少； 有效地使用了多种衔接手法，内容连贯、流畅，层次清晰。
第四档 （13～16 分）	较好地完成了试题规定的任务： 原文理解较为准确，基本包含所有要点，评论较为合理； 绝大部分使用了自己的语言，语法结构和词汇比较丰富； 语法结构和词汇有少量错误，但不影响意义表达； 比较有效地使用了一些衔接手法，内容较连贯，层次较清晰。
第三档 （9～12 分）	基本完成了试题规定的任务： 原文理解基本准确，包含多数要点，评论基本合理； 基本使用自己的语言，少数词组或句子抄自原文； 有一些语法结构和词汇错误，但基本不影响意义表达； 使用了简单的衔接手法，内容基本连贯，层次基本清晰。
第二档 （5～8 分）	未能按要求完成试题规定的任务： 原文理解有偏差，遗漏部分要点，评论缺乏合理性； 语法结构和词汇单调，一些词组或句子抄自原文； 有较多语法结构和词汇错误，影响了意义的表达； 未使用必要的衔接手法，内容缺少连贯性。
第一档 （1～4 分）	未能完成试题规定的任务： 原文理解有较多偏差，总结和评论不当，与题目要求不符； 语法结构和词汇很单调，较多词组或句子抄自原文； 语法结构和词汇错误很多，严重影响了意义的表达； 缺乏衔接手法，内容不连贯，缺少组织、分段。
0 分	白卷、内容太少无法评判或所写内容与题目要求无关。

（三）Part B 具体评分细则（对三档及三档以上作文的具体要求）及样题

具体评分细则：

内容：作者应总结出所给短文的大意，对其进行分析，发表自己的见解。

准确性：文章语句完整，表达准确，用词和语法结构正确，单词拼写和标点使用没有错误。

多样性：词汇丰富，能够使用较复杂的表达方式，句式变化多样。

连贯性：总结和评论有条理、合乎逻辑。采用必要的衔接手法，层次清晰，行文流畅。

格式与语域：采用叙述性和议论性语言。

目标读者：通过作者的总结和评论，读者可了解原文主要内容，并了解作者的观点。

【样题】

Directions:

Read the text below. Write an essay in about 120 words, in which you should summarize the key points of the text and make comments on them. Try to use your own words.

Mary's son Luke continued to argue with her. She didn't demand very much from him. "Study hard, get the best grades you can," she told him. She tried to get it into his head that she didn't have the money to pay for his college education. Instead of studying harder, however, Luke spent hour after hour playing video games on his computer. He waited until the last minute before school tests, and then stayed up all night stuffing as much as possible into his head. When Mary tried to remind him that he needed good grades so that he could get a scholarship, he would get angry. He said it was her responsibility to take care of him financially until he graduated from college.

When Mary's friend John heard about all this, he was shocked. "Where did he get that idea?" he asked. "You' ve raised him for 10 years all by yourself. You don't owe him a thing. He should be glad you haven't kicked him out of the apartment. He is graduating from high school next year. When I was in the eleventh grade, my father made it clear to me that I was expected to leave home after graduation from high school. Yet Luke thinks you have to pay his way through college!"

Mary was worried, for she didn't know what to do.

【解析】

考生在阅读材料时要重点关注段落的“首二末”，即每段的第一句、第二句及最后一句，因为这些位置的句子往往是段落的中心。此外，考生还需特别关注表示转折的词语，如 but，however，yet 等，转折后的内容通常更为重要。

这篇样题文章是记叙文，从第一段首句“Mary's son Luke continued to argue with her.”考生可以得到 Mary 母子长期争吵这一信息。第一段第三句“Instead of studying harder, however, Luke spent hour after hour playing video games on his computer.”既包含转折词 however，也包含连接相反关系的词语 instead of，考生应重点关注。该句给出了 Mary 母子争吵的原因，儿子 Luke 不但不努力学习，还沉迷网络游戏。最后一句“He said it was her responsibility to take care of him financially until he graduated from college.”给出了母子争吵的另一个原因，儿子认为母亲要承担他大学毕业前的各项花销。

第二段首句“When Mary's friend John heard about all this, he was shocked.”给出了母亲朋友 John 对此事的看法：很震惊。紧接着描述了 John 自己的做法，最后一句“Yet Luke thinks you have to pay his way through college!”再次表明 John 对儿子做法的不认同。

最后一段只有一句话，Mary 现在很担心，不知道应该怎么做。

（四）各档范文评分（第三档及第三档以上）

以下是三位考生（考生 A、考生 B、考生 C）的文章、点评及评分档。

1. 考生 A

In this passage, Mary's son Luke is involved in video games and focuses little on study. It makes Mary very worried.

In my opinion, for students, it's their duties to spare every efforts studying. Only in this way can they get a bigger future. Addionallys, it's also important for them to develop the ability to live independently. Playing video games all day will make them hard to adapt into the society.

For Mary, she ought to communicate with Luke more. It's hard to skip the generation gap. After communication, Luke will understand the hard of making living and the importance of learning.

It's never easy to solve the problem. Only with enough communication can they better deal with it.

【点评】

内容：简单总结了原文大意，评论基本合理。

准确性：基本使用自己的语言，有一些错误和表达不当之处，如：“spare every efforts studying”“Luke will understand the hard of making living”等。

多样性：应用的语法结构和词汇基本满足任务要求。

连贯性：分段基本合理，意思基本连贯。

格式与语域：格式和语域恰当。

目标读者：读者可基本了解原文要点及作者的观点。

档次：第三档

2. 考生 B

Mary is a mother who suffered from arguing with her son. Her son Luke thought it was her responsibility to take care of him financially, but he refused to study hard, staying up all night playing video games. Mary's friend John got independent at the age of eleven and was very grateful to his family.

As far as my concerned, Mary's case is not an exception but a common situation. Many college students waste their time and money with no sense of guilty. At the same time, their parents make many sacrifices for their children's education.

I suggest Mary cut down Luke's expenses. He must take his responsibility to study hard. He must learn to pay cost on his own. Only in this way can he have the possibility of becoming an independent man in the future.

【点评】

内容：总结涵盖了大部分要点，评论较为合理。

准确性：绝大部分使用了自己的语言，有少量表达不当之处，如“As far as my concerned”“pay cost on his own”等。

多样性：使用了较为丰富的词汇及表达方式，如“suffered from arguing”“make many sacrifices”等。

连贯性：分段合理，语义基本连贯，有效地使用了一些衔接手法，如“but”“At the same time”等。

格式与语域：格式和语域恰当。

目标读者：读者能够清楚地了解原文要点和作者的观点。

档次：第四档

3. 考生 C

Mary worked hard to earn money for her son Luke, but the boy didn't understand his mother's sacrifice. He was addicted to playing computer games, and spent little time on his study. Mary's friend John was shocked at the boy's behavior and advised Mary to be hard on him. Mary seemed reluctant to do so.

Luke's problem also prevails among Chinese families. Parents sacrifice everything for their children, whereas many children don't cherish at all the opportunities they get. In my opinion, it is really unwise of parents to indulge their children too much or satisfy their children's unreasonable demands. As for Mary, she should treat her son more strictly from now on, otherwise the boy would never grow up to be an independent person.

【点评】

内容：对原文理解准确，涵盖全部要点，评论合理。

准确性：语言运用准确熟练，基本没有错误。

多样性：使用了丰富多样的表达方式，如“was addicted to”“reluctant to”“it is really unwise of parents to indulge...”等。

连贯性：分段合理，结构紧凑，语义连贯，有效使用了多种衔接手法，如“but”“whereas”“otherwise”等。

格式与语域：格式与语域恰当。

目标读者：读者可充分了解原文要点和作者的观点。

档次：第五档

总的来说，综合写作的评分重点包括：完整性、多样性、准确性、连贯性。完整性指对短文的理解完全、准确，对短文的总结包含所有要点，对短文的评论合理到位。

多样性指考生完全没有抄写短文内容，自身呈现的语言丰富多样，包括多样化的词汇、句式、语法结构等。准确性指考生在写作中是否能够在正确的语境下使用词汇、短语等，是否正确地使用了句式结构、语法结构等。同时，准确性也包括对拼写、标点等方面的要求。连贯性指正确地使用连接词等衔接手段，实现前后段落间、上下文句子间的衔接，并以此达到文章层次清晰、内容连贯流畅的要求。在备考练习时，考生应牢记这四个评价标准，有针对性的进行练习。

三、应试技巧

（一）审题

仔细分析题干给出的信息和任务要求，重点阅读文章的首末段或段落的首末句。切忌“提笔就写”。

1. 审题干要求

57. *Directions*: *Read the text below. Write an essay in about* 120 *words*, *in which you should summarize the key points of the text and make comments on them. Try to use your own words.*

综合写作的题干基本固定，要求考生先总结文章主要观点，再发表自己的观点。

2. 审文章内容

考生应尽可能快速地阅读短文，注意利用段落“首二末”及表示转折等逻辑关系的词汇。考生在阅读短文后首先要判断文章体裁，通常来说记叙文和说明文比较常见。如果短文是记叙文，则应找到人物关系，事情的起因、经过、结果及事件带来了什么启发。如果是说明文，则应关注说明事物或问题是什么、为什么、怎么样，以及短文的中心思想是什么。

（二）列出文章基本框架

在开始写作之前，考生应简单地列出文章框架，包括有几个段落，每段写什么。

1. 总结文章观点

考生应在作文的第一段简明扼要地概述短文的主要内容。概述时，不同体裁的总结要点不同（具体总结方法在后文将详细解说）。同时，考生应注意尽量避免使用短文原有的词汇、句式等，以免被扣分。

2. 表达自己观点

综合写作要求考生在总结文章内容后，发表自己的评论，因此，考生需要明确表达自己的观点。为了达到层次清晰的要求，考生的观点即作文的论点可以放在第一段的最后一句或者第二段的第一句，而且必须要在其中一处清晰的表明自己的观点。在作文的第二段，考生可根据论点写作分论点，并展开细节进行支撑。结尾段可根据主体段内容进行总结概括。

3. 达到字数要求

因为综合写作明确将字数限制在 120 词左右，且文章过短（80 词以下）或过长（160 词以上）会被额外扣 2 分，所以考生在备考是最好能够掌握自己大约写多少句能够达到 80 词、120 词、160 词，以避免不必要的丢分。

（三）根据列好的提纲，套用基本框架写作

段落之间、句子之间用连接词衔接，使内容连贯流畅，层次清晰。上下文如需表达相同意思，注意使用同义词、句式转写等方式避免重复。

（四）检查

在时间允许的情况下，考生在写作完成后应进行检查。从语法方面查看是否存在句子的时态、语态、主谓一致的错误，名词单复数是否对应。从词汇方面检查是否存在段落及上下句连接词使用不当、固定短语搭配、词性误用、单词拼写错误。同时，考生还应注意是否存在大小写、标点符号等方面的错误，尤其注意句末逗号是否使用正确、书写清晰。

此外，考生还应注意卷面书写清晰。如书写较差，以致影响交际，分数将被降低一个档次。在写作过程中，不要进行大篇幅的修改、更不要因为修改破坏卷面的整洁。

四、作文结构及论证展开

作文结构及论证展开

综合写作出题方式相对固定，即考生在阅读一篇 200 ~ 250 词的英语文章后，应写出一篇约 120 词（标点符号不计算在内）的作文。在作文中要首先概括文章中心内容，然后围绕中心内容，进行有深度、有根据的评论。

通常来说，一篇作文要包含开头段、主体段、结尾段三个部分。结合综合写作的题目要求，考生写作时可参照如下作文结构：

（一）开头段

开头段要求包括两部分内容：概述短文中心内容，表明考生自己的观点即文章的中心句。

1. 概述短文

作文的第一句话，考生应开门见山地总结短文内容。在总结短文中心内容时，考生应注意避免使用原文词句，因评分标准明确提出“没有抄写”的要求。同时，考生应尽量概括性地表达短文中心，避免过多细节性的描述。但也要注意完整性要求，不能遗漏重要信息。

① 说明文。如果阅读短文是说明文，通常是对某一事物或现象进行说明解释。考生在概括中心内容时，首先应该找到短文的中心词，即说明对象是什么。短文的中心词一定是多次提及的，应该和每个段落的中心词一致。在寻找中心词时，考生要注意中心词很可能被进行了各种形式的转写以避免重复。此外，考生还应关注短文是否提

及为什么会出现某现象或问题，怎么样解决某问题等。此外，考生还可以根据每段的大意（通常位于段落的第一句、第二句和最后一句）总结短文中心。

范文 1（利用是什么、为什么、怎么样进行概括）（2017 年 9 月真题）

It seems the nation's younger citizens are finally favoring the beauty of the natural world over the cries of amateur singers.

The BBC has confirmed that the first three episodes of *Planet Earth II* have attracted more viewers in the 16 to 34 age group than *The X Factor*. The best ratings so far were for the second episode, which brought in 1. 8 million young viewers compared to *The X Factor*'s 1. 4 million.

The show's narrator, Sir David Atenborough, credited improvements in technology with the show's increased success in its second season, which have brought animals close to the viewer and made their environments look real.

"You feel like the camera is with the animals," said producer Mike Gunton. "It's very active. For example, you see a monkey leaping through the forest. Normally you'll stand back to film that. But here the monkey almost jumps over your shoulder. The camera is running with it. Visually, *Planet Earth* told you to look down on the Earth and see the scale of the planet. What *Planet Earth II* is doing is saying 'Let's get ourselves into the lives of the animals, and see it from their perspective .' "

"The music of Hans Zimmer is also a big factor," added Atenborough. "That pleases me enormously."

Besides technology and music, Atenborough said that viewers are "reconnecting with a planet whose beauty is spoiled and whose health is failing." He believes the young are learning that their future is linked to that of the environment.

这篇短文的第一句比较了自然美景和业余歌手：这个国家的年轻人似乎更加喜欢自然的美景，而不是业余歌手的歌声（It seems the nation's younger citizens are finally favoring the beauty of the natural world over the cries of amateur singers.）。

在第二段作者说明了这两者分别代表着两个节目，Planet Earth II（《地球脉动第二季》是 BBC 制作的自然纪录片）和 The X Factor（《X 音素》，是一档音乐选秀节目），Planet Earth II 在 16 至 34 岁的年轻观众中，比 The X Factor 更受欢迎。

在接下去的几个段落里，文章写了对 Planet Earth II 一些工作人员的采访，通过阅读段落的首尾句，考生可以知道这部纪录片的成功得益于技术的提升和音效的使用。最后一段升华了中心，指出该纪录片提升了年轻人的环保意识。

对于这篇文章的概括，考生应先把握中心词（Planet Earth II），而后说明这是什么（是 BBC 关于地球和动物的节目），怎么了（在年轻人中大受欢迎，并提升了年轻人的环保意识），为什么会这样（技术和音效进步）。

The Planet Earth II is a program about planet and animals produced by BBC. This program is very popular among young people because of improvements in technology and music. By watching this program, young people's awareness of environmental protection has been aroused.

范文 2（利用段落中心句进行概括）（2018 年 3 月真题）

Internet is getting into people's life and becoming more and more popular. Experts are now working on setting up a national long-distance educational system in China to provide educational opportunities via Internet.

In reality, the educational via Internet plan has been taking shape. Some universities have already got involved in regional long-distance education, catching the attention of many educators and computer experts worldwide. Others have just connected their campus computers for teaching and research, and provided more opportunities for learners.

The Internet education will be developing dramatically. It's estimated that computerized long-distance teaching networks will be available by 2010 for postgraduate education, vocational programs, teachers' training and employees' training. Moreover, it will soon cover all the corners of China and eventually win the worldwide popularity.

该文的中心词是 Internet education（网络教育），在短文中其同义表达还包括：long-distance educational system, the educational via Internet, long-distance education, computerized long-distance teaching。

该文第一段第一句进行了社会背景介绍：网络已经深入人们的生活并且越来越重要（Internet is getting into people's life and becoming more and more popular.）。紧接着在第二句点明文章的中心：internet education，专家们现在致力于在中国建立一个全国性的远程教育系统，通过网络提供教育机会（Experts are now working on setting up a national long-distance educational system in China to provide educational opportunities via Internet.）。

短文第二、三段的首句分别是这两个段落的中心句。第二段首句写到，事实上，网络教育计划已经成型（In reality, the educational via Internet plan has been taking shape.），其后用一些大学网络教育目前的发展情况来支撑。第三段首句提到，网络教育将迅速发展（The Internet education will be developing dramatically.），其后用未来发展趋势进行说明。

在写这篇短文总结时，考生应结合短文第一段的第二句，第二、三段的第一句进行概括：Internet education provides more educational chances. It has been applied in a number of universities. It will be used widely both in China and all over the world in the future.

② 记叙文。如果阅读短文是记叙文，考生应重点关注记叙事件的时间、地点、人物、经过。如果出现人物较多，考生应抓住主人公，结合故事情节对主要人物加以介绍。对于其他人物，如有必要可简单说明其与主人公之间的关系，次要人物可忽略。

介绍完人物之后考生应总结短文叙述之事的起因、经过、结果。如果故事有转折性的情节，注意不要遗漏。事件经过部分考生无须进行过于细节化的描述，以免出现短文总结过长、评论过短或作文超出字数限制的情况。

范文 3（2017 年 3 月真题）

Lee Rocdriguez-Espada, 12, was late to the Wegmans Family 5k Sunday in Rochester, New York. To save time, her mom dropped her near the starting line before parking the car. Lee rushed to the starting line only to realize the race had already begun. She was told to just start running and quickly fell into pace with the others. Meanwhile her mom found a spot at the finish line, expecting to congratulate her daughter within the hour.

Concentrating on running, Lee didn't realize until mile 4 that the finish line was nowhere in sight. Turning to another runner, she asked how much further. "That's when it stuck me I was in the half marathon instead of the 5k," Lee said afterwards. Instead of dropping out, she decided to keep running.

Realizing Lee wasn't among the runners crossing the 5k finish line, her mom alerted race officials and the police. A police officer eventually found Lee on the course of the Flower City Half Marathon. The girl said she knew her family was worried but she couldn' t quit. She needed to finish the race. And as she finally crossed the finish line, after running 10 miles more than she had planned, her mother cried tears of joy. " I see her with a medal and I thought, ' Oh my gosh, she ran the other one, like for real, '" she said. "She decided to just keep running and not give up. " "I'm really proud," said Lee, whose next race is this weekend.

这篇记叙文讲述了主人公 Lee Rocdriguez-Espada 意外地完成半马比赛的故事。除了主人公之外，故事还出现了 her mom 这个重要人物及次要人物 police officer，考生应抓住主要人物之间的关系，概述主要故事情节。

考生在概述时可以主人公作为开头进行展开：Lee Rocdriguez-Espada was a 12-year-old girl who planned to join a 5k race. She was dropped in a half marathon race by her mother. However, she did not give up and finished the race.

"Lee Rocdriguez-Espada was a 12-year-old girl"是人物介绍，"who planned to join a 5k race"介绍了事件的起因，这个女孩只想参加一个 5 公里跑步比赛。事情的经过是"She was dropped in a half marathon race by her mother. "，然而，"she did not give up"。事情的结果是"finished the race. "

范文 4（2016 年 3 月真题）

Dear Sally,

It was amazing to see your dance performance last weekend. I felt so proud of you when your teacher and schoolmates congratulated you upon your completion of the performance.

While you continue to enjoy the moment, I'd like to share with you a small quote from Abraham Lincoln, "This, too, shall pass away. " I want these words to be your guide at every turning point in your life.

When you're feeling very proud of yourself at an achievement, knowing no bounds at that moment, remember that "This, too, shall pass away."

When you' re at a difficult moment in your life and don't know what to do, find comfort in the same words- "This, too, shall pass away."

I'm not saying that the ache of some losses and setbacks will completely go away from your life. In fact, often the memories of painful events will hit you unexpectedly like tons of bricks and take your breath away years after they happen.

But, like all humans, you have an almost infinite capacity to adapt to life's changes and a great ability to bounce back from trying times. This understanding should give you a spark of hope When you're in a season of despair; it should also build up your confidence for taking risks in the future.

Sally, our lives are made up of several peaks and several valleys. That's the nature of life. Live each moment as it comes. And always remember "This, too, shall pass away."

Love,

Papa

这是一份父亲写给女儿的信，属于记叙文。父亲在信中首先对女儿完成舞蹈表演表示了骄傲，而后和女儿分享了一句格言。

考生可以以 father 或者 daughter 作概述的开头，也可以从叙述者的角度来写：The writer of the letter, who feels proud of his daughter's dance performance, congratulates her on her success and tells her a quote, "This, too, shall pass away." He tells her daughter to remember it either when achieving success or in difficulty.

2. *表明观点*

考生的观点可以是强调重要性。说明文的中心句可以是“我认为，在当今社会，……对我们的日常生活/学习很重要/有很大影响。”记叙文的中心句可以写成“我认为这个故事/这封信告诉我们，……对我们的日常生活/学习很重要/有很大影响。”

“我认为，在当今社会”及其相近意思可以用如下句式：

In my opinion, nowadays/these days, it seems that...

我认为，现在看起来……

As far as I am concerned, in contemporary society, there is no denying that...

在我看来，在当今社会，……是不可否认的。

In my view, recently, it is universally acknowledged that...

我认为，最近大家普遍认为……

From my perspective, at present, there is no doubt that...

从我的角度来看，现在……是毫无疑问的。

Personally, today, there is no exaggerating to say that...

我个人认为，现在，……是毫不夸张的。

“我认为这个故事/这封信告诉我们”等可以用如下句式表达：

In my opinion, the story /this letter/it shows/demonstrates/reveals/illustrates/tells that...

在写这个句子时，考生应注意主谓一致。通常短文是一个故事或是一封信，在写这个句式时，如果用“一个故事或是一封信”做主语，谓语动词要用第三人称单数，加 s。

“……对我们的日常生活/学习很重要/有很大影响”等可以用如下句式表达：

... plays an increasingly/more and more important/significant/essential/crucial/vital/critical/irreplaceable role in people's life/study.

……在人们的生活/学习中承担着越来越重要/重大/必要/关键/至关重要/极为重要/不可替代的角色。

... is particularly/ really/actually very/extremely important in people's life/study.

……对人们的生活/学习是特别/及其重要的。

... has a profound impact on people's daily life.

……对人们的日常生活有重要影响。

除了强调重要性之外，考生也可以从分析原因的角度点明中心，可用如下句式引入：

A number of/ A variety of factors/ reasons are accountable for this situation.

这个情况可以归于很多原因。

A large number of factors might contribute to / lead to/ account for the issue.

很多原因可以用来解释这个问题。

In my opinion, the problem/ phenomenon/ change in... is mainly/ largely attributable to...

在我看来，这个问题/现象/……变化的原因主要是因为……

The reasons to explain this situation can be listed as follows.

解释这个情况的原因有如下几点。

结合这些句式，这几篇范文中心句可写为：

范文 1 的中心句可写为：From my perspective, it reveals that environmental protection is extremely crucial in our life.

范文 2 的中心句可写为：As far as I am concerned, it is widely acknowledged that Internet education plays an increasingly important role in modern society.

范文 3 的中心句可写为：In my opinion, this story shows that persistence is really essential in our daily life.

范文 4 的中心句可写为：In my view, it illustrates that everything will pass away, no matter good or bad.

（二）主体段

在首段表明观点后考生应展开论证，证明自己的观点是有道理的。通常可以从原因、优势等角度进行构思。

1. 分论点

考生应围绕分论点展开主体段论证。那么需要几个分论点？写几个主体段呢？这主要决定于考生在考场上的构思。如果每个分论点能够想到的支撑细节较多，则选择两个分论点，分别写作两个主体段。如果短时间内能想到的支撑细节较少，则建议考生至少写出三个分论点，不需分段，写一个主体段即可。

特别提醒考生注意：如果是写两个主体段，一定要在每段的第一句开门见山地给出分论点，即该主体段的中心句，让阅卷老师能够在第一时间获知该段的中心思想。此外，不管是写两个主体段还是一个主体段，都建议考生在写作前一定要构思好整体框架，切勿边写边想，甚至写完一个段落全部划掉重写，既浪费时间又影响卷面。

以范文 2 为例，该文的中心句是“As far as I am concerned, it is widely acknowledged that Internet education plays an increasingly important role in modern society.”考生可以从网络学习带来的好处展开，如，“网络学习很方便”“网络学习的信息量大”。那么这篇文章的分论点即主体段第一句则应该围绕这两点写作。

2. 根据分论点展开论证

考生应该在构思框架时就已经想好用哪种方式进行展开论证，并根据写作的难易程度调整顺序。建议考生先写比较容易展开论证的分论点，相对不好展开的后写或者合并在一个主体段里。论证展开方式主要有如下 7 种：

① 说理展开。对中心句加以解释说明，使之更加具体化，但注意不能是简单的重复。可用如下句式引入：

That means...

To put it differently, ...

That is to say, ...

In other words, ...

② 举例展开。用事例证明中心句。考生在用例证法时应注意举例不宜过长、过于细节化，举例后最好能够再说明一下例子为什么能够证明中心句。可用如下句式引入：

A good example of this is...

Take... for example, ...

Consider... for example, ...

For example, ...

For instance, ...

... such as ...

... like...

③ 因果展开。利用因果关系展开论证。可用如下句式引入：

表示原因：The reason is...

... is the reason/element/factor.

be responsible for...

be connected with...

表示结果：Therefore, ...

As a consequence, ...

Consequently, ...

As a result, ...

④ 对比展开。从对比的角度展开论证，如对比传统教学方式和网络教学。可用如下句式引入：

By/In contrast, ...

On the contrary/Contrary to/Instead...

While/Whilst/Whereas...

Rather than/Instead of...

⑤ 类比展开。类比是另一种比较方式，是比较两者或多个事物之间的相似之处，如类比水污染和空气污染对环境的破坏。可用如下句式引入：

Similarly, ...

Likewise, ...

Like...

The same is true of...

⑥ 让步展开。用让步关系进行上下文的展开，可用如下句式引入：

Despite/In spite of/Notwithstanding...

(后面跟名词或从句)

Nonetheless/Nevertheless...

(后面跟完整的句子)

Even though/Although...

(后面跟从句，表示对已经存在的状况让步)

Even if...

(后面跟从句，表示对还未发生的状况让步)

No matter...

(后面跟从句)

⑦ 假设展开。假设条件进行展开，可用如下句式引入：

If...

Provided that...

Unless...

Otherwise...

Without... , ... would...

以范文 2 为例，假设考生在构思提纲时只想到了“网络学习的信息量大”、“网络学习很方便”两个分论点，那么便适合用两个主体段的方式展开。此时考生应该考虑每个主体段用哪种方式展开。关于“信息量大”，考生可能会想到网络上有大量的课程可供选择，可以用说理的方法展开。关于“方便”，考生可以举例比如没时间上课时怎么办。那么这篇文章的两个主体段可以参照下文展开：

Firstly, it is obvious that students can have access to more information via online learning.（中心句，开门见山点明信息量大。）This means that they are exposed to a large number of courses given by different teachers, and they could choose according to their needs and interest.（用说理的方法进一步阐述具体理由：网络上有大量课程可供选择。）So compared with traditional learning, Internet education provides students with more learning resources.（回应中心句，但不能简单重复。此句使用了对比的方法。）

Moreover, Internet learning brings a great convenience to people.（第二个原因，即中心句：网络学习很方便。）For example, if a student is occupied with an emergency and can not take the class on time, he or she could watch the class video whenever they are free.（用举例的方法展开论证：比如没时间上课时，可以有空时再看课程视频。）Therefore, with Internet education, people could take class at anytime and anyplace, which is totally different from traditional class.（解释例子为什么能够证明该段中心：和传统教育不同，人们可以在任何时候任何地方上课。）

（三）结尾段

考生应在结尾段再次表明观点，但是要注意不能和开头段的表述重复，可以转写或升华。结尾段最好不要只有一句话，在表明观点后，考生可将主体段内容用单词或简短的词组加以概括。如范文 2 可作如下结尾：

In conclusion, Internet education is particularly crucial at present.（再次点明中心，网络学习在当今是十分重要的。）It is not only informative, but also convenient.（informative 和 convenient 两个词分别总结两个主体段的内容：信息量大、方便。）

此外，结尾段还可以提出建议，同时对采纳该建议可能出现的结果做出预测，如 We could... , Only by doing that can we...（我们可以做……只有那样做了我们才能……）。

（四）有效衔接

综合写作评分标准要求考生要能够“有效使用多种衔接手段，内容连贯流畅，层次清晰”。

1. 主体段常用衔接表达

句子与句子之间需要使用衔接词使得上下文更加的流畅。句间衔接词可参照前文主体段展开方式用词。段落之间同样也需要使用有效地衔接使得段落之间层次更加清晰，过渡更加自然。主体段之间可用如下句式引入：

First, ... Second, ... Finally, ...

First of all, ... Secondly, ...　The third reason is that...

To start with, ... In the second place, ...　Eventually...

One is that... , Secondly, ... A third reason is...

To start with, ... Then, ... Moreover, ... Furthermore, ... In addition, ...　Finally, ...

2. 结尾段常用衔接表达

结尾段作为文章的最后一部分，是对文章的总结。可用如下方式引入结尾段：

In a word, ...

In summary, ...

All in all, ...

In brief, ...

In short, ...

From what has been discussed above, we can easily come to the conclusion that...

通过刚才所讨论的一切，我们可以很容易就得出结论……

It is high time that effective measures were taken to stop... For example, ... In addition... All these measures will certainly...

是我们采取有效措施来阻止……的时候了。比如说……；另外……。所有这些方法肯定会……

It is necessary that... steps should be taken to...

采取一些措施来……是有必要的。

三、PETS–3 真题及解析

全国英语等级考试第三级
2019 年 9 月笔试真题（改编版）

笔试部分答题时间：120 分钟

2019. 9

SECTION I Listening

(25 minutes)

Directions:

This section is designed to test your ability to understand spoken English. You will hear a selection of recorded materials and you must answer the questions that accompany them. There are two parts in this section, Part A and Part B.

Remember, while you are doing the test, you should first put down your answers in your test booklet. At the end of the listening section, you will have 3 *minutes to transfer all your answers from your test booklet to your ANSWER SHEET.*

If you have any questions, you may raise your hand now as you will not be allowed to speak once the test has started.

Now look at Part A in your test booklet.

Part A

Directions:

You will hear 10 *short dialogues. For each dialogue, there is one question and four possible answers. Choose the correct answer-A, B, C or D, and mark it in your test booklet. You will have* 15 *seconds to answer the question and you will hear each dialogue* ***only once****.*

Example:

You will hear:

W: Could you please tell me if the Beijing flight will be arriving on time?

M: Yes, Madam. It should be arriving in about ten minutes.

You will read:

Who do you think the woman is talking to?

[A] A bus conductor.

[B] A clerk at the airport.

[C] A taxi driver.

[D] A clerk at the station.

From the dialogue, we know that only a clerk at the airport is most likely to know the arrival time of a flight, so you should choose answer [B] and mark it in your test booklet.

Sample Answer: [A] ■ [C] [D]

Now look at question 1.

1. What will the woman do?

[A] Play basketball. [B] Have a rest.

[C] Go to the library. [D] Prepare for the examination.

2. Why couldn't the woman get through to the man?

[A] His mobile was stolen. [B] His mobile didn't work.

[C] His mobile was powered off. [D] He wasn't at home.

3. What is the man?

[A] A waiter. [B] A taxi driver.

[C] A conductor. [D] A policeman.

4. Why does the man refused the woman?

[A] He doesn't have a bike.

[B] He'll use his bike.

[C] He had lent his bike to others.

[D] He doesn't want to lend his bike to her.

5. What is probably the relationship between the two speakers?

[A] Sister and brother. [B] Mother and son.

[C] Teacher and pupil. [D] Friends.

6. What does the woman plan to do tomorrow?

[A] Sleep late. [B] Do some washing up.

[C] Cook breakfast herself. [D] Go shopping with her friends.

7. What can be inferred about the woman?

[A] She is going to drop the class too.

[B] She doesn't know how to swim.

[C] It took her a long time to learn to swim.

[D] She doesn't like to swim.

8. What does the doctor imply?

[A] The man should continue using the medicine.

[B] The man should stop using the medicine.

[C] She'll be away from the office for two days.

[D] The man doesn't need anything for his cough.

9. Where does the conversation probably take place?

[A] In a hospital. [B] In a school.

[C] Outside a house. [D] On the road.

10. What does the woman mean?

[A] The machine was just repaired.

[B] The clerk doesn't like to be bothered.

[C] The man shouldn't make any copies.

[D] She can teach the man to operate the machine.

Part B

Directions:

You will hear four dialogues or monologues. Before listening to each one, you will have 5 *seconds to read each of the questions which accompany it. While listening, answer each question by choosing A, B, C or D. After listening, you will have* 10 *seconds to check your answer to each question. You will hear the recording* ***only once.***

Questions 11 – 13 *are based on the following dialogue.*

11. Why is the woman so happy?

[A] She started carrying a credit card. [B] She got an ID card of her own.

[C] She's got some money belonging to her. [D] She met something interesting.

12. What advice does the man give the woman?

[A] She must have enough money with her.

[B] She should not buy everything she wants.

[C] She must care about her credit card and ID card.

[D] She shouldn't use the card.

13. How much can the woman spend at most with her credit card?

[A] \$ 500. [B] \$ 1,500.

[C] \$ 50. [D] \$ 15.

Questions 14 – 17 *are based on the following dialogue.*

14. How long will Anna still have to stay in London?

[A] At least 40 days. [B] At least 35 days.

[C] At least 30 days. [D] At least 25 days.

15. What does Anna do in the afternoon?

[A] Taking classes. [B] Doing homework.

[C] Going sightseeing. [D] Playing games.

16. Why does Anna want to improve English?

[A] To get a promotion soon.

[B] To communicate with her customers better.

[C] To make friends with British people.

[D] To make use of her spare time.

17. What do we know about Anna?

[A] She has never been to London before.

[B] She knows little English before coming to London.

[C] She practices English with her roommates.

[D] She has met many English people in London.

Questions 18 – 21 *are based on the following dialogue.*

18. What was the woman doing these days?

[A] She was doing nothing. [B] She was going shopping.

[C] She was studying. [D] She was going sightseeing.

19. What does the woman want the man to do?

[A] Be a tour guide for her. [B] Be a shopping guide for her.

[C] Buy some presents for her. [D] See her off the next day.

20. What does the woman want to buy for herself?

[A] A tartan jacket. [B] A book and a record.

[C] Skirts and socks. [D] Expensive perfume.

21. What is the woman going to do after the conversation?

[A] Return to the hotel and have a rest. [B] Go sightseeing at Piccadilly.

[C] Buy a cup of coffee for the man. [D] Treat a friend at a restaurant.

Questions 22 – 25 *are based on the following monologue.*

22. What does the speaker mainly talking about?

[A] Pollution. [B] Human voice.

[C] Good old days. [D] None of the above.

23. What does the saying "you can't hear yourself think" mean?

[A] You have head trouble. [B] You are too stressed.

[C] It's very noisy. [D] There is something wrong with your ears.

24. How many ways of reducing harm are mentioned?

[A] Five. [B] Four.

[C] Three. [D] Two.

25. What is the main purpose of the speech?

[A] To explain scientific knowledge. [B] To explain this phenomenon.

[C] To call on people to act. [D] To introduce a saying.

You now have 3 *minutes to transfer all your answers from your test booklet to your ANSWER SHEET.*

That is the end of listening section.

SECTION Ⅱ Reading

(50 minutes)

Part A

Directions:

Read the following two texts. Answer the questions on each text by choosing A, B, C or D. Mark your answers on your ANSWER SHEET.

Text 1

"Family" is of course an elastic word. And in different countries it has different meanings. But when British people say that their society is based on family life, they are thinking of "family" in its narrow, peculiarly European sense of mother, father and children living together in their own house as an economic and social unit. Thus, every British marriage indicates the beginning of a new and independent family—hence the tremendous importance of marriage in British life. For both man and woman, marriage means leaving one's parents and starting one's own life. The man's first duty will then be to his wife, and the wife's to her husband. He will be entirely responsible for her financial support, and she for the running of the new home. Their children will be their common responsibility and their alone. Neither the wife's parents nor the husband's, nor their brothers or sisters, aunts or uncles, have any right to interfere with them—they are their own masters.

Readers of novels like Jane Austen's *Pride and Prejudice* will know that in former times, marriage among wealthy families were arranged by the girl's parents, that is, it was the parents' duty to find a suitable husband for their daughter, preferably a rich one, and by skillful encouragement to lead him eventually to ask their permission to marry her. Until that time, the girl was protected and maintained in the parents' home, and the financial relief of getting rid of her could be seen in their giving the newly married pair a sum of money called a dowry (嫁妆). It is very different today. Most girls of today get a job when they leave school and become financially independent before their marriage. This has had two results. A girl chooses her own husband, and she gets no dowry. Every coin has two sides: independence for girls is no exception. But it may be a good thing for all of the girls, as their social status are much higher and they are no longer the subordinate (部下，下级) of their parents and husbands.

26. What does the author mean by "Family is of course an elastic word"?

[A] Different families have different ways of life.

[B] Different definitions could be given to the word.

[C] Different nations have different families.

[D] Different times produce different families.

27. For an English family, the husband's duty is ________

[A] supporting the family while the wife is working out

[B] defending the family while the wife is running the home

[C] providing financial support while the wife is running the home

[D] independent while his wife is also independent

28. Everything is decided in a family ________.

[A] by the couple [B] with the help of their parents

[C] by brothers and sisters [D] with the help of aunts and uncles

29. What is TRUE concerning the book Pride and Prejudice?

[A] It is the best book on marriage.

[B] It is a handbook on marriage.

[C] It gives some idea of English social life in the past.

[D] It provides a lot of information of former-time wealthy families.

30. With regard to marriage in Britain, present-day girls differ from former-time girls in ________.

[A] the right family [B] more parental support

[C] choosing husbands [D] social position

Text 2

I don't think there is anything wrong with your blood. The key to your problem is that long nap after dinner. If you didn't sleep for hours during the early part of the evening, you would be more ready to sleep at bedtime. If you didn't nap after dinner, you would not want to stay up so late, and you would not feel the need to take a sleeping pill. The pill is still working in your system when you get up in the morning. This helps account for the fact that you feel tired all day. You should get out of the habit of sleeping during the evening. Right after your evening meal, engage in some sort of physical activity—a sport such as bowling, perhaps. Or get together with friends for an evening of cards and conversation. Then go to bed at your usual time or a little earlier, and you should be able to get a good night's rest without taking a pill.

If you can get into the habit of spending your evenings this way, I am sure you will feel less tired during the day. At first it may be hard for you to go to sleep without taking a pill. If so, get up and watch television or do some jobs around your house until you feel sleepy. If you fall asleep and then wake up a few hours later, get up but do not take a sleeping pill. Read a while or listen to the radio, and make yourself a few hours' sleep that night, you will feel better in the morning than you usually feel after taking a pill. The next night you will be ready to sleep at an earlier hour. The most important thing is to avoid taking that nap right after dinner and avoid taking pills.

31. According to the writer, it is difficult for you to go to sleep because ________.

[A] you get the habit of staying up late
[B] you haven't taken sleeping pills
[C] you sleep for hours after dinner
[D] you fail to do some exercises

32. Which of the following is NOT true if you want to get out of the habit of sleeping during the evening?

[A] Go to bed earlier than usual.
[B] Talk with friends after dinner.
[C] Stay with friends after dinner.
[D] Do some physical labor.

33. You feel tired all day probably because ________.

[A] you stay up too late
[B] you get up too early in the morning
[C] you take sleeping pills
[D] you wake up too frequently at night

34. Which of the following is true according to the passage?

[A] You mustn't take sleeping pills in order to get a good night's sleep.
[B] You should stay up if you want to sleep effectively.
[C] Food is necessary at night if you fail to go to sleep.
[D] It is very important to get out of the habit of taking a nap after dinner.

35. We may infer that the author is most probably a ________.

[A] doctor [B] scientist [C] reporter [D] professor

Part B

Read the following paragraphs in which five people talked about language learning. For questions 36 – 40, match the name of each person to one of the statements (A – G) given below. Mark your answers on your ANSWER SHEET.

Gary:

It is generally held that one can pick up a foreign language easily when under the age of eight. If you immerse a child (under 8) in a foreign language, then he or she will pick it up within months. When a child is under 5, this can be a matter of weeks. This, very simply, is because the part of the brain that learns language is still developing and that it is easy for that child to pick up and copy sounds.

William:

It seems that the older you get, the more rigid your brain becomes, so that it is much harder to learn a new language, for example you were a teenager. I think that as a child you learn a language intuitively, just absorbing the language around. As you get older, you have to study the language more intensively and analytically, studying grammar and such.

Arthur:

We learn our first language not for any other reason than solving problems (communicating is a problem, and we develop our patterns to do so), when we have "covered" that need we don't go further, unless we have an extra need (it could be the desire of having more languages). It is fascinating how we are motivated by those needs, which combined with proper exposure makes us learn a new language.

Joyce:

My own theory is that language learning is very attitude or self-image dependent. Each person's self-image governs to what extent they are willing to absorb a new language. Clearly, children before they become self-conscious are far less inhibited than young teenagers who have begun to worry what others think about them. I've come across examples of self-conscious inhibition in adults when teaching pronunciation. Whereas children, who are still forming their own identity, seek to conform to their peers, adults, on the other hand, with an already firmly established self-image feel foolish when making unfamiliar tongue and lip movements.

Mary:

Besides self-image, children and adults experience different types of pressure from those of the same age or status. Young children are often placed in a completely foreign language environment by their parents—leaving them with little choice but to learn the new language. Peer pressure is pushing them to learn. Adults on the other hand, almost never completely separate themselves from the native culture. When it comes too hard they can easily break away from the foreign group and revert to their native language. Depending on the person's culture, peer pressure can push them not to learn.

Now match the name of each person (36-40) to the appropriate statement.

Note: there are two extra statements.

Statements

36. Gary
37. William
38. Arthur
39. Joyce
40. Mary

[A] Stress around you affects foreign language achievement.

[B] Learning strategies determine one's foreign language learning achievements.

[C] Ideas about your qualities and abilities affect a new language learning.

[D] Practical needs often have positive impact on a new language learning.

[E] The older one is, the harder it will be to learn a new language.

[F] Personality produces difference in the development of a new language learning.

[G] Younger children enjoy an advantage in learning a foreign language.

Part C

Directions:

Read the following text from which five sentences have been removed. Choose from the sentences A-G the most suitable one to fill each numbered gap in the text (41 –45). *There are TWO extra sentences that you do not need to use. Mark your answer in your* ***ANSWER SHEET.***

__41__ The Daily Mirror and the Daily Express both sell about four million copies every day. Apart from the national papers, there is, __42__ Local newspapers have a weekly circulation of 13 million. Almost every town and country area has one. Nearly all of them hold their own financially and many of them are very profitable.

These papers are written almost entirely for readers interested in local events, birth, deaths, council meetings and sports. __43__ Editors prefer to rely on a small staff of people who all know the district well. A great deal of local news is regularly supplied by clubs and churches in the neighborhood and it does not get out of date as quickly as national news. If there is no room for it in this week's edition, an item can sometimes be held over until the following week.

The editor must never forget that the success of any newspaper depends on advertising. __44__ But if the newspaper is well written and the news items have been carefully chosen to attract local readers, the businessmen are grateful for the opportunity to keep their products in the public eyes.

Local newspapers do not often comment on problems of national importance and editors rarely hold with taking sides on political questions. __45__ A newspaper can sometimes persuade the council to take action to provide better shopping facilities, improve transport in the area, and so on.

[A] Newspapers in Britain usually have great profits.

[B] So local businesses are very interested in advertising in local papers.

[C] The content is naturally influenced by the kind of community they serve.

[D] For this reason, he is keen to keep the good will of local businessmen.

[E] However, another branch of the British press which sells almost as many as copies.

[F] But they can often be of service to the community in expressing public feelings on local issues.

[G] Visitors to Britain are sometimes surprised to learn that newspapers there have such a large circulation.

Part D

Directions:

Read the following text from which 10 *words have been removed. Choose from the words A-O the most suitable one to fill each numbered gap in the text* (46 –55). *There are FIVE extra words that you do not need to use. Mark your answers on your ANSWER SHEET.*

With the world's population estimated to grow from six to nine billion by 2050, researchers, businesses and governments are already dealing with the impact, this increase will have on everything from food and water to infrastructure and jobs. Underlying all this __46__ will be the demand for energy, which is expected to double over the next 40 years.

Finding the resources to meet this demand in a __47__, sustainable way is the cornerstone of our nation's energy security, and will be one of the major __48__ of the 21st century. Alternative forms of energy-bio-fuels, wind and solar, to name a few are __49__ being funded and developed, and will play a growing __50__ in the world's energy supply. But experts say that even when __51__, alternative energy sources will likely meet only about 30% of the world's energy needs by 2050.

For example, even with __52__ investments, such as the $ 93 million for wind energy development __53__ in the American Recovery and Reinvestment Act, important alternative energy sources such as wind and bio-fuels __54__ only about 1% of the market today.

Energy and sustainability experts say the answer to our future energy needs will likely come from a lot of __55__ both traditional and alternative.

[A] consist	[B] solutions	[C] certainly
[D] stable	[E] comprise	[F] competitions
[G] exactly	[H] growth	[I] included
[J] role	[K] progress	[L] marvelous
[M] challenges	[N] combined	[O] significant

SECTION Ⅲ Writing

(45 minutes)

Directions:

You should write your responses to both Part A and Part B of this section on your ANSWER SHEET.

Part A

56.

You are preparing for an English test and are in need of some reference books. Write a letter to the sales department of a bookstore to ask for:

(1) detailed information about the books you want;

(2) methods of payment;

(3) time and way of delivery.

You should write about 100 words. Do not sign your own name at the end of your letter. Use "Wang Lin" instead.

Part B

57.

Directions:

Read the text below. Write an essay in about 120 words, in which you should summarize the key points of the text and make comments on them. Try to use your own words.

It's the graduation season again. According to a latest survey, most Chinese graduates have high salary expectations, and thus prefer working for foreign companies or state-owned enterprises in first-tier cities.

The survey was conducted by *renren. com*, a Chinese social media site, which is similar to Facebook. The results show that among 1,510 respondents, more than 64.7 percent want to work in first-tier cities.

In addition, 29.4 percent of the graduates who were born in the 1990s want to work for foreign companies, 25.5 percent for SOEs and 23.5 percent for private companies.

One interesting revelation is that although there are less than 100 days before graduation and more than half of the respondents have yet to get a job offer, they are not lowering their salary expectations. Apparently, 41.2 percent aim for 8000-10000 yuan ($ 1279- $ 1599) per month and 31.4 percent for 4000-6000 yuan.

According to the data released by the Chinese Academy of Social Sciences, the average monthly salary in Beijing was 5826 yuan ($ 931) last year, while the numbers for Shanghai, Tianjin and Chongqing were 5380, 4058 and 3995 yuan respectively.

A sample of comments in Weibo: "Are the survey results only jokes for April Fools' Day? Don't daydream anymore! Please check if you have a good command of English and professional skills that deserve a decent job with a high pay." On other comments says: "Some of my classmates got offers from foreign banks, international accounting firms and other famous foreign companies. They are told their yearly salary can reach 100, 000 yuan ($ 15,990)."

THAT IS THE END OF THE TEST.

全国英语等级考试第三级
2019 年 9 月笔试真题（改编版）答案及解析

SECTION Ⅰ　Listening

Part A

1. D　　2. B　　3. B　　4. B　　5. C

6. B　　7. C　　8. A　　9. C　　10. D

【原文及解析】

1. M: Will you be joining us later in the basketball game?

W: No, thanks. I have to prepare for my tomorrow's examination.

D **【解析】** 问题：女士将会干什么？男士邀请女士参加稍后的篮球比赛，女士拒绝了。根据画线部分可得知，她得为明天的考试做准备，故答案是［D］Prepare for the examination.

2. W: I dialed your phone number many times yesterday, but I couldn't get through. What's the matter?

M: Oh, there was something wrong with my mobile. I will have to buy a new one.

B **【解析】** 问题：为什么女士无法打通男士的电话？根据画线部分可得知男士的电话坏了，他得买一个新的。选项［C］His mobile was powered off. 的意思是手机没电了，不符合对话内容。答案是［B］His mobile didn't work.

3. M: This is River Street. What number do you want to go to?

W: Let me get off there in front of that tree. That's fine.

B **【解析】** 问题：该男士是干什么的？根据男士说的话可知，他先报了目前的方位，并问女士要去几号。女士回答说要在那棵树前下车。由此可以推断该男士是一个司机，故答案是［B］A taxi driver.

4. W: Would you mind if I borrowed your bike just over the weekend?

M: I'm sorry, but it's just not possible, because I'm visiting my mother this weekend.

B **【解析】** 问题：为什么男士拒绝了女士？女士想跟男士借用自行车在周末使用，男士拒绝了，说不可能。根据画线部分可得知拒绝的原因是本周末他要去拜访母亲，言下之意是他自己要在周末使用自行车，故答案是［B］He'll use his bike.

5. M: If you touch me I'll tell my father.

W：Go ahead and tell him. He has asked me to punish you whenever you interrupt this class.

C【解析】问题：对话双方可能的关系是什么？男士警告女士说：如果你碰我一下，我就告诉我的父亲。画线部分出现了 class，女士的意思是：你的父亲已经授权我，如果你打断上课的话，我就可以惩罚你。由此我们推断本题是学校场景，对话双方是师生关系。故答案是［C］Teacher and pupil. Pupil 一般指小学生。

6. M：What are your plans for tomorrow, Brenda?

W：Well, first, I'm going to do the washing up.

M：Poor you! While you're doing the washing up, I'll be having breakfast in bed.

W：It's all right for some people.

B【解析】问题：明天女士计划做什么？根据画线部分可得知，女士首先得做些洗洗涮涮的事，男士表示同情，故答案是［B］Do some washing up.

7. M：I'm thinking of dropping my swimming class. I am just not catching on.

W：Stick with it. I did and I learned how to swim eventually.

C【解析】问题：关于女士我们可以推断出什么？男士想要放弃游泳课了，因为他跟不上。女士鼓励他坚持住。在这里，"drop sth." 指放弃某事物，"stick with sth." 指坚持某事物。根据画线部分可得知，女士以前坚持住了，最终学会了游泳，言下之意是她学游泳也不容易，花了很长时间，故答案是［C］It took her a long time to learn to swim.

8. M：Doctor, this cough medicine doesn't seem to be helping. Can you give me a different prescription?

W：Let's give it another day or two to see how you are doing then.

A【解析】问题：医生暗示什么？男士（病人）告诉女士（医生）咳嗽药好像不管用，要求给他开不同的处方。根据画线部分可得知，女士（医生）建议再试一两天看看情况，故答案是［A］The man should continue using the medicine.

9. W：Help! Help! Fire!

M：Please step aside. Everything will be all right.

W：Oh, sir, there is still a baby inside, who is sleeping.

M：Don't worry. We'll find her at once.

C【解析】问题：对话很有可能发生在什么地方？女士开始时说的话显示发生了火灾，根据画线部分可得知里面还有一个正在睡觉的宝宝，我们可以推断男士是消防员，两人在着火的房子外面对话，故答案是［C］Outside a house.

10. M：I'm still waiting for the clerk to come back and make some copies of this paper for me.

W：Why bother him? I'll show you how easy it is to operate the machine.

M：Thank you very much. You know, I'm not good at operating machines.

D【解析】问题：女士是什么意思？男士说他还在等办事员回来为他复印这篇论文，女士回应说："为什么要麻烦他？我来给你展示操作复印机是多么的容易。"根据画线部分可得知，女士能教男士使用复印机，故答案是［D］She can teach the man to operate the machine.

Part B

11. A	12. C	13. B	14. D	15. C
16. B	17. A	18. D	19. B	20. C
21. C	22. A	23. C	24. D	25. C

【原文及解析】

Questions 11 – 13

W：(11) I am happy I started carrying the credit card that the bank gave us.

M：Why is that, Kate? Did you use it to buy something?

W：I surely did. On my way home I stopped at the store to buy some beef for dinner because I didn't have any cash with me.

M：And they permitted you to pay with the card?

W：Yes. They didn't even ask me to give the ID.

M：(12) You have to be careful. If you lose them and someone finds them, the bank will charge you for what you buy.

W：(13) How much has the bank allowed us to spend with the card?

M：(13) Fifteen hundred dollars. The bank encourages us to use the card, but they will also require us to pay them back.

W：You are right, Henry. I'll remember that. But the card surely makes it easy to spend money.

11. 问题：这位女士为什么感到高兴？

A【解析】细节辨认题。对话的开头女士提到："我开始随身携带银行办的信用卡了，这让我很高兴。"因此 A 是正确选项。女士提到她用信用卡买牛肉的时候身上没带现金（I didn't have any cash with me.）刷卡的时候："他们甚至都没要求我出示身份证(They didn't even ask me to give the ID)。"故 B、C 都是干扰项，D 对话中未提及。

12. 问题：男士给了女士什么建议？

C【解析】细节辨认题。男士建议说："你得小心点。如果你的卡丢了被别人捡到，银行会认定是你买的东西并向你收费。"与 C 选项表达的意思一致，因此 C 是正确选项。

13. 问题：女士的信用卡最多可以透支多少钱？

B【解析】细节辨认题。本题考查英文中数字的表达。女士问："银行最多允许我们用卡透支多少钱？"男士回答："1,500 美元。"B 是正确选项。

Questions 14 – 17

M：Er，Anna，tell me，how long have you been here in London？

W：I arrived ten days ago.

M：(14) I understand you are taking an English course at this school.

W：Yes，that's right.

M：(14) When did the course start？

W：(14) It started... er，five days ago.

M：(14) How long does it last？

W：(14) It lasts a month，and there are three hours of classes every morning. (15) In the afternoon there are trips to places of interest in London.

M：I see. (16) Why did you decide to take this course？

W：(16) For two reasons，really. You see，I work in the Sales Department of a computer company，and I often have to speak English to customers，so I wanted to improve my spoken English.

M：You speak very well.

W：Thank you.

M：(16) And the second reason？

W：(16) It was a good excuse to see London.

M：(17) Is this the first time you've been here？

W：(17) Yes.

M：And are you living with an English family here in London？

W：No，I'm living in a hotel，but I think it's better to live with a family. There are five French people staying at the hotel，so we speak French together. I haven't met many English people yet！

14. 问题：安娜还要在伦敦待多久？

D【解析】细节辨认题。从男士说："我知道你在这所学校上英语课。"可推断安娜来伦敦的目的是上英语课。男士问："课程是什么时候开始的？"安娜说："大概五天前开始的。""课程将持续多久？"安娜说："一个月。"经过简单的加减计算，可知D是正确选项。

15. 问题：安娜下午一般做什么？

C【解析】细节辨认题。对话中提到安娜每天上午有三小时的课程，下午有伦敦名胜的参观活动。going sightseeing 是 there are trips to places of interest 的同义转述。C 是正确选项。

16. 问题：为什么安娜想要提高英语水平？

B【解析】细节辨认题。男士问："为什么你决定要学这门课程？"安娜说有两个原因。"我在一家电脑公司的销售部工作，经常要用英语和客户交流，所以我想提高我的英语口语。”原因二则是“这是个参观伦敦的好借口。”B 选项与原因一相同，因此是正确选项。get a promotion 得到晋升，make use of her spare time 充分利用业余时间。

17. 问题：我们可得知安娜的哪些信息？

A【解析】细节辨认题。男士问：“这是你第一次来到这里吗？”安娜说：“是的。”A 是正确选项。对话的最后，安娜说：“我们五个人都住在那家旅馆，所以我们在一起说法语。我到现在还没认识几个英国人呢！”因此，C、D 选项与原文相反。从上文中可知安娜工作中经常需要说英文，因此她来伦敦前并非对英文一窍不通，排除 B。

必背词汇

places of interest　名胜古迹

get a promotion　得到晋升

spare time　业余时间

Questions 18 – 21

W：(19) Hey, Tom. I wonder if you can help me. (18) I've been so busy sightseeing these days and I haven't done any shopping. Now it's almost the end of my tour and I'm leaving tomorrow. (19) I need to buy some presents for my family members but I don't know where to get them.

M：I'm glad to be of any help. Do you have anything particular in mind?

W：Well, I need to buy a warm jumper for my mother so that she can wear it in winter. My sister likes perfume. And then some wine or aftershave for my brother.

M：Can we stop for a moment so I can tell you where you may get those things. Have you got a map there? Well, there's a Scorch Wale shop here on the left side as you go down Regent Street from the hotel you are staying. They have all kinds of jumpers and tartan skirts and...

W：(20) Oh, tartan skirts? That's what I want for myself. I love those skirts. And do they also sell socks? I'd like to buy some too.

M：I'm not sure, but there is a sock shop on the opposite side of the street in fact. Now, as to perfume...

W：No. I've changed my mind. I think a book for sister and a record for my brother may be better. Can I get those near Piccadilly?

M：Oh, yes. There is big record shop. And not far from there, you will find a good selection of books at Harcher's.

W：Ah, I see. Well, that's about everything then. Thank you, Tom. (21) Now let's go to have a cup of coffee first. My treat.

18. 问题：这位女士这几天在做什么？

D【解析】细节辨认题。对话的开头，女士提到：“我这几天忙着观光，还没去购物。”因此 D 是正确选项。

19. 问题：女士想请这位男士做什么？

B【解析】细节辨认题。对话的开头，女士对男士说：“不知你能不能帮我个忙？……我需要给家人买些礼物，但我不知道在哪里能买到。”因此 B 是正确选项。

20. 问题：女士想给自己买什么？

C【解析】细节辨认题。对话中，女士说：“哦，格纹裙？这是我自己想要的。我喜欢那些裙子。他们也卖袜子吗？我也想买一些。”tartan n.（尤指源自苏格兰织物的）花格图案，方格花纹。女士起初想给妈妈买套头毛衣 jumper，给妹妹买香水 perfume，给哥哥买红酒或须后水 wine or aftershave，后来又改变了主意，打算给妹妹买本书，给哥哥买张唱片。因此正确答案是 C。

21. 问题：对话结束后女士打算做什么？

C【解析】细节辨认题。在对话的最后，女士说：“现在我们先去喝杯咖啡吧。我请客。”treat 在这个语境中表示“请客，做东”。因此正确答案是 C。

Questions 22 – 25

The sense of hearing is one of our most important means of knowing what is going on around us. We are warned of danger by sound. Sounds serve to please us in music. It has a waste product, too, in the form of noise. (22) Noise has been called unwanted sound. Noise is growing and it may get much worse before it gets any better. Automobiles, trucks, buses, motorcycles, airplanes, boats, factories, bands—all these things make noise. They bother not only our ears but our minds and bodies as well.

(23) There is a saying about it being so noisy that you can't hear yourself think. Doctors who study noise believe that we must sometimes hear ourselves think. If we don't, we may have headaches, other aches and pains, or even worse mental problems. Noise adds stress to our society that already faces enough.

(24) There are two ways to cut down on the harm caused by noise. One is to cut down on the amount of noise. The other is to protect ourselves against the noise we can't stop.

Ways of making less noise are now being tested. There are groups for the prevention of noise in this country. There is even a law controlling noise. (25) We cannot return to the "good old days" of peace and quiet. But we can reduce noise—if we shout loudly enough about it.

22. 问题：演讲者发言的主题是什么？

A【解析】主旨归纳题。演讲的开头通过听觉的重要性，引出了主题：“噪音被称为不必要的声音。现在噪音变得越来越大，在这个问题好转之前噪音问题可能会变得更糟。”接下来列举了一系列交通工具、工厂的噪音等。演讲者介绍了噪音的危害、如何减少噪音的危害以及如何降低噪音。因此，本文的主题是讨论噪音污染，应选择 A。

23. 问题：谚语“你听不到自己的想法”表达的是什么意思？

C【解析】语义理解题。在这句谚语的上文中提到“噪音不仅困扰着我们的耳朵，也困扰着我们的身心。”接着演讲者提到了这句谚语并用医生的话说明了噪音的危害。“you can't hear yourself think.”这句谚语表示“如果你听不到自己在想什么，你就不能把注意力放在任何事情上，因为噪音太大了。”应选择 C。

24. 问题：演讲者提到了几种减少噪音危害的方法？

D【解析】细节辨认题。演讲者说：“有两种方法可以减少噪音造成的危害，一种是减少噪音。另一个是既然我们无法控制噪音，就要保护自己不受它的影响。”应选择 D。

25. 问题：演讲的主要目的是什么？

C【解析】主旨推断题。在引出问题—科普危害—介绍解决方案之后，演讲者在最后表达了意见和建议：“我们不能回到和平与宁静的‘美好的旧时光’。但是我们可以减少噪音——如果我们大声呼吁的话。”因此可推断本文的主要目的是唤起人们改变噪音现状的意识。应选择 C。

SECTION Ⅱ Reading

Part A

Text 1

26. B【解析】句意理解题。由题干的“Family is of course an elastic word”直接定位到原文第一段第一句。elastic 本意为“有弹性的，可伸缩的”。由后句“And in different countries it has different meanings.”可知“它在不同的国家有不同的含义”，因此此句是说家庭的含义很灵活，故选 B。A 选项“不同的家庭有不同的生活方式”、C 选项“不同的国家有不同的家庭”、D 选项“不同的时代产生不同的家庭”原文都没有提及，因此排除。

27. C【解析】细节题。由题干的“For an English family, the husband's duty is”定位至原文第一段中间，由“He will be entirely responsible for her financial support, and she for the running of the new home.”可知，丈夫要完全负责妻子经济上的开销，妻子要操持整个新家。因此，C 选项是对原文的同义转述。

28. A【解析】细节题。由题干的“Everything is decided in a family”定位到原文第一段最后一句“Neither the wife's parents nor the husband's, nor their brothers or sisters, aunts or uncles, have any right to interfere with them-they are their own masters.”“男女双方的父母、兄弟、姐妹、姑姑和叔叔都不能干扰夫妻两人的生活——他们是自己的主人”可知家里一切事务都由夫妻二人自己决定。故选 A。

29. C【解析】推论题。由题干的“concerning the book Pride and Prejudice”定位到原文第二段，本段提到小说《傲慢与偏见》中有对旧时代富裕人家的女孩的婚姻状况的描写，写作的目的是为了描述当时英国社会生活的一个方面。故选 C。

30. D【解析】细节题。由题干的“present-day girls differ from former-time girls”定

位至原文最后一段，由最后一段最后一句“as their social status are much higher and they are no longer the subordinate（部下，下级）of their parents and husbands”. 可知，和以前相比，现在的女孩经济独立，社会地位提高了。故选 D。

【参考译文】

“家庭”是一个意思很灵活的词语，在不同的国家有着不同的含义。但是当英国人说他们的社会是建立在家庭生活上时，他们指的是狭义的、特别是对于欧洲特有的观念，即爸爸、妈妈和孩子作为一种经济和社会单位住在自己的房子里。因此，每一个英国婚姻都意味着独立而崭新的家庭生活开始了，所以婚姻对于英国人来说有着非比寻常的重要意义。无论是对于男人还是女人，结婚都意味着离开自己的父母开始自己的生活。丈夫的首要责任是照顾妻子，而妻子的首要责任是照顾丈夫。丈夫要完全负责妻子经济上的开销，妻子要操持整个新家。孩子是他们共同的责任，也只能是他们的责任。男女双方的父母、兄弟、姐妹、姑姑和叔叔都不能干扰夫妻两人的生活——他们是自己的主人。

读过简·奥斯汀的小说《傲慢与偏见》的人都知道，从前富裕人家的女孩的婚姻都是由她们的父母安排的。也就是说，为女儿找个合适的、最好是有钱的夫君是父母的责任。他们会游说那个年轻人主动向他们女儿求婚。那个时代，女孩还被保护在父母的家中。把女儿嫁出去时，他们要给新婚夫妇经济补贴，即嫁妆。现在跟以前不同了。现如今，大多数的女孩子毕业之后都有工作，且结婚之前经济独立。这样会导致两种结果：女孩可以自己选择丈夫，但是她也没有了嫁妆。凡事都有两面性，女孩独立这件事也不例外。但这对于女孩来说也许是件好事情，因为她们的社会地位提高了，她们不再是父母和丈夫的附属品。

Text 2

31. C【解析】细节题。由题干的“it is difficult for you to go to sleep because”定位到文章第一段第三句“If you didn't sleep for hours during the early part of the evening, you would be more ready to sleep at bedtime.”可知，如果你在晚上的早些时候没有睡好几个小时的话，你就会在睡觉时间更容易入睡。也就是说如果在晚上早些时候睡了的话，睡觉时间就难以入睡。C 项“你在晚饭后睡了几个小时”是对本句的同义转述，故选 C。

32. D【解析】细节题。由题干定位至文章第一段第七句到最后一句“You should get out of the habit of sleeping during the evening. Right after your evening meal, engage in some sort of physical activity—a sport such as bowling, perhaps. Or get together with friends for an evening of cards and conversation. Then go to bed at your usual time or a little earlier, and you should be able to get a good night's rest without taking a pill.”可知，你应该改掉晚上睡觉的习惯。晚饭后，就去参加一些体育活动，比如保龄球。晚上和朋友们一起打牌聊天。然后在你平常的时间或稍早一点上床睡觉，你应该可以在不吃药的情况下得到很好的休息。A 项“比平时早一些睡觉”，B 项“晚饭后和朋友聊天”和 C 项“晚饭

后和朋友待在一起”与文章原文表述一致。D 项“做一些体力劳动”与原文中的“physical activities（身体活动）”表述不符，故选 D。

33. C【解析】细节题。由题干的“You feel tired all day”定位至文章第一段第五、第六句“ The pill is still working in your system when you get up in the morning. This helps account for the fact that you feel tired all day.”可知，当你早上起床的时候，药片还在你的体内发挥作用。这有助于解释你整天感到疲劳这个事实。由此可知，整天感觉到很疲倦可能是因为“服用了安眠药”，C 选项符合题意，故选 C。

34. D【解析】推断题。通读全文可知，D 选项“摆脱晚饭后睡一小会的习惯是重要的”，与文章第一段和第三段中相关表述一致，故选 D。A 选项“为了获得好的夜晚睡眠，你千万不能吃安眠药”表达太过绝对，可排除；B 选项“如果你想要睡眠更有效率，你应该熬夜”与文章表述不符，排除；C 选项“如果你晚上失眠了，食物是必不可少的”在文章中并未提及，排除。

35. A【解析】推断题。根据文章首句“I don't think there is anything wrong with your blood”，即“我不认为你的血液有什么问题”，并结合全文，文章的主题是关于就寝前小睡对睡眠和休息的影响，可以推断出作者的职业可能是一位医生，故选 A。

【参考译文】

我认为你的血液没有什么问题。你问题的关键是晚饭后长时间的小睡。如果你在晚上的早些时候没有连续睡上好几个小时的话，那么在就寝时间你会更容易入睡。如果你晚饭后不打盹，你就不会想熬夜这么晚，你也不会觉得有必要吃安眠药。当你早上起床的时候，药丸还在你的身体里起作用。这有助于解释你一整天都感到疲倦的事实。你应该改掉晚上睡觉的习惯。晚饭后，就去参加一些体育活动，比如保龄球。晚上和朋友们一起打牌聊天。然后在你平常的时间或稍早一点上床睡觉，你应该可以在不吃药的情况下得到很好的休息。

如果你能养成这样度过晚上的习惯，我相信你白天不会感到那么累。一开始你可能很难不吃药就入睡。如果是这样的话，起床看电视或者在家里做些工作直到你感到困倦。如果你睡着了，然后几小时后醒来，起床，但不要服用安眠药。看一会儿书或者听听广播，晚上让自己睡几个小时，早上你会感觉比你吃药后感觉更好。第二天晚上你就很容易在较早的时候睡觉了。最重要的是避免在晚饭后小睡，而且避免吃安眠药。

Part B

【要求解析】

从“Read the following paragraphs in which five people talked about language learning.”可以得知五段文章是五个人对学习语言的不同看法。

【选项解析】

选项 A：来自周围的压力会影响你的外语学习。可用 Stress 作关键词。

选项 B：学习策略决定着一个人的外语学习成绩。可用 strategies 作关键词。

选项 C：有关素质和能力的想法影响着你学习新语言。可用 qualities and abilities 作关键词。

选项 D：通常来说，实际需求对学习一门新的语言有积极影响。可用 Practical needs 作关键词。

选项 E：年纪越大，就越难学习一门新语言。可用 older，harder 作关键词。

选项 F：个性在学习新语言的发展过程中会产生不同影响。可用 Personality 作关键词。

选项 G：年幼的孩子在学习外语方面具有优势。可用 Younger 作关键词。

【题目解析】

36. G **【解析】** 主旨题。该段第一句是主旨句，表明 8 岁以下的孩子学习外语很容易。后文提及 8 岁以下，5 岁以下的孩子学习外语的情况。最后一句是为什么孩子学外语更容易的原因。这些都与选项 G “Younger” 对应，“enjoy an advantage” 虽然没有相对应的表达，但该词组是对整段意思的概括。

37. E **【解析】** 主旨题。该段第一句是主旨句，表明年纪越大，大脑就会变得越僵化，学习一门新的语言就越困难。其中 “older，harder” 在选项 E 中直接出现，整句话语义也与该段落相符。

38. D **【解析】** 主旨题。该段第一句是主旨句，表明我们学习第一语言的原因无他，就是为了解决问题（交流是一种问题，我们发展了我们的交流模式），当我们满足了这个需求后我们便不再前进，直到我们又有了额外需求。第二句也提到了我们是被需求所激励着（we are motivated by those needs），“need” 一词在文章中反复出现，在选项 D 中也直接出现。选项 D 中 “对学习一门新语言有积极影响（have positive impact on a new language learning）” 对应文章 “激励（motivated）”，该段第一句也含有积极影响之意。

39. C **【解析】** 主旨题。该段第一句是主旨句，表明 Joyce 个人的理论是语言学习是非常依赖于态度和自我形象（very attitude or self-image dependent）。第二句解释了原因，每个人的自我形象都决定着他们在多大程度上希望吸收一门新的语言。第三句对比了孩子和青少年，孩子们在他们变得有自我意识之前，受抑制的程度小得多（before they become self-conscious are far less inhibited），而青少年则开始担心别人怎么看他们（have begun to worry what others think about them）。后文对比了孩子和成年人，也说明关注自我形象对语言学习的影响。文章中 “self-image” 对应选项 C “qualities and abilities”，指自身素质和能力的表现在别人面前留下了怎样的形象。

40. A **【解析】** 主旨题。该段第一句是主旨，表明孩子和成人都会经历不同类型的压力，这些压力来自相同年龄和地位的人们。文章中 “pressure” 对应选项 A “Stress” “those of the same age or status” 对应 “around you”。

【参考译文】

加里：

人们普遍认为，8 岁以下的孩子学习外语很容易。如果你把一个孩子（8 岁以下）放到一个外语环境里，他/她能在数月内很快学会这门外语。如果孩子的年龄是在 5 岁以下，那可能只需要几个星期就能学会了。原因其实很简单，孩子们大脑中语言学习的部分还在发展中，所以对他们来说，习得、模仿发音很容易。

威廉：

似乎你的年纪越大，大脑就会变得越僵化，所以学习一门新的语言就越困难，比如在你青少年时期。我认为，在你小时候，你能凭直觉学会一门语言，就吸收周围的语言就可以了。当你渐渐长大了，你就要深入地、分析地学习语言，学习语法等。

亚瑟：

我们学习第一语言的原因无他，就是为了解决问题（交流是一种问题，我们发展了我们的交流模式），当我们“满足”了这个需求后我们便不再前进，直到我们又有了额外需求（这可能是学习更多语言的渴望）。令人着迷的是，我们是如何被这些需求所激励，并将这些需求和适当的接触相结合，学会一门新语言的。

乔伊斯：

我个人的理论是语言学习是非常依赖于态度和自我形象。每个人的自我形象都决定着他们在多大程度上希望吸收一门新的语言。显然，孩子们在变得有自我意识之前，受抑制的程度比开始担心别人怎么看自己的青少年小得多。在我教授发音的时候，遇到过很多成年人有自我意识地抑制自己的例子。然而，还处在形成自我认知时期的孩子，想方设法地和同龄人保持一致。另外，成年人已经完全建立起自我形象，觉得做出不熟悉的舌头和唇部动作，看起来有点愚蠢。

玛丽：

除了自我形象，孩子和成人都会经历不同类型的压力，这些压力来自相同年龄和地位的人们。父母经常会把小孩子放到一个完全的外语环境中，孩子们没有选择的余地，只能学习这门新语言。来自同龄人的压力也逼着他们去学习。另外，成年人几乎从来没有完全从母语文化中分离。一旦发现困难，他们可以很轻易地从外国群体脱离，重新回到母语环境。因为依赖于个人文化，同伴的压力会促使他们停止学习。

Part C

【答案及解析】

41. G【解析】空格为文章第一段第一句话，起着统领全文的作用，因此应该填入一个可以做主题句的句子。结合空格后的内容，提到了英国两家报纸巨大的发行量，《每日镜报》和《每日快报》两份报纸每天都销售约 400 万份。后面又说本地报纸发行量同样惊人，G 选项“到英国访问的人有时会惊奇地发现英国报纸有如此大的发行量”符合，故选 C。

42. E【解析】空格前提到“Apart from the national papers（除了全国性报纸）”，

由此可知下文将要开始谈除了全国发行的报纸以外的另一种报纸，空格后又提到了 local newspapers 发行量也很巨大，E 选项“然而，英国媒体的另一部分也能发行如此多份”可以起到承前启后的作用，符合要求，故选 E。

43. C【解析】空格前一句为“these papers are written almost entirely for readers interested in local events, birth, deaths, council meetings and sports.”“本地报纸所写的几乎全是读者感兴趣的当地事件、出生、死亡、议会会议和体育”。因此本句是关于本地报纸的内容，C 选项“其内容自然也受到他们所服务社区的影响”符合文章逻辑，故选 C。

44. D【解析】由第三段开头“The editor must never forget that the success of any newspaper depends on advertising...”可知，编辑决不能忘记任何报纸的成功都离不开广告，所以编辑也要获得商人的好感，D 项“由于这个原因，编辑渴望获得当地商人的好感”能够体现出这种因果关系，故选 D。

45. F【解析】由最后一段第一句“Local newspapers do not often comment on problems of national importance and editors rarely hold with taking sides on political questions”可知，本地报纸通常不对国家的重大事件发表意见，并且编辑们也几乎不在政治问题上表明自己的立场。空格后却提到有时候报纸能够说服本地的理事会采取一些行动，空格前后是转折关系，所以应该填入一个表示转折的句子。F 选项“但是，在表达公众对地方问题的看法方面，它们通常能够为社区提供服务”符合要求，故选 F。

【参考译文】

(41)［G］到英国访问的人有时会惊奇地发现当地的报纸有这么大的发行量。《每日镜报》和《每日快报》两份报纸每天都销售约 400 万份。(42)［E］除了在全国发行的报纸外，然而，其实还有其他的小报业公司卖得不比他们少。本地报纸每周发行量有 1300 万份。基本上每个镇和乡村都有自己的报纸，而且几乎全部都能经营得不错，其中很大一部分还非常赚钱。

这些报纸所写的几乎全是读者感兴趣的当地事件，包括出生、死亡、市镇会议和体育，(43)［C］其内容自然也受到它们所服务的社区的影响。编辑们更愿意依靠很了解当地情况的人。报纸附近地区的俱乐部和教堂会定期提供大量的当地新闻，这些消息并不像国家新闻有较强的时效性。如果有时本周的报纸已经没有版面了，一条消息会被延期至下周刊登。

编辑们必须永远记住，任何报纸的成功都要依靠广告。(44)［D］由于这个原因，编辑渴望获得当地商人的好感。但是如果报纸办得好，而且新闻都经过仔细挑选去吸引读者，商人们也非常高兴有机会使公众了解他们的产品。

地区报纸通常不对国家的重大问题发表评论，编辑们也几乎不在政治问题上表明自己的立场。(45)［F］但是，在表达公众对地方问题的看法方面，他们通常能够为社区提供服务。有时候报纸能够说服理事会采取行动来提供更好的购物设施、改善当地交通，而且很快。

［A］英国的报纸通常都有很大的利润。

［B］因此，当地企业对当地报纸的广告都很感兴趣。

［C］其内容自然也受到它们所服务的社区的影响。

［D］由于这个原因，编辑渴望获得当地商人的好感。

［E］然而，英国媒体的另一部分也能发行如此多份。

［F］但是，在表达公众对地方问题的看法方面，他们通常能够为社区提供服务。

［G］到英国访问的人有时会惊奇地发现当地的报纸有这么大的发行量。

Part D

【答案及解析】

46.［H］growth

【解析】本句是倒装句，原顺序应为 The demand for energy，which is expected to double over the next 40 years，will be underlying all this ________. 由空格前的指示代词 this 可知，空格中应填入单数名词。单数名词选项有 H、J、K。this 是对上文的概括，指的是上文提到的人口增长，因此空格处应填入与上文 increase 近义的词，［H］growth “增长”，符合文义，故 H 为正确答案。

47.［D］stable

【解析】根据空格前的冠词 a 和逗号后的 sustainable 一词可知，空格处需填入形容词，与 sustainable 并列共同修饰名词 way，且空格里的单词要与 sustainable “可持续的”逻辑一致。［D］stable “稳定的” 与 sustainable 语义相近，符合语境，故 D 为正确答案。

48.［M］challenges

【解析】根据空格前的 one of the major 可推断出，空格处需填入名词的复数形式，名词的复数形式有选项 B、F、M。上文提到能源需求不断增加，空格所在段段末谈及可替换能源或许只能满足世界能源需求的 30% 左右，由此可见，要找到充足的能源是一种“挑战”，因此［M］challenges 符合文义，为正确答案。［F］competitions 多指人或机构为了某种利益而竞争，这里没有“争夺能源”这种语境，故排除。

49.［C］certainly

【解析】分析句子结构可知，空格处需填入副词，修饰空格后的动词词组 being funded and developed。副词选项只有 C 和 G。下文谈到了可替代能源在世界能源供给中扮演越来越重要的角色，由此可以推断资助发展可替代能源是理所当然的事情，故选项［C］certainly 符合文义需要，为正确答案。另一个副词［G］exactly “确切地；精确地；恰恰” 不符合句意，故排除。

50.［J］role

【解析】由空格前的 a growing 可知，空格处应填入名词的单数形式。play a role in 为固定搭配，意为“在……中起作用”，符合文义需要，故选项 J 为正确答案。

51.［N］combined

【解析】 通过分析句子结构可知，when 引导的时间状语从句省略了主语和 be 动词，空格处填入的动词应该和主语 alternative energy sources 构成被动关系，因此空格处应填入动词的过去分词形式。动词的过去分词形式选项只有 I 和 N。结合该句句意可以推断，空格处所填的词有“结合”的意思，意指各种替代能源结合起来，故选项［N］combined“使结合，联合”符合句意，为正确答案。

52. ［O］significant

【解析】 根据空格前的介词 with 和空格后的名词 investments 可知，空格处需填入一个形容词。剩余的形容词选项只剩下了 L 和 O。下文用 such as 举例提到了 9300 万美元，由此可知投资数额是比较大的，选项［O］significant“相当数量的；重要的；显著的；意味深长的”符合文义，故 O 为正确答案。

53. ［I］included

【解析】 通过分析此处的句子结构可知，空格处需填入动词的过去分词形式，该分词需要跟介词 in 构成搭配，一起作 $ 93million for wind energy development 的后置定语。空格后的内容是一项法案，由此可以推断，风能开发的投资应该是被包含在法案当中的，因此［I］included 符合句意，be included in 意为“被包含在……内”，故 I 为正确答案。并且，此时选项 I 是唯一的动词的过去分词选项。

54. ［E］comprise

【解析】 通过分析此处的句子结构可知，空格处需填入谓语动词，由主语 alternative energy sources 为复数形式及句末的 today 可知，空格处应是动词原形。动词原形选项只有［A］consist 和［E］comprise，两者都有“包含，组成”的意思，但 consist 需后接介词 of 才能跟宾语，此处 1% 是数词作宾语，故［E］comprise 为正确答案。此时考生应该能意识到［A］consist 是作为一个干扰项存在的，可以直接画掉。

55. ［B］solutions

【解析】 由空格前的 a lot of 可知，空格处需填入名词，空格后面的部分 both traditional and alternative 作为后置定语修饰空格内的名词。剩余的名词选项只有 B 和 F。结合前文的 the answer to... “解决……的方法”可知，［B］solutions“解决方法，处理手段”符合语意，为正确答案。

【参考译文】

据估计，到 2050 年，世界人口将从 60 亿增长至 90 亿，研究人员、企业和各国政府已经开始着手应对人口增长会对从食物、水资源到基础设施及就业等各方面带来的影响。在这一<u>(46)［H］增长</u>的背后将是对能源的需求，这种需求预计在未来的 40 年内翻一番。

找到能够<u>(47)［D］稳定</u>而持续地满足这种需求的资源是我们国家能源安全的基石，也将是 21 世纪的主要<u>(48)［M］挑战</u>之一。这些可替代能源，如生物燃料、风能和太阳能，<u>(49)［C］肯定</u>将会得到投资和发展，并且将在世界能源供应中扮演着越来越重要的<u>(50)［J］角色</u>。但是专家指出，即使将所有可替代能源都<u>(51)［N］结合</u>

起来，到2050年，或许只能满足世界能源需求的30%左右。

例如，即便有了(52)［O］大额投资，比如(53)［I］包含在《美国复苏与再投资法案》中的为开发风能投资的9300万美元，像风能和生物燃料这样重要的可替代能源却仅(54)［E］占了当今市场份额的1%。

能源和可持续发展方面的专家称，要满足将来的能源需求，可能要依赖于多种(55)［B］解决方法，既包括传统能源又包括可替代能源。

干扰项：

［A］consist：不及物动词，意为“由……组成，由……构成”，consist 需后接介词 of 才能跟宾语，如：A week consists of seven days. 类似的近义短语还有：be made up of, be composed of，comprise 等。表示组成、构成的表达有 constitute, make up, comprise 等。考生要注意整体和部分在句子中的位置关系，如：A whole consists of parts and the parts constitute the whole.

［F］competitions：名词 competition 的复数形式，意为“比赛；竞争”。

［G］exactly：副词，意为“确切地；精确地；恰恰”。

［K］progress：（1）名词，意为“进步；前进；（生物学）进化；（向更高方向）增长”；（2）动词，意为“发展；（使）进步，（使）进行；促进”。

［L］marvelous：形容词，意为“不可思议的；非凡的；引起惊异的”。

SECTION Ⅲ　Writing

Part A

【写作思路】

本篇文章属于应用文文体写作，首先要注意英文书信的格式。完整的英文书信应由三个部分构成：称呼、主体内容、信末礼貌用语及署名。本文的收信人是书店的销售部，不知收信人的具体名字和性别，称呼用 Dear Sir or Madam，语言应简洁、正式。正文一定要覆盖题目中所列出的三项要点，即自己所需书籍的详细信息、付款方式、送货时间和方式。注意最后的写信人名字要写“Wang Lin”。

【参考范文】

Dear Sir or Madam,

As I am planning to take College English Test Band 4 (CET-4), I have decided to place an order of some reference books. Therefore, I would very much appreciated if you could supply me with the following information.

Firstly, could you please send me a booklist with detailed information, including authors, publishing houses and prices? Secondly, I also need to know methods of payment. Do you accept online orders via Ali Pay? Thirdly, how many days will it take to get the books? I would like to know if you could deliver them by post to 118 Fuxing Road, Shanghai?

I would appreciate your early response.

Yours sincerely,

Wang Lin

(115 *words*)

Part B

【短文分析】

这篇短文是关于中国毕业生对工作地点和工资的要求。短文开头就写到根据最近调查，大多数中国毕业生都对薪水期望较高，想要到一线城市的外企、国企工作（most Chinese graduates have high salary expectations, and thus prefer working for foreign companies or state-owned enterprises in first-tier cities），第二、三段用调查数据进一步加以证明。

第四、五段主要写了虽然还有不到 100 天就要毕业了，超过半数的受访者还没有找到工作，但他们不愿意降低工资要求（although there are less than 100 days before graduation and more than half of the respondents have yet to get a job offer, they are not lowering their salary expectations），随后的数据表明他们对工资的要求：41.2% 的人想要拿到 8000 ~ 10000 元月薪，31.4% 的人想要拿到 4000 ~ 6000 元的月薪［41.2 percent aim for 8000 ~ 10000 yuan（$ 1279 ~ $ 1599）per month and 31.4 percent for 4000 ~ 6000 yuan］，高于目前北京、上海等城市的平均工资水平。

最后一段点明主题：不要做白日梦了！看看你自己英语水平高不高，专业技能怎么样，是否够得上高薪工作的要求（Don't daydream anymore! Please check if you have a good command of English and professional skills that deserve a decent job with a high pay.）。

在阅读短文时，考生应注意抓重点，略细节。数据等内容是中心主旨的支撑细节，不必仔细阅读。

短文总结思路：

这篇短文通过一些网络调查及发言反映了中国毕业生中“眼高手低”的现象。这是一篇说明文，考生可以从是什么、怎么样两个方面加以说明。首先，短文说明的是什么？是大学毕业生想在一线城市找高薪工作，而且即使临近毕业没有找到工作也不降低薪资要求。那么现实是怎么样的呢？北京、上海等大城市的平均工资水平都低于大学生们的要求。

评论展开思路：

这篇短文是关于毕业生对工作、薪水的要求，考生可以从哪些因素能够带来高薪的角度展开评论，如自身能力水平、工作经验等。

【参考范文】

A recent survey reveals that a large percent of Chinese graduates choose to hunt jobs in metropolis, where they could get more opportunities for good working condition and high salary. And it is interesting to find that they don't lower their expectations in salary even when they can't find jobs soon before graduation. However, to their disappointment, the average monthly salary in some big cities such as Beijing, Shanghai and so on is not as much as they expect.

According to the comments online, students should equip themselves well first. I totally agree with this idea. As students, we should acquire more academic knowledge, develop a wide range of skills, and improve our proficiency in foreign language. Only by doing so can we prepare ourselves better for employment. What's more, experience is important. As a fresh graduate, we should not expect too much.

In summary, students should endeavor to increase their employability and make expectations according to their ability.

(165 *words*)

全国英语等级考试第三级
2019 年 3 月笔试真题（改编版）

笔试部分答题时间：120 分钟

SECTION Ⅰ　Listening

(25 minutes)

2019.3

Directions:

This section is designed to test your ability to understand spoken English. You will hear a selection of recorded materials and you must answer the questions that accompany them. There are two parts in this section, Part A and Part B.

Remember, while you are doing the test, you should first put down your answers in your test booklet. At the end of the listening section, you will have 3 minutes to transfer all your answers from your test booklet to your ANSWER SHEET.

If you have any questions, you may raise your hand now as you will not be allowed to speak once the test has started.

Now look at Part A in your test booklet.

Part A

Directions:

You will hear 10 short dialogues. For each dialogue, there is one question and four possible answers. Choose the correct answer-A, B, C or D, and mark it in your test booklet. You will have 15 seconds to answer the question and you will hear each dialogue ***only once.***

Example:

You will hear:

W: Could you please tell me if the Beijing flight will be arriving on time?

M: Yes, Madam. It should be arriving in about ten minutes.

You will read:

Who do you think the woman is talking to?

[A] A bus conductor.

[B] A clerk at the airport.

[C] A taxi driver.

[D] A clerk at the station.

From the dialogue, we know that only a clerk at the airport is most likely to know the arrival time of a flight, so you should choose answer [B] and mark it in your test booklet.

Sample Answer: [A] ■ [C] [D]

Now look at question 1.

1. Where are the two speakers?

[A] In a department store. [B] In a restaurant.

[C] In a clothes factory. [D] On a playground.

2. What's the man doing?

[A] He's working in a hotel. [B] He's visiting a young couple.

[C] He's playing games. [D] He's traveling around.

3. What does the man need?

[A] A rest. [B] A bigger room.

[C] More air. [D] More food.

4. What time is it now?

[A] It is 8: 55. [B] It is 8: 35.

[C] It is 8: 05. [D] It is 8: 15.

5. How many bank robbers were there altogether?

[A] 2. [B] 3. [C] 4. [D] 5.

6. What's the probable relationship between the two speakers?

[A] Husband and wife. [B] Father and daughter.

[C] Doctor and patient. [D] Doctor and nurse.

7. What is the woman going to do?

[A] She will join a contest next time. [B] She won't join the contest.

[C] She doesn't know what to do. [D] She will take part in the contest.

8. How did the woman feel about the film?

[A] Enjoyable. [B] Inspiring.

[C] Terrible. [D] Dull.

9. What does the woman mean?

[A] She is interested in reading novels.

[B] She read only part of the book.

[C] She seldom reads books from cover to cover.

[D] She was eager to know what the book was about.

10. What does the woman suggest Jim do?

[A] He should buy an apartment right away.

[B] He should start to find a new apartment right now.

[C] He should start to find a new apartment in a few weeks.

[D] He should buy an apartment near the campus.

Part B

Directions:

You will hear four dialogues or monologues. Before listening to each one, you will have 5 *seconds to read each of the questions which accompany it. While listening, answer each question by choosing A, B, C or D. After listening, you will have* 10 *seconds to check your answer to each question. You will hear the recording* ***only once***.

Questions 11 – 13 *are based on the following dialogue.*

11. What kind of weather is normal for March?

[A] Cold. [B] Very hot.

[C] Cooler than that day. [D] Hotter than that day.

12. Where was the man born?

[A] Florida. [B] New York.

[C] California. [D] Indiana.

13. How often is the bus scheduled to pass their stop?

[A] Every ten minutes. [B] Every thirty minutes.

[C] Once a day. [D] At twenty to one.

Questions 14 – 17 *are based on the following dialogue between two friends.*

14. Why is the woman in New York?

[A] Because she likes the city. [B] Because the man is ill.

[C] Because she has a project there. [D] Because she wants to visit the man.

15. What's wrong with the man?

[A] He has got a cold. [B] He wants to die.

[C] His dog is sick. [D] He throws up seriously.

16. Where does the man live?

[A] At 903 Haven Avenue in the 116th Street.

[B] At 903 Haven Avenue in the 168th Street.

[C] At 904 Haven Avenue in the 168th Street.

[D] At 904 Haven Avenue in the 116th Street.

17. What will the woman do for the man?

[A] Buy some food for him. [B] Give him some medicine.

[C] Send him to the hospital. [D] Bring some vegetables to him.

Questions 18 – 21 *are based on the following dialogue.*

18. What's the relationship between the two speakers?

[A] Husband and wife. [B] Waiter and customer.

[C] Good friends. [D] Colleagues.

19. Why does the woman think the man is kind?

[A] The man does her a favor.

[B] The man decides to treat her to a meal.

[C] The man is very patient to her questions.

[D] The man recommends her many good foods.

20. Which of the following statements is true about the man's country?

[A] It is famous for the different recipes.

[B] Many people emigrated out of his country.

[C] It prevents foreign languages from getting in.

[D] There were not many Chinese restaurants before.

21. What does the man think of the woman?

[A] He hates to choose between Chinese cuisine and French cuisine.

[B] He cannot understand why the woman always speaks nonsense.

[C] He believes the woman is capable of being promoted soon.

[D] He doesn't think the woman knows how to enjoy herself.

Questions 22 – 25 *are based on the following monologue.*

22. Who is the speaker?

[A] A store manager. [B] A class president.

[C] A sales representative. [D] A committee chairperson.

23. What's the purpose of the meeting?

[A] To choose the chairperson of the ceremonies.

[B] To begin planning the graduation ceremonies.

[C] To determine who will graduate this year.

[D] To discuss the seating arrangements.

24. What should the students write on the paper?

[A] The names and addresses of their guests.

[B] Their dormitory names, addresses and phone numbers.

[C] Their names, phone numbers and job preference.

[D] The names and genders.

25. When is the next meeting?

[A] Next week. [B] Next year.

[C] In an hour. [D] In one month.

You now have 3 *minutes to transfer all your answers from your test booklet to your ANSWER*

SHEET.

That is the end of listening section.

SECTION Ⅱ Reading

(50 minutes)

Part A

Directions:

Read the following two texts. Answer the questions on each text by choosing A, B, C or D. Mark your answers on your ANSWER SHEET.

Text 1

Elizabeth Freeman was born about in 1742 to African American parents who were slaves. At the age of six months she was acquired, along with her sister, by John Ashley, a wealthy Massachusetts slaveholders. She became known as "Mumbet" or "Mum Bett."

For nearly 30 years Mumbet served the Ashley family. One day, Ashley's wife tried to strike Mumbet's sister with a spade. Mumbet protected her sister and took the blow instead. Furious, she left the house and refused to come back. When the Ashleys tried to make her return, Mumbet consulted a lawyer, Theodore Sedgewick. With his help, Mumbet sued (起诉) for her freedom.

While serving the Ashleys, Mumbet had listened to many discussions of the new Massachusetts constitution. If the constitution said that all people were free and equal, then she thought it should apply to her. Eventually, Mumbet won her freedom—the first slave in Massachusetts to do so under the new constitution.

Strangely enough, after the trial, the Ashleys asked Mumbet to come back and work for them as a paid employee. She declined and instead went to work for Segdewick. Mumbet died in 1829, but her legacy lived on in her many descendants (后裔). One of her great-grandchildren was W. E. B. Du Bois, one of the founder of the NAACP, and an important writer and spokesperson for African American civil rights.

Mumbet's tombstone still stands in the Massachusetts cemetery where she was buried. It reads, in part: "She was born a slave and remained a slave for nearly thirty years. She could neither read nor write, yet in her own sphere she had no superior or equal."

26. What do we know about Mumbet according to Paragraph 1?

[A] She was born a slave. [B] She was a slaveholder.

[C] She had a famous sister. [D] She was born into a rich family.

27. Why did Mumbet run away from the Ashleys?

[A] She found an employer.
[B] She was hit and got angry.
[C] She wanted to be a lawyer.
[D] She had to take care of her sister.

28. What did Mumbet learn from discussions about the new consititution?

[A] How to apply for a job.

[B] How to be a good servant.

[C] She should always obey her owners' orders.

[D] She should be as free and equal as whites.

29. What did Mumbet do after the trial?

[A] She founded the NAACP.

[B] She chose to work for a lawyer.

[C] She continued to serve the Ashleys.

[D] She went to live with her grandchildren.

30. What is the test mainly about?

[A] A story of a famous writer and spokesperson.

[B] The friendship between a lawyer and a slave.

[C] The life of a brave African American woman.

[D] A trial that shocked the whole world.

Text 2

"We are not about to enter the Information Age, but instead are rather well into it." Present predictions are that by 1990, about thirty million jobs in the United States, or about thirty percent of the job market, will be computer-related. In 1980, only twenty-one percent of all American high schools owned one or two computers for student use. In the fall of 1985, a new study showed that half of United States secondary schools have fifteen or more computers for student use. And now educational experts, administrators, and even the general public are demanding that all students become "computer literate". By the year 2000, knowledge of computers will be necessary in over eighty percent of all occupations. Soon those people not educated in computer use will be compared to those who are "print-illiterate" today.

What is "computer literacy"? The term itself seems to imply some degree of "knowing" about computers, but knowing what? The present opinion seems to be that this should include a general knowledge, of what computers are, plus a little of their history and something of how they operate.

Therefore, it is important that educators everywhere take a careful look not only at what is being done, but also at what should be done in the field of computer education. Today most adults are able to use a motor car without the slightest knowledge of how the internal combustion engine works. We effectively use all types of electrical equipment without being able to tell their histories or to explain how they work.

Business people for years have made good use of typewriters and adding machines, yet few have ever known how to repair them. Why, then, attempt to teach computers by teaching how or why they work?

Rather, we first must fix our mind on teaching the effective use of the computer as the tool is. "Knowing how to use a computer is what's going to be important. We don't talk about 'automobile literacy'. We just get in our cars and drive them."

31. In 1990, the number of jobs having nothing to do with computers in the United States will be reduced to ________.

[A] 30 million　　[B] 70 million

[C] 79 million　　[D] 100 million

32. The underlined part "print-illiterate" in the text refers to ________.

[A] one who has never learnt to read

[B] one who has never learnt to drive

[C] one who is not a computer literate

[D] one who is not able to use a typewriter

33. What is the first paragraph mainly about?

[A] The wide of computers in schools

[B] Public interest in computers

[C] The urgency of computers education

[D] Recent predictions of computer-related jobs

34. According to the author, the effective way to spread the use of computers is to teach ________.

[A] what computers use　　[B] how computers work

[C] how to use computers　　[D] where computers can be used

35. From the text, we can infer that ________.

[A] illiteracy rate will be down

[B] computers will be easy to operate

[C] computers will be set in automobiles

[D] automobiles will be more comfortable

Part B

Read the texts in which five people wrote about their ideas towards workaholism. For questions 36 – 40, match the name of each person to one of the statements (A – G) given below. Mark your answers on your ANSWER SHEET.

Martin:

I work not because I like it but that I have to, so I often count the minutes until stopping work or holidays. However, my sister is totally different. She enjoys her work so much that she often spends extra time on her job even takes work home with her. I think she is so crazy about work just as some people are about drugs or alcohol. I could hardly understand it.

Joseph:

Work is a core element of our lives. It gives us a sense of identity in the larger world outside the personal circle of family and friends. However, there are some people for whom work occupies an even more central place in their lives. Workaholics are a stereotype of modern life, and they are both praised and criticized. On the one hand, it may be the accepted way of earning promotion. On the other hand, workaholics are often viewed as neglecting aspects of life such as family and leisure that are important for maintaining a healthy equilibrium.

Malcolm:

In cities, workaholism is so common that people do not regard it as unusual. I think workaholics prefer to work rather than do anything else because they don't know how to kill time if they don't work. They can only get pleasure from work. Work is everything for them.

Emily:

Workaholism is dangerous in a sense because it can cause some problems. First of all, workaholics often have health problems because they don't have time to relax and keep themselves occupied all the time. Secondly, their family life is not happy since they spend little time with their family. Their marriage may even end in divorce.

Linda:

Being a workaholic can mean you achieve great things, but more people achieve great things without being addicted to work. Workaholics need time away from work and when I say "away from" I mean psychologically distanced from it as well as physically. If you are still obsessing about work when you should be focused on your loved ones or an outside of work activity then you are still basically working.

Now match the name of each person (36 – 40) to the appropriate statement.

Note: there are two extra statements.

Statements

36. Martin
37. Joseph
38. Malcolm
39. Emily
40. Linda

[A] If you don't get rid of workaholism, you may get ill.

[B] To get promotion, you need to be a workaholic.

[C] Workaholics' behaviors are hard to understand.

[D] Workaholics had better have some time with no work.

[E] Workaholics don't know how to enjoy themselves except working.

[F] It's hard for workaholics to be away from work psychologically.

[G] Some people appreciate those who pay almost all their attention to work.

Part C

Directions:

Read the following text from which five sentences have been removed. Choose from the sentences A – G the most suitable one to fill each numbered gap in the text (41 – 45). *There are TWO extra sentences that you do not need to use. Mark your answer in your ANSWER SHEET.*

Everyone needs a break, and vacations are not meant for serious study. __41__ The Spring Festival is coming up so this is the perfect time to discuss some great English language literature to take on a long train journey.

Before getting into the recommendations, we need to determine your English reading comprehension level. If you're at the beginner level, there are two options: reading a children's book or reading a book that you've read in Chinese translation. __42__ If you're at the intermediate level, popular books like pop fiction, mysteries and thrillers are good option. For advanced readers, science fiction, classic works of literature or contemporary prize winners (Nobel, Pulitzer) are good options. __43__ When I pick up a new book I like, even though the first few chapters are always really hard to get through, I would get accustomed to the way the language the author uses. Generally, after the first few chapters, things get a lot easier, especially if I get involved in the story.

Another great way to keep yourself motivated is to find a friend who's interested in reading the same book. You can make goals that you both want to achieve. __44__

Some quick recommendations: *Harry Potter*, start with the first book and go on from there; the Narnia series; anything by US writer Michael Crichton; and if you like horror, US writer Stephen King is always unusual and fun. __45__ Happy reading!

[A] Instead, they're a great way to take a break and enjoy a good book.

[B] If you pick a book which is so challenging, it will be too stressful.

[C] You may also enjoy your reading when hanging out with your family.

[D] The most important thing is to pick a book that you're really interested in.

[E] You can also discuss plot lines or vocabulary issues with each other by SMS or e-mail.

[F] You should just find a topic or author you're interested in, and the rest will go from there.

[G] This will help you get over any unfamiliar words or phrases, since you're already familiar with the story.

Part D

Directions:

Read the following text from which 10 *words have been removed. Choose from the words A – O the most suitable one to fill each numbered gap in the text* (46 – 55). *There are FIVE extra words that you do not need to use. Mark your answers on your ANSWER SHEET.*

Women with low literacy suffer disproportionately more than men, encountering more ___46___ in finding a well-paying job and being twice as likely to end up in the group of lowest wage earners, a study released on Wednesday said.

Analysis by the Institute for Women's Policy Research (IWPR) found women at all levels of ___47___ tend to earn less than men, but it's at the lowest literacy levels that the wage gap between genders is most ___48___.

Women with low literacy are twice as likely as men at the same skill level to be among the lowest earners, bringing in $ 300 a week or less, the report said.

"Because women start off so low in terms of wages, having higher literacy and more skills really ___49___ a big difference," said Kevin Miller, a ___50___ research associate at IWPR and co-author of the study.

"Women need to go ___51___ in their training and education level to earn the same as men", Miller said.

The ___52___ was based on 2003 National Assessment of Adult Literacy surveys, the most recent data ___53___, and focused on reading skills, not writing and numeric literacy. That data was ___54___ from a nationally representative sample of 19714 people aged 16 and older, living in households or prisons.

Data showed about one-third of American adults have low literacy levels, and more than 36 percent of men and 33 percent of women fall into that ___55___, the institute said.

[A] pattern	[B] independent	[C] makes
[D] difficulties	[E] collected	[F] conducted
[G] available	[H] category	[I] positions
[J] striking	[K] literacy	[L] analysis
[M] senior	[N] further	[O] longer

SECTION Ⅲ Writing

(45 minutes)

Directions:

You should write your responses to both Part A and Part B of this section on your ANSWER SHEET.

Part A

56.

Suppose you are a major in Art of Central Academy of Fine Arts. After graduation you decide to pursue your study in the graduate school in Yale University. Write a letter of application for admission, which should include the following points:

(1) make an application;

(2) provide your personal information and academic documents;

(3) express your hope for a reply.

You should write about 100 words. Do not sign your own name at the end of your letter. Use "Wang Lin" instead.

Part B

57.

Directions:

Read the text below. Write an essay in about 120 *words, in which you should summarize the key points of the text and make comments on them. Try to use your own words.*

In the 1960s, medical researchers Thomas Holmes and Richard Rahe developed a checklist of stressful events. They appreciated the tricky point that any major change can be stressful. Negative events like "serious illness of a family member" were high on the list, but so were some positive life-changing events, like marriage. When you take the Holmes-Rahe test you must remember that the score does not reflect how you deal with stress—it only shows how much you have to deal with. And we now know that the way you handle these events dramatically affects your chances of staying healthy.

By the early 1970s, hundreds of similar studies had followed Holmes and Rahe. And millions of Americans who work and live under stress worried over the reports. Somehow, the research got boiled down to a memorable message. Women's magazines ran headlines like "Stress causes illness!" If you want to stay physically and mentally healthy, the articles said, avoid stressful events.

But such simplistic advice is impossible to follow. Even if stressful events are dangerous, many—like the death of a loved one—are impossible to avoid. Moreover, any warning to avoid all stressful events is a prescription for staying away from opportunities as well as trouble. Since any change can be stressful, a person who wanted to be completely free of stress would never marry, have a child, take a new job or move.

The notion that all stress makes you sick also ignores a lot of what we know about people. It assumes we're all vulnerable and passive in the face of adversity. But what about human initiative and creativity? Many come through periods of stress with more physical and mental vigor than they had before. We also know that a long time without change or challenge can lead to boredom, and physical and mental strain.

THAT IS THE END OF THE TEST.

全国英语等级考试第三级
2019 年 3 月笔试真题（改编版）答案及解析

SECTION I　Listening

Part A

1. A　2. D　3. C　4. B　5. D

6. C　7. D　8. D　9. B　10. B

【原文及解析】

1. M：May I help you?

W：Yes, I'd like to try on some sports jackets. I prefer something like the one I'm wearing.

A【解析】问题：两位说话者在哪里？男士说的"May I help you?"是典型的服务行业的语言。根据画线部分可得知，女士想要试一些运动夹克，她喜欢类似于穿在身上的这种，所以可以推测对话发生在百货商店，故答案是"In a department store."

2. W：So, how long have you been here?

M：Just a couple of days actually. I'm on a big journey. You know, I'm visiting all the places of interest here.

D【解析】问题：男士正在干什么？根据画线部分可得知男士正在旅行，在此地拜访所有的旅游景点，故答案是"He's traveling around."

3. W：It's terribly hot in this small room.

M：I agree. Would you mind raising the window a bit more?

C【解析】问题：男士需要什么？女士说这个小房间里非常热，男士表示同意。根据画线部分可得知，男士希望女士把窗户往上抬一些，可以推测目的是通风降温，故答案是 More air.

4. W：When will the film begin?

M：It begins at 8：55. We only have 20 minutes left. Let's go now.

B【解析】问题：现在几点钟？根据画线部分可得知电影在 8：55 开始，他们只剩下 20 分钟了，因此现在的时间是 8：35，故答案是 It is 8：35.

5. M：Did you know the news about the bank robbers?

W：Yes, but I don't know whether they have been caught or not.

M：All except one. He escaped while the police were searching the hotel where the other four were hidden.

D【解析】问题：总共有多少个银行劫匪？根据画线部分可得知，只有一个劫匪在警察搜索另外 4 个藏匿在宾馆的劫匪时逃脱了，所以一共有 5 个劫匪，故答案是 5。

6. W：Need I take some medicine?

M：Yes. And I strongly advise you to go on a low-fat diet.

W：Do you really think that's really important?

M：Of course. If you don't, you might have a heart attack some day.

W：Well, I think I should follow your advice. You have been very helpful. Thanks.

C【解析】问题：这两个说话者可能的关系是什么？画线部分的表达都与看医生有关，所以我们推测二人是医患关系，故答案是"Doctor and patient."

7. W：Do you think I should join the English speech contest?

M：Why not? Your English is very good.

W：But I don't think I'm that good. Besides, there are so many others who are a lot better than me.

M：Come on, you're as good as them, if not better. I'm sure you'll do well.

W：Well, I guess it won't hurt to try. I'll enter my name tomorrow.

D【解析】问题：这位女士打算做什么？女士就是否应该参加英语演讲比赛的问题向男士征求意见，男士给与鼓励。根据画线部分可得知，女士最后说尝试不会造成任何伤害，决定明天报名。enter one's name 意为报名，故答案是"She will take part in the contest."

8. M：Did you watch the midnight film last night?

W：Yes, I watched part of it.

M：I really liked it. I thought it was really exciting.

W：Exciting? I fell asleep during the film.

D【解析】问题：女士对于这部电影的感觉如何？男士表示对电影的喜爱，女士表示异议。根据画线部分可得知她在看电影的过程中睡着了，可以推测电影对她来说很无聊。Enjoyable"有乐趣的；令人愉快的"；Inspiring"鼓舞人心的；启发灵感的"；Terrible"可怕的；很糟糕的"，都不符合。故答案是 Dull"枯燥无味的"。

9. M：Hi, Susan! Have you finished reading the book Professor Johnson recommended?

W：Oh, I haven't read it through the way I read a novel. I just read a few chapters which interested me.

B【解析】问题：女士是什么意思？男士问女士是否已经看完了教授推荐的书，根据画线部分可得知，她读这本书的方式和读小说不同，她只读了她感兴趣的几个章节，故答案是"She read only part of the book."

10. M：Jim needs to find another place to live.

W：What's wrong?

M：The apartment he rents now has been sold to a new owner.

W：He'd better start looking right away. When all the students come back in a few weeks, he won't find any near the campus.

D【解析】问题：女士建议 Jim 做什么？男士告知女士，因为公寓已经卖给了新主人，Jim 得另找地方居住了。根据画线部分可得知，女士认为 Jim 最好马上开始找地方。当学生在几周后回来后，他在校园附近就租不到了。句型 "had better do something" 表示：应该做某事；最好还是做某事。故答案是 He should start to find a new apartment right now.

Part B

11. C	12. B	13. B	14. C	15. D
16. C	17. B	18. C	19. B	20. D
21. C	22. D	23. B	24. C	25. A

【听力理解原文】

Questions 11 – 13

M：Excuse me. Have you been waiting here long?

W：Yes, about ten minutes.

M：Did you notice whether the No. 7 bus has passed by?

W：Not while I've been standing here.

M：Good. Hot today, isn't it?

W：Yes, it is. I wish that it would rain and cool off.

M：Me too. (11) This is unusual for March. I don't remember it ever being so hot and dry in March before.

W：You're from Florida then.

M：(12) Not really. I was born in New York, but I've lived here for ten years now.

W：My mother and I have just moved here from Indiana.

M：Pretty cold in Indiana, isn't it?

W：Yes. That's why we moved. But we didn't know that it would be so hot here. We should have gone to California. Do you think that we've missed the bus?

M：No, it's always a little late.

W：It's twenty to one, but my watch is a little faster.

M：Take it easy. (13) It never comes exactly every half hour like it should.

11. 问题：三月份通常是怎样的？

C【解析】细节辨认题。女士说："我希望能下点雨，天气变凉快些。"男士说："我也是。这样的天气在三月份不常见。我不记得以前三月份天气会这么又热又干燥。"注意 cold 指气温低，寒冷，而 cool 表示凉的，凉爽。因此选项 C "比那天凉快" 与原文相符，是正确选项。

12. 问题：男士的出生地是哪里？

B【解析】细节辨认题。女士说：“你是从佛罗里达州来的吧？”男士回答：“并不是。我在纽约出生，但已经在这里生活了十年。”故 B 是正确答案。

13. 问题：按照时刻表，公共汽车每隔多久会经过他们的车站？

B【解析】细节辨认题。本题要注意英文中时间的表达方式。be scheduled to 表示预定，按计划。在对话的最后，女士说：“现在是一点四十，但是我的表快了一点。”男士说：“别担心。这班车从来没有按预计的那样每隔半小时就准点到站。”选项 B“每隔三十分钟”是原文 every half hour 的转述，故 B 是正确选项。

Questions 14 – 17

W：Hi，this is Emily. Do you know where I am now?

M：Of course I don't.

W：It's so exciting I am here in New York！(14) My company sends me here for a project. And I think maybe we could get together today.

M：(15) I'd love to，but I'm sick as a dog.

W：You do sound awful. Do you have a cold or the flu?

M：(15) I don't know. All I know is that I want to die. I'm burning up and throwing up all over the place.

W：Oh，you men are such babies when you're sick. Listen，I'm at the 116th Street. Just tell me how to get to your place and I'll come up to visit you.

M：(16) Take the 104 bus uptown and get off at the 168th Street. I'm at 904 Haven Avenue，apartment 3A on the third floor.

W：I'll be there in less than an hour.

M：I'll probably be dead by then.

W：Oh，stop it. Do you have any food in the house?

M：I don't know.

W：Never mind. (17) I'll bring you some Chinese medicine I have in my bag and make some soup for you.

M：Thanks.

14. 问题：这位女士为什么来纽约？

C【解析】细节辨认题。女士说：“我到纽约了，这太令人兴奋了！公司派我来做一个项目。我想今天我俩可以聚一聚。”由此判断，女士来纽约的目的是工作，顺便拜访这位男士。因此 C 是正确选项。

15. 问题：这位男士怎么了？

D【解析】语义理解题。“sick as a dog”意思是“病得很严重”；“burn up”意思是“发烧”；“throw up”意思是“呕吐”。男士说：“我很想去见你，但是我病得很严重。”女士问：“你的声音听起来不太好。是感冒了吗，还是得了流感？”男士说：“我不知道。我只感到难受得要命。我发烧了，还吐得到处都是。”因此 D 是正确选项。

16. 问题：这位男士住在哪里？

C【解析】细节辨认题。本题需注意数字的表达，以排除干扰项。女士说：“听着，我在 116 街。告诉我怎么去你住的地方，我去看望你。”男士答：“乘 104 路公共汽车到上城区，在 168 街下车。我在海文大道 904 号三楼 3A 公寓。”因此 C 是正确选项。

17. 问题：这位女士将会帮男士做些什么？

B【解析】细节辨认题。女士最后说：“我给你拿些我包里带的中药，再给你煮点汤。”因此 B 是正确选项。

必背词汇

awful *adj.* 糟糕的，可怕的

sick as a dog 病得很严重

burn up 发烧

throw up 呕吐

avenue *n.* （城镇的）大街

Questions 18 – 21

M：What are you going to have?

W：I have no idea. Could you help me with the menu?

M：Yes, sure. These are starters, and these are main courses and these are desserts. See?

W：What's the alternative?

M：The alternative is to order a complete dinner. For a set price you get your choice of soup or juice, one dish with potato and vegetable, salad, bread and butter and sometimes coffee and sometimes dessert.

W：And you pay the price listed next to the main course?

M：Right. Like the roast beef dinner is $ 7.85—plus tax and tip, of course.

W：(19) It all looks pretty expensive to me.

M：(19) It's not. This is only a bit more expensive than McDonald's. So enjoy yourself. (18) We're celebrating, remember?

W：(19) You're kind.

M：(18) Friends are friends. I cannot get promoted often. Are you ready to order?

W：Ah, can you tell me what Hot Fudge Sundae is?

M：That's a dessert. It's an English specialty. It's a kind of ice cream with a hot sticky sauce over the top—very sweet and fattening!

W：I don't really like the sound of that. How come here is English food? I thought we agreed to eat American food.

M：(20) Our country is made up of people from all over the world, so besides collected words and phrases from every language, we've also absorbed recipes. We even have a lot of Chinese restaurants now.

W：Which is better, French or Chinese cuisine?

M：I'd say it's a toss-up. I love them both.

W：I didn't know you were so fond of foreign foods. (21) When my boss promotes me, I will take you to a French restaurant near my company. The food there is delicious.

M：(21) Oh, we will have a second dinner soon.

18. 问题：两位对话者之间是什么关系？

C【解析】场景/人物关系推断题。本题需要结合全文大意进行推断。从对话开头的 menu 菜单，starters 开胃小吃，main course 主菜，dessert 甜品，order a complete dinner 点一份完整的套餐以及他们提到的各种食物名称，可推断场景是在餐厅，两人在商量点什么菜。接着男士提到"We're celebrating, remember?""要记得我们是来庆祝的。""Friends are friends. I cannot get promoted often. Are you ready to order?""朋友就是朋友。我可不是经常升职的。你想好点什么了吗？"由此可推断他们不是服务员与顾客的关系，而是朋友。男士请女士吃饭，庆祝自己升职。在对话的末尾，女士说："When my boss promotes me, I will take you to a French restaurant near my company.""当我的老板提拔我时，我请你去公司附近的一家法国餐馆。"可进一步得知他们不是同事关系。因此 C 选项为正确答案

19. 问题：为什么这位女士认为男士人很好？

B【解析】语义推断题。在对话的开头，男士为女士详细介绍了菜单上的内容及套餐，女士觉得价格太贵了"It all looks pretty expensive to me."，男士说："不贵的。只是比麦当劳稍微贵一点儿而已。要记得我们是来庆祝的。"女士说："You're kind.""你人真好。"由此推断，因为男士请她吃大餐，女士想表达感谢。选项 A 中的短语 do sb. a favor 表示"帮某人一个忙"；选项 B 中的短语 treat sb. a meal 表示"请某人吃饭"。因此 B 是正确选项。

20. 问题：关于这个人的祖国，以下哪项陈述是正确的？

D【解析】语义理解题。男士提到自己的国家时说："我们的国家是由来自世界各地的人组成的，所以除了融合各种语言的单词和短语外，还吸纳了各种食谱。我们现在甚至有很多中餐馆。"D 选项的意思是"以前中餐馆不多"，与原文中提到的现状形成对比，因此是正确的陈述。词汇辨析：B 选项中 emigrate 表示移居海外，与原文不符；immigrate 表示（从外国）移居；作为移民定居。

21. 问题：这位男士是对这位女士的看法是怎样的？

C【解析】语义推断题。在对话的末尾女士说："当我的老板提拔我时，我请你去

公司附近的一家法国餐馆。那里的食物很好吃。”男士说：“哦，那我们很快就要吃第二次大餐了。”这里暗示对方应很快就有升职的机会，因此C选项为正确答案。

必背词汇

starter *n.* （主菜之前的）开胃小吃

main course *n.* 主菜

dessert *n.*（饭后）甜点

alternative *n.* 可供选择的事物

promote *v.* 升职

specialty *n.* （某个地方的）特色食品，特产

sauce *n.* 味汁；酱汁

fattening *adj.* （食物）要使人发胖的

recipe *n.* 食谱

cuisine *n.* 烹饪，烹调法；菜肴

emigrate *vt.* 移居国外

Questions 22 – 25

OK, everybody. Can we start the meeting now? (22) I'm Jeff Milton, the chairperson of the Graduation Committee for this year. (23) You've all been selected as representatives to plan the graduation ceremonies. (24) I'm sending around the sheet of paper for you to fill in your name and telephone number.

(24) Also, please write down what part of the ceremonies you would like to work on. Think about it carefully before you decide. Do what you are good at and do remember, as a representative, you will have a lot of responsibilities. Surely we have a lot to prepare for the ceremonies. The job you are going to do is not easy, but it's going to be very interesting that we will work together and solve all kinds of problems. Besides, you will make a lot of new friends in this committee. It will take up a lot of your spare time, mostly on weekends. So only sign up if you feel you have the time to participate.

And if you have any questions about anything concerning ceremonies or about the committee, do not hesitate to ask me. When everyone has finished writing down the information, please return the paper to me. (25) At our next meeting one week from today, we'll start to discuss the details of the ceremonies.

The next meeting will begin with a self-introduction to let us be familiar with each other, which is the first step to do our jobs. So if you decide to come, do not miss the first meeting.

22. 问题：发言者是谁？

D【解析】细节辨认题。开头第二句话：“可以开始会议了吗？”得知本文是一次会议发言。第三句话是发言者对自己身份的介绍：“我是杰夫·米尔顿，今年毕业委员

会的主席。”因此 D 是正确选项。

23. 问题：会议的目的是什么？

B【解析】细节推断题。发言者对听众说：“你们都是被选为策划毕业典礼的代表。”可以推断本次会议的目的是进行毕业典礼的策划工作。因此 B 是正确选项。

24. 问题：学生们应该在纸上填写什么内容？

C【解析】细节辨认题。会议主持人在交代填写内容时说：“现在给每人发一张纸，请填写你的名字和电话号码。另外，请写下你想参加哪部分典礼的准备工作。”“job preference”表示“工作偏好”，C 选项包含了原文中提及的完整信息，因此 C 是正确选项。

25. 问题：下一次会议是什么时间？

A【解析】细节辨认题。会议主持人在最后提到下一次会议的安排：“在一周后的下一次会议上，我们将开始讨论仪式的细节。”因此 A 是正确选项。

必背词汇

committee *n.* 委员会；
representative *n.* 代表
ceremony *n.* 典礼，仪式
participate *v.* 参与
preference *n.* 偏爱；优先权

SECTION Ⅱ Reading

26. A	27. B	28. D	29. B	30. C
31. B	32. D	33. C	34. C	35. B
36. C	37. G	38. E	39. A	40. D
41. A	42. G	43. D	44. E	45. F
46. D	47. K	48. J	49. C	50. M
51. N	52. L	53. G	54. E	55. H

Part A

Text 1

26. A【解析】细节题。由题干的“according to Paragraph 1”直接定位到第一段，从第一段第一句“Elizabeth Freeman was born about ... who were slaves.”可知，Mumbet 出生在一个奴隶家庭里，所以她也是一个奴隶。由第一段最后一句可知，Elizabeth Freeman 就是题目中的 Mumbet，所以 Mumbet 出生在一个奴隶家庭，A 选项“她生来就是奴隶”表达符合原文，故选 A。B 项“她是奴隶主”与原文表达的意思相反、C 项“她有一个著名的姐姐”原文没有提及，D 项“她出生于一个富裕的家庭”与原文意思相反，故排除。

27. B【解析】细节题。由题干的“... run away from Ashley”定位到原文的第二段，从第二段的第三句“Mumbet protected her sister... ”和第四句“Furious, she left the house and refused to come back.”可知，Mumbet 在奴隶主暴打姐姐的时候因为保护姐姐而被打，她因为愤怒而离开了奴隶主家。故选 B。A 项“她找到一个雇主”、C 项“她想成为一名律师”、D 项“她不得不照顾姐姐”原文都没有提及，故不选。

28. D【解析】细节题。由题干的“... discussion about the new constitution”定位到原文第三段。由第三段的第二句“If the constitution said that all... she thought it should apply to her”可知，宪法规定所有人都是自由平等的，那么她认为这也应该适用于她。最终，Mumbet 赢得了她的自由——成为新宪法下马萨诸塞州第一个获得自由的奴隶。故选 D“她应该跟白人一样自由和平等”。A 项“怎样申请一份工作”、B 项“怎样成为一个好仆人”、C 项“她应该一直遵守主人的命令”都与原文不符，故排除。

29. B【解析】细节题。由题干的“trial”定位到原文第四段，从第四段“She declined and instead went to work for Segdewick”可知，Mumbet 在审判之后拒绝了 Ashleys 家的聘用，而是去为律师 Sedgewick 工作，故选 B。

30. C【解析】主旨题。这是一篇人物传记，人物传记是记叙文体的一种，主要描写某人的生平事迹、趣闻轶事、生活背景、个性特征、成长奋斗历程等，包含记叙文的时间、地点、人物、事件等要素。其特点是以时间的先后或事件的发展为主线，空间或逻辑线索贯穿文章始终，脉络清楚。由文章第四段第一、第二句“Strangely enough, after the trial, the Ashleys asked Mumbet to come back and work for them as a paid employee. She declined and instead went to work for Segdewick.”可知，奇怪的是，在审判结束后，阿什利一家要求 Mumbet 作为一名带薪的员工回来，继续为他们工作。Mumbet 拒绝了，转而去了律师塞奇威克那里工作。因此，本文讲述的是一位勇敢的奴隶为了获得自由而做出的努力。故选 C。

【参考译文】

伊丽莎白·弗里曼大约出生于 1742 年，她的父母是非洲裔美国人，都是奴隶。六个月大的时候，她和她的姐姐一起被马萨诸塞州一个富有的奴隶主约翰·阿什利买下。她被称为妈妈贝特。

妈妈贝特为阿什利家族服务了近 30 年。有一天，阿什利的妻子试图用铁锹打妈妈贝特的姐姐。贝特保护了她的姐姐，并接受了这一打击。她怒气冲冲地离开了家，拒绝再回来。当阿什利一家试图让她回来时，她咨询了一位名叫西奥多·塞奇威克的律师。在他的帮助下，贝特起诉要求她的自由。

在为阿什利一家提供服务期间，妈妈贝特也听取了许多关于新马萨诸塞州新宪法的讨论。如果宪法规定所有人都是自由平等的，那么她认为这也应该适用于她。最终，妈妈贝特赢得了她的自由——成为新宪法下马萨诸塞州第一个获得自由的奴隶。

奇怪的是，在审判结束后，阿什利一家要求妈妈贝特作为一名带薪的员工回来，继续为他们工作。妈妈贝特拒绝了，转而去了塞奇威克那里工作。虽然妈妈贝特于1829 年去世，但她的许多后代继承了她的遗志。W. E. B・杜波依斯是她的曾孙辈后代之一，他是 NAACP 的创始人之一，也是美国黑人民权运动的一位重要作家和发言人。

她的墓碑仍然矗立在她的安葬地——马萨诸塞州的公墓里。墓碑上的部分文字是这样写的："她生来就是奴隶，并在将近 30 年的时间里一直是奴隶。她既不会读书也不会写字，在她自己的领域里也不出众或得不到平等对待。"

Text 2

31. B【解析】细节题。根据题干中的时间 In 1990 可定位至文章第一段第二句 "Present predictions are that by 1990, about thirty million jobs in the United States, or about thirty percent of the job market, will be computer-related." "目前的预测是，到 1990 年，在美国大约 3000 万的工作或大约 30% 的工作市场将和电脑相关。"换句话说，就是 7000 万的工作将和电脑没有关系，因此 B 选项为正确答案。

32. D【解析】词义推断题。由题干的"print-illiterate"定位到原文第一段最后一句话，因为本文的主题是跟电脑相关，根据"Soon those people not educated in computer use will be compared to those who are print-illiterate today."可知，很快那些不会使用电脑的人将会被比作今日的"打字文盲"，故 D 选项为正确答案。

33. C【解析】主旨大意题。由题干直接定位到原文第一段，由第一段可知，信息时代电脑必不可少，不懂电脑相当于"文盲"，现在教育专家、行政人员甚至普通大众正要求所有学生懂电脑。到 2000 年，电脑知识将在超过 80% 的职业中成为必然要求。很快那些不会使用电脑的人将会被比作今日的"打字文盲"。因此本段旨在呼吁加强电脑教育，故 C 选项为正确答案。

34. C【解析】推断题。由题干的"... the effective way to spread the use of computers is to teach..."定位到原文第三段和第四段，文章第三、四段中以现代人会骑摩托车和生意人学用打印机为例，告诉了我们学习电脑的最有效方法就是学会如何使用电脑，故 C 选项为正确答案。

35. B【解析】推断题。由文章最后一段"Knowing how to use a computer is what's going to be important. We don't talk about 'automobile literacy'. We just get in our cars and drive them."可知，知道如何使用电脑是很重要的……就像我们坐在车里开车一样，由此可以推断，学会操作电脑也不是太难，故 B 选项为正确答案。

【参考译文】

"我们不是将要进入信息时代，而是置身其中的感觉相当好。"目前的预测是，到 1990 年，美国将有大约 3000 万个工作岗位，或者说大约占就业市场 30% 的工作将和电脑相关。1980 年，只有 21% 的美国高中拥有一两台供学生用的电脑。而在 1985 年秋季，一项新的研究表明，美国一半的中等学校拥有十五台或者更多的供学生用的电脑。现在教育专家、行政人员甚至普通大众正要求所有学生懂电脑。到 2000 年，电脑知识将在超过 80% 的职业中成为必然要求。很快那些不会使用电脑的人将会被比作今日的

"打字文盲"。

什么是"计算机素养"？这个词本身似乎在某种程度"了解"计算机，但是了解什么呢？目前的观点似乎是，它应该包括一个关于什么是计算机的一般知识，再加上一点计算机的历史和如何操作的知识。

因此，每个地方的教育者不仅要留心观察正在做的事情，而且要注意在电脑教育领域什么应该做。今天，大部分成年人都能在根本不了解内燃机如何运作的情况下驾驶一辆汽车。在无法讲出它们的历史或解释它们如何运作的情况下，我们也能够有效地使用各种电器设备。

生意人已经充分利用打字机和加法机很多年了，但很少有人知道怎样维修它们。那么为什么试图教电脑要通过教它们内部构造及电脑运行的原理呢？

相反，我们首先必须把注意力放在教他们如何有效地使用电脑这一工具。"知道怎样使用电脑将会变得很重要。我们不是在讨论'汽车知识'。我们只需上车并且驾驶就可以。"

Part B

【要求解析】

从"Read the texts in which five people wrote about their ideas towards workaholism."可以得知五段文章是五个人对工作狂的不同看法。

【选项解析】

选项 A：如果你不摆脱工作狂的行为，你可能会生病。可用 ill 作关键词。

选项 B：为了升职，你要做一个工作狂。可用 promotion 作关键词。

选项 C：工作狂的行为是很难被理解的。可用 hard to understand 作关键词。

选项 D：工作狂需要有一些不工作的时间。可用 time with no work 作关键词。

选项 E：除了工作，工作狂不知道怎样享受生活。可用 enjoy themselves 作关键词。

选项 F：工作狂很难从心理上远离工作。可用 away from work psychologically 作关键词。

选项 G：有人欣赏那些几乎把所有精力都投入工作的人。可用 appreciate 作关键词。

【题目解析】

36. C【解析】细节题。第一句 Martin 首先讲了自己对工作的态度。第二句转折写到他姐姐是完全不同的，她经常额外花时间在工作上甚至把工作带回家做（she often spends extra time on her job even takes work home with her）。该题的考点在最后一句，文章中"I could hardly understand it（我几乎无法理解这种行为）"对应选项 C"hard to understand（难以理解）"。

37. G【解析】主旨题。该段的第一句和第四句都是段落中心。第一句表明，工作是我们生活的核心。第三句转折说到有些人的工作在生活中占据了更加核心的位置（occupies an even more central place in their lives），第四句提出人们对工作狂的态度是褒贬不一的（they are both praised and criticized）。该句中"praised"对应选项 G

“appreciate”，但与之并列的另一词“criticized”在选项中未提及，属于文章出现并列两者或以上，但题目只考察其中一个或部分的情况。在这种情况下，只有提及对象相关信息与文章一致，该选项便是正确答案。

38. E【解析】细节题。文章中提到，如果不工作要怎么消磨时间（how to kill time if they don't work）对应选项 E 除了工作要怎样享受生活（how to enjoy themselves except working）。在解答该题时，考生应注意“time”虽然在选项 D 也出现了，但选项 D 的意思是工作狂需要有一些不工作的时间，与段落意思不相符。

39. A【解析】细节题。该段的第一句是主旨句，提出工作狂是危险的，因为这会带来很多问题。后文说明了具体有健康和婚姻两个方面的问题。文章中工作狂经常会有健康问题（workaholics often have health problems）对应选项 A 你可能会生病（you may get ill）。此外，考生应注意文章中“they don't have time to relax”会提示到选项 D “time”，但该选项意为“工作狂需要有一些不工作的时间”，和该段不符。

40. D【解析】细节题。该段的第一句是主旨句，告诉人们不能沉迷工作，在后文具体说明要有身心都远离工作的时间。文章中提出，工作狂需要一些远离工作的时间（Workaholics need time away from work）对应选项 D，工作狂需要有一些不工作的时间。

【参考译文】

马丁：

我不是因为喜欢而工作，我只是不得不工作，所以我经常数着时间直到下班或放假。但是，我的姐姐却完全不同。她经常额外花时间在工作上甚至把工作带回家做。我觉得她对待工作是疯狂的，就像那些对毒品或者酒精上瘾的人。我几乎无法理解这种行为。

约瑟夫：

工作是我们生活的核心。在亲人和朋友间的个人交际圈之外，工作赋予我们在更广阔的世界的身份认同感。然而对于有些人，工作在他们生活中占据了更加核心的位置。工作狂是现代生活的固定模式，人们对此褒贬不一。一方面，为了升职，疯狂工作是一条可行之路。另一方面，人们认为工作狂忽视了生活，比如忽视家庭，不会休闲，这些都对保持健康平衡很重要。

马尔科姆：

在城市里，工作狂是很常见的，以至于人们并不认为这有什么特别。我认为工作狂对工作的喜爱超过了其他任何事情，是因为他们不知道如果不工作要怎么消磨时间。他们只能从工作中获得快乐。对他们来说，工作就是一切。

艾米丽：

在某种意义上，工作狂是危险的，因为这会带来很多问题。首先，工作狂经常会有健康问题，因为他们没有时间放松，他们把所有的时间都投入到工作中了。其次，因为他们没时间陪家人，他们的家庭生活并不幸福，甚至可能会以离婚收场。

琳达：

做一个工作狂意味着你会有很大成就，但是很多取得成就的人并没有沉迷工作。工作狂需要一些远离工作的时间，我所说的“远离”是指心理上和身体上都保持一定距离。如果你在应该关注所爱之人的时候，在应该做工作之外事情的时候，都想着工作，那么你基本上仍然在工作。

Part C

【答案及解析】

41. A【解析】由文章的第一句“Everyone needs a break, and vacations are not meant for serious study.”即“每个人都需要休息一下，而且假期不是为了严肃而认真地学习”，并结合空格后面一句话“春节就要到了，所以这正是个绝佳时机来谈谈可以带上火车旅途的英语语言文学作品”可知，用 Instead 转折引出下文最为合适，故 A 选项“假期却是一个可以休息一下，读本好书的好时候”承上启下，符合文义，为正确答案。

42. G【解析】根据空格前“... there are two options: reading a children's book or reading a book that you've read in Chinese translation.”可知，如果读过中译本，就会对故事感到熟悉，故 G 选项“这能帮助你克服生词和短语的障碍，因为你已经熟悉故事内容了”与上文意思相符，为正确答案。

43. D【解析】该空格位于段落首句，由此可以推断，填入句应具有概括性，可以总结概括该段主旨。由空格后的“When I pick up a book I like, even though the first few chapters are really hard to get through...”可知，作者建议应该选择感兴趣的书，故 D 选项“最重要的是，要选一本你自己真正感兴趣的书。”符合文义，为正确答案。

44. E【解析】空格前一句“Another great way to keep yourself motivated is to find a friend who's interested in reading the same book. You can make goals that you both want to achieve”“另一个让自己保持动机的好方法就是找一个跟自己对同一本书感兴趣的朋友，你们可以制定一些两个人都想要完成的目标”换句话说，主要讲了和朋友一起读书能做的事，这与 E 选项中“plot lines or vocabulary issues”相对应，故 E 为正确答案。

45. F【解析】空格前提到了“Harry Porter, the Narnia series, Michael Crichton, Stephen King”，这些都是推荐读的书目及作者，而且也提到了 horror“惊悚”，属于一个主题。对比选项，只有 F 选项包含上述提到的所有内容，意为“你应该找到一个自己感兴趣的话题或作者，接下来的一切就顺理成章了”。符合文义需要，故 F 为正确答案。

【参考译文】

每个人都需要休息一下，而且假期不是为了严肃而认真地学习。(41)［A］相反，假期却是个可以休息一下读本好书的好时候。春节就要到了，所以这正是个绝佳时机来谈谈可以带上火车旅途的英语语言文学作品。

在开始推荐之前，你需要确定你的英语阅读和理解水平。如果你处于初学者阶段，你有两种选择：读儿童书籍或者读你已经看过中文译本的书，(42)［G］这能帮助你克服生词和短语的障碍，因为你已经熟悉故事内容了。如果你处于中级水平，一些流行的读物比如畅销小说、悬疑和惊悚故事都是很好的选择。对于水平较高的读者，科幻小说、经典文学作品或者现代获奖作品（诺贝尔奖、普利策奖）都是不错的选择。

(43)［D］最重要的是，要选一本你自己真正感兴趣的书。当我选的是一本自己喜欢的书时，即便开始的几章真的很难读懂，我也会努力适应作者使用的语言。一般来说，读过几章之后，继续读就会简单不少，尤其是当我被故事所吸引的时候。

另一个让自己保持动机的好方法就是找一个跟自己对同一本书感兴趣的朋友，你们可以制定一些两个人都想要完成的目标。(44)［E］你们也可以通过短信或者电子邮件讨论情节或者词汇。

迅速来推荐几本：《哈利波特》，从第一本开始读然后一直读下去；《纳尼亚传奇》；美国作者迈克尔·克莱顿的所有作品；如果你喜欢惊悚故事，美国作家斯蒂芬·金的书一直不失其特点和幽默。

(45)［F］你应该找到一个自己感兴趣的话题或作者，接下来的一切就顺理成章了。祝你阅读愉快！

［A］相反，假期却是个可以休息一下，读本好书的好时候。

［B］如果你挑选了一本有挑战的书，你就会感到很有压力。

［C］如果你和家人闲逛的时候你也可以享受阅读。

［D］最重要的是，要选一本你自己真正感兴趣的书。

［E］你们也可以通过短信或者电子邮件讨论情节或者词汇。

［F］你应该找到一个自己感兴趣的话题或作者，接下来的一切就顺理成章了。

［G］这能帮助你克服生词和短语的障碍，因为你已经熟悉故事内容了。

Part D

【答案及解析】

46.［D］difficulties

【解析】根据空格前的 more 和空格后的 in finding a well-paying job 可知，空格处应填入名词复数形式。备选项中只有［D］difficulties 和［I］positions 是名词复数形式，将它们分别代入空格处，只有［D］difficulties“困难”语义最为恰当，意为“与男性相比，文化水平低的女性在寻求高薪工作的过程中会遇到更多困难”，故 D 为正确答案。

47.［K］literacy

【解析】由空格前的 at all levels of 和空格后的 tend to earn less than men 可知，空格处应填入名词。剩余的名词选项有［A］pattern、［H］category、［I］positions、［K］literacy 和［L］analysis。由本文的第一句话 Women with low literacy suffer disproportionately more than men... 得知，本文主要探讨的是女性的文化程度与其收入的关系，［K］literacy 意为“文化；识字率；教养”，且 literacy level 在下文中也紧接着出现，故这里应该是 at all levels of literacy 最为恰当，意为“不同的文化水平”，故选项 K

为正确答案。

48. [J] striking

【解析】由空格前的 is most 可知，空格处应填入形容词原形，与空格前的 most 结合成形容词的最高级形式，以此说明 the wage gap 劳动报酬的差距。形容词备选项 [B] independent “独立的”、[G] available “可获得的”、[J] striking “显著的，引人注目的”、[M] senior “高级的；年长的” 都是形容词原形。其中 [M] senior 无比较级和最高级形式，却含有比较的含义，可排除。对比剩余选项，只有 [J] striking “显著的，引人注目的” 语义最为恰当，意为“在文化水平最低的人群中，男女收入差距最显著。”，故选项 J 为正确答案。

49. [C] makes

【解析】通过分析此处的句子结构可知，空格前的现在分词结构 having higher literacy and more skills 为该句主语，再结合副词 really 和空格后的 a big difference，可知空格处应填入动词作谓语，且该动词应为第三人称单数形式。符合语法要求的只有 [C] makes，而且 make a difference 是一个经常被考查的固定搭配，意为“有影响，起作用”，符合本题语义需要，故选项 C 为正确答案。

50. [M] senior

【解析】由空格前的冠词 a 和空格后的名词短语 research associate 可知，空格处应填入形容词原形。剩余的备选形容词原形有 [B] independent、[G] available、[M] senior，经过对比只有 [M] senior “资深的，高级的” 最符合文意，意为“资深助理研究员”，故选项 M 为正确答案。

51. [N] further

【解析】根据空格前的 Women need to go 和空格后的 in their training and education level 可知，空格处应填入副词。纵观所有选项，只有 [N] further 是副词，意为“进一步地”，代入文中，意为“米勒说，要想和男性赚得一样多，女性需要进一步地接受培训和教育”，故选项 N 为正确答案。

52. [L] analysis

【解析】由空格前的 The 和空格后的 was based on 可知，空格处应填入名词的单数形式，做主语。剩余的名词单数形式选项有 [A] pattern、 [H] category 和 [L] analysis。对比选项，只有 [L] analysis “分析” 最符合文意需要，意为“这一分析是基于《2003 年全国成人文化评估调查》得出的”，故选项 L 为正确答案。

53. [G] available

【解析】本句前半部分 The analysis was based on 2003 National Assessment of Adult Literacy surveys 结构完整，空格部分 the most recent data ________ 是作为前面 2003 National Assessment of Adult Literacy surveys 的同位语，进一步说明 2003 年的调查是最新的数据。空格处需要填入后置定语来修饰 data，浏览剩余选项，[E] collected “被收集的” 作为后置定语似乎可以，但是当做到 54 题的时候就会发现，the data was collected from... 是必然的选择，由于每个选项只能使用一次，故本题不能选 E。而［G］available “可获得的，可用的” 代入文中，the most recent data available 意为 “最新的可获得的/可用的数据”，符合此处句意，故选项 G 为正确答案。

54. ［E］collected

【解析】通过此处的分析句子结构，结合空格前的 That data was 和空格后的 from a nationally representative sample 可知，空格处应填入动词的过去分词形式，构成被动语态。［E］collected “收集” 和［F］conducted “实施；引导；执行” 都是动词的过去分词形式，但［E］collected 最符合文义，意为 “该报告收集了来自全国具有代表性的 19714 人的数据……”，故选项 E 为正确答案。

55. ［H］category

【解析】由空格前的 fall into that 和空格后的逗号可知，空格处应填入名词的单数形式。剩余备选项中的名词只有［A］pattern “模式；范例；图案”、［H］category “种类，类别” 可供考查，fall into that category 为常用搭配，意为 “属于这一类别”，故选项 H 为正确答案。

【参考译文】

周三发布的一项研究称，文化程度低的女性比那些文化程度低的男性吃的亏更大，在寻求高薪工作的过程中会遇到更多(46)［D］困难，而且最终沦为最低收入阶层的概率是男性的两倍。女性政策研究所（IWPR）的分析发现，各个(47)［K］文化层次的女性收入一般都比相同文化程度的男性要低，在文化水平最低的人群中，男女收入差距最为(48)［J］显著。

报告称，文化程度低的女性成为最低收入者（每周工资不超过 300 美元）的概率是同一文化水平的男性的两倍。

IWPR 的(50)［M］资深助理研究员、研究论文的合著者凯文·米勒（Kevin Miller）说，“因为女性工资的起点太低，提高文化水平和技能确实(49)［C］带来很大差异。”

米勒说，要想和男性挣得一样多，女性需要(51)［N］进一步地接受培训和教育。

这一(52)［L］分析是基于《2003 年全国成人文化评估调查》得出的，这一调查收集了最新的(53)［G］可用的数据，而且更注重阅读技能，而不是写作能力和算术能力。该报告(54)［E］收集了来自全国具有代表性的 19714 人的数据，这些人都年满 16 岁，有住在家中的，也有正在坐牢的。

该研究称，数据显示约三分之一的美国成年人文化程度较低，超过 36% 的男性和 33% 的女性属于这一(55)［H］类别。

干扰项：

［A］pattern：名词，意为 “模式；图案；样品”。

［B］independent：形容词，意为 “独立的；单独的；无党派的；不受约束的”。

［F］conducted：动词 conduct 的过去式或过去分词形式，意为 “管理；引导；指挥”。

［I］positions：名词 position 的复数形式，意为“位置，定位”。

［O］longer：形容词 long 的比较级形式，意为“比较久的；（距离，长度）长的；长时间的”。

SECTION Ⅲ　Writing

Part A

【解析】

题目要求考生向耶鲁大学研究生院写一封入学申请书。

1．入学申请书在正文开头交代写信的目的，即申请入学。

2．介绍个人的基本情况，包括学历、专业、工作或实习经验，进行的研究情况及在校成绩等。可说明自己的经济资助情况，是否准备申请奖学金等。内容要实事求是，言简意赅。

3．结尾可提出自己的需求，希望获得更多入学信息等，对对方可能给予的帮助表示感谢，表达期望得到对方回复，并附上自己的联系方式。

入学申请书属于正式文体写作，要注意信件格式和语言表达，避免出现语法、句法等失误。

【参考范文】

Dear Sir or Madam,

I am writing to apply for admission to your program for postgraduate studies.

Currently, I am a senior in Art at Central Academy of Fine Arts, China. I have completed all the required undergraduate courses with satisfactory scores. My diligence and love for challenges have earned me several awards for excellent students in our university. Official copies of my transcript and of my TOEFL scores are being sent from the offices concerned. I would also like to know about the possibility of receiving financial support, for example, a scholarship, from your university.

Please contact me by e-mail at wanglin@ sina. com. Thank you very much in advance for your attention to these matters. I look forward to hearing from you soon.

Yours sincerely,

Wang Lin

(128 words)

【常用句型】

I am writing to apply for...

If further information is needed, please (do not hesitate to) let me know.

I have enclosed (details of) ... for your convenience.

I look forward to hearing from you soon.

Part B

【短文分析】

这篇短文主要讲了变化带来的压力与健康的关系。第一段通过20世纪60年代的一个研究表明任何重大的变化都是有压力的（any major change can be stressful），这些变化包括消极的（negative）和积极的（positive）变化，人们处理这些变化的方式会极大地影响健康（the way you handle these events dramatically affects your chances of staying healthy）。

第二段提及到了70年代，处于工作和生活压力之下的人们对这些报告更加担忧了（work and live under stress worried over the reports），有杂志以“压力导致疾病（Stress causes illness!）”为标题，告诉人们要远离压力（avoid stressful events）。

第三段开头转折，提出避免压力是无法做到的。一些压力是无法避免的（impossible to avoid）。同时，避免麻烦的同时也失去了机会（staying away from opportunities as well as trouble），如段末提及的结婚生子等。

第四段批判性地质疑了这些研究报告，提出这些报告假设人们在面对困境时是脆弱的、被动的（It assumes we're all vulnerable and passive in the face of adversity），但人类是有主动性和创造性的（human initiative and creativity），如果长期没有变化或挑战反而会觉得无聊，身心紧张（We also know that a long time without change or challenge can lead to boredom, and physical and mental strain.）。

【短文总结思路】

这篇短文以20世纪60年代的研究报告开头，主要讲了变化带来的压力和健康之间的关系。这是一篇说明文，考生可以从“是什么”和“怎么样”两个方面概述。首先短文说明的“是什么”。短文说明了研究报告提出的生活中的改变会带来压力进而影响健康。其次，变化是怎样影响人们生活的呢？报告建议人们要远离变化，避免压力。但是，如果没有变化，人们将失去很多机会。长期没有变化的生活会使人们感觉到很无聊，反而会导致压力。所以避免变化是很难做到的。

【评论展开思路】

考生可以从变化的不可避免性、如何处理变化、缓解其带来的压力及健康问题几方面展开评论。

【参考范文】

According to a medical report in the 1960s, any positive or negative changes in life might lead to stress, which could cause health problem. So it was suggested that people should keep away from stressful situation. However, it is easier said than done. For one thing, opportunity is often followed by stress. For another, human beings are not so vulnerable when facing troubles. We are creative, so life without challenge makes us feel bored and stressful.

Personally, I think that changes are inevitable in our lives. There are so many people around us, including our families, friends, and classmates and so on. They are uncontrollable factors that bring us different things. What's more, not every change leads to stress or even health issue because we have the ability to cope with the potential stress.

In conclusion, changes will be with us. We should not only accept them but also deal with different changes creatively. That is the way to stay healthy.

(163 words)

全国英语等级考试第三级
2018 年 9 月笔试真题（改编版）

笔试部分答题时间：120 分钟

SECTION Ⅰ　Listening

（25 minutes）

2018.9

Directions:

This section is designed to test your ability to understand spoken English. You will hear a selection of recorded materials and you must answer the questions that accompany them. There are two parts in this section, Part A and Part B.

Remember, while you are doing the test, you should first put down your answers in your test booklet. At the end of the listening section, you will have 3 minutes to transfer all your answers from your test booklet to your ANSWER SHEET.

If you have any questions, you may raise your hand now as you will not be allowed to speak once the test has started.

Now look at Part A in your test booklet.

Part A

Directions:

You will hear 10 short dialogues. For each dialogue, there is one question and four possible answers. Choose the correct answer-A, B, C or D, and mark it in your test booklet. You will have 15 seconds to answer the question and you will hear each dialogue ***only once.***

Example:

You will hear:

W: Could you please tell me if the Beijing flight will be arriving on time?

M: Yes, Madam. It should be arriving in about ten minutes.

You will read:

Who do you think the woman is talking to?

[A] A bus conductor.

[B] A clerk at the airport.

[C] A taxi driver.

[D] A clerk at the station.

From the dialogue, we know that only a clerk at the airport is most likely to know the arrival time of a flight, so you should choose answer [B] and mark it in your test booklet.

Sample Answer: [A] ■ [C] [D]

Now look at question 1.

1. What does the man want to do?

[A] Interview the manager. [B] Apply for a job.

[C] Visit a woman. [D] Travel.

2. What does the mother want the boy to do?

[A] Read a book. [B] Climb the mountain.

[C] Wait for her. [D] Wash the clothes.

3. What are the speakers talking about?

[A] Driving. [B] The Internet.

[C] Their jobs. [D] Their friends

4. What is the man going to do?

[A] Look for a job. [B] Watch movie.

[C] Give up his job. [D] Go shopping.

5. Why did the woman fail to come to class?

[A] She didn't catch the bus. [B] The class began too early.

[C] She didn't find the campus. [D] She is ill with headache.

6. What do we know about Sheila?

[A] She talks a lot. [B] People are persuaded in her speeches.

[C] She stops talking to people. [D] She likes to make friends.

7. What's the probable relationship between the speakers?

[A] Husband and wife. [B] Boss and secretary.

[C] Host and guest. [D] Teacher and student.

8. What does the woman mean?

[A] Be quick. [B] Run for a while.

[C] Sometimes. [D] Take the next bus.

9. What is the woman unhappy about?

[A] Her neighbor's keeping a cat. [B] Her neighbor's walking on her grass.

[C] Her neighbor's not keeping her word. [D] Her neighbor's walking on her street.

10. Why does the man like that type of music?

[A] Because he likes the instruments. [B] Because Rock interests him.

[C] Because the music is wonderful. [D] Because the music is terrible.

Part B

Directions:

You will hear four dialogues or monologues. Before listening to each one, you will have 5 *seconds to read each of the questions which accompany it. While listening, answer each question by choosing A, B, C or D. After listening, you will have* 10 *seconds to check your answer to each question. You will hear the recording* ***only once***.

Questions 11 – 13 *are based on the following dialogue.*

11. How long will the man be away?

[A] A month. [B] Nearly a week.

[C] Three days. [D] Two days.

12. Who will take care of Roger?

[A] His father. [B] His mother.

[C] The woman. [D] The stranger.

13. What do we know about the woman?

[A] She is a teacher. [B] She still works.

[C] She likes children. [D] She is a doctor.

Questions 14 – 17 *are based on the following conversation between a man and woman about taking a vacation.*

14. What does the man think of Curacao?

[A] It is difficult to reach. [B] It is a tourist paradise.

[C] It is a perfect place for sports. [D] It is an ordinary tropical island.

15. Why does the woman hesitate to make her decision to go to Curacao?

[A] She thinks it is too far. [B] She thinks it is too quiet.

[C] It is safe to go there. [D] It is the right time to go there.

16. What is the woman probably going to do?

[A] Pack up for the trip. [B] Make her reservations.

[C] Contact her travel agent. [D] Book her airline ticket.

17. Who is the woman talking to?

[A] Her friend. [B] Her son.

[C] Her travel agent. [D] Her husband.

Questions 18 – 21 *are based on the following conversation about renting a handbag.*

18. Why does the woman want to buy a handbag?

[A] To attend Mary's wedding with it. [B] To carry it on her wedding.

[C] To give it to Mary as a gift.

[D] To celebrate her birthday.

19. What do we learn about Handbag Hire?

[A] It is the largest handbag dealer.　[B] It specializes in renting handbags.

[C] It designs expensive handbags.　[D] It is a famous handbag company.

20. How will the woman place her order?

[A] By post.　[B] In person.

[C] By telephone.　[D] On the Internet.

21. How many days will the woman have to wait for her order?

[A] 2.　[B] 6.　[C] 4.　[D] 7.

Questions 22 – 25 are based on the following discussion about job applicants at an employment agency.

22. What kind of position is to be offered?

[A] A doctor.　[B] A director.

[C] A teacher.　[D] A programmer.

23. What do the two speakers say about Anderson?

[A] He is dependable.　[B] He is well-trained.

[C] He is experienced.　[D] He is hard-working.

24. Why does the man think Logan is the best candidate?

[A] She is devoted.　[B] She is shy.

[C] She is considerate.　[D] She is outgoing.

25. How many applicants do the speakers mention?

[A] 1.　[B] 3.　[C] 4.　[D] 6.

You now have 3 minutes to transfer all your answers from your test booklet to your ANSWER SHEET.

That is the end of listening section.

SECTION Ⅱ Reading

(50 minutes)

Part A

Directions:

Read the following two texts. Answer the questions on each text by choosing A, B, C or D. Mark your answers on your ANSWER SHEET.

Text 1

Whole life is permanent insurance protection that protects you for your whole life, from the day you purchase the policy until you die, as long as you pay the premiums.

Whole life can be a solid foundation. Upon this foundation you can build a long-term financial plan, because it guarantees lifetime protection for your family or business.

Whole life insurance provides basic insurance protection, plus Mortgage protection, Estate preservation, Retirement funding, Charitable giving, Business needs...

A life insurance agent will help you determine an amount of insurance needed to protect your family or business in the event of your death.

Generally after the first year, the policy begins to increase cash value. The amount of cash value in your policy usually increases every year. This money can be used to help purchase a home, fund a child's education, add to retirement income, or for any other purpose. You may also choose to leave it in the policy and allow it to grow.

A whole life policy can earn dividends. Dividends are determined by the company's board of directors each year and are not guaranteed. When a dividend is payable, you may choose to take it in cash, use it to buy more insurance or to pay or reduce your premiums.

When you die, the company will pay your beneficiaries the death benefit, usually the face amount of the policy plus any dividend. This money is generally received by the beneficiaries free from income tax.

26. What is whole life insurance?

[A] It's permanent insurance protection from the day you were born until you die.

[B] It's permanent insurance protection that protects you for your whole life, from the day you buy it until you die.

[C] It's insurance protection for your whole family members.

[D] It's income protection insurance.

27. What can whole life insurance do for you?

[A] It only provides basic insurance protection.

[B] It provides Mortgage protection and Estate preservation.

[C] It offers Retirement funding, Charitable giving, Business needs.

[D] It not only offers basic insurance protection, but also provides Mortgage protection, Estate preservation, Retirement funding, Charitable giving and Business needs.

28. According to the passage, who will help you determine an amount of insurance needed?

[A] A life insurance agent. [B] Nobody except yourself.

[C] Your family members. [D] Your lawyer.

29. The word "policy" in the fifth paragraph probably means ________.

[A] 政策 [B] 保险

[C] 彩票 [D] 策略，方法

30. When you die, the death benefits of your life insurance will ________.

[A] be lost

[B] be paid to your beneficiaries

[C] be possessed by the insurance company

[D] will be given to the government

Text 2

You must have been troubled by when to say "I love you" because it is one of the greatest puzzles in our life.

What if you say it first and your partner doesn't love you back? Or if they do say it but you don't feel they mean it? Being the first to declare your love can be nerve racking and risky and can leave you feeling as vulnerable as a turtle with no shell. But is the person who says it first really in a position of weakness? Doesn't it pay to hold back, play it cool and wait until the other half has shown their hand fast?

"A really good relationship should be about being fair and being equal," says psychologist Sidney Crown. "But love is seldom equal." All relationships go through power struggles but, he says, if a love imbalance continues for years, the rot will set in. "That feeling of 'I've always loved you more' may be subverted for a time, but it never goes away completely and it often emerges in squabbling." In love, at least, the silent, withholding type is not always the most powerful. "The strongest one in a relationship is often the person who feels confident enough to talk about their feelings," says educational psychologist Ingrid Collins. Psychosexual therapist Paula Hall agrees. "The one with the upper hand is often the person who takes the initiative. In fact, the person who says 'I love you' first may also be the one who says 'I'm bored with you' first." Hall believes that much depends on how "I love you" is said and the motivation of the person saying it. "Is it said when they're drunk? Is it said before their partner files off on holiday, and what it really means is 'Please don't be unfaithful to me'?" By saying 'I love you', they are really saying 'Do you love me'? If so, wouldn't it just be more honest to say that. Collins agrees that intention is everything. "It's not what is said, but how it's said. What it comes down to is the sincerity of the speaker."

31. What is the main idea of this passage?

[A] The importance of "I love you".

[B] The meaning of "I love you".

[C] The time of saying "I love you".

[D] The place of saying "I love you".

32. In the first sentence the author means that ________.

[A] it is easy to say "I love you"

[B] it is hard to say "I love you"

[C] we have many troubles in our life

[D] people usually do not know when to say "I love you".

33. According to the expert, a good relationship should be ________.

[A] fair and equal　　[B] fair and kind

[C] powerful and equal　　[D] confident and fair

34. In the third paragraph, the phrase "with the upper hand" means ________.

[A] being low in spirit　　[B] having only one hand

[C] being active　　[D] being passive

35. What is the most important for you to consider when somebody says "I love you" to you?

[A] The intention.　　[B] The place.

[C] The time.　　[D] The determination.

Part B

Directions:

Read the texts from a magazine in which five people voice their different opinions in response to an article on Facebook. For questions 36-40, match the name of each person to one of the statements (A-G) given below. Mark your answers on ANSWER SHEET.

Helen Smith:

What better way to start of my senior year in high school than by reading something I am entirely familiar with? I couldn't have described this online revolution any better. The expansion of Facebook and its continuing success make me more interested in the world of computers and web design and the career choices they offer. Thanks, Mark Zuckerberg, for "poking" me into Facebook.

Kevin Stuart:

Rather than seeing Facebook as the hottest connection tool, I think it's more like the latest way to make an already impersonal world even more impersonal. How sad that our society is so isolated that we need a computer to "connect" with others. No, thanks! I'm going to continue hanging out on the street corner, and hope someone builds a village square someday. Now, there's a radical idea!

Robert Meyer:

Isn't it a contradiction that so many Americans criticize the government measures for national security purposes as an invasion of privacy when many of these same people feel free to lay bare their private lives to public exposure on Facebook? Perhaps it reveals shallow minds or shallow lives. Or worse, does it reveal a lack of concern about the security of our country? Sad indeed.

James Brown:

I eagerly returned from vacation so I could see my nieces who were home from college, only to find them with their "faces" in Facebook almost all day. They no longer communicate much with others face to face. No more hanging out at someone's home. I wonder what effect this societal isolation will have on all of us. I hope this isn't a trend, I remember all the fun face-to-face contact used to be.

Laura Lee:

I love email. I live and die by Google, but I will never understand the appeal of Facebook and its vast community of friends. In fact, I'm rather shocked. There are thousands out there who would like to be your friend and demand your time: they're called books. Pick one up. Life is short. Save your few real friendships for coffee over at Starbucks or invest yourself in a local cause that will form meaningful, lifelong relationships.

Now match the name of each person (36-40) to the appropriate statement.

Note: there are two extra statements.

Statements

36. Helen Smith
37. Kevin Stuart
38. Robert Meyer
39. James Brown
40. Laura Lee

[A] Facebook has built up my confidence in my study.

[B] Facebook raises individual awareness of privacy protection.

[C] Facebook serves as an eye-opener for my future work pursuit.

[D] Facebook worsens, instead of bettering, interpersonal relations.

[E] I miss the good old days when people met and talked to each other in person.

[F] Mind your own behavior online before you blame others for privacy interference.

[G] Don't waste your time on Facebook when you can do something more significant.

Part C

Directions:

Read the following text from which five sentences have been removed. Choose from the sentences A – G the most suitable one to fill each numbered gap in the text (41 – 45). There are TWO extra sentences that you do not need to use. Mark your answer in your ANSWER SHEET.

I love reading novels, especially those classics. My favorite writer is Jane Austen, the one who wrote *pride and prejudice*. __41__ it was watched by a record 18 million British viewers. The series was then sold to 18 countries round the world, from America to Australia, from Iceland to Israel, there are Jane Austen fans in all corners of the globe, and even special Jane Austen discussion groups on the internet.

__42__. When she died a spinster in 1817, only four of her six novels had been published, all anonymous and she earned a grand total of 648. 65 pounds from her books.

Now, nearly 200 years later, sales of her novels rival modern bestsellers, reaching 35, 000 a week. There have been film and television productions of not only *pride and prejudice*, but also *Emma*, *Persuasion*, and the Oscar-winning *Sense and Sensibility*. __43__

She was born in 1775, the seventh of eight children. Her father was the reverend George Austen. They were not well off, and lived in a village. By the time when she was 12, Jane was writing stories about heroines imprisoned in haunted castles, being rescued by glamorous heroes. __44__ The first was a handsome Irish law student called Tom Lefroy, who she met in 1795, but who had to return to Ireland a year later. The second, in 1801, was a young man called Samuel Blackall who she fell in love with when on holiday in Devon, but who tragically died suddenly soon after. The third was a large young man called Harries whose proposal she briefly accepted in 1802, "but he had nothing to recommend him but his size," so she changed her mind.

In 1801 the family moved to Bath, where she was very unhappy. To make matters worse, in 1805 her father died, leaving his widow, Jane and her only sister Cassandra, also unmarried, even poorer than before. For four years they had to move from house to house, often staying with relatives. __45__ only a few miles from Steventon where she had grown up. Here she was much happier, despite being the poor relation, dependent on charity. She not only revised her earlier novel but was able to write new ones, using her experiences to satirize and make fun of the social inequalities she saw around her. At last in 1811, *Sense and Sensibility* was the first of her novels to be published.

[A] Her house in Chawton in Hampshire is visited by 200 people a day.

[B] Jane Austen never once traveled abroad in her life time and she hardly ever left the south of England.

[C] The remarkable Chicago bull presented a striking contrast to its opponent, and the crowd just went wild.

[D] When BBC screened its latest adaption of Jane Austen's novel *Pride and Prejudice*.

[E] Finally in 1809, her brother Edward allowed them to live in a house on his estate in Chawton.

[F] In Jane's own life there were three romantic attachments.

[G] Sports can really get me away from a stressful day and exercise my brain.

Part D

Directions:

Read the following text from which 10 words have been removed. Choose from the words A-O the most suitable one to fill each numbered gap in the text (46-55). There are FIVE extra words that you do not need to use. Mark your answers on your ANSWER SHEET.

To get a sense of how women have progressed in science, take a quick tour of the physics department at the University of California, Berkeley. This is a storied place, the ___46___ of some of the most important discoveries in modern science-starting with Ernest Lawrence's invention of the cyclotron in 1931. A generation ago, female faces were ___47___ and, even today, visitors walking through the first floor of LeConte Hall will see a full corridor of exhibits ___48___ the many distinguished physicists who made history here, ___49___ all of them white males.

But climb up to the third floor and you'll see a ___50___ display. There, among the photos of current faculty members and students, are portraits of the ___51___ head of the department, whose research ___52___ everything from the mechanics Marjorie Shapiro, and four other women of the universe to the smallest particles of matter. A sixth woman was hired just two weeks ago. Although they're still only about 10 percent of the physics faculty, women are clearly a presence here. And the real ___53___ may be in the smaller photos to the right: graduate and undergraduate students, about 20 percent of them female. Every year Berkeley sends its fresh female physics PhDs to the country's top universities. That makes Shapiro optimistic, but also ___54___. "I believe things are getting better," she says, "but they're not getting better as ___55___ as I would like."

[A] circumstance	[B] confidence	[C] covers
[D] current	[E] deals	[F] different
[G] exposing	[H] fast	[I] honoring
[J] hope	[K] presently	[L] rare
[M] realistic	[N] site	[O] virtually

SECTION Ⅲ Writing

Directions:

You should write your responses to both Part A and Part B of this section on your ANSWER SHEET.

Part A

56.

You have made an appointment with Prof. Wang, but failed to keep it. Write a letter to

(1) apologize for your failure to keep the appointment.

(2) explain your reason to your teacher.

(3) express your wish to make another appointment.

You should write about 100 words. Do not sign your name at the end of your letter. Use "Li Ming" instead. You do not need to write the address.

Part B

57.

Directions:

Read the text below. Write an essay in about 120 words, in which you should summarize the key points of the text and make comments on them. Try to use your own words.

You might think that good-looking men have every advantage in life.

But new study suggests being handsome may not always work in a man's favour-at least when it comes to his career.

The research claims that attractive men are less likely to be given a job in a competitive workplace because they intimidate bosses. "It's not always an advantage to be pretty," says Marko Pitesa, an assistant professor at the University of Maryland. "It can backfire if you are perceived as a threat."

Interestingly, in Pitesa's study, it was male attractiveness in particular, rather than female beauty, that made the most difference. If the interviewer expected to work with the candidate as part of a team, then he preferred good-looking men. However, if the interviewer saw the candidate as a potential competitor, the interviewer discriminated in favour of unattractive men.

The results suggest that interviewers were not blinded by beauty, and instead calculated which candidate would further their own career.

"The dominant theoretical perspective in the social sciences for several decades has been that biases and discrimination are caused by irrational prejudice," Pitesa says. "The way we explain it here, pretty men just seem more competent, so it is actually subjectively rational to discriminate for or against them."

"On a deeper level," she adds, "the behaviour remains irrational, since there's no evidence that a real link exists between looks and competence."

THAT IS THE END OF THE TEST.

全国英语等级考试第三级
2018年9月笔试真题（改编版）答案及解析

SECTION I Listening

Part A

1. B　2. A　3. C　4. A　5. A

6. B　7. A　8. D　9. C　10. A

【原文及解析】

1. M：Good morning. I'm here for an interview. Can you tell me where the manager's office is?

W：The manager's office is down the passage, to the left.

M：Thank you.

B【解析】问题：男士想干什么？根据画线部分可得知男士是来工作面试的，他问经理的办公室在哪里，故答案是［B］Apply for a job.

2. M：Every boy and every girl is going to climb the mountain tomorrow. Can I go with them, Mom?

W：I'm afraid not. Wait till you have finished reading the book, dear.

A【解析】问题：这位妈妈想要男孩做什么？男孩说明天大家都要去爬山，他也想去，根据画线部分可得知女士拒绝了他的请求，要求他必须先读完那本书，故答案是［A］Read a book.

3. M：I'm so bored. I have nothing to do at work. I just surf the Internet all day long.

W：Damn！I'm so busy at work, and it's driving me crazy. I really wish I had your job.

C【解析】问题：两位说话者在讨论什么？男士说他很无聊，工作没什么可做的，仅仅上了一天网。女士则相反，她很忙，快忙疯了。"I really wish I had your job."是虚拟语气，意为：我真想做你的工作。男女双方都是在围绕工作交谈，故答案是［C］Their jobs.

4. W：How is your day going?

M：I'm looking for a job. The job market does not look that great, but I can't give up.

A【解析】问题：男士打算做什么？根据画线部分可得知男士正在找工作，劳动力市场看起来不怎么样，但是他不会放弃，故答案是［A］Look for a job.

5. M：Why you didn't come to class yesterday?

W：I missed the bus and by the time I got to campus，class was already over.

A【解析】问题：为什么女士没能来上课？动词短语 fail to do 表示没做成某件事。根据画线部分可得知她错过了公交车，当她抵达校园的时候，已经下课了，故答案是［A］She didn't catch the bus.

6. M：Sheila is a very persuasive speaker. When she talks，people stop and listen.

W：That's right. A lot of people even change their opinions after talking to her.

B【解析】问题：关于 Sheila 我们了解什么？男士说 Sheila 是一个非常具有说服力的演讲者。当她讲话的时候，别人都会停下来倾听。女士表示同意，在和 Sheila 交谈之后，许多人甚至会改变他们的观点。对话的重点是 Sheila 的说服力强，故答案是［B］People are persuaded in her speeches.

7. M：Cathy，this is Mike. I am telephoning because I am going to meet some guests at the airport. So I will be absent for lunch.

W：That is OK. I will wait for you at supper time.

M：See you then.

A【解析】问题：两位说话者可能是什么关系？两人正在打电话，男士说他打电话的原因是他要去机场接人，所以他会缺席午餐。女士说好的，她会在晚餐的时候等他。浏览选项的四种关系，最有可能的是夫妻关系，故答案是［A］Husband and wife.

8. M：Look！Here comes the bus. Let's hurry.

W：Why run? There is no need to be in such a hurry. There will be another one in two or three minutes.

D【解析】问题：女士是什么意思？男士提议要快点赶上公交车，女士说：为什么要跑？没有必要这么着急，两三分钟后会有另外一班公交车。根据画线部分可推断，女士不想太赶，想搭下一班公交车，故答案是［D］Take the next bus.

9. M：What made you so upset?

W：My neighbour gave me her word that she would keep her cat off my grass，but she hasn't.

M：That's too bad.

C【解析】问题：女士对什么表示不高兴？give sb. one's word 的意思是向某人承诺。根据画线部分可得知，女士的邻居向她承诺让猫远离草坪，结果没有做到，所以她不高兴，故答案是［C］Her neighbor's not keeping her word.

10. W：What kind of music do you enjoy listening to?

M：I like to listen to Rock.

W：Why do you like that type of music?

M：I like the kinds of instruments that they use.

W：I think that's an excellent reason to like something.

M：Thanks，I feel the same way.

A【解析】问题：为什么男士喜欢那种音乐？男士喜欢听摇滚乐，根据画线部分可得知喜欢摇滚乐的原因是他喜欢摇滚乐的乐器，故答案是［A］Because he likes the instruments.

Part B

1. B	12. C	13. C	14. B	15. A
16. C	17. A	18. A	19. B	20. D
21. A	22. D	23. C	24. A	25. B

【原文及解析】

Questions 11 –13

W：Simon，you look worried. What's wrong with you?

M：I'm all right. But it's my son，Roger.

W：What has happened to him? Can I do something for you?

M：Well，I'm going to New York in three days. And my wife is in London，and she will not return until the end of the month.

W：Oh，I see. You want someone to take care of Roger，don't you?

M：Yes. But it's hard work. He is too naughty.

W：（12）Please don't worry. I'll look after him during your stay in New York.

M：（11）I'll be away for nearly a week. I think there will be too much trouble for you.

W：It doesn't matter.（13）You see，I was a teacher before I retired. I like children very much.

M：Thank you very much.

11. 问题：这位男士要离开多久？

B【解析】细节辨认题。在对话的末尾，男士说："我要离家将近一周。"因此B是正确选项。要注意表示时间的干扰项。在前面的对话中，男士说："三天后（in three days）我要去纽约。但这与离开多久无关。

12. 问题：谁来照顾罗杰？

C【解析】细节辨认题。女士说："你想找个人来照顾罗杰，是吗？"男士说："是的，但这很难。他太淘气了。"女士说："别担心。你去纽约的时候我来照顾他。"因此C是正确选项。

13. 问题：我们可以得知这位女士的哪些信息？

C【解析】语义理解题。在对话的末尾，女士说："你看，我退休前是个老师。我非常喜欢孩子。"因此C是正确选项。注意A选项的时态，"She is a teacher."表示她现在是老师。

Questions 14 –17

W：I really need a vacation. I just can't decide where to go.

M：Have you ever been to Curacao?

W：(15) No, I haven't. It's so far.

M：(14) Oh, come on! In this day and age, nothing is far. Besides, once you get there, it's like being in paradise. I really think you should consider it. In fact, I suggest you ask your travel agent about it.

W：What's so great about Curacao? (15) It's just another tropical island with a pretty beach.

M：Just another tropical island? Bright sunny days with blue water rolling upon to the clean white sand. Gentle winds blowing through the palm trees of clear move at night. Come on! It's a tremendous place to go.

W：Oh, I don't know.

M：Look, You can go wherever you want. But it's important that you relax during your vacation. And Curacao is the perfect place for that. I mean, you can do all the things you like to do. Play tennis, swim, read, rest, not to mention eat well and get a great suntan. Why are you so hesitant? Come on! Be adventurous.

W：You're certainly making it sound better by the minute. (16) OK, maybe I'll check it out with my travel agent.

M：I suggest you hurry. This is a very busy time of the year. And reservations aren't always easy to get. And it is absolutely necessary that you have reservations.

14. 问题：这位男士觉得库拉索岛怎么样？

B【解析】语义理解题。对话中的女士认为库拉索岛太远了，男士说：“哦，来吧！在这个时代，没有什么地方是遥远的。”排除 A 选项，difficult to reach 表示路途遥远，难以到达；男士接着说：“况且，一旦你到了那里，就像在天堂一样。”tourist paradise 旅游天堂；因此 B 是正确选项。在后面的对话中男士虽然提到了可以打网球和游泳，但并没说是这个地方特别适合运动，排除 C；女士说：“这只不过是另一个有美丽海滩的热带岛屿罢了。”男士用了反问的语气回应，并说：“这是个极好的旅游目的地。”所以 D 也不符合题意。

15. 问题：为什么女士对去库拉索岛的决定犹豫不决？

A【解析】语义理解题。在对话中女士有两处表示迟疑，第一次她说：“我没去过这个地方。那儿太远了。”第二次她说：“这只不过是另一个有美丽海滩的热带岛屿罢了。”因此，只有 A 符合文中的表述，正确选项是 A。

16. 问题：那位女士接下来有可能做什么？

C【解析】语义推断题。经过男士的一番推荐和描述，女士说：“好吧，也许可以让我的旅行社查一下。”因此 C 是正确选项。本题考查了和旅行相关的短语 pack up“打包行李”，make a reservation“预订”。

17. 问题：那位女士在和谁说话？

A【解析】场景/身份关系推断题。对话中未出现明显表示场景或身份的词汇，但从最后女士打算联系她的旅行社，可推断不是旅行社员工和顾客的对话；男士只是给她推荐旅行目的地，没有打算一起去，可排除是家人，他们可能是朋友关系。因此 A 是正确选项。

必背词汇

paradise *n.* 天堂；乐园

travel agent *n.* 旅行代办人

tropical island *n.* 热带岛屿

tremendous *adj.* 极好的

suntan *n.* 晒成古铜色的皮肤

adventurous *adj.* 爱冒险的；新奇的

Questions 18 – 21

W：John, shall we go to Sun Store?（18）I have decided to buy that Murrberry handbag. Anyway, I'm not carrying this one to Mary's wedding.

M：（19）But, Jane, why not rent one with Handbag Hire? Instead of $ 990, pay $ 50, and you have it for a whole week.

W：Sounds great, but I never knew I can rent a handbag.

M：Handbag Hire is a new business. It was founded two months ago. Its collection covers many designer handbags.

W：So, for the price of one Murrberry, I can use a different bag each week for twenty weeks?

M：Absolutely. And if you like one of them, you can choose to buy it at a discounted rate. Of course the price varies by age and condition. For example, a $ 1500 Murrberry bag can sell for just $ 750.

W：Great, but how do I rent? By telephone? Or in person?

M：Either.（20）And more conveniently, it accepts online orders.

W：（20）I'll do it online now. I still have one more question. Mary's wedding is next Saturday. There are only five days left. Do I have enough time?

M：Don't worry.（21）It promises that customers receive their orders by post within two days. Three more days to go.

W：Oh, I'd better order one right now.

18. 问题：女士为什么想去买一个手提包？

A【解析】细节辨认题。女士在对话开头提到："我已经决定去买那只 Murrberry 牌的手提包。无论如何，我不会背现在这个包去参加玛丽的婚礼。"因此 A 是正确选项。

19. 问题：对话中有哪些关于 Handbag Hire 的信息？

B【解析】语义推断题。男士建议说："但是，简，你为什么不从 Handbag Hire 那儿租一个手提包呢？不用花 990 美元，只要支付 50 美元，你就可以整整一个星期都使用它。"由此推断 Handbag Hire 是一个皮包租赁公司。因此 B 是正确选项。

20. 问题：女士将用什么方式下订单？

D【解析】细节辨认题。从对话中得知，通过电话或当面预订都可以，男士还说："更方便的是他们接受网络订单。"女士说："那我就在网上订。"因此 D 是正确选项。

21. 问题：女士要等几天才能收到她订的货？

A【解析】细节辨认题。男士说："它承诺顾客在两天内收到他们的订单。"因此 A 是正确选项。

必背词汇

dealer *n.* 经销商

specialize in 专门从事……

hire *v.* 租用；*n.* 租赁

convenient *adj.* 实用的；方便的

Questions 22 – 25

W：(22) I don't think Poppas is right for this position.

M：I agree. (22) He's got experience as a computer operator but he has very little training in programming. (23) What about Anderson?

W：I like him. (23) He seems very enthusiastic and he knows a lot about programming.

M：That's true. (23) Do you think he is dependable enough? He's already had two different jobs this year. He might work for a couple of months and then decide to leave.

W：I suppose so. But his last supervisor wrote a three-page letter of recommendation. He says Anderson is an excellent programmer.

M：He probably is. But we don't want him to leave after we've spent a lot of time training him. Actually, I think Logan is the best candidate.

W：She hasn't worked since she got married, hasn't she?

M：She's been taking care of her family. (24) But she is really devoted.

W：Oh, yes. The letter from her principal says she did a wonderful job. Do you think she'll be a good programmer?

M：I bet she will. She has an excellent letter of recommendation from her teacher at the institute she attended.

W：That's true.

M：And Logan seems more professional. She was well-dressed and seemed to have a very positive attitude about working for us.

22. 问题：他们提供的是什么职位？

D【解析】细节辨认题。对话中的两个人正在讨论应聘的人选。从 computer operator“电脑操作员”、training in programming“编程培训”等词汇可以判断他们要找的是程序员。因此 D 是正确选项。

23. 问题：两位发言者口中的安德森是怎样的？

C【解析】细节辨认题。本题考查描述人物品质特征的形容词，dependable“可靠的”，well-trained“训练有素的”，experienced“有经验的”，hard-working“勤奋的”。关于安德森的描述有：“他看起来很热情，对编程也很在行。”“你认为他足够可靠吗？他今年已经换了有两份不同的工作了。他可能会工作几个月，然后决定离开。”“他说安德森是个优秀的程序员。”因此 C 是最符合题意的选项。

24. 问题：为什么男士认为洛根是最好的候选人？

A【解析】细节辨认题。本题考查描述人物品质特征的形容词 devoted“专心的”，shy“害羞的”，considerate“考虑周到的”，outgoing“开朗的”。关于洛根的描述有：really devoted“非常专注”，has an excellent letter of recommendation“有优秀的推荐信”，seems more professional“看上去更专业”，well-dressed“打扮得体”，seemed to have a very positive attitude about working for us“看起来工作态度积极”。A 符合文中的描述，是正确选项。

25. How many applicants do the speakers mention?

B【解析】细节辨认题。对话中共提到了 3 个候选人的名字，分别是 Poppas，Anderson 和 Logan。因此 B 是正确选项。

必背词汇

programmer *n.* 程序员
dependable *adj.* 可信赖的，可靠的
well-trained *adj.* 训练有素的
experienced *adj.* 有经验的
hard-working *adj.* 勤奋的
devoted *adj.* 忠诚的，专心的
considerate *adj.* 考虑周到的；体贴的；
outgoing *adj.* 对人友好的，开朗的

SECTION Ⅱ Reading

Part A

Text 1

26. B【解析】细节题。由题干的“the whole life insurance”定位到原文的第一段，从原文第一段第一句话“Whole life is permanent insurance protection that protects you for

your whole life, from the day you purchase the policy until you die”，可以得知，终身人寿保险期限是从你购买保险的那天开始直至死亡之日的，因此 B 项是对原文的同义转述，故选 B。A 项“终身人寿保险保护期限是从你出生直到死亡”、C 项“终身人寿保险保护全家人”、D 项“它是收入保护保险”都跟原文不符，故排除。

27. D【解析】细节题。由题干可以定位到原文第三段，从第三段“Whole life insurance provides basic insurance protection, plus Mortgage protection, Estate preservation, Retirement funding, Charitable giving, Business needs”可知，终身人寿保险的作用是提供基本保险保障，外加抵押贷款保护、房产保值、退休基金、慈善捐赠、商业需求等六项。故选 D。其他三项不完整。故不选。

28. A【解析】细节题。由题干的关键词“help you determine an amount of insurance”可以定位到原文第四段第一句“A life insurance agent will help you determine an amount of insurance needed”，人寿保险代理将会协助你确定，在你死亡以后，为了保护你的家人或者企业所需的保险金额。故选 A。

29. B【解析】释义题。由题干可以直接定位到原文第五段。纵观全文，文章的主题都是跟保险有关，通过上下文提示，可以判断 policy 在这里的意思是“保险单”。其他选项“政策”、“彩票”及“策略、方法”都与原文主题不符，故不选。

30. B【解析】细节题。由题干的“When you die, the company will... ”定位到原文最后一段第一句话“When you die, the company will pay your beneficiaries the death benefit”，说明在投保人死后，保险公司把死亡抚恤金交给受益人。故选 B。A 项“丢失”、C 项“为保险公司拥有”、D 项“给政府”都与本句意思不符，故排除。

【参考译文】

终身保险是一种永久性的保险保障，从你购买保险单的第 21 天起直到你死亡，只要你支付保险费，就可以终身保护你。

终身保险可以是坚实的基础。在此基础上，你可以建立一个长期的财务计划，因为它保证终身保护你的家庭或企业。

终身寿险提供基本保险保障，外加抵押贷款保护、房产保值、退休基金、慈善捐赠、商业需求……

人寿保险代理将会协助你确定，在你死亡以后，为了保护你的家人或者企业所需的保险金额。

通常在第一年之后，保险单就会开始增加现金价值。你保单中的现金金额通常每年都会增加。这些资金可以用来购买房屋，投资孩子的教育，增加到退休收入中或者用于任何其他目的。你也可以让它存在保险单中继续增值。

终身人寿保险可以获得红利。红利的分配是由每年召开的公司董事会决定的，它并不是有保障的。如果红利应该得到偿付，那么你可以选择拿现金用它来购买更多的保险或者支付和减少你的保险费。

如果你不幸死亡，我们公司会向你的受益人支付死亡抚恤金，它通常是保险面额外加任何可能的红利。这些资金通常是由受益人享用的，它们都不需要付所得税。

Text 2

31. C【解析】由题干可以定位至全文，这是一道主旨大意题，纵观全文，第一段用什么时候说“我爱你”是我们生活中最大的难题之一而引出话题，从第二段讨论了应该先说“我爱你”还是忍住不要主动。第三段是关于良好的两性关系应该是什么样的，因此这篇文章主要讲述的是说“我爱你”的时机，是先说“我爱你”采取主动还是等待对方先说处于被动，以及说话者的动机，故选 C。A 项“‘我爱你’的重要性”、B 项“‘我爱你’的意思”、D 项“‘我爱你’的地方”都与原文的主题不符，因此排除。

32. D【解析】由题干“the first sentence”定位至原文第一句话。“You must have been troubled by when to say ‘I love you’ because it is one of the greatest puzzles in our life.”也就是说人们为何时说“我爱你”而烦恼。故选 D。A 项“‘我爱你’很容易说出”、B 项“‘我爱你’很难说出”原文都没有提到，C 项“我们生活中有很多烦恼”是对原文的过度解读，故不选。

33. A【解析】由题干的“a good relationship”定位到原文第三段第一句，“A really good relationship should be about being fair and being equal”，真正良好的两性关系应该是公平和平等的。A 项是原文的直接表达，故选 A。

34. C【解析】由题干的直接定位到原文第三段，此题是词义解析，联系上下文，意思是在两性关系中掌握主动的一方，因此选项 C“占了上风”符合题意。

35. A【解析】由题干的“what is the most important for you”定位到原文第三段的最后一句话，从第三段末“It’s not what is said, but how it’s said. What it comes down to is the sincerity of the speaker.”可知，“重要的不在于说话内容而在于说话的方式。归根到底是说话人的真诚。”因此，选 A。

【参考译文】

你一定曾经为什么时候说“我爱你”而烦恼过，因为这是我们生活中的最大的难题之一。

如果你先说“我爱你”而对方却没有说这句话，或者如果他们说了但你觉得他们不是认真的，那该怎么办？第一个表白爱的人会让人紧张，而且也很冒险，它会让你觉得像没了硬壳的海龟那样脆弱。但先说出爱的人真的是处于劣势吗？忍住，冷静地等待，让对方采取主动值得吗？

“真正良好的关系应该是公平和平等的，”心理学家悉德尼·克朗说，“但爱情很少是平等的。”所有的关系都会经历权力的斗争，但是，他说，如果爱情不平衡持续多年，就会开始出现问题。那种“我对你的爱更多”的感觉暂时会被颠覆，但这种感觉却不会完全消失，且常常会在争吵中出现。”至少在爱情上，沉默含蓄的那种类型并不总是强有力的。“两性关系中强大的一方常常是感觉自信地说出自己的感受的人。”教育心理学家因格瑞·柯林斯说。性心理治疗学家波拉·霍尔赞同说，“占上风的常常是主动出击的人。实际上，先说‘我爱你’的人往往也是先说‘我讨厌你’的人。”霍尔认为，很大程度上取决于说“我爱你”的方式和说话人的动机。“他们是在喝醉时说的吗？是在对方乘飞机度假前说的吗？而其真正的含义是——‘请一定要对我忠诚’？是不是表面上说：‘我爱你’，而真正想说的却是‘你爱我吗？’如果这样，直截了当地说不是更诚实吗?”考林也认为你的动机决定一切。“重要的不在于说话内容而在于说话的方式。归根到底是说话人的真诚。”

Part B

【要求解析】

从“Directions: Read the texts from a magazine in which five people voice their different opinions in response to an article on Facebook.”可以得知五段文章是五个人对一篇有关“脸书”的文章的不同看法。

【选项解析】

选项 A：在学习方面，脸书帮助我建立了信心。可用 confidence 作关键词。

选项 B：脸书提升了人们保护隐私的意识。可用 privacy protection 作关键词，不宜用 individual awareness 作关键词，因为这个词组较为抽象。

选项 C：脸书拓宽了我对未来的工作追求的眼界。可用 eye-opener，work pursuit 作关键词。

选项 D：脸书不但没有改善人际关系，反而使其更加糟糕。可用 interpersonal relations 作关键词。

选项 E：我怀念过去的美好时光，那时候人们彼此见面交谈的。可用 good old days 作关键词。

选项 F：在你责备别人侵犯隐私前，先注意你自己在网络上的行为表现。可用 privacy interference 作关键词。

选项 G：如果你能做一些更重要的事情，就不要在脸书上浪费时间。可用 waste your time 作关键词。

【题目解析】

40. C**【解析】**细节题。该段第一句是一个问句，Helen Smith 问：“还有什么比读一些我完全熟悉的东西开始高三生活更好的呢?”紧接着第二句回答了这个问题：我想不到比这场网络革命更好的了（I couldn't have described this online revolution any better.），也是本段的主旨句。后文进一步做出解释：脸书的扩张和持续成功使我对计算机世界、网页设计及其提供的职业选择更加感兴趣（The expansion of Facebook and its continuing success make me more interested in the world of computers and web design and the career choices they offer.），该句“expansion”对应选项 C 中“eye-opener”，“career choices”对应选项 C 中“work pursuit”。

41. D**【解析】**主旨题。该段第一句是主旨句。其中词组“Rather than”对应选项 D“instead of”，都表示对后面词组的否定，在文章中表示 Kevin Stuart 并未将脸书看作是最受欢迎的联系工具（seeing Facebook as the hottest connection tool）。后半句对脸书做出了否定：我认为它更像是把已经冷漠的世界变得更加淡薄的最新方式（I think it's more like the latest way to make an already impersonal world even more impersonal.），与选项 D 相符。

42. F【解析】推断题。该段第一句表示，许多美国人批评政府为了国家安全的目的侵犯个人隐私的做法，但其中很多人又认为把自己的私生活完全公开地暴露在脸书上也无所谓，这难道不是很矛盾吗？根据这句话可以推断出选项 F，人们在责备别人侵犯以隐私之前，先注意你自己在网络上的行为表现，其中“privacy interference”对应文章“an invasion of privacy”。

43. E【解析】细节题。James Brow 发现自己的侄子们整天在玩脸书，于是他在段末感叹：我希望这不是趋势，我记得过去面对面交谈时的所有快乐（I hope this isn't a trend, I remember all the fun face-to-face contact used to be.）。该句中“used to be”对应选项 E 中“old days”“remember”对应“miss”“face-to-face contact”对应“people met and talked to each other in person”。

44. G【解析】细节题。第二句转折后 Laura Lee 提出自己对脸书的看法：我永远无法理解脸书及其庞大的社区好友的吸引力（I will never understand the appeal of Facebook and its vast community of friends.）。文章的后半段是主旨：在脸书之外有许许多多想成为你朋友、需要你花时间的，那就是书（There are thousands out there who would like to be your friend and demand your time： they're called books.），人们要建立有意义的、终身的关系（form meaningful, lifelong relationships）。由此可知作者认为脸书是在浪费人们时间，人们要做更有意义的事情，对应选项 G。

【参考译文】

海伦·史密斯：

还有什么比读一些我完全熟悉的东西开始高三生活更好的呢？我想不到比这场网络革命更好的了。脸书的扩张和持续成功使我对计算机世界、网页设计及其提供的职业选择更加感兴趣。感谢马克. 扎克伯格，带我进入脸书。

凯文·斯图尔特：

我并没有将脸书看作是最受欢迎的联系工具，我认为它更像是把已经冷漠的世界变得更加淡薄的最新方式。我们的社会是如此孤立以至于需要计算机“联系”彼此，这是多么可悲啊。不用了，谢谢！我要继续在街角闲逛，希望有一天有人建立一个村庄广场。现在，这可真是个不同凡响的想法！

罗伯特·梅尔：

许多美国人批评政府为了国家安全的目的侵犯个人隐私的做法，但其中很多人又认为把自己的私生活完全公开地暴露在脸书上也无所谓，这难道不是很矛盾吗？也许这暴露了浅薄的想法和浅薄的生活。或者更糟糕的是，这是否暴露了人们对国家安全的漠不关心呢？真是悲哀。

詹姆斯·布朗：

我急匆匆地度假回来，就是想看见我那几个从大学放假回来的侄子们，结果发现他们几乎天天是在脸书上“见面”。他们不再面对面彼此交流，不再约在谁家一起玩了。我不禁思考这种社会孤立感会给我们每个人带来怎样的后果。我希望这不是趋势，我记得过去面对面交谈时的所有快乐。

劳拉·李：

我喜欢电子邮件。谷歌决定着我的生活，但我永远无法理解脸书及其庞大的社区好友的吸引力。事实上，我对此感觉到很震惊。脸书之外有许许多多想成为你朋友、需要你花时间的，那就是书。拿起一本书吧！生命很短，把你的时间节省下来，去星巴克和为数不多的真朋友喝一杯咖啡，或者投身到地区事业中，这些将建立有意义的、终身的关系。

Part C

41. D【**解析**】本题考查的是对上下文之间意义关系的理解和对文章细节的把握。根据空格后的句子“it was watched by a record 18 million British viewers”，“当时创下了1800万英国观众的收看记录”可知，空格部分应该与Jane Austen的作品有关，只有D项“当BBC（英国广播公司）上映简·奥斯丁的《傲慢与偏见》小说的最终改写本时”谈到了奥斯丁的作品，因此最符合题意，故选D。

42. B【**解析**】本题考查的是对段落主旨的理解和对文章细节的把握。空格在句首，因此要起统领整段的作用，分析空格后的句子“When she died a spinster in 1817...”可知空格部分应该与主人公的生平有关，B选项“简·奥斯丁在她的一生中没有出过一次国，甚至从未离开过英国的南部”最符合题意，故选B。

43. A【**解析**】本题考查的是对段落主旨的理解和对文章细节的把握。空格在段落最后一句话，起着总结整段的作用。根据分析本段内容，前半部分主要讲作家生平，而后半部分主要讲Jane Austen的作品成就，以及受欢迎的程度，并列举一系列数字加以说明，A选项“她在汉普郡Chawton的家，每天都不低于200人参观拜访”也是讲她的受欢迎程度，因此最符合题意，故选A。

44. F【**解析**】本题考查的是对上下文之间意义关系的理解和对文章细节的把握。根据第三段内容可知本段主要讲述Jane Austen的感情生活，根据空格后内容“The first was... The second... . The third was...”可知Jane Austen有三段感情生活，F选项“在简的生命中，有三次浪漫的情感历程”是对下文的概括，逻辑关系明确，故选F。

45. E【**解析**】本题考查的是对上下文之间意义关系的理解和对文章细节的把握。第四段内容主要讲述Jane Austen生活环境的变化，空格前提到“For four years they had to move from house to house, often staying with relatives”“四年来他们不得不到处搬家，经常在亲戚家逗留”可知，Jane Austen生活居住靠亲戚维系，E选项“终于在1809年，她的兄弟爱德华同意她们住进他在Chawton作为不动产的房子”最符合题意，故选E。

【参考译文】

我喜欢看小说，特别是那些经典名著。我最喜欢的一个作家是简·奥斯丁，她写过一部小说叫《傲慢与偏见》。41. ［D］当 BBC（英国广播公司）上映简·奥斯丁的《傲慢与偏见》小说的最终改写本时，当时创下了 1800 万英国观众的收看记录。之后，一系列的丛书出售到全世界 18 个国家，从美国到澳大利亚，从冰岛到以色列，全世界到处到有简·奥斯丁的书迷，甚至在互联网上还有专门的简·奥斯丁的讨论组。

42. ［B］简·奥斯丁在她的一生中没有出过一次国，甚至从未离开过英国的南部。在 1817 年她过世的时候，还是个未婚女子，她的六部小说只有四部已经出版，并且全部是匿名的，她从书中总共赚了 648. 65 英镑。如今，也就是此后将近 200 年后，她小说的销量可与现代畅销书媲美，每周达到 35000 英镑的收益。已经成为电影、电视作品的不仅仅是《傲慢与偏见》，还有《爱玛》《劝导》和奥斯卡获奖影片《理智与情感》。43. ［A］她在汉普郡 Chawton 的家，每天都不低于 200 人参观拜访。

简·奥斯丁出生于 1775 年，是家里八个孩子中的第七个。她的父亲是受人尊敬的牧师乔治·奥斯丁。她们家不富裕，而且住在一个乡村里。直到她十二岁的那年，简·奥斯丁一直在写关于女主人公被关押在魔鬼城堡的故事，直到被魅力英雄拯救出来。44. ［F］在简的生命中，有三次浪漫的情感历程。第一次，是与一个英俊的爱尔兰法律系的学生，名叫 Tom Lefroy，她是在 1795 年遇到他的，但他不得不在一年之后返回爱尔兰。第二次是在 1801 年，一个名叫 Samuel Blackall 的年青男子在德尔郡的假日里让她坠入爱河。但是那个男子没过多久，突然悲惨地死去了。第三次是与一个名叫 Harries 大个子年青人，在 1802 年他向她求婚的时候，她暂且允诺了他，“但是他除了体型高大之外，一无所长”，于是她改变了主意。

1801 年，她们家搬迁到了巴思，她在那儿过得非常不幸。更为糟糕的是，她父亲在 1805 年撇下她们撒手人寰了，简和她同样未完婚的妹妹卡珊德娜比以前更加贫困。四年以来，她们到处搬家，经常在亲戚家逗留。

45. ［E］终于在 1809 年，她的兄弟爱德华同意她们住进他在 Chawton 作为不动产的房子，只离她成长的 Steventon 这个地方几英里的距离。在这儿她生活幸福得多，尽管是依靠贫弱的亲戚施舍维系。她不仅修正了她以前的小说，而且还创作出了新的作品，用她个人的经历和见闻来嘲讽社会的不平等。最终在 1811 年，《理智与情感》作为她的第一部小说被出版了。

［A］她在汉普郡 Chawton 的家，每天都不低于 200 人参观拜访。

［B］简·奥斯丁在她的一生中没有出过一次国，甚至从未离开过英国的南部。

［C］那只非凡的西班牙公牛与它的对手形成鲜明的对比，人群已开始疯狂起来。

［D］当 BBC（英国广播公司）上映简·奥斯丁的《傲慢与偏见》小说的最终改写本时。

［E］终于在 1809 年，她的兄弟爱德华同意她们住进他在 Chawton 作为不动产的房子。

［F］在简的生命中，有三次浪漫的情感历程。

［G］运动真的可以让我摆脱紧张的一天，锻炼我的大脑。

Part D

46. ［N］site

【解析】名词辨析题。空格前面是定冠词 the，后面是介词 of，因此空格处需要填入一个名词。空格所在部分为空格前的 a storied place 的同位语，根据句意可知，空格处填入的词意思应与“place”相接近。结合名词备选名词 A、B、D、J、N 可知，选项［N］site“场所，地点”符合题意。

47. ［L］rare

【解析】形容词辨析题。空格前面是 be 动词 were，因此空格处应填入形容词或名词作表语。结合空格后的内容可知，LeConte 大厅一楼物理学家的展览中，几乎全部都是白人男性。而空格所在部分介绍的是“a generation ago”的情况，再根据“female faces”，可知这里说的是女性面孔少。结合形容词备选项 D、F、H、L、M 可知，［L］rare“稀少的；罕见的；珍贵的”，符合题意，故为答案。

48. ［I］honoring

【解析】动词辨析题。分析句子结构可知，空格前 visitors... exhibits 部分主谓宾结构完整，空格前面是名词 exhibits“展品”，后面是名词短语 the many distinguished physicists“许多杰出的物理学家”，因此空格处应填入动词的现在分词形式，G 和 I 是动词的现在分词形式。再结合句意可知，展览应当是为了纪念这些物理学家而举办的，由此确定本题答案为［I］honoring“纪念”。

49. ［O］virtually

【解析】副词辨析题。空格前的句子结构完整，空格后是 all of them white males，由此可以推断，空格处应填副词。结合上下文可知，这里说的是女性物理学家人数少，男性白人多，再结合副词备选项 H、K、O，可知［O］virtually“几乎，差不多”符合题意，故为答案。

50. ［F］different

【解析】形容词辨析题。空格前是冠词 a，后面是名词 display，因此空格处应填形容词。结合上下文可知，文章第一段末句讲的是一楼的情况（几乎全是白人男性），本段讲三楼的情况（很多女性），因此三楼的展览和一楼的是不一样的。结合剩余的形容词备选项 D、F、H、M，因此本题答案为［F］different“不同的”。

51. ［D］current

【解析】形容词辨析题。空格前是定冠词 the，后面是名词短语 head of the department“系主任”，因此空格处应填入形容词。短语 the head of the department 本身意思就是完整的，所以填入的形容词应当是对其身份的更准确的描述，结合剩余的形容词备选项 D、H、M 可知，［D］current“当前的”符合题意，the current head of the department 意为“现任系主任”。

52. [C] covers

【解析】动词辨析题。空格前是 whose research，空格后是 everything from... to...，因此空格处应填入及物动词，作 whose 引导的定语从句的谓语，该动词应为三单形式。结合备选三单动词选项 C 和 E 可知，[C] covers“包含，覆盖”，符合题意，故为答案。

53. [J] hope

【解析】名词辨析题。空格前是 the real，后面是 may be，因此空格处应填名词。剩余的名词选项有 A、B、D、J。上文提到，教职人员中有 6 位女性，女性在三楼很有存在感。下文则指出，学生中女性的比例占到 20%，由此可以推测，空格所在句表达的是女学生的数量才是真正的希望所在，由此确定本题答案为 [J] hope“希望”。

54. [M] realistic

【解析】形容词辨析题。分析句子结构可知，空格所在句中有 make Shapiro optimistic 这一结构。由空格前的 but 可知，空格填入的词应是与形容词 optimistic 是相对意思的形容词。再结合备选形容词可知，[M] realistic“现实的，实际的”，符合题意，故为答案。

55. [H] fast

【解析】副词辨析题。空格前是 not getting better as，空格后是 as I would like，可知此空格处应填入副词。上文提到，Shapiro 的态度既乐观又实际，所以她认为事情正在好转，但没有像她想要的那样好转，结合剩余的备选副词 H、K 可知，[H] fast“快速地”，符合题意，故为答案。

干扰项：

[A] circumstance：名词，意为：“环境；情况；事件；境遇”。

[B] confidence：名词，意为：“信心；自信；秘密”。

[E] deals：名词复数形式，意为：“（一笔）交易（deal）”。

[G] exposing：expose 的现在分词形式，意为：“暴露；揭露；曝光”。

[K] presently：副词，意为：“目前；不久；马上”。

【参考译文】

想要了解女性在科学上取得了怎样的进步，就去快速地逛一下加利福尼亚大学伯克利分校的物理系吧。这是一个很有名的地方，是一些现代科学最重要的发现的(46) [N] 诞生地——最早的是 1931 年 Ernest Lawrence 发明的回旋加速器。那时候，女性的面孔还很(47) [L] 少见。即便是现在，游客走遍 LeConte 大厅一楼，会看到整个走廊里都是(48) [I] 纪念这些创造历史的著名的物理学家的展览，而这些人(49) [O] 几乎全部都是白人男性。

但爬上三楼，你会看到一个(50) [F] 不一样的展览。在那里展出的在职教职工和学生的照片中(52) [C] 包括 (51) [D] 现任系主任 Marjorie Shapiro 女士和另外四位女士，她们的研究从宇宙力学到最小的物质颗粒，可谓是无所不包。就在两周前，系里聘请了第六位女士。尽管她们只占物理系教职工的 10%，但很明显她们已不可小觑。真正的(53)［J］希望也许在于右边那些小一点的照片：研究生和本科生，他们中有20%是女性。每年，伯克利都将刚刚毕业的女物理博士生送往国内顶尖的大学。对此，Shapiro女士的态度很(54)［M］乐观也很现实，她说：“我认为事情正在好转，但是好转的速度并没有像我希望的(55)［H］那样快。”

SECTION Ⅲ Writing

Part A

【写作思路】

【解析】

本题要求写一封给老师的道歉信。

1. 道歉信在正文开头应直接交代写信的目的，诚恳地向对方表示歉意。
2. 第二段应具体解释未能赴约的原因，内容应简洁明了，语气要诚恳。
3. 最后再次表示歉意，恳切邀请老师重新预约见面时间，并期待对方答复。

此外，要注意书信格式，注意信件后面的写信人名字要写“Li Ming”。

【参考范文】

Dear Prof. Wang,

I am writing to apologize for not being able to keep our appointment. It was inconsiderate of me not to tell you earlier that I could not make it.

I remembered very well that Tuesday morning was the regular time for our appointment. Unfortunately, I had a bad cold and fainted on the bus and was sent to the hospital at once. I should have called to inform you when I recovered. But I found that my mobile phone was lost in the chaos.

Please accept my sincere apology for any inconvenience I have caused. I would be grateful if you could make another appointment with me later this week. I am looking forward to hearing from you.

Yours sincerely,

Li Ming

(125 *words*)

【常用句型】

I am writing to apologize for...

Let me apologize for any inconvenience that I have caused.

To make up for my impolite behavior, I want to...

Part B

【短文分析】

这篇短文主要写的是外貌和能力是否相关。短文开头提出，你也许认为长得帅的男人在生活中处处都有优势，该句中“You might think”暗示转折，随后话锋一转，表示最新的研究表明长得帅对男人来说也许不总是有利的，至少在事业方面（But new study suggests being handsome may not always work in a man's favour—at least when it comes to his career.）。通过这两句话考生可以大致了解短文的中心词“good-looking”。第三段通过研究证明：男人长得帅不一定对事业有帮助。第四段首句表明，长得帅的男人，而不是长得美的女人，更不具有优势，其后用合作者和竞争对手的不同情况加以证明。第五段根据第四段下结论：面试官不会被外表所蒙蔽，他们会判断谁能够帮助其发展事业。第六段分析了这种想法出现的原因：认为长得好看的人更加有能力其实是人们的主观偏见。最后一段再次通过研究者的话语表明：这种行为是不理智的，因为没有证据表明外貌和能力之间有真正的联系（the behaviour remains irrational, since there's no evidence that a real link exists between looks and competence.）。

【短文总结思路】

这篇短文是说明文，整体内容较多，考生应注意不要有遗漏。考生可以从是什么、为什么、怎么样三个方面总结。首先，短文说明的是什么？是人们的一种错误观念，认为长得帅的男人更有优势。但研究证实至少在事业方面不是如此。其次，为什么会有这样的看法？这是人们的主观偏见，没有证据表明外貌和能力之间有真正的联系。最后，人们怎么样做的呢？外貌有时并不是优势，尤其是在竞争对手面前。面试官不会被外表所蒙蔽，他们会判断谁能够帮助其发展事业。

【评论展开思路】

短文是关于外貌的影响，特别是和能力是否有关。考生可以分别分析外貌和能力的获得方式，以及哪些因素有助于个人能力提升。

Part B

【参考范文】

Some people hold the idea that the more good-looking a man is, the more capable he is. They have unreasonable discrimination on the effect of people's looks. However, a research reveals that there is no connection between appearance and ability, at least when it is about career. A handsome man may loose his opportunity if the interviewer considers him as a competitor. Capacity is what will be considered as the priority.

In my opinion, a person's competence is not determined by his appearance. Appearance is greatly influenced by parents genetically. Differently, competence is what could be fostered via study and developed through one's effort. It is affected by many factors, such as parenting, education, personality, experience and so on, but looks are not in this list.

In a word, people should not pay too much attention to appearance. What they should do is to improve themselves to be more capable.

（156 *words*）

全国英语等级考试第三级
2018 年 3 月笔试真题（改编版）

笔试部分答题时间：120 分钟

SECTION I　Listening

(25 minutes)

2018. 3

Directions:

This section is designed to test your ability to understand spoken English. You will hear a selection of recorded materials and you must answer the questions that accompany them. There are two parts in this section, Part A and Part B.

Remember, while you are doing the test, you should first put down your answers in your test booklet. At the end of the listening section, you will have 3 minutes to transfer all your answers from your test booklet to your ANSWER SHEET.

If you have any questions, you may raise your hand now as you will not be allowed to speak once the test has started.

Now look at Part A in your test booklet.

Part A

Directions:

You will hear 10 short dialogues. For each dialogue, there is one question and four possible answers. Choose the correct answer-A, B, C or D, and mark it in your test booklet. You will have 15 seconds to answer the question and you will hear each dialogue ***only once.***

Example:

You will hear:

W: Could you please tell me if the Beijing flight will be arriving on time?

M: Yes, Madam. It should be arriving in about ten minutes.

You will read:

Who do you think the woman is talking to?

[A] A bus conductor.　　　　[B] A clerk at the airport.

[C] A taxi driver.　　[D] A clerk at the station.

From the dialogue, we know that only a clerk at the airport is most likely to know the arrival time of a flight, so you should choose answer [B] and mark it in your test booklet.

Sample Answer: [A] ■ [C] [D]

Now look at question 1.

1. What will the woman do tomorrow?

[A] Hold a party.　　[B] See Mr. Smith.

[C] Work overtime.　　[D] Attend a wedding.

2. Who is Mr. Johnson according to the speakers?

[A] Their former colleague.　　[B] Their former neighbor.

[C] Their former teacher.　　[D] Their former client.

3. What are the speakers talking about?

[A] A job interview.　　[B] A reporter's work.

[C] How to impress people.　　[D] How to handle an interview.

4. How many flights to Sydney will there be next Tuesday afternoon?

[A] One.　　[B] Two.　　[C] Four.　　[D] Five.

5. What did the man's teacher tell him to do?

[A] Polish his essay.　　[B] Hand in his essay.

[C] Rewrite his essay.　　[D] Write a shorter essay.

6. What can we learn about the woman's son?

[A] He often talks with his mother.　　[B] He often drives in a careless way.

[C] He is willing to listen to his mother.　　[D] He is worried about his driving skills.

7. What do we know about Jack?

[A] He is a company manager.　　[B] He makes emergency calls.

[C] He records emergency calls.　　[D] He is a company technician.

8. What can we learn from this conversation?

[A] The woman is paying the bill.

[B] Bill's phone number is 510-1520-20.

[C] The man pays 20 dollars to the woman.

[D] The woman has a 20-dollar bill changed.

9. What does the woman mean?

[A] The dentist's is at a convenient place.

[B] The dentist's is close to Times Square.

[C] It was comfortable to sit at the dentist's.

[D] It was not so terrible a visit to the dentist's.

10. What do we know about the woman?

[A] She is going to deliver a lecture.

[B] She spent a year in the rain forest.

[C] She is looking forward to the lecture.

[D] She will finish her report this weekend.

Part B

Directions:

You will hear four dialogues or monologues. Before listening to each one, you will have 5 seconds to read each of the questions which accompany it. While listening, answer each question by choosing A, B, C or D. After listening, you will have 10 seconds to check your answer to each question. You will hear the recording ***only once****.*

Questions 11 – 13 are based on the following conversation between a reporter and a female writer.

11. What do we know about the woman's family?

[A] They kept a lot of birds. [B] They lived in a big house.

[C] They owned a small farm. [D] They suffered from poverty.

12. What did the woman's mother impress her with?

[A] Her love. [B] Her success.

[C] Her ambition. [D] Her knowledge.

13. What did the woman's mother wish her to do?

[A] Go to college. [B] Become a writer.

[C] Have a better life. [D] Support her family.

Questions 14 – 17 are based on the following conversation.

14. Whom is the man probably complaining to?

[A] A receptionist. [B] A travel agent.

[C] A coach driver. [D] A hotel staff member.

15. Why did the man wait in the heat for two hours?

[A] The coach had to be replaced. [B] The coach driver felt sick.

[C] The hotel rooms were full. [D] The hotel had to be cleaned.

16. What did the man mention in his complaint?

[A] Impolite hotel cleaners. [B] Dark light and dirty rooms.

[C] Rude people living downstairs. [D] Disturbing noise and poor food.

17. How did the man feel about the woman's apology?

[A] Amusing. [B] Annoying.

[C] Desirable. [D] Reasonable.

Questions 18 – 21 are based on the following interview with John Smith, chairman of National Weight and Health Association (NWHA).

18. What did the NWHA survey aim to explore?

[A] The incidences of obesity. [B] Popular views on obesity.

[C] Ways to fight obesity. [D] The causes of obesity.

19. How many people in the world are rated as being overweight?

[A] 16 million. [B] 18 million.

[C] 1.6 billion. [D] 1.8 billion.

20. In which country do people feel the most pressure to be thin?

[A] Brazil. [B] India.

[C] France. [D] America.

21. Who are most likely to blame their parents for obesity?

[A] The French. [B] The Swiss.

[C] Germans. [D] Russians.

Questions 22 – 25 are based on the following interview with Emily Galash, a high school student who works part-time as a trendspotter.

22. What do trendspotters do?

[A] Take pictures of youth culture. [B] Write reports on youth culture.

[C] Sell products to young people. [D] Create websites for young people.

23. What does Look-Look concentrate on?

[A] Recruiting trendspotters for its clients.

[B] Providing advice to young trendspotters.

[C] Organizing sales networks for its clients.

[D] Dealing in information about youth trends.

24. Why do some companies use Look-Look's images on their websites?

[A] To promote visits to Look-Look.com.

[B] To attract young people to their new products.

[C] To learn about what makes young people buy.

[D] To encourage young people to be photographed.

25. Why is it difficult for trendspotters to catch original styles?

[A] Many young people like to show off.

[B] Many young people stick to the rules.

[C] Many young people try to copy trends.

[D] Many young people refuse to take pictures.

You now have 3 minutes to transfer all your answers from your test booklet to your ANSWER SHEET.

That is the end of listening section.

SECTION Ⅱ Reading

(50 minutes)

Part A

Directions:

Read the following two texts. Answer the questions on each text by choosing A, B, C or D. Mark your answers on your ANSWER SHEET.

Text 1

In 1997, 25 Japanese citizens, all older than 60, launched Jeeba (the name means "old man and old woman") to make senior-friendly products. They knew they were making history when they coined their company motto: "Of the elderly, by the elderly and for the elderly." They do not hire young people, and the oldest of their workers is 75.

Firms run by senior citizens are still a rarity, in Japan and worldwide. But the elderly have numbers on their side. Healthier and longer-living seniors, born immediately after World War II, are reaching retirement age in huge numbers all over the developed world. Extremely low birthrates in those same countries mean there are far fewer young workers to take their place. One likely consequence is now clear: shrinking work forces.

While the streamlining effects of international competition are focusing attention on the need to create and keep good jobs, those fears will eventually give way to worries about the growing shortage of young workers. One unavoidable solution: putting older people back to work, whether they like it or not. Indeed, advanced economies like those of Finland and Denmark have already raised their retirement ages. Others are under severe pressure to follow suit, as both the European Commission and the Organization for Economic Cooperation and Development have recently warned their members that their future prosperity depends on a growing contribution from the elderly.

Whether these changes are good or bad news to workers depends on whether they anticipate retirement with eagerness or dread. In the United States, half of working-age Americans now expect to work into their 70s, whether by financial necessity or by lifestyle choice, according to a new study by Putnam Investments.

Contrary to still widespread assumptions, there is very little hard evidence to suggest that companies cannot stay competitive with a rising share of older workers. At British hardware chain B&Q, its "elder worker" stores in Manchester and Exmouth were 18 percent more profitable than its regular outlets—due in part, the company says, to six times less employee turnover and 60 percent less shoplifting and breakage.

26. Jeeba's difference from a conventional company mainly lies in ________.

[A] the age of its employees [B] the number of its owners

[C] the quality of its products [D] the scope of its operations

27. In the developed world, compared with young people, the elderly ________.

[A] are better at business [B] are greater in number

[C] have healthier lifestyles [D] have more job opportunities

28. According to the writer, in the current situation companies are faced with the tough task of ________.

[A] creating good positions [B] employing retired workers

[C] filling vacant positions [D] replacing unskilled workers

29. For future prosperity, many European countries will have to ________.

[A] increase the number of young workers [B] offer many senior-friendly jobs

[C] improve services for seniors [D] raise their retirement ages

30. B&Q's "elder worker" stores are mentioned to show that the employment of older workers ________.

[A] does not reduce a company's competitiveness

[B] does not affect older workers' lifestyle choices

[C] is not a usual practice among competitive firms

[D] is not good news to those who are eager to retire

Text 2

One important thing during the pre-Christmas rush at our house was the arrival of my daughter's kindergarten report card. She got high praise for her reading, vocabulary and overall enthusiasm. On the other hand, we learnt that she has work to do on her numbers and facility with the computer, though the detailed handwritten report her teachers prepared is absent of any words that might be interpreted as negative in describing her efforts. A number system indicates how she's measuring up in each area without any mention of passing or failing.

All of which seems to make my daughter's school neither fish nor fowl when it comes to the debate over the merits of giving formal grades to kids. At one level, the advantages and disadvantages are obvious. A grade system provides a straightforward standard by which to measure how your child is progressing at school and how he or she is getting on compared to other children. But as writer Sue Ferguson notes, "Grades can deceive." The aim should be "to measure learning, not simply what a student can recall on a test." The two aren't the same and if you doubt that as an adult, ask yourself whether you could sit down without any preparation and still pass those high school level examinations.

If you're old enough, you've lived through this debate before. At one time, it was considered unfair to put children in direct competition with one another if it could be avoided.

The intention behind that may have been good, but it ignored the fact that competition, and the will to come out on top, are essential components of the human condition.

This time around, educators working with a no-grades approach are emphasizing different reasons. The thing is, that approach is much more commonplace in the adult workplace than in the traditional pass-fail system we place on our children. Many workplaces conduct regular employee evaluations. There are usually fairly strict limits to what an employer can tell an employee in those evaluations and even then, negative evaluations can be challenged by the employee. No matter where you sit in the debate over the grade system, then, the real question is this: if it's so good for kids, why isn't that also true for adults?

31. The school report indicates that the writer's daughter ________.

[A] lacks interest in her school work

[B] ranks among the best at language

[C] has some trouble with her handwriting

[D] needs to improve in math and computer skills

32. We can learn that the girl's school tries to deliver the report ________.

[A] in a positive way [B] in a scientific way

[C] in an attractive way [D] in an enthusiastic way

33. Sue Ferguson seems dissatisfied with the grade system for its focus on ________.

[A] the process of getting the knowledge

[B] the capability of memorizing for the test

[C] the procedure of measuring learning

[D] the standard of comparing schools

34. The writer would agree that cutting children off from competition is ________.

[A] fit for human development [B] fit for their age and experience

[C] against a key part of human nature [D] out of consideration for children

35. It can be learned that today's educators supporting the no-grades approach insist that ________.

[A] kids be allowed to challenge the negative evaluations

[B] the traditional teacher-student relationship be changed

[C] the evaluation system for kids be similar to that for adults

[D] strict rules be set up in evaluating school children

Part B

Directions:

Read the texts from a magazine in which five people voice their different opinions in response to an article on the issue of praising. For questions 36–40, match the name of each person to one of the statements (A-G) given below. Mark your answers on ANSWER SHEET.

Mike

Praise often and sincerely—it's as simple as that. Employees want to feel needed and appreciated. By offering sincere praise with examples about what they did right, you'll go far in creating an energetic team. Meanwhile, I don't agree with the assertion that "to focus on what needs improving isn't good management." In fact, it's the balance of praise along with constructive criticism that drives employees to work smarter and reach higher.

Frank

This article makes a valid point that needs to be understood, especially for the new generation of workers, my generation. We don't see ourselves as parts in the machine to be put in the dark to work. My generation needs respect in return from our employer. We need to feel appreciated beyond just a pay check. It's the difference between being fulfilled at our career and being sad at our job.

Joyce

One skill missing in today's workplace is the ability to build effective business relationships. At the core of that relationship is the need for consistent feedback. "How am I doing?" is a question that should be answered consistently. When you tell an employee once a year what is needed to improve, you have not done your job as a leader—build skills, provide feedback and help the employee grow and develop.

Ellen

I don't see a problem with praising employees when it's truly deserved (insincere praise is entirely different story). It's a cost-free "benefit", if you will, in that it allows employees to see that their efforts are both noticed and valued. In the work world there are always people available to tell that you are doing something wrong and far too few occasions when employees are told that they've done something right!

Diana

Praise what the employee did. Be specific about why it was helpful. An employee who continually earns your praise also deserves your attention as to how else to reward their behavior. Meaningful praise encourages people beyond anything else. Written comments are available for later review. They give them confidence that they can "do it again." I never regretted praising an employee who deserved it but often kicked myself for missing an opportunity.

Now match the name of each person (36 – 40) to the appropriate statement.

Note: there are two extra statements.

Statements

	[A]	Praise combined with criticism is helpful.
36. Mike	[B]	Praise can bring about many kinds of desired behavior.
37. Frank	[C]	Employees may feel it hard to accept insincere praise.
38. Joyce	[D]	Let employees know exactly for what they are praised.
39. Ellen	[E]	In my opinion, we are not generous enough to give praise.
40. Diana	[F]	Employees need helpful advice on a regular basis.
	[G]	Money alone cannot guarantee a sense of career fulfillment for me.

Part C

Directions:

Read the following text from which five sentences have been removed. Choose from the sentences A-G the most suitable one to fill each numbered gap in the text (41 –45). *There are TWO extra sentences that you do not need to use. Mark your answer in your ANSWER SHEET.*

At 21, Ricardo Semler became boss of his father's business in Brazil, Semco, which sold parts for ships. Semler Junior worked like a madman, from 7: 30 a. m. , until midnight every day. One afternoon, while touring a factory in New York, he collapsed. The doctor who treated him said, "There's nothing wrong with you. But if you continue like this, you'll find a new home in our hospital." Semler got the message. He changed the way he worked. In fact, he changed the way his employees worked too.

He let his workers take more responsibility so that they would be the ones worrying when things went wrong. He allowed them to set their own salaries, and he cut all the jobs he thought were unnecessary, like receptionists and secretaries. (41) ________________ "Everyone at Semco, even top managers, meets guests in reception, does the photocopying, sends faxes, types letters and dials the phone."

He completely reorganized the office: instead of walls, they have plants at Semco, so bosses can't shut themselves away from everyone else. (42) ________________ As for uniforms, some people wear suits and others wear T-shirts.

Semler says, "We have a sales manager named Rubin Agater who sits there reading the newspaper hour after hour. He doesn't even pretend to be busy. But when a Semco pump on the other side of the world fails millions of gallons of oil are about to spill into the sea, Rubin springs into action. (43) ________________ That's when he earns his salary. No one cares if he doesn't look busy the rest of the time."

Semco has flexible working hours: the employees decide when they need to arrive at work. (44) ________________

It sounds perfect, but does it work? The answer is in the numbers: in the last six years, Semco's revenues have gone from \$ 35 million to \$ 212 million. The company has grown from eight hundred employees to 3,000. Why?

Semler says it's because of "peer pressure". Peer pressure makes everyone work hard for everyone else. (45) ________________ In other words, Ricardo Semler treats his workers like adults and expects them to act like adults. And they do.

[A] This saved money and brought more equality to the company.

[B] He knows everything there is to know about our pumps and how to fix them.

[C] And the workers are free to decorate their workspace as they want.

[D] Most managers spend their time making it difficult for workers to work.

[E] If someone isn't doing his job well, the other workers will not allow the situation to continue.

[F] Also, Semco lets its workers use the company's machines for their own projects, and makes them take holidays for at least thirty days a year.

[G] After years of hard-working, he tired.

Part D

Directions:

Read the following text from which 10 *words have been removed. Choose from the words A-O the most suitable one to fill each numbered gap in the text* (46 – 55). *There are FIVE extra words that you do not need to use. Mark your answers on your ANSWER SHEET.*

America's Internet is faster than ever before, but people still complain about their Internet being too slow.

New York's Attorney General's office __46__ an investigation in the fall into whether or not Verizon, Cablevision and Time Warner are delivering broadband that's as fast as the providers __47__ it is. Earlier this month, the office asked for the public's help to measure their speed results, saying consumers __48__ to get the speeds they were promised. "Too many of us may be paying for one thing, and getting another," the Attorney General said.

If the investigation uncovers anything, it wouldn't be the first time a telecom provider got into __49__ over the broadband speeds it promised and delivered customers. Back in June, the Federal Communications Commission fined AT&T $ 100 million over __50__ that the carrier secretly reduced wireless speeds after customers consumed a certain amount of __51__.

Even when they stay on the right side of the law, Internet providers arouse customers' anger over bandwidth speed and cost. Just this week, an investigation found that media and telecom giant Comcast is the most __52__ provider. Over 10 months, Comcast received nearly 12,000 customer complaints, many __53__ to its monthly data cap and overage charges.

Some Americans are getting so __54__ with Internet providers they're just giving up. A recent study found that the number of Americans with high-speed Internet at home today __55__ fell during the last two years, and 15% of people now consider themselves to be "cord-cutters".

[A] accusations	[B] actually	[C] claim
[D] communicating	[E] complain	[F] data
[G] deserved	[H] frustrated	[I] hated
[J] launched	[K] relating	[L] times
[M] trouble	[N] usually	[O] worried

SECTION Ⅲ Writing

Directions:

You should write your responses to both Part A and Part B of this section on your ANSWER SHEET.

Part A

56. Write a letter to Andy and tell her about your situation. The letter must include:

(1) your family;

(2) your school or work;

(3) your hobby.

You should write about 100 words. Do not sign your own name at the end of the letter. Use "Wang Lin" instead.

Part B

57.

Directions:

Read the text below. Write an essay in about 120 *words, in which you should summarize the key points of the text and make comments on them. Try to use your own words.*

Internet is getting into people's life and becoming more and more popular. Experts are now working on setting up a national long-distance educational system in China to provide educational opportunities via Internet.

In reality, the educational via Internet plan has been taking shape. Some universities have already got involved in regional long-distance education, catching the attention of many educators and computer experts worldwide. Others have just connected their campus computers for teaching and research, and provided more opportunities for learners.

The Internet education will be developing dramatically. It's estimated that computerized long-distance teaching networks will be available by 2010 for postgraduate education, vocational programs, teachers'training and employees'training. Moreover, it will soon cover all the corners of China and eventually win the worldwide popularity.

THAT IS THE END OF THE TEST.

全国英语等级考试第三级
2018 年 3 月笔试真题（改编版）答案及解析

SECTION I　Listening

Part A

1. A　2. B　3. A　4. A　5. C

6. B　7. D　8. D　9. D　10. C

【原文及解析】

1. W：Oh，I'm sorry，Mr. Smith.

M：What's up，Mary?

W：I'm afraid I can't work overtime tomorrow. John and I are holding a party for the 5th anniversary of our wedding.

M：That's all right. Enjoy yourselves.

A【解析】问题：明天女士将会干什么？根据画线部分可得知，她明天不能加班，她和约翰要举办结婚五周年派对，故答案是［A］Hold a party.

2. W：Guess who I met at the grocery store this morning?

M：Well，I can't imagine.

W：Do you remember Mr. Johnson? He used to live in the building next to ours.

M：Oh，yes，now I remember. He had dark hair and wore glasses.

B【解析】问题：谁是 Mr. Johnson？由画线部分可得知，他曾经住在隔壁楼内，也就是说他是他们以前的邻居，故答案是［B］Their former neighbor.

3. M：I've just been interviewed for a reporter's job on the evening paper.

W：What's your overall feeling about how it went?

M：Well，I think I made a good impression. It seems that they were interested in me because I've worked as a reporter before.

A【解析】问题：说话者在讨论什么？由画线部分可以得知男士接受了晚报的记者工作的面试，故答案为［A］A job interview.

4. W：Northwest Airways，good morning. Can I help you?

M：Yes，do you have any flights to Sydney next Tuesday afternoon?

W：Yes，there is a flight at 6：45 and one at 18：00.

M：That's fine. Could you tell me how much return flight costs?

W：That would be 418 dollars.

A【解析】问题：下周二下午有几班航班飞去悉尼？由画线部分可以得知一班在6：45，是上午的航班。另一班在18：00，是下午的航班，故答案为［A］One.

5. W：You look tired, John. What have you been doing?

M：My teacher wasn't happy with my mid-term essay. She told me to do it all over again.

W：At least, she gave you a second chance.

M：Yeah, I have to admit that.

C【解析】问题：男士的老师让他干什么？由画线部分可以得知老师对他的期中论文不满意，叫他重写。故答案为［C］Rewrite his essay.

6. W：I'm worried about my son at driving, but he won't listen to me.

M：Well, teenagers always think they won't get hurt, but the fact is just the opposite.

W：What should I do?

M：Keep talking with him and lead by an example. Parents always matter.

B【解析】问题：关于女士的儿子我们了解什么？由画线部分可以得知，女士担心儿子开车的事，但是她的儿子不听她的意见。［A］He often talks with his mother. 和［C］He is willing to listen to his mother. 与画线部分内容不符，可排除。选项［D］He is worried about his driving skills. 具有一定迷惑性，是妈妈担心，而不是儿子担心自己的驾驶技术，所以也可以排除。选项［B］He often drives in a careless way. 是合理的推测，因此B是正确答案。

7. W：Where is Jack? His manager is trying to catch him several times but has always just missed him.

M：That's because he is being in and out all day.

W：What's been going on?

M：It has been many emergency calls and he is the only technician available to go out and deal with them.

D【解析】问题：关于Jack，我了解什么？由画线部分可以得知紧急电话太多了，他是唯一可以用的技术员。故［D］He is a company technician. 是正确答案。

8. W：Can you change the bill for me please?

M：Sure, 5, 10, 15, 20. OK, 20.

W：Can I have some coins? I need them for a phone call.

M：Here you are.

D【解析】问题：从这个对话我们了解什么？由画线部分可以得知女士要求男士帮她兑换零钱，她需要一些硬币用来打电话。故［D］The woman has a 20-dollar bill changed. 是正确答案。

9. W：I went to the dentist's to get my teeth polished this morning.

M：How terrible!

W：Well, the chair was so cleverly placed. I got a terrific view of Times Square down below. He finished the job before I knew it.

D【解析】问题：女士是什么意思？由画线部分可以得知牙科诊所的椅子摆放的位置非常巧妙。她能看到下面的时代广场的美丽景色。在她意识到结束之前牙医就完成了工作。由此可以推断女士的意思是这次看牙医没有男士想象得那么恐怖，故［D］It was not so terrible a visit to the dentist's. 是正确答案。选项［B］The dentist's is close to Times Square. 非常具有迷惑性，和对话的内容相符，但不是女士想要表达的重点。

10. M：I hear the guy who is going to deliver the lecture this weekend spend a year living in the rainforest.

W：Great. I'm doing a report on the rainforest. Maybe I can get some new information to add to it.

C【解析】问题：关于女士我们了解什么？男士告诉女士本周末将做讲座的人曾经在雨林里度过了一年，由画线部分可以得知女士听到这个消息很高兴，她正在写一份关于雨林的报告，或许从讲座中可以得到一些新的信息加到报告中去。由此可以推断她非常期待这次讲座，所以选项［C］She is looking forward to the lecture. 是正确答案。

Part B

11. D	12. A	13. C	14. B	15. A
16. D	17. B	18. B	19. C	20. A
21. D	22. A	23. D	24. B	25. C

【原文及解析】

Questions 11 – 13

M：Your readers are interested in your childhood. What was it like?

W：I grew up in a small town. We lived in very poor housing but we lived always in very beautiful settings, so I have favorite trees and I have contacted with birds. My parents were farm workers. (11) Though we were poor for most of part, I think I was often happy.

M：It would not have been expected from that background that you'll become a literary figure. Was your mother ambitious with you?

W：Well, my mother wasn't especially ambitious with me in the sense of going to college when I grew up. (12) I think her greatest contribution was simply that she loved me very much. No matter what happened, I had my mother with me.

M：She gave you confidence.

W：Oh, she did. She earned very little money, offering about $10 a week and never more than $20 a week. And in spite of that, she managed to buy a typewriter for me. She managed to buy me my first toothpaste when I left home. (13) She just wanted me to be able to do things that she couldn't do even she didn't know what they were.

11. 问题：这位女士的家庭是怎样的？

D【解析】细节推断题。对话中提到 poor housing 表示这位女士小时候家中住房条件很差，排除 B 选项；A 选项 kept a lot of birds 表示养许多鸟，而对话中提到的 have contact with birds 表示可以接触到鸟类，排除 A 选项；My parents were farm workers 意思是“父母在农场务工”与 own a small farm “拥有一个小型农场”不同，排除 C 选项；we were poor for most of part 意思是“我们大部分时间都处在贫困之中”，故 D 选项 suffered from poverty 遭受着贫困为正确答案。

12. 问题：那位女士的母亲给她留下了什么印象？

A【解析】观点辨认题。问题中 impress sb. with 表示“给予某人深刻的印象”。男士问及你母亲是否对你抱有很高的期望（be ambitious with sb.），女士否认了。但她提到母亲对她最大的帮助是给予了她深厚的母爱。故 A 为正确选项。

13. 问题：那位女士的母亲希望她将来做什么？

C【解析】语义推断题。问题中提到 wish her to do 即母亲对她的期望，对话最后一句提到母亲只是期望她能比自己过得更好一些，实现一些母亲无法做到的事情。故选择 C。

必背词汇

housing *n.* 住房，住宅

setting *n.* 环境

suffer from 因……而受苦

literary figure 作家的身份

ambitious *adj.* 有抱负的，有雄心的

ambition *n.* 追求，理想

impress sb. with sth. 给（某人）留下深刻印象

Questions 14 – 17

W：Good morning. Can I help you?

M：(14) I'd like to make a complaint about my holiday in Paris last week.

W：I'm sorry to hear that. What exactly was the problem?

M：First of all, (15) the coach taking us to the hotel broke down and we had to wait for over 2 hours in the terrible heat before our replacement arrived. Then when we got to the hotel, we found our room hadn't been cleaned.

W：Oh, dear. Did you complain to the hotel staff?

M：Of course, but we were told all the cleaners were off duty. Anyway, that's not all. (16) The people in room above sounded like they were having all night parties every night. I demanded another room but the receptionist told me the hotel was full.

W：Oh，I see.

M：（16）And the worst thing was the food in the restaurant was awful. It was so bad we had to eat out all the time despite having paid for meals in the price of our holiday.

W：I do apologize. I'd like to offer you a 20% discount on the price of one of our autumn breaks as a gesture of good will.

M：（17）A 20% discount? You must be joking. I want to see the manager.

14. 问题：男士可能在向谁抱怨？

B【解析】场景推断题。男士说的第一句为："我想就上周我在巴黎度假的经历进行投诉（make a complaint）。"故选择 B。

15. 问题：那个人为什么在高温下等了两个小时？

A【解析】事实细节题。男士中提到因为旅游大巴车（coach）坏了，在接替的车到达前，他们不得不在高温中等了两小时。故选择 A。

16. 问题：那人在投诉中提到了什么？

D【解析】细节辨认题。在男士投诉的细节中提及当他们到达时房间仍未打扫，但所有清洁工都下班了，楼上的住客每晚都发出类似开派对的噪音；想换房间但酒店客满了，最糟糕的是餐厅的食物非常差。A、B、C 选项与原文不一致，D 符合以上表述中的两项，故为正确答案。

17. 问题：这位男士对女士所提出的道歉方式是什么态度？

B【解析】态度推断题。女士提出可以提供以八折优惠价购买该旅社的秋季行程，以示友好。而男士对此表示极为不满，要求见经理。在态度推断题中，要留意说话者的语气和语调。

必背词汇

make a complaint　投诉

receptionist　*n.*　接待员

travel agent　*n.*　旅行代办人

coach　*n.*　长途汽车

replacement　*n.*　接替者，替代者

off duty　不当班；不值班

discount　*n.*　折扣

Questions 18 – 21

W：Good evening. Welcome back to *Miss Know It All*. For today's program, Mr. John Smith, chairman of National Weight and Heath Association, has come with findings from our recent NWHA survey on obesity. Now, Mr. Smith, what is the purpose of your survey?

M：（18）We wanted to explore how people around the world view obesity or being overweight. Actually, obesity has gone global.

W：How did you do it？

M：We interviewed 16 000 people in 16 countries.

W：How large is the overweight population of the world according to your estimates？

M：（19）1.6 billion including 18 million children under age 5.

W：Really surprising，isn't it？And what are your findings about people's attitudes regarding obesity？

M：（20）Our survey found that people in Brazil feel the most pressure to be thin，83% of Brazilians think there is too much emphasis placed on weight. French are most likely to blame Americans. They use American's fast food as an excuse for their overweight problem.（21）Russians are most likely to blame their parents for obesity. They are followed by Germans and Indians. When asked who encouraged them to try to lose weight，the Swiss tend to exclude their doctor.

W：Stay tuned for more about the NWHA survey，we will be back soon after the break.

18. 问题：NWHA 调查的目的是什么？

B【解析】语义理解题。这是一个访谈节目，主持人的提问往往为答案定位点。主持人的第一个问题中提到 purpose，为题目中 aim 的同义替换。接下来男士的回答了他们调查的目的是找出全世界人们是如何看待肥胖这一问题的，因此 B 为正确答案。

19. 问题：世界上有多少人属于超重人群？

C【解析】细节辨认题。主持人问："根据你的估计，全世界有多少超重人口？"男士回答："16 亿，包括 1800 万 5 岁以下儿童。"由此得知提到的第一个数字应是答案，故正确选项为 C。

20. 问题：哪个国家的人觉得减肥的压力最大？

A【解析】细节辨认题。男士说："我们的调查发现，觉得减肥压力最大的是巴西人。"注意表述中使用了最高级 feel the most pressure。因此 A 为正确选项，其他选项虽然在文中提及，但语义不符，为干扰项。

21. 问题：谁最有可能把肥胖归咎于父母？

D【解析】细节辨认题。男士说："俄罗斯人最有可能把肥胖归咎于父母。"注意表述中使用了最高级 be most likely to。因此 D 为正确选项。其他选项虽然在文中提及，但语义不符，为干扰项。

必背词汇

survey *n.* 民意调查

obesity *n.* 肥胖；肥胖症

overweight *adj.* 太胖的；超重的

purpose *n.* 意图；目的

incidence *n.* 发生率；影响范围

blame sb. for sth. 把某事归咎于某人

exclude *v.* 把……排除在外

Questions 22 – 25

M：Emily, what do you do as a trendspotter?

W：Very simple, (22) Take digital photos of youth culture and send them to my company. It's called Look-Look.

M：What kind of company is it?

W：It's a youth culture marketing and trend forecasting film in Hollywood, I'm one of Look Look's 65, 000 trendspotters worldwide.

M：(23) Look-Look gets a lot of information about the ever shifting tastes of the youth market by these images.

W：Yes, its clients are mostly companies. They get information about trends from Look-Look and develop their products. (24) They also use their images of Look-Look on their websites to impress young people and promote their newly designed products.

M：But are there any people who don't like their pictures to be used on the website?

W：I always have my subjects'permission before I take their pictures and put up their images onto Look-Look. com.

M：Where do you find your best subjects?

W：At school, in the park, at local supermarkets and near many music clubs.

M：What is difficult about this job?

W：To catch our original styles because so many young people try hard to stand out. (25) You have to be able to find the difference between someone who is copying trends and someone who is truly inventing a new look.

M：Thank you for talking with us, Emily.

22. 问题：潮流发现者的任务是什么？

A【**解析**】事实细节题。女生提到工作任务是拍下青少年文化的数码照片，然后发回公司。pictures 是 digital photos 是同义转述，故正确选项是 A。

23. 问题：Look-Look 公司的主要关注点是什么？

D【**解析**】语义理解题。原文中提到 Look-Look 通过这些图片获得了大量关于不断变化着的年轻人市场品味的信息。选项 A 是为客户招募潮流发现者。选项 B 是为年轻的潮流发现者提供建议。选项 C 是为客户组织销售网络。选项 D 意思与原文一致，为正确选项。

24. 问题：为什么有些公司在他们的网站上使用 Look-Look 的图片？

B【**解析**】语义理解题。原文中提到两点理由：他们从 Look-Look 获得潮流趋势信息并开发产品；他们还利用自己网站上的形象来打动年轻人，推销他们新设计的产品。选项 A 是增加 Look-Look 网站的访问量。选项 B 是吸引年轻人购买他们的新产品。原文中的 promote 是推销的意思，因此 B 是正确答案。选项 C 是了解年轻人购买的动机。选项 D 的意思是鼓励年轻人成为拍摄对象。

25. 问题：为什么潮流发现者很难捕捉到原创风格？

C【解析】语义理解题。最后一句话提到：你必须能够分辨出模仿潮流的人和真正发明新造型的人，故 C 为正确选项。

必背词汇

trend *n.* 趋势;风尚
spotter *n.* 观察者
digital *adj.* 数码的;数字式的
image *n.* 影像
taste *n.* 品味;爱好
client *n.* 客户
promote *v.* 促销
permission *n.* 准许

SECTION Ⅱ Reading

Part A

Text 1

26. A【解析】细节题。由题干的 Jeeba 可以定位到原文第一段，根据文章第一段 "all older than 60" "the name means old man and old woman" "Of the elderly, by the elderly and for the elderly" "They do not hire young people, and the oldest of their workers is 75" 可以看出，Jeeba 是由日本的老年市民发起的运动，其目的和公司格言主要体现的是老年人这个特点。由此可知，Jeeba 与传统公司的主要区别就体现在员工的年龄上，故选 A。B 项"所有者的数量"、C 项"产品质量"、D 项"经营的范围"原文都没有提及，故不选。

27. B【解析】细节题。由题干的"in the developed world"定位到原文的第二段，从第二段第四句话"Extremely low birthrates in those same countries mean there are far fewer young workers to take their place."在出生率极低的发达国家，接替退休老年人工作的年轻人的数量少得多。由此可以看出，老年人跟年轻人相比，数量更多。故选 B。A 项"更擅长做生意"没有提到、C 项"生活方式更健康"虽然提到，但只是说二战后老年人的身体状况、D 项"工作机会更多"没有提及，因此都不符合题意，故不选。

28. B【解析】推断题。由题干可以定位到原文第三段，从第三段第一、二句话："While the streamlining effects of international competition are focusing attention on the need to create and keep good jobs, those fears will eventually give way to worries about the growing

short-age of young workers. One unavoidable solution：puking older people back to work, whether they like it or not.” 和最后一句话：“... their future prosperity depends on a growing contribution from the elderly.” 可知，对创造和维持好工作需求的担忧最终会转变为对日益缺少的年轻劳动力的担心，对此担心的解决方法就是需要让老年人回到工作岗位，公司未来的发展繁荣依赖于老年人的不断贡献。由此可推测，在当前形势下，公司面临的严峻任务就是雇佣退休的员工，故选 B。A 项“创造更好的岗位”、C 项“填补空白岗位”、D 项“替换不熟练的员工”都不是公司当前面临的最困难的任务，故不选。

29. D【解析】细节题。根据题干的“many European countries”定位到原文的第三段最后两句话。“Advanced economies like those of Finland and Denmark have already raised their retirement ages” “their future prosperity depends on a growing contribution from the elderly”可以看出：像芬兰和丹麦这样的经济发达国家，已经延迟了退休年龄，他们未来的繁荣依赖于老年人的不断奉献。最后一句继而说公司的繁荣离不开老年人的贡献，故选 D。A 项“增加年轻员工的数量”、B 项“提供很多适合老年人的工作”、C 项“提高对老年人的服务”都不是本句的主旨，故不选。

30. A【解析】推断题。根据题干“B&Q's ‘elder worker’ store”定位到原文最后一段，从最后一段第二句话“At British hardware chain B&Q, its ‘elder worker’ stores... were l8 percent more profitable than its regular outlets...”可知，B&Q 的“高龄者”商店比其一般商店多盈利 18%。由此可以推断，公司雇佣高龄工作者并不会降低公司的竞争力，故选 A。B 项“没有影响老年员工的生活方式的选择”、C 项“不是有竞争力的公司的通常的做法”、D 项“对于那些急于退休的人来说不是好消息”原文没有提到，故不选。

【参考译文】

1997 年，年龄都超过 60 岁的 25 名日本市民发起了一场 Jeeba 运动（Jeeba 意为老年男性与女性），生产方便于老年人使用的产品。当他们编撰出公司的格言“老年人所有，老年人制造，为了老年人”时，他们知道他们正在创造历史。他们不雇佣年轻人，公司里最年长的员工年龄高达 75 岁。

不管是在日本还是全世界，由高龄者经营的公司仍然为数不多。但是老年人人口数量巨大。第二次世界大战以后出生的人们，现在到了退休年龄，这些老年人更加健康、长寿，他们人数众多，遍布世界各地。在出生率极低的那些发达国家，接替老年人工作的年轻人更少了。一个可能出现的结果现在变得清楚了：劳动力日益缩减。

国际竞争的精简效应正集中注意力于创造和维持好工作的需求上，这些担心最终会转变为对日益缺少的年轻劳动力的担心。一个不可避免的解决方法是，让老年人回归工作，不管他们喜不喜欢。确实如此，像芬兰和丹麦这样的经济发达国家，已经延迟了退休年龄。其他一些国家正处在顺应潮流的高压下，因为欧盟委员会和经济合作与发展组织最近告诫其成员，他们未来的繁荣依赖于老年人的不断奉献。

这些改变是否是好消息取决于工人们在退休的时候是怀着急切的还是恐惧的心情。

据百能投资的一项新研究显示，在美国，不论是由于经济需要还是生活方式的选择，现在有一半处在工作年龄的美国人期待着能工作到 70 多岁。

与一直广泛传播的想法相反，几乎没有确凿的证据表明，公司里高龄工作者增多会导致公司不再有竞争力。在英国硬件连锁企业 B&Q 里，位于曼彻斯特和埃克斯茅斯的“高龄者”商店比其一般商店多盈利 18%，公司说部分原因是员工流动减少了 6 倍，商店偷窃和商品损坏事件减少了 60%。

Text 2

31. D【解析】细节题。由题干的“the school report”定位到原文第一段，文章第一段第三句话“on the other hand, we learnt that she has work to do on her numbers and facility with the computer, though the detailed handwritten report her teachers prepared is absent of any words that might be interpreted as negative in describing her effort.”可知，作者从成绩单上面了解到女儿在数字和计算机应用能力方面仍要做很多工作，也就是说女儿需要在这两方面加强和提高，故 D 项符合文义。而根据第一段第二句话“She got high praise for her reading, vocabulary and over-all enthusiasm.”只能得知，作者从成绩单上面了解到女儿在语言方面得到很高的评价，因此 B 选项表述与原文不符。A 项“对学校功课缺乏兴趣”、B 项“在语言方面排名最好”原文没有涉及，故选 D。

32. A【解析】推断题。由题干的“the girl's school tries to deliver the report”可以定位到文章第一段，从第一段来看，作者收到女儿学校的成绩单，上面写的全是表扬的话，而作者自己知道，女儿在数字运算等方面还需要学习，由此可推断女儿学校只是努力从正面的角度赞扬女儿在学校的表现，故选 A。

33. B【解析】细节题。由题干的“Sue Ferguson”可以定位到原文第二段，从文章第二段第五句“The aim should be ‘to measure learning, not simply what a student can recall on a test’”可知苏·弗格森对评级体系不满意的原因是它强调测试学生的记忆能力，而非学习本身，故选 B。

34. C【解析】细节题。由题干的“cutting children off from competition”可以定位到原文第三段，从文章第三段最后一句话“... but it ignored the fact that competition, and the will to come out on top, are essential components of the human condition”可知，作者认为让孩子们远离竞争是违反了人类生存本质的，故选 C。

35. B【解析】推断题。由题干的“today's educators supporting the no-grades approach”可以定位到原文的最后一段，通过排除法，A 项说允许孩子质疑消极的测评结果，与原文不符，原文是作者拿成年人举例，并提出疑问，为什么成年人不能用不评级的体系，故排除 A 项和 C 项。D 项说应该建立严格的规章制度来测评学生，这个文章中更没有提及，亦排除，故选 B。

【参考译文】

在繁忙的圣诞节来临前，我们家一件重要的事情就是，收到了女儿幼儿园的成绩单。她在阅读、词汇和整体学习热情方面得到高度评价。另一方面，我们了解到，她需要好好练习数字运算和计算机操作，尽管女儿的老师准备的这份手写的详细成绩单上没有出现任何可能显示女儿消极学习的话语。一项计数法暗示了女儿在每一个学科的成绩情况，虽然没有任何通过或不及格的说明。

当谈到给小学生正常评级的好处的争论时，所有这些似乎表明女儿的学校不伦不类。在一个层面上，优点和缺点不言而喻。评级系统提供了一个直接的标准，通过这个标准可以衡量你的孩子在学校的进步情况，以及相对于其他孩子来说，自家孩子的表现情况。但正如苏·弗格森作家写的那样“成绩是可以欺骗人的”。目的应该是“衡量学习情况，而不是简单地测试学生在考试时能记得多少东西”。这两者并不一样。如果作为一个成年人，你对此感到质疑，那么你可以问问你自己，是否可以在不做任何准备的情况下仍然通过那些高中阶段的考试。

如果你足够大了，你以前就经历过了这样的辩论。曾经有人一度认为，在可以避免的情况下，让孩子们置于彼此之间直接竞争的环境中是不公平的。这个想法背后的意图或许是好的，但它忽略了一个事实：竞争和出类拔萃的愿望构成了人类生存环境的核心部分。

现在，用不给成绩的教育方法工作的教育家们在强调不同的原因。问题是，比起传统的施加在孩子身上的“过或不过”体系，这个方法在我们成人工作中更普遍。许多工作采用常规的员工测评方法。在这些测评中，通常有严格的规定限制雇主可以告知雇员的内容，即便如此，员工还是可以质疑消极的测评结果。不管你是处在关于评级体系争论的哪一方，真正的问题是：如果不给成绩的方式对孩子来说有这么多好处，为什么对成年人来说却并非如此呢?

Part B

【要求解析】

从“Directions：Read the texts from a magazine in which five people voice their different opinions in response to an article on the issue of praising.”可以得知五段文章是五个人对一篇有关“表扬”的文章的不同看法。

【选项解析】

选项 A：结合批评的表扬是有帮助的。可用 criticism 作关键词。

选项 B：表扬可以引发许多好的行为表现。可用 many kinds of desired behavior 作关键词。

选项 C：员工可能会觉得很难接受不诚意的表扬。可用 Employees，insincere praise 作关键词。

选项 D：要让员工确切知道他们为什么被表扬。可用 know exactly 作关键词。

选项 E：我认为我们表扬别人时不够慷慨（做不到经常表扬别人）。可用 not generous enough to give praise 作关键词。

选项 F：员工需要定期得到有用的建议。可用 helpful advice，on a regular basis 作关键词。

选项 G：对于我来说，仅仅获得金钱是无法保障职业满足感的。可用 Money，career fulfillment 作关键词。

【题目解析】

36. A【解析】细节题。Mike 这段文章第一句是该段主旨句，提出要经常并真诚地给予表扬（Praise often and sincerely—it's as simple as that.）。其中“often”与选项 F 中“on a regular basis（经常性的）”是同义转换，“sincerely”一词在选项 C 中出现了反义词“insincere”，但是这两个选项的其他部分在该段未被提及，因此都不是正确答案。段落中间出现“Meanwhile（同时）”一词提示并列关系，衔接段落的第二个主旨句：“我并不同意关注需要改进之处就不是好的管理之道这一说法”（I don't agree with the assertion that “to focus on what needs improving isn't good management”.）。但同第一个主旨句一样，此句也并未设置考点。该题考点在其后支撑细节句，文章中“表扬和积极的批评（praise along with constructive criticism）”对应选项 A“结合批评的表扬（Praise combined with criticism）”，文章中“使得员工工作更加有效，取得更大的进步（drives employees to work smarter and reach higher）”对应选项 A 中 helpful 一词。

37. G【解析】主旨题。该段的最后一句是段落主旨句，提出我们这一代人（My generation）除了需要一份工资（a pay check），更多的是需要从雇主那里得到尊重作为回报（respect in return from our employer）及感觉被赏识（feel appreciated），这些是实现事业满足感（being fulfilled at our career）和痛苦地工作（being sad at our job）之间的区别。选项 G 与此句含义相对应。

38. F【解析】主旨题。该段的第二句是主旨句，提出建立有效商业关系的核心是持续性的反馈（consistent feedback）。“持续性”一词表示频率，提示选项 F 中“经常性的（on a regular basis）”，两者之间互为同义词。段末给员工提供反馈，帮助他们成长进步（provide feedback and help the employee grow and develop）对应选项 F 员工需要有用的建议（Employees need helpful advice）。

39. E【解析】主旨题。该段的第一句为主旨句，提出当员工值得表扬时，给予他们表扬是没有问题的（但不真诚的表扬就另当别论了）。“insincere praise”在选项 C 出现，但选项 C 中难以接受（feel it hard to accept）并未在这句及此段出现，因此可将选项 C 做迷惑项排除。段落的最后一句进一步说明在职场上，总是有人告诉你你做错事了，但是极少数情况会有人告诉你你做对了，对应选项 E，人们在给予表扬的时候太不慷慨了。

40. D【解析】细节题。该段的第一句是主旨句，指出要表扬员工所做的事，后文说明了各种表扬的细节，如具体化（Be specific），有意义的表扬（Meaningful praise），书面形式的评价（Written comments）等。段落第二句具体的（specific）对应选项 D“exactly”，这为什么有帮助（why it was helpful）对应选项 D 他们为了什么而被表扬（for what they are praised）。

【参考译文】

麦克：

经常性、真诚地给予表扬——事情就是这么简单。员工们希望被需要和被赏识。对员工们正确行事的事例给予真诚的表扬，你就离创立一个富有活力的团队不远了。同时，我并不同意“关注需要改进之处就不是好的管理之道”这一说法。事实上，正是表扬和积极的批评之间的平衡促使员工更加有效地开展工作并取得更大的进步。

弗兰克：

这篇文章提出一个需要被理解的合理观点，尤其是对新一代工作者，我们这一代人。我们不把自己看作是放置在黑暗里工作的机器的一部分。我们这代人需要从雇主那里得到尊重作为回报，除了一份工资单，我们还需要被赏识的感觉。这是实现事业满足感和痛苦地工作之间的区别。

乔伊斯：

当今职场中缺失的一种技能是建立有效商业关系的能力。这一关系的核心是对持续性反馈的需求。“我做得怎么样?”是一个应该经常被回答的问题。如果你一年中只有一次只告诉某员工他需要如何改进，那么你便没有能够完成作为领导的工作——培训技能，提供反馈，帮助员工成长发展。

艾伦：

当员工确实值得表扬时，给予他们表扬是没有问题的（但不真诚的表扬就另当别论了）。这是没有成本的“利益”，如果你这样做了，你的员工们会看到自己付出的努力得到了关注，是值得的。在职场上，总是有人告诉你你做错事了，但是极少数情况会有人告诉你你做得对!

戴安娜：

表扬员工所做的事。具体说明为什么其所做之事是有助的。一个经常得到你表扬的员工也值得你关注如何奖励他们的行为表现。有意义的表扬比任何其他形式都更能鼓励人。书面评价可以用于日后回顾。这些给了他们“再做一次”的信心。我从来没后悔过表扬一个值得表扬的原因，但经常责怪自己错过了表扬的机会。

Part C

【答案及解析】

41．A【解析】本题考查的是对上下文之间意义关系的理解和对文章细节的把握。上一句说到“他允许他们自己制定薪水，但会削减他认为不必要的，比如像接待员和秘书这样的工作”，这些都是公司采取的措施，按照行文逻辑，下一句应该解释这种做法的原因。而选项 A 说明“这样可以减少开支，并给公司带来更多平等”，与上下文联系最符合逻辑，因此选 A。

42．C【解析】本题考查的是对段落主旨的理解和对文章细节的把握。本段主要讲 semler 如何改造公司：办公室没有墙，而是植物，因此老板不能与其他人隔开，而选项中只有 C 提到这方面的内容，“员工可以随意装饰自己的工作空间”放在这里是和前后两句话的并列。因此选 C。

43. B【解析】本题考查的是对上下文之间意义关系的理解和对文章细节的把握。上一句说到“但如果 Semco 在地球另一端的油泵坏了，上百万加仑的油即将注入大海时，Robin 就会立刻跳起来行动”，下一句需要说到 Robin 怎样行动，因此选项 B“他了解关于我们公司油泵的任何事情，并能修理”符合题目要求。

44. F【解析】本题考查的是对段落主旨的理解和对文章细节的把握。这一段讲述了 Semco 给予员工的自由，而选项中只有 F“Semco 也允许员工用公司的机器做自己的项目，并且一年至少能休假 30 天”与此内容相关，因此选 F。

45. E【解析】本题考查的是对上下文之间意义关系的理解。上一句说到同伴的压力让员工努力为他人工作，而下一句应具体解释这种压力如何发挥作用。选项 E“如果有人表现不好，其他人会制止这一局面”延续了这一句的内容。因此选 E。

【参考译文】

21 岁时，Ricardo Semler 就成为父亲在巴西的公司 Semco 的老板，该公司出售轮船部件。年少的 Semler 每天从早上七点半直到深夜疯狂地工作着。有天下午当他在纽约参观工厂时晕倒了，治疗医生说：“你身体没有什么毛病，但你若一直这样工作，你会长期待在医院的。”Semler 听从了医生的话。他改变了自己的工作方式，事实上也改变了员工的工作方式。

他让员工担负更多责任，让他们为事情偏离轨道而担忧。他允许他们自己制定薪水，但会削减他认为不必要的，比如像接待员和秘书这样的工作。(41)［A］这样可以减少开支，并给公司带来更多平等。Semco 的每个人，甚至高管都要自己接待客人，复印、发传真、打字和打电话。

他完全改造了 Semco：办公室没有墙，而是植物，因此老板不能与其他人隔开。(42)［C］员工可以随意装饰自己的工作空间。制服方面，则有人穿西装，有人穿 T 恤。

Semler 说：“我们有个坐在那里看几个小时报纸的销售经理，叫 Rubin Agater。他甚至不用去装很忙碌的样子。但如果 Semco 在地球另一端的油泵坏了，上百万加仑的油即将注入大海时，Robin 就会立刻跳起来行动。”(43)［B］他了解关于我们公司油泵的任何事情，并能修理。这就是他挣工资的时候，别人并不关心其他时间他是否看上去忙忙碌碌。

Semco 有弹性工作时间：员工自己决定什么时候来上班，并且一年要两次评估老板。(44)［F］Semco 也允许员工用公司的机器做自己的项目，并且一年至少能休假 30 天。

听上去很好？但这一切都起作用了么？答案在数字中：在过去的六年里，Semco 的收入从三千五百万美元上升到两亿一千二百万美元。公司员工数量从 800 增长到 3000。为什么会发生这一切？

Semler 认为这是因为“同伴的压力”。同伴的压力让员工努力为他人工作。

45［E］如果有人表现不好，其他人会制止这一局面。换句话说，Ricardo Semler 给员工以成人的待遇，并希望他们有成人的行为。他们都做到了。

［A］这样可以减少开支，并给公司带来更多平等。

［B］他了解关于我们公司油泵的任何事情，并能修理。

［C］员工可以随意装饰自己的工作空间。

［D］大部分经理都把时间花在了给工人们的工作增加难度上。

［E］如果有人表现不好，其他人会制止这一局面。

［F］Semco 也允许员工用公司的机器做自己的项目，并且一年至少能休假 30 天。

［G］多年的努力工作后，他累了。

Part D

46.［J］launched

【解析】动词辨析题。空格位于主语 office 之后，名词 an investigation 之前，应填入动词作谓语。根据上下文的语境，此句应为一般过去时。本句意为：纽约总检察长办公室于秋天________一项调查。由此推断，空格处应填入含有“开展”含义的动词，故本题答案为［J］launched。launch an investigation 意为：开展一项调查，是一个非常常见的搭配，经常被考查。在备选动词过去式中，［G］deserved，“应得，值得”；［H］frustrated，“沮丧”；［I］hated，“憎恨”；［O］worried，“担忧”都不能与 investigation 搭配，因此排除。

47.［C］claim

【解析】动词辨析题。空格位于于从句 it is 之前，应填入动词，作为 the providers 的谓语。本句意为：Verizon 公司、有线电视公司和时代华纳公司提供的宽带网速是否与他们________一样快。由本段最后一句可知，许多消费者花的钱和获得的东西并不一致，所以这些网络服务商真实提供的网速与他们所说的可能不一致，故本题答案为［C］claim，意思为“宣称”。空格后的从句用的是一般现在时，且前面的 providers 是复数形式，所以空格处应填入动词原形。备选动词原形中的［E］complain“抱怨”；［M］trouble“使烦恼”，均与句意不符，因此排除。

48.［G］deserved

【解析】动词辨析题。空格所在部分是 saying 的宾语从句，而且空格位于主语 consumers 之后，应填入动词作谓语。由本句中 asked for 和 they were promised 可推断，空格处应填入动词的过去式。本句意为：本月早些时候，总检察长办公室呼吁公众帮助测试网速，说消费者________享受到服务商承诺的网速。由本段大意可知，纽约总检察长办公室认为网络服务商存在欺诈消费者的嫌疑，而消费者既然已经花了钱，就有权享受服务商承诺的网速。由此推断，空格处应填入“有权获得，应得”等类似含义的动词，故答案为［G］deserved。备选项中的［H］frustrated、［I］hated、［O］worried 都不符合句意，因此排除。［J］launched 已经成为 46 题答案，已不在此题的考查范围内。

49. ［M］trouble

【解析】名词辨析题。空格位于介词 into 之后，应填入名词。本句意为：如果该调查有所发现的话，这也不会是电信服务商第一次因为其承诺的宽带速度和实际提供给顾客的网速不一致而陷入________中。结合本段第二句美国电话电报公司被罚款的例子可知，如果该调查有所发现，第二段提到的这几家公司肯定会遭受麻烦，故答案为［M］trouble。get into trouble 是一个常见的搭配，意为：陷入麻烦。备选名词中，［A］accusations 意为指控，程度过重了，电信服务商不一定会因此被指控，而［F］data“数据”和［L］times“次数”，都不符合句意，因此排除。

50. ［A］accusations

【解析】名词辨析题。空格位于介词 over 之后，应填入名词。本句意为：早在六月份，联邦通讯委员会对 AT&T 公司处以 1 亿美元的罚款________该公司在顾客使用一定量的__51__后私自降低无线网速。由此可知，AT&T 公司被政府监管部门处以巨额罚款，应该是触犯了法律。那么空格处应填入与法律相关，且含有“控告”意思的名词，故答案为［A］accusations。fine... over... 意为：因为……而罚款……。备选名词中，剩下的［F］data 和［L］times 都不符合句意，可以排除。

51. ［F］data

【解析】名词辨析题。本题在 50 题 accusations 的同位语从句中，空格位于介词 of 之后，应填入名词。意为：该公司在顾客使用一定量的________后私自降低无线网速。结合全文可知，顾客在此使用的是网络，进一步说是网络中的数据，故本题答案为［F］data。a certain amount of 后面接不可数名词，在备选名词中，只有［F］data 符合要求。data 是 datum 的复数形式，但是在实际应用中常常作为不可数名词来应用，类似的词还有 media。

52. ［I］hated

【解析】形容词辨析题。空格位于 the most 之后，名词 provider 之前，应填入形容词。本句意为：就在本周，一项调查发现，媒体和电信巨头 Comcast 公司是最________的服务商。而前一句提到，即使没有触犯法律，网络服务商也会因为宽带速度和收费激起消费者的怒气。下一句提到 Comcast 公司收到很多消费者投诉。结合这两句可以推断，Comcast 公司并不受消费者欢迎，故答案为［I］hated“被憎恨的；被讨厌的”。在形容词备选形容词中［H］frustrated 和［O］worried 都不符合句意，因此排除。

53. ［K］relating

【解析】动词辨析题。空格所在部分与前面的句子用逗号隔开，而且位于代词 many（complaints）之后，因此应填入动词的现在分词形式。本句意为：历经 10 个多月，Comcast 公司收到了近 12000 份消费者投诉，很多都与其每月数据限额和超额收费________。前一句提到，Comcast 公司是电信业巨头，因此得知消费者投诉肯定是与数据限额有关的，故答案为［K］relating。relate to 表示与……有关，空格处于非谓语结构中，因此用 ing 形式。备选动词中，只有［D］communicating 和［K］relating 是现在分词形式，而 communicating 意为交流，与句意不符，因此排除。

54. ［H］ frustrated

【解析】形容词辨析题。空格位于 getting so 之后，应填入形容词。本句意为：有些美国人对网络服务商越来越感到如此的________，以至于他们正在放弃使用。由句意可知，人们因为失望、不满才会放弃使用网络，故本题答案为 H，短语 get frustrated with... 意为：对……失望。在剩余的形容词备选形容词中，［O］ worried 意为：担忧的，且不能与 with 连用，因此排除。

55. ［B］ actually

【解析】副词辨析题。分析空格所在句的句子成分可知，本句有完整的主谓结构，而且空格处又位于动词 fell 之前，因此应填入副词来修饰动词 fell。本句意为：一项最近的研究表明，在过去两年里，家中有高速网络的美国人的数量________下降了。结合前一句可知，一些美国人放弃使用网络，因此使用人数实际上是下降的，故本题答案为［B］ actually。在备选副词选项中，［N］ usually 意为：通常地，常常地，不符合句意，因此排除。

干扰项：

［D］ communicating：动词 communicate 的现在分词，意为“交流；通讯；传达；表达”。

［E］ complain：动词，意为“抱怨，诉苦；投诉”。

［L］ times：名词 time 的复数形式，意为“时代；次数；时间”。

［N］ usually：表示频率的副词，意为“通常，经常”。

［O］ worried：worry 的过去式或过去分词形式，有时也作为形容词使用，意为“担忧；担心的；苦恼的”。

【参考译文】

美国的网速比以往任何时候都要快，但是人们仍然抱怨网速太慢了。

纽约总检察长办公室在秋天(46) ［J］ 发起了一项调查，以查明 Verizon 公司、有线电视公司和时代华纳公司提供的宽带速度与其(47) ［C］ 声称的是否一致。本月早些时候，总检察长办公室呼吁公众帮助测试网速，称消费者 (48) ［G］ 理应享受到服务商承诺的网速。“我们中的太多人付的钱和买到的产品完全是两码事，”总检察长说道。

如果该调查有所发现的话，这也不会是电信服务商第一次因为其承诺的宽带速度和实际提供给顾客的网速不一致而陷入(49) ［M］ 麻烦中。早在六月份，联邦通讯委员会对美国电话电报公司处以 1 亿美元的罚款，(50) ［A］ 指控该公司在顾客使用一定量的(51) ［F］ 数据后私自降低无线网速。

即便网络服务商没有犯法，也会因为宽带速度和收费激起消费者的怒气。就在本周，一项调查发现，媒体和电信巨头 Comcast 公司是最(52) ［I］ 令人憎恨的服务商。历经 10 个多月，Comcast 公司收到了近 12000 份消费者投诉，很多都与其每月数据限额和超额收费(53)［K］有关。

一些美国人对网络服务商变得越来越(54)［H］失望，他们正在放弃使用。一项最近的研究表明，在过去两年里家中有高速网络的美国人的数量(55)［B］实际上下降了，并且 15% 的人现在认为自己是“剪线族”。

SECTION Ⅲ Writing

Part A

【写作思路】

首先要注意英文书信的格式。完整的英文书信应由三个部分构成：称呼，主体内容，信末礼貌用语及署名。

称呼：如果收信人是商务伙伴或组织机构，不知对方的具体名字和性别，可以用 Dear Sir or Madam，或 Dear 加收信人头衔，如 Dear Editor；如知道收信人的姓名和性别，但不是亲密的朋友，一般使用 Dear Mr. /Mrs. /Miss/Ms. Surname，如 Dear Mr. Green；如果是熟悉的朋友或家人，则通常使用 Dear First name，如 Dear Andy。根据题目要求，本文开头称呼应为“Dear Andy,”。

主体内容：正文的开头通常用简洁的陈述性文字表明写作背景。信件主体部分要紧扣题目中列出的写作任务（通常有三个要求），不能遗漏。另外，文章布局尽量合理，篇幅上不要过于偏重某个方面，可一一回应题目中要求写出的要点。最后注意落款以及全文字数是否足够。

信末礼貌用语及署名：根据应用场合，如果是正式书信，如商务信函等，通常可用 Yours sincerely；介于正式与非正式之间，可用 Best wishes；写给熟悉的朋友或家人，可用 Lots of love 等。根据题目要求，本文署名一律用 Wang Lin.

【参考范文】

Dear Andy,

I hope this finds you and your family well. I'm writing now to let you know about my recent situation.

My grandparents came to live with us last month. It's a great fun to live with them. I really admire the relationship between my mother and my grandmother. Besides, I applied for a job at a new company. Although the competition was fierce, I was admitted as a senior manager! The pay is better and the workplace is within 10 minutes' walk from home! On weekends, I would enjoy some leisure time. I'm quite keen on swimming and watching movies.

How are you getting on these days? Expect to hear from you!

With love,

Wang Lin

(118 words)

词汇拓展

family

relationship *n.* 关系；血缘关系

family gathering 家庭聚会

connection 人脉；亲戚

teenager *n.* 青少年

adult *n.* 成年人

endure *v.* 忍耐；容忍；

work

career *n.* 生涯；职业

candidate *n.* 候选人；应试者

colleague *n.* 同事

income *n.* 收入

interview *n.* 面试

workplace *n.* 工作场所

school

assignment *n.* 作业

curriculum *n.* 课程

lecture *n.* 讲座

scholarship *n.* 奖学金

academic *adj.* 学术的，学业的

review *v.* 复习

hobby

be interested in 对……感兴趣

be keen on 对……有兴趣；喜爱……

take pleasure in 对……有兴趣；

have a wide range of interests 兴趣广泛

go fishing/hiking/shopping 去钓鱼/徒步旅行/购物

Part B

【短文分析】

该文的中心词是 Internet education（网络教育），在短文中其同义表达还包括：long-distance educational system, the educational via Internet, long-distance education, computerized long-distance teaching。

该文第一段第一句“Internet is getting into people's life and becoming more and more popular.（网络已经深入人们的生活并且越来越重要。）”先进行了社会背景介绍。紧接

着第二句 “Experts are now working on setting up a national long-distance educational system in China to provide educational opportunities via Internet. （专家们现在致力于在中国建立一个全国性的远程教育系统，通过网络提供教育机会。）” 点明文章的中心：Internet education。

短文第二、三段的首句分别是这两个段落的中心句。第二段首句 “In reality, the educational via Internet plan has been taking shape. （事实上，网络教育计划已经成型。）”，其后用一些大学网络教育目前的发展来支撑。第三段首句 “The Internet education will be developing dramatically. （网络教育将迅速发展。）”，其后用未来发展趋势进行说明。

【短文总结思路】

在写这篇短文总结时，考生应结合短文第一段的第二句，第二、三段的第一句进行概括：Internet education provides more educational chances. It has been applied in a number of universities. It will be used widely both in China and all over the world in the future.

【评论展开思路】

这是一篇关于网络教育的短文，建议考生从积极的方面评论其优点，如网络课程提供了更大量的信息、网络学习更加方便等。可以分两个主题段用不同的方法展开论证。

【参考范文】

As a popular and wide-spread assistance of traditional education, Internet education is becoming more and more important in China. And it is estimated that this new form of education will develop fast in the future. In my opinion, nowadays, Internet education has a profound impact on modern education.

Firstly, students have a wide range of options of online courses. They even could choose different courses or teachers according to their needs or preferences. This is totally different from traditional education. Moreover, it is more convenient for online learners to balance their life and study. They could watch online courses when they are not busy.

In conclusion, Internet education brings learners not only more options but also much convenience. It will be particularly important in our future life.

（156 *words*）

四、PETS–3 实战演练

全国英语等级考试第三级
2016 年 3 月笔试真题（改编版）

笔试部分答题时间：120 分钟

SECTION Ⅰ　Listening

（25 minutes）

2016. 3

Directions:

This section is designed to test your ability to understand spoken English. You will hear a selection of recorded materials and you must answer the questions that accompany them. There are two parts in this section, Part A and Part B.

Remember, while you are doing the test, you should first put down your answers in your test booklet. At the end of the listening section, you will have 3 *minutes to transfer your answers from your test booklet onto your ANSWER SHEET.*

If you have any questions, you may raise your hand now as you will not be allowed to speak once the test has started.

Now look at Part A in your test booklet.

Part A

Directions:

You will hear 10 *short dialogues. For each dialogue, there is one question and four possible answers. Choose the correct answer – A, B, C or D, and mark it in your test booklet. You will have* 15 *seconds to answer the question and you will hear each dialogue* ***only once.***

Example:

You will hear:

W: Could you please tell me if the Beijing flight will be arriving on time?

M: Yes, Madam. It should be arriving in about ten minutes.

You will read:

Who do you think the woman is talking to?

[A] A bus conductor.

[B] A clerk at the airport.

[C] A taxi driver.

[D] A clerk at the station.

From the dialogue, we know that only a clerk at the airport is most likely to know the arrival time of a flight, so you should choose answer [B] and mark it in your test booklet.

Sample Answer: [A] ■ [C] [D]

Now look at question 1.

1. What is the woman doing at the moment?

[A] Having a break. [B] Having a coffee.

[C] Writing a report. [D] Visiting the man.

2. What does the woman ask the man to do?

[A] Repair her windows. [B] Take care of her house.

[C] Take a rest for a few days. [D] Go to the seaside with her.

3. What do we learn about the woman from the dialogue?

[A] She bought a suitable skirt. [B] She wanted to purchase a skirt.

[C] She returned a skirt to the shop. [D] She complained about the service.

4. What does the man say to the woman?

[A] He envies her a lot. [B] He enjoys cooking.

[C] He usually eats out. [D] He runs a restaurant.

5. What are the speakers talking about?

[A] Gardening. [B] Air quality.

[C] Hot weather. [D] Lack of rain.

6. Why is the woman angry with her son?

[A] He ignored traffic signals. [B] He failed to repair her car.

[C] He didn't attend his class. [D] He didn't take her advice.

7. Why does the man feel sorry?

[A] He forgot his dad's birthday.

[B] He didn't buy a birthday present.

[C] He didn't put the cake in the fridge.

[D] He arrived late for his dad's birthday.

8. Where is the man's house located?

[A] Near a park. [B] By a restaurant.

[C] Close to a highway. [D] In a Chinese neighborhood.

9. What does the woman say about the data in the article?

[A] It is original. [B] It is reliable.

[C] It is questionable.
[D] It is authoritative.

10. What does the man tell the woman?

[A] The best time for job interviews.

[B] The strategies for job interviews.

[C] His comments on her recent work.

[D] His congratulations on her good luck.

Part B

Directions:

You will hear four dialogues or monologues. Before listening to each one, you will have 5 seconds to read each of the questions which accompany it. While listening, answer each question by choosing A, B, C or D. After listening, you will have 10 seconds to check your answer to each question. You will hear the recording ***only once***.

Question: 11 – 13 *are based on the following interview with John Smith, a psychologist on office behavior.*

11. What is the man's first tip on a productive workday?

[A] Arrive at the office earlier.

[B] Jump into paper work first.

[C] Start with less difficult tasks.

[D] Get ready within 15 minutes.

12. Why should personal phone calls be avoided?

[A] They may take a lot of time.
[B] They may reduce social time.

[C] They may spoil a great mood.
[D] They may cause errors in work.

13. Why should an alarm be set?

[A] To give a go-home signal.
[B] To remind people to relax.

[C] To make people work fast.
[D] To warn people of an emergency.

Questions 14 – 17 *are based on the following conversation between two friends.*

14. What news does Renee share with Tom?

[A] She met a high school classmate.
[B] She found an old friend's address.

[C] She paid a visit to her high school.
[D] She got in touch with an old friend.

15. Why did Renee and her friend lose contact?

[A] Her friend's family left for another city.

[B] Her friend transferred to another school.

[C] They had an argument and drifted apart.

[D] They were too busy to write to each other.

16. What does Tom say about his old friends?

[A] He has lost touch with all of them.

[B] He maintains contact with most of them.

[C] He has regained contact with a few of them.

[D] He keeps in touch with one or two of them.

17. How did Renee's friend set her email address?

[A] From an old address book.

[B] From one of their former teachers.

[C] From another high school classmate.

[D] From the website of Renee's company.

Questions 18 –21 *are based on a conversation between Lisa and her former neighbor John.*

18. Why did the woman decide to cancel her vacation?

[A] She had trouble with her health.

[B] She had trouble with her investment.

[C] She had to attend a financial course.

[D] She had to attend a conference in Paris.

19. What did the woman do after she graduated from college?

[A] She worked as a stock trader.

[B] She worked as a stock analyst.

[C] She worked as a finance teacher.

[D] She worked as a company manager.

20. Why did the woman want to start her own company?

[A] To make more money.

[B] To have more time for herself.

[C] To find more business opportunities.

[D] To know more about the stock market.

21. How does the woman feel about the present economic stimulating package?

[A] Relieved. [B] Optimistic.

[C] Unconfident. [D] Disappointed.

Questions 22 –25 *are based on the following interview between a reporter and Mr. Smith on his website.*

22. Which industry is the man's website concerned with?

[A] News. [B] Music. [C] Education. [D] Television.

23. Whom is the man's website mainly meant for?

[A] College students in Asia. [B] English learners of all ages.

[C] Teenagers and young adults. [D] Any visitors for entertainment.

24. What does the website want its visitors to get familiar with?

[A] Classic films. [B] Western music.

[C] English accents. [D] Public speeches.

25. What does the man hope his website will do in three years?

[A] Fulfill its short-term goal. [B] Get a big market in Asia.

[C] Become self-financed. [D] Get more investments.

Now you have 3 minutes to transfer your answers from your test booklet to your ANSWER SHEET.

That is the end of listening section.

SECTION Ⅱ Reading

(50minutes)

Part A

Directions:

Read the following two texts. Answer the questions on each text by choosing A, B, C or D. Mark your answers on your ANSWER SHEET.

Text 1

Isabel has turned down two job offers in the past year. In 2006, she started her own consulting practice, but by 2008, most of her larger clients had to drop her because of the economy. In 2011, she was undertaking irregular assignments and knew she needed a steady job. The first job she considered was Director of HR for a company in Utah. After the initial interviews, she felt the job fit her except for the location. Still, she flew west to meet the hiring manager. The hiring manager explained that Isabel was the top candidate for the job but that, before she continued with the process, she should better understand the firm's culture. She directed Isabel to several videos of the company's CEO, who regularly appeared in front of the company in costume as part of morale building exercises and expected his senior leaders to do the same. "Even though I was desperate for a job, I knew I couldn't do that," Isabel says. She called the recruiter to turn down the job and explained that she didn't feel there was a cultural fit.

A few months later, she interviewed for another job: a director of employee relations at a local university. After several interviews, the hiring manager told her the job was hers if she wanted it. The job had many positives: it was a low-stress environment, it offered great benefits, and the university was an employee-friendly place. But the job was relatively junior despite the title and Isabel worried it wouldn't be challenging enough. Finally, she turned it down. "It would be great to have a paycheck and great benefits but I would definitely have trouble sleeping at night," she says.

In both cases, she was frank with the hiring managers about why she wasn't taking the jobs. "In the past, it felt like dating. I was worried about hurting people's feelings," she says. However, they appreciated her frankness and thanked her for her honesty. She says it was hard to turn down the jobs and it was a risk for her financially but she felt she had to.

26. In 2011, Isabel ________.

[A] did consulting now and then

[B] found a job close to her home

[C] refused several job interviews

[D] ran a successful consulting firm

27. Isabel turned down the first job offer mainly because of its ________.

[A] CEO [B] culture [C] location [D] recruiter

28. Isabel was dissatisfied with the second job due to its ________.

[A] junior title [B] low benefits

[C] environment [D] lack of challenge

29. Isabel believed that her rejection of the jobs was ________.

[A] harmful [B] surprising [C] justifiable [D] troublesome

30. According to Isabel, it is important to ________.

[A] look for jobs with little stress [B] look for jobs with great benefits

[C] be truthful in declining job offers [D] be cautious in declining job offers

Text 2

You do not usually get something for nothing. Now, a new study reveals that the evolution of an improved learning ability could come at a particularly high price: an earlier death.

Past experiments have demonstrated that it is relatively easy through selective breeding to make rats, honey bees and—that great favourite of researchers—fruit flies a lot better at learning. Animals that are better learners should be competitive and, thus, over time, come to dominate a population by natural selection. But improved learning ability does not get selected amongst these animals in the wild. No one really understands why.

Tadeusz Kawecki and his colleagues at the University of Fribourg in Switzerland have measured the effects of improved leaning on the lives of fruit flies. The flies were given two different fruits as egg-laying sites. One of these was laced with a bitter additive that could be detected only on contact. The flies were then given the same fruit but without an additive. Flies that avoided the fruit which had been bitter were deemed to have learned from their experience. Their children were reared and the experiment was run again.

After repeating the experiment for 30 generations, the children of the learned flies were compared with normal flies. The researchers report in a forthcoming edition of *Evolution* that although learning ability could be bred into a population of fruit flies, it shortened their lives by

15%. When the researchers compared their learned flies colonies selectively bred to live long lives, they found even greater differences. Whereas learned flies had reduced their life spans, the long-lived flies learned less well than even average flies.

The authors suggest that evolving an improved learning ability may require a greater investment in the nervous system which takes resources away from processes that delay ageing. However, Dr. Kawecki thinks the effect could also be a by-product of greater brain activity increasing the production of Reactive Oxygen Species (ROS), which can increase oxidation in the body and damage health.

No one knows whether the phenomenon holds true for other animals. So, biologists, at least, still have a lot to learn.

31. Past experiments prove selective breeding can make animals better ________.

[A] commanders [B] competitors

[C] survivors [D] learners

32. In this experiment, scientists observed that ________.

[A] some flies avoided the fruit without an addictive

[B] some flies preferred the fruit with an addictive

[C] the eggs of the flies were not damaged

[D] the impact on the flies did not last long

33. The forthcoming report says that ________.

[A] long-lived flies are better at laying eggs

[B] long-lived flies are poorer in learning

[C] learned flies have a relatively long life

[D] learned flies live as long as average ones

34. According to Dr. Kawecki, greater brain activity ________.

[A] reduces oxygen consumption [B] regulates the nervous system

[C] speeds up the ageing process [D] stabilizes the ageing process

35. We learn from the text that ________.

[A] the research findings need to be tested further

[B] biologists are doing similar research on other animals

[C] the animal world usually follows the same universal laws

[D] biologists are applying their findings to other areas

Part B

Directions:

Read the texts from a magazine article in which five people talked about tipping in a restaurant. For questions 36 – 40, *match the name of each person to one of the statements* (*A* – *G*) *given below. Mark your answers on your ANSWER SHEET.*

Richard:

I've always viewed tipping as a way of saying "thank you" to the one who serves me. I believe what is bad is when no tip is left at all. The better the service is, the higher the tip is. Unless the service is literally perfect, I never tip more than 10% of the bill. Much like the harder teachers in school. I never give an easy "A." My assessment is honest.

Daniel:

A tip is a "thank you," but in truth, a tip is payment for service, 20% is a standard tip. Servers deserve it for their hard work. Restaurants will never pay more for labor unless they are forced to do so by new laws. Tips make up about 97% of a server's total income. Those tips are needed for survival. So, before servers are paid a living wage, tip 20%.

Kate:

Why should I pay the difference between what the restaurant is willing to pay the employee and what an acceptable wage is? I do pay 20%, but I hate it. A friend of mine left Europe for New York City, found a job in a restaurant there and ended up making $ 5, 500 a month. Enough above minimum wage? How about miners, construction workers, resident doctors, etc.? Do they get tipped?

Patricia:

18 – 20% for good service is today's standard. The restaurant and its employees are too polite to tell you this or to put it on their menus, but that is their expectation and you need to understand that. I believe it is good manners to respect this. To do otherwise is to be openly rude. If you disagree, you are wise to eat elsewhere, as you are hurting a hardworking professional.

Michael:

Tipping has gotten out of control. I always had thought it was 15%, and now suddenly servers have made it 20%. I tip 15%, and that's it. If the service is really superior, then I work higher from there. Interesting to be told, "If you can't afford to tip 20%, then you should eat at home." If all those people stayed away, the restaurant would not even be in business.

Now match the name of each person (36 – 40) to the appropriate statement.

Note: there are two extra statements.

Statements

36. Richard [A] It's rude not to tip.
37. Daniel [B] I do tip, though I don't like it.
38. Kate [C] Tipping shouldn't be compulsory.
39. Patricia [D] Tips are essential to servers' survival.
40. Michael [E] If you don't tip, you are punishing the server.

[F] I think the current tipping standard is too high.

[G] My tip faithfully reflects how good the service is.

Part C

Directions:

Read the following text from which five sentences have been removed. Choose from the sentences A – G the most suitable one to fill each numbered gap in the text (41 – 45). There are TWO extra sentences that you do not need to use. Mark your answers on your ANSWER SHEET.

In 2009, the number of hungry people in the world reached one billion for the first time. It's difficult not to be shocked by the fact that more than one in seven people in the world do not have enough to eat. __41__ Hunger kills more people per year than diseases such as AIDS, malaria and TB combined.

The UN estimates that almost two thirds of the world's hungry people are in Asia, which is of course the world's most populous continent. __42__ Although this region has a much lower population than Asia, it has the highest percentage of hungry people. Almost all of the rest are in Latin America, North Africa and the Caribbean. In the richest regions of the world there are only a tiny number of people who don't have enough to eat.

There are many reasons for world hunger. They include wars, droughts, floods, and the overuse of farming land. __43__ Many people also blame greedy businessmen for pushing up the prices of basic foods in the global market. But the most important reason, quite simply, is poverty, which has increased recently due to the financial crisis of 2008.

Although many people make the obvious point that there would be less hunger if the global population were smaller, few people would argue that there is not enough food to go around. __44__ In the last 50 years, global food production has risen even more quickly than the global population. There are many areas of the world in which people generally have more than enough food. __45__ The answer to world hunger, therefore, may be a balanced food distribution around the whole world. Everyone will have enough to eat, but not overeat.

[A] The basic problem seems to be not a lack of food, but its distribution.

[B] More than a quarter are in sub-Saharan Africa.

[C] All these factors affect food production.

[D] It takes the effort of every country to fight against world hunger.

[E] In those places, obesity is a far bigger problem than hunger.

[F] Those places need far more food than they actually get.

[G] By the end of this year, more than 35 million people will have died as a result of not having enough to eat.

Part D

Directions:

Read the following text from which 10 *words have been removed. Choose from the words A – O the most suitable one to fill each numbered gap in the text* (46 – 55). *There are FIVE extra words that you do not need to use. Mark your answers on your ANSWER SHEET.*

I can't believe the kind of rubbish that some people call art. Yesterday, my girlfriend dragged me to a modern art __46__ to see an exhibition she had read about in the paper. It was five or six so-called installations made of bits of plastic, wood and paper that __47__ just to have been thrown on the floor. It was a mess, basically—just like the floor in my sister's house when my two-year-old nephew's left all his toys out, but less __48__ . Come to think of it, __49__ you had given those bits of plastic, wood and paper to my nephew, he could probably have __50__ something just as good. I guess, sometimes, the cleaners end up throwing art like that in the bins at the end of the day, __51__ they must find it hard to work out what's an exhibit and what's just __52__ . I think that if a painting or an installation looks like something I could have done myself in fifteen minutes, it doesn't __53__ to be called art. But when I say that, people like my girlfriend say I'm "uncultured." I think a lot of people who say they __54__ the kind of stuff we saw yesterday are just pretending—deep down they know it's rubbish but they don't want to be the first one to admit it, unlike me, they're __55__ of being looked down on.

[A] afraid	[B] appreciate	[C] because
[D] colorful	[E] created	[F] deserve
[G] dislike	[H] gallery	[I] if
[J] litter	[K] object	[L] proved
[M] seemed	[N] serious	[O] when

SECTION Ⅲ Writing

(45 minutes)

Directions:

You should write your responses to both Part A and Part B of this section on your ANSWER SHEET.

Part A

56.

You have just had a terrible trip to a foreign country. Post a message to an English online forum:

(1) telling other travelers some of your bad experiences;

(2) giving them some suggestions about taking a trip.

You should write about 100 words. Do not sign your own name at the end of your message. Use "Wang Lin" instead.

Part B

57.

Directions:

Read the text below. Write an essay in about 120 words, in which you should summarize the key points of the text and make comments on them. Try to use your own words.

Dear Sally,

It was amazing to see your dance performance last weekend. I felt so proud of you when your teacher and schoolmates congratulated you upon your completion of the performance.

While you continue to enjoy the moment, I'd like to share with you a small quote from Abraham Lincoln, "This, too, shall pass away." I want these words to be your guide at every turning point in your life.

When you're feeling very proud of yourself at an achievement, knowing no bounds at that moment, remember that "This, too, shall pass away."

When you're at a difficult moment in your life and don't know what to do, find comfort in the same words— "This, too, shall pass away."

I'm not saying that the ache of some losses and setbacks will completely go away from your life. In fact, often the memories of painful events will hit you unexpectedly like tons of bricks and take your breath away years after they happen.

But, like all humans, you have an almost infinite capacity to adapt to life's changes and a great ability to bounce back from trying times. This understanding should give you a spark of hope when you're in a season of despair; it should also build up your confidence for taking risks in the future.

Sally, our lives are made up of several peaks and several valleys. That's the nature of life. Live each moment as it comes. And always remember "This, too, shall pass away."

Love,

Papa

THAT IS THE END OF THE TEST.

全国英语等级考试第三级
2016年3月笔试真题（改编版）答案

SECTION Ⅰ Listening

Part A

1. C	2. B	3. B	4. C	5. D
6. D	7. D	8. A	9. C	10. A

Part B

11. D	12. A	13. B	14. D	15. A
16. D	17. D	18. B	19. B	20. B
21. C	22. C	23. C	24. C	25. B

SECTION Ⅱ Reading

Part A

Text 1

26. A	27. B	28. D	29. A	30. C

Text 2

31. D	32. A	33. B	34. C	35. A

Part B

36. G	37. D	38. B	39. A	40. F

Part C

41. G	42. B	43. C	44. A	45. E

Part D

46. H	47. M	48. D	49. I	50. E
51. C	52. J	53. F	54. B	55. A

SECTION Ⅲ Writing

Part A

【参考范文】

56.

Recently, I had a trip that I would rather forget. Let me tell you the details. It was the first time I'd been to France. We'd crossed the English Channel at night, the coach taking us to the hotel broke down and we had to wait for over 2 hours before our replacement arrived. It was really cold and dark outside. Then when we got to the hotel, we found our room hadn't been cleaned. We wanted to complain to the hotel staff, but none of them speaks English!

If you plan to visit a foreign country, please make sure the travelling conditions are good, for example, a comfortable mode of transportation, knowledge of the country's language and always make a backup plan beforehand.

Wang Lin

(126 *words*)

Part B

【参考范文】

57.

Sally's father wrote her a letter to congratulate her on her recent success in the dance performance. In the letter, her father also gave some suggestions on life by quoting from Abraham Lincoln: "This, too, shall pass away."

This sentence expressed a life philosophy, which is true and appropriate in all times and situations. Sally's father wanted to remind her that any success or setback would only last a short period of life. He hoped his daughter should neither be carried away by success nor lose hope in difficulties.

It is widely agreed that life is full of ups and downs. You will never fully appreciate the ups unless you have some downs. Provided that we are optimistic and take a positive attitude, we will be more likely to enjoy our life to the fullest.

(139 *words*)

全国英语等级考试第三级
2015 年 9 月笔试真题（改编版）

笔试部分答题时间：120 分钟

SECTION I　Listening

（25 minutes）

2015. 9

Directions:

This section is designed to test your ability to understand spoken English. You will hear a selection of recorded materials and you must answer the questions that accompany them. There are two parts in this section, Part A and Part B.

Remember, while you are doing the test, you should first put down your answers in your test booklet. At the end of the listening section, you will have 3 minutes to transfer all your answers from your test booklet to your ANSWER SHEET.

If you have any questions, you may raise your hand now as you will not be allowed to speak once the test has started.

Now look at Part A in your test booklet.

Part A

Directions:

You will hear 10 short dialogues. For each dialogue, there is one question and four possible answers. Choose the correct answer – A, B, C or D, and mark it in your test booklet. You will have 15 seconds to answer the question and you will hear each dialogue ***only once***.

Example:

You will hear:

W: Could you please tell me if the Beijing flight will be arriving on time?

M: Yes, Madam. It should be arriving in about ten minutes.

You will read:

Who do you think the woman is talking to?

[A] A bus conductor.　　　　[B] A clerk at the airport.

[C] A taxi driver. [D] A clerk at the station.

From the dialogue, we know that only a clerk at the airport is most likely to know the arrival time of a flight, so you should choose answer [B] and mark it in your test booklet.

Sample Answer: [A] ■ [C] [D]

Now look at question 1.

1. Where does the conversation most probably take place?

[A] In a post office. [B] In a hotel.

[C] In a bank. [D] In a supermarket.

2. When will the bank open on Sundays?

[A] From 8: 30 a. m. to 8: 30p. m. [B] From 9: 30a. m. to 6: 30p. m.

[C] From 8: 30 a. m. to 6: 30p. m. [D] From 9: 30a. m. to 3: 30p. m.

3. What did the man ask the woman to do?

[A] Go on a diet. [B] Have a snack.

[C] Play some tennis. [D] Stop screaming.

4. Where are the two speakers?

[A] In a hotel. [B] At a dinner table.

[C] In the street. [D] At the man's house.

5. What can we assume from this conversation?

[A] The man is a judge.

[B] It's an interviewer.

[C] The man agrees with the woman.

[D] The man believes that Jack will quit his job.

6. Why can't they meet on Thursday?

[A] Because she wants to meet him on Wednesday.

[B] Because she has to go out of town.

[C] Because she is in charge of the project.

[D] Because she has another meeting.

7. What does the woman mean?

[A] The man should not expect her to go along.

[B] She doesn't think she has enough money.

[C] She will go even though the movie is bad.

[D] The man should count the number of people going.

8. What does the woman mean?

[A] She is asking for a higher pay.

[B] She is introducing a new friend.

[C] She is too busy.

[D] She's got some problems.

9. Who is the man?

[A] A judge. [B] An interviewer.

[C] A professor. [D] A counselor.

10. What are they talking about?

[A] City is better than countryside. [B] Changes in the city.

[C] Going camping. [D] Life in the summer.

Part B

Directions:

You will hear four dialogues or monologues. Before listening to each one, you will have 5 seconds to read each of the questions which accompany it. While listening, answer each question by choosing A, B, C or D. After listening, you will have 10 seconds to check your answer to each question. You will hear the recording ***only once****.*

Questions 11 – 13 are based on the following dialogue between an employer and an employee.

11. How old is Katie?

[A] 16. [B] 17. [C] 18. [D] 19.

12. What kind of job is Katie looking for?

[A] A part-time job for a school magazine.

[B] A full-time job at a college.

[C] A permanent job at Johnson's Imports.

[D] A short-term job in an office.

13. What qualifications does Katie have for the job?

[A] Her extra classes in sport at school.

[B] She has computer skills and used to working with people.

[C] She's adaptable.

[D] Her work experience in the school newspaper.

Questions 14 – 17 are based on the following dialogue between a lawyer and his customer.

14. How long have they not met each other?

[A] Half a year. [B] Two years.

[C] Three or four years. [D] More than five years.

15. What's the purpose of Mr. Tim's visiting this time?

[A] He wants to make some changes in his will.

[B] He wants the woman's help in buying a land and building a house.

[C] He wants the woman to see the architect for him.

[D] He asks the woman to find a plot for him.

16. When did Mr. Tim go to see the plot chosen by his son?

[A] Last Friday. [B] Last Saturday.

[C] Two days ago. [D] Yesterday.

17. Which material should the house be built of?

[A] Stone. [B] Brick. [C] Cement. [D] Wood.

Questions 18 – 21 *are based on the following dialogue in a travel agency.*

18. Which city is the man going to visit?

[A] Oxford. [B] Paris. [C] Shaftsbury. [D] London.

19. Which tourist attraction is NOT mentioned in the dialogue?

[A] Buckingham Palace. [B] Shops and restaurants.

[C] Tower of London. [D] The British Museum.

20. What is NOT listed on the man's schedule?

[A] Shopping. [B] Watching a show.

[C] Meeting friends. [D] Visiting art galleries.

21. What can you infer from the dialogue?

[A] The visitor will see very little of the city.

[B] The visitor's schedule is tight.

[C] The visitor will enjoy his time.

[D] The visitor will leave for another city the next time.

Questions 22 – 25 *are based on the following monologue on smoking.*

22. Why are so many people dependent on cigarette?

[A] Because they like the taste of tar.

[B] Because smoking makes them feel relaxed.

[C] Because smoking is funny.

[D] Because smoking cures disease.

23. Which substance in cigarette causes cancer?

[A] Cigarette ashes. [B] Nicotine.

[C] Tar. [D] Not mentioned here.

24. What do experts suggest people to do?

[A] To buy cigarettes with less tar. [B] To smoke only a few cigarettes a day.

[C] To smoke only during a break. [D] To give up smoking.

25. Why do smokers like low tar cigarettes?

[A] Because they are less harmful. [B] Because they cost less.

[C] Because they taste better. [D] Because they last longer.

Now you have 3 *minutes to transfer your answers from your test booklet to your ANSWER SHEET.*

That is the end of Listening Comprehension.

SECTION Ⅱ　Reading

(50 minutes)

Part A

Directions:

Read the following two texts. Answer the questions on each text by choosing A, B, C or D. Mark your answers on your ANSWER SHEET.

Text 1

Five-year-old Elia arrived at school with a big box of colored pencils. Her friend, Anna, offered to exchange her set of markers for the brand-new pencils. Elia agreed, but soon discovered that the markers were dried up. "That's not fair!" cried Elia to her teacher. "I want my new pencils back." After some tears and negotiation, the teacher helped the girls set things right by returning the items to their original owners.

Later that day, at story time, the teacher shared the picture book classic *A Bargain for Frances*. Though the conflict in the story is just over a broken tea set, the message about fair play was not lost on the children. The book was helpful in exploring a small, yet significant, life lesson.

Stories are vital to the way we process and experience life events and the feelings that surround us. The ability to create, share, and respond to stories is one of the vital characteristics of being human. In fact, the human brain is programmed to see patterns and become fascinated in the plot development of stories, finally storing them in long-term memory. As a result, the brain is a remarkably effective processor of stories, both real and fictional.

High-quality picture books are a good blend of art and literature that attracts kids' imagination and communicates an idea in an effective way. These books are perfect teaching tools, as they deal with the powerful emotions that kids feel, model effective coping strategies, and present complex concepts in appropriate ways. In addition, according to brain research, the picture book complements words with what leaves the most permanent impression: images. The pictures in books are distinctive from the fleeting images kids see on television in that they remain on the page, ready to be revisited, touched, and commented upon.

Whether we share stories about families, historical events, or emotions, stories are a way to sum up life's memorable moments and lasting lessons. We can control the power of literature and use it to develop positive character in young kids by reading often, choosing suitable books, and enjoying stories together.

26. Elia cried "That's not fair!" as she thought that she was ________.

[A] cheated by her friend
[B] defeated by her friend
[C] ignored by her teacher
[D] scolded by her teacher

27. *A Bargain for Frances* is intended to teach kids how to ________.

[A] play fair in life
[B] organize things
[C] win in conflicts
[D] write a message

28. According to the text, stories can help kids ________.

[A] realize their potential
[B] improve their memory
[C] concentrate on reading
[D] understand the human world

29. In comparison with pictures in books, television images ________.

[A] are frequently commented on
[B] stay temporarily with children
[C] blend art and literature vividly
[D] communicate ideas effectively

30. The power of literature can help kids develop their ________.

[A] positive character
[B] interest in history
[C] passion for stories
[D] learning strategies

Text 2

We have heard a lot about the health benefits of tea, especially green tea. It is high in polyphenols, compounds with strong antioxidant activity that in test-tube and animal models show anti-cancer and heart-protective effects. Good clinical studies are few, however, and although physicians tell their patients to drink green tea, there hasn't been any definite proof of the value of that advice.

A team of Japanese researchers was able to link green tea consumption with decreased mortality from many causes-including heart disease. The researchers tracked 40, 530 healthy adults ages 40 to 79 in a region of northeastern Japan where most people drink green tea, following them for up to 11 years. Those who drank five or more cups of green tea a day had significantly lower mortality rates than those who drank less than one cup a day. There were also fewer deaths from cardiovascular disease.

But no such association was seen with deaths from cancer. Nor was consumption of Oolong or black tea connected with any decrease in mortality. Those teas are easier to be combined with oxygen in processing, which not only darkens the color of the leaves and changes their flavor but also reduces their polyphenol content.

Coffee is more complicated. It has received both gold stars and black marks in medical literature. It, too, contains antioxidants, although they are less well studied than tea polyphenols. Evidence for the health benefits of coffee is growing, however. A group of investigators from Finland, Italy and the Netherlands reports that coffee seems to protect against age-related decline in mental capacity. The scientists studied 676 healthy men born from 1900 to 1920 and followed them for 10 years, using standardized measures of brain function. Their conclusion: the men who consumed coffee had significantly less decline in mental capacity than those who didn't. Three cups a day seemed to provide the most protection.

Population studies like those help us form assumptions about relationships between dietary habits and long-term health. We still have to test our suppositions in controlled conditions, and measure the effects of coffee and tea on various systems of the body.

31. Physicians often tell their patients to drink green tea because ________.

[A] its medical value has been proved

[B] it is believed to be good for one's health

[C] it has long since been used clinically

[D] its effectiveness has been shown in animals

32. The Japanese study seems to have confirmed the positive effect of green tea on ________.

[A] young adults　　[B] Asian people

[C] patients with cancer　　[D] patients with heart disease

33. The text indicates that black tea differs from green tea in that ________.

[A] it can retain the color of its leaves

[B] it can reduce cancer-related deaths

[C] it contains less polyphenol content

[D] it is stronger in flavor than the latter

34. Coffee is beneficial to one's health because ________.

[A] it has more antioxidants than green

[B] it slows down the rate of brain aging

[C] it lowers the rate of natural mortality

[D] it keeps systems of the body active

35. The text indicates that the relationships between dietary habits and long-term health ________.

[A] are a falsely perceived supposition

[B] are a conflicting issue among people

[C] deserve further scientific research

[D] deserve to be tested on a larger population

Part B

Directions:

Read the texts from a magazine section called "Letters" in which five people wrote about online shopping. For questions 36 – 40, match the name of each person to one of the statements (A – G) given below. Mark your answers on ANSWER SHEET.

Jennifer:

In your article about online shopping being the newest and easiest way to shop, you said that computers will replace shopping malls sooner or later because they make buying things faster and cheaper. But don't you think that the entire point of shopping is to spend leisure time with friends while doing something necessary. Shopping is not just a quick task. It is, in fact, an entire way of life.

Paul:

I am a great collector of all manner of hard-to-find items such as out-of-print books and antiques. Purchasing in physical stores would mean round-the-world travel and years of effort. I can get the same result in a few hours on eBay, and often at bargain prices. I am quite well-off, but very few consumer items available in regular shops. I have many friends and acquaintances with the same approach.

Mike:

My wife buys online often. I have not heard complaints or dissatisfaction. She can compare with different online vendors' prices after she has decided what she wants. It's delivered to the door, a big time savings and gas savings. If I need something, I check online first and see what it costs and then decide where to buy, local stores or online. Online has the advantage most of the time.

Henry:

Virtually all online stores make you register. But, I don't need another username and password to remember. I will only buy online if I cannot find something locally. Even though shipping is fast, I'd rather drive across town and pay more to be able to bring home a new gadget the same day. And, most of the time, there is no difference in price between local stores and online stores.

Jeff:

I you think the prices are the same online as they are locally, you're dealing with the wrong online retailers. I'm an online shopping veteran and I always save quite a bit on my large-dollar purchases. With a little research experience, I've easily saved thousands of dollars over the last several years. Besides, shipping on most items is reasonable and you don't even pay taxes 99.9% of the time.

Now match the name of each person (36 – 40) to the appropriate statement.

Note: there are two extra statements.

Statements

36. Jennifer	[A] I'll buy online only when I have to.
37. Paul	[B] You can enjoy steep discounts with most online sellers.
38. Mike	[C] I shift between buying on or off line depending on what suits me.
39. Henry	[D] Shopping is not only a necessary task but a sociable pleasure.
40. Jeff	[E] Online selling helps to satisfy my special needs in buying.
	[F] Buying online is far from being as good as it is boasted to be.
	[G] Buying online can save you a lot only if you find the right online sellers.

Part C

Directions:

Read the following text from which five sentences have been removed. Choose from the sentences A – G the most suitable one to fill each numbered gap in the text (41 – 45). *There are TWO extra sentences that you do not need to use. Mark your answer in your ANSWER SHEET.*

"Any apples today?" Effie asked cheerfully at my window. I followed her to her truck and bought a kilo. On credit, of course. __41__ "Pay me whenever you like," said Effie, climbing back to her truck.

All pretense of payment was dropped when our funds, food and fuel decreased to alarming lows. Effie came often, always bringing some gift: a jar of peaches or some firewood. There were other generosities. Our baby was not doing well, so Effie financed my wife's trip to New York for consultation with a specialist.

__42__ Her income, derived from investments she had made while running an interior decorating shop, had never exceeded \$ 200 a month, which she supplemented by selling her apples. But she always managed to help someone poorer.

Years passed before I was able to return the money Effie had given me from time to time. She was ill now and had aged rapidly in the last year. "Here, darling," I said, "is what I owe you." "Don't give it to me all at once," she said. "__43__" I think she believed there was magic in the slow discharge of a love debt.

The simple fact is that I never repaid the whole amount to Effie, for she died a few weeks later. __44__ But a curious thing began to happen.

Whenever I saw a fellow human in financial trouble, I was moved to help him. I can't afford to do this always, but in the ten years since Effie's death, I have indirectly repaid my debt to her.

The oddest part of the whole affair is that people whom I help often help others later on. __45__ So the account can never be marked closed, for Effie's love will go on in hearts that have never known her.

[A] At that time, it seemed that my debt would forever go unsettled.

[B] Give your help to those in greater need.

[C] Effie was not a rich woman.

[D] Effie worked diligently all her life.

[E] Cash was the one thing in the world I lacked just then.

[F] By now, the few dollars Effie gave me have been multiplied many times.

[G] Give it back as I gave it to you—a little at a time.

Part D

Directions:

Read the following text from which 10 words have been removed. Choose from the words A – O the most suitable one to fill each numbered gap in the text (46 – 55). There are FIVE extra words that you do not need to use. Mark your answers on your ANSWER SHEET.

It can be a special experience to go on a family trip during the holiday season, but one reason that many parents __46__ to stay home is the cost of travel. Here are some ways of reducing your travel __47__ .

Flying is a fast way to arrive at your destination, but the cost of airline tickets can really add up if you are buying flights for the whole family. Often, it is cheaper to pay for gas __48__ the whole family can fit in the car, __49__ with the current decreases in gas prices.

If your destination is too far to drive to, you should look at a variety of __50__ for your flight times. For example, it is often cheaper to fly on Christmas day instead of flying a few days before Christmas. Also, __51__ early morning flights is cheaper than traveling during peak times during the day.

Eating out __52__ you are on the road can quickly increase the trip cost, and it's much cheaper to stop at the grocery store, planning your own food __53__ . If you plan to eat out, it's usually cheaper to eat at a restaurant during breakfast or lunch, __54__ you to skip the higher dinner prices.

Also, it might be cheaper to visit an all-inclusive resort. These resorts include all the meal and a variety of activities, and many of them have children's activities so that the kids can __55__ entertained during the trip.

[A] allowing	[B] if	[C] begin
[D] choose	[E] driving	[F] especially
[G] expense	[H] instead	[I] before
[J] options	[K] stay	[L] taking
[M] too	[N] troubles	[O] while

SECTION Ⅲ Writing

(45 minutes)

Directions:

You should write your responses to both Part A and Part B of this section on your ANSWER SHEET.

Part A

56.

Your friend Paul wants to know in detail about the part-time job you took at a restaurant during the summer vacation. Write an email to Paul, telling him about:

(1) what you did on the job;

(2) how you felt about the working environment and co-workers;

(3) what you learned from the job.

You should write about 100 words. Do not sign your own name at the end of your email. Use "Wang Lin" instead.

Part B

57.

Directions:

Read the text below. Write an essay in about 120 *words, in which you should summarize the key points of the text and make comments on them. Try to use your own words.*

Lori Schneider knows a few things about fear. "We were crossing a ridge that dropped off 8,000 feet on both sides," says the 53-year-old climber of ascending Mount Everest last spring. "The wind was blowing at 60 miles an hour. If there was ever a moment to panic, this was it."

But she didn't. An hour later, she reached the peak—the last step in her personal challenge to scale the highest mountains on all seven continents.

Ten years earlier, she'd come face-to-face with a different type of fear, when she was unable to feel anything in the right side of her body. After learning she had multiple sclerosis (MS)—a serious illness that gradually makes a person weak and unable to move or see, she left her marriage, job, and home: "I ran from my whole life."

It was just before climbing South America's Mount Aconcagua in 2000 that she set her sights on the Seven Summits. After training by pulling 50-pound bags of dog food up the ski slopes near her home, she topped Europe's Mount Elbrus in 2002, North America's McKinley in 2006, and Australia's Kosciuszko and Antarctica's Vinson Massif in 2008. She'd scaled

Africa's Kilimanjaro in 1993. That left Asia's Everest, the highest of all.

And there she stood, on a ridge at 28, 800 feet. "When I trained, I told myself to take one step at a time by spelling out words," she says. "So I spelled out 'Don't let fear in.'". It got her to the top.

She's the first person with MS to conquer the Seven Summits. With her condition stable, she plans a return to Kilimanjaro—this time with 15 others with MS by her side.

THAT IS THE END OF THE TEST

全国英语等级考试第三级
2015 年 9 月笔试真题（改编版）答案

SECTION Ⅰ Listening

Part A

1. C	2. D	3. B	4. A	5. D
6. D	7. A	8. A	9. B	10. C

Part B

11. C	12. D	13. B	14. C	15. B
16. C	17. A	18. D	19. C	20. C
21. B	22. B	23. C	24. D	25. A

SECTION Ⅱ Reading

Part A

Text 1

26. A	27. A	28. D	29. B	30. A

Text 2

31. B	32. D	33. C	34. B	35. C

Part B

36. D	37. E	38. C	39. A	40. G

Part C

41. E	42. C	43. G	44. F	45. A

Part D

46. D	47. G	48. B	49. F	50. J
51. L	52. O	53. H	54. A	55. K

SECTION Ⅲ　Writing

Part A

【参考范文】

56.

Dear Paul,

I am very happy to share my experience of doing part-time job with you. In this summer holiday, I worked as a waiter in a restaurant. My job includes cleaning the table, placing orders and so on.

It is a fast food restaurant but the environment is very comfortable. And I get along well with my co-workers. We even get in touch with each other now.

I have learned a lot from this job. The most important one that I'd like to share with you is to be patient and polite to customers. I think this is the key to be a waiter.

I'm looking forward to seeing you soon.

Yours Sincerely,

Wang Lin

(122 *words*)

Part B

【参考范文】

57.

Lori Schneider is a 53-year-old woman. Being a patient suffering from multiple sclerosis, she has scaled the highest mountains on the Seven Summits. It is difficult for healthy people, let alone a person with such serious disease. How great she is! What should we do to overcome difficulty?

First of all, we should learn to calm down while we are in trouble. Fear does not help in this situation. Only calm could make us deal with problems successfully. If we are panic, we will only make things worse.

Then, it is time to think what should be done to solve the problem. We may analyze what leads to it. Could we handle it ourselves? If we couldn't, is there anyone could help?

In a word, when facing obstacles, we should not be afraid of it. Try to make a plan calmly by ourselves or with the help of our families or friends.

(153 *words*)

全国英语等级考试第三级
2015 年 3 月笔试真题（改编版）

笔试部分答题时间：120 分钟

SECTION I　Listening

（25 minutes）

2015. 3

Directions:

This section is designed to test your ability to understand spoken English. You will hear a selection of recorded materials and you must answer the questions that accompany them. There are two parts in this section, Part A and Part B.

Remember, while you are doing the test, you should first put down your answers in your test booklet. At the end of the listening section, you will have 3 minutes to transfer all your answers from your test booklet to your ANSWER SHEET.

If you have any questions, you may raise your hand now as you will not be allowed to speak once the test has started.

Now look at Part A in your test booklet.

Part A

Directions:

You will hear 10 short dialogues. For each dialogue, there is one question and four possible answers. Choose the correct answer – A, B, C or D, and mark it in your test booklet. You will have 15 seconds to answer the question and you will hear each dialogue ***only once.***

Example:

You will hear:

W: Could you please tell me if the Beijing flight will be arriving on time?

M: Yes, Madam. It should be arriving in about ten minutes.

You will read:

Who do you think the woman is talking to?

[A] A bus conductor.　　　　[B] A clerk at the airport.

[C] A taxi driver. [D] A clerk at the station.

From the dialogue, we know that only a clerk at the airport is most likely to know the arrival time of a flight, so you should choose answer [B] and mark it in your test booklet.

Sample Answer: [A] ■ [C] [D]

Now look at question 1.

1. What does the woman mean?

[A] She prefers the artists she has studied.

[B] She hopes they will take some of the paintings away.

[C] She hasn't gone to see the exhibits yet.

[D] She doesn't want to describe the exhibit.

2. What is the woman's reply?

[A] She knows Professor Arnold has come.

[B] She thinks Professor Arnold has checked in.

[C] She is sure that Professor Arnold has arrived.

[D] She doesn't know whether Professor Arnold has arrived.

3. Who answered the phone?

[A] James Clock. [B] Mary. [C] Sue. [D] Not mentioned.

4. How does the man feel about his grade?

[A] It was an improvement. [B] It was disappointing.

[C] It was unfair. [D] It was satisfying.

5. What does the woman mean?

[A] They're ready for the snow. [B] Once it starts, it'll snow a lot.

[C] It has been snowing for some time. [D] The winter has just begun.

6. What subject does the man teach now?

[A] English. [B] Chemistry. [C] History. [D] Chinese.

7. Which subject does the woman like most?

[A] Science. [B] Maths.

[C] History. [D] Computer programming.

8. What does the man mean?

[A] The library no longer had the book on reserve.

[B] The library closed earlier than he'd expected.

[C] The professor had chosen a mystery book for him instead.

[D] The homework assignment isn't clear.

9. What does the man mean?

[A] He must hand in a full report on the exhibition.

[B] He is too busy to go along.

[C] He has to wash his hands first.

[D] He has already seen the show.

10. Where does this conversation most probably take place?

[A] In a library. [B] In a hospital. [C] At a bank. [D] In a store.

Part B

Directions:

You will hear four dialogues or monologues. Before listening to each one, you will have 5 seconds to read each of the questions which accompany it. While listening, answer each question by choosing A, B, C or D. After listening, you will have 10 seconds to check your answer to each question. You will hear the recording ***only once***.

Questions 11 – 13 are based on a dialogue between a clerk of Air-ticket Booking office and a customer.

11. How long has the woman been with the company?

[A] Only two years. [B] Only one year.

[C] More than two years. [D] One year and a half.

12. Why hasn't the woman got the new job, according to the man?

[A] Because she is a woman.

[B] Because of her clothes.

[C] Because she is not capable enough.

[D] Because she dislikes the job.

13. What can we learn from the dialogue?

[A] Carl Drexler is a good manager.

[B] The man thought the woman was too proud.

[C] The woman is not confident enough.

[D] The woman thinks that capability is the most important thing.

Questions 14 – 17 are based on the following dialogue.

14. Where is the Bank of English created?

[A] At the University of Buckingham.

[B] At the Oxford University.

[C] At the Cambridge University.

[D] At the University of Birmingham.

15. How many words are there in the Bank of English?

[A] 120 million. [B] 112 million. [C] 7,000. [D] 20 million.

16. Which of the following is NOT mentioned in the use of the Bank of English?

[A] The way ordinary people use English.

[B] The way language is developing.

[C] The way people communicate.

[D] The way psychologists treat the mentally diseased people.

17. What does Professor John Sinclair say about one of the findings coming out of the studies?

[A] "Ex" and "former" are often associated with "lover".

[B] "Her lover" is more often used than "his lover".

[C] English language is used wittily and lively.

[D] Ordinary people use English language more frequently.

Questions 18 –21 *are based on the following dialogue.*

18. What is probably the man's position?

[A] Dean of Students.

[B] Lecturer in Speech Communication.

[C] Professor of Business Administration.

[D] Chairman of the Journalism Department.

19. What does she have to take before she begins, practical training?

[A] English sociology. [B] Journalism 121.

[C] Freshman French. [D] Journalism 112.

20. How many courses did she take last semester?

[A] 3. [B] 4. [C] 5. [D] 6.

21. What year is the woman going to be in?

[A] The junior year. [B] The freshman year.

[C] The senior year. [D] The sophomore year.

Questions 22 –25 *are based on the following TV interview program.*

22. Why did the woman eat the berries even though she was not sure whether they were poisonous?

[A] Because she was so hungry.

[B] Because the berries were delicious.

[C] Because she had lost the faith to live.

[D] Because the berries were beautiful.

23. Why is finding a river important for people lost in the forest?

[A] Because it can supply water to people.

[B] Because it can lead people out of the forest.

[C] Because people can take a bath in it.

[D] Both A and B.

24. Was the woman far away from a river? Did she find it?

[A] Yes, she was miles away from a river but she found it at last.

[B] No, she was near a river and she found it without efforts.

[C] Yes, she was far away from a river and she didn't find it.

[D] No, she was near a river but she didn't notice it.

25. What saved her life at last?

[A] A local hunter. [B] A dog. [C] A bear. [D] A monkey.

Now you have 3 minutes to transfer your answers from your test booklet to your ANSWER SHEET.

That is the end of Listening Comprehension.

SECTION Ⅱ Reading

(50 minutes)

Part A

Directions:

Read the following two texts. Answer the questions on each text by choosing A, B, C or D. Mark your answers on your ANSWER SHEET.

Text 1

Sometime in the middle of the 15th century, a well-to-do merchant from London buried more than 6, 700 gold and silver coins on a sloping, hillside in Surrey. He was fleeing the War of the Roses and planned to return during better times. But he never did. The coins lay undisturbed until one September evening in 1990, when local resident Roger Mintey chanced upon them with a metal detector, a device used to determine the presence of metals. Mintey's find, much of which now sits in the British Museum-earned him roughly $ 350,000, enough to quit his job with a small manufacturer and spend more time pursuing lost treasure.

But digging up the past is controversial in Britain. In many European countries, metal detectorists, or people using metal detectors, face tough regulations. In the U. K., however, officials introduced a scheme in 1997 encouraging hobbyists to report their discoveries (except for those falling under the definition of treasure, like Mintey's find, which they are required to report) – but allowing them to keep what they find, or receive a reward. Last year, a hidden store was uncovered in a field outside Birmingham. It consists of more than 1, 500 gold and silver objects from the seventh century and was valued at more than $ 4. 5 million. While local museums hurry to raise enough money to keep the find off the open market, it sits in limbo, owned by the Crown but facing claims by the landowner and the metal detectorist who found it.

The find marks the latest battleground in the increasingly heated conflict between the country's 10,000 – 20,000 metal detectorists and the museum workers determined to protect its precious old objects. Supporters say the scheme stems the loss of valuable information about precious old objects, while opponents argue that metal detectorists don't report everything.

The debate centers on the larger question of who owns the past. "There's been a slow move over the centuries that precious old things belong to us all." says Professor Christopher Chippindale of Cambridge University. But in Britain at least, the temptation of buried treasure could change all that.

26. According to the first paragraph, the coins in Surrey were ________.

[A] worth roughly $ 350,000
[B] possessed by a local resident
[C] unearthed about 500 years ago
[D] left by a merchant during a war

27. What do we know about Roger Mintey?

[A] He produces metal detectors.
[B] He owns a manufacturing firm.
[C] He works for the British Museum.
[D] He seeks buried treasure as a hobby.

28. In the U. K., metal detectorists ________.

[A] are rewarded for whatever they find
[B] are forced to obey tough regulations
[C] may keep what they have discovered
[D] should report whatever they discover

29. As for the find outside Birmingham, it is still unclear ________.

[A] how much it is worth
[B] how it was discovered
[C] who is entitled to it
[D] what it is made up of

30. According to Professor Christopher Chippindale, buried treasure ________.

[A] is owned by the public
[B] is debated in a heated way
[C] remains a big temptation
[D] turns precious over time

Text 2

Every year for more than a decade I've gone with some good male friends to the music festival. Women are not invited, but they do prepare a picnic for our trip. The better the food, the more likely we are to continue our annual tradition and give them peace at least one week out of the year.

When we're not eating, we sit around in circles and talk about many stuff: women, mostly. After years of this special journey I have figured out women are different from us, especially when it comes to how we communicate. Women don't need to manufacture reasons to chat, but guys need excuses like outings or organized events.

And I've noticed that when women are in groups there can be several conversations going on at once. When men are in a group, one man talks, and everybody else listens. It's like bluegrass jamming in a way; one musician plays the lead, and the rest try to follow.

I've had more heartfelt conversations with other men at the festival than I've had at any other time in my life, partly because there are no women there, and partly because we're all a little drunk. It was males bonding over whatever parts we still had left. The festival is also the only place I've ever cried in front of other men.

As the years have slipped by, some in our group have lost parents and grandparents, some have divorced, and others have changed careers, not always on purpose. It seems that every year something distressing has happened to at least one member of our crew, and the rest of us are there to listen and offer support.

I hope that this column can offer some comfort to women: if your man heads out on a bowling or poker night with the guys, be happy. Chances are good he's not fleeing you and the kids, but he's running toward the conversations he can only have with other men, and he'll come home the better for it.

31. It is implied in the first paragraph that ________.

[A] the trip is a relief for both men and women

[B] the trip will continue in spite of everything

[C] the quality of the picnic needs improvement

[D] the women can rarely get peace themselves

32. Men and women differ in the way they talk in that ________.

[A] men like to play the lead in conversations

[B] women can strike up a talk for any reason

[C] men can be engaged in several talks at once

[D] women are good listeners in conversations

33. That the author cried in front of other men reveals ________.

[A] the effect of bluegrass music upon men

[B] the effect of alcohol on men's behaviors

[C] men's need to release their deep emotions

[D] men's need to cultivate intimate friendship

34. What is the idea that the author wants to convey in paragraph 5 ?

[A] Life is doomed to be full of distresses

[B] Changes are the constant theme of life

[C] Friendship stays despite changes in life

[D] Life consists of sweating and harvesting

35. In the last paragraph, the author advises women to ________.

[A] encourage their husbands to improve their life style

[B] encourage their husbands to go bowling or play poker

[C] give their husbands chances to flee from housework

[D] give their husbands chances for male communication

Part B

Directions:

Read the texts from a magazine in which five people talked about the future of reading. For questions 36 – 40, match the name of each person to one of the statements (A – G) given below. Mark your answers on ANSWER SHEET.

Paul:

I think books will be more affordable. They are pretty expensive. Publishers are so silly because they focus on "We're not going to be selling so many hardcover books at $ 26. " But you're going to sell infinitely more electronically, so what are you complaining about? I view it as a greater opportunity. My e-reader is great because I travel, and I don't want to carry a billion things with me.

David:

I don't own an e-reader, and I've never read a page on an e-reader. I do everything I can to avoid more screen time. Not to play down the value of a physical book, when it comes to somebody investing in one, it's something you want to keep. You have to give readers a choice, between a richer experience with physical books, and a more lifeless experience through an electronic reader.

James:

The new immigrants don't shoot the old inhabitants when they come in. One technology tends to supplement rather than substitute. How you read is not as important as: Will you read? Will you read something that's a book-the sustained train of thought of one person speaking to another? Search techniques are embedded in e-books that invite people to dip into something rather than follow a full train of thought.

Alex:

We've maintained in the last few years there will be fewer bookstores. We have the best business model in the world. Books are still a majority of what we sell in stores, but they are becoming less and less. About 50 percent of physical books are sold in non-bookstore outlets, like drugstores and club stores. There are people with agendas in this industry, but the physical book is going no-where.

William:

E-readers take out the paper middleman and give me what I want from books: the words. My e-reader has allowed me to read more than ever. When I travel I can take five books with me all without cutting down a single tree or using any extra jet fuel. Books made of paper can be beautiful, but they are never as beautiful as the words in the best of them.

Now match the name of each person (36 – 40) to the appropriate statement.

Note: there are two extra statements.

Statements

	[A] I prefer physical books to e-books.
36. Paul	[B] E-books are environmentally friendly.
37. David	[C] The market for physical books is shrinking.
38. James	[D] What counts is not how but how well you read.
39. Alex	[E] E-reading will benefit, rather than harm, publishers.
40. William	[F] The price of hardcover books will be greatly lowered.
	[G] Non-bookstore outlets add to the growth of physical books.

Part C

Directions:

Read the following text from which five sentences have been removed. Choose from the sentences A – G the most suitable one to fill each numbered gap in the text (41 – 45). *There are TWO extra sentences that you do not need to use. Mark your answer in your ANSWER SHEET.*

The whole of the United States cheered its latest hero, Ashley Smith, with the Federal Bureau of Investigation saying it was planning to give a big reward to her for having a brave heart and wise mind.

__41__ She was moving into her apartment in Atlanta, Georgia early on the morning of March 12, when a man followed her to her door and put a gun to her side. "I started walking to my door, and I felt really, really afraid," she said in a TV interview last week. The man was Brian Nichols, 33. He was suspected of killing three people at an Atlanta courthouse (法院) on March, 11 and later of killing a federal agent. __42__

Nichols tied Smith up with tape, but released her after she repeatedly begged him not to take her life. "I told him if he hurt me, my little girl wouldn't have a mummy," she said. In order to calm the man down, she read to him from *The Purpose-Driven Life*, a best-selling religious book. He asked her to repeat a paragraph " about what you thought your purpose in life was—what talents were you given." __43__

"I basically just talked to him and tried to gain his trust," Smith said.

Smith said she asked Nichols why he chose her. "He said he thought I was an angel sent from God, and we were Christian sister and brother," she said. "And that he was lost, and that God led him to me to tell him that he had hurt a lot of people." __44__ She said Nichols was surprised when she made him breakfast and that the two of them watched television coverage (报道) of the police hunt for him. "I cannot believe that's me," Nichols told the woman. Then, Nichols asked Smith what she thought he should do. She said, "I think you should turn yourself in. If you don' t, lots of more people are going to get hurt."

Eventually, he let her go. __45__ A $ 60, 000 reward had been posted for Nichol's capture. Authorities said they did not yet know if Smith would be eligible (有资格的) for that money.

[A] She even cooked breakfast for the man before he allowed her to leave.

[B] Smith thanked the man for his kindness.

[C] Smith tried very hard to kill Nichols.

[D] The local police were searching for him.

[E] And the two of them discussed this topic.

[F] Then she called the police.

[G] Smith is a 26-year-old single mother with a daughter.

Part D

Directions:

Read the following text from which 10 words have been removed. Choose from the words A – O the most suitable one to fill each numbered gap in the text (46 – 55). There are FIVE extra words that you do not need to use. Mark your answers on your ANSWER SHEET.

One in six. Believe it or not, that's the number of Americans who struggle with hunger. To make tomorrow a little better, Feeding America, the nation's largest __46__ hunger-relief organization, has chosen September as Hunger Action Month. As part of its 30 Ways in 30 Days program, it's asking __47__ across the country to help the more than 200 food banks and 61,000 agencies in its network provide low-income individuals and families with the fuel they need to __48__.

It's the kind of work that's done every day at St. Andrew's Episcopal Church in San Antonio. People who __49__ at its front door on the first and third Thursdays of each month aren't looking for God-they're there for something to eat. St. Andrew's runs a food pantry (食品室) that __50__ the city and several of the __51__ towns. Janet Drane is its manager.

In the wake of the __52__, the number of families in need of food assistance began to grow. It is __53__ that 49 million Americans are unsure of where they will find their next meal. What's most surprising is that 36% of them live in __54__ where at least one adult is working. "It used to be that one job was all you needed," says St. Andrew's Drane. "The people we see now have three or four part-time jobs and they're still right on the edge __55__."

[A] accumulate	[B] circling	[C] communities
[D] competition	[E] domestic	[F] financially
[G] formally	[H] gather	[I] households
[J] recession	[K] reported	[L] reviewed
[M] serves	[N] surrounding	[O] survive

SECTION Ⅲ Writing

(45 minutes)

Directions:

You should write your responses to both Part A and Part B of this section on your ANSWER SHEET.

Part A

56.

You are the organizer of an English speech contest, and you want to invite a foreign teacher in your school to be a judge. Write an email to him,

(1) telling him about the contest (time, location, topic, etc.);

(2) expressing your hope for his participation and his reply to your message.

You should write approximately 100 words. Do not use your own name at the end of your email. Use "Wang Lin" instead.

Part B

57.

Directions:

Read the text below. Write an essay in about 120 *words, in which you should summarize the key points of the text and make comments on them. Try to use your own words.*

The Princess of Cambridge has finally been revealed to the world as Charlotte Elizabeth Dianna a touching nod to her grandfather, her grandmother and her great-grandmother.

The name has a long tradition which can be traced hack to the royal background. Charlotte, derived from French name, pays tribute to her grandfather, prince of Wales. And Charlotte is also Kate's sister, Pippa Middleton's middle name.

Kensington Palace revealed the royal baby's full name yesterday after days of speculation and close friends of Princess Diana immediately said the choice means the spirit of Prince William's beloved mother "lives on".

William was, however, clear that his baby girl should not have Diana as a first name. "It would have been a millstone around her neck," said one of the princess's longtime friends.

Within minutes of the name being announced this afternoon, Diana's closest friend Rosa Monckton said: "Diana's spirit lives on in her sons, and now her name lives on in her granddaughter 'Charlotte Elizabeth Diana'." Diana was the godmother of Mrs. Monckton's daughter Dominica.

The British citizens show their satisfaction with this name via Internet. They said it is the perfect name for their lovely princess.

THAT IS THE END OF THE TEST.

全国英语等级考试第三级
2015 年 3 月笔试真题（改编版）答案

SECTION Ⅰ Listening

Part A

1. C	2. D	3. D	4. B	5. C
6. C	7. D	8. B	9. B	10. A

Part B

11. C	12. B	13. D	14. D	15. A
16. D	17. C	18. D	19. B	20. C
21. D	22. A	23. D	24. C	25. D

SECTION Ⅱ Reading

Part A

Text 1

26. D	27. D	28. C	29. C	30. A

Text 2

31. A	32. B	33. C	34. C	35. D

Part B

36. E	37. A	38. D	39. C	40. B

Part C

41. G	42. D	43. E	44. A	45. F

Part D

46. E	47. C	48. O	49. H	50. M
51. N	52. J	53. K	54. I	55. F

SECTION Ⅲ　Writing

Part A

【参考范文】

56.

Dear Mr. Smith,

The students' Union of our Faculty plans to hold an English speech contest from 2 p. m. to 4 p. m. on Saturday, Oct. 8, 2020 at the school club. This year's contest focuses on the topic "The importance of recycling". Because I have been selected as a representative to prepare for the contest, I am very glad to invite you to be the judge of this contest. Anyone with your experience and proficiency would be the perfect person to undertake this task.

If you accept our sincere invitation, please inform us at your earliest convenience, enabling us to make the necessary preparations.

Yours Sincerely,

Wang Lin

(109 *words*)

Part B

【参考范文】

57.

All the British people and even the world were looking forward and anticipating the new princess of Cambridge. The princess' name was finally revealed as Charlotte Elizabeth Diana, which is named after her grandfather, her grandmother and her great-grandmother.

One probability is that the name of Diana, which is also the name of the princess' grandmother, means the eternal love between the princess' grander parents. And princess William, the princess' father announced that they didn't use Diana as her first name because they don't want to give her too much pressure, by living under her grandmother's fame.

In my opinion, it is unimportant what this little girl's name was as it is just a call for people to recognize her. The most important thing is that the girl can grow up in a harmonious environment. May this little girl be happy every day.

(142 *words*)

全国英语等级考试第三级
2014 年 9 月笔试真题（改编版）

笔试部分答题时间：120 分钟

SECTION Ⅰ　Listening

（25 minutes）

2014. 9

Directions:

This section is designed to test your ability to understand spoken English. You will hear a selection of recorded materials and you must answer the questions that accompany them. There are two parts in this section, Part A and Part B.

Remember, while you are doing the test, you should first put down your answers in your test booklet. At the end of the listening section, you will have 3 minutes to transfer all your answers from your test booklet to your ANSWER SHEET.

If you have any questions, you may raise your hand now as you will not be allowed to speak once the test has started.

Now look at Part A in your test booklet.

Part A

Directions:

You will hear 10 short dialogues. For each dialogue, there is one question and four possible answers. Choose the correct answer – A, B, C or D, and mark it in your test booklet. You will have 15 seconds to answer the question and you will hear each dialogue ***only once.***

Example:

You will hear:

W: Could you please tell me if the Beijing flight will be arriving on time?

M: Yes, Madam. It should be arriving in about ten minutes.

You will read:

Who do you think the woman is talking to?

[A] A bus conductor.　　　　[B] A clerk at the airport.

[C] A taxi driver. [D] A clerk at the station.

From the dialogue, we know that only a clerk at the airport is most likely to know the arrival time of a flight, so you should choose answer [B] and mark it in your test booklet.

Sample Answer: [A] ■ [C] [D]

Now look at question 1.

1. What does the man ask the woman to do?

[A] To help him with his paper. [B] To play with him.

[C] To go to see a play with him. [D] To visit him tomorrow.

2. What will the two speakers do first?

[A] Look for sports clothes.

[B] Move the desk.

[C] Paint the wall.

[D] Ask someone to help them move the desk.

3. When did the concert begin?

[A] 7: 15. [B] 7: 30. [C] 7: 50. [D] 7: 35.

4. Why does the man want the woman to give up drinking?

[A] Because he doesn't want the woman to relax.

[B] Because he thinks it is bad for her health.

[C] Because the woman is going to have a baby.

[D] Because it's a bad example to the children.

5. What does the woman mean?

[A] Professor Zhang couldn't be in the lab.

[B] Professor Zhang forgot to turn off the lights in the lab.

[C] Professor Zhang went home a long time ago.

[D] Professor Zhang was the last one to leave the lab.

6. What does the man imply?

[A] Jane will certainly be glad to hear about Bill's promotion.

[B] Jane has lost her job.

[C] Jane probably won't feel pleased with Bill's promotion.

[D] Jane should have got the promotion.

7. What does the man mean?

[A] It is impossible for Toby to pass the exam.

[B] He doesn't know whether Toby will pass the exam or not.

[C] Toby will certainly pass the exam.

[D] Toby doesn't know the way to the classroom.

8. What does the woman say about the course?

[A] It is more difficult than everyone says.

[B] It is not interesting at all.

[C] She doesn't believe the course is difficult.

[D] It is as difficult as everyone says.

9. How did the man travel?

[A] By plane. [B] By bus. [C] By train. [D] By car.

10. What does the man suggest they should do?

[A] Put another bookshelf in the room.

[B] Put the bookshelf in the kitchen.

[C] Move the old dining table out of the room.

[D] Put the old dining table in the room.

Part B

Directions:

You will hear four dialogues or monologues. Before listening to each one, you will have 5 *seconds to read each of the questions which accompany it. While listening, answer each question by choosing A, B, C or D. After listening, you will have* 10 *seconds to check your answer to each question. You will hear the recording* ***only once***.

Questions 11 – 13 *are based on a dialogue between a clerk of Air-ticket Booking office and a customer.*

11. Where does the conversation take place?

[A] At an airport. [B] On the phone.

[C] In a ticket office. [D] We don't know.

12. Which flight will the man take?

[A] 3: 45 flight. [B] 1: 30 flight.

[C] 5: 00 flight. [D] Either 3: 45 flight or 5: 00 flight.

13. How much money does the man have to pay for the tickets?

[A] 450 dollars. [B] 900 dollars.

[C] 1,350 dollars. [D] 1,800 dollars.

Questions 14 – 17 *are based on the following dialogue.*

14. What does Nancy think of her new neighbors?

[A] They are not polite. [B] They seem nice.

[C] They are crazy. [D] They don't talk much.

15. What bothers Nancy about her new neighbors' son?

[A] He sings in the mid-night. [B] He drives too fast.

[C] His radio wakes her children. [D] He comes back too late.

16. What is the most probable relationship between the two speakers?

[A] Neighbors. [B] Colleagues.

[C] Husband and wife. [D] Classmates.

17. What suggestion does the man give?

[A] Nancy should visit her neighbors and make some complaints.

[B] Nancy should talk about her children with her neighbors.

[C] Nancy should let the neighbors' son stop playing the radio.

[D] Nancy should say hello to the neighbors whenever she comes across them.

Questions 18 – 21 are based on the following dialogue.

18. How does David go back home from the store?

[A] On foot. [B] By bike.

[C] By car. [D] Jane offers him a lift.

19. Why did David go to the store?

[A] Because he wanted to buy some bags.

[B] Because he wanted to buy some grocery for a dinner.

[C] Because he wanted to meet with the Jane.

[D] Because he wanted to buy the Kremers some gifts.

20. What can we learn about the Kremers from the dialogue?

[A] They are coming home from a vacation.

[B] They are David's relatives.

[C] They asked David to prepare dinner before they arrived at home.

[D] They rent a room to David in their house.

21. What do we know about David?

[A] He is working in a school.

[B] He is grateful to the Kremers.

[C] He has little money and can't afford to pay the house rent.

[D] He is inviting some of his friends to the dinner.

Questions 22 – 25 are based on a passage about London taxi drivers.

22. Why are London taxi drivers efficient?

[A] Because they all grow up in London.

[B] Because they have a special license.

[C] Because they all have gone through a very tough training period.

[D] Because they drive at a high speed.

23. How long does the training period last?

[A] Two years. [B] Three years.

[C] Four years. [D] Two to four years.

24. Why do learner drivers have to keep their present jobs?

[A] Because they want to earn more money.

[B] Because they are not allowed to earn money as drivers without a license.

[C] Because they don't want to leave the jobs.

[D] Because they are asked to do so.

25. What can we learn from the passage?

[A] London taxi drivers always take a map of London with them.

[B] Streets in London are quite small.

[C] Learner taxi drivers use cars during the training.

[D] The exams during the training period are not easy.

Now you have 3 minutes to transfer your answers from your test booklet to your ANSWER SHEET.

That is the end of Listening Comprehension.

SECTION Ⅱ Reading

(50 minutes)

Part A

Directions:

Read the following two texts. Answer the questions on each text by choosing A, B, C or D. Mark your answers on your ANSWER SHEET.

Text 1

Today there are three different kinds of New Yorkers: the people who act as if they were born here; the people who are here and wish to be elsewhere; and the collection of virtual New Yorkers all over the world, who wish they were living in New York. These are the three states of mind and what they have in common are longing and illusion. In fact, it's a city of dreamers.

What makes New York special? New Yorkers are convinced of its specialness—but Toronto is more diverse, London is larger, Washington is more powerful. So why does New York think it's the capital of the world?

People often explain the problems in European cities by citing inequality. But New York today is one of the most unequal cities in America. In 2010, 1 percent of New Yorkers earned 45 percent of its income. That works out to an average of $ 3.7 million a year for the city's top 34,500 households. The average daily income of this group is greater than the average annual income of the city's bottom 10 percent.

So why would people still come to try their luck in this tough place? Is it opportunity or illusion that draws them?

They come because any newcomer can find a place in the hierarchy of New York. If you look at a New York City restaurant, for example, the cook might be French, the people washing dishes might be Mexican, the hostess might be Russian, the owner might be British. They are not all equal. They earn different rates. But they work together to get food to hungry people.

What New York demonstrates is this: immigration works. The city can use its immigrants, even the illegal ones. Though they broke the law by illegally crossing the borders, the city's economy would be a shell of itself had they not, and it would collapse if they were deported. Attracted here by the founding myth of the city, each immigrant is seeking to escape from history, personal and political. For him, New York is the city of the second chance.

26. The writer mentions the three kinds of New Yorkers to stress that ________.

[A] they share the same longing　　[B] they are in pursuit of dreams

[C] they are proud of their birthplace　　[D] they wish to live in another place

27. In the eyes of New Yorkers, their city is ________.

[A] powerful　　[B] diverse　　[C] special　　[D] large

28. The figures in paragraph 3 are given to show that New York ________.

[A] favors the lucky　　[B] favors the locals

[C] is a city of inequality　　[D] is a city of opportunities

29. People keep coming to New York because they can find jobs that ________.

[A] challenge them　　[B] suit them well

[C] pay them well　　[D] raise their status

30. It is implied in the text that New York is ________.

[A] a tolerant city　　[B] a wealthy city

[C] a mythical city　　[D] a historical city

Text 2

We've read how babies stare longer and cry less when held by pretty people, and heard tales of handsome children doing better in school, given special attention by their teachers. In life, as in love, beautiful people seem to have it awfully easy. But what if we told you that when it comes to online dating, good looks could actually hurt you?

According to a recent survey of 43,000 users by OK Cupid, an online dating site, the more men disagree about a woman's looks, the more they end up liking her. What does that mean for ladies looking for a match? "We now have mathematical evidence that minimizing your 'weaknesses' is the opposite of what you should do," says the site's co-founder, Christian Rudder. "If you' re a little fat, play it up. If you have a big nose, play it up. Statistically, the guys who don't like it can only help you, and the ones who do like it will be all the more excited."

The results of this study end up highlighting an idea that recent scientific research does indeed support. Which is this: the beautiful may have it good, but online, as in work and life, women who are too attractive don't always have an advantage.

Beauty creates more competition among women, taught they must out-look each other for men and jobs and everyday satisfaction; and among men, who are competing for the most attractive prize. All of which might help explain why 47 percent of corporate recruiters believe it's possible for a woman to suffer for being "too good-looking"; why attractive women tend to face heightened examination from their female peers; or, finally, why men on OK Cupid end up contacting women who may ultimately be less attractive because it removes the opposition. "If you suspect other men are uninterested, it means less competition," explains Rudder. "You might start thinking: maybe she's lonely... maybe she's just waiting to find a guy who appreciates her... at least I won't get lost in the crowd."

In the end, being beautiful will always have its blessings but sometimes, there's more to an advantage than meets the eye.

31. It is generally believed that beautiful people ________.

[A] have less difficulty in life
[B] are less worried about love
[C] pay less attention to others
[D] like to gaze at lovely babies

32. The OK Cupid survey found that men's arguments over a woman's looks ________.

[A] have little meaning
[B] benefit online dating
[C] will actually hurt her
[D] add to her popularity

33. Christian Rudder advises women to ________.

[A] play up their physical advantages
[B] view their popularity scientifically
[C] highlight their physical weaknesses
[D] accept guys who are willing to help

34. The attitude of women toward their attractive peers is ________.

[A] critical
[B] friendly
[C] conservative
[D] straightforward

35. The main idea of the text is that a woman's good looks ________.

[A] help to shape ideas of beauty
[B] can put her at a disadvantage
[C] end up with blessings for her
[D] will always appeal to the eye

Part B

Directions:

Read the texts in which five people wrote about being a vegetarian. For questions 36 – 40, *match the name of each person to one of the statements* (*A – G*) *given below. Mark your answers on ANSWER SHEET.*

Laurie:

It is encouraging to see that, whether out of sympathy for animals or a concern for their own health or both, people are starting to realize that it does not pay to eat too far up on the food chain. Meat needs not be what is for dinner. Factory farming is barbaric and cruel. Every person who reduces the use of animals in his life is performing a lifesaving act.

Jeff:

I am ready to be a vegetarian, but in our country, farmers, food producers, restaurants and supermarkets are not prepared to support me. We all know that it is much easier and less expensive to get a hamburger at McDonald's or Chinese takeout or a roast chicken from the supermarket than it is to take the time to shop for, assemble and cook a tasty, nutritious and fulfilling vegetarian meal.

Rod:

I've heard another term for vegetarians: beady-eyed vegetarians. They'll eat things with beady eyes (fish, chicken) but not with big, sad eyes (cows, lambs). A friend of mine explained it by saying he would eat only things he thought he could kill himself. He figures he can kill a fish but not a cow. That seems like a more honest and consistent rational than some of the others I've heard.

Jerry:

As a moral vegetarian, I have found that there is great misunderstanding about vegetarian principles in our society. While some vegetarians keep of animals as a matter of health, we moral vegetarians don't want other animals to live for us, nor do we want other animals to die for us, as they do for food, clothing and wasteful scientific research. All animals live for their own sake, not for mine.

Ellen:

Why do some people think that animals and human beings are the same? In my opinion, a human life is worth a lot more than an animal's. I think that we must stop thinking of meat eaters as killers. Vegetarians also kill vegetable life. Is there any difference? Eat vegetables and meat; both help you to be healthy and allow you to have all the nutrients your bodies need.

Now match the name of each person (36 – 40) to the appropriate statement.

Note: there are two extra statements.

Statements

36. Laurie
37. Jeff
38. Rod
39. Jerry
40. Ellen

[A] All animals have the right to live for themselves.
[B] Some vegetarians in fact eat small-sized animals.
[C] Vegetarians need to do more to save animals' lives.
[D] Some people have overstressed the rights of animals.
[E] Vegetarians should be consistent in their eating habits.
[F] How can I become a vegetarian without a favorable environment?
[G] Eating less meat saves not only the life of animals but also that of your own.

Part C

Directions:

Read the following text from which five sentences have been removed. Choose from the sentences A – G the most suitable one to fill each numbered gap in the text (41 –45). *There are TWO extra sentences that you do not need to use. Mark your answer in your ANSWER SHEET.*

In shopping malls, the assistants try to push you into buying "a gift to thank her for her unselfish love". When you log onto a website, a small pop-up invites you to book a bouquet for her. Commercial warmth and gratitude are the atmosphere being spread around for this special Sunday in May.

__41__ The popularity of Mother's Day around the world suggests that Jarvis got all she wanted. In fact, she got more-enough to make her horrified.

__42__ They buy, among other things, 132 million cards. Mother's Day is the No 1 holiday for flower purchases. Then there are the various commodities, ranging from jewelry and clothes to cosmetics and washing powder, that take advantage of the promotion opportunities. Because of this, Jarvis spent the last 40 years of her life trying to stop Mother's Day. One protest against the commercialization of Mother's Day even got her arrested for disturbing the peace, interestingly.

__43__ As Ralph Fevre, a reporter at the UK newspaper *The Guardian*, observe, traditionally "motherhood is something that we do because we think it's right." But in the logic of commercialism, people need something in exchange for their time and energy. A career serves this purpose better.

__44__ So they work hard and play hard. Becoming a mother, however, inevitably handicaps career anticipation.

__45__ According to *The Guardian*, there are twice as many child-free young women as there were a generation ago. Or, they put off the responsibility of parenting until later in their lives.

So, Fevre writes that the meaning of celebrating Mother's Day needs to be updated: "It is to persuade people that parenting is a good idea and to honor people for their attempt to be good people."

[A] According to a research by the US card company Hallmark, 96 percent of American consumers celebrate the holiday.

[B] But what's more, commercialism changes young people's attitude towards motherhood.

[C] Obviously, the best gift will be a phone call or a visit.

[D] The American version of Mother's Day was thought up as early as 1905, by Anna Jarvis, as a way of recognizing the real value of motherhood.

[E] In addition, women are being encouraged to pursue any career they desire.

[F] As a result, motherhood has suffered a huge drop in status since the 1950s.

[G] Nowadays Mother's Day become more and more commercialization.

Part D

Directions:

Read the following text from which 10 words have been removed. Choose from the words A – O the most suitable one to fill each numbered gap in the text (46 – 55). There are FIVE extra words that you do not need to use. Mark your answers on your ANSWER SHEET.

Children do not think the way adults do. For most of the first year of life, if something is out of sight, it's out of mind. If you cover a baby's __46__ toy with a piece of cloth, the baby thinks the toy has disappeared and stops looking for it. A 4-year-old may __47__ that a sister has more fruit juice when it is only the shapes of the glasses that differ, not the __48__ of juice.

Yet children are smart in their own way. Like good little scientists, children are always testing their child-sized __49__ about how things work. When your child throws her spoon on the floor for the sixth time as you try to feed her, and you say, "That's enough! I will not pick up your spoon again!" The child will __50__ test your claim. Are you serious? Are you angry? What will happen if she throws the spoon again? She is not doing this to drive you __51__; rather, she is learning that her desires and yours can differ, and that sometimes those __52__ are important and sometimes they are not.

How and why does children's thinking change? In the 1920s, Swiss psychologist Jean Piaget proposed that children's cognitive abilities unfold __53__, like the blooming of a flower, almost independent of what else is __54__ in their lives. Although many of his specific conclusions have been __55__ or modified over the years, his ideas inspired thousands of studies by investigators all over the world.

[A] advocate	[B] amount	[C] confirmed
[D] crazy	[E] definite	[F] differences
[G] favorite	[H] happening	[I] immediately
[J] naturally	[K] obtaining	[L] primarily
[M] protest	[N] rejected	[O] theories

SECTION Ⅲ Writing

Directions:

You should write your responses to both Part A and Part B of this section on your ANSWER SHEET.

Part A

56.

Your friend Paul is coming to visit you next month. In his last email, he asked you about the interesting places in your hometown. Write an email back to Paul, telling him about:

(1) some interesting places you would recommend;

(2) things necessary for the travel.

You should write approximately 100 words. Do not use your own name at the end of your email. Use "Wang Lin" instead.

Part B

57.

Directions:

Read the text below. Write an essay in about 120 *words, in which you should summarize the key points of the text and make comments on them. Try to use you own words.*

A 23-year-old Chinese woman has died after her mobile phone exploded while it was being charged.

Miss Zhao was found dead in Shijiazhuang, the capital city of northeast China's Hebei province. She was talking to her boyfriend on her mobile phone, but suddenly went silent.

After the boyfriend failed to get a response in a prolonged period of time, he rushed to Zhao's home. It was already too late, as the phone had clearly exploded in her hands, and her entire chest had been burned.

This piece of news draws public attention to the using safety of electronic devices, especially the most commonly used mobile phone, and provides information that will be of great value in assessing the safety of cell phone use.

Liang Guangchuan, a researcher from Hebei University of Technology, says the tragedy could be caused by a faulty charger and electric leakage of the lithium battery. He suggests that to be on the safe side, one should avoid using his or her mobile phone while it is being charged.

This accident caused great response in the population of cell phone users. A cell phone user replied in an interview, "I swear, after I post this comment, I will never play with my mobile phone again when the battery is still being charged." A sample of comments on Weibo: "Should the cell phone producer be responsible for this accident and make effort to broadcast the knowledge of cell phone using safety?"

THAT IS THE END OF THE TEST

全国英语等级考试第三级
2014 年 9 月笔试真题（改编版）答案

SECTION Ⅰ Listening

Part A

1. C	2. B	3. B	4. D	5. A
6. C	7. A	8. A	9. D	10. C

Part B

11. B	12. A	13. A	14. B	15. C
16. B	17. B	18. A	19. B	20. A
21. B	22. C	23. D	24. B	25. D

SECTION Ⅱ Reading

Part A

Text 1

26. B	27. C	28. C	29. B	30. A

Text 2

31. A	32. D	33. C	34. A	35. B

Part B

36. G	37. F	38. B	39. A	40. D

Part C

41. D	42. A	43. B	44. E	45. F

Part D

46. G	47. M	48. B	49. O	50. I
51. D	52. F	53. J	54. H	55. N

SECTION Ⅲ Writing

Part A

【参考范文】

56.

Dear Paul,

I was very glad to learn that you will visit Shanghai. I wish the following information will help you enjoy your stay in my hometown.

Shanghai is a large and busy city. I am aware that you are interested in art and history. So firstly, I suggest you pay a visit to Shanghai Museum. Secondly, not far from the museum is the famous Bund, where you will always have a terrific view of Pudong, the Oriental Pearl TV Tower, and Jinmao Tower, which is the third tallest building in the world!

I hope these suggestions will be helpful. I'm looking forward to meeting you here.

Yours Sincerely,

Wang Lin

(113 *words*)

Part B

【参考范文】

57.

Recently, a tragedy took place in Hebei province, China. A young girl died of cell phone explosion. Her cell phone exploded when she was talking to her boyfriend in the evening via cell phone, which is being charged.

The sad news aroused public discussion all over the country. Experts and researchers claimed that cell phone users should avoid of using cell phone when charging them in case of accidents.

Those people who frequently use cell phones are concerned about the safety of cell phone using. Most users are frightened by this news and promised that they would never use cell phones when they were being charged. However, someone intended to question the liability of the phone producers and want to get safety assurance from them.

From my perspective, as many cautionary tales as I have heard, I will try to get rid of the problem of cell phone addiction and find other things to do when it is being charged.

(161 *words*)

附录一　语法项目表

一、词类

1. 名词

（1）普通名词和专有名词

（2）可数名词和不可数名词

（3）名词的复数形式

（4）所有格

2. 代词

（1）人称代词

（2）物主代词

（3）反身代词

（4）相互代词

（5）指示代词

（6）不定代词

（7）疑问代词

（8）关系代词

3. 限定词

（1）冠词：定冠词、不定冠词

（2）物主限定词

（3）指示限定词

（4）数量限定词

（5）疑问限定词

（6）关系限定词

4. 数词

（1）基数词

（2）序数词

（3）分数

（4）小数

（5）百分比

5. 形容词

（1）形容词作定语、表语、宾语补足语

（2）比较等级：原级/比较级/最高级

6. 副词

（1）表示方式、地点、时间、程度、观点、连接等

（2）比较等级：原级/比较级/最高级

7. 介词

8. 连词

（1）并列连词

（2）从属连词

9. 感叹词

10. 动词

（1）动词的基本形式

A. 原形：用于现在时（第三人称单数除外）、不定式、祈使语气等

B. -s 形式：用于现在时第三人称单数

C. -ing 分词：用于进行体、动名词、非谓语形式等

D. 过去式：用于过去时

E. -ed 分词：用于完成体、被动态、非谓语形式等

F. 不规则动词的过去式和-ed 分词

（2）动词的种类

A. 行为动词：及物动词和不及物动词

B. 助动词：be，do，have 等

C. 情态助动词：can，could，may，might，must，will，would，shall，should 等

D. 半情态助动词：be going to，used to，had better，have（got）to，ought to 等

E. 连系动词：be，seem，look，sound，get，turn，grow，become 等

（3）短语动词：动词 + 小词（副词、介词）

（4）时态

A. 一般现在时

B. 现在进行时

C. 一般过去时

D. 过去进行时

E. 现在完成时

F. 过去完成时

G. 现在完成进行时

H. 过去完成进行时

I. 过去将来时

J. 一般将来时

K. 将来进行时

L. 将来完成时

M. 将来完成进行时

（5）被动态

A. 被动态的不同时态

B. 带情态动词的被动态

（6）动词非谓语形式

A. 不定式

B. -ing 分词

C. -ed 分词

（7）虚拟语气

二、句子

1. 句子的成分

（1）主语

（2）谓语

（3）宾语（直接和间接宾语）

（4）补语

（5）表语

（6）定语

（7）状语：修饰性、评注性、连接性

（8）插入语、呼唤语、感叹语

2. 句子的种类

（1）陈述句

（2）疑问句

（3）祈使句

（4）感叹句

3. 句子的肯定与否定

4. 简单句的基本句型

5. 主谓一致

6. 并列复合句

7. 主从复合句

（1）宾语从句

（2）状语从句

（3）定语从句（关系从句）

（4）主语从句

（5）表语从句

8. 直接引语和间接引语

9. 省略

10. 替代

11. 强调

12. 标点符号

三、构词法

1. 转化

2. 合成

3. 派生

4. 缩写

附录二　PETS-3 必备词汇表

A

a [ei,ə] *art.* 一(个);每一(个)
abandon [əˈbændən] *vt.* 丢弃;放弃,抛弃;*n.* 放纵
ability [əˈbiliti] *n.* 能力,本领
able [ˈeibl] *adj.* 能干的,有能力的;出色的
aboard [əˈbɔːd] *prep.* 上船,上飞机,上车;*adv.* 在船(车)上,在火车上,在飞机上
abolish [əˈbɒlɪʃ] *vt.* 废除,废止(法律、制度、习俗等)
abort[əˈbɔːt] *vt.* 使流产;小产;(使)夭折;中止(尤指很可能失败的事情)
about [ˈəbaut] *prep.* 关于;在……周围;*adv.* 大约
above [əˈbʌv] *prep.* 在……上面;超过,高于;*adj.* 上面的;*adv.* 在上面;超过
above[əˈbʌv] *prep.* 在(或向)……上面;(数目、数量、水平、年龄)超过;多于;(重要性、质量)超过,胜过;*adv.* 在(或向)上面;在(或向)较高处;(数目、数量、水平、年龄)超过;*adj.* 前文述及的;上述的
abroad [əˈbrɔːd] *adv.* (在)国外　海外;到国外
abrupt [əˈbrʌpt] *adj.* 突然的;意外的;(言语、行为)粗鲁的,莽撞的,唐突的;生硬的
absence [ˈæbsəns] *n.* 缺席,不在场;缺乏
absent [ˈæbsənt] *adj.* 缺席的,不在场的;缺乏的
absolute [ˈæbsəluːt] *adj.* 绝对的;纯粹的,完全的
absorb [əbˈsɔːb] *vt.* 吸收,吸纳;吸引……的注意;使专心
abstract [ˈæbstrækt] *adj.* 抽象的;*n.* 摘要;抽象的东西;*vt.* 做摘要
absurd[əbˈsɜːd] *adj.* 荒谬的;荒唐的
abundant [əˈbʌndənt] *adj.* 丰富的,充裕的,大量的
abuse [əˈbjuːz] *vt.* 滥用;辱骂;虐待;*n.* 滥用
academic [ˌækəˈdemik] *adj.* 学院的;学术性的;*n.* 教学人员,学术人员
accelerate [əkˈseləreit] *vt.* (使)加快;促进;加速
accent [ˈæksənt] *n.* 口音;重音;强调;*vt.* 重读;强调
accept [əkˈsept] *vt.* 接受,同意
access [ˈækses] *n.* 进入、接近(的机会);使用之权;通道入口;*vt.* 进入
accident [ˈæksidənt] *n.* 意外的事故
accommodate [əˈkɔmədeit] *vt.* 容纳;供应,供给,提供方便;*vi.* 使自己适应
accommodation [əˌkɔməˈdeiʃən] *n.* 招待设备;预定铺位;住处;膳宿;适应
accompany [əˈkʌmpəni] *vt.* 陪伴陪同;伴随;*vi.* 给……伴奏
accomplish [əˈkʌmpliʃ] *vt.* 达到(目的);完成
according (to) [əˈkɔːdɪŋ] *prep.* 给予,赠予,授予(权力、地位、某种待遇);(与……)一致,符合,配合
account [əˈkaunt] *n.* 记述;解释;理由;账目;报告;*vt.* 认为,视为
accurate [ˈækjərət] *adj.* 准确的;正确无误的
accuse [əˈkjuːz] *vt.* 指责,责备;控告;归咎于
ache [eɪk] *vi.* 疼痛;隐痛;*n.* (身体某部位的)疼痛
achieve [əˈtʃiːv] *vt.* 完成;实现,达到;*vi.* 达到目的
acid [ˈæsid] *n.* 酸,酸味物质;*adj.* 酸的,酸性的
acknowledge[əkˈnɒlɪdʒ] *vt.* 承认(属实);承认(权威、地位);告知,收悉
acquaint [əˈkweɪnt] *vt.* 使熟悉;使了解
acquaintance [əˈkweintəns] *n.* 认识,了解;熟人
acquire [əˈkwaiə] *vt.* 占有;取得,获得;学到
acre [ˈeikə] *n.* 英亩(=6.07 亩)
across [əˈkrɔs] *prep.* 横过,穿过;在……对面;

adv. 横过；使……被理解（或接受）
act [ækt] *vi.* 行动；表演；表现；充当；*vt.* 表演，扮演；*n.* 行为，行动；法案；（戏剧、歌剧等的）一幕
action [ˈækʃən] *n.* 行动；作用，功能；活动
active [ˈæktiv] *adj.* 活跃的；积极的，主动的
activity [ækˈtiviti] *n.* 活动；活跃；行动
actor [ˈæktə] *n.* 男演员
actress [ˈæktris] *n.* 女演员
actual [ˈæktjuəl] *adj.* 实际的，真实的
adapt [əˈdæpt] *vt.* 使适应；改编；*vi.* 适应；适合
add [æd] *vt.* 添加，附加；增加
addict [ˈædɪkt] *n.* 吸毒成瘾的人；对……入迷的人
addition [əˈdɪʃn] *n.* 加；加法；增加物；增加；添加
address [əˈdres] *n.* 地址，住址；致辞，讲话，演说；*vt.* 发表演说；写地址；称呼
adhere [ədˈhɪə(r)] *v.* 黏附；附着
adjust [əˈdʒʌst] *vt.* 调整，调节；校正；使……适于；*vi.* 适应
administration [ədminisˈtreiʃən] *n.* 管理，行政；管理部门
admire [ədˈmaiə] *vt.* 钦佩，羡慕；赞赏
admit [ədˈmit] *vt.* 承认；准许……进入；*vi.* 允许进入；允许；承认
adolescent [ˌædəˈlesnt] *n.* 青少年
adopt [əˈdɔpt] *vt.* 收养；采用；采取；接受
adult [əˈdʌlt，ˈædʌlt] *n.* 成年人；*adj.* 成年的；成人的；成熟的
advance [ədˈvɑːns] *n.* 前进，进展；进步；*vt.* 前进；预先；*vi.* 前进；提高，提升；*adj.* 预先的，提前的
advanced [ədˈvɑːnst] *adj.* 先进的；高级的
advantage [ədˈvɑːntidʒ] *n.* 优点，优势；有利条件；好处；*vt.* 有利于
adventure [ədˈventʃə] *n.* 冒险；奇遇；惊险活动；*vt.* 冒险；尝试；*vi.* 大胆进行；冒险
advertise [ˈædvətaɪz] *v.* （为……）做广告；登广告
advice [ədˈvais] *n.* 劝告，忠告；意见，建议
advise [ədˈvaiz] *vt.* 劝告；建议；*vi.* 劝告；与……商量
advocate [ˈædvəkeɪt，ˈædvəkət] *v.* 拥护；支持；提倡；*n.* 拥护者；支持者；提倡者
affair [əˈfɛə] *n.* 事情，事件；绯闻
affect [əˈfekt] *vt.* 影响；感动；作用
affection [əˈfekʃən] *n.* 慈爱，爱；爱慕；影响；喜爱；感情
afford [əˈfɔːd] *vt.* 担负得起；提供；给予
afraid [əˈfreid] *adj.* 害怕的，担心的
after [ˈɑːftə] *adj.* 以后的；*adv.* 以后，后来；*conj.* 在……以后；*prep.* 在……以后；次于
afternoon [ˈɑːftəˈnuːn] *n.* 下午，午后；*int.* 下午好
afterward(s) [ˈɑːftəwədz] *adv.* 后来；以后
again [əˈgein] *adv.* 又一次；而且；又，再
against [əˈgenst，əˈgeinst] *prep.* 倚在，倚靠；逆；对着；反对，违背；防御；相比，相对
age [eidʒ] *n.* 年龄；时代，时期；*vt.* （使）变老；*vi.* 变老；（使）变成熟
agency [ˈeidʒənsi] *n.* 经办，代理；代理处；政府机构
agenda [əˈdʒendə] *n.* （会议的）议程表，议事日程
agent [ˈeidʒənt] *n.* 代理人，代理商；特工人员
aggressive [əˈgresiv] *adj.* 侵略的；好斗的，攻击性的；有进取心的
ago [əˈgəu] *adv.* 以前
agony [ˈægəni] *n.* 极度痛苦
agree [əˈgriː] *vt.* 同意，赞成；承认；*vi.* 同意；一致；符合
agreement [əˈgriːmənt] *n.* 协定，协议；同意；一致
agriculture [ˈægrikʌltʃə] *n.* 农业；农艺；农学
ahead [əˈhed] *adv.* 在前，向前，提前
aid [eid] *n.* 帮助；救护；助手，辅助物；*v.* 援助，帮助；救护
aim [eim] *n.* 目标；对准；*vt.* 瞄准；针对；*vi.* 瞄准；针对；旨在
air [ɛə] *n.* 空气，空中；气氛；态度；*vt.* 晾干；使通风；广播
aircraft [ˈeəkrɑːft] *n.* 飞机，飞行器
airline [ˈeəlain] *n.* 航空公司；航线
airmail [ˈeəmeɪl] *n.* 航空邮递
airplane [ˈeəplein] *n.* 飞机 = aeroplane（英）
airport [ˈeəpɔːt] *n.* 机场，航空站
alarm [əˈlɑːm] *n.* 惊恐，惊慌；忧虑；警报，警告，报警器；*vt.* 使……惊慌；警告，装报警器
album [ˈælbəm] *n.* 相册；影集；集邮簿；（唱片或盒式磁带等上的）音乐专辑，歌曲专辑
alcohol [ˈælkəhɔl] *n.* 酒精，乙醇
alert [əˈlɜːt] *adj.* 警觉的；警惕的；戒备的；*vt.* 向……报警；使警觉；使警惕；使戒备；*n.* 警戒；戒备；警惕；警报
alien [ˈeɪliən] *adj.* 陌生的；不熟悉；外国的；异域的；不相容；相抵触；格格不入；*n.* 外国人；外

侨;外星人;外星生物

alike [ə·laik] *adj.* 同样的,相同的,相似的;*adv.* 相似地;同样地

alive [ə·laiv] *adj.* 活着的;有活力,活跃的

all [ɔːl] *adv.* 全部,所有;*pron.* 全部,所有

allergic [ə·lɜːdʒɪk] *adj.* 过敏的;过敏性的;对……十分反感;厌恶

allied[·ælaɪd,ə·laɪd] *adj.* (国与国协同作战)结盟的,联盟的;共存的;有关联的

allow [ə·lau] *vi.* (for)考虑到;*vt.* 允许,准许;承认;给予

alloy [·ælɔi] *n.* 合金

almost [·ɔːlməust] *adv.* 几乎,差不多

alone [ə·ləun] *adj.* 单独的;仅仅,独自一人

along [ə·lɔŋ] *prep.* 沿着

alongside [əˌlɒŋ·saɪd] *prep.* 在……旁边;沿着……的边;与……一起;与……同时

aloud [ə·laud] *adv.* 出声地,大声地

already [ɔːl·redi] *adv.* 早已,已经

also [·ɔːlsəu] *adv.* 亦,也;而且;还

alter [·ɔːltə] *vt.* 改变,变更

alternate [·ɔːltəneɪt] *adj.* 交替的;轮流的;间隔的;每隔(……天等)的;*v.* 使交替;使轮流;交替;轮流;*n.* 代替者;代理人;候补者

alternative [ɔːl·təːnətiv] *adj.* 两者择一的,供选择的;*n.* 替换物;取舍,抉择

although [ɔːl·ðəu] *conj.* 尽管,虽然

altogether [ˌɔːltə·geðə] *adv.* 完全;总共;总而言之

always [·ɔːlweiz] *adv.* 总是,一直;永远

amateur [·æmətə(r)] *n.* 业余爱好者;业余运动员;生手;外行;*adj.* 业余爱好的;业余的

amaze [ə·meiz] *vt.* 使惊奇,使惊愕

ambassador[æm·bæsədə(r)] *n.* 大使;使节

ambiguous[æm·bɪgjuəs] *adj.* 模棱两可的;含混不清的;不明确的

ambition [æm·biʃən] *n.* 雄心,抱负;野心;精力

ambitious [æm·bɪʃəs] *adj.* 有野心的;有雄心的

ambulance [·æmbjuləns] *n.* 救护车;野战医院

amongst [ə·mʌŋst] *prep.* 在……之中,在……之间(= among)

amount [ə·maunt] *n.* 总数;数量,总额;和;*vi.* 总计等于

ample[·æmpl] *adj.* 足够的;丰裕的;丰满的;硕大的

amuse [ə·mjuːz] *vt.* 逗乐;给……娱乐,消遣

analogy [ə·nælədʒi] *n.* 类比;比拟;比喻;类推

analyse(-ze) [·ænəlaiz] *vt.* 分析;分解;解析

analysis [ə·næləsis] *n.* 分析;分解;解析

ancestor [·ænsəstə] *n.* 祖宗,祖先;原种

anchor [·æŋkə] *n.* 铁锚;*vi.* 抛锚;停泊,用锚系住主持(广播电视新闻节目)

ancient [·einʃənt] *adj.* 古代的,古老的

and [ənd,ænd] *conj.* 和,又,并

angel [·eindʒəl] *n.* 天使,天使般的人;(名)安琪儿

anger [·æŋgə] *n.* 怒,愤怒;*vt.* 使发怒;激怒

angle [·æŋgl] *n.* 角;角度;角落;*vt.* 斜移;转变角度

angry [·æŋgri] *adj.* 愤怒的,生气的

animal [·ænimәl] *n.* 动物;兽,兽性

ankle [·æŋkəl] *n.* 踝,踝关节

anniversary [ˌænɪ·vɜːsəri] *n.* 周年纪念日

announce [ə·nauns] *vi.* 宣称;*vt.* 宣布,宣告;发表;通知

annoy [ə·nɔi] *vt.* 使恼怒,使生气;打搅;骚扰;使……苦恼

annual [·ænjuəl] *adj.* 每年的,年度的;*n.* 年报,年刊,年鉴

another [ə·nʌðə] *pron.* 另一个;又一,再一;不同的(人或事物)

answer [·ɑːŋsə] *n.* 答案;回答;反驳;回应;*vi.* 回答;*vt.* 回答,响应

ant [ænt] *n.* 蚂蚁

anticipate [æn·tisipeit] *vt.* 预料,预期;期望

antique [æn·tiːk] *adj.* 古老的;古董的;*n.* 文物;古物;古董;古玩

anxiety [æŋ·zaiəti] *n.* 焦虑,忧虑;渴望;担心

anxious [·æŋkʃəs] *adj.* 焦急的,忧虑的;渴望的

any [·eni] *adv.* (用于否定句或疑问句中,加强语气)完全(不),丝毫(不);*pron.* 任何数量;任一,任何一些

anybody [·eni. bɔdi,·enibədi] *pron.* 任何人

anyhow [·eniː. hau] *adv.* 无论如何,不管怎样

anyone [·eniwʌn] *pron.* 任何人

anything [·eni. θiŋ] *pron.* 任何事物,一切

anyway [·eniwei] *adv.* 无论如何,不管怎样

anywhere [·eniweə] *adv.* 在什么地方;任何地方

apart [ə·pɑːt] *adv.* 相隔,分开;分别地;有区别地

apartment [ə·pɑːtmənt] *n.* 一套公寓房间

apologise(-ze) [ə·pɔlədʒaiz] *vi.* 道歉,谢罪,认错

apology [ə·pɔlədʒi] *n.* 道歉,认错,谢罪

apparent [ə·pærənt] *adj.* 表面上的;明显的

appeal [əˈpiːl] *n.* 呼吁;申述;恳求;上诉;吸引力;*vi.* 求助;诉请;呼吁;申述;吸引
appear [əˈpiə] *vi.* 出现,来到,抵达;似乎,显得;出版
appearance [əˈpiərəns] *n.* 出现,出场,来到;外观
appendix [əˈpendɪks] *n.* 阑尾;(书、文件的)附录
appetite [ˈæpitait] *n.* 食欲,胃口;欲望
applaud [əˈplɔːd] *vt.* 鼓掌;称赞;赞许;赞赏
apple [ˈæpəl] *n.* 苹果,苹果树
application [ˌæpliˈkeiʃən] *n.* 应用;请求,申请;施用;应用软件程序
apply [əˈplai] *vt.* 应用,实施;使用;涂;使专心从事;*vi.* 申请
appoint [əˈpɔint] *vt.* 任命,委任;约定,指定;预约
appointment [əˈpɔintmənt] *n.* 任命;约定,约会;预约;委派官职
appreciate [əˈpriːʃieit] *vt.* 欣赏;感激;赏识;领会;感谢
approach [əˈprəutʃ] *n.* 接近;途径;方法;*vt.* 向……靠近,接近;动手处理
appropriate [əˈprəupriːət] *adj.* 适当的,恰当的,相称的;*vt.* 拨出(款项);占用
approval [əˈpruːvəl] *n.* 赞成,同意;批准;认可
approve [əˈpruːv] *vt.* 赞成;称许;批准,核准;证实;*vi.* 赞同
approximate [əˈprɔksimət] *adj.* 近似的,大约的;*vt.* 近似,接近,约等于
arch [ɑːtʃ] *n.* 拱(支撑如桥梁或房屋上部的弧形结构);拱门;足背;足弓;*vt.* (使)成弓形
architect [ˈɑːkɪtekt] *n.* 建筑师;设计师;缔造者;创造者
architecture [ˈɑːkitektʃə] *n.* 建筑学,建筑式样;建筑业;建筑物结构;[总称]建筑物;建筑风格
area [ˈeəriə] *n.* 面积;地区,区域,领域;方面
argue [ˈɑːgjuː] *vt.* 争论,辩论;争吵;劝说;表明;*vi.* 提出理由;争论,争辩,辩论
argument [ˈɑːgjumənt] *n.* 争论,辩论;理由,论点(据)
arise [əˈraiz] *vi.* 出现;由……引起;上升
arm [ɑːm] *n.* 手臂,臂状物;武器;扶手;袖子;*vt.* 装备;*vi.* 武装自己
army [ˈɑːmi] *n.* 军队,陆军;大群
around [əˈraund] *adj.* 大约;*adv.* 大约;到处;在周围;*prep.* 在……周围,在……附近;到处
arouse [əˈrauz] *vt.* 引起,唤起,唤醒;激发,激起;*vi.* 唤醒
arrange [əˈreindʒ] *vt.* 筹备,整理;安排;*vi.* 协商;计划
arrest [əˈrest] *n.* 逮捕,监禁;*vt.* 逮捕,拘留
arrival [əˈraivəl] *n.* 到达,到来,到达者
arrive [əˈraiv] *vi.* 到达,来临,达到
arrow [ˈærəu] *n.* 箭,箭头,箭状物
art [ɑːt] *n.* 艺术,美术
article [ˈɑːtikəl] *n.* 文章;条款;物品;冠词
artificial [ˈɑːtiˈfiʃəl] *adj.* 人工的,人造的;虚伪的;武断的;矫揉造作的
artist [ˈɑːtist] *n.* 艺术家,美术家,艺人
artistic [ɑːˈtistik] *adj.* 艺术的,艺术家的
as [æs] *adv.* 同样地,像;*prep.* 当作;*conj.* 当……的时候;像……一样;因为
ash [æʃ] *n.* 灰,灰烬,灰末,骨灰
ashamed [əˈʃeimd] *adj.* 惭愧(的),羞耻(的),感到惭愧,感到害臊
aside [əˈsaid] *adv.* 在旁边,到旁边;在一边
ask [ɑːsk] *vt.* 问,询问;要求;邀请,请求;开价;*vi.* 询问;恳求
asleep [əˈsliːp] *adj.* 睡着的,睡熟的;不活跃的,麻木的
aspect [ˈæspekt] *n.* 方面;样子,外表;外貌,外观;方位,方向
assemble [əˈsembəl] *vt.* 集合,召集;装配;*vi.* 集合,聚集
assembly [əˈsembli] *n.* 集合,集会;装配
assert [əˈsɜːt] *vt.* 明确肯定;断言;坚持自己的主张;表现坚定;维护自己的权利(或权威)
assess [əˈses] *vt.* 对(财产等)估价,估定,评定
asset [ˈæset] *n.* 有价值的人(或事物);有用的人(或事物);资产;财产
assignment [əˈsainmənt] *n.* 分配;功课,任务,被指定的(课外)作业;委派
assist [əˈsist] *vt.* 援助,帮助;*vi.* 帮助,协助
assistance [əˈsɪstəns] *n.* 帮助;援助;支持
assistant [əˈsistənt] *n.* 助手,助理,助教;*adj.* 副的,助理的
associate [əˈsəuʃieit] *vt.* 联合;联想;*vi.* 交往;陪同;*n.* 伙伴,同事,合伙人;准学士学位获得者;*adj.* 副的;有联系的
association [ə. səusiˈeiʃən] *n.* 协会;团体,社团;联合,结合;交往;联想
assume [əˈsjuːm] *vt.* 假定;设想;承担;呈现;(想当然的)认为
assure [əˈʃuə] *vt.* 使确信;向……保证;保险;保

证;确信;担保
astonish [əsˈtɔniʃ] *vt.* 使惊讶,使吃惊
at [æt] *prep.* 在……里,在……时
athlete [ˈæθlit,ˈæθliːt] *n.* 运动员,田径运动员
atmosphere [ˈætməsfiə] *n.* 大气,空气;气氛,格调
atom [ˈætəm] *n.* 原子,微粒,微量
attach [əˈtætʃ] *vt.* 缚,系,贴;附加;使依恋
attack [əˈtæk] *n.* 攻击,抨击;*vt.* 攻击,动手;疾病发作;*vi.* 发动攻击
attain [əˈtein] *vt.* 达到;获得;完成
attempt [əˈtempt] *vi.* 努力;尝试;*n.* 企图
attend [əˈtend] *vt.* 出席;照顾,护理,照料;参加;注意;*vi.* 专心;留意
attendant [əˈtendənt] *n.* 服务员;侍者;(要人的)侍从,随从;(病人的)护理者;*adj.* 伴随的;随之而来的
attention [əˈtenʃən] *n.* 注意(力);留心,关心;立正
attitude [ˈætitjuːd] *n.* 态度,看法;姿势
attorney [əˈtɜːni] *n.* 律师(尤指代表当事人出庭者);(业务或法律事务上的)代理人
attract [əˈtrækt] *vt.* 吸引;引起;诱惑,有吸引力
attractive [əˈtræktiv] *adj.* 有吸引力的,引起注意的
attribute [ˈætribjuːt,əˈtribjuːt] *vt.* 把……归因于;属于;*n.* 属性,特征
audience [ˈɔːdiəns] *n.* 听众,观众;读者;拥护
aunt [ɑːnt] *n.* 伯母,婶母,姑母,姨
aural [ˈɔːrəl] *adj.* 耳的,听觉的
authentic [ɔːˈθentɪk] *adj.* 真正的;真品的;真迹的;真实的;逼真的
author [ˈɔːθə] *n.* 作者;作家;创造者;*vt.* 著作;写作
authority [əˈθɔriti] *n.* 当局,官方;权力,权威;专家,权威人士
auto(mobile) [ˈɔːtəməbiːl] *n.* 汽车
automatic [ˌɔːtəˈmætik] *adj.* 自动的;机械的;半自动化的;*n.* 自动装置,半自动武器
autumn [ˈɔːtəm] *n.* 秋,秋季,秋天
available [əˈveiləbəl] *adj.* 可利用的,可得到的;有用的,有效的,通用的
avenue [ˈævənjuː,ˈævinjuː] *n.* 林荫道,道路,大街;途径,手段
average [ˈævəridʒ] *n.* 平均数,平均水平;
adj. 平均的;一般的,通常的;*vt.* 取平均值,达到平均水平
avoid [əˈvɔid] *vt.* 避免;躲开,逃避;撤销
await [əˈweit] *vt.* 等候;期待;准备……以待
awake [əˈweik] *adj.* 醒着的;警惕的;*vt.* 唤醒,唤起;激发;*vi.* 醒来,恢复意识
award [əˈwɔːd] *n.* 奖,奖品;判定;*vi.* 授予,给予;*vt.* 授予
aware [əˈweə] *adj.* 知道的,意识到的
away [əˈwei] *adv.* 离开,远离;出去;遥远地
awful [ˈɔːfl] *adj.* 令人不愉快的;可怕的,畏惧的;*adv.* 极其

B

baby [ˈbeibi] *adj.* 小型的;幼嫩的;*n.* 婴儿;孩子气的人,像婴儿的人;*vt.* 溺爱
bachelor [ˈbætʃələ(r)] *n.* 未婚男子;单身汉;学士
back [bæk] *adj.* 后面的;过时的;向后的;
adv. 在后;回原处;向后地;*n.* 后背,背脊;后面;靠背;*vt.* 后退;支持;*vi.* 后退
background [ˈbækgraund] *n.* 背景;经历
backward(s) [ˈbækwədz] *adv.* 倒,向后
bacon [ˈbeɪkən] *n.* 咸猪肉;熏猪肉
bad [bæd] *adj.* 坏的,恶的;严重的;令人不满意的;有害的;*n.* 坏人,坏事
badly [ˈbædli] *adv.* 坏,差;严重地;恶劣地;极度地
badminton [ˈbædmintən] *n.* 羽毛球
bag [bæg] *n.* 袋,包;钱包;背包;*vt.* 把……装入袋中
baggage [ˈbægidʒ] *n.* 行李
bake [beik] *vt.* 烤,烘焙;烧硬;*vi.* 烘焙,烤;变得炎热
bakery [ˈbeɪkəri] *n.* 面包(糕饼)店;面包(糕饼)烘房;面包厂
balance [ˈbæləns] *vt.* 使平衡;称重量;权衡;抵消;*vi.* 平衡,均衡;*n.* 平衡
balcony [ˈbælkəni] *n.* 阳台;(剧院的)楼厅,楼座
bald [bɔːld] *adj.* 秃顶的;秃头的;无毛的;无茸毛的;光秃的;不加赘述的;简单的;赤裸裸的
ball [bɔːl] *n.* 球,球状物;舞会;*v.* (把……捏)成球状

ballet[ˈbæleɪ] *n.* 芭蕾舞;芭蕾舞剧;芭蕾舞团
balloon [bəˈluːn] *n.* 气球,玩具气球;*vt.* 使膨胀;*vi.* 如气球般膨胀,激增
ban [bæn] *v.* 明令禁止;取缔;禁止(某人)做某事(或去某处等);*n.* 禁令
banana [bəˈnɑːnə] *n.* 香蕉
band [bænd] *n.* 乐队;带;波段;队;*vt.* 分等级,划分档次
bandage [ˈbændɪdʒ] *n.* 绷带;*v.* 用绷带包扎
bang [bæŋ] *n.* (突然)巨响;枪声;猛击,重击;*vt.* 重击;敲;*vi.* 大声敲击,发出巨响
bank [bæŋk] *n.* 银行;库;岩堤;*vt.* 堆积;*vi.* 开户,把……存入银行
bankrupt[ˈbæŋkrʌpt] *adj.* 破产;倒闭;*n.* (经法院判决的)破产者;*v.* 使破产
banner [ˈbænə] *n.* 旗,旗帜;横幅;大标题
banquet [ˈbæŋkwɪt] *n.* 宴会;盛宴;筵席
bar [bɑː] *n.* 酒吧间;条,杆,栅,横木;*vt.* 禁止,阻挠
barbecue [ˈbɑːbɪkjuː] *n.* (户外烧烤用的)烤架;户外烧烤;*v.* (在烤架上)烤,烧烤
barber [ˈbɑːbə] *n.* 理发师
bare [bɛə] *adj.* 赤裸的;显露的;仅够的;最基本的;*vt.* 使赤裸露出
barely [ˈbeəli] *adv.* 仅仅;刚刚;勉强可能;几乎不;几乎没有
bargain [ˈbɑːgən] *n.* 交易;物美价廉的东西;*vi.* 议价;成交
bark [bɑːk] *n.* 吠叫声,狗叫;咆哮;厉声说话;*vi.* 吠;叫;咆哮;急促地说
barn [bɑːn] *n.* 谷仓;牲口棚
barrel[ˈbærəl] *n.* 桶,圆筒;枪管,炮管,笔管;一桶的量;汽油桶;*vt.* 高速行进,飞奔
barrier [ˈbæriə] *n.* 栅栏;屏障,障碍,障碍物;界线
base [beis] *n.* 基础,底层;基地;(支持、收入、力量等的)基础;*vt.* 以……作基础;*adj.* 卑鄙的,不道德的
baseball[ˈbeɪsbɔːl] *n.* 棒球运动;棒球
basement [ˈbeɪsmənt] *n.* 地下室
basic [ˈbeisik] *n.* 基本,实质性的东西;基础训练;*adj.* 基本的;基础的
basin [ˈbeisən] *n.* 盆,洗脸盆;盆地;水池
basis [ˈbeisis] *n.* 基础;根据;主要成分
basket [ˈbɑːskit] *n.* 篮,篓,筐;篮球筐
basketball [ˈbɑːskitbɔːl] *n.* 篮球,篮球运动
bat [bæt] *n.* 球拍;短棍,棒;击打;蝙蝠;*v.* 用棒击打
bath [bɑːθ] *n.* 浴,洗澡;洗澡水;浴缸,浴室;*vt.* 洗澡
bathe [beið] *vt.* 给……洗澡;弄湿;沐浴,用水洗;沉浸
bathroom [ˈbɑːθrum,-ruːm] *n.* 浴室,盥洗室
battery [ˈbætəri] *n.* 电池;一套,一组,一系列;排炮
battle [ˈbætl] *n.* 战役,斗争;争论;*vi.* 与……作战,与……斗争
bay[beɪ] *n.* (海或湖的)湾;分隔间(户外或室内的,用以停放车辆、存放货物等);*vi.* (尤指捕猎时)发出长嗥,低沉地吠叫;*adj.* 深棕色的;枣红色的
Be(**am**,**is**,**are**) [biː] aux. *v.* & *vi.* 是;在;做;有
beach [biːtʃ] *n.* 海滩,湖滩,河滩;*vt.* 拖(船)上岸
beam [biːm] *n.* 梁,横梁;束;柱;光线;电波;笑容;*vi.* 微笑;发光
bean [biːn] *n.* 豆,菜豆;豆科植物
bear [beə(r)] *n.* 熊;*vt.* 忍受;负荷;结果实;生子女
beard [biəd] *n.* 胡须,络腮胡子
beast [biːst] *n.* 兽,野兽,牲畜;凶残的人;令人厌憎的人
beat [biːt] *n.* 打,敲打声;拍子;*vt.* & *vi.* 打,敲;打败
beautiful [ˈbjuːtifəl] *adj.* 美的,美丽的,漂亮的
beauty [ˈbjuːti] *n.* 美,美丽;美人,美的东西
because [biˈkɔz] *conj.* 由于;因为
become [biˈkʌm] *vt.* 变得;*vi.* 变成,成为,变得
bed [bed] *n.* 床,床位;圃;河床;层,基座;*vt.* 铺床;*vi.* 铺床;去睡觉
bedroom [ˈbedruːm] *n.* 卧室;
bee [biː] *n.* 蜂,蜜蜂;忙碌的人
beef [biːf] *n.* 牛肉;*v.* 抱怨;诉苦
beer [biə] *n.* 啤酒
before [biˈfɔː] *adv.* 以前;在……之前;*prep.* & *conj.* 在……以前向……
beg [beg] *vt.* 乞讨;恳求;*vi.* 行乞,乞求
begin [biˈgin] *vi.* 开始,起初是
beginning [biˈginiŋ] *n.* 开始,开端,起源;早期
behalf [biˈhɑːf] *n.* 代表(或代替)某人;为了某人
behave [biˈheiv] *vi.* 表现,举止,行为;举止端正;运转
behavior [biˈheivjə] *n.* 行为,举止;态度
behind [biˈhaind] *adv.* 在后面,落后,迟地;*n.* 屁股;*prep.* 在……后面,落后于

being [ˈbiːiŋ] *n.* 存在;生物,生命,人
belief [biˈliːf] *n.* 信任,相信;信念,信仰
believe [biˈliːv] *vt.* 相信,认为
bell [bel] *n.* 钟,铃,门铃,钟声;花冠
belong [biˈlɔŋ] *vi.* 属于;附属
beloved [biˈlʌvid] *adj.* 为……的爱的,心爱的;*n.* 心爱的人
below [biˈləu] *adv.* 在下面;向下;下级;*prep.* 在……下面(以下);(级别、重要性)低于
belt [belt] *n.* 带(状物);腰带,皮带;区;*vt.* 击打
bench [bentʃ] *n.* 长凳,条凳;工作台;梯田
bend [bend] *vt.* 使弯曲;*vi.* 弯曲;屈服;*n.* 弯曲(物);弯道
beneath [biˈniːθ] *prep.* 在……下方,在……之下
benefit [ˈbenifit] *n.* 利益,恩惠;津贴;义卖,义演;*vt.* 有益于;*vi.* 得益
beside [biˈsaid] *prep.* 在……旁边
besides [biˈsaidz] *adv.* 而且;也;此外;*prep.* 除……之外
best [best] *adj.* 最好的,最合适的;*adv.* 最,最好地;*n.* 最好的人(或物);*vt.* 打败,胜过
bet [bet] *n.* 打赌,赌注;最大的可能;*vi.* 下注;*vt.* 打赌
betray [biˈtrei] *vt.* 出卖,背叛;辜负
better [ˈbetə] *adj.* 较好的,更好的;*adv.* 更好地;*v.* 使……更好,超越;*n.* 更好的事物
between [biˈtwiːn] *adv.* 在中间;*prep.* 在……中间
beverage[ˈbevərɪdʒ] *n.* (除水以外的)饮料
beyond [biˈjɔnd] *adv.* 在更远处;另外;*prep.* 在……的那边;超出,越过;另外
bias[ˈbaɪəs] *n.* 偏见;偏心;偏向;偏爱;特殊能力;*vt.* 使有偏见;使偏心;使偏向
Bible [ˈbaibl] *n.* 基督教的《圣经》
bicycle(=**bike**) [ˈbaisik(ə)l] *n.* 自行车,脚踏车;*v.* 骑自行车
bid [bɪd] *vi.* 出(价);(尤指拍卖中)喊价;投标;努力争取;企图获得;*n.* 买方的出价;投标;努力争取
big [big] *adj.* 大的;巨大的;重要的;*adv.* 大大地;给人印象深刻地
bill [bil] *n.* 账单;钞票;招贴;票据,清单;议案,法案;*vt.* 开账单;用海报宣传
billion [ˈbiljən] num.　十亿
bind [baind] *vt.* 捆绑,包扎;装订;约束,约束
biology [baiˈɔlədʒi] *n.* 生物学,生态学
bird [bəːd] *n.* 鸟,家禽
birth [bəːθ] *n.* 分娩,出生,诞生;出身,血统;起源
birthday [ˈbəːθdei] *n.* 生日,诞生的日期
biscuit [ˈbiskit] *n.* (英)饼干;(美)软饼
bit [bit] *n.* 一点,少量,一些,小片;比特(二进位制信息单位),位
bite [bait] *n.* 咬;一口,少量食物;咬伤的伤口;*vt.* 咬,叮,螯;刺穿;*vi.* 咬(饵);使剧痛;紧抓
bitter [ˈbitə] *adj.* 苦的,痛苦的;剧烈的;严寒的;*n.* 苦涩的东西
black [blæk] *adj.* 黑的,暗的;邪恶的;阴沉的;*n.* 黑色东西,黑色;黑人;*v.* (使)变黑,抹黑
blackboard [ˈblækbɔːd] *n.* 黑板
blade [bleid] *n.* 刀刃,刀片;叶片;刀锋
blame [bleim] *n.* 过失;责备;*vt.* 责备,把……归咎于
blank [blæŋk] *adj.* 空白的;茫然的,面无表情的;*n.* 空白(处),空隙;空虚;*vt.* 使模糊不清
blanket [ˈblæŋkit] *n.* 毛毯,羊毛毯;覆盖物;*vt.* 用毯子裹;挡风;覆盖
blast [blɑːst] *n.* 爆炸;冲击波,气流;一阵;汽笛声;*vi.* 爆破;突然发出声音
bleed [bliːd] *vi.* 出血,流血;*vt.* 放血;勒索钱财;使……流血
blend [blend] *vt.* & *vi.* 混合;*n.* 混合物
bless [bles] *vt.* 为……祝福,赐福;祈佑;称颂上帝,
blind [blaind] *adj.* 瞎的;盲目的;未察觉的;*n.* 百叶窗;*vt.* 使失明;*adv.* 盲目地
block [blɔk] *n.* 街区;木块;石块;阻塞(物),障碍(物);*vt.* 堵塞拦阻
blog [blɒg] *n.* 网志;博客
blood [blʌd] *n.* 血,血液;血统
bloody [ˈblʌdi] *adj.* 血腥的;残暴的;血淋淋的;流血的
bloom [bluːm] *n.* 花,开花,开花期;兴旺;*vi.* 开花
blossom [ˈblɔsəm] *n.* 花,开花,全盛期;*vi.* 开花
blouse[blaʊz] *n.* (女式)短上衣,衬衫
blow [bləu] *vi.* 吹,吹动;吹响;打击,殴打;*vt.* 吹,风吹;擤(鼻子)
blue [bluː] *adj.* 蓝色的;沮丧的,忧郁的;*n.* 蓝色
blush [blʌʃ] *vi.* (因尴尬或害羞)脸红,涨红了脸;(因某事)羞愧,尴尬;*n.* (因难堪、羞愧)面部泛起的红晕
board [bɔːd] *n.* 板,木板,甲板;董事会;伙食;船舷;*vt.* 上(飞机、船、车等)用木板覆盖;*vi.* 有

偿提供食宿
boast [bəust] *n.* 吹牛;*vi.* 吹牛,自夸;*vt.* 吹牛,吹嘘
boat [bəut] *n.* 小船,艇,渔船,船型物体
body [ˈbɔdi] *n.* 身体;主体;尸体;正文
boil [bɔil] *n.* 沸腾;沸点;*vi.* 沸腾;*vt.* 煮沸
bold [bəuld] *adj.* 大胆的,冒失的;粗体的,醒目的;无礼的;陡峭的
bomb [bɔm] *n.* 炸弹;轰炸;*vt.* 轰炸
bond [bɔnd] *n.* 联结,联系,结合;公债,债券
bone [bəun] *n.* 骨,骨骼;核心;*vt.* 除去骨头
bonus [ˈbəʊnəs] *n.* 奖金;红利;意外收获
book [buk] *n.* 书,书籍;*vt.* 预定;登记;
vi. 通过……预订
boom [buːm] *n.* (贸易和经济活动的)激增,繁荣;(某种体育运动、音乐等)突然风靡的时期;
vi. 轰鸣;轰响;迅速发展;激增;繁荣昌盛
boost [buːst] *vt.* 使增长;使兴旺;*n.* 帮助;激励;增长;提高
boot [buːt] *n.* 靴子,长筒靴;(英)汽车行李箱;
vt. 踢
booth [buːθ] *n.* 货摊;公用电话亭;小间
border [ˈbɔːdə] *n.* 边,边缘;边界;*vt.* 和……毗邻;与……接壤
bore [bɔː] *vt.* 忍受(动词 bear 过去式);*n.* 令人讨厌的人;*vt.* 使厌烦;钻,挖;*vi.* 挖掘,开凿
bored [bɔːd] *adj.* (对某人/事物)厌倦的;烦闷的
boring [ˈbɔːrɪŋ] *adj.* 没趣的;令人厌倦(或厌烦)的
born [bɔːn] 动词 bear 的过去分词;*adj.* 天生的;出生的;与生俱来的
borrow [ˈbɔrəu] *vt.* 借,借用,借入
boss [bɔs] *n.* 老板,上司;*vt.* 指挥;控制
botany [ˈbɒtəni] *n.* 植物学
both [bəuθ] *pron.* 两者(都)
bother [ˈbɔðe] *vt.* 烦扰;迷惑;*vi.* 烦扰;操心;
n. 麻烦;烦扰
bottle [ˈbɔtl] *n.* 瓶,酒瓶;一瓶;*vt.* 装瓶
bottom [ˈbɔtəm] *n.* 底,底部,根基;臀部;水底;低洼地;尽头;*adj.* 底部的;*vi.* 降到最低点
bounce [bauns] *n.* 跳,弹力;*vt.* 弹跳;*vi.* 反跳,弹起,跳起
bound [baund] *n.* 跳跃;*adj.* 一定的,必定的;有义务的,受约束的
boundary [ˈbaundri] *n.* 分界线,边界
bow [bəu,bau] *n.* 弓;蝴蝶结;鞠躬;船头;
vi. 鞠躬;成弓形;弯腰;屈服,听从;*vt.* 使弯曲;低头
bowl [bəul] *n.* 碗,钵,碗状物;*vi.* 快速移动;
vt. 投球;投球得分
bowling [ˈbəʊlɪŋ] *n.* 保龄球运动
box [bɔks] *n.* 箱,盒,包箱;专席;*vt.* 装……入盒中;用拳击打……
boy [bɔi] *n.* 男孩;儿子;家伙
brain [brein] *n.* 脑,脑髓;脑力,智力;
vt. 打……的脑袋
brake [breik] *n.* 闸;刹车;制动器;
vt. & vi. 制动;刹车
branch [brɑːntʃ] *n.* 分支;树枝;分部;
vt. & vi. 分支,分岔
brand [brænd] *n.* 商标,牌子;烙印;类型;
vt. 铭刻;打烙印
brass [brɑːs] *n.* 黄铜(制品),黄铜器;铜管(乐器)
brave [breiv] *adj.* 勇敢的;*n.* 勇敢的人
bread [bred] *n.* 面包;食物,粮食;生计
break [breik] *n.* 休息;中断;破裂;*vt.* 打破;损坏,弄破,弄坏,破坏
breakdown [ˈbreɪkdaʊn] *n.* (车辆或机器的)故障,损坏;(关系的)破裂;(讨论、系统的)失败
breakfast [ˈbrekfəst] *n.* 早饭,早餐;*vi.* 吃早餐
breakthrough [ˈbreɪkθruː] *n.* 重大进展;突破
breast [brest] *n.* 乳房;胸脯,胸膛
breath [breθ] *n.* 气息,呼吸;气味
breathe [briːe] *vi.* 呼吸;*vt.* 呼吸
breed [briːd] *n.* 品种,族类;*vt.* 使繁殖,养育,繁殖;*vi.* 繁殖
brick [brik] *n.* 砖,砖块,砖状物;积木;
vt. (up)用砖砌补,用砖堵住
bride [braɪd] *n.* 新娘
bridegroom [ˈbraɪdgruːm] *n.* 新郎
bridge [bridʒ] *n.* 桥,桥梁;桥牌;鼻梁;
vt. 渡过;架桥
brief [briːf] *n.* 摘要;简报;*adj.* 简短的,简洁的;短暂的;*vt.* 作简报;简单讨论
bright [brait] *adj.* 明亮的,阳光的;生动的;聪明的;*adv.* 光亮地;明亮地
brilliant [ˈbriljənt] *adj.* 光辉的;卓越的;灿烂的;有才气的,杰出的
bring [briŋ] *vt.* 带来;引出;促使;劝诱
broad [brɔːd] *adj.* 宽广的,阔的;广泛的;明显的
broadcast [ˈbrɔːdkɑːst] *n.* 广播,广播节目,播音;*vt. & vi.* 广播
brochure [ˈbrəʊʃə(r)] *n.* 资料(或广告)手册

broom [bruːm] *n.* 扫帚
brother [ˈbrʌðə] *n.* 兄弟;同事;同胞
brow [brau] *n.* 额;额头
brown [braun] *adj.* 褐色的;棕色的;*n.* 褐色;棕色
brush [brʌʃ] *n.* 刷子,毛刷;画笔;轻擦;*vt.* 用刷子清洗;画;拭去;*vi.* 轻擦,拂拭
bubble [ˈbʌbl] *n.* 泡,泡沫,气泡;幻想;*vi.* 冒泡,沸腾起泡;*vt.* 使冒泡
bud [bʌd] *n.* 芽,萌芽,蓓蕾;*vi.* 发芽,萌芽
budget [ˈbʌdʒɪt] *n.* 预算;政府的年度预算;*vt.* 谨慎花钱;把……编入预算;*adj.* 价格低廉的;花钱少的
buffet[ˈbʌfeɪ, ˈbʌfɪt] *n.* 自助餐;(火车)饮食柜台;(车站)快餐部;
build [bild] *vt. & vi.* 建筑;建立,创立;建造;开发;逐渐增强;*n.* 体格,身材
building [ˈbildiŋ] *n.* 建筑物,大楼;建筑
bulb [bʌlb] *n.* 电灯泡;球状物
bull [bul] *n.* 公牛;斗牛犬
bullet [ˈbulit] *n.* 枪弹,子弹,弹丸
bulletin [ˈbʊlətɪn] *n.* (电台或电视台的)新闻简报;公告;布告;(机构或组织的)简报
bunch [bʌntʃ] *n.* 束,串,一群,一组;大量;*vi.* 使成一束(或一群等)
bundle [ˈbʌndl] *n.* 捆,包,束;包袱;一批;*vt.* 捆
burden [ˈbəːdn] *n.* 担子,负担,重担;装载量;*vt.* 使负重;装载烦扰
bureau [ˈbjuərəu] *n.* 局,司,处,社,所,办公处
burn [bəːn] *vt. & vi.* 烧;燃烧;烧着;烧毁;灼伤;*n.* 烧伤;灼伤
burst [bəːst] *n.* 破裂;阵;爆发;*vt. & vi.* 爆裂;突发
bury [ˈberi] *vt.* 埋葬;埋藏
bus [bʌs] *n.* 公共汽车
bush [buʃ] *n.* 灌木,灌木丛;矮树
business [ˈbiznis] *n.* 商业;生意;事务
busy [ˈbizi] *adj.* 忙的,繁忙的;*vt.* 使忙于做某事
but [bʌt] *adv.* 仅仅,只;*conj.* 但是,可是;*prep.* 除……以外
butter [ˈbʌtə] *n.* 黄油;*vt.* 涂黄油
butterfly [ˈbʌtəflai] *n.* 蝴蝶,蝶状物;蝶泳
button [ˈbʌtn] *n.* 扣子;按钮;像纽扣的东西;*vt.* 扣紧;用纽扣装饰,钉纽扣;*vi.* 扣上
buy [bai] *n.* 购买;购买的东西;*vt.* 买,购买;收买
by [bai] *prep.* 在……旁;被;由,经由;在……之前;根据;*adv.* 靠近;经过;放在一旁地
bye [baɪ] int. 再见;再会

C

cab [kæb] *n.* 出租汽车;计程车;的士
cabbage [ˈkæbidʒ] *n.* 洋白菜　卷心菜
cabin [ˈkæbin] *n.* 小木屋;船舱;机舱
cabinet [ˈkæbinit] *n.* 橱,柜;内阁
cable [ˈkeibl] *n.* 缆,索,电缆;电报;*vt.* 打电报;*vi.* 打电报
cafe [ˈkæfei] *n.* 咖啡馆,小餐厅
cafeteria [ˌkæfiˈtiəriə] *n.* 自助食堂
cage [keidʒ] *n.* 笼,鸟笼;囚笼,监狱;笼状结构;*vt.* 关入笼中
cake [keik] *n.* 饼,糕,蛋糕;块状物;小菜一碟(容易做成的事)
calculate [ˈkælkjuleit] *vt.* 计算,估计;考虑;推测
calendar [ˈkælində] *n.* 日历,月历;日程表;历书,历法
call [kɑːl] *n.* 呼叫;访问;打电话;请求;把……看作;*vt.* 把……叫作;叫喊,呼叫;访问;打电话;*vi.* (短暂的)拜访;呼叫
calm [kɑːm] *n.* 平稳;宁静的状态;*adj.* 静的,平静的;冷静的;*vt. & vi.* 平静下来,镇静
calorie[ˈkæləri] *n.* 卡,卡路里(热量单位)
camel [ˈkæməl] *n.* 骆驼
camera [ˈkæmərə] *n.* 照相机,摄影机
camp [kæmp] *n.* 野营,营地;兵营;露营;训练营;*vt. & vi.* 露营,扎营
campaign [kæmˈpein] *n.* 战役;运动;活动;*vt.* 参加竞赛;*vi.* (从事、组织)活动
campus [ˈkæmpəs] *n.* 校园;学校场地
can [kæn] aux. *v.* 能,会;可能;*n.* 罐头,听,容器;*vt.* 罐装
canal [kəˈnæl] *n.* 运河;沟渠;管,气管,食管
cancel [ˈkænsl] *vt.* 取消,撤销;删去;*vi.* 抵消
cancer [ˈkænsə] *n.* 癌,癌症,肿瘤
candidate [ˈkændidit] *n.* 候选人;投考者;求职者

candle [ˈkændl] *n.* 蜡烛,烛形物;烛光
candy [ˈkændi] *n.* 糖果
canteen [kænˈtiːn] *n.* 食堂
cap [kæp] *n.* 帽子,便帽,帽状物;盖子;顶;*vt.* 覆盖顶端
capable [ˈkeipəbl] *adj.* 有能力的,有才能的;足以胜任的
capacity [kəˈpæsiti] *n.* 容量;能力;能量;容积;
capital [ˈkæpitl] *n.* 资本,资金;首都;大写字母;*adj.* 大写的
capsule [ˈkæpsjuːl] *n.* (装药物的)胶囊;(装物或装液体的)小塑料容器;太空舱;航天舱
captain [ˈkæptin] *n.* 陆军上尉;队长;船长;首领;*vt.* 担任队长(或船长)
capture [ˈkæptʃə] *n.* 抓取;战利品,捕获之物;*vt.* 捕获,俘获,夺得;抓取,获得;迷住
car [kɑː] *n.* 汽车,小汽车,轿车
carbon [ˈkɑːbən] *n.* 碳;复写纸
card [kɑːd] *n.* 卡,卡片;名片;纸牌
care [k ɛə] *n.* 小心;照料;忧虑;*vi.* 关心;照顾;喜爱;*vt.* 介意
career [kəˈriə] *n.* 生涯;职业,事业;经历
careful [ˈkɛəfəl] *adj.* 小心的,仔细的;细致的
careless [ˈkɛəlis] *adj.* 粗心的,漫不经心的,疏忽的
cargo [ˈkɑːgəu] *n.* 船货,货物
carpet [ˈkɑːpit] *n.* 地毯,毡毯,毛毯;*vt.* 铺以地毯,铺盖
carriage [ˈkæridʒ] *n.* 客车厢;四轮马车
carrot [ˈkærət] *n.* 胡萝卜
carry [ˈkæri] *vt.* 负载,承担;携带;运载;传送,传播
cart [kɑːt] *n.* (二轮或四轮)运货马车;手推车;*vt.* 用马车装载
cartoon [kɑːˈtuːn] *n.* (报刊中与政治或时事有关的)漫画,讽刺画;动画片;卡通片;草图
carve [kɑːv] *vt.* 刻,雕刻;切开;*vi.* 雕刻;切割
case [keis] *n.* 情况;事实,实情;病例;箱(子),盒(子);案例
cash [kæʃ] *n.* 现金,现款;*vt.* 兑现,付现款
cashier [kæˈʃɪə(r)] *n.* 出纳员
cassette [kəˈset] *n.* 盒式录音带
cast [kɑːst] *n.* 演员阵容;投掷;*vt.* 投,扔,抛
castle [ˈkɑːsl] *n.* 城堡;巨大建筑物
casual [ˈkæʒjuəl] *adj.* 偶然的;随便的,非正式;漫不经心的
casualty [ˈkæʒuəlti] *n.* (战争或事故的)伤员,亡者,遇难者;受害者;毁坏物;损坏物
cat [kæt] *n.* 猫,猫科
catalog [ˈkætələːg] *n.* 目录,目录册;商品型录;*vt.* 做目录,分类说明;名入列表
catch [kætʃ] *n.* 捕捉;陷阱;捕获物;接(球等);*vt.* 捉住,赶上;领会,了解;感染;察觉
category [ˈkætəgəri] *n.* (人或事物的)类别,种类
Catholic [ˈkæθlɪk] *n.* 天主教信徒
cattle [ˈkætl] *n.* 牛,牲口,家畜;牲畜(复数)
cause [kɔːz] *n.* 原因,理由;事业;*vt.* 引起,使发生
caution [ˈkɔːʃn] *n.* 谨慎;小心;慎重;;(对危险或风险的)警告,告诫;*vt.* 警告;告诫;提醒;
cautious [ˈkɔːʃəs] *adj.* 小心的;谨慎的
cave [keiv] *n.* 山洞,洞穴,窑洞;*vi.* 塌落
cease [siːs] *vi.* & *vi.* 停止,终了,停息
ceiling [ˈsiːliŋ] *n.* 天花板,顶篷
celebrate [ˈselibreit] *vt.* 庆祝;歌颂,赞美;*vi.* 庆祝,祝贺;颂扬
celebrity [səˈlebrəti] *n.* 名人;名流;名望;名誉;著名
cell [sel] *n.* 细胞;小房间;电池;小组;单人牢房;(蜂房的)巢室;手机
cellar [ˈselə] *n.* 地窖,地下室
cellphone (= **cellular phone**) [ˈselfəʊn] *n.* 手机;移动电话
cement [siˈment] *n.* 水泥;胶泥;接合剂;*vt.* 黏结,接合;用水泥涂
cent [sent] *n.* 分,分币;百(分之)
centigrade [ˈsentigreid] *adj.* 百分度的;摄氏的
centimetre [ˈsenti. miːtə] *n.* 厘米 = centimeter(美)
central [ˈsentrəl] *adj.* 中心的;主要的;基本的;中枢的
centre (er) [ˈsentə] *n.* 中心;中枢;聚集点;*vt.* 集中;置于中央;关注于
century [ˈsentʃuri] *n.* 世纪,一百年;成百的东西
ceremony [ˈseriməni] *n.* 典礼,仪式;礼节,礼仪
certain [ˈsəːtn] *adj.* 确实的,肯定的;必然的;特定的;*pron.* 某几个,某些
certainly [ˈsəːtənli] *adv.* 一定,必定,当然
certainty [ˈsəːtnti] *n.* 必然,肯定,确定,确实的事情
certificate [səˈtifikit] *n.* 证(明)书,证件;执照;*vt.* 批准,认可;发结业(或职业培训)证书给……
chain [tʃein] *n.* 链,链条;项圈;连锁;束缚;*vt.* 用铁链锁住;束缚囚禁

chair [tʃɛə] *n.* 椅子;主席;席位;要职;*vt.* 上任,使担任(某事务)的主席;主持

chairman [ˈtʃɛəmən] *n.* 主席;议长;会长

chalk [tʃɔːk] *n.* 白垩;粉笔;*v.* 用粉笔写;记录

challenge [ˈtʃælindʒ] *n.* 挑战;要求,需要;*v.* 向……挑战

chamber [ˈtʃeimbə] *n.* 会议室;房间,会所,室;腔

champion [ˈtʃæmpjən] *n.* 冠军,得胜者;拥护者;勇士;*vt.* 保卫;拥护

chance [tʃɑːns] *n.* 机会;运气;风险;可能性;*vi.* 偶然发生;*vt.* 偶然发生;冒险

chancellor [ˈtʃɑːnsələ(r)] *n.* (德国或奥地利的)总理;(英国大学的)名誉校长;(某些美国大学的)校长

change [tʃeindʒ] *n.* 改变,变化;零钱;*vt. & vi.* 改变

channel [ˈtʃænl] *n.* 海峡;渠道;通道;频道;方法;*vt.* 引导;开导;形成河道;输送

chaos [ˈkeɪɒs] *n.* 混乱;杂乱;紊乱

chapter [ˈtʃæptə] *n.* 章,回,篇

character [ˈkæriktə] *n.* 性格,个性;品质,特性;角色;字符,人物

characterise (-ze) [ˈkærəktəraɪz] *vt.* 是……的特征;以……为典型;使……具有特点(或最引人注目的特征);描述,表现(……的特征、特点)

characteristic [ˌkæriktəˈristik] *adj.* 特有的;典型的;*n.* 特性;特征;特色

charge [tʃɑːdʒ] *vt. & vi.* 索价;控告;加罪于;要价;充电;*n.* 电荷;指控;费用;照管;主管

charity [ˈtʃæriti] *n.* 施舍;慈善事业;慈善,慈善机构(团体);仁慈,宽厚

charm[tʃɑːm] *n.* 魅力;魔力;吸引力;迷人的特征;吸引人的特性;妩媚

charming [ˈtʃɑːmɪŋ] *adj.* 令人着迷的;迷人的;吸引人的

chart [tʃɑːt] *n.* 图,图表;海图;*vt.* 记录,跟踪(进展);制订计划

chase [tʃeis] *n.* 追逐,追赶;追求;狩猎;争取;*vt.* 追捕,狩猎;努力获得,争取

chat[tʃæt] *vi.* 闲聊;闲谈;聊天;(尤指在网上聊天室)闲聊,交谈;*n.* 闲聊;闲谈;聊天;(尤指非正式的)谈话,讲话

cheap [tʃiːp] *adj.* 廉价的,便宜的;劣质的,品质低的

cheat [tʃiːt] *n.* 骗子;欺骗行为;*vt.* 骗取,哄;作弊;*vi.* 行骗作弊

check [tʃek] *vt.* 检查;核对;*n.* 检查;支票;账单

cheek [tʃiːk] *n.* 面颊,脸蛋;*vt.* 粗鲁地向……讲

cheer [tʃiə] *n.* 愉快;激励;欢呼;*vt.* 欢呼;加油;鼓舞;*vi.* 欢呼

cheese [tʃiːz] *n.* 乳酪,干酪

chef [ʃef] *n.* 厨师;(尤指餐馆、饭店等的)主厨,厨师长

chemical [ˈkemikəl] *adj.* 化学的;*n.* 化学制品

chemist [ˈkemist] *n.* 化学家,药剂师

chemistry [ˈkemistri] *n.* 化学

cheque [tʃek] *n.* 支票

cherish [ˈtʃerɪʃ] *vt.* 珍爱;钟爱;爱护;抱有(信念、希望);怀有(好感);怀念

cherry [ˈtʃeri] *n.* 樱桃,樱桃树,樱桃色;*adj.* 樱桃色的;鲜红色的

chess [tʃes] *n.* 国际象棋

chest [tʃest] *n.* 胸腔,胸膛

chew [tʃuː] *vt.* 咀嚼,嚼碎;损坏;*vi.* 咀嚼;*n.* 咀嚼,口香糖,糖果

chicken [ˈtʃikin] *n.* 小鸡;鸡肉;*adj.* 懦弱的;胆小的

chief [tʃiːf] *adj.* 主要的;首席的;*n.* 首领

child [tʃaild] *n.* 小孩,儿童;儿子,女儿

childhood [ˈtʃaildhud] *n.* 童年,幼年;孩童时期

chill [tʃil] *vt.* 使变冷,使……寒心;冷冻;使……惊恐;*n.* 寒冷,寒意;*adj.* 寒冷的

chimney [ˈtʃimni] *n.* 烟囱,烟筒

chin [tʃin] *n.* 颏,下巴

china [ˈtʃainə] *n.* 瓷器,瓷料

chip [tʃɪp] *n.* (木头、玻璃等的)缺口,缺损处;(木头、玻璃等上掉下来的)碎屑,碎片,碎渣;油炸土豆条;炸薯条;*vt. & vi.* 打破;弄缺;被损坏;切下,削下,凿下(碎片、屑片)

chocolate [ˈtʃɔkəlit] *n.* 巧克力,巧克力糖,巧克力饮品

choice [tʃɔis] *n.* 选择,挑选;抉择;*adj.* (尤指食物)优质的,优选的;上等的;精选的

choke [tʃəuk] *vt.* 使(某人)停止呼吸;塞满;*vi.* 窒息;阻塞;*n.* 窒息;阻风门开关,阻塞

choose [tʃuːz] *vt.* 选择,挑选;*vi.* 选择

chopsticks[ˈtʃɒpstɪks] *n.* 筷子

chorus[ˈkɔːrəs] *n.* 合唱曲;合唱团;*v.* 合唱;齐声说;异口同声地说

Christian [ˈkristʃən] *n.* 基督教徒,信徒;*adj.* 基督教(徒)的,信奉基督教的;仁慈的

Christmas [ˈkrisməs] *n.* 圣诞节

chronic [ˈkrɒnɪk] *adj.* 长期的;慢性的;难以治愈(或根除)的;长期患病的

church [tʃəːtʃ] *n.* 教堂,礼拜堂;礼拜仪式;

教会
cigar[sɪˈɡɑː(r)] *n.* 雪茄烟
cigarette [ˌsigəˈret] *n.* 香烟,纸烟,卷烟
cinema [ˈsinimə] *n.* 电影院;电影艺术,电影制片业
circle [ˈsəːkl] *n.* 圆,圆周;圈子,社交圈;循环;*vt. & vi.* 包围;盘旋,环绕
circular [ˈsəːkjulə] *adj.* 圆的;环形的;*n.* 传单,通报
circulate [ˈsəːkjuleit] *vt.* 使循环,使流通;*vi.* 流通;循环;传播
circumstance [ˈsəːkəmstəns] *n.* 情况,条件;境遇;环境(复数);境况
circus [ˈsɜːkəs] *n.* 马戏团;马戏表演(常在大帐篷里进行);引人注意的人(或事);热闹场面
cite [saɪt] *vt.* 提及(原因);举出(示例);列举;引用;引述;援引;传唤;传讯
citizen [ˈsitizn] *n.* 公民,市民,居民
city [ˈsiti] *n.* 城市,都市
civil [ˈsivil] *adj.* 国内的;公民的;有礼貌的;民事的
civilisation (**-zation**) [ˌsivilaiˈzeiʃən] *n.* 文明,文化,开化
civilise (**-ze**) [ˈsivilaiz] *vt.* 使文明;教育
claim [kleim] *vt.* 要求,请求;声称;主张,断言;索取;*n.* 要求,要求权;主张;断言,声称;要求物
clap [klæp] *vi.* 拍手;*vt.* 拍,轻拍,轻敲鼓掌,击掌;*n.* 拍手,拍手声
clarify [ˈklærifai] *vt.* 澄清;阐明,使……明晰
class [klɑːs] *n.* 班,班级;(等)阶级;种类;*vt.* 分类
classic [ˈklæsɪk] *adj.* 最优秀的;第一流的;有代表性的;典型的;(风格或设计)典雅的,古朴的;传统的;*n.* (书、电影或歌曲的)经典作品,名著,杰作;优秀的典范
classical [ˈklæsikəl] *adj.* 古典的;经典的;典雅的
classify [ˈklæsifai] *vt.* 把……分类,分类,归类
classmate [ˈklɑːsmeit] *n.* 同班同学
classroom [ˈklɑːsrum] *n.* 教室;课堂
clay [klei] *n.* 黏土;泥土;肉体
clean [kliːn] *adj.* 清洁的,干净的;纯洁的;正当的;*adv.* 完全地;*n.* 清洁;*vt. & vi.* 打扫;清扫
clear [kliə] *adj.* 清晰的,清楚的,明确;澄清的,头脑清醒的;*vt.* 清除,清除障碍;澄清;使明亮;明确;*vi.* 变清晰;(烟、雾等)消失;放晴;*adv.* 离开,不靠近,不能;一直(到远处)
clerk [klɑːk] *n.* 店员;办事员,职员
clever [ˈklevə] *adj.* 聪明的,机敏的
click [klɪk] *vi.* 使发出咔嗒声;使咔嗒(或咔嚓)响;(在计算机屏幕上用鼠标)点击,单击;被突然明白;*n.* 短而尖的声音;咔嗒声;(对计算机鼠标的)点按,单击
client[ˈklaɪənt] *n.* 委托人;当事人
cliff [klif] *n.* 悬崖,峭壁
climate [ˈklaimit] *n.* 气候;风土;气氛
climax [ˈklaɪmæks] *n.* (重要事情或时刻的)高潮;极点,顶点;(戏剧、音乐等通常接近结束时出现的)高潮;*vi. & vt.* 达成(或形成)极点(或顶点、高潮)
climb [klaim] *vt. & vi.* 攀登,爬;上升;*n.* 攀登;攀登用的时间
cling [klɪŋ] *vi. & vt.* 抓紧;紧握;紧抱;粘住;附着;(尤指情感上)依恋,依附
clinic[ˈklɪnɪk] *n.* 诊所;(医院的)门诊部;私人诊所;专科医院
clock [klɔk] *n.* 钟,时钟;计时器;仪表
clone [kləʊn] *n.* 克隆动物(或植物);无性繁殖动物(或植物);复制动物(或植物);复制品;仿造品;*vt.* 以无性繁殖技术复制;克隆;
close [kləus, kləuz] *vt.* 关闭;结束;靠近;*vi.* 关;停业;*n.* 完结;*adj.* 靠近的;亲近的;几乎;密切的;势均力敌的;*adv.* 紧挨着;紧紧地
cloth [klɔθ] *n.* 布,衣料;桌布
clothes [kləuðz] *n.* 衣服,服装
clothing [ˈkləuðiŋ] *n.* (总称)衣服
cloud [klaud] *n.* 云,云状物;云状的烟;阴影;*vt.* 使……模糊;以云遮蔽,笼罩;使……混淆
cloudy [ˈklaudi] *adj.* 多云的;云一般的
club [klʌb] *n.* 俱乐部,夜总会;扑克牌中的梅花;*vt.* 用棍棒打
clue [kluː] *n.* 线索;暗示,提示;*vt.* 给(某人)提供最新信息
clumsy [ˈklʌmzi] *adj.* 笨拙的;笨重的;愚笨的;不得体的
clutch[klʌtʃ] *vt. & vi.* 紧握;抱紧;抓紧;(因害怕或痛苦)突然抓住;*n.* (汽车等起换挡功能的)离合器踏板;一群(人或动物);一批(物品)
coach [kəutʃ] *n.* 长途公共汽车;大巴;教练;(火车)客车车厢四轮马车;经济舱;*vt.* & 训练,指导
coal [kəul] *n.* 煤,煤块;木炭
coarse [kɔːs] *adj.* 粗的,粗糙的;非精制的;粗俗的
coast [kəust] *n.* 海岸,海滨(地区);*vi.* 下滑
coat [kəut] *n.* 外套,上衣;表皮,动物皮毛;一

层;*vt.* 外面覆盖盖上毛衣
cock [kɔk] *n.* 公鸡;雄禽;*vt.* 立起;竖起
code [kəud] *n.* 码,密码;法规,准则;法典;代码;*vt.* 把……编码
coffee [ˈkɔfi] *n.* 咖啡,咖啡粉
coherent[kəʊˈhɪərənt] *adj.* 合乎逻辑的;有条理的;清楚易懂的;
coil [kɔɪl] *vt.* (使)缠绕,盘绕;*n.* (绳索、金属线等的)圈,卷,盘;一圈(绳索、金属线等);线圈
coin [kɔin] *n.* 硬币;金钱;货币;铸造(硬币);*vt.* 制造钱币;创造
coincide [ˌkəʊɪnˈsaɪd] *vi.* 同时发生;相同;相符;极为类似;相接;相交;同位;位置重合;重叠
coke [kəʊk] *n.* 焦炭
cold [kəuld] *adj.* 冷的;冷淡的,漠然的;*n.* 冷,感冒;低温;*adv.* 唐突地;即兴地
collaborate [kəˈlæbəreɪt] *vi.* 合作;协作;通敌;勾结敌人
collapse [kəˈlæps] *vi.* 倒坍;崩溃,瓦解;*n.* 崩溃;倒塌;暴跌
collar [ˈkɔlə] *n.* 衣领;项圈;*vt.* 抓住;捉住
colleague [ˈkɔliːg] *n.* 同事,同僚
collect [ˈkɔlekt,kəˈlekt] *vt.* 收集;募捐;*vi.* 聚集;积累;*adj.* & *adv.* 对方付费(的)
collection [kəˈlekʃən] *n.* 搜集,收集;收藏品;作品集
collective [kəˈlektiv] *adj.* 集体的;共同的;集合性的;*n.* 集体
college [ˈkɔlidʒ] *n.* 学院;学校;社团;
collision [kəˈliʒən] *n.* 碰撞;冲突
color [ˈkʌlə] *n.* 颜色;彩色;颜料;气色;*vt.* 把……涂颜色粉饰;*vi.* 脸红
colonial[kəˈləʊniəl] *adj.* 殖民的;殖民国家的
colony [ˈkɒləni] *n.* 殖民地;殖民地定居者群体;(来自同一地方,职业或兴趣相同的)聚居人群
comb [kəum] *n.* 梳子,梳状物;鸡冠;*vt.* 梳理;用梳子梳;*vi.* 搜寻
combat [ˈkɒmbæt] *n.* 搏斗;打仗;战斗;*vt.* 防止;减轻;战斗;与……搏斗
combination [ˌkɔmbiˈneiʃən] *n.* 结合,联合;联合体
combine [kəmˈbain] *vt.* 使结合;兼有;融合;联结;*vi.* 结合;联合
come [kʌm] *vi.* 来,来到;达到;出现;发生;进入
comedy[ˈkɒmədi] *n.* 喜剧;喜剧片;滑稽;幽默;诙谐
comfort[ˈkʌmfət] *n.* 舒适;安慰;令人感到安慰的人或事物;*vt.* 安慰
comic[ˈkɒmɪk] *adj.* 滑稽的;使人发笑的;喜剧的;*n.* 喜剧演员;(尤指儿童看的)连环画杂志;(报刊上的)连环漫画栏
command [kəˈmɑːnd] *vt.* 命令;指挥;控制;支配;*n.* 命令;指挥;控制
comment [ˈkɔment] *n.* 评论;意见;注释;闲话;*vi.* & *vt.* 注释;评论
commerce [ˈkɔməːs] *n.* 商业,贸易
commercial [kəˈməːʃəl] *adj.* 商业的,商品化的;*n.* 商业广告
commission [kəˈmiʃən] *n.* 委员会;佣金;*vt.* 委任;委托
commit [kəˈmit] *vt.* 犯(错误);干(坏事);委托(托付)
committee [kəˈmiti] *n.* 委员会;全体委员
commodity [kəˈmɒdəti] *n.* 商品;有用的东西
common [ˈkɔmən] *adj.* 普通的;共同的;平常的;*n.* 公共用地
communicate [kəˈmjuːnikeit] *vt.* & *vi.* 通讯;传达;传播沟通
communication [kəˌmjuːniˈkeiʃən] *n.* 通讯;传达;交通;信息;[计算机]通信
communism [ˈkɔmjunizəm] *n.* 共产主义
communist [ˈkɔmjunist] *n.* 共产党员;共产主义者
community [kəˈmjuːniti] *n.* 社区;团体;社会;公社;群落(生)
compact [kəmˈpækt, ˈkɒmpækt] *adj.* 小型的;袖珍的;紧凑的;体积小的;紧密的;坚实的;*n.* 协定;协议;契约;合约;*v.* 把……紧压在一起(或压实)
companion [kəmˈpænjən] *n.* 同伴;同事,共事者;伴侣
company [ˈkʌmpəni] *n.* 公司,商号;同伴;客人;一群人;
comparable [ˈkɒmpərəbl] *adj.* 类似的;可比较的
comparative[kəmˈpærətiv] *adj.* 比较的;相对的;*n.* (语法)比较级
compare [kəmˈpɛə] *vt.* & *vi.* 比较;对照;比作,比喻;*n.* 比较;对照
comparison [kəmˈpærisn] *n.* 比较;对照;
compartment [kəmˈpɑːtmənt] *n.* (铁路客车车厢分隔成的)隔间;(家具或设备等的)分隔间,隔层
compass [ˈkʌmpəs] *n.* 罗盘,指南针;圆规
compel [kəmˈpel] *vt.* 强迫,迫使屈服
compensate[ˈkɒmpenseɪt] *vt.* & *vi.* 补偿;弥补;

给(某人)赔偿(或赔款)
compete [kəm'piːt] *vi.* 比赛,竞争,对抗
competent ['kɔmpitənt] *adj.* 有能力的,胜任的;足够的
competition [ˌkɔmpi'tiʃən] *n.* 竞争,比赛
competitor [kəm'petɪtə(r)] *n.* (尤指商业方面的)竞争者,对手;参赛者;竞赛者
complain [kəm'plein] *vi.* 抱怨,诉苦;悲叹;控告,控诉
complaint [kəm'pleint] *n.* 抱怨,怨言;控告
complement ['kɒmplɪment] *vt.* 补充;补足;*n.* 补充物;补足物;足数;足额;补足语;补语
complete [kəm'pliːt] *adj.* 完整的;完成的;彻底的;*vt.* 完成使圆满
complex ['kɔmpleks] *adj.* 结合的;复杂的;*n.* 复合体
complicate ['kɔmplikeit] *vt.* 使复杂;使陷入;使错综
complicated ['kəmplikeitid] *adj.* 复杂的,难懂的
comply [kəm'plaɪ] *vi.* 遵从;服从;顺从
component [kəm'pəunənt] *n.* 组成部分;组件,元件;成分
compose [kəm'pəuz] *vt.* 组成,构成;创作,写作;作曲;使镇静
composition [ˌkɔmpə'ziʃən] *n.* 构成;作品;写作,作文,著作;成分
compound ['kɔmpaund, kɔm'paund] *n.* 化合物,混合物;复合词;*adj.* 复(混)合的;*vt.* 使加重;使恶化;*vi.* 混合
comprehend [ˌkɒmprɪ'hend] *vt.* & *vi.* 理解;领悟;懂
comprehension [ˌkɔmpri'henʃən] *n.* 理解,理解力;领悟
comprehensive [ˌkɔmpri'hensiv] *adj.* 综合的;全部的
compress ['kɔmpres, kəm'pres] *vt.* 压紧,压缩
comprise [kəm'praiz] *vt.* 包含,包括;构成
compromise ['kɔmprəmaiz] *n.* 妥协,让步,和解;折中,折中方案;*vt.* 使受到怀疑;*vi.* 妥协;让步
compulsory [kəm'pʌlsəri] *adj.* (因法律或规则而)必须做的,强制的,强迫的
compute [kəm'pjuːt] *vt.* 计算,估计,估算
computer [kəm'pjuːtə] *n.* 计算机,电脑
conceal [kən'siːl] *vt.* 把……隐藏起来,掩盖
concentrate ['kɔnsentreit] *vt.* 集中;专心;聚集;浓缩;*n.* 浓缩物;精选
concept ['kɔnsept] *n.* 概念,观念,设想
concern [kən'səːn] *n.* 关心(人或事);忧虑;挂念;关系;*vt.* 涉及;影响;关心;担忧
concerning [kən'səːniŋ] *prep.* 关于
concert ['kɔnsət] *n.* 音乐会,演奏会
concession [kən'seʃn] *n.* 让步;妥协;承认;给予
concise [kən'saɪs] *adj.* 简明的;简练的;简洁的;简略的;简缩的
conclude [kən'kluːd] *vt.* 推断出;使结束;缔结;断定,得出结论;*vi.* 做出决定;推断
conclusion [kən'kluːʒən] *n.* 结论,推论;结尾
concrete ['kɔnkriːt] *n.* 水泥,混凝土;*adj.* 具体的,实在的;混凝土制的;*vt.* 用混凝土覆盖
condemn [kən'dem] *vt.* 谴责,指责;判刑
condition [kən'diʃən] *n.* 状况,状态;环境,条件;*v.* 训练;使适应;影响;保持……健康
conditional [kən'dɪʃənl] *adj.* 附带条件的;依……而定的;条件的;*n.* 条件句
conduct [kən'dʌkt] *n.* 举止,行为,品行;*vt.* 导电;传热,组织,实施安排;指挥
conductor [kən'dʌktə] *n.* 售票员;(乐队)指挥;导体
confer [kən'fɜː(r)] *vi.* 商讨;协商;交换意见;*vt.* 授予(奖项、学位、荣誉或权利)
conference ['kɔnfərəns] *n.* 会议,讨论会
confess [kən'fes] *vt.* 供认,承认,坦白;告白;忏悔
confidence ['kɔnfidəns] *n.* 信任,信赖;信心
confident ['kɔnfidənt] *adj.* 确信的,自信的
confidential [ˌkɒnfɪ'denʃl] *adj.* 机密的;保密的;秘密的;隐秘的;受信任的;委以机密的
confine [kən'fain] *vt.* 限制;禁闭
confirm [kən'fəːm] *vt.* 证实,肯定;批准;确定
conflict ['kɔnflikt] *n.* 争论;冲突;斗争,战斗;矛盾;*vi.* 争执;冲突
conform [kən'fɔːm] *vi.* 顺从,顺应(大多数人或社会);遵守,遵从,服从(规则、法律等);相一致;相符合;相吻合
confront [kən'frʌnt] *v.* 使……无法回避;降临于;处理,解决(问题或困境);面对;对抗;与(某人)对峙
confuse [kən'fjuːz] *vt.* 使混乱,混淆;困惑
congratulate [kən'grætju. leit] *vt.* 祝贺;向……道喜
congratulation [kən. grætju'leiʃən] *n.* 祝贺,祝贺词
congress ['kɔŋgres] *n.* 大会;国会,议会;集会
connect [kə'nekt] *vt.* 连接,联结;联通;联系,使

有联系
conquer [ˌkɔŋkə] *vt.* 征服,战胜,克服
conquest [ˈkɔŋkwest] *n.* 攻取,征服
conscience [ˈkɔnʃəns] *n.* 良心,道德心,责任心
conscious [ˈkɔnʃəs] *adj.* 意识到的;神志清醒的;自觉的
consent [kənˈsent] *n.* 同意,赞成;许可;*vi.* 同意;承诺
consequence [ˈkɔnsikwəns] *n.* 结果,后果
consequently [ˈkɔnsikwəntli] *adv.* 因此,因而,所以
conservation [ˌkɔnsəːˈveiʃən] *n.* 保存;保护
conservative [kənˈsəːvətiv] *adj.* 保守的,守旧的;*n.* 保守的人,保守派(党)
consider [kənˈsidə] *vt.* 认为;考虑,思考;关心
considerable [kənˈsidərəbl] *adj.* 相当大的;重要的;可观的
considerate [kənˈsidərit] *adj.* 考虑周到的;体谅的
consideration [kənsidəˈreiʃən] *n.* 考虑,思考;体贴;考虑因素
consist [kənˈsist] *vi.* 由……组成
consistent [kənˈsistənt] *adj.* 一贯的,始终如一的,一致的
consolidate [kənˈsɒlɪdeɪt] *vt.* 使加强;使巩固;(使)结成一体,合并
conspicuous [kənˈspɪkjuəs] *adj.* 易见的;明显的;惹人注意的
constant [ˈkɔnstənt] *adj.* 连续发生的;恒定的;不变的;*n.* 常数,恒量
constitution [ˌkɔnstiˈtjuːʃən] *n.* 章程;体质;构造;组织;宪法
construct [ˈkɔnstrʌkt, kənˈstrʌkt] *vt.* 建造,建设,构筑;绘制;想出;*n.* 构想,建造物
consult [kənˈsʌlt] *vt.* 向……请教;查阅;商讨
consultant [kənˈsʌltənt] *n.* 顾问;高级顾问医师;会诊医师
consume [kənˈsjuːm] *vt.* 消耗;消费;消灭,毁灭;吃、喝、挥霍
contact [ˈkɔntækt] *vt.* 使接触,与……联系;*n.* 接触;联系;联系人
contain [kənˈtein] *vt.* 包含;容纳;克制,抑制
container [kənˈteinə] *n.* 容器;集装箱
contemporary [kənˈtempərəri] *adj.* 当代的,同时代的,现代的;*n.* 同时代的人
contend [kənˈtend] *v.* (尤指在争论中)声称,主张,认为;竞争;争夺
content [ˈkɔntent, kənˈtent] *n.* 内容;目录;容量;*adj.* 满足的,满意的;*vt.* 使……满足;使……安心
contest [ˈkɔntest, kənˈtest] *vt.* 争夺,争取;辩驳;竞赛;*n.* 竞赛;比赛
continent [ˈkɔntinənt] *n.* 大陆,陆地;洲;(the Continent)欧洲大陆
continual [kənˈtinjuəl] *adj.* 不断的;连续的;频繁的
continue [kənˈtinjuː] *vt. & vi.* 继续,连续
continuous [kənˈtinjuəs] *adj.* 连续不断的,连续的,继续的,连绵不断的;持续的
contract [ˈkɔntrækt, kənˈtrækt] *n.* 契约,合同书,合同;*vi.* 缩短;缩小;*vt.* 订约
contradict [ˌkɒntrəˈdɪkt] *vt.* 反驳;驳斥;批驳;相抵触;相矛盾;相反
contrast [ˈkɔntræst, kənˈtræst] *n.* 对比,对照;悬殊,差别;*vi. & vt.* 对比,成对照
contrary [ˈkɒntrəri, kənˈtreəri] *adj.* 与之相异的;相对立的;相反的;(在性质或方向上)截然不同的,完全相反的;*n.* 相反的事实(或事情、情况)
contribute [kənˈtribjuːt] *vt.* 捐献,捐助;投稿;*vi.* 投稿;贡献;是……原因之一
control [kənˈtrəul] *vt.* 控制;克制;掌管,支配;*n.* 管理权,控制权;控制能力
controversial [ˌkɒntrəˈvɜːʃl] *adj.* 引起争论的;有争议的
convenience [kənˈviːnjəns] *n.* 便利,方便,便利设施;
convenient [kənˈviːnjənt] *adj.* 便利的,近便的,方便的
convention [kənˈvenʃən] *n.* 习俗,惯例;公约;大会协定
conversation [ˌkɔnvəˈseiʃən] *n.* 会话,谈话,非正式会谈
convert [ˈkɔnvəːt, kənˈvəːt] *vt.* 使转变,使改变;倒置;*n.* 皈依者
convict [kənˈvɪkt, kɒnvɪkt] *vt.* 定罪;宣判……有罪;*n.* 服刑囚犯
conviction [kənˈvɪkʃn] *n.* 判罪;定罪;证明有罪;坚定的看法(或信念)
convince [kənˈvins] *vt.* 使确信,使信服;说服,使……相信
cook [kuk] *vt.* 烹调,煮;编造,虚构;烧(菜);*vi.* 烧菜;密谋;*n.* 厨师
cookie [ˈkuki] *n.* 曲奇饼
cool [kuːl] *adj.* 凉的;冷静的;冷色系的;*n.* 凉气;凉快的地方;*vt. & vi.* (使)变凉(使)冷静

cooperate [kəu'ɔpəreit] *vi.* 合作,协作,配合
coordinate [kəu'ɔːdneit, kəu'ɔːdnit] *vt.* 使协调;调节;整合,使一致;*n.* 同等的人物(色调 图案 样式等)配套服装;坐标
cope [kəup] *vi.* 对付,应付;对抗
copper ['kɔpə] *n.* 铜,铜币;铜制器
copy ['kɔpi] *n.* 抄件,副本;一册;稿件;*vt.* 抄写;复制,复印;*vi.* 抄袭;*n.* 复制,拷贝
core [kɔː] *n.* 果实的心;核心,要点;*vt.* 挖去果核
corn [kɔːn] *n.* 谷物,谷粒;鸡眼
corner ['kɔːnə] *n.* 角,角落,转角;边远地区;偏僻住所;*vt.* 使……走投无路,使……陷入绝境;转弯
corporation [ˌkɔːpə'reiʃən] *n.* 公司;法人;集团;企业;社团
correct [kə'rekt] *adj.* 正确的;*vt. & vi.* 改正;纠正
correspond [ˌkɔris'pɔnd] *vi.* 相符合,相当;通信
correspondence [ˌkɔri'spɔndəns] *n.* 来往信件;往来书信;通信;通信联系;相关;相似
correspondent [ˌkɔri'spɔndənt] *n.* 通信者,通讯记者,通讯员
corresponding [ˌkɔri'spɔndiŋ] *adj.* 相应的;符合的,一致的;相同的;相当的
corridor ['kɔridɔː] *n.* 走廊,回廊;通路
corrupt [kə'rʌpt] *adj.* 贪污的;受贿的;腐败的;营私舞弊的;不诚实的;不道德的;*v.* 使腐化;使堕落;破坏;损坏
cost [kɔst] *n.* 价格;代价;成本,费用;*vt.* 花费;使付出
costly ['kɔstli] *adj.* 昂贵的,价值高的,代价高的
costume ['kɒstjuːm] *n.* (某地或某历史时期的)服装,装束;(戏剧或电影的)戏装,服装;*v.* 给(某人)穿上特殊服装
cottage ['kɔtidʒ] *n.* 村舍,小屋
cotton ['kɔtn] *n.* 棉,棉花;棉线;棉布
cough [kɔf] *vt. & vi.* 咳,咳嗽;*n.* 咳嗽
could [kud] *aux. v.* (can 的过去式)
council ['kaunsil] *n.* 理事会;委员会;商议
counsel ['kaʊnsl] *n.* (尤指年长者或专家的)劝告,忠告,建议;法律顾问;律师;*vt.* 提供专业咨询;建议,劝告(做某事)
count [kaunt] *vt.* 计算;视为;依赖;*vi.* 数,计数;*n.* 计数
counter ['kauntə] *n.* 柜台;计数器;计算者;*adv.* 相反地;*vt.* 反对;反击;抵制;抵消
country ['kʌntri] *n.* 国家;国土;农村;*adj.* 国家(的);农村(的)
countryside ['kʌntri'said] *n.* 乡下,农村
county ['kaunti] *n.* 英国的郡,美国的县
couple ['kʌpl] *n.* 夫妇;(一)对;几个,数个;*v.* 加倍;成双;联结
courage ['kʌridʒ] *n.* 勇气;胆量,胆识
course [kɔːs] *n.* 课程;讲座;过程;路线;一道菜
court [kɔːt] *n.* 法院,法庭;庭院;球场;*v.* 献殷勤,追求
courtyard ['kɔːtjɑːd] *n.* (通常为城堡、大宅第等的)庭院,院子,天井
cousin ['kʌzn] *n.* 堂(或表)兄弟(姐妹)
cover ['kʌvə] *vt.* 盖,覆盖;包括;涉及,包含;*n.* 盖子,封面;表面
cow [kau] *n.* 母牛,奶牛;母兽
coward ['kauəd] *n.* 懦夫,胆怯者;*adj.* 胆小的
crack [kræk] *n.* 裂缝,裂纹;声变;*vi.* 爆裂,破裂
craft [krɑːft] *n.* 工艺,手艺;行业;航空器
crane [krein] *n.* 起重机;摄影升降机;鹤;*vt.* 伸长(脖子等)
crash [kræʃ] *vi.* 碰撞,坠落;猛使……破碎;迫降;*n.* 碰撞,猛撞;轰隆声;崩溃;破产,垮台
crawl [krɔːl] *vi.* 爬,爬行;*n.* 爬行,匍匐而行
crazy ['kreizi] *adj.* 疯狂的;荒唐的
cream [kriːm] *n.* 奶油,乳酪,乳脂;奶油色;面霜;精华
create [kri'eit] *vt.* 创造;引起,产生
creature ['kriːtʃə] *n.* 生物;动物;家畜;人
credit ['kredit] *n.* 信用贷款;信用,荣誉;学分;*vt.* 归功于;赞颂;信任
creep [kriːp] *vi.* 爬行,缓慢地行进;蔓延;*n.* 爬;徐行;蠕动
crew [kruː] *n.* 全体船员;全体乘务员;*vi.* 当(尤指船上的)工作人员;
crime [kraim] *n.* 罪,罪行;犯罪;羞耻
criminal ['kriminəl] *n.* 犯人,罪犯,刑事犯;*adj.* 犯罪的;刑事的
crisis ['kraisis] *n.* 危机,存亡之际
crisp [krɪsp] *adj.* 脆的;酥脆的;鲜脆的;脆嫩的;洁净的;挺括的;*n.* 油炸土豆片,炸薯片(有多种风味,袋装);*vt.* (使)变脆
criterion [kraɪ'tɪəriən] *n.* (评判或作决定的)标准,准则,原则
critic ['kritik] *n.* 批评家,评论家;爱挑剔的人
critical ['kritikəl] *adj.* 决定性的;批评的;危险的;挑剔的

criticize [ˈkritisaiz] *vt.* 批评；评论；非难，吹毛求疵
crop [krɔp] *n.* 农作物，庄稼；收成；*vt.* 修剪，剪短；收割；使谷物生长；*vi.* 种植谷物
cross [krɔs] *vt.* 穿过；划叉剔除；画横线于；*vi.* 穿越；*n.* 十字架，十字架形物件；交叉，交叉路；*adj.* 生气的
crossing [ˈkrɒsɪŋ] *n.* 人行横道；渡口；(从一国到另一国的)过境处；(线的)交叉点；(道路的)十字路口；(轨道的)交叉道口
crowd [kraud] *n.* 群；大众；一伙人；一堆；*vi.* 拥挤；挤满；挤进；*vt.* 挤满，将……塞进
crown [kraun] *n.* 王冠，冕；王权；顶点；花冠；*vt.* 使……成王，加冕；使完美
crucial [ˈkruːʃl] *adj.* 至关重要的；关键性的
crude [kruːd] *adj.* 简陋的；天然的，未加工的；粗鲁的；*n.* 原油
cruel [ˈkruːəl] *adj.* 残忍的，残酷的；引起痛苦的
crush [krʌʃ] *n.* 拥挤的人群；迷恋；*vt.* 压破；征服；挤入；镇压
cry [krai] *vi.* 哭，哭泣，叫喊；强烈要求；*vt.* 大声叫喊；*n.* 叫，哭，喊；叫卖声
crystal [ˈkristl] *n.* 水晶，结晶体，晶粒
cube [kjuːb] *n.* 立方体，立方；*vt.* 求……的立方
cucumber [ˈkjuːkəmbə] *n.* 黄瓜
cue [kjuː] *n.* 暗示；提示；信号；(戏剧的)提示 *v.* 给(某人)暗示(或提示)
cultivate [ˈkʌltiveit] *vt.* 耕，种植；培养，栽培；结交(朋友)；促进增长；教养
culture [ˈkʌltʃə] *n.* 文化，文明；教养；种植；*vt.* 培养
cup [kʌp] *n.* 杯子，(一)杯；奖杯；*vt.* 使(手)窝成杯状；使(双手)成圆状托起
cupboard [ˈkʌbəd] *n.* 碗柜，碗碟橱，食橱
cure [kjuə] *vt.* 医治；消除；*vt.* 治疗，治愈；改正；*n.* 药；药物；疗程；治疗法
curious [ˈkjuəriəs] *adj.* 好奇的；奇特的，稀奇古怪的
curl [kəːl] *n.* 卷发；螺旋；*vt. & vi.* 卷曲，弄卷，弯曲
currency [ˈkʌrənsi] *n.* 通货；货币；通用；流行；流传
current [ˈkʌrənt] *adj.* 当前的，现在的；最近的；通用的；流通的；*n.* (水、气、电)流；趋势
curriculum [kəˈrɪkjələm] *n.* (学校等的)全部课程
curse [kəːs] *n.* 诅咒，咒骂；天谴；祸端；*vt.* 咒骂；*vi.* 诅咒
curtain [ˈkəːtn] *n.* 帘，窗帘；幕(布)；遮蔽物；*vt.* 用窗帘装饰遮蔽
curve [kəːv] *n.* 曲线；弯，弯曲；*vt.* 弄弯，使……弯曲；*vi.* 弯曲
cushion [ˈkuʃən] *n.* 垫子，坐垫，橡皮软垫；缓冲；*vt.* 起缓冲作用
custom [ˈkʌstəm] *n.* 习惯，风俗
customer [ˈkʌstəmə] *n.* 顾客，主顾；家伙
cut [kʌt] *vt.* 切，割，剪；减少；停止，修剪；*vi.* 切割；*n.* 切口，割伤；降低；删节
cute [kjuːt] *adj.* 可爱的；漂亮迷人的；有性吸引力的；性感的；精明的；机灵的
cycle [ˈsaikl] *n.* 自行车；循环；周期；长期；圈；*vi.* 骑自行车

D

dad [dæd] *n.* 爸爸
daily [ˈdeili] *adj.* 每日的；按天计算的；日常的；*adv.* 每日，天天；*n.* 日报
dairy [ˈdɛəri] *n.* 牛奶场；乳制品；乳品店；*adj.* 牛奶的
dam [dæm] *n.* 水坝，水堤；*vt.* 筑坝
damage [ˈdæmidʒ] *vt.* 损害，毁坏；*n.* (*pl.*)赔偿；损坏，毁坏，损害
damp [dæmp] *adj.* 潮湿的，有湿气的；*n.* 潮湿，湿气；*vt.* 抑制；使潮湿
dance [dɑːns] *vi.* 跳舞；雀跃；*vt.* 跳……舞；*n.* 舞，跳舞，舞蹈；舞会；舞步
danger [ˈdeindʒə] *n.* 危险，危险事物
dangerous [ˈdeindʒərəs] *adj.* 危险的，不安全的，引起危险的
dare [dɛə] *vt. & vi.* & aux. *v.* 敢，竟敢，敢于；*n.* 挑战
dark [dɑːk] *adj.* 暗的，黑色的；*n.* 黑暗，暗处
darling [ˈdɑːliŋ] *n.* 亲爱的，宝贝；宠儿；*adj.* 可爱的，亲爱的
dash [dæʃ] *vt.* 使猛撞，猛掷；急奔，猛冲；*vi.* 猛冲，猛撞；*n.* 猛冲，冲撞；破折号；短跑；冲劲
data [ˈdeitə] *n.* (datum 的复数)数据，资料
database [ˈdeɪtəbeɪs] *n.* (储存在计算机中的)数据库
date [deit] *n.* 日期；约会；枣椰子；*vt.* 约会；

定……日期；*vi.* 追溯到
daughter[ˈdɔːtə] *n.* 女儿
dawn [dɔːn] *n.* 黎明，破晓；开端；*vi.* 开始；逐渐明白
day [dei] *n.* （一）天，白昼，白天
daylight [ˈdeilait] *n.* 白昼，日光；黎明
daytime [ˈdeɪtaɪm] *n.* 白天；白昼；日间
dead [ded] *adj.* 死的，无生命的；萧条的；精疲力竭的，用完的，无趣的；*adv.* 完全地，确实地；非常；*n.* 死者；死
deadline [ˈdedlaɪn] *n.* 最后期限；截止日期
deadly [ˈdedli] *adj.* 致命的，致死的；极度的，十足的；*adv.* 非常地
deaf [def] *adj.* 聋的；不愿听的
deal [diːl] *n.* 买卖；待遇；交易；协定；分量；
vt. （dealt dealt[delt]）处理，应付
dealer [ˈdiːlə(r)] *n.* 交易商；贸易商；贩毒者；毒品贩子
dean [diːn] *n.* 座堂主任牧师；（乡间主管若干教堂牧师的）主任牧师；（大学的）学院院长，系主任
dear [diə] *adj.* 严重的；珍贵的；亲爱的；昂贵的；*adv.* 高价地；*n.* 亲爱的人，可爱的人；
int. 啊，哎呀
death [deθ] *n.* 死，死亡，灭亡，死神
debate [diˈbeit] *vt.* & *vi.* 争论，辩论；商讨；
n. 争论；思考
debt [det] *n.* 债，债务，欠债，负债状态
decade [ˈdekeid] *n.* 十年，十年期
decay [diˈkei] *vt.* & *vi.* 腐烂；衰败；*n.* 腐烂；衰退
deceit [diˈsiːt] *n.* 欺骗，欺诈；诡计
deceive [diˈsiːv] *vt.* 欺骗，蒙蔽，行骗
December [diˈsembə] *n.* 十二月
decent [ˈdiːsnt] *adj.* 正派的，体面的；有分寸的，得体的
decide [diˈsaid] *vt.* & *vi.* 决定，决心；解决；做出抉择
decision [diˈsiʒən] *n.* 决定，决心；果断；决策
deck [dek] *n.* 甲板；舱面；层面；桥面；楼层；
vt. 装饰
declaration [ˌdekləˈreɪʃn] *n.* 公告；宣告；宣言；声明（书）；宣布；表白；宣称；申报（单）
declare [diˈklɛə] *vt.* & *vi.* 断言，声明；表明；宣布；申报
decline [dɪˈklaɪn] *n.* （数量、价值、质量等的）减少，下降，衰落，衰退；*vt.* & *vi.* 减少；下降；衰弱；衰退；谢绝；婉言拒绝；
decorate [ˈdekəreit] *vt.* 装饰，装潢；修饰；授予某人奖章或其他奖状
decrease [ˈdiːkriːs, diːˈkriːs] *vi.* & *n.* 减少
dedicate [ˈdedɪkeɪt] *v.* 把……奉献给；（在书、音乐或作品的前部）题献词；为……举行奉献典礼；为（建筑物等）举行落成典礼
deed [diːd] *n.* 行为，事迹；功绩；（尤指房产）契约；证书
deem [diːm] *vt.* 认为；视为；相信
deep [diːp] *adj.* 深的；深奥的；纵深的；
adv. 深深地；*n.* 海，海洋
deer [diə] *n.* 鹿
defeat [diˈfiːt] *vt.* 战胜，击败，挫败；*n.* 败北，失败
defect [diˈfekt] *n.* 缺点，缺陷，欠缺；*vi.* 背叛
defence [diˈfens] *n.* 防御，防务；辩护；答辩
defend [diˈfend] *vt.* & *vi.* 防护；辩护；防卫，保卫，防守
deficit [ˈdefɪsɪt] *n.* 赤字；逆差；亏损；不足额；缺款额；缺少
define [diˈfain] *vt.* 给……下定义；限定；解释
definite [ˈdefinit] *adj.* 明确的；肯定的，一定的
degree [diˈgriː] *n.* 程度；度，度数；学位
delay [diˈlei] *vt.* 推迟，耽搁，延误；*vi.* 耽搁；
n. 耽搁，迟滞
delegate [ˈdelɪgət, ˈdelɪgeɪt] *n.* 代表；会议代表；*vt.* 授（权）；把（工作、权力等）委托（给下级）；选派（某人做某事）
delegation [ˌdeliˈgeiʃən] *n.* 代表团；委派
delete [dɪˈliːt] *vt.* 删去；删除
deliberate [dɪˈlɪbərət, dɪˈlɪbəreɪt] *adj.* 故意的；蓄意的；存心的；不慌不忙的；小心翼翼的；从容不迫的；*vi.* 仔细考虑；深思熟虑；反复思考
delicate [ˈdelikit] *adj.* 纤细的；易碎的；精美的；微妙的；美味的；脆弱的；敏锐的
delicious [diˈliʃəs] *adj.* 美味的，可口的；怡人的
delight [diˈlait] *n.* 快乐，快乐；*vt.* 使高兴
deliver [diˈlivə] *vt.* 投递，递送，送交；发表；表达；释放
demand [diˈmɑːnd] *vt.* 要求，需要；*n.* 要求，需求
democracy [diˈmɔkrəsi] *n.* 民主，民主制，民主国家
demonstrate [ˈdemənstreit] *vt.* 说明；论证，证明；表露；示范，演示；*vi.* 示威
denial [dɪˈnaɪəl] *n.* 否认；否定；拒绝给予，剥夺（应有的权利）；否认（令人不快、痛苦的事）
dense [dens] *adj.* 密集的；浓厚；愚钝的；不易看

懂的
density [ˈdensiti] *n.* 密集,稠密;密度;透明度
dentist[ˈdentɪst] *n.* 牙科医生;牙科诊所
deny [diˈnai] *vt.* 否定;拒绝相信,拒绝;反对;克制
depart [diˈpɑːt] *vi.* 离开,起程;出发;违反,背离(常规);*vt.* 离职
department [diˈpɑːtmənt] *n.* 部,司,局,处,系;部门
departure [diˈpɑːtʃə] *n.* 离开;出发,起程;分歧
depend [diˈpend] *vi.* 依靠,依赖;相信;指望
deposit [diˈpɔzit] *vt.* 使沉淀;存放;*n.* 存款;定金
depress [diˈpres] *vt.* 使沮丧;降低
depth [depθ] *n.* 深度;深厚;深处;强度
deputy [ˈdepjuti] *n.* 副手;副职;代理;(某些国家的)议员;(美国协助地方治安官办案的)警官
derive [diˈraiv] *vt.* 取得;得自;起源
descend [diˈsend] & *vi.* 降临;下来,下降,下倾
describe [diˈskraib] *vt.* 形容;描写,描绘,描述
description [diˈskripʃən] *n.* 描写,描述;说明书
desert [ˈdezət, diˈzəːt] *n.* 沙漠,荒地;应得(的惩罚或奖励);*vt.* 离弃;擅离;遗弃;*vi.* 擅离职守
deserve [diˈzəːv] *vt.* 应受,值得
design [diˈzain] *vt.* 设计;想象;计划;*n.* 设计图样
desirable [diˈzaiərəbl] *adj.* 可取的;值得有的;令人满意的;有吸引力的
desire [diˈzaiə] *vt.* 要求;向往;请求;渴望;*n.* 愿望;欲望
desk [desk] *n.* 书桌,办公桌
despair [diˈspεə] *n.* 绝望,失望;*vi.* 绝望,失望
desperate [ˈdespərit] *adj.* 拼死的,绝望的,不顾一切的,极想得到的
despite [diˈspait] *prep.* 不管;尽管;不顾;*v.* 憎恨;轻视
dessert [dɪˈzɜːt] *n.* (饭后)甜点,甜食
destination [ˌdestiˈneiʃən] *n.* 目的地,终点;目标
destroy [disˈtrɔi] *vt.* & *vi.* 破坏;消灭;打破
destruction [diˈstrʌkʃən] *n.* 破坏,毁灭,消灭;破坏者
detach [dɪˈtætʃ] *v.* 拆卸;(使)分开,脱离;挣脱;摆脱;离开;派遣;分遣;分派
detail [ˈdiːteil] *n.* 细节,详情;部分;分派;枝节;零件;*vt.* 详述;
detain[dɪˈteɪn] *v.* 拘留;扣押;耽搁;留住;阻留
detect [diˈtekt] *vt.* 察觉,发觉;侦察;发现,探测信息
detective [dɪˈtektɪv] *n.* 侦探;警探;私人侦探
determine [diˈtəːmin] *vt.* 决定;查明;决心
develop [diˈveləp] *vt.* 发展,形成;开发;冲洗照片;*vi.* 加剧,加重
device [diˈvais] *n.* 器械,装置,设备;设计
devise [diˈvaiz] *vt.* 设计;发明
devote [diˈvəut] *vt.* 将……奉献;致力于,投入于,献身
diagnosis [ˌdaɪəgˈnəʊsɪs] *n.* 诊断;(问题原因的)判断
diagram [ˈdaiəgræm] *n.* 图解,图表,简图
dial [ˈdaiəl] *n.* 钟面;拨号盘;刻度盘;*vt.* 拨
dialog(ue) [ˈdaiəlɔg] *n.* 对话,对白
diameter [daiˈæmitə] *n.* 直径
diamond [ˈdaiəmənd] *n.* 金刚石,钻石;菱形;像钻石的物质;纸牌的方块;棒球内场
diary [ˈdaiəri] *n.* 日记,日记簿
dictate [ˈdikteit, dikˈteit] *vt.* & *vi.* 口授;命令;*n.* 命令;指挥;指令
dictation [dikˈteiʃən] *n.* 口授笔录;听写
dictionary [ˈdikʃəneri] *n.* 词典,字典,辞典
die [dai] *vi.* 死,死亡,灭亡
diet [ˈdaɪət] *n.* 日常饮食;日常食物;规定饮食(为健康或减肥等目的);规定饮食的时期;*vi.* 节食;进规定饮食
differ [ˈdifə] *vi.* 不同(意见)相异,不一致
difference [ˈdifərəns] *n.* 差别;分歧
different [ˈdifərənt] *adj.* 差异的;各种的;不同的,与众不同的
difficult [ˈdifikəlt] *adj.* 困难的;难对付的;(人)难取悦的,难相处的
difficulty [ˈdifikəlti] *n.* 困难;争议;麻烦;难事;困境
dig [dig] *vt.* 掘,挖,翻土,采掘
digest [daiˈdʒest] *vt.* 消化;领会,理解;*vi.* 消化;*n.* 文摘,摘要
digital [ˈdidʒitəl] *adj.* 数字的,计数的;数码的,电子的
dignity [ˈdɪgnəti] *n.* 庄重;庄严;尊严;尊贵;高贵;高尚;自尊;自重
dilemma [dɪˈlemə] *n.* (进退两难的)窘境,困境
diligent [ˈdilidʒənt] *adj.* 勤勉的,勤奋的,用功的
dim [dim] *adj.* 昏暗的,暗淡的;朦胧的,模糊的;*vt.* 使暗淡,使失去光泽;*vi.* 变暗
dimension [diˈmenʃən] *n.* 尺寸;尺度;面积
dine [dain] *vi.* 吃饭,进餐;*vt.* 设宴款待,请客

dinner [ˈdinə] *n.* 正餐;主餐;宴会;晚宴
dip [dip] *vt.* 浸;蘸;*vi.* 浸一浸;下降;向下倾斜;*n.* 减少;低洼处;
diploma [diˈpləumə] *n.* 毕业文凭;学位证书;公文;奖状
diplomatic [ˌdipləˈmætik] *adj.* 外交上的;外交人员的
direct [diˈrekt] *adj.* 直接的;直率的;笔直的;坦白的;*vt.* 指挥命令;负责;*vi.* 指导;指出
direction [diˈrekʃən] *n.* 方向,方位;指导;用法说明
directly [diˈrektli] *adv.* 直接地;立即;完全
director [diˈrektə, daiˈrektə] *n.* 指导者;理事,董事;经理
directory [dəˈrektəri] *n.* 人名地址录;(电话)号码簿
dirt [dəːt] *n.* 尘土;污垢;泥土
dirty [ˈdəːti] *adj.* 脏的 *vt.* 使……变脏;*vi.* 弄脏
disable [disˈeibl] *vt.* 使无能;使伤残;使……失去能力
disadvantage [disədˈvæntidʒ] *n.* 不利,不利地位,不利条件损害;损失
disagree [disəˈgriː] *vi.* 有分歧;不一致;不适应,不适宜
disappear [disəˈpiə] *vi.* 不见,失踪,消失;灭绝
disappoint [disəˈpɔint] *vt. & vi.* 使失望;使受挫折
disaster [diˈzɑːstə] *n.* 灾难,灾祸;天灾
disk(= **disc**) [disk] *n.* 圆盘;唱片,光盘;盘形物;[计算机]磁盘
discard [ˈdiskɑːd, disˈkɑːd] *vt.* 丢弃,抛弃,遗弃;*n.* 被抛弃的人(或物)
discharge [disˈtʃɑːdʒ] *vt.* 准许(某人)离开;排出,放出;放(电),发(力)
discipline [ˈdisiplin] *n.* 纪律;训练;惩罚;学科;*vt.* 训练;惩罚
disclose [disˈkləuz] *vt.* 揭开;揭发;透露
discount [ˈdɪskaʊnt, dɪsˈkaʊnt] *n.* 折扣;*v.* 打折
discourage [disˈkʌridʒ] *vt.* 使泄气;使灰心;阻碍
discover [disˈkʌvə] *vt. & vi.* 发现;暴露
discovery [disˈkʌvəri] *n.* 发现;被发现的事物
discuss [diˈskʌs] *vt.* 讨论,谈论;论述
discussion [diˈskʌʃən] *n.* 讨论,谈论;辩论;论述
disease [diˈziːz] *n.* 病,疾病,病害
disguise [disˈgaiz] *vt.* 假装,假扮;掩饰;*n.* 假装;伪装物
disgust [disˈgʌst] *n.* 厌恶,憎恶,嫌恶;*vt.* 令人厌恶
dish [diʃ] *n.* 碟;盘子;菜肴;*vt.* 装盘
dishonour [disˈɔnə] *n.* 不光彩,丢脸的人;耻辱;*vt.* 使丢脸;侮辱
dislike [disˈlaik] *vt. & n.* 不喜爱;厌恶;反感
dismiss [disˈmis] *vt.* 解雇,开除;解散
disorder [disˈɔːdə] *n.* 混乱,杂乱;骚乱
display [diˈsplei] *vt.* 陈列,展览;显示;炫耀;*vt.* 显示;表现
disposal [diˈspəuzəl] *n.* 丢掉;处理;销毁
dispose [diˈspəuz] *vi.* 去掉;丢掉;销毁;*vt.* 处置
displease [disˈpliːz] *vt.* 使不愉快;使生气
dispute [diˈspjuːt] *vi.* 争论,争执;*vt.* 争论;质疑;*n.* 争论;争吵
dissatisfy [disˈsætisfai] *vi.* 使不满;使不平
dissolve [diˈzɔlv] *vt.* 使溶解;解散;消除;解决(问题);*vi.* 消散;溶解;解散
distance [ˈdistəns] *n.* 距离,间距;远处;(人际关系的)疏远;*vt.* 使疏远;与……保持距离
distant [ˈdistənt] *adj.* 在远处的;疏远的;陌生的;远行的
distinct [diˈstiŋkt] *adj.* 与其他不同的;不同的;明显的(from);独特的;清楚的
distinction [diˈstiŋkʃən] *n.* 差别,不同;区分;对比;杰出
distinguish [diˈstiŋgwiʃ] *vt.* 区别,辨别;*vi.* 区别
distress [diˈstres] *n.* 忧虑,悲伤;不幸,苦恼;贫困;忧郁;*vt.* 使……苦恼
distribute [diˈstribjut] *vt. & vi.* 分发,分送;分布;分配
distribution [ˌdistriˈbjuːʃən] *n.* 分发,分配;分布;散布
district [ˈdistrikt] *n.* 区;地区;区域;行政区
disturb [disˈtəːb] *vt.* 打扰;扰乱;弄乱;妨碍;使……不安
ditch [ditʃ] *n.* 沟,沟渠;渠道
dive [daiv] *vi.* 跳水;潜水;俯冲;把……伸入;*vt.* 跳水;俯冲
diverse [daiˈvəːs] *adj.* 不一样的,相异的,不同的;多种多样的
divide [diˈvaid] *vt.* 分,分配;分开(组)
division [diˈviʒən] *n.* 分,分配;除法;划分,分开;部门
divorce [diˈvɔːs] *n.* 离婚,离异;*vi. vt.* 离婚,与……办离婚

dizzy [ˈdizi] *adj.* 头昏眼花的；使人眩晕的，引起头晕的
do [duː] aux. *v. vt. & vi.* 做；干；办
dock [dɔk] *n.* 船坞；码头；*vt.* 进港；
doctor [ˈdɔktə] *n.* 医生，医师；博士；*vt.* 医治
document [ˈdɔkjumənt，ˈdɔkjument] *n.* 公文；文件；证件；[计算机]文档；*vt.* 记载；用文件等证明
dog [dɔg] *n.* 狗，犬；犬科动物
doll [dɔl] *n.* (口技演员使用的)木偶；玩偶；*vt.* 把……打扮漂亮
dollar [ˈdɔlə] *n.* 美元(货币单位)
domain [dəˈmeɪn] *n.* 范围，领域；领土，疆土；管辖范围；[计]域名
dome [dəʊm] *n.* 圆屋顶；像圆屋顶一样的东西；圆顶体育场
domestic [dəˈmestik] *adj.* 本国的；国内的；家庭的；驯养的；*n.* 家仆，佣人
dominate [ˈdɔmɪneɪt] *v.* 支配，影响；占有优势；在……中具有最重要的特色；在……中拥有最重要的位置
donate [dəʊˈneɪt] *v.* 赠送；捐献；
donkey [ˈdɔŋki] *n.* 驴；笨蛋
door [dɔː] *n.* 门；通道；一家
dorm [dɔːm] *n.* (集体)宿舍
dormitory [ˈdɔːmitri] *n.* 集体寝室，宿舍
dose [dəus] *n.* 剂量，用量；一剂；*vt.* 给……服药
dot [dɔt] *n.* 点，圆点；少量；小东西[计算机]点；*vt.* 作小点记号；点缀
double [ˈdʌbl] *adj.* 两倍的；成双的；双重的；连续两个的；供两人用的；*adv.* 成双地；*v.* (使)加倍；*n.* 两倍；双人房
doubt [daut] *n.* 怀疑，疑虑；不信任；*vt.* 怀疑；不信任
doubtful [ˈdautfəl] *adj.* 难以预测的；怀疑的，疑心的；不确定的
doubtless [ˈdautlis] *adv.* 无疑地；很可能；确定地
dove 英 [dəuv，dʌv] *n.* 鸽；*v.* 潜水(dive 的过去式)
down [daun] *adv.* 向下；在下面；下跌；在南方；*adj.* 向下的；降低的；情绪低落；停止运行；*prep.* 沿着……而下
download [ˌdaʊnˈləud，ˈdaʊnləʊd] *v.* 下载；*n.* 已下载的数据资料
downstairs [ˌdaunˈstɛəz] *adv.* 在楼下；向楼下；*n.* 楼下
downtown [ˈdaʊntaʊn，ˌdaʊnˈtaʊn] *adv.* 在市中心的
downward(s) [ˈdaunwəd] *adj.* 向下的；*adv.* 向下地
dozen [ˈdʌzn] *n.* 一打，十二个；*adj.* 一打的；十二个的
draft [dræft] *n.* 草稿；草图；汇票；征兵；*vt.* 起草；征兵；选派，抽调
drag [dræg] *vt.* 拖，拉，拖曳；拖累；拖拉(动)；*vi.* 拖拉(动)；缓慢地行走；*n.* 用来拖拉的东西；拖累
dragon [ˈdrægən] *n.* 龙
drain [drein] *vt.* 排去；放水；耗尽；排出；排干；喝光；*vi.* 变干；排出；排水；*n.* 下水道；排水沟；消耗；耗竭
drama [ˈdrɑːmə] *n.* 一出戏剧；剧本；戏剧；戏剧性情节
dramatic [drəˈmætik] *adj.* 引人注目的；戏剧的；给人深刻印象的
draw [drɔː] *vt.* (drew drawn) 拉，拖；挨近；提取；画，绘制；划；拨出；*n.* 拉，拽；吸引人的事物
drawback [ˈdrɔːbæk] *n.* 缺点，劣势
drawer [ˈdrɔːə] *n.* 抽屉
drawing [ˈdrɔːiŋ] *n.* 图画；素描，绘图
dread [dred] *n.* 畏惧；恐怖；可怕的人；可怕的事；*vt.* 惧怕，恐惧；*adj.* 可怕的，恐怖的
dreadful [ˈdredfl] *adj.* 可怕的；令人畏惧的；讨厌的，糟透了的，丑陋的；糟糕的
dream [driːm] *n.* 梦，梦想；*vt. & vi.* 做梦；想象
dress [dres] *n.* 女服；童装；服装；*vt. & vi.* 穿着
drift [drift] *vi.* 漂流；漂泊；*n.* 漂流；漂移；漂流物；*vt.* 使漂流
drill [dril] *n.* 钻头；钻孔机；钻子；操练；*vi.* 钻孔；*vt.* 训练；钻孔
drink [driŋk] *vt. & vi.* 饮，喝；喝酒；*n.* 饮料
drip [drip] *vi.* 滴下；漏水；*n.* 水滴；滴；点滴
drive [draiv] *vt. & vi.* 驾驶；驱使；*n.* 驾车；快车道；推进力；驱使；[计算机]驱动器
driver [ˈdraivə] *n.* 驾驶员，司机
drop [drɔp] *vt.* 使落下；降低；减少；*vi.* 落下；减少；减弱；*n.* 滴；微量；落下
drought [draut] *n.* 旱灾，干旱
drown [draun] *vi.* 淹死，溺死；*vt.* 淹死；沉浸于
drug [drʌg] *n.* 药，药物，药材；毒品；*vt.* 下药
drum [drʌm] *n.* 鼓；鼓声；鼓状物；圆桶；*vi.* 击鼓；作鼓声；*vt.* 连续击打
drunk [drʌŋk] *adj.* 醉的；陶醉的；*n.* 醉汉，酒鬼，酗酒者；*v.* 喝(酒)(drink 的过去分词)；饮；

喝酒,(尤指)酗酒
dry [drai] *adj.* 干的;干燥的;干旱的;
vt. 把……弄干;*vi.* (使)变干
duck [dʌk] *n.* 鸭;鸭肉
due [djuː] *adj.* 预期的;应给的;到期的
dull [dʌl] *adj.* 枯燥的;不鲜明的;呆滞的;迟钝的;无趣的;钝的;暗的;*vt.* 使变钝;*vi.* 变钝
dumb [dʌm] *adj.* 哑的;无言的;沉默的;愚蠢的;*vt.* 使人沉默
dump [dʌmp] *vt.* 倾卸,倾倒;倾销;丢弃;抛售;导出;*vi.* 骤降;扔垃圾;*n.* 垃圾场;堆放处
durable [ˈdjuərəbl] *adj.* 耐久的,耐用的
duration [djuˈreiʃən] *n.* 持续,持久;持续时间;期间
during [ˈdjuəriŋ] *prep.* 在……期间
dusk [dʌsk] *n.* 薄暮,黄昏;幽暗
dust [dʌst] *n.* 尘土,灰尘;*vt.* 拂去灰尘;撒上粉状物体;*vi.* 擦拭灰尘
dusty [ˈdʌsti] *adj.* 布满灰尘的;尘状的
duty [ˈdjuːti] *n.* 职责;责任;义务;税;*adj.* 值班的;作为一种义务的
dwelling [ˈdweliŋ] *n.* 住处,寓所
dye [dai] *vt.* 染;*vi.* 染色;*n.* 染料;染色
dying [ˈdaiiŋ] *adj.* 垂死的,临终的;*n.* 死;死亡
dynamic [daiˈnæmik] *adj.* 有活力的;动态的;(有)动力的;(有)力的;*n.* 动力;力学
dynasty [ˈdinəsti] *n.* 王朝;朝代

E

each [iːtʃ] *pron.* (两个或两个以上的人或物中)各自;各个;每个
eager [ˈiːgə] *adj.* 渴望的;热切的
eagle [ˈiːgl] *n.* 鹰
ear [iə] *n.* 耳朵;听力,听觉;倾听
early [ˈəːli] *adv.* 早;*adj.* 早的;早期的
earn [əːn] *vt.* 赚得,挣得,获得;赢得;生利
earnest [ˈəːnist] *adj.* 认真的;诚恳的;重要的;*n.* 真诚;重要的东西
earth [əːθ] *n.* 地球;陆地;地面,大地;泥土;世间;地球人
earthquake [ˈəːθkweik] *n.* 地震;大震荡
ease [iːz] *n.* 容易;舒适,安乐;*n.* 安逸;悠闲;*vt.* 缓和;使……安心;使……安心;*v.* 减轻;放松
easily [ˈiːzili] *adv.* 容易地;舒适的;无疑地
east [iːst] *n.* 东,东部;*adv.* 在东方;向东方;*adj.* 东方的
Easter [ˈiːstə(r)] *n.* <宗>复活节
eastern [ˈiːstən] *adj.* 东部的;东方的;朝东的
easy [ˈiːzi] *adj.* 容易的;安逸的;不费力的;*adv.* 慢慢地;当心地
eat [iːt] *vt.* 吃;喝;消耗;*vi.* 吃饭;侵蚀
echo [ˈekəu] *n.* 回声,回音;回波;反响;共鸣
vi. 重复发回声;回响;仿效
ecology [iˈkɔlədʒi] *n.* 生态(学)
economic [ˌiːkəˈnɔmik] *adj.* 经济的;经济学的;*n.* [-s]经济学(状况等)
economical [ˌiːkəˈnɔmikəl] *adj.* 节约的,节俭的;经济的;合算的;经济学的
economy [iˈkɔnəmi] *n.* 经济;节约,节省;*adj.* 经济型的
edge [edʒ] *n.* 边缘,边;刀口;*vt.* 给……加上边
edition [iˈdiʃən] *n.* 版,版本,版次
editor [ˈeditə] *n.* 编辑,编者;校订者
editorial [ˌedɪˈtɔːriəl] *adj.* 编辑的,主笔的
educate [ˈedjukeit] *vt.* 教育;培养;训练
education [ˌedjukeiʃn] *n.* 教育;培养;训导;教育学
effect [iˈfekt] *n.* 结果;效果;效力;影响;
vt. 招致;引起;实现;达到
effective [iˈfektiv] *adj.* 有效的;有影响的
efficiency [iˈfiʃənsi] *n.* 效率;功效;效能
efficient [iˈfiʃənt] *adj.* 效率高的;有能力的;胜任的
effort [ˈefət] *n.* 努力;努力的成果
egg [eg] *n.* 蛋,鸡蛋;卵
eight [eit] *num.* 八;八个
eighteen [ˈeiˈtiːn] *num.* 十八;十八个
eighth [eitθ] *num.* 第八;*n.* 八分之一
eighty [ˈeiti] *num.* 八十;八十个
either [ˈiːðə] *pron.* (两者)任何一个;*adv.* 也
elaborate [iˈlæbəreit] *adj.* 复杂的;精心制作的;精细的,精心的;详尽的;*v.* 详细地说明;用心地作;推敲
elastic [iˈlæstik] *n.* 橡皮圈;有松紧的东西;松紧带;*adj.* 有弹性的;灵活的;可变的
elbow [ˈelbəu] *n.* 肘,肘部;*v.* 用手肘推开;推挤
elder [ˈeldə] *adj.* 年龄较大的,年长的;*n.* 长者;长辈
eldest [ˈeldist] *adj.* 最年长的,最老的;年事最

高的(old 的最高级)
elect [iˈlekt] *vt.* 选举,推选;选择;*adj.* 被选的,选出的
election [iˈlekʃən] *n.* 选举;选择权;当选
electric [iˈlektrik] *adj.* 电的,电动的;*n.* 供电
electrical [iˈlektrikəl] *adj.* 电的;电气科学的;与电有关的
electricity [ˌilekˈtrisiti] *n.* 电;电学;电流
electron [iˈlektrɔn] *n.* 电子
electronic [ilekˈtrɔnik] *adj.* 电子的
electronics [ilekˈtrɔniks] *n.* 电子学;电子器件
elegant [ˈelɪɡənt] *adj.* 优美的;典雅的;简洁的
element [ˈelimənt] *n.* 成分;要素;元素
elementary [ˌeləˈmentəri] *adj.* 基本的;初级的;元素的
elephant [ˈelifənt] *n.* 大象
elevator [ˈeliveitə] *n.* 电梯;升降机
else [els] *adv.* 其他,另外;否则
elsewhere [ˈelsˈwεə] ad. 在别处;向别处
email [ˈiːmeɪl] *n.* 电子邮件;*vt.* 给……发电子邮件
embarrass [imˈbærəs] *vt.* 使窘迫;使为难;阻碍;*vi.* 变得困窘
embassy [ˈembəsi] *n.* 大使馆;大使馆全体成员;大使的职务(地位)
embrace [imˈbreis] *vt.* 拥抱;包括,包含;包围;信奉;*n.* 拥抱
emerge [iˈməːdʒ] *vi.* 出现,涌现;冒出;(由某种状态)脱出;(事实)显现出来
emergency [iˈməːdʒnsi] *n.* 紧急情况,突然事件
emigrate [ˈemiɡreit] *vt.* 移居国外
emit [iˈmit] *vt.* 散发;发射;发表;发出;放射;吐露
emotion [iˈməuʃən] *n.* 情感,感情;情绪;激动
emotional [iˈməuʃənl] *adj.* 感情的;情绪的
emperor [ˈempərə] *n.* 皇帝
emphasis [ˈemfəsis] *n.* 强调,重点;重要性
emphasize [ˈemfəsaiz] *vt.* 强调;着重
empire [ˈempaiə] *n.* 帝国
employ [imˈplɔi] *vi.* 雇用;使用;使忙于
employee [ˌemplɔiˈiː] *n.* 受雇者,雇员,雇工
employer [imˈplɔiə] *n.* 雇佣者,雇主
employment [imˈplɔimənt] *n.* 工业;雇用;使用;职业
empty [ˈempti] a. 空的;空洞的
enable [iˈneibl] *vt.* 使能够;使可能
enclose [inˈkləuz] *vt.* 围住,圈起;附上;放入封套
encounter [inˈkauntə] *vt.* & *vi.* 遭遇,遇到;偶然碰到;*n.* 遭遇意外的相见
encourage [inˈkʌridʒ] *vt.* 鼓励,支持;助长;激励
encyclop(a)edia [enˌsaikləuˈpiːdjə] *n.* 百科全书,大全
end [end] *n.* 末端;终点;目标;结束;
vt. & *vi.* 结束,终结;*adj.* 最终的
endeavo(u)r [inˈdevə(r)] *n.* 尽力,竭力;
v. 努力;尽力;竭力
ending [ˈendiŋ] *n.* 结尾,结局;死亡
endless [ˈendlis] *adj.* 无止境的;没完没了的
endure [inˈdjuə] *vt.* 忍受,容忍;*vi.* 持久,持续
enemy [ˈenimi] *n.* 敌人,仇敌;敌兵;敌对势力
energetic [ˌenəˈdʒetik] *adj.* 积极主动的;精力旺盛的
energy [ˈenədʒi] *n.* 活力;精力;能力;能量
enforce [inˈfɔːs] *vt.* 实施,执行;强制,强迫;加强
engage [inˈgeidʒ] *vt.* 使从事于;聘用;答应;预定;使忙碌;订婚
engine [ˈendʒin] *n.* 发动机;引擎;机车;火车头;*vt.* 装引擎
engineer [ˌendʒiˈniə] *n.* 工程师,技师,机械师;*vt.* 设计;建造
engineering [ˌendʒiˈniəriŋ] *n.* 工程,工程学
enhance[inˈhɑːns] *v.* 提高,增强;改进
enjoy [inˈdʒɔi] *vt.* & *vi.* 享受;欣赏;喜爱
enlarge [inˈlɑːdʒ] *vt.* 扩大,扩展;增大;放大
enormous [iˈnɔːməs] *adj.* 巨大的,庞大的
enough [iˈnʌf] *adv.* 足够地;完全地;
pron. 足够;受够
enquire (in-) [ɪnˈkwaɪə(r)] *vi.* 打听;询问;问问题;查问
enrich [ɪnˈrɪtʃ] *vt.* 使富裕,使富有
ensure [inˈʃuə] *vt.* 保证;保护;赋予
enter [ˈentə] *vt.* 走进,进入;参加;报名;开始;加入;*vi.* 进入;参加;开始
entertain [ˌentəˈtein] *vt.* & *vi.* 使欢乐;招待;怀抱
enthusiasm [inˈθjuːziæzəm] *n.* 热情,热心,热忱;热衷的事物
enthusiastic [in. θjuːziˈæstik] *adj.* 热情的,热心的
entire [inˈtaiə] *adj.* 全部的,整个的,完整的;同性质的;纯正的;全面的
entitle [inˈtaitl] *vt.* 给……权利(或资格);取名为;使有权利

entrance [ˈentrəns, inˈtrɑːns] *n.* 入口，门口；进入；登场
entry [ˈentri] *n.* 入口处；登记；进入，入口
envelope [ˈenviləup] *n.* 信封；封套，封皮
environment [inˈvaiərənmənt] *n.* 环境；外界；围绕
envy [ˈenvi] *vt. & vi. & n.* 妒忌，嫉妒；羡慕
equal [ˈiːkwəl] *adj.* 相等的；平等的；*n.* 对手；匹敌；同辈；*vt.* 等于；比得上
equality [iːˈkwɔliti] *n.* 等同；平等；相等
equation [iˈkweiʃən] *n.* 方程(式)；等式；均衡；相等
equip [iˈkwip] *vt.* 装备；配备；设备
equipment [iˈkwipmənt] *n.* 装备，设备；配备
equivalent [iˈkwivələnt] *adj.* 相等的；等量的；*n.* 相等物
era [ˈiərə] *n.* 时代；年代；纪元
erect [iˈrekt] *vt.* 建，建立；使竖立；*adj.* 直立的；竖立的；笔直的
error [ˈerə] *n.* 错误，谬误；差错
esp. [isˈpeʃəl] *adj.* (= especial)特别的，特殊的；尤其；*adv.* (= especially)特别，特殊
escape [isˈkeip] *vt. & vi.* 逃跑，逃脱；避开；*n.* 逃跑，逃亡
especially [isˈpeʃəli] *adv.* 特别，尤其；格外
essay [ˈesei, eˈsei] *n.* 短文；散文；论文；小品文
essential [iˈsenʃəl] *adj.* 必要的；重要的；本质的；*n.* 要素；要点
establish [iˈstæbliʃ] *vt.* 建立；设立；确立；创办
establishment [isˈtæbliʃmənt] *n.* 建立；设立；确立；设施
estimate [ˈestimeit] *vt.* 估计；估价；评价；*n.* 估计；估价
etc. [etˈsetərə] *n.* 附加的人；附加物；以及其他；等等 = etcetera
Europe [ˈjuərəp] *n.* 欧洲
European [ˌjuərəˈpi(ː)ən] *adj.* 欧洲的；*n.* 欧洲人
evaluate [iˈvæljueit] *vt.* 评估；评价；估……的价
evaporate [iˈvæpəreit] *vt.* 使蒸发；*vi.* 蒸发；失去水分；消失
eve [iːv] *n.* 前夜，前夕；前一刻
even [ˈiːvən] *adv.* 甚至；甚至更；还；恰好；正当；*adj.* 偶数的；相等的；均匀的；*v.* 相等
evening [ˈiːvniŋ] *n.* 傍晚，黄昏；晚上
event [iˈvent] *n.* 事件，大事；事变；项目；活动
eventually [iˈventjuəli] *adv.* 终于，最后
ever [ˈevə] *adv.* 在任何时候；曾经；永远
every [ˈevri] *adj.* 每一的；每隔……的
everybody [ˈevribɔdi] *pron.* 每人，人人，各人
everyday [ˈevriˈdei] *adj.* 每天的；日常的；平常的
everyone [ˈevriwʌn] *pron.* 每人，人人；*n.* 每个人
everything [ˈevriθiŋ] *pron.* 每件事，事事；一切
everywhere [ˈevriwɛə] *adv.* 到处，处处；无论何处
evidence [ˈevidəns] *n.* 根据；证据；证人；*vt. & vi.* 证实；证明
evident [ˈevidənt] *adj.* 明显的；明白的
evil [ˈiːvl] *n.* 邪恶；罪恶；祸害；*adj.* 邪恶的；坏的
evolution [ˌiːvəˈluːʃən] *n.* 进化，演化；发展
evolve [iˈvɔlv] *vt. & vi.* 使进化；使发展；展开
exact [igˈzækt] *adj.* 确切的；精确的；*vt.* 强求；要求；索取
exactly [igˈzæktli] *adv.* 确切地；恰恰正是
exaggerate [igˈzædʒəreit] *vt. & vi.* 夸大，夸张
exam [igˈzæm] *n.* 考试；检查；细查 = examination 考试
examination [ig. zæmiˈneiʃən] *n.* 考试；检查；细查；审讯
examine [igˈzæmin] *vt.* 检查；仔细观察；调查；考试；*vi.* 调查
example [igˈzɑːmpl] *n.* 例子，实例；模范，榜样；*vt.* 把……作为例子
exceed [ikˈsiːd] *vt.* 超过，超出；胜过；超出界限；*vi.* 领先
exceedingly [ikˈsiːdiŋli] *adv.* 极端地；非常；很
excellent [ˈeksələnt] *adj.* 优秀的；杰出的
except [ikˈsept] *prep. & conj.* 除了……之外；若不是；除非；*vt.* 除；除外
exception [ikˈsepʃən] *n.* 例外；除外
excess [ikˈses] *n.* 超越；过量，过度；*adj.* 过量的；额外的
excessive [ikˈsesiv] *adj.* 过多的；过分的；极度的
exchange [iksˈtʃeindʒ] *vt. & vi.* 交换，交流；交易；兑换；*n.* 交换，交换物；汇兑；交易所
excite [ikˈsait] *vt.* 使激动；引起；刺激；激励
exciting [ikˈsaitiŋ] *adj.* 令人兴奋的
exclaim [iksˈkleim] *vi.* 呼喊；惊叫；大声叫
exclude [iksˈkluːd] *vt.* 把……排除在外；拒绝
exclusively [iksˈkluːsivli] *adv.* 专门地；排他地(独占地；专门地；仅仅；只)
excursion [iksˈkəːʃən] *n.* 远足；短途旅行
excuse [iksˈkjuːz] *vt.* 原谅；免除；辩解；*n.* 借口；理由

execute [ˈeksikjuːt] *vt.* 将……处死;实施;执行;完成
executive [igˈzekjutiv] *adj.* 执行的;行政的;决策的;经营的;*n.* 执行者;主管;行政部门
exercise [ˈeksəsaiz] *n.* 锻炼,运动;训练;练习,作业;*vi.* 练习;锻炼;*vt.* 运用
exert [igˈzəːt] *vt.* 尽(力);运用;施加(压力影响等)
exhaust [igˈzɔːst] *vt.* 使筋疲力尽;用尽;排空;*vi.* 耗尽;*n.* 排气;排气装置
exhibit [igˈzibit] *vt.* 陈列,展览;展现;*vi.* 展览;*n.* 展览品;展览;物证
exhibition [ˌeksiˈbiʃən] *n.* 展览,陈列,展示;展览会
exist [igˈzist] *vi.* 存在;生存,生活
existence [igˈzistəns] *n.* 存在,实在;生存
exit [ˈeksit] *n.* 出口;退场,离去;
vi. 退出;*vt.* 离开
expand [iksˈpænd] *vt.* 扩大;增加;详述;扩展;使膨胀;*vi.* 扩展;增加;详述
expansion [iksˈpænʃən] *n.* 扩大;扩充;扩张;膨胀
expect [iksˈpekt] *vt.* 预料,预期;等待,盼望
expectation [ˌekspekˈteiʃən] *n.* 期待,期望;预期
expedition [ˌekspəˈdɪʃn] *n.* 考察,远航;考察队,(短途的)旅行
expense [iksˈpens] *n.* 花费,消费;费用;代价
expensive [iksˈpensiv] *adj.* 昂贵的,花钱多的;豪华的
experience [iksˈpiəriəns] *n.* 经验;感受;经历;*vt.* 经历 体验
experiment [iksˈperimənt] *n.* 实验,试验;尝试;*vi.* 做实验;尝试
experimental [iks. periˈmentl] adj 实验(性)的,试验(性)的
expert [ˈekspəːt] *n.* 专家;能手;*adj.* 熟练的;内行的
explain [iksˈplein] *vt. & vi.* 解释;说明;为……辩解
explanation [ˌekspləˈneiʃən] *n.* 解释;说明;辩解
explicit [ɪkˈsplɪsɪt] *adj.* 易于理解的;明确的;直言的
explode [iksˈpləud] *vt.* 使爆炸;驳倒;*vi.* 爆炸;爆发(感情);激增
exploit [ˈeksplɔit, iksˈplɔit] *vt. & vi.* 剥削;利用;开拓;开发
explore [iksˈplɔː] *vt. & vi.* 探险;探索;探测;探究;
explosion [iksˈpləuʒən] *n.* 爆炸;爆发;炸裂;激增
explosive [iksˈpləusiv] *n.* 炸药;*adj.* 爆炸(性)的
export [ˈekspɔːt, eksˈpɔːt] *vt.* 输出;出口;运走;*n.* 出口;输出品;*vi.* 传播;输出
expose [ikˈspəuz] *vt.* 使暴露;揭露,揭穿;使遭受(危险或不快)
exposure [iksˈpəuʒə] *n.* 暴露;揭露;显露;曝光;面临(困难)
express [iksˈpres] *vt.* 表达;表示;挤压出;快递;*n.* 快车;快递;专使;*adj.* 急速的;明确的;直接的;*adv.* 用快递;特意地
expression [iksˈpreʃən] *n.* 词句;措辞;表达;表示;表现;表情
extend [iksˈtend] *vt.* 延长,延伸,伸展;扩大,扩充;扩展
extension [iksˈtenʃən] *n.* 延长部分;伸展;扩充;范围
extensive [iksˈtensiv] *adj.* 广阔的;广泛的
extent [iksˈtent] *n.* 广度;范围;程度;宽度;长度;大小;
exterior [eksˈtiəriə] *adj.* 外部的,外在的;表面的;对外的;*n.* 外部;表面;外形
external [eksˈtəːnl] *adj.* 外部的,外面的;外用的;客观的;表面的
extra [ˈekstrə] *adj.* 额外的;*ad.* 特别地;*n.* 额外的事物
extraordinary [iksˈtrɔːdnri] *adj.* 非同寻常的;特别的;非凡的
extreme [iksˈtriːm] *adj.* 极度的;极端的;严重的;*n.* 极端;极限
extremely [iksˈtriːmli] *adv.* 极端;极其;非常
eye [ai] *n.* 眼睛;眼力;鉴赏力;*v.* 看,注视
eyesight [ˈaisait] *n.* 视力,目力

F

fable [ˈfeɪbl] *n.* 寓言,童话;传说
fabric [ˈfæbrɪk] *n.* 织物;布;构造

face [feɪs] *n.* 面容;表面;脸;*vt.* 面对;面向……;正视;面临……
facility [fəˈsiliti] *n.* 设备;容易;便利;灵巧;容易;熟练
fact [fækt] *n.* 事实;实际;实情
factor [ˈfæktə] *n.* 因素;因子;
factory [ˈfæktəri] *n.* 工厂,制造厂
faculty [ˈfækəlti] *n.* 才能,能力;(大学的)系;科;全体教员
fade [feid] *vi.* 褪色;逐渐消失;凋谢;*vt.* 使褪色
Fahrenheit [ˈfærənhait, ˈfɑːr-] *n.* 华氏温度计;*adj.* 华氏的
fail [feil] *vi.* 失败;失灵;不能;衰退;不及格;*vt.* 辜负;缺少;未能做;*n.* 不及格
failure [ˈfeiljə] *n.* 失败;失败的人或事
faint [feint] *adj.* 微弱的;虚弱的;无力的;模糊的;*vi.* 昏倒;*n.* 昏厥,昏倒
fair [fɛə] *adj.* 公平的;晴朗的;美丽的;相当的;(皮肤;毛发等)浅色的;白皙的;*n.* 展览会;市集,定期集市;*adv.* 公平地;直接地
fairly [ˈfɛəli] *adv.* 相当;公平地,公正地;合法地;适当地
faith [feiθ] *n.* 信任;信心;信仰
faithful [ˈfeiθfəl] *adj.* 忠诚的;如实的
fake [feɪk] *vt.* 伪造;篡改;对……做手脚;仿造,假装;*n.* 骗子;冒牌货,赝品;冒充,诈骗;*adj.* 假的,冒充的
fall [fɔːl] *vi.* 落下;跌倒,倒下;陷落;来临;*n.* 秋天;落下;瀑布
false [fɔːls] *adj.* 不真实的,伪造的;人造的;假的;错误的;虚伪的
fame [feim] *n.* 名声,名望
familiar [fəˈmiljə] *adj.* 熟悉的,熟知的
family [ˈfæmili] *n.* 家,家庭,家族;*adj.* 家庭的
famine [ˈfæmin] *n.* 饥荒;严重的缺乏
famous [ˈfeiməs] *adj.* 著名的,出名的;一流的
fan [fæn] *n.* (运动等)狂热爱好者;风扇;扇形物;*vt.* 吹拂;煽吹,煽动;向扇子一样展开
fancy [ˈfænsi] *n.* 想象力;设想,幻想;爱好,喜好;爱;*adj.* 想象的;时髦的;华丽装饰的;奢侈的;*vt.* 想象;自认为;喜好
far [fɑː] *adj.* 远的;*adv.* 远 遥远;*n.* 远处
fare [fɛə] *n.* 车费,船费;票价;费用
farewell [ˈfɛəˈwel] *n.* 告别
farm [fɑːm] *n.* 农场,农庄,农田;饲养场;*vt.* 务农;*vi.* 务农
farmer [ˈfɑːmə] *n.* 农民,农夫;农场主
farther [ˈfɑːðə] *adv.* 更远地;进一步地;*adj.* 更远的;进一步的
fascinate [ˈfæsɪneɪt] *v.* 深深吸引;入迷
fashion [ˈfæʃən] *n.* 样子;方式;风尚,流行;时装
fashionable [ˈfæʃənəbl] *adj.* 流行的,时髦的
fast [fɑːst] *adj.* 快速的,偏快的;*adv.* 快,很快地
fasten [ˈfæsn] *vt.* 扎牢;扣住,拴紧,使固定,系;强加于;*vi.* 固定,系紧;抓紧
fat [fæt] *adj.* 肥的;胖的;厚的;*n.* 脂肪;肥肉
fatal [ˈfeitl] *adj.* 致命的;毁灭性的;决定性的;命运的
fate [feit] *n.* 命运;天数,天意;*vt.* 注定
father [ˈfɑːðə] *n.* 父亲;神父;创始人;鼻祖;*vt.* 成为父亲
father-in-law [ˈfɑːðərinlɔː] *n.* 岳父;公公
fatigue [fəˈtiːg] *n.* 疲劳,劳累;累活
fault [fɔːlt] *n.* 缺点;过失;故障;*vt. & vi.* 挑剔;指责;发现错误
faulty [ˈfɔːlti] *adj.* 有错误的;有缺点的
favo(u)r [ˈfeivə] *n.* 好感;赞同;恩惠;好意;喜爱;偏爱;*vt.* 关心;偏爱;支持;利于
favo(u)rable [ˈfeivərəbl] *adj.* 有利的;有用的;良好的;赞成的
favo(u)rite [ˈfeivərit] *adj.* 特别受喜爱的;特别喜爱的;*n.* 特别喜爱的人(或物)
fax [fæks] *n.* 传真;*vt.* 传真;传真;传输
fear [fiə] *n.* 害怕;担心;敬畏;不安的原因;*vt.* 害怕;敬畏
fearful [ˈfiəfəl] *adj.* 害怕的,可怕的;担心的
feasible [ˈfiːzəbl] *adj.* 可行的;可能的
feast [fiːst] *n.* 盛宴,宴会,酒席,筵席;节日;节会;*vt. & vi.* 款宴;享乐;请客
feather [ˈfeðə] *n.* 羽毛,翎毛,羽状物;
feature [fiːtʃə] *n.* 特征,特色;面貌;*vt.* 以……为特色;*vi.* 起重要作用
February [ˈfebruəri] *n.* 二月
federal [ˈfedərəl] *adj.* 联邦(制)的,联邦政府的;联盟的,同盟的;*n.* 联邦主义者;同盟盟友
fee [fiː] *n.* 费 酬金,赏金
feeble [fiːbl] *adj.* 虚弱的;微弱的;无力的
feed [fiːd] *vt.* 喂(养),饲养;靠……为生;*vi.* 吃饲料;进食;*n.* 饲养;饲料;一餐
feedback [ˈfiːdbæk] *n.* 回授;反馈,反应;成果
feel [fiːl] *vi.* 有知觉;似乎;同情;*vt.* 触摸;感觉,觉得;*n.* 感觉;触觉;直觉;氛围
feeling [ˈfiːliŋ] *n.* 感情;感觉;知觉;意识;气氛;*adj.* 有感情的;富于同情心的;含情脉脉的

fellow [ˈfeləu] *n.* 人;家伙;伙伴,朋友;同类;*adj.* 同类的;同事的;同伴的
female [ˈfiːmeil] *n.* 雌性的动植物;女子;*adj.* 雌的;女(性)的
fence [fens] *n.* 栅栏;围墙;*vt.* 用篱笆围住;防护
ferry [ˈferi] *n.* 渡船;渡口;摆渡;用船渡运;*vt.* (乘渡船)渡过(河等);渡运;*vi.* 摆渡
fertile [ˈfəːtail] *adj.* 肥沃的;多产的;能繁殖的
fertilise(-ze) [ˈfəːtilaiz] *v.* 施肥;使丰饶
fertiliser(-zer) [ˈfəːtilaizə] *n.* 肥料
festival [ˈfestəvəl] *n.* 节日;音乐节;庆祝及祭祀;欢宴
fetch [fetʃ] *vt.* 拿来;请来;接去;航行到达;*vi.* 取回
fever [ˈfiːvə] *n.* 发热,发烧;狂热
few [fjuː] *adj.* 很少的;少数的;*pron.* 少数
fibre [ˈfaibə] *n.* 纤维,纤维质,纤维组织;织地
fiction [ˈfikʃən] *n.* 小说;虚构,杜撰
field [fiːld] *n.* 田野,田地,原野;牧场;场地;领域
fierce [fiəs] *adj.* 凶猛的,猛烈的;残暴的;强烈的;狂热的
fifteen [ˈfifˈtiːn] num. 十五;十五个
fifth [fifθ] num. 第五;*n.* 五分之一
fifty [ˈfifti] num. 五十;五十个
fight [fait] *vi.* 打架(仗);斗争,战斗;斗志;*vt.* 对抗;打架;*vi.* 斗争;奋斗
figure [ˈfigə] *n.* 数字;外形;人物;图形;形状;体型;*v.* 认为;领会到
file [fail] *n.* 档案;公文箱;*vt.* 把……归档
fill [fil] *vt.* 装满,盛满,占满;填充
film [film] *n.* 影片;胶卷;*vt.* 把……拍成电影;*vi.* 从事电影拍摄
filter [ˈfiltə] *vt.* & *vi.* 过滤;渗透;*n.* 滤纸;筛选;滤波器;过滤器;滤色镜;
final [ˈfainl] *adj.* 最后的;决定性的;*n.* 决赛;期末考试
finally [ˈfainəli] *adv.* 最后,最终;不可更改的
finance [faiˈnæns] *n.* 财政,金融;财源;*vt.* 给……提供资金
financial [faiˈnænʃəl] *adj.* 财政的,金融的
find [faind] *vt.* & *vi.* 找到,找出;发觉,感觉到;认为;*n.* 发现物
finding [ˈfaindiŋ] *n.* 发现,发现物;调查(或研究)的结果
fine [fain] *adj.* 美好的;优质的;精致的;晴朗的;健康的;*adv.* 恰好地;合适地;*n.* 罚款;罚金;结尾;*vt.* 罚款
finger [ˈfiŋgə] *n.* 手指;指针;指状物;*vt.* 用手指触碰(演奏);(用手)指;*vi.* 触摸
finish [ˈfiniʃ] *vt.* 完成,结束;*vi.* 终结,完成;*n.* 结束,完成
fire [ˈfaiə] *n.* 火;火灾;射击;*vi.* 点燃;解职;开枪,开火
fireman [ˈfaiəmən] *n.* 消防队员
firm [fəːm] *n.* 商行,商号,公司;*vt.* (使)变得坚实;定案;*vi.* 变硬;*adj.* 坚定的,坚固的;结实的;*adv.* 稳固地;坚定地
first [fəːst] *num.* 第一;*adv.* 最初;首先;第一;优先;*adj.* 第一的;最早的;一流的;*n.* (序数词)第一;第一个人或事物;(大学学位的)最优等成绩
fish [fiʃ] *n.* 鱼,鱼肉;*vi.* 钓鱼,捕鱼
fisherman [ˈfiʃəmən] *n.* 渔民,渔夫,打鱼人;渔船
fist [fist] *n.* 拳(头);抓住;*vt.* 紧握;用拳头打
fit [fit] *vt.* 适合;安装;*vi.* 适合;*n.* 适宜;*adj.* 适宜的;健壮的
five [faiv] num. 五;五个
fix [fiks] *vt.* & *vi.* 使固定;决定;修理;准备
flag [flæg] *n.* 旗,旗帜,旗标,信号旗;旗舰旗
flame [fleim] *n.* 火焰,火舌;鲜红色;热情;*vi.* 焚烧;面红
flare [flɛə] *vi.* 闪耀,闪光;*vt.* 使闪亮;*n.* 闪光,闪耀
flash [flæʃ] *n.* 闪光,闪现,闪烁物;花哨;一瞬间;电脑动画技术;*vi.* 闪,闪现,闪烁;*vt.* 传送;流露出;*adj.* 花哨的;炫耀的;
flat [flæt] *adj.* 平的,扁平的,平坦的;单调的;*adv.* 平直地;干脆地;*n.* 一套房间;单元住宅;[英]公寓
flavour [ˈfleivə] *n.* 味,味道,风味;香味;*vt.* 给……加味
fleet [fliːt] *n.* 舰队,船队;团队;机群;*vt.* & *vi.* 飞过;掠过;*adj.* 跑得快的
flesh [fleʃ] *n.* 肉,肌肉,肉体;人性;*vt.* 用肉喂;赋予血肉;使长肉;*vi.* 变胖
flexible [ˈfleksəbl] *adj.* 易弯曲的,灵活的,柔韧的;可变通的
flight [flait] *n.* 航班;飞行;逃跑;航程;*vi.* 滑行;*vt.* 冲
float [fləut] *vi.* 漂浮,游荡,飘;*vt.* 使漂浮;提出;*n.* 漂流物
flock [flɔk] *n.* 羊群;群;大量;*vi.* 成群而行;聚集

flood [flʌd] *n.* 洪水,水灾;*vt. & vi.* 灌溉;淹没;泛滥
floor [flɔː] *n.* 地板;楼层;底部;地面
flour [flauə] *n.* 面粉;粉,粉状物质;*vt. & vi.* 在……上撒(面)粉
flourish [ˈflʌriʃ] *vi.* 繁荣,兴旺;茂盛;活跃;*vt.* 挥舞;*n.* 挥舞;茂盛;兴旺
flow [fləu] *vi.* 流动;飘垂;涨潮;*vt.* 使流动;淹没;*n.* 流;水流;循环;顺畅;涨潮
flower [ˈflauə] *n.* 花,花卉;华丽;*vi.* 成熟;开花
flu [fluː] *n.* 流行性感冒
fluent [ˈfluːənt] *adj.* 流利的;流畅的
fluid [ˈfluːid] *n.* 流体;液体;*adj.* 流畅优美的;流体的;流动的;不稳定的
flush [flʌʃ] *vi.* 奔流;(脸)发红;冲刷;*vt.* 用水冲洗惊起(一群鸟);*n.* 流溢;面红;旺盛;冲水(尤指冲马桶)
fly [flai] *n.* 蝇,苍蝇;飞行;升高;*vt. & vi.* 飞行;飞翔
focus [ˈfəukəs] *vi.* 聚焦;注视;集中,聚集,使集中;*n.* 焦点;焦距
fog [fɔg] *n.* 雾,烟雾,尘雾;朦胧;喷雾;*vt. & vi.* 以雾笼罩;使模糊
fold [fəuld] *vt.* 折叠;合拢;包;*n.* 褶;折层,折痕
folk [fəuk] *n.* 人们;家属,亲属;*adj.* 民间的
follow [ˈfɔləu] *vt.* 跟随;沿行;遵循;听得懂;结果是;*vi.* 跟着做;之后是
following [ˈfɔləuiŋ] *adj.* 接着的;下列的;其次的;*n.* 下列各项;部下
fond [fɔnd] *adj.* 喜爱的,溺爱的;渴望的
food [fuːd] *n.* 食物,食品;养料
fool [fuːl] *n.* 蠢人,傻子;*vt.* 欺骗,愚弄;*vi.* 干傻事;开玩笑;*adj.* 愚蠢的
foolish [ˈfuːliʃ] *adj.* 愚蠢的;鲁莽的;荒谬的;可笑的
foot [fut] *n.* 脚;最下部;英尺;山脚;最底部;*vi.* 跳舞;步行
football [ˈfutbɔːl] *n.* 足球比赛,足球;橄榄球
footstep [ˈfutstep] *n.* 脚步,脚步声,足迹
for [fɔː] *prep.* 为;给;因为;关于;代表;支持;往;*conj.* 因为
forbid [fəˈbid] *vt.* 禁止,不许,阻止;妨碍
force [fɔːs] *vt.* 强迫,施暴,强夺;加压力;*n.* 力,力量;武力;暴力;影响力
forecast [ˈfɔːkɑːst] *n.* 预测,预报;*vt. & vi.* 预示;预测
forehead [ˈfɔːhed] *n.* 额头;前部
foreign [ˈfɔrin] *adj.* 外国的,外来的;外交的
foreigner [ˈfɔːrinə] *n.* 外国人
foremost [ˈfɔːməust] *adj.* 最初的;第一流的;*adv.* 在最前面
forest [ˈfɔrist] *n.* 森林,森林地带;园林;*vt.* 用树林覆盖植树
forever [fəˈrevə] *adv.* 永远;总是,老是;*n.* 漫长时间
forget [fəˈget] *vt. & vi.* 忘记,遗忘;忽略
forgive [fəˈgiv] *vt. & vi.* 原谅,饶恕,宽恕
fork [fɔːk] *n.* 餐叉,叉,叉状物;*vt. & vi.* 叉起;耙;成叉状
form [fɔːm] *n.* 形式;形状;表格;*vt.* 形成,组成;建立
formal [ˈfɔːməl] *adj.* 正式的;礼仪上的;形式的;*n.* 正式(活动)
format [ˈfɔːmæt] *n.* (出版物的)版式 *vt.* 使格式化;安排……的格局;设计……的版面;*vi.* 设计一个版式
formation [fɔːˈmeiʃən] *n.* 形成,构成,形成物;编队
former [ˈfɔːmə] *adj.* 在前的,以前的;前任的;*n.* 前者;形成的原因
formula [ˈfɔːmjulə] *n.* 公式;式;配方;规则;*adj.* (赛车的)级的;方程式的
forth [fɔːθ] *adv.* 向前;向外,往外
fortnight [ˈfɔːtnait] *n.* 两星期,十四天
fortunate [ˈfɔːtʃənit] *adj.* 幸运的,侥幸的
fortunately [ˈfɔitʃənitli] *adv.* 幸运地,幸亏
fortune [ˈfɔːtʃən] *n.* 命运,运气;财产
forty [ˈfɔːti] *pron.* 四十(个 只……)
forum [ˈfɔːrəm] *n.* 论坛,讨论会,专题讨论节目;集会的公共场所;提供公开讨论的媒体;法庭
forward [ˈfɔːwəd] *adv.* 向前;今后,往后;*adj.* 向前的;早的;迅速的;前锋;*v.* 转交;促进;运送
found [faund] *vt.* 创立,创办,建立;打地基;铸造;*vt.* 寻找(find 的过去分词)
foundation [faunˈdeiʃən] *n.* 基础;根据;建立;地基;基金
fountain [ˈfauntin] *n.* 泉水,喷泉;源泉;储水容器
four [fɔː] *num.* 四,四个
fourteen [ˌfɔːˈtiːn] *num.* 十四,第十四
fourth [fɔːθ] num. 第四,四分之一
fox [fɔks] *n.* 狐狸;狡猾的人;*v.* 把……难住;使上当;使迷惑
fraction [ˈfrækʃən] *n.* 小部分;片断;分数;破片

fragile [ˈfrædʒaɪl] *adj.* 脆弱的；易碎的；精巧的；虚弱的
fragment [ˈfrægmənt] *n.* 碎片，破片，碎块；*vt. & vi.* 变成碎片；
fragrant [ˈfreɪgrənt] *adj.* 芳香的，香的；愉快的；喷香；芳菲
frame [freim] *n.* 框架，框子，构架
framework [ˈfreimwəːk] *n.* 框架，构架，结构；骨架
France [frɑːns] *n.* 法国，法兰西
frank [fræŋk] *adj.* 坦白的，直率的；无误的
free [friː] *adj.* 自由的；空闲的；大方的；免费的；*vt.* 释放；解放；*adv.* 自由地；免费地
freedom [ˈfriːdəm] *n.* 自由，自主
freely [ˈfriːli] *adv.* 自由地；免费地；直率地
freeze [friːz] *vi.* 冻，结冻，冷动；僵硬；*vt.* 使结冰
freight [freit] *n.* 货运，货物；运费；船货；*vt.* 装货；运送
French [frentʃ] *adj.* 法国(人)的，法语的；*n.* 法国人；法语
frequency [ˈfriːkwənsi] *n.* 屡次；次数，频率，频繁
frequent [ˈfriːkwənt] *adj.* 时常发生的，经常的，频繁的；*vt.* 常到，常去
frequently [ˈfriːkwəntli] *adv.* 时常，常常，经常地，频繁地
fresh [freʃ] *adj.* 新的，新鲜的；无经验的；淡(水)的；精神饱满的
freshman [ˈfreʃmən] *n.* （中学或大学的）一年级学生；新手
friction [ˈfrikʃən] *n.* 摩擦，摩擦力；分歧
Friday [ˈfraidi] *n.* 星期五
fridge [fridʒ] *n.* 电冰箱
friend [frend] *n.* 朋友，友人；赞助者；支持者
friendly [ˈfrendli] *adj.* 友好的，友谊的；*n.* 友好者
friendship [ˈfrendʃip] *n.* 友谊，友好
fright [fraɪt] *n.* 恐怖；惊吓；可怕的东西
frighten [ˈfraitən] *vt.* 使惊恐，吓唬，惊恐
frog [frɔg] *n.* 蛙；
from [frɔm] *prep.* 从……来；
front [frʌnt] *adj.* 前面的；*n.* 前部，前面；开头；前线；*vt.* 面对，朝向；*vi.* 面朝
frontier [ˈfrʌntjə] *n.* 边境，边界，边疆；新领域；尖端；边缘
frost [frɔst] *n.* 冰冻，严寒；霜；*vt. & vi.* 覆着霜，结霜；冻结
frown [fraun] *vt. & vi.* 皱眉，蹙额；不同意；*n.* 皱眉，不悦
frozen [ˈfrəʊzn] *adj.* 冷冻的；冰封的；冻硬的；呆若木鸡的；*v.* 结冰(freeze 的过去分词)；冷藏；冻结；冻住
fruit [fruːt] *n.* 水果，果实；成果；*vt. & vi.* 结果实
fruitful [ˈfruːtfəl] *adj.* 多产的；肥沃的；富有成效的
frustrate [frʌˈstreɪt] *vt.* 挫败；阻挠；使受挫折
fry [frai] *vt.* 油煎，油炸，油炒，炸焦；*vi.* 油炸；烧焦；*n.* （美）法式炸薯条
fuel [ˈfjuəl] *n.* 燃料，木炭；*vt.* 给……加燃料；*vi.* 加燃料
fulfil [ful. fil] *vt.* 履行；满足；完成；实践
full [ful] *adj.* 满的；完全的；充满的；丰富的；*adv.* 完全地；整整
fun [fʌn] *n.* 乐趣，娱乐；玩笑；有趣的人或事物；*adj.* 充满乐趣的；令人愉悦的
function [ˈfʌŋkʃən] *n.* 功能；职务；*vi.* 运行起作用
fund [fʌnd] *n.* 资金；基金；存款；储备；*vt.* 为……提供资金
fundamental [ˌfʌndəˈmentl] *adj.* 基础的，基本的；根本的；重要的；*n.* 基本原理；基础
funeral [ˈfjuːnərəl] *n.* 葬礼，丧礼，丧葬
funny [ˈfʌni] *adj.* 古怪的；滑稽的；有趣的
fur [fəː] *n.* 软毛；毛皮，裘皮；毛皮服饰；毛皮制品
furious [ˈfjuəriəs] *adj.* 狂怒的；狂暴的；猛烈的
furnace [ˈfəːnis] *n.* 炉子，熔炉
furnish [ˈfəːniʃ] *vt.* 供应，提供；布置
furniture [ˈfəːnitʃə] *n.* 家具；装置；设备
further [ˈfəːðə] *adv.* 更远地；此外；进一步地；*adj.* 更多的；更进一步的；*vt.* 促进
furthermore [ˈfəːðəˈmɔː] *adv.* 而且；此外
future [ˈfjuːtʃə] *n.* 将来，未来；前途，前程；*adj.* 将来的

G

gain [gein] *vt.* 获得，得到；增进，增加；*vi.* 增加；得到；*n.* 增进，增益；利润

gallery [ˈgæləri] *n.* 长廊，游廊，画廊，美术馆
gallon [ˈgælən] *n.* 加仑（容量单位）
gamble [ˈgæmbl] *vi.* 赌博；投机，冒风险；孤注一掷；打赌；*vt.* 赌博，下赌注；使冒风险；*n.* 赌博或其他投机；冒险
game [geim] *n.* 游戏；比赛
gang [gæŋ] *n.* 一帮，一伙；队，群，帮；*vt. & vi.* 结一组；联合在一起
gap [gæp] *n.* 缺口；间隔；差距；缝隙；漏洞
garage [ˈgærɑːʒ] *n.* 车库；加油站；汽车修理厂；*vt.* 把……放入车库
garbage [ˈgɑːbidʒ] *n.* 垃圾，污物；废料，废物
garden [ˈgɑːdn] *n.* 花园，菜园，果园，菜园；草地；公园；*vi.* 栽培花木；从事园艺工作；*vt.* 造园；以花园装饰
gardener [ˈgɑːdnə] *n.* 园丁，花匠；园艺家
garment [ˈgɑːmənt] *n.* 衣服；服装
gas [gæs] *n.* 煤气；气体；汽油；*vt.* 给……加汽油；*vi.* 加汽油
gaseous [ˈgæsiəs] *adj.* 气体的，气态的
gasoline [ˈgæsəliːn] *n.* （美）汽油
gasp [gɑːsp] *vi.* 气喘，喘息
gate [geit] *n.* 大门，入口
gather [ˈgæðə] *vi.* 聚集，集合；渐增；*vt.* 收集；使聚集
gay [gei] *adj.* 快乐的，欢快的；鲜明的，色彩鲜艳的；同性恋的；*n.* 同性恋者
gaze [geiz] *vi.* 凝视，盯，注视；*n.* 凝视
gear [giə (r)] *n.* 齿轮；排挡；传动装置
gender [ˈdʒendə (r)] *n.* 性别
gene [dʒiːn] *n.* 基因
general [ˈdʒenərəl] *adj.* 总的；一般的，普遍的；全体的；*n.* 将军；一般；大体
generally [ˈdʒenərəli] *adv.* 一般地；通常地
generate [ˈdʒenəreit] *vt.* 发生，产生，引起；生殖
generation [ˌdʒenəˈreiʃən] *n.* 一代，一代人；产生
generator [ˈdʒenəreitə] *n.* 发电机；发生器；电力公司
generous [ˈdʒenərəs] *adj.* 慷慨的；宽厚的，宽宏大量的
genius [ˈdʒiːnjəs] *n.* 天才，天赋，天资，高智力
gentle [ˈdʒentl] *adj.* 和蔼的，温和的；轻柔的；文雅的；
gentleman [ˈdʒentlmən] *n.* 绅士，先生；有教养的人
gently [ˈdʒentli] ad. 有礼貌地；柔和地，轻轻地，温柔地
genuine [ˈdʒenjuin] *adj.* 真的，真正的，真实的；诚恳的
geography [dʒiˈɔgrəfi] *n.* 地理，地理学
geometry [dʒiˈɔmitri] *n.* 几何，几何学
germ [dʒəːm] *n.* 微生物；细菌；幼芽
German [ˈdʒəːmən] *adj.* 德国（人）的，德语的，日耳曼的；*n.* 德国人，德语，日耳曼人
Germany [ˈdʒəːməni] *n.* 德意志，德国
gesture [ˈdʒestʃə] *n.* 姿势，手势，姿态；*vt. & vi.* 做手势表达
get [get] *vi.* 变得，成为；到达；能够；离开；*vt.* 得到；准备抓住；克服；激怒；使得
ghost [gəust] *n.* 鬼，灵魂，幽灵，鬼魂；*vt. & vi.* 像（鬼一样）地行进
giant [ˈdʒaiənt] *n.* 巨人；伟人；巨大的东西；*adj.* 巨大的
gift [gift] *n.* 礼物，赠品；天赋；赋予；*vt.* 赠送；赋予
girl [gəːl] *n.* 女孩子，姑娘，女儿
give [giv] *vt.* 做，作；送给
glad [glæd] *adj.* 高兴的，乐意的
glance [glɑːns] *vi.* 看一下；瞥闪，瞥见；反光；浏览；*vt.* 瞥见；反光；*n.* 一瞥；闪光；一滑
glare [glɛə] *vi.* 瞪眼；发眩目的光；*n.* 瞪眼；闪耀光；刺眼的光
glass [glɑːs] *n.* 玻璃，玻璃杯，玻璃器皿；窗户；（复）眼镜；透镜；*vt.* 用玻璃把……盖（或罩、围）住；给……装上玻璃
glide [glaid] *vi.* 滑动，滑翔；溜走；消逝；*n.* 滑行，滑动，滑过流水
glimpse [glimps] *vt. & vi.* 瞥见，一瞥；闪烁；*n.* 一瞥，一看；一闪
glitter [ˈglitə] *vi.* 闪闪发光，闪烁；灿烂；辉耀；*n.* 闪光，闪烁；灿烂；辉耀
global [ˈgləʊbl] *adj.* 全球的；整体的；全面的
globe [gləub] *n.* 地球，世界；地界仪；球体
gloomy [ˈgluːmi] *adj.* 黑暗的，阴暗的；令人沮丧的；抑沉的，忧闷的
glorious [ˈglɔːriəs] *adj.* 光荣的；壮丽的；辉煌的
glory [ˈglɔːri] *n.* 光荣，荣誉；壮丽；赞颂；荣誉的事；*vi.* 为……而骄傲自豪
glove [glʌv] *n.* 手套；*vt.* 给……戴手套
glow [gləu] *n.* 微弱稳定的光，暗淡的光；（运动高兴或激动时）脸通红；喜悦；满足的心情；*vi.* 发出暗淡的光；（运动或激动）脸发红；色彩鲜艳
glue [gluː] *n.* 胶，胶水；黏性之物；*vt.* 胶合，粘；

紧附于……
go [gəu] *vi.* 去,走;变为;进行;放;通往;消失;*vt.* 走过
goal [gəul] *n.* 球门;得分;目的;目标
goat [gəut] *n.* 山羊
god [gɔd] *n.* 神,神像;上帝
gold [gəuld] *n.* 金,金子,金币;金黄色;金牌;钱财;*adj.* 金制的;金色的
golden [ˈgəuldən] *adj.* 金(黄)色的;极好的
golf [gɔlf] *n.* 高尔夫球
good [gud] *adj.* 好的,优良的,上等的;有本事的;*n.* 善行;好处;[*pl.*]商品
goodbye [ˌgudˈbai] int. 再见,再会
goodness [ˈgudnis] *n.* 优良;德行,美德;仁慈,善良;精华 *int.* 天哪
goods [gudz] *n.* 货物;商品
goose [guːs] *n.* 鹅,雌鹅,鹅肉
gossip [ˈgɔsip] *n.* 流言蜚语;闲话;爱说长道短的人;*v.* 说闲话;
govern [ˈgʌvən] *vt.* 统治,治理;支配;管理;规定;*vi.* 统治;执行
government [ˈgʌvənmənt] *n.* 政府,政体;统治,治理;政治
governor [ˈgʌvənə] *n.* 州长;主管人员;统治者;管理者
gown [gaun] *n.* 长袍,长外衣
grab [græb] *v.* 攫取;抢夺;抓住(机会);匆忙取;赚取;*n.* 攫取,争取
grace [greis] *n.* 优美,文雅,雅致;魅力;恩惠;慈悲
graceful [ˈgreisfəl] *adj.* 优美的,优雅的
gracious [ˈgreiʃəs] *adj.* 有礼貌的,仁慈的;亲切的;高尚的
grade [greid] *vt.* & *vi.* 给……分等级;记成绩;*n.* 等级,年级;阶段
gradual [ˈgrædjuəl] *adj.* 逐渐的,渐进的
gradually [ˈgrædjuəli] *adv.* 逐渐地,逐步地
graduate [ˈgrædjueit] *n.* 毕业生;*vi.* 大学毕业,获学位;*vt.* 毕业;
grain [grein] *n.* 谷物,谷粒;颗粒,细粒
gram(me) [græm] *n.* 克(重量单位) = gram
grammar [ˈgræmə] *n.* 语法,语法书
grammatical [grəˈmætikəl] *adj.* 语法上的;合乎文法的
grand [grænd] *adj.* 宏伟的,壮丽的;重大的;豪华的;主要的
granddaughter [ˈgræn. dɔːtə] *n.* 孙女,外孙女
grandfather [ˈgrænd. fɑːðə] *n.* 祖父,外祖父
grandmother [ˈgrænd. mʌðə] *n.* 祖母,外祖母
grandson [ˈgrændsʌn] *n.* 孙子,外孙子
grant [grɑːnt] *n.* 授给物;补助金;同意;给予;财产转让;*vt.* 授予;同意;承认
grape [greip] *n.* 葡萄,葡萄藤;[色彩]深紫色
graph [græf,grɑːf] *n.* (曲线)图,图表
grasp [grɑːsp] *vt.* 抓紧,抓住,紧握;掌握,领会;*n.* 抓,抓紧;把握,领会
grass [grɑːs] *n.* 草,牧草,草地;*vt.* 覆盖着草
grateful [ˈgreitfəl] *adj.* 感激的,感谢的;令人愉快的
gratitude [ˈgrætitjuːd] *n.* 感恩之心感谢
grave [greiv] *n.* 坟墓
gravity [ˈgræviti] *n.* 重力,引力;庄重,严肃
gray = grey [grei] *adj.* 灰色的;阴沉的;黯淡的;*n.* 灰色;*v.* 变灰色
great [greit] *adj.* 大的,伟大的;大量的;很好的,美好的;重要的;*adv.* (口语)好极了
greatly [ˈgreitli] *adv.* 大大地;非常,很
greedy [ˈgriːdi] *adj.* 贪吃的,贪婪的
Greek [griːk] *adj.* 希腊(人)的;*n.* 希腊人,希腊语
green [griːn] *adj.* 绿色的;长满绿草的;温和的;未成熟的;*n.* 绿色;*vt.* & *vi.* 变绿
greenhouse [ˈgriːnhaus] *n.* 温室,玻璃暖房
greet [griːt] *vt.* 问候,招呼;反应;致敬;欢迎
greeting [ˈgriːti] *n.* 问候,招呼;致敬
grief [ˌgriːf] *n.* 悲伤;悲痛;悲伤的事
grieve [griːv] *vt.* 使悲痛;*vi.* 悲痛
grind [graind] *n.* 磨(碎),碾;磨快;*vt.* 磨,碾
grip [grip] *vt.* 握紧,抓牢;*n.* 紧握;了解;手柄
groan [grəun] *vi.* 哼 呻吟;*n.* 呻吟
grocer [ˈgrəusə] *n.* 食品商,杂货商
grocery [ˈgrəusəri] *n.* 食品杂货店
gross [grəus] *adj.* 总的;*n.* 总量;*vt.* 总共赚得
ground [graund] *n.* 土地,场地;战场;*vt.* 放在地上
group [gruːp] *n.* 小组,群,团,团体;
vt. & *vi.* 聚合,成群,聚集
grow [grəu] *vt.* & *vi.* 生长;变得,变成;增长;种植;逐渐开始
grown-up [ˌgrəʊnˈʌp,ˈgrəʊnʌp] *adj.* 成年的,成人的;成熟的;适合于成人的
growth [grəuθ] *n.* 增长,增长量;生长,生长物
guarantee [ˌgærənˈtiː] *n.* 保证(书),担保(书);担保人;担保物,抵押品;*vt.* 保证,担保
guard [gɑːd] *vt.* & *vi.* 守卫,看守,保卫;警惕;*n.* 卫兵,守卫者,护卫队;警戒;保护

guess [ges] *vt. & vi. & n.* 猜测,推测,猜想
guest [gest] *n.* 客人,宾客;旅客;客串演员;特邀来宾;*vi.* 做特邀嘉宾;做客串
guidance [ˈgaidəns] *n.* 引导,指导;领导;导航系统
guide [gaid] *n.* 导游者;领路者;指南;路标;*vt.* 给……导游;领路指导;*vi.* 作导游
guideline [ˈgaidlain] *n.* 指导方针;指导原则
guilty [ˈgilti] *adj.* 内疚的;有罪的
guitar [giˈtaː(r)] *n.* 吉他;六弦琴
gulf [gʌlf] *n.* 海湾
gum [gʌm] *n.* 口香糖,树胶;黏性物质;*vi.* 形成胶质;发黏
gun [gʌn] *n.* 枪,炮,手枪
guy [gaɪ] *n.* 男人;家伙;一群男人/女人
gunpowder [ˈgʌn. paudə] *n.* 黑色火药,有烟火药
gym (= **gymnasium**) [dʒimˈneiziəm] *n.* 体育馆,健身房

H

habit [ˈhæbit] *n.* 习惯,习性;长袍
habitual [həˈbitjuəl] *adj.* 习惯性的,惯常的
hair [hɛə] *n.* 头发,毛发,毛,毛织物
haircut[ˈhɛəkʌt] *n.* 理发,发式
half [hɑːf] *n.* 半,一半;*adv.* 一半地
hall [hɔːl] *n.* 门厅;过道;会堂,礼堂
halt [hɔːlt] *vi.* 停止;立定;*vt.* 使……停止;*n.* 停住
ham [hæm] *n.* 火腿;
hamburger [ˈhæmbəːgə] *n.* 汉堡包,牛肉饼
hammer [ˈhæmə] *n.* 锤,榔头;*vt.* 锤击,锤打;*vi.* 锤击,反复敲打
hand [hænd] *n.* 手,人手;协助;*vt.* 交递,给
handbook [ˈhændbʊk] *n.* 手册;指南
handful [ˈhændful] *n.* 一把,少数,一小撮
handicap [ˈhændikæp] *n.* 障碍;缺陷;不利条件;*vt.* 妨碍,使不利;使(某人)行动和生活不正常
handkerchief [ˈhæŋkətʃif] *n.* 手帕
handle [ˈhændl] *n.* 柄,把手;*vt.* 处理,操作;*vi.* 驾驭
handsome [ˈhænsəm] *adj.* 英俊的
handwriting [ˈhænd. raitiŋ] *n.* 笔迹,手迹;书法
handy [ˈhændi] *adj.* 手边的;方便的;便于使用的
hang [hæŋ] *n.* 挂,悬,悬挂方式;*vt.* (hanged hanged)悬挂;绞死;*vi.* (使)低垂;悬浮(在空中);悬挂
happen [ˈhæpən] *vi.* 发生;碰巧,恰好;出现;偶然遇到
happiness [ˈhæpinis] *n.* 幸福;幸运;快乐;适当
happy [ˈhæpi] *adj.* 快乐的,幸福的
harbor(u)r [ˈhɑːbə] *n.* 海港,港口;*vt.* 庇护;停泊
hard [hɑːd] *adj.* 硬的,困难的;艰难的;苛刻的;*adv.* 努力地;猛烈地;坚定地
harden [ˈhɑːdn] *vt.* 使变硬;(使)坚强;*vi.* 变硬
hardly [ˈhɑːdli] ad. 几乎不;简直不
hardship [ˈhɑːdʃip] *n.* 艰难,困苦
hard-working [ˈhɑːdˈwɜːkɪŋ] *adj.* 辛勤的
hardware [ˈhɑːdwɛə] *n.* 五金器具;(计算机)硬件
hare [hɛə] *n.* 野兔
harm [hɑːm] *n.* 伤害,损害;*vt.* 伤害,损害
harmful [ˈhɑːmfəl] *adj.* 有害的
harmony [ˈhɑːməni] *n.* 调和,协调;和谐;和弦;和睦
harness [ˈhɑːnis] *vt.* 治理;束以马具;利用(产生动力);*n.* 马具;系在身上的绳子
harsh [hɑːʃ] *adj.* 严厉的;刺耳的;粗糙的;使人不舒服的;大约的
harvest [ˈhɑːvist] *n.* 收获(期),收获物;成果收成;*vt. & vi.* 收割,收获
haste [heist] *n.* 急速,急忙;草率
hasten [ˈheisn] *vt.* 催促,赶快,急忙;*vi.* 赶紧,赶快,急忙
hasty [ˈheisti] *adj.* 急速的,急忙的,仓促的,匆匆的;轻率的
hat [hæt] *n.* 帽子(一般指有边的)
hatch [hætʃ] *vt.* 孵出;*vi.* (蛋)孵化,破壳;*n.* 孵化;舱口
hate [heit] *vt.* 恨,憎恨;不喜欢;不愿;*vi.* 表示憎恨;*n.* 憎恨,厌恶;厌恶的人或事
hateful [ˈheitfəl] *adj.* 可恨的,可恶的
hatred [ˈheitrid] *n.* 憎恶,憎恨,仇恨
have(**has**, **had**, **had**) [hæv] *v. aux.* 已经,曾经;*vt.* 有;吃;从事;得到;雇用;享有允许

hawk [hɔːk] *n.* 鹰,隼;掠夺别人的人
hay [hei] *n.* 干草
hazard [ˈhæzəd] *n.* 危险,危害,公害;冒险;*vt.* 冒险,赌运气
he [hiː] *pron.* (主格)他
head [hed] *n.* 头,头脑;领袖;*vt.* & *vi.* 率领;为首;朝向;前进
headache [ˈhedeik] *n.* 头痛;头痛的事
heading [ˈhediŋ] *n.* 标题;题词,题名
headline [ˈhedlain] *n.* (*pl.*)新闻提要;大字标题
headmaster [ˈhedˈmɑːstə] *n.* (中小学的)校长
headquarters [ˈhedˈkwɔːtəz] *n.* 司令部,指挥部,总部
heal [hiːl] *vt.* 治愈;使和解;痊愈;恢复;*vi.* 痊愈
health [helθ] *n.* 健康,健康状况;卫生,保健
healthy [ˈhelθi] *adj.* 健康的,有益健康的
heap [hiːp] *n.* (一)堆,大量,许多;累积;*vt.* 使成堆 装满
hear [hiə] *vt.* & *vi.* 听见,听说,听到;审讯;得知;倾听;听证
heart [hɑːt] *n.* 心,内心;中心
heat [hiːt] *n.* 热,炎热,热度;*vi.* 变热,变暖;因热变质;*vt.* 使……变热
heating [ˈhiːtiŋ] *n.* 加热;供暖,暖气装置
heaven [ˈhevn] *n.* 天堂;天,天空
heavily [ˈhevili] *adv.* 重重地,很重地;沉重地,沉闷地;大量地
heavy [ˈhevi] *adj.* 重的;大(量)的;沉闷的;*adv.* 密集地
hedge [hedʒ] *n.* 篱笆,树篱;障碍物;*vt.* 包围;限制;*vi.* 种树篱
heel [hiːl] *n.* 脚后跟,踵,后跟;*v.* 倾侧
height [hait] *n.* 高,高度;高处;身高;最高峰;极点
heighten [ˈhaitn] *vt.* & *vi.* (使)变高;(使)加强
heir [ɛə] *n.* 后嗣,继承人
helicopter [ˈhelikɔptə] *n.* 直升机
hell [hel] *n.* 地狱;极大的痛苦
hello [həˈləu] int. 喂;*n.* (见面打招呼或打电话用语)喂,哈罗
helmet [ˈhelmit] *n.* 头盔,钢盔;遮阳帽
help [help] *vt.* & *vi.* 帮助,援助;改善;*n.* 帮手;帮助,援助
helpful [ˈhelpfəl] *adj.* 给予帮助的;有用的,有益的
helpless [ˈhelplis] *adj.* 无助的;无能的;无依靠的
hen [hen] *n.* 母鸡;雌禽
hence [hens] *ad.* 因此;从此;所以,今后
henceforth [ˌhensˈfɔːθ] *adv.* 从今以后,今后
her [həː] *pron.* (宾格)她,她的;*adj.* 她的
herd [həːd] *n.* 兽群,牧群;人群,牧人;*vt.* 放牧;群集;使……成群;*vi.* 使向……移动
here [hiə] *adv.* 这里,向这里;*n.* 这里
heritage [ˈherɪtɪdʒ] *n.* 遗产;传统
hero [ˈhiərəu] *n.* 男主角;英雄,勇士
heroic [hiˈrəuik] *adj.* 英雄的,英勇的
heroin [ˈherəʊɪn] *n.* 海洛因;吗啡
heroine [ˈherəuin] *n.* 女主角;女英雄
hers [həːz] *pron.* 她的(所有物)
herself [həːˈself] *pron.* 她自己;她亲自
hesitate [ˈheziteit] *vi.* 犹豫;踌躇;含糊;停顿;口吃;迟疑;*vt.* 用犹疑的态度表示
hi(= **hey**) [hai] *ini.* 嗨(表示问候等);引人注意时的喊声;打招呼
hide [haid] *vt.* & *vi.* 把……藏起来;隐瞒;遮蔽;*n.* 藏身之处
high [hai] *adj.* 高的;高级的;轻微变质的;高尚的;*adv.* 高;好;*n.* 高地;上天;高气压;高度;兴奋
highlight [ˈhaɪlaɪt] *v.* 突出,强调;(使)醒目;*n.* 最好的部分;强光部分
highly [ˈhaili] *adv.* 高度地;很;非常
highway [ˈhaiwei] *n.* 公路,大路
hijack(= **highjack**) [ˈhaidʒæk] *v.* 抢劫(走私卡车等),劫持
hike [haik] *n.* 徒步旅行;远足;*vi.* 徒步旅行
hill [hil] *n.* 小山,小堆,斜坡,山冈,丘陵
hillside [ˈhilˈsaid] *n.* (小山)山腰,山坡
him [him] *pron.* (宾格)他
himself [himˈself] *pron.* 他自己;他亲自
hint [hint] *n.* 暗示,提示,示意;建议;*vt.* & *vi.* 暗示,示意
hire [ˈhaiə] *vt.* 租借,出租;雇请;*n.* 租用;雇用
his [hiz] *pron.* 他的;他的东西
historic [hɪˈstɔrɪk] *adj.* 历史(性)的;有历史记载的
historical [hisˈtɔːrikəl] *adj.* 历史的;有关历史的
history [ˈhistəri] *n.* 历史;个人经历
hit [hit] *vt.* 打(击) 碰撞;*vi.* 打(击),袭击;达到;*n.* 打(击); 冲撞
hobby [ˈhɔbi] *n.* 业余爱好;癖好
hold [həuld] *vt.* 拿住;掌握;拥有,持有;举行;*n.* 把握,控制
hole [həul] *n.* 洞,孔眼;裂开处;穴;*vt.* & *vi.* 挖洞,掘坑;进洞
holiday [ˈhɔlədi] *n.* 假日,节日,假期;*vi.* 度假

hollow [ˈhɔləu] *adj.* 空的，空洞的；虚伪的；空腹的；*vt.* 形成空洞，挖空；*n.* 洞；窟窿；山谷
holy [ˈhəuli] *adj.* 神圣的，圣洁的；令人敬仰的
home [həum] *n.* 家，家乡；住所；国内的；养老院；*adj.* 家庭的，家(乡)的；*adv.* 回家，在家
hometown [ˈhəʊmtaʊn] *n.* 家乡，故乡
homework [ˈhəʊmwɜːk] *n.* 家庭作业；功课
honest [ˈɔnist] *adj.* 诚实的；可敬的；正直的
honesty [ˈɔnisti] *n.* 诚实，正直
honey [ˈhʌni] *n.* 蜜，(复数)蜂蜜；甜，甜蜜；宝贝；爱人
honeymoon [ˈhʌnimuːn] *n.* 蜜月；*vi.* 度蜜月
hono(u)r [ˈɔnə] *n.* 光荣；尊敬；敬意；荣誉，荣幸；头衔；*vt.* 尊敬
hono(u)rable [ˈɔnərəbl] *adj.* 诚实的；光荣的，荣誉的；可敬的；体面的
hook [huk] *n.* 钩，挂钩，钩子；勾拳；*vt.* & *vi.* 钩住
hope [həup] *n.* & *vt.* & *vi.* 希望
hopeful [ˈhəupfəl] *adj.* 有希望的
hopeless [ˈhəuplisli] *adj.* 没有希望的，绝望的；无可救药的
horizon [həˈraizn] *n.* 地平线；眼界，见识，视野
horizontal [ˌhɔriˈzɔntl] *adj.* 地平的，水平的；横的；*n.* 水平线；水平面
horn [hɔːn] *n.* 号角；警报器；角，动物角，触角，角状物；喇叭；力量源泉
horrible [ˈhɔrəbl] *adj.* 讨厌的；令人震惊的；极严重的
horror [ˈhɔrə] *n.* 恐怖，战栗；憎恶，厌恶
horse [hɔːs] *n.* 马，马科动物
horsepower [ˈhɔːspauə] *n.* 马力(功率单位)
hospital [ˈhɔspitl] *n.* 医院
hospitality [ˌhɔspɪˈtæləti] *n.* 殷勤好客；招待，款待；(气候，环境等的)宜人，适宜
host [həust] *n.* 主人，东道主；主持人；主机；*vt.* 主持；做东
hostage [ˈhɔstɪdʒ] *n.* 人质；抵押品
hostess [ˈhəustis] *n.* 女主人；空姐
hostile [ˈhɔstail] *adj.* 敌方的；不友善的，怀敌意的
hot [hɔt] *adj.* 热的；热情的；刺激的；辣的；性感的；*v.* 激烈起来，活跃
hotel [həuˈtel] *n.* 旅馆，宾馆，酒店，饭店
hour [auə] *n.* 小时；时间，时刻；钟点
house [haus] *n.* 房屋；住宅；*vt.* 提供住处，安置，收容
household [ˈhaushəuld] *n.* 家庭，户；家务；*adj.* 家庭的；家喻户晓的
housewife [ˈhauswaif] *n.* 家庭主妇
housework [ˈhauswəːk] *n.* 家务劳动
how [hau] *adv.* 如何，怎么，怎样；多少；*conj.* 如何，怎样，以……方式；*n.* 方式
however [hauˈevə] *adv.* 然而；不管怎样
hug [hʌg] *v.* 拥抱；抱住；紧挨；缠紧；*n.* 拥抱
huge [hjuːdʒ] *adj.* 巨大的，庞大的；程度高的
human [ˈhjuːmən] *adj.* 人的，人类的；*n.* 人
humble [ˈhʌmbl] *adj.* 谦逊的；地位低下的，卑下的；粗陋的；*vt.* 使……卑下；贬低
humid [ˈhjuːmid] *adj.* 湿的，湿气重的，潮湿的
humo(u)r [ˈhjuːmə] *n.* 幽默，诙谐，幽默感
humoro(u)s [ˈhjuːmərəs] *adj.* 富于幽默的，诙谐的
hundred [ˈhʌndrəd] num. 百，百个，百位；*n.* 许多
hunger [ˈhʌŋgə] *n.* 饿，饥饿；渴望；*v.* 渴望；渴求
hungry [ˈhʌŋgri] *adj.* 饥饿的；渴望的
hunt [hʌnt] *n.* 打猎，狩猎；搜寻，追捕；*vt.* 追猎，狩猎，打猎；搜索
hurricane [ˈhʌrɪkən] *n.* 飓风
hurry [ˈhʌri] *vi.* 赶紧；快速移动；*vt.* 催促；加快；迅速处理；*n.* 匆忙；急需
hurt [həːt] *vt.* 使受伤；使痛心；伤害；(使)疼痛；损害；*vi.* 受疼痛；破坏；*n.* 打击；创伤
husband [ˈhʌzbənd] *n.* 丈夫
hut [hʌt] *n.* 小屋，棚屋
hydrogen [ˈhaidridʒən] *n.* 氢

I

I [ai] *pron.* (主格)我
ice [ais] *n.* 冰，冰块；*vt.* 冰冻，结冰
ice-cream [ˈaiskriːm] *n.* 冰淇淋
idea [aiˈdiə] *n.* 想法，思想；意见；观念
ideal [aiˈdiəl] *adj.* 理想的；观念的；完美的；高尚的；*n.* 理想；典范；目标
identical [aiˈdentikəl] *adj.* 完全相同的，同一的
identify [aiˈdentifai] *vt.* 认出，识别，鉴定；*vi.* 认同，感同身受
identity [aiˈdentəti] *n.* 身份；个性；一致

idiom [ˈidiəm] *n.* 习语,成语,惯用语;方言;风格,特色
idle [ˈaidl] *adj.* 空闲的;懒散的;无目的的,无聊的;
idol [ˈaidl] *n.* 偶像,崇拜物
if [if] *conj.* 假如,如果;是否;即使;*n.* 不确定的情况
ignorant [ˈignərənt] *adj.* 不知道的,无知的,愚昧的
ignore [igˈnɔː] *vt.* 不顾,不理;忽视
ill [il] *adj.* 有病的;坏的;引起痛苦的;敌意的;*adv.* 坏,恶劣地;*n.* 问题,疾病,祸害;不幸
illegal [iˈliːgəl] *adj.* 不合法的,非法的;*n.* 非法移民
illness [ˈilnis] *n.* 病,疾病
illustrate [ˈiləstreit] *vt.* (用图等)说明,举例说明;作图解
illustration [i. ləsˈtreiʃən] *n.* 说明;图解,插图;例证
image [ˈimidʒ] *n.* 像,形象,映象,图像;影像;肖像;想象;*vt.* 想象;描绘;反映
imaginary [iˈmædʒinəri] *adj.* 想象中的,假想的,虚构的
imagination [i. mædʒiˈneiʃən] *n.* 想象,想象力,空想
imaginc [iˈmœdʒin] *vt.* 想象,设想;料想,幻想,猜测;认为
imitate [ˈimiteit] *vt.* 模仿,仿效,仿制
immediate [iˈmiːdjət] *adj.* 立即的,即刻的;直接的
immediately [iˈmiːdiətli] *adv.* 立即;直接地;*conj.* 一……(就)
immense [iˈmens] *adj.* 巨大的,广大的
immigrant [ˈimigrənt] *n.* 移民,侨民
immune [ɪˈmjuːn] *adj.* 免疫的;有免疫力的;不受影响的;免除……的
impact [ˈimpækt, imˈpækt] *n.* 影响(力);作用;冲击(力);冲突;*vt.* 撞击;对…… 发生影响
impatient [imˈpeiʃənt] *adj.* 不耐烦的;急躁的
implement [ˈɪmplɪment, ˈɪmplɪmənt] *vt.* 实施,执行;使生效,实现 *n.* 工具,器械;家具;手段
implication [ˌimpliˈkeiʃən] *n.* 含义;暗示,暗指
imply [imˈplai] *vt.* 暗示;意指
import [ˈimpɔːt, imˈpɔːt] *vt. & vi. & n.* 输入,进口
importance [imˈpɔːtəns] *n.* 重要,重要性
important [imˈpɔːtənt] *adj.* 重要的,影响很大的;有势力的
impose [imˈpəuz] *vt.* 把……强加;加上;强迫
impossible [imˈpɔsəbl] *adj.* 不可能的,办不到的
impress [imˈpres] *vt.* 给……深刻印象;影响;印刻;传送
impression [imˈpreʃən] *n.* 印,印象;印记;效果
impressive [imˈpresiv] *adj.* 给人印象深刻的
imprison [imˈprizn] *vt.* 关押,监禁;限制,束缚
improve [imˈpruːv] *vt.* 使更好,改进;利用;(提高)价值;*vi.* 改善,改进
improvement [imˈpruːvmənt] *n.* 改进,改善,改进处
in [in] *prep.* 在……里,在;穿着;参与;在……方面;*adv.* 进入
inch [intʃ] *n.* 英寸;少量
incident [ˈinsidənt] *n.* 发生的事,事件,事变
incline [ˈinklain, inˈklain] *n.* 倾斜,斜坡,斜面;*vt.* 使倾斜,使 ……倾向;爱好;易于
include [inˈkluːd] *vt.* 包括,包含
income [ˈin. kʌm] *n.* 收入,所得,收益,进款
incorrect [ˌinkəˈrekt] *adj.* 不正确的,错误的
increase [ˈinkriːs, inˈkriːs] *vt. & vi.* 增加,提高;*n.* 增加,增强,提高
increasingly [inˈkriːsiŋli] *adv.* 越来越多地,逐渐地;渐增地
incredible [ɪnˈkredəbl] *adj.* 不可思议的;惊人的;难以置信的;未必可能的
indeed [inˈdiːd] *adv.* 真正地;确实,的确;事实上
indefinite [inˈdefinit] *adj.* 不明确的,模糊的,不定的
independence [ˌindiˈpendəns] *n.* 独立,自主,自立
independent [ˌindiˈpendənt] *adj.* 独立的,自主的;私立的;无偏见的
index [ˈindeks] *n.* 索引;指数,指标;指针;*vt.* 编入索引中;指出
India [ˈindiə] *n.* 印度
Indian [ˈindjən] *adj.* 印度的,印度人的,印第安人的;*n.* 印度人印第安人
indicate [ˈindikeit] *vt.* 标示,表示,指明,表明;*v.* 显示;象征;指示
indication [ˌindiˈkeiʃən] *n.* 指示,表示,象征,表明
indifferent [inˈdifrənt] *adj.* 冷漠的,漠不关心的;不积极的;无重要性的;中立的
indignant [inˈdignənt] *adj.* 愤慨的,义愤的,愤愤不平的
indirect [ˌindiˈrekt] *adj.* 间接的;不坦率的;迂

回的;次要的
indispensable [ˌindisˈpensəbl] *adj.* 必不可少的,必需的
individual [ˌindiˈvidjuəl] *adj.* 个别的,独特的;*n.* 个人,个体
indoor [ˈɪndɔː(r)] *adj.* 室内的,户内的;在室内使用的;待在家里的
indoors [ˈinˈdɔːz] *adv.* 在室内,在屋里
industrial [inˈdʌstriəl] *adj.* 工业的,产业的
industrialize [inˈdʌstriəlaiz] *vt.* (使)工业化
industry [ˈindəstri] *n.* 工业,产业;勤劳
inefficient [ˌiniˈfiʃənt] *adj.* 效率低的,无效率的;不称职的;无能的
inevitable [inˈevitəbl] *adj.* 不可避免的,必然(发生)的
inexpensive [ˌinikˈspensiv] *adj.* 花费不多的,廉价的
infant [ˈinfənt] *n.* 婴儿,幼儿;*adj.* 婴儿的;幼稚的;初期的
infect [inˈfekt] *vt.* 传染,感染
infer [inˈfəː] *vt.* 推论,推断;猜想;暗示;*vi.* 推论
inferior [inˈfiəriə] *adj.* 下等的,劣等的,次等的;较低的;不如的
infinite [ˈinfinit] *adj.* 无限的,无穷的,无数的;*n.* 无限
inflation [ɪnˈfleɪʃn] *n.* 膨胀;通货膨胀;夸张
influence [ˈinfluəns] *n.* 影响,影响力;势力,权势;有影响的人(或事物);*vt.* 影响;感化
influential [ˌinfluˈenʃəl] *adj.* 有影响的;有权势的;*n.* 有影响力的人物
inform [inˈfɔːm] *vt.* 通知,向……报告,告诉,告发
information [ˌinfəˈmeiʃən] *n.* 消息,信息,通知;情报;新闻;资料;询问
ingredient [ɪnˈgriːdiənt] *n.* (混合物的)组成部分;(烹调的)原料;(构成)要素;因素
inhabit [inˈhæbit] *vt.* 居住于,栖息于;占据
inhabitant [inˈhæbitənt] *n.* 居民,住户
inherent [ɪnˈhɪərənt] *adj.* 固有的,内在的;天生
inherit [inˈherit] *vt.* 继承(传统等),遗传;*vi.* 继承
initial [iˌniʃəl] *n.* 首字母;*adj.* 开始的,最初的;字首的;*vt.* 签姓名的首字母于
initiate [ɪˈnɪʃieɪt, ɪˈnɪʃiət] *vt.* 开始,发起;传授;创始,开辟
initiative [ɪˈnɪʃətɪv] *n.* 主动性;主动精神;倡议;主动权
injection [inˈdʒekʃən] *n.* 注射,注入,注射物
injure [ˈindʒə] *vt.* 伤害,损害,损伤
injury [ˈindʒəri] *n.* 损害,伤害;受伤处
ink [iŋk] *n.* 墨水,油墨
inn [in] *n.* 客栈,小旅店,小酒店
inner [ˈinə] *adj.* 内部的;内心的,里面的
innocent [ˈinəsnt] *adj.* 清白的,无罪的;无辜的
innovate [ˈɪnəveɪt] *vi.* 改革,创新;*vt.* 引入(新事物、思想或方法)
input [ˈinput] *n.* 输入;投入的资金
inquire [inˈkwaiə] *vt.* 打听,询问;调查;*vi.* 询问;查究
inquiry [inˈkwaiəri] *n.* 询问,打听;调查;查问
insect [ˈinsekt] *n.* 昆虫,虫
insert [inˈsəːt] *vt.* 插入,嵌入;*n.* 插入物
inside [ˈinˈsaid] *prep.* 在……里面;*n.* 内部;*adj.* 里面的;*adv.* 在里面
insight [ˈinsait] *n.* 洞察力;领悟;了解
insist [inˈsist] *vi.* 坚持;强调;坚持要求
inspect [inˈspekt] *vt.* 检查,审查,调查;检阅;*vi.* 调查
inspection [inˈspekʃən] *n.* 检查,审查,检阅;视察
inspire [inˈspair] *vt.* 鼓舞;给……以灵感
install [inˈstɔːl] *vt.* 安装;设置;安置;使……就职
installation [ˌinstəˈleiʃən] *n.* 安装;装置;设施
instance [ˈinstəns] *n.* 例子,实例,事例;阶段;情况;*vt.* 举例说明
instant [ˈinstənt] *n.* 瞬间,片刻;*adj.* 立即的,即时的
instantly [ˈinstəntli] *adv.* 立即,即刻
instead [inˈsted] *adv.* 代替,顶替;反而
instinct [ˈinstiŋkt] *n.* 本能,直觉;生性,天性
institute [ˈinstitjuːt] *n.* 研究所,学院,学会,协会
institution [ˌinstiˈtjuːʃən] *n.* 协会,制度;习俗;机构;创立
instruct [inˈstrʌkt] *vt.* 教;指示;通知;命令;指导
instruction [inˈstrʌkʃən] *n.* 命令,指令;教学;教训;说明;须知
instructor [ɪnˈstrʌktə(r)] *n.* 指导者,教师
instrument [ˈinstrumənt] *n.* 仪器,工具;乐器;器械
insufficient [ˌinsəˈfiʃənt] *adj.* 不足的;不适当的
insult [ˈinsʌlt, inˈsʌlt] *vt.* & *n.* 侮辱,凌辱
insurance [inˈʃuərəns] *n.* 保险,保险费

insure [inˈʃuə] *vt.* 给……保险;确保
intellectual [ˌintilˈektʃuəl] *n.* 知识分子;*adj.* 智力的,聪明的
intelligence [inˈtelidʒəns] *n.* 智力,理解力
intelligent [inˈtelidʒənt] *adj.* 聪明的;理智的
intend [inˈtend] *vt.* 想要,打算,计划;意指
intense [inˈtens] *adj.* 强烈的;紧张的;剧烈的;热情的;激烈的
intensity [inˈtensiti] *n.* 强烈;剧烈;强度
intensive [inˈtensiv] *adj.* 加强的;精耕细作的;强烈的;密集的;精细的;强调的
intention [inˈtenʃən] *n.* 意图,意向;目的
intentional [inˈtenʃənəl] *adj.* 故意的,有意识的;策划的;企图的
interact[ˌɪntərˈækt] *v.* 交流,互动;相互作用
interaction *n.* 相互作用,相互影响;互动交流;干扰
interest [ˈintərist] *n.* 兴趣;利益;利息;嗜好;股份;*vt.* 使……感兴趣
interesting [ˈintəristiŋ] *adj.* 有趣的;引人入胜的
interfere [ˌintəˈfiə] *vi.* 干涉,干预;妨碍;冲突
interference [ˌintəˈfiərəns] *n.* 干涉,干预,干扰;阻碍
interior [inˈtiəriə] *adj.* 内的,内地的;国内的;内部的;*n.* 内部,内在
intermediate [ˌintəˈmiːdiət] *adj.* 中间的,中级的
internal [inˈtəːnəl] *adj.* 内的,内在的;国内的;身体内部的
international [ˌintəˈnæʃənəl] *adj.* 国际的,世界(性)的
Internet [ˈɪntənet] *n.* 互联网
interpret [inˈtəːprit] *vt.* 解释,说明;口译,翻译;演出
interpretation [in. təːpriˈteiʃən] *n.* 解释;口译,翻译;演出
interpreter [inˈtəːpritə] *n.* 译员,口译者
interrupt [ˌintəˈrʌpt] *vt.* 打断,打扰;中止,妨碍;*vi.* 插嘴
interruption [ˌintəˈrʌpʃən] *n.* 中断,打断;障碍物
interval [ˈintəvəl] *n.* 间隔;休息,休息时间
interview [ˈintəvjuː] *n.* 接见,会见;面谈;访问;*vt.* 接见;对…… 进行面谈(试);*vi.* 面试;采访
intimate [ˈintimeit, ˈintimit] *adj.* 亲密的;个人的,私人的;秘密的;*n.* 密友
into [ˈintuː] *prep.* 进入,进入到,到……里
introduce [ˌintrəˈdjuːs] *vt.* 介绍;引进,传入;采用;提出,提倡;放入
introduction [ˌintrəˈdʌkʃən] *n.* 介绍;引进;引言,导论,序言
invade [inˈveid] *vt.* 入侵,侵略,侵害,侵袭
invasion [inˈveiʒən] *n.* 入侵,侵略,侵犯
invent [inˈvent] *vt.* 发明,创造;捏造
invention [inˈvenʃən] *n.* 发明,发明物;虚构,虚构物;创造,捏造
inventor [inˈventə] *n.* 发明者,发明家,创造者
invest [inˈvest] *vt.* 投资,投入;花费;*vi.* 投资
investigate [inˈvestigeit] *vt. & vi.* 调查,研究
investigation [in. vestiˈgeiʃən] *n.* 调查,调查研究
investment [inˈvestmənt] *n.* 投资,投资额,投入
invisible [inˈvizəbl] *adj.* 看不见的,无形的
invitation [ˌinviˈteiʃən] *n.* 邀请,招待;请柬
invite [inˈvait] *vt.* 邀请,聘请;招待;要求;*n.* 邀请;请柬
involve [inˈvɔlv] *vt.* 使卷入,使陷入;使忙于;牵涉;包含
inward [ˈinwəd] *adj.* 里面的,内心的;向内的;*adv.* 向内
iron [ˈaiən] *n.* 铁,烙铁,熨斗;铁制物;*vt.* 烫(衣);用铁装备;*vi.* 熨烫(平);*adj.* 刚强的
irregular [iˈregjulə] *adj.* 不规则的,不整齐的;*n.* 不合规格之物
island [ˈailənd] *n.* 岛,岛屿
isolate [ˈaisəleit] *vt.* 使隔离;使孤立
issue [ˈiʃjuː] *n.* 问题;争论点;发行,发行物;*vi. & vt.* 发行;流出
it [it] *pron.* 它
Italian[iˈtæljən] *adj.* 意大利;*n.* 意大利人
Italy [ˈitəli] *n.* 意大利
item [ˈaitəm] *n.* 条,条款;一条,项目;一件商品(或物品)
its [its] *pron.* (it 的所有格)它的
itself [itˈself] *pron.* 它;自己;它本身;自身

J

jacket [ˈdʒækit] *n.* 短上衣,夹克衫
jail [dʒeil] *n.* 监狱,监狱,拘留所;*vt.* 监禁,下狱
jam [dʒæm] *n.* 果酱;拥塞之物,堵塞;窘境;

vt. 使塞满;使堵塞
January [ˈdʒænjuəri] *n.* 一月
Japan [dʒəˈpæn] *n.* 日本,日本国;
Japanese [dʒæpəˈniːz] *adj.* 日本的,日本人的,日语的;*n.* 日本人,日语
jar [dʒɑː] *n.* 罐子, 坛子, 广口瓶
jaw [dʒɔː] *n.* 颌, 颚
jazz [dʒæz] *n.* 爵士音乐, 爵士舞(曲)
jealous [ˈdʒeləs] *adj.* 妒忌的,猜疑的;戒备的
jeans [dʒiːnz] *n.* 牛仔裤;瘦腿紧身裤
jeep [dʒiːp] *n.* 吉普车
jet [dʒet] *n.* 喷气式飞机;喷嘴;喷射, 喷出
Jew [dʒuː] *n.* 犹太人
jewel [ˈdʒuːəl] *n.* 宝石,宝石饰物
jewelry(=jewellery) [ˈdʒuːəlri] *n.* 珠宝,首饰
job [dʒɔb] *n.* 职业,工作,零活;职责,任务
jog [dʒɔg] *v.* 慢跑,慢步长跑;*n.* 慢跑(尤指锻炼)
join [dʒɔin] *vt.* 参加;结合,联合;加入;连接
joint [dʒɔint] *n.* 接头, 接缝; 关节; 接合处; *adj.* 联合的,共同的;合资的, 连带的;*v.* 连接,贴合
joke [dʒəuk] *n.* 笑话, 玩笑;*vi.* 说笑话, 开玩笑
jolly [ˈdʒɔli] *v.* 恭维; 哄;开玩笑,戏谑;*n.* 欢乐,欢庆
journal [ˈdʒəːnl] *n.* 日报,期刊,杂志,日志
journalist [ˈdʒəːnəlist] *n.* 记者,新闻工作者
journey [ˈdʒəːni] *n.* 旅行,旅程,行程;*v.* 旅行
joy [dʒɔi] *n.* 欢乐,喜悦,乐趣,乐事
joyful [ˈdʒɔifəl] *adj.* 十分喜悦的,快乐的
judge [dʒʌdʒ] *n.* 法官,裁判员;*v.* 断定,判断,估计
judgement [ˈdʒʌdʒmənt] *n.* 意见;审判;判断
juice [dʒuːs] *n.* (水果等)汁,液, 果汁
July [dʒu(ː)ˈlai] *n.* 七月
jump [dʒʌmp] *vi.* & *vt.* 跳,跳过, 跳越, 惊跳;暴涨,突升;*n.* 跳跃, 跳动; 上涨
June [dʒuːn] *n.* 六月;琼(女子名)
jungle [ˈdʒʌŋgl] *n.* 丛林,密林, 莽丛
junior [ˈdʒuːnjə] *adj.* 年少的;下级的;后进的;*n.* 晚辈;年少者地位较低者;大学三年级学生
jury [ˈdʒuəri] *n.* 陪审团,评委会, 评奖团
junk [dʒʌŋk] *n.* 废旧物品,破烂物;便宜货,假货;废话,哄骗;*vt.* 丢弃,废弃
just [dʒʌst] *adv.* 刚才;只是;正好, 恰好;*adj.* 公正的,公平的;恰当的
justice [ˈdʒʌstis] *n.* 正义,公正;司法;上诉法庭的法官
justify [ˈdʒʌstifai] *vt.* 证明……是正当的,替……辩护

K

keen [kiːn] *adj.* 热心的;激烈的;敏锐的;强烈的; 精明的;热衷于
keep [kiːp] *vi.* 保持, 坚持, 保存;维持,继续;保有;记录;*n.* 生计维持
keeper [ˈkiːpə] *n.* 看护人;饲养员;保管人
kettle [ˈketl] *n.* 水壶,水锅;坑穴
key [kiː] *n.* 钥匙; 关键; 答案; 按键; 音调;*adj.* 主要的, 关键的
keyboard [ˈkiːbɔːd] *n.* 键盘;*vt.* 用键盘输入
kick [kik] *n.* 踢; *vt.* 踢;*vi.* 踢
kid [kid] *n.* 小孩,儿童,少年
kill [kil] *vt.* 杀死, 扼杀;消磨,消减; 破坏;*n.* 杀, 杀戮
kilo[ˈkiːləʊ] *n.* 千克;公斤
kilogram(me) [ˈkiləgræm] *n.* 千克,公斤
kilometer(-er) [ˈkilə. miːtə] *n.* 千米, 公里
kind [kaind] *n.* 种类; 本质;*adj.* 仁慈的, 友好的,和蔼的
kindergarten [ˈkɪndəgɑːtn] *n.* 学前班;幼儿园
kindness [ˈkaindnis] *n.* 仁慈, 好意
king [kiŋ] *n.* 国王,君主
kingdom [ˈkiŋdəm] *n.* 王国;领域;界
kiss [kis] *vt.* 吻;轻触;*vi.* 接吻; 轻触;*n.* 吻
kitchen [ˈkɪtʃɪn] *n.* 厨房,灶间
kite [kait] *n.* 风筝
knee [niː] *n.* 膝, 膝盖, 膝关节;*vt.* 用膝盖顶
kneel [niːl] *vi.* 跪,跪下,跪着
knife [naif] *n.* 小刀, 刀, 餐刀;*vt.* 用刀切割
knit [nit] *vt.* 把……编结, 编织, 密接; 结合;*vi.* 编织, 变得紧凑; 愈合;*n.* 编织的衣服
knob [nɔb] *n.* 门把, 拉手,旋钮
knock [nɔk] *vi.* & *vt.* 敲, 击, 打, 互撞, 攻击;*n.* 敲, 敲打, 敲门
knot [nɔt] *n.* (绳的)结(树的)节,*vi.* 打结,把…… 打成结;*vt.* 系牢, 捆扎
know [nəu] *vt.* 知道,认识,通晓;*n.* 知情,熟悉内幕
knowledge [ˈnɔlidʒ] *n.* 知识,学识;知道;了解

L

lab(ortory) [læb] *n.* 实验室,研究室
label [ˈleibl] *n.* 标签,签条,标记;符号;商标; *vt.* 贴标签于,分类,把……称为
laboratory [ˈlæbrətɔːri] *n.* 实验室,研究室,实验大楼
labo(u)r [ˈleibə] *n.* 工作,劳动,劳力,劳方; *vi.* 苦干,劳动
labour [ˈleibə] *n.* 劳动,工作;劳工
lace [leis] *n.* 鞋带,系带;花边;饰带;缎带; *vt.* 结带子;饰以花边
lack [læk] *vi.* & *vi.* &*n.* 缺乏,不足,无
ladder [ˈlædə] *n.* 梯子,阶梯,梯状物
lady [ˈleidi] *n.* 女士,夫人;贵妇人
lag [læg] *vi.* 走得慢,落后;*n.* 落后,滞后
lake [leik] *n.* 湖
lamb [læm] *n.* 羔羊,小羊,羔羊肉;*v.* 产羊羔
lame [leim] *adj.* 跛的,瘸的
lamp [læmp] *n.* 灯
land [lænd] *n.* 陆地;国土;土地;*vi.* 降落,着陆;跌落;*vt.* (飞机或船)着陆,登陆
landing [ˈlændiŋ] *n.* 上岸,登陆,着陆;楼梯平台
landlady [ˈlænd. leidi] *n.* 女房东,女地主
landlord [ˈlændlɔːd] *n.* 地主,房东;店主
lane [lein] *n.* (乡间)小路,小巷,行车道,跑道
language [ˈlæŋgwidʒ] *n.* 语言,语言课程
lantern [ˈlæntən] *n.* 提灯,灯笼
lap [læp] *n.* 膝部,膝盖
laptop [ˈlæptɔp] *n.* 便携式电脑
large [lɑːdʒ] *adj.* 大的,巨大的;广泛的;强烈的;普遍地;大量地
largely[ˈlɑːdʒli] *adv.* 大部分地,主要地;大规模地;丰富地
laser [ˈleizə] *n.* 激光
last [lɑːst] *adv.* 最后,最新;*n.* 最后来的人(或发生的事);*vi.* 持续,持久;耐久
late [leit] *adj.* 迟的,晚的;已故的;*adv.* 迟,很迟,晚
lately [ˈleitli] *adv.* 最近,不久前
later [ˈleitə] *adv.* 后来,过一会儿,稍后,后来; *adj.* 更迟的,后面的
Latin [ˈlætin] *adj.* 拉丁的,拉丁人的,拉丁语系国家的;*n.* 拉丁语,拉丁人
latter [ˈlætə] *adj.* (两者中)后者的,后面的
laugh [lɑːf] *vi.* 笑,发笑;*n.* 笑(声),笑料
laughter [ˈlɑːftə] *n.* 笑,笑声
launch [lɔːntʃ] *vt.* & *n.* 发射,投射;发动;下水;开始;升天
laundry [ˈlɔːndri] *n.* 洗衣房,洗衣店;要洗的衣服;洗衣物的活
lavatory [ˈlævətəri] *n.* 盥洗室,厕所
law [lɔː] *n.* 法律,法令,起诉,法则;规律; *vi.* 起诉
lawn [lɔːn] *n.* 草地,草坪,草场
lawyer [ˈlɔːjə] *n.* 律师,法学家
lay [lei] *vt.* 置放,铺设,设置;击;产卵;使平静;压平;*vi.* 生蛋;打赌;*adj.* 世俗的;外行的
layer [ˈleiə] *n.* 层,层次;铺设者;*vt.* 把……分层堆放
layout [ˈleiaut] *n.* 布局;安排;设计
lazy [ˈleizi] *adj.* 懒惰的;懒散的
lead [led,liːd] *vt.* 为……带路;领导,引导;带领;过……(的生活);*n.* 领引;榜样
leader [ˈliːdə] *n.* 领袖,领导人;首领
leaf [liːf] *n.* 叶,叶子,树叶;页;活动桌板;花瓣; *vt.* 翻页;*vi.* 翻页浏览
league [liːg] *n.* 同盟;联盟;联合会;社团
lean [liːn] *vi.* 倾斜;屈身;倚靠;依赖;*vt.* 使倾斜;*n.* 瘦肉;*adj.* 瘦的;贫乏的;歉收的
leap [liːp] *vi.* 跳;跃;跳跃;猛冲;*vt.* 跃过; *n.* 跳跃;剧增;急变
learn [ləːn] *vi.* 学;学习;了解;习得;获悉; *vt.* 学;学习
least [liːst] *pron.* 最少的;最小的;*adv.* 最少;最小
leather [ˈleðə] *n.* 皮革;皮革制品
leave [liːv] *vi.* 离去;*vt.* 离开;告假;遗留;听任;使处于某种状态;*n.* 许可;准假;告别
lecture [ˈlektʃə] *n.* (通常指大学里的)讲座,讲课,演讲;(冗长的)教训,训斥,遣责;*vi.* (尤指在大学里)开讲座,讲授,讲课;*vt.* (尤指恼人地)指责,训斥,告诫
left [left] *adj.* 左边的;*ad.* 在左边;*n.* 左边
leg [leg] *n.* 腿;腿部;支柱;裤脚管;*vi.* 跑,(尤指)逃跑
legal [ˈliːgəl] *adj.* 法律的;合法的;法定的
leisure [ˈliːʒə] *n.* 空闲时间;悠闲;闲暇;休闲
lemon [ˈlemən] *n.* 柠檬;柠檬树
lend [lend] *vt.* 把……借给;贷(款);给予;增添
length [leŋθ] *n.* 长度;篇幅;时间的长短;

有……长度的；一节
less [les] *adv.* 更少地；更小地；*pron.* 较少，更少；*prep.* 减去；少掉；不足
lesson [ˈlesn] *n.* 功课；课；课程；教训
lest [lest] *conj.* 唯恐；以免
let [let] *vt.* 允许；让；使；释放；出租；承包；*n.* 出租；租借；(发球时的)擦网球
letter [ˈletə] *n.* 信；字母；*vt.* 用字母标明；写字母于
level [ˈlevl] *n.* 水平面；水平；等级；标准；层次；*adj.* 齐平的；平的；地位相等的；平稳的；*vt.* 压平；使同等；瞄准；夷为平地
liberate [ˈlibəreit] *vt.* 解放；释放；使获自由
liberty [ˈlibəti] *n.* (自己选择生活方式的)自由；行动自由；人身自由；冒犯行为(或言语)
librarian [laiˈbrεəriən] *n.* 图书馆馆长
library [ˈlaibrəri] *n.* 图书馆
licence(-se) [ˈlaisns] *n.* 许可；批准；批准；执照；许可证；*vt.* 准许；特许
lid [lid] *n.* 盖子；盖
lie [lai] *vi.* 躺；平放；位于；说谎；欺骗；*n.* 谎言
life [laif] *n.* 生命；生存；(总称)生物；性命；寿命；人生阶段；生活；世事；人生；(机器等的)使用期，有效期
lifetime [ˈlaiftaim] *n.* 一生；终身；寿命；使用期限
lift [lift] *vt.* 提起；提高；升高；举起；还清；取消；偷窃；运送；*vi.* 提升；*n.* 电梯；举起；帮助；提升；电梯；搭便车
light [lait] *n.* 光；光线；灯；光源；启发；眼光；*adj.* 轻的；不重要的；明亮的；淡色的；少量的；*vi.* 点燃；着火；*vt.* 点燃；照亮；*adv.* 轻地；轻便的
lightly [ˈlaitli] *adv.* 轻轻地；轻松地；轻快地；轻蔑地；轻率地；轻微地
lightning [ˈlaitniŋ] *n.* 闪电；闪电放电；*adj.* 闪电般的；快速的
like [laik] *vt.* 喜欢；喜爱；愿意；想；*adj.* 相似的；同样的；*prep.* 像；如同；像要；*n.* 喜好；类似的事物/人；种类；*adv.* 大概；和……一样；*conj.* 像……一样；好像
likely [ˈlaikli] *adj.* 可能的；*adv.* 很可能
likewise [ˈlaikwaiz] *ad.* 同样地；也，而且；
limb [lim] *n.* 肢；臂；腿；翼
lime [laim] *n.* 石灰；酸橙；酸橙树；*vt.* 撒石灰于
limit [ˈlimit] *n.* 限度；限制；范围；*vt.* 限制；限定
limitation [ˌlimiˈteiʃən] *n.* 限制；限度；局限
limited [ˈlimitid] *adj.* 有限的；被限制住的
line [lain] *n.* 线；排；路线；线条；行；航线；*vt.* 用做衬里；排成一行；顺……排列；*vi.* 排成一行；顺……排列；画线于
linen [ˈlinin] *n.* 亚麻布；亚麻线；亚麻织物；亚麻制品
link [liŋk] *vt.* 有环连接；连接；联系；*n.* 环；环节；联系(链的)环圈
lion [ˈlaiən] *n.* 狮子；勇猛的人
lip [lip] *n.* 嘴唇
liquid [ˈlikwid] *n.* 液体；*a.* 液体的；液态的
list [list] *n.* 清单；(船)倾斜；*v.* 列举；把……列入单子；(尤指船)倾侧；
listen [ˈlisn] *vi.* 听；留神听；听从；倾听；*n.* 听；倾听
literally [ˈlɪtərəli] *adv.* 逐字地；照字面地；确实地；真正地
literary [ˈlitərəri] *adj.* 文学的；适于文学作品的；爱好文学的；书面的
literature [ˈlitərətʃə] *n.* 文学；文献
liter [ˈliːtə(r)] *n.* [计量] 公升(容量单位)
litter [ˈlɪtə(r)] *n.* 废弃物，垃圾；杂乱的一堆；*v.* 使凌乱；乱扔
little [ˈlitl] *adj.* 小的；少；幼小的；*adv.* 毫不；少量地；*pron.* 几乎没有(指数量或程度等)
live [laiv, liv] *vi.* 居住；活；过着；*adj.* 活的；生动的；精力充沛的；*adv.* 直播的
lively [ˈlaivli] *adj.* 活泼的；活跃的；栩栩如生的；真实的；逼真的
living-room [ˈliviŋˌruːm] *n.* 起居室
load [ləud] *vt.* 装；装满；装载；装填；担负；给(枪)装子弹 [计算机] 装入；*n.* 负载；负荷；重担；装载量
loaf [ləuf] *n.* 一条面包；*vi.* 游手好闲；虚掷光阴
loan [ləun] *n.* 贷款；暂借；借出；债权人；*vt.* 借出；借给；供应货款
local [ˈləukəl] *adj.* 地方的；局部的；地方性的；当地的；*n.* 当地人
locate [ləuˈkeit] *vt.* 探明；找出；查出；设于；位于；建立
location [ləuˈkeiʃən] *n.* 位置；场所；地点；定位；(电影的)外景拍摄地
lock [lɔk] *n.* 锁；刹车；水闸；牢牢紧握；一束；一缕；*vt.* 锁上；锁住；抓牢；使固定
lodge [lɔdʒ] *vi.* 暂住；借宿；投宿；临时住宿；安顿；*n.* 小屋；门房；支部
log [lɔg] *n.* 原木；木料；记录；日志；计程仪；*vt.* 伐木；切；记录航行；度过(时间)
logical [ˈlɔdʒikəl] *adj.* 逻辑的；符合逻辑的；有推理能力的

lonely [ˈləunli] *adj.* 孤独的;荒凉的;寂寞的
long [lɔŋ] *adj.* 长的;远的;很久的;冗长的;*adv.* 长久;长期地;远地;*vi.* 渴望;热望;极想念
look [luk] *vi.* 看;显得;注意;*vt.* 打量;注视;用眼神或脸色表示;期待;*n.* 看;神色;样子;脸色
loose [luːs] *adj.* 松的;宽松的;不牢固的;不精确的;*n.* 解放;放任;放纵;*v.* 释放;放枪;开船
lord [lɔːd] *n.* 贵族;上帝;基督;主
lorry [ˈlɔri] *n.* 运货汽车;卡车
lose [luːz] *vt.* 失去;遗失;迷失;输掉;失败;损失
loss [lɔs] *n.* 遗失;损失;失败;丧失;损耗;亏损
lot [lɔt] *n.* 许多;大量;签;抽签;小组;场地;命运;*adv.* 很,非常;*pron.* 大量
loud [laud] *adj.* 响亮的;吵闹的;大声的;难闻的;*adv.* 响亮地;大声地
loudspeaker [ˈlaudˈspiːkə] *n.* 扬声器;喇叭
love [lʌv] *vt.* 爱;爱慕;热爱;喜欢;*vi.* 爱;*n.* 爱;恋爱;爱情;情人
lovely [ˈlʌvli] *adj.* 可爱的;令人愉快的;*n.* 美人,佳人
lover [ˈlʌvə] *n.* 爱好者;情人;情侣
low [ləu] *adj.* 低的,矮小的;楼下的,低洼的;沮丧的;下贱的;*adv.* 向下;向……底部;*n.* 低点;低水平;牛的叫声(一生或事业中的)艰难时期,低谷 *vi.* (牛)哞哞叫;
lower [ˈləuə, ˈlauə] *adj.* 下方的;底部的;朝海岸的;向南的;较小的;较低级的;*vt.* 放下;降低;跌落;减弱;贬低;*vi.* 皱眉;降低
loyal [ˈlɔiəl] *adj.* 忠诚的;忠心的
loyalty [ˈlɔiəlti] *n.* 忠诚;忠心
luck [lʌk] *n.* 运气;好运;幸运;吉祥之物;*vi.* 走运,交好运
lucky [ˈlʌki] *adj.* 幸运的;带来好运的;吉祥的
luggage [ˈlʌgidʒ] *n.* 行李;皮箱;皮包
lump [lʌmp] *n.* 块,团;肿块;许多,大量;笨拙的人;*vt.* 使成团,使成块;使团结在一起;把……混在一起;
lunch [lʌntʃ] *n.* 午餐 (美)便餐;*vi.* 吃午餐;供给午餐;
lung [lʌŋ] *n.* 肺脏;肺
luxury [ˈlʌkʃəri] *n.* 奢侈;奢华;奢侈品

M

machine [məˈʃiːn] *n.* 机器,机械;机械般的人;核心机构;*vt.* 加工成型
machinery [məˈʃiːnəri] *n.* 机器;机械装置;组织;机构;体制
mad [mæd] *adj.* 发疯的;恼火的;狂热的;生气的
madam [ˈmædəm] *n.* 夫人;女士;太太
magazine [ˌmægəˈziːn] *n.* 杂志;期刊
magic [ˈmædʒik] *n.* 魔法;巫术;戏法;*adj.* 有魔力的;神奇的
magnificent[mægˈnɪfɪsnt] *adj.* 壮丽的;宏伟的;值得赞扬的
maid [meid] *n.* 女佣;女仆;侍女;少女
mail [meil] *n.* 邮件;邮政;*vt.* 邮寄
mailbox [meilbɔks] *n.* 信箱
main [mein] *adj.* 主要的;最重要的;*n.* 主要部分;干线(水、煤气、电等)供应系统
mainland [ˈmeinlənd] *n.* 大陆;本土
maintain [meinˈtein] *vt.* 维持;赡养;维修;保养
major [ˈmeidʒə] *adj.* 较大的;主要的;较多的;大部分的;*n.* 专业主修;成年人;陆军少校;*vi.* 主修
majority [məˈdʒɔːriti] *n.* 多数;大多数
make [meik] *vt.* 使;做;制造;*vi.* 生产;*n.* 牌子;型号
makeup[ˈmeɪkʌp] *n.* 化妆;补充;构造
male [meil] *adj.* 男性的;雄性的;有力的;*n.* 男;雄性动物
man [mæn] *n.* 男人;人;人类
manage [ˈmænidʒ] *vt.* 管理;设法;对付;处理;维持;达成;经营;*vi.* 管理;达成
management [ˈmænidʒmənt] *n.* 管理(层);经营;处理
manager [ˈmænidʒə] *n.* 经理;管理人
mankind [mænˈkaind] *n.* 人类
manly [ˈmænli] *adj.* 男子气概的;强壮的
manner [ˈmænə] *n.* 方式;态度,举止;礼貌;习俗
manual [ˈmænjuəl] *adj.* 体力的;手工的;*n.* 手册,指南
manufacture [ˌmænjuˈfæktʃə] *vt.* 制造,生产,加工;捏造,虚构;从事制造;*n.* 大量制造;批量生产;工业品;
many [ˈmeni] *pron.* 许多人或物;许多的
map [mæp] *n.* 地图;*vt.* 绘制地图;计划
marathon [ˈmærəθən] *n.* 马拉松赛跑;

adj. 马拉松式的；
marble [ˈmɑːbl] *n.* 大理石
march [mɑːtʃ] *n.* (March)三月；示威游行；*vt.* 使同行；强迫(某人)一起走；*vi.* 齐步走，行进；进军；游行示威
margin [ˈmɑːdʒin] *n.* 页边的空白；边缘；差额；利润
mark [mɑːk] *n.* 斑点；污迹；记号；标记；分数；*vt.* 标明；做标记于；留意；打分数；留下污痕
market [ˈmɑːkit] *n.* 市场；集市；交易；推销地区；*vt.* 推销，促销
marriage [ˈmæridʒ] *n.* 结婚；婚姻；婚礼
marry [ˈmæri] *vt.* 娶；嫁；*vi.* 结婚；结合
Marxism [ˈmɑːksizəm] *n.* 马克思主义
mask [mɑːsk] *n.* 面具；伪装；口罩；掩饰；面膜
mass [mæs] *n.* 一团；大堆；大量；块；群众；平民百姓；大部分；充满；*adj.* 大批的，数量极多的
massive [ˈmæsɪv] *adj.* 巨大的；大而重的；(疾病)非常严重的；
master [ˈmɑːstə] *n.* 主人；能手；硕士学位；专家；*adj.* 最重要的，最大的；*vt.* 控制；精通
match [mætʃ] *n.* 比赛；竞赛；火柴；相配的人(或物)；*v.* 般配；与……相匹敌；相配；适应，满足
mate [meit] *n.* 伙伴；同事；配偶；助手
material [məˈtiəriəl] *n.* 布料；材料；素材；*adj.* 物质的
maths [mæθs] *n.* (英)数学 =mathematics(英)
matter [ˈmætə] *n.* 事情；物质；原因；*vi.* 要紧；有关系
mature [məˈtjuə] *adj.* 成熟的；到期的；充分发育的；考虑周到的
maximum [ˈmæksiməm] *n.* 最大量；最大限度；最大高度；*adj.* 最大的；最高的；最大极限的
may [mei，me] *v. aux.* 可能；可以；祝愿；*n.* (May) 五月；
maybe [ˈmeibi] *adv.* 大概；或许；也许；*n.* 不确定性
mayor [ˈmeə(r)] *n.* 市长
me [miː] *pron.* (宾格)我
meadow [ˈmedəu] *n.* 草地；牧场
meal [miːl] *n.* 一顿饭；一餐
mean [miːn] *vt.* 作……解释；意指；意谓；想要；意欲；*adj.* 低劣的；卑鄙的；吝啬的
meaning [ˈmiːniŋ] *n.* 意义；意思；含义；意图
means [miːnz] *n.* 方法；手段；工具
meantime [ˈmiːnˈtaim] *n.* 其时；其间；*adv.* 当时；与此同时
meanwhile [ˈmiːnˈwail] *adv.* 同时；当时；*n.* 其时；其间
measure [ˈmeʒə] *v.* 度量；测量；(尺寸、长短、数量等)量度为……；估量；*n.* 措施；尺度；判断
meat [miːt] *n.* 肉
mechanic [miˈkænik] *n.* 机械机；机修工
mechanics [miˈkæniks] *n.* 力学；机械学
mechanism [ˈmekənɪzəm] *n.* [生]机制，机能；(机械)结构，机械装置[作用]
medal [ˈmedl] *n.* 奖章；勋章；纪念章
medical [ˈmedikəl] *adj.* 医学的；医疗的
medicine [ˈmedisin] *n.* 内服药；医学
medium [ˈmiːdiəm] *n.* 媒质；方法；媒介；中间；*adj.* 中等的 适中的
meet [miːt] *vt.* 遇见；引见；经历；结识；满足；*vi.* 相遇；集合；交锋；相交
meeting [ˈmiːtiŋ] *n.* 聚集；会合；会见；会议
melon [ˈmelən] *n.* 瓜；甜瓜
melt [melt] *vi.* 融化；熔化；溶解；软化；*vt.* 使融化
member [ˈmembə] *n.* 成员；会员
membership[ˈmembəʃɪp] *n.* 会员身份
memo [ˈmeməʊ] *n.* 备忘录
memorial [miˈmɔːriəl] *adj.* 纪念的；追悼的；记忆的；*n.* 纪念碑(堂) 纪念仪式
memory [ˈmeməri] *n.* 记忆；回忆；存储；内存
mend [mend] *vt.* 修理；缝补
mental [ˈmentl] *adj.* 思想的；精神健康的
mention [ˈmenʃən] *vt.* & *n.* 提及；说起
menu [ˈmenjuː] *n.* 菜单
merchant [ˈməːtʃənt] *n.* 商人；店主
mercy [ˈməːsi] *n.* 仁慈；慈悲；恩惠；怜悯
mere [miə] *adj.* 仅仅的；纯粹的；微小的
merely [ˈmiəli] *adv.* 仅仅；只不过
merit [ˈmerit] *n.* 长处；优点；功过；功绩；价值
merry [ˈmeri] *adj.* 欢乐的；愉快的
mess [mes] *n.* 脏乱；困境；不整洁的人；粪便；*v.* 弄乱
message [ˈmesidʒ] *n.* 信息；消息；启示；要点
metal [ˈmetl] *n.* 金属
method [ˈmeθəd] *n.* 方法；办法；教学法；条理
metre(-er) [ˈmiːtə] *n.* 米；计量器
microwave [ˈmaɪkrəweɪv] *n.* 微波炉；微波；*v.* 用微波炉烹调(或加热)；
midday [ˈmiddei] *n.* 正午；中午
middle [ˈmidl] *n.* 中部；中间；腰；中项；*adj.* 中部的；中等的；中间的；中期的
midnight [ˈmidnait] *n.* 午夜；子夜
midst [midst] *n.* 中部；中间；当中；

prep. (= amidst)在……当中
might [mait] *v.* aux. 可能;会;也许;*n.* 力量;威力;能力;*v.* 或许可以
mighty [ˈmaɪti] *adj.* 巨大的;强有力的
mild [maild] *adj.* 和缓的;温柔的;味淡的;轻微的;温和的
mile [mail] *n.* 英里
military [ˈmilitəri] *adj.* 军事的;军人的;*n.* 军队
milk [milk] *n.* 乳;乳状物;牛奶;*vt.* 挤(奶);产乳
mill [mil] *n.* 磨坊;磨粉机;工厂
millimetre [ˈmili. miːtə] *n.* 毫米 = millimeter(美)
million [ˈmiljən] *num.* 百万;*n.* 许多;百万(the millions);群众;*adj.* 百万的;无数的
mind [maind] *n.* 头脑;记忆力;思考能力;聪明的人;*vt.* 留心注意;介意;照顾;*vi.* 留心;关心
mine [main] *pron.* 我的;*n.* 地雷;矿;*vt.* 采矿;埋地雷
mineral [ˈminərəl] *n.* 矿物;矿石;*adj.* 矿物的
minimum [ˈminiməm] *n.* 最小量;最低限度;*adj.* 最低的;最小的
minister [ˈministə] *n.* 部长;大臣;公使
ministry [ˈministri] *n.* (政府的)部
minor [ˈmainə] *adj.* 较小的;较次要的
minority [maiˈnɔːriti] *n.* 少数;少数民族
minus [ˈmainəs] *adj.* 负的;减的;*prep.* 减(去);*n.* 减号;负数
minute [ˈminit] *n.* 分钟;一会儿
[maɪˈnjuːt] *adj.* 微小的;不重要的;详细的
miracle [ˈmirəkl] *n.* 奇迹;令人惊奇的人
mirror [ˈmirə] *n.* 镜子;*vt.* 反映;反射
misery [ˈmɪzəri] *n.* 痛苦;不幸;穷困;悲惨的境遇
misfortune [ˌmɪsˈfɔːtʃuːn] *n.* 不幸,厄运;灾难;不幸事故
miss [mis] *n.* 小姐;*vt.* 想念;惦念;漏掉;错过;未看到
missile [ˈmisail] *n.* 发射物;导弹
missing [ˈmisiŋ] a. 丢失的;失去的;失踪的
mission [ˈmiʃən] *n.* 代表团;使命;官方使命;*v.* 给……交代任务;派遣;把任务交给
mist [mist] *n.* 薄雾;迷蒙;朦胧不清
mistake [miˈsteik] *n.* 错误;误会;*vt.* 误解;看错;
Mister [ˈmistə] *n.* 先生
mistress [ˈmistris] *n.* 女主人;主妇
misunderstand [ˈmisʌndəˈstænd] *vt.* 误解;误会;曲解
mix [miks] *vt.* 混合;调配;*n.* 混合;混杂
mixture [ˈmikstʃə] *n.* 混合;混合物
mo(u)ld [məʊld] *n.* 铸模;模型;性格;霉;*vt.* 用模子做;形成;陶冶,训练(人格)
mobile [ˈməubail] *adj.* 运动的;流动的;可移动的;易变的;迁徙的
mobilise(-ze) [ˈməʊbɪlaɪz] *vt. & vi.* 动员起来,调动,鼓动起;
mock[mɒk] *vt. & vi.* 愚弄,嘲弄;*vt.* 使受挫折;不尊重,蔑视;*adj.* 仿制的;模拟的;虚假的;不诚实的;*n.* (英国)模拟考试;
mode [məud] *n.* 方式;样式;模式;风格;[音乐]调式
model [ˈmɔdl] *n.* 模型;模式;模特儿;模范
moderate [ˈmɔdəreit, ˈmɔdərit] *a.* 温和的;适度的;中等的;*v.* 使……适中;使……缓和
modern [ˈmɔdən] *a.* 现代的;近代的;时髦的;*n.* 现代人;时尚人士
modest [ˈmɔdist] *adj.* 谦虚的;适度的;庄重的
modify [ˈmɔdifai] *vt.* 更改;修改;修饰;调正;缓和;*vi.* 修改
module [ˈmɒdjuːl] *n.* 模块;组件;(宇宙飞船上各个独立的)舱
moist [mɔist] *adj.* 湿润的;潮湿的
mom [mɒm] *n.* <美>妈妈 = mum
moment [ˈməʊmənt] *n.* 片刻;时刻;时机
monetary[ˈmʌnɪtri] *adj.* 货币的,钱的(尤指一国的金融)
money [ˈmʌni] *n.* 钱;薪水;钞票
monitor [ˈmɔnitə] *n.* 班长;监视器;[计算机]显示器;监视器;*v.* 监视;监听;监督
monkey [ˈmʌŋki] *n.* 猴子;猿
monopoly [məˈnɒpəli] *n.* 垄断;垄断者
monster [ˈmɒnstə(r)] *adj.* 巨大的;*n.* 怪物;庞然大物;
month [mʌnθ] *n.* 月;月份
monthly [ˈmʌnθli] *adj.* 每月的;持续一个月的;每月发生的;*adv.* 每月;按月;*n.* 月刊
monument [ˈmɔnjumənt] *n.* 纪念碑;纪念馆;历史遗迹;丰碑;永久的典范
mood [muːd] *n.* 心情;情绪;语气
moon [muːn] *n.* 月球;月亮;卫星
moral [ˈmɔrəl] *adj.* 道德(上)的;合乎道德的;*n.* 品行;寓意;道德
more [mɔː] a. 更多的;程度较大的;更大的;*adv.* 更;更多;进一步;*n.* 更多;附加,添加

moreover [mɔːr'əuvə] *adv.* 再者;加之;此外;而且
morning ['mɔːniŋ] *n.* 早晨;上午
mortal ['mɔːtl] *adj.* 终有一死的;人世间的;致命的;终有一死的;*n.* 凡人,人类;
mortgage ['mɔːgɪdʒ] *n.* 按揭贷款;*vt.* 抵押;
most [məust] *adj.* 最多的;大多数的;几乎全部的;*adv.* 最;最多;极其;*n.* 最多;最大;*pron.* 大多数
mostly ['məustli] *adv.* 主要的;大部分;大概
mother ['mʌðə] *n.* 母亲;妈妈;*adj.* 母亲的;母体的;*vt.* 生育;像母亲一样关爱
motion ['məuʃən] *n.* 运动;手势;动机,意向;请求;*vt.* 打手势;向某人点头或摇头示意;打手势要求[指示];*vi.* 运动;打手势
motivate ['məutiveit] *vt.* 促动;激励;激发(兴趣或欲望);给予动机
motive ['məutiv] *n.* 动机;目的;主题;*adj.* 发动的;运动的;积极的;动机的;*vt.* 促使;使有动机
motor ['məutə] *n.* 发动机;马达;*adj.* 机动的;有引擎的;*v.* (用引擎)驱动
mount [maunt] *v.* 攀登;增加;骑上;安装;组织;开展;*n.* 山峰
mountain ['mauntin] *n.* 山;山岳;山脉
mountainous ['maʊntənəs] *adj.* 多山的;巨大的;山一般的
mouse [maus] *n.* 老鼠;鼠标;羞怯[胆小]的人
mouth [mauθ] *n.* 口;出入口
move [muːv] *v.* 移动;改变位置;进步;采取行动;搬家;调动;走棋;动摇;感动;提议;*n.* 行动;移动;改变;搬家;步骤;一步(棋)
movement ['muːvmənt] *n.* 动作;活动;移动;运动;变动
movie ['muːvi] *n.* 电影;电影院
much [mʌtʃ] *adv.* 非常;很;*adj.* 许多的;*pron. & n.* 许多
mud [mʌd] *n.* 软泥;泥浆;*vt.* 弄脏
multiple ['mʌltipl] *adj.* 复合的;并联的;许多;多种多样的
multiply ['mʌltiplai] *vt.* 使增加;乘;*vi.* 扩大;繁衍;做乘法;*adv.* 多样地;多重地
municipal [mjuː'nɪsɪpl] *adj.* 市政的;地方政府的
murder ['məːdə] *n.* 谋杀;凶杀;*vt.* 谋杀;凶杀;*vi.* 谋杀;凶杀
muscle ['mʌsl] *n.* 肌肉
museum [mjuː'ziəm] *n.* 博物馆;展览馆
mushroom ['mʌʃrum] *n.* 蘑菇;菌类植物;*vi.* 扩张;迅速增加;采蘑菇
music ['mjuːzik] *n.* 音乐;乐曲;乐谱
musical ['mjuːzikəl] *adj.* 音乐的;和谐的;*n.* 音乐片
musician [mjuː'ziʃən] *n.* 音乐家;作曲家
must [mʌst] modal. 必须;一定;应该;一定要;*n.* 必须做的事
mutual ['mjuːtʃuəl] *adj.* 相互的;共同的
my [mai] *pron.* 我的;*adj.* 我的(I 的所有格形式);*int.* 哎哟(用于表示惊讶的感叹词)
myself [mai'self] *pron.* 我自己;我亲自
mysterious [mis'tiəriəs] *adj.* 神秘的;难以理解的;不可思议的
mystery ['mistəri] *n.* 神秘;秘密;神秘的人或事物
myth [mɪθ] *n.* 神话;神话故事;虚构的事

N

nail [neil] *n.* 钉子;指甲;*vt.* 钉;使牢固
naive[naɪ'iːv] *adj.* 幼稚的;天真的;单纯的
naked ['neikid] *adj.* 裸体的;无遮蔽的;不加掩饰的
name [neim] *n.* 名字;名声;名人;*v.* 给……取名;叫出……的名称;确定;提名
namely ['neimli] *adv.* 即;也就是
nap [næp] *n.* (日间的)小睡;打盹;*vi.* 小睡;疏忽;*vt.* 使……起毛
napkin ['næpkɪn] *n.* 餐巾,餐巾纸;尿布
narrow ['nærəu] *adj.* 狭窄的;严格的(种类或数目);有限的;*vt.* 变窄;使……狭窄;*vi.* 变窄
nation ['neiʃən] *n.* 民族;国家
national ['næʃənəl] *adj.* 民族的;国家的;*n.* 国民
nationality [ˌnæʃə'næliti] *n.* 国籍;民族;族
native ['neitiv] *adj.* 本土的;本国的;出生地的;天生的;*n.* 本地人;土著人
natural ['nætʃərəl] *adj.* 自然界的;天然的;正常的;天生的;*n.* 有天赋的人
nature ['neitʃə] *n.* 大自然;自然界;自然状态;本性;性质;类型
naughty ['nɔːti] *adj.* 顽皮的;淘气的;粗俗的
navigation [ˌnævi'geiʃən] *n.* 航行;航海术;导航
navy ['neivi] *n.* 海军;船队;深蓝色
near [niə] *prep.* 靠近,在……附近;接近,临近;

濒临,快要;近似于;*adj.* 不远的;不久以后;差不多的;*adv.* 在附近;不久以后;几乎;*v.* 接近,靠近,临近

nearby [ˈniəbai] *adj.* 附近的;*adv.* 在附近;*prep.* 在……附近

nearly [ˈniəli] *adv.* 几乎;差不多

neat [niːt] *adj.* 整洁的;爱整洁的;小巧优雅的;灵巧的;干净利落的;很好的

necessary [ˈnesə. səri] *adj.* 必要的;必然的;*n.* 必需品

necessity [niˈsesiti] *n.* 必要,需要;必需品;不可避免的情况

neck [nek] *n.* 颈;脖子

necklace [ˈneklis] *n.* 项链;项圈

need [niːd] *v.* 需要;有必要;(modal verb)需要;*n.* 必要;迫切要求;欲望;短缺

needle [ˈniːdl] *n.* 针;缝补;编织针;*vt.* 用针缝;*vi.* 缝纫

needless [ˈniːdlis] *adj.* 不需要的;无用的

negative [ˈnegətiv] *adj.* 消极的;否定的;负的;阴极的;*v.* 拒绝;否定;*n.* 底片;(化验或科学试验中的)阴性结果;坏的事情

neglect [niˈglekt] *v.* 疏忽;忽视;*n.* 忽略;怠慢

negotiate [nɪˈgəʊieɪt] *vi.* 谈判,协商,交涉;*vt.* 谈判达成

neighbor(u)r [ˈneibə] *n.* 邻居;邻近的人[物];邻国

neighbor(u)rhood [ˈneibəhud] *n.* 邻居关系

neither [ˈniːðə] *adj.* (两者)都不的;皆不;*int.* 两者都不;*conj.* 既非,既不

nephew [ˈnefjuː] *n.* 侄子;外甥

nerve [nəːv] *n.* 神经;勇气,胆量

nervous [ˈnəːvəs] *adj.* 神经(质)的;易激动的;紧张的;焦虑的

nest [nest] *n.* 巢;窝;穴;*vt.* 嵌入;*vi.* 筑巢

net [net] *n.* 网;球网;网罩;*vt.* 用网捕;捕获;净赚;*adj.* 净的;净得的;最后的

network [ˈnetwəːk] *n.* 网;网络系统;广播网;关系网;人际网 *vt. & vi.* 将……连接成网络;建立工作关系;*vt.* 把(地方节目)编排到广播网(或电视网)联播;使(全国)联播;(如)用网覆盖;广泛分布;*vi.* 沟通,互助;

neutral [ˈnjuːtrəl] *adj.* 中立的;中性的;*n.* 中立者

never [ˈnevə] *adv.* 永不;决不;不

nevertheless = nonetheless[ˌnevəðəˈles] *conj.* 然而;不过;*adv.* 仍然;不过

new [njuː] *adj.* 新的;新近出现的;附加的;*adv.* 新的

news [njuːz] *n.* 新闻;消息

newspaper [ˈnjuːz. peipə] *n.* 报纸;报;报社;新闻纸;*v.* 从事新闻工作

next [ˈnekst] *adj.* 紧接的;贴近的;下一个的;*adv.* 其次;*n.* 下一个;*prep.* 靠近

nice [nais] *adj.* 令人愉快的;好心的;友好的

nickname [ˈnɪkneɪm] *n.* 绰号;诨名;昵称;*vt.* 给……起绰号;

niece [niːs] *n.* 侄女;外甥女

night [nait] *n.* 夜;夜间

nightmare [ˈnaɪtmeə(r)] *n.* 噩梦

no [nəu] *adv.* 不;并不;*adj.* 没有;不是;绝非;*n.* 不;拒绝;否决票

noble [ˈnəubl] *adj.* 品质高尚的;贵族的;崇高的;*n.* 出生高贵

nobody [ˈnəubɔdi] *pron.* 谁也不;无人;没有人;*n.* 无足轻重的人;小人物

nod [nɔd] *vt.* 点(头);点头表示;打盹;*v.* 点头;打盹

noise [nɔiz] *n.* 噪音;喧闹声;响声;干扰信息

noisy [ˈnɔizi] *adj.* 嘈杂的;喧闹的;发出噪声的

none [nʌn] *pron.* 没有人;没有任何东西;*adv.* 毫不;一点也不

nonsense [ˈnɔnsəns] *n.* 胡说;废话;荒唐

noodle [ˈnuːdl] *n.* 面条

noon [nuːn] *n.* 正午;中午

nor [nɔː] *conj.* 也不;也不是;和 neither 或 not 连用

normal [ˈnɔːməl] *adj.* 正常的;正规的;普通的;*n.* 常态;标准

north [nɔːθ] *n.* 北,北方;*adj.* 北方的;*adv.* 向北方

northern [ˈnɔːðən] *adj.* 北方的;北部的

nose [nəuz] *n.* 鼻子;嗅觉 *vi.* 小心翼翼地向前移动

not [nɔt] *adv.* 不,没有

notable [ˈnəʊtəbl] *adj.* 值得注意的;显著的;著名的;*n.* 名人;显要人物;

note [nəut] *n.* 笔记;便条;注释;备忘录;音符;音调;票据;纸币;*vt.* 记录;注解;注意

notebook [ˈnəutbuk] *n.* 笔记;便笺;音符;钞票;*vt.* 注意;记录;对……加注释;指出

nothing [ˈnʌθɪŋ] *pron.* 没有什么;无关紧要的事物/人;零;不值钱;*adv.* 一点都不像……;简直是……

notice [ˈnəutis] *vt.* 注意;通知;留心;*n.* 通知;注意;布告

notify[ˈnəʊtɪfaɪ] *vt.* 通知；布告
notion [ˈnəuʃn] *n.* 观念；信念；理解
novel [ˈnɔvəl] *n.* 小说；*adj.* 新的；新奇的
now [nau] *adv.* 现在，此刻；从现在开始；（语气词）喂，好，哦；*conj.* 既然；由于
nowadays [ˈnaʊədeɪz] *adv.* 现今
nowhere [ˈnəuwɛə] *adv.* 无处；哪里都不
nuclear [ˈnjuːkliə] *adj.* 原子核的；原子能的
number [ˈnʌmbə] *n.* 数字；编号；号码；数量；期，号 *v.* 总计；把……算作；把……编号
numerous [ˈnjuːmərəs] *adj.* 为数众多的；许多
nurse [nəːs] *n.* 保姆；护士；*vt.* 看护；哺乳；*vi.* 看护；照顾栽培
nursery [ˈnəːsəri] *n.* 托儿所；苗圃
nut [nʌt] *n.* 坚果；螺母；螺帽；难对付的人（事）
nutrition [njuˈtrɪʃn] *n.* 营养
nylon [ˈnailɔn] *n.* 尼龙；耐纶（复数 nylons）：女长袜

O

obesity[əʊˈbiːsɪti] *n.* 肥胖，过胖；肥胖症
obey [əˈbei] *vt.* 顺从；*vi.* 服从；听从
object [ˈɔbdʒikt] *n.* 物；物体；目的；目标；宾语；*v.* 反对；提出……作为反对的理由；反感
objective [əbˈdʒektiv] *adj.* 客观的；基于事实的；宾格的；*n.* 目标；宾语
obligation[ɔˈblɪˈgeɪʃn] *n.* 义务，责任；证券，契约；债务；恩惠
oblige [əˈblaidʒ] *vt.* 强制，强迫
observation [ˌɔbzəˈveiʃən] *n.* 观察；观测；监视
observe [əbˈzəːv] *vt.* 遵守；看到；注意到；说；观察
obstacle [ˈɔbstəkl] *n.* 障碍；障碍物；绊脚石
obtain [əbˈtein] *vt.* 获得；得到；买到；*vi.* 通用；流行；存在
obvious [ˈɔbviəs] *adj.* 明显的；显而易见的
occasion [əˈkeiʒən] *n.* 场合；时刻；时机；机会；理由
occupation [ˌɔkjuˈpeiʃən] *n.* 职业，工作；占有，占领；（土地、房屋、建筑等的）使用
occupy [ˈɔkjupai] *vt.* 居住；占用；占领；担任；使忙于（做某事）；占……
occur [əˈkəː] *vi.* 发生；出现；存在；想到
ocean [ˈəuʃən] *n.* 海洋；洋
o'clock [əˈklɔk] *ad.* = of the clock ……点钟
odd [ɔd] *adj.* 奇数的；单只的；古怪的；剩余的
odds [ɒdz] *n.* 希望，可能性；几率，胜算；逆境；不利条件
odo(u)r [ˈəudə] *n.* 气味；香气；味道
of [əv] *prep.* 关于；属于……的；由……制成
off [ɔːf] *adv.* （离）开；（停）止；出发；减价的 *adj.* 不热情；冷淡；*prep.* 离开；偏离
offend [əˈfend] *vt.* 冒犯；犯罪；*vi.* 犯过错；令人不适；违反
offense(-ce) [əˈfens] *n.* 进攻；冒犯
offer [ˈɔːfə] *v.* 提供；表示愿意；*n.* 建议；提供；出价；减价
office [ˈɔːfis] *n.* 办公室；职务；事务；处；局；社
officer [ˈɔːfisə] *n.* 军官，警官；高级职员；公务员
official [əˈfiʃəl] *adj.* 官方的；公务的；公开的；公务的；*n.* 官员；裁判员
often [ˈɔːfən] *adv.* 经常；常常
oil [ɔil] *n.* 油；石油；油画；燃油；*vt.* 给……加油
old [əuld] *adj.* 老的；古老的；以前的；（用于指称被替代的东西）原来的
Olympic [əˈlɪmpɪk] *adj.* 奥林匹斯山的，奥林匹克运动会的；*n.* 奥林匹克运动会比赛项目；[用复数] [the Olympic] = Olympic Games
omit [əuˈmit] *vt.* 省略；省去；遗漏；疏忽
on [ɔn] *prep.* （表示方向）向；（表示对象）对；（表示位置）在……上；（表示时间）在……之时；*adv.* （放，穿，连接）上；向前，（继续）下去
once [wʌns] *adv.* 一次；每一次；每隔……一次；曾经；*conj.* 一……就
oneself [wʌnˈself] *pron.* 自己；亲自
onion [ˈʌnjən] *n.* 洋葱；洋葱头
only [ˈəunli] *adv.* 只；仅仅；专门地；唯一地；刚才；*adj.* 最好的；唯一的；出众的；*conj.* 除非；但是；然而；毕竟
onto [ˈɔntuː] *prep.* 到……上
open [ˈəupən] *adj.* 展开；开放；张开的；敞开的；营业，开放；坦诚；思想开明的；*vt.* 开；打开；公开；开放；开始；*vi.* 开；通行；大叫；*n.* 公开；户外；空旷
opening [ˈəupəniŋ] *n.* 开幕，开始；空缺的职位；[商] 开盘，交易开始时间；（职位的）空缺；*adj.* 首次的，开始的；*v.* （打）开（ open 的现在分词）；开始；睁开；启动
opera [ˈɔpərə] *n.* 歌剧

operate [ˈɔpəreit] *vi.* 操作;施行手术;运转;*vt.* 起作用;动手术

operation [ˌɔpəˈreiʃən] *n.* 操作;手术;运算;行动;活动

operator [ˈɒpəreɪtə(r)] *n.* 经营者;操作员;电话接线员

opinion [əˈpinjən] *n.* 意见;看法;主张;判断

opponent [əˈpəunənt] *n.* 对手;敌手;对抗者;反对者;*adj.* 敌对的;反对的

opportunity [ˌɔpəˈtjuːniti] *n.* 机会;时机;良机

oppose [əˈpəuz] *vt.* 反对;抵制;阻挠;(在竞赛中)与……角逐

opposite [ˈɔpəzit] *prep.* 在……的对面;与……合演;*adj.* 对面的;截然相反的;*n.* 对立物;

optimistic [ˌɔptiˈmistik] *adj.* 乐观的;乐观主义的

option [ˈɔpʃən] *n.* 选择;选择权;可选物

or [ɔː, ə] *conj.* 或;或者;即;还是;否则

oral [ˈɔːrəl] *adj.* 口头的;口的;*n.* 口试

orange [ˈɔːrindʒ] *n.* 橘子,橙子;[植]橘树;橙色;橘色;橙汁;*adj.* 橙色的;橘色的;橘红色的

orbit [ˈɔːbit] *vt. & vi.* 在……轨道上运行,环绕轨道运行

order [ˈɔːdə] *n.* 次序;条理;治安;命令;订货;点菜;付款指令;秩序;阶层;(生物分类的)目;修会;授勋的人;勋章;社团;汇票;*v.* 命令;订货;点菜;组织

orderly [ˈɔːdəli] *adj.* 整洁的;有秩序的;一丝不苟的;和平的;*adv.* 有秩序地;有条理地;依次地;*n.* 勤务兵(医院的)勤务工

ordinary [ˈɔːdnrɪ] *adj.* 平常的;平凡的;普通的

organ [ˈɔːgən] *n.* 器官;机构;管风琴

organic [ɔːˈgænik] *adj.* 有机体的;器官的;有机的,不使用化肥的

organisation(-zation) [ˌɔːgənaiˈzeiʃən] *n.* 组织;团体;机构;*adj.* 有组织的

organize(-ze) [ˈɔːgənaiz] *vt.* 组织;编组;*vi.* 组织起来

orient [ˈɔːrient] *vt.* 确定方向;使熟悉或适应;朝向;面对

origin [ˈɔridʒin] *n.* 起源;由来;出身

original [əˈridʒənl] *adj.* 最初的;新颖的;原始的;有独创性的;原版的;*n.* 原件;原稿;有独创性的人

ornament [ˈɔːnəmənt] *n.* 装饰物;装饰

other [ˈʌðə] *adj.* 其他的;另外的;额外的;另一的;余下的;别人的;*pron.* 另外,其他;另一个;其他的

otherwise [ˈʌðəwaiz] *adv.* 否则;除此以外;与之不同地;以其他方式

ought [ɔːt] *v.* aux. 应当;应该;*conj.* 应该;大概

ounce [auns] *n.* 盎司;英两

our [ˈauə] *pron.* 我们的;*adj.* 我们的

ours [ˈauəz] *pron.* 我们的

ourselves [ˌauəˈselvz] *pron.* 我们自己

out [aut] *adv.* 出局;在外,在外部;完全,彻底;出版;*prep.* (表示来源)从;(从……里)出来;(表示不在原状态)脱离;离去;*vt.* 使熄灭;揭露;驱逐;*n.* 不流行;出局

outbreak [ˈaʊtbreɪk] *n.* (战争,怒气等的)爆发;突然发生

outcome [ˈautkʌm] *n.* 结果;后果;成果

outdoor [ˈautdɔː] *adj.* 户外的;室外的;野外的;露天的

outdoors [autˈdɔːz] *adv.* 在户外;在野外;*n.* 露天;野外;名词 outdoor 的复数形式

outer [ˈautə] *adj.* 外部的;外面的

outgoing [ˈaʊtgəʊɪŋ] *adj.* 对人友好的,开朗的;出发的,外出的;即将离职的

outline [ˈautlain] *n.* 轮廓;略图;大纲;概要;素描;*vt.* 描画轮廓描述要点

outlook [ˈautluk] *n.* 观点;看法;展望;前景;景色

output [ˈautput] *n.* 产量;输出量;输出;输出功率;输出端;*vt.* 输出(信息等)

outside [autˈsaid] *n.* 外部;外表;*adj.* 外部的;*adv.* 在外面;*prep.* 在……外;*pron.* 在……外边

outstanding [autˈstændiŋ] *adj.* 突出的;杰出的;显著的

oven [ˈʌvən] *n.* 炉;灶;烤炉

over [ˈəuvə] *prep.* 在……上方;超过;表示能控制;在……期间;*adj.* 结束的;超过的;多余的;*adv.* 结束;落下;穿过;完全覆盖;*vt.* 越过

overall [əuvəˈrɔːl] *n.* 工装裤;防护服;罩衫;*adj.* 全面的;全部的全体的;一切在内的;*adv.* 总的来说;全部地

overcoat [ˈəuvəkəut] *n.* 外衣;大衣

overcome [ˌəuvəˈkʌm] *vt.* 克服;解决;受到……的极大影响

overhead [ˈəuvəˈhed] *adj.* 上面的,高架的;头顶上的;经费的;管理费用的;*adv.* 在头顶上;在空中

overlook [ˌəuvəˈluk] *v.* 俯瞰;忽略;不理会;不考虑

overnight [ˈəuvəˈnait] *adv.* 在晚上;一夜之间;

adj. 夜间的；突然的

overseas [ˌəuvəˈsiːz] *adv.* 在海外；*adj.* 在海外的

overtake [ˌəuvəˈteik] *vt.* 追上；赶上；大于，超过；(不愉快的事情)突然发生

overtime [ˈəuvətaim] *adj.* 超时的；加班的；*adv.* 在规定时间之外(超出时间地)；*n.* 加班时间(加班加点费)

overview[ˈəʊvəvjuː] *n.* 概观；总的看法；回顾，复习

owe [əu] *vt.* 欠(债等)；应把……归功于；*vi.* 欠钱

owing [ˈəuɪŋ] *adj.* 欠着的，应付的，未付的；*v.* 感激(owe 的现在分词)；应把……归功于；欠……债

owl [aul] *n.* 猫头鹰

own [əun] *adj.* 自己的；*vt.* 有；拥有；承认；*vi.* 承认；*pron.* 自己的

owner [ˈəunə] *n.* 物主；所有人

ownership [ˈəunəʃip] *n.* 所有(权)；所有制

ox [ɔks] *n.* 牛，公牛

oxygen [ˈɒksɪdʒən] *n.* 氧(气)

P

pace [peɪs] *n.* 速度；节奏；步速；迅速出现；*v.* 踱步；确定速度；调整节奏

pack[pæk] *v.* 收拾行李；将……打包；保存；挤满；压实；佩枪；夹带；*n.* 纸盒；全套东西；一捆……；背包

package[ˈpækɪdʒ] *n.* 包裹；包装盒；一套建议；软件包；包价；*v.* 包装；使改头换面

packet[ˈpækɪt] *n.* 小包；信息包；邮船；大笔款项；*vt.* 包装，打包；用邮船运送

pad [pæd] *vt.* 给……装衬垫，加垫子；填塞；踏平；*vi.* 步行，放轻脚步走；*n.* 垫，衬垫；护具；便签本

page[peɪdʒ] *n.* 页；(计算机的)页面；年史；*vt.* 标记……的页数；翻页；*vi.* 翻书页；浏览

pain[peɪn] *n.* 痛；痛苦；讨厌的人/事；*v.* 使痛苦；使苦恼

painful [ˈpeɪnfl] *adj.* 令人疼痛的；令人痛苦的；不愉快的

paint [peɪnt] *n.* 油漆；涂层；绘画颜料；*v.* 给……上油漆；(用颜料)绘画；涂，抹；描绘

painter[ˈpeɪntə(r)] *n.* 画家，着色者；油漆匠；(系船的)缆绳

painting[ˈpeɪntɪŋ] *n.* 绘画；油画；上色，着色；颜料，油漆

pair [peə(r)] *n.* 一双；分两个相连接部分的物体；一对(两个……)；*v.* 使配对

palace [ˈpæləs] *n.* 宫殿；王室；豪宅；大的公共建筑

pale [peɪl] *adj.* 浅色的；苍白的；暗淡的

palm [pɑːm] *n.* 手掌；手心；棕榈树

pan[pæn] *n.* 平底锅；盘状的器皿

panda[ˈpændə] *n.* 熊猫

panel [ˈpænl] *n.* 专门小组；(门等的)镶板，嵌板；仪表板，面板

panic[ˈpænɪk] *n.* 恐慌；恐慌局面；*v.* 使惊慌失措

pants [pænts] *n.* <英>(紧身的)短裤；<美>裤子

paper [ˈpeɪpə(r)] *n.* 纸；报纸；材料；壁纸；论文；试卷；文件；*adj.* 书面的；纸质的

parade [pəˈreɪd] *v.* 游行；检阅；阅兵；夸示；炫耀；*n.* 检阅；游行；炫耀

paradise[ˈpærədaɪs] *n.* 天堂；伊甸园；乐园

paragraph[ˈpærəgrɑːf] *n.* 段落

parallel [ˈpærəlel] *adj.* 平行的；相同的，类似的；*n.* 相似物；相似特征；纬线；*vt.* 与……媲美；与……相比；与……相似

parcel[ˈpɑːsl] *n.* 包袱，包裹；(土地的)一块；*vt.* 包；裹好；打包

pardon[ˈpɑːdn] *vt.* 宽恕；原谅；赦免，劳驾；*n.* 饶恕，原谅；赦免；*int.* (用于请求别人重复某事)什么，请再说一遍

parent[ˈpeərənt] *n.* 父亲(或母亲)(动植物的)亲本，亲代；创始机构

park[pɑːk] *n.* 公园；停车场；*vi.* 泊车，停车；*vt.* 将……放置在某处；停车

parliament [ˈpɑːləmənt] *n.* 议会，国会

part[pɑːt] *n.* 部分；零件；角色；成员；部位；参与；声部；*v.* 离开；分离；解散；*adv.* 部分地

partial [ˈpɑːʃl] *adj.* 部分的；偏袒的；钟爱的

participate [pɑːˈtɪsəpeət] *v.* 参与

particular[pəˈtɪkjələ(r)] *adj.* 特定的；特殊的；格外的；挑剔的

partly [ˈpɑːtli] *adv.* 部分地；某种程度地

partner [ˈpɑːtnə(r)] *n.* 配偶；同伴；合伙人；盟友；*v.* 做……的伙伴；与……配对

party [ˈpɑːti] *n.* 社交聚会;党,党派;当事人;同类,伙伴;*v.* 为……举行社交聚会;为……请客;参加社交聚会
pass[pɑːs] *v.* 使经过;通过;超过;转交;转变;消逝,度过;*n.* 合格;通行证;传球;关口;飞跃;阶段
passage [ˈpæsɪdʒ] *n.* 通道,走廊;段落;流逝;通过;旅程;通行许可
passenger[ˈpæsɪndʒə(r)] *n.* 乘客;闲散人员;*adj.* 乘客的
passerby[ˈpɑːsəˈbaɪ] *n.* 过路人,行人
passion[ˈpæʃn] *n.* 热情;热恋;强烈的情感;酷爱;热衷的爱好(或活动等)
passive[ˈpæsɪv] *adj.* 消极的;被动的;被动语态的;*n.* 被动语态
passport[ˈpɑːspɔːt] *n.* 护照;途径,手段
past [pɑːst] *adj.* 过去的,以前的;结束的;前任的;*n.* 过去,过往;往事;[语]过去时;*prep.* 超过,超出;远于;越过;*adv.* 经过,超过
paste [peɪst] *n.* 面团;糨糊;肉(或鱼等)酱(作涂抹料或烹饪用);*vt.* 粘贴,张贴;以……覆盖于
pastime[ˈpɑːstaɪm] *n.* 消遣,娱乐
pasture [ˈpɑːstʃə(r)] *n.* 牧草地,牧场;*vt.* & *vi.* 放牧
pat [pæt] *v.* 轻拍;*n.* 轻拍;*adj.* 过于简单的
patent [ˈpætnt,ˈpeɪtnt] *n.* 专利权;*v.* 得到专利权;*adj.* 有专利的;专利生产的;明显的
path [pɑːθ] *n.* 小路;路线,道路;行动计划
patience [ˈpeɪʃns] *n.* 容忍;毅力
patient [ˈpeɪʃnt] *n.* 病人,患者;*adj.* 有耐心的,能忍耐的
pattern [ˈpætn] *n.* 模式;范例;图案;模型;样品;*v.* 构成图案;使形成
pause[pɔːz] *v.* 停顿;暂停放音;*n.* 停顿;延长记号;暂停键
pavement [ˈpeɪvmənt] *n.* 人行道;石板铺的地面;路面
pay[peɪ] *v.* 付款;偿还;盈利;划算;付代价;*n.* 薪水
payment [ˈpeɪmənt] *n.* 支付,付款;款项;报答
pea [piː] *n.* 豌豆,豌豆粒
peace [piːs] *n.* 和平;宁静;平静;和谐
peaceful[ˈpiːsfl] *adj.* 和平的;平和的;宁静的;寻求和平的
peach [piːtʃ] *n.* 桃子;桃红色;*adj.* 桃红色的;粉红色的
peak [piːk] *n.* 山峰;最高点;尖端;帽檐;*v.* 达到高峰;达到最高值;*adj.* 最高度的;巅峰状态的
peanut[ˈpiːnʌt] *n.* 花生
pear [peə(r)] *n.* 梨(树);梨树
pearl [pɜːl] *n.* 珍珠;珠状物;*adj.* 如珍珠般的
peasant [ˈpeznt] *n.* 农民;农夫;佃农
peculiar[pɪˈkjuːliə(r)] *adj.* 奇怪的,古怪的;不寻常的;特有的,特殊的
pedestrian [pəˈdestriən] *n.* 步行者;*adj.* 行人的
pedlar(=**peddler**) [ˈpedlə(r)] *n.* 流动小贩,商贩
peel [piːl] *vt.* 剥皮;覆盖层脱落,剥落;*vi.* 剥落;脱落;揭掉;表面起皮;*n.* 果皮,蔬菜皮;长柄木铲
peer[pɪə(r)] *vi.* 仔细看;端详;*n.* 同辈,同等的人
pen [pen] *n.* 笔,钢笔;*vt.* 写;把……关入栏中
penalty[ˈpenəlti] *n.* 惩罚;刑罚;害处;足球点球
pencil [ˈpensl] *n.* 铅笔;*vt.* 用铅笔写(或画、做记号)
penny [ˈpeni] *n.* 便士;(美国、加拿大的)一分钱;少量的钱
pension [ˈpenʃn] *n.* 养老金
people [ˈpiːpl] *n.* 人,人类;居民;人民;种族;*vt.* 居住于,使住满人
pepper[ˈpepə(r)] *n.* 胡椒粉;*v.* 撒胡椒粉
per[pə(r)] *prep.* 由;(表示根据)依照;(表示比率)(尤指数量,价格,时间)每
perceive[pəˈsiːv] *v.* 意识到;察觉,发觉;理解为;认为
percent[pəˈsent] *n.* 百分比;*adj.* & *adv.* 每一百中
percentage [pəˈsentɪdʒ] *n.* 百分比;提成
perfect [ˈpɜːfɪkt, pəˈfekt] *adj.* 完美的;十分适合的;完美无缺的;十足的;(动词)完成时的;*n.* (动词的)完成时(态);*v.* 使完善/完美/完备
perform[pəˈfɔːm] *v.* 执行;履行;演出;工作,运转(好/不好)
performance [pəˈfɔːməns] *n.* 表演;演出;表现;性能;执行
perfume[ˈpɜːfjuːm] *n.* 香水;香精;芳香;*v.* 使香气弥漫;为……增加香味;抹香水
perhaps [pəˈhæps] *adv.* 可能;也许;或者;大概
period [ˈpɪəriəd] *n.* 一段时间;阶段;时期;句号;*adj.* 具有每个时代特征的;*adv.* 到此为止
perish[ˈperɪʃ] *vi.* 死亡,丧生;毁灭;腐烂,枯萎;老化;*vt.* 使麻木;使毁坏
permanent [ˈpɜːmənənt] *adj.* 永久的;不断出现的;终生的;固定的
permission[pəˈmɪʃn] *n.* 准许;许可证
permit [pəˈmɪt, ˈpɜːmɪt] *v.* 允许;使有可能;破

例做;*n.* 许可证
persist[pəˈsɪst] *v.* 坚持;固执;存留;继续存在
person [ˈpɜːsn] *n.* 人;(语法)人称;身体;容貌
personal [ˈpɜːsənl] *adj.* 个人的;亲自的;人际的;个别的;针对个人的;身体的;私人的
personality[ˌpɜːsəˈnæləti] *n.* 性格,气质;特征;名人;性格鲜明的人
personnel [ˌpəˈsəˈnel] *n.* 人员;人事部门
perspective[pəˈspektɪv] *n.* 态度;观点,思考方法;客观判断力
persuade[pəˈsweɪd] *v.* 劝说;使信服
persuasion[pəˈsweɪʒn] *n.* 劝说,说服(力)
pet [pet] *n.* 宠物;宠儿;受宠的人;*adj.* 宠爱的,钟爱的;*vt.* 宠爱;爱抚,亲抚
petrol [ˈpetrəl] *n.* 汽油
petroleum [pəˈtrəʊliəm] *n.* 石油
phase [feiz] *n.* 阶段;时期
phenomenon [fəˈnɔminən] *n.* 现象;非凡的人或事物
philosopher [fiˈlɔsəfə] *n.* 哲学家;思想家
philosophy [fiˈlɔsəfi] *n.* 哲学;哲理;人生观
phone(= **telephone**) [fəun] *n.* 电话;听筒;(发声或使用声音的)工具 *vt. & vi.* 打电话(给某人)
photo(= **photograph**) [ˈfəutəgrɑːf] *n.* 照片 相片;*vi.* 照相 摄影;*vt.* 给……照相
physical [ˈfizikəl] *adj.* 身体的;物质的;物理的
physician [fiˈziʃən] *n.* 医生;内科医生
physicist [ˈfizisist] *n.* 物理学家
physics [ˈfiziks] *n.* 物理学
piano [piˈænəu,piˈɑːnəu] *n.* 钢琴
pick [pik] *v.* 挑选;采;剔除;*n.* 挑选;选中的人/事物;精华
picnic [ˈpiknik] *n.* 野餐郊游;供野餐吃的食品;*vi.* 野餐
picture [ˈpiktʃə] *n.* 照片,画像;图画,图片;影片;情景;*vt.* 构想,想象;描绘,画;描述
pie [pai] *n.* (西点)馅饼
piece [piːs] *n.* 碎片;块;片;一篇,一首,一支(新闻传媒的)文章,报道
pig [pig] *n.* 猪
pigeon [ˈpidʒin] *n.* 鸽子
pile [pail] *n.* 堆;桩;大量;*vt.* 堆叠;堆积;*vi.* 形成堆;拥挤进入
pill [pil] *n.* 药丸;丸剂
pillow [ˈpiləu] *n.* 枕头;*vt.* 枕;搁 垫
pilot [ˈpailət] *n.* 领航员;飞行员;引航员;*vt.* 领航;驾驶;向导;*adj.* 引导的;示范的
pin [pin] *n.* 针;饰针;大头针;拴(有别针的)徽章;*vt.* 将……用针别住;钉住;压住;*adj.* 别针的
pine [pain] *n.* 松树;松木
pink [piŋk] *adj.* 粉红色的;淡红色的;*n.* 粉红色;典范;香石竹
pioneer [ˌpaiəˈniə] *n.* 拓荒者;先驱者;先锋;*vt.* 提倡;开辟;*vi.* 做先驱
pipe [paip] *n.* 管子;导管;烟斗;笛
pirate [ˈpaɪrət] *n.* 海盗;海盗船;侵害版权者;盗版者;*vt.* 抢劫(海上船只);剽窃,盗用
pistol [ˈpistl] *n.* 手枪;*vt.* 用手枪射击
pit [pit] *n.* 坑;地坑;煤矿;深坑;矿井
pitch [pitʃ] *n.* (体育比赛的场地)球场;程度;强度;音高;*vt.* 投掷;颠簸;扎牢;搭帐篷;定调;*vi.* 用沥青覆盖;投掷
pity [ˈpiti] *n.* 怜悯;遗憾;遗憾的事;*vt.* 同情;怜悯
place [pleis] *n.* 地方;地点;住所;职位;获奖的名次;*vt.* 放置;任命;安排;*vi.* 获得名次
plain [plein] *n.* 平原;草原;*adj.* 清楚的;坦白的;简单的;平坦的平常的;纯的
plan [plæn] *n.* 计划;策略;方法;*vt.* 计划;设计;打算;*vi.* 打算
plane [plein] *n.* 平面;飞机;木工刨;*adj.* 平的,平坦的
planet [ˈplænit] *n.* 行星
plant [plɑːnt] *n.* 植物;工厂;(工业用的大型)设备;*vt.* 栽种;种植;建立;设立
plastic [ˈplæstik] *adj.* 塑料的;*n.* 塑料
plate [pleit] *n.* 板;片;盘;碟;金属板;板块
platform [ˈplætfɔːm] *n.* 平台;站台;讲台;月台
play [plei] *n.* 比赛;游戏;戏剧;赌博;*vt. & vi.* 玩;演奏;演出;参加比赛;*vt.* 扮演;担任,充当……的角色;演出;装扮;*vi.* 玩耍,游戏;[游戏]参加游戏;赌博;闹着玩
player [ˈpleiə] *n.* 游戏的人;比赛者;演奏者;演员;播放器
playground [ˈpleigraund] *n.* 操场;运动场
plead [pliːd] *vi.* 恳求;辩论;*vt.* 以……为理由;陈述案情;申辩,认罪,辩护;*vt. & vi.* 申诉,答辩,为……辩护
pleasant [ˈpleznt] *adj.* 令人愉快的 舒适的;*vi.* 满意;喜欢;*vt.* 使高兴
please [pliːz] *vt.* 取悦;使高兴;合心意;请;*vi.* 取悦;满意;*adv.* 请
pleased [pliːzd] *adj.* 高兴的;乐于做的
pleasure [ˈpleʒə] *n.* 愉快;快乐;乐事
plentiful [ˈplentifəl] *adj.* 丰富的;富裕的;多的
plenty [ˈplenti] *n.* 丰富;充足;大量;繁荣;

adj. 充足的；*adv.* 非常
plot [plɔt] *n.* 小块土地；阴谋；情节；图；
vt. 密谋；绘图；计划；标示位置
plug [plʌg] *n.* 塞子；插头；消防栓；
vt. & *vi.* 插上插头
plunge [plʌndʒ] *vt.* 使投入；使陷入；*vi.* 投入；骤降；使……陷入全神贯注于；*n.* 突然跌落；跳水
plural [ˈpluərəl] *adj.* 复数的；*n.* 复数
plus [plʌs] *prep.* 加；加上；另外；*adj.* 正的；略高于；*n.* 加号；正号；优势；*conj.* 并且
pocket [ˈpɔkit] *n.* 衣袋；口袋；钱；*vt.* 装……在口袋里隐藏；私吞
poem [ˈpəuim] *n.* 诗；韵文
poet[ˈpəuit] *n.* 诗人
poetry [ˈpəuitri] *n.* 诗；诗歌；诗作
point [pɔint] *n.* 论点；观点；要点；意图；目的；得分；尖端；细节；目标；时刻；关头；地点
poison[ˈpɔizn] *n.* 毒；毒药；败坏道德之事；毒害；*vt.* 毒害；摧毁
poisonous [ˈpɔizənəs] *adj.* 有毒的；有害的
polar [ˈpəulə(r)] *adj.* 极地的；磁极的；完全相反的
pole [pəul] *n.* 杆；柱；极(点)；磁极；电极
police [pəˈliːs] *n.* 警察；警察当局；警方；
vt. 管辖；维持治安
policeman [pəˈliːsmən] *n.* 警察
policy [ˈpɔlisi] *n.* 政策；方针；保险单
polish [ˈpɔliʃ] *vt.* 磨光；擦亮；使优美；推敲；完善；*vi.* 变光亮；*n.* 光泽；上光剂；优雅；精良
polite [pəˈlait] *adj.* 有礼貌的；有教养的；客气的
political [pəˈlitikəl] *adj.* 政治的；政治上的；政党的；对政治感兴趣的；争权夺利的
politician [ˌpɔliˈtiʃən] *n.* 政治家；政客
politics [ˈpɔlitiks] *n.* 政治；政治学；政纲；政策；政治活动；政见
pollute [pəˈluːt] *vt.* 弄脏；污染；沾污
pollution [pəˈluːʃən] *n.* 污染；污染物
pond [pɔnd] *n.* 池塘
pool [puːl] *n.* 水塘；游泳池；水池
poor [puə] *adj.* 贫穷的；贫乏的；可怜的；缺乏的；拙劣的
pop [pɔp] *vi.* (意外地、突然地)出现；突然出现；发出爆裂声；(突然地)行动；*vt.* (突然地)伸出；(突然地)提出问题；(把准备好的东西)突然拿出来；敲击；*n.* 流行音乐；汽水；(尤用作称呼)爸；(迅速打上的)记号；*adj.* 流行音乐的；通俗风格的；通俗的；现代的
popular [ˈpɔpjulə] *adj.* 民众的；受喜爱的；当红的；通俗的；大众文化的
population [ˌpɔpjuˈleiʃən] *n.* 人口；人口数量
porch [pɔːtʃ] *n.* 门廊；入口处
pork [pɔːk] *n.* 猪肉
port [pɔːt] *n.* 港；港口；舱门；码头；机场；(船，飞机的)左舷
porter [ˈpɔːtə] 看门人；行李员；列车服务生；护工；搬运工
portion [ˈpɔːʃən] *n.* 一部分；一份；分担的责任
portrait [ˈpɔːtrit] *n.* 肖像；画像
pose [pəʊz] *v.* 摆姿势；假装；炫耀；引起；提问；*n.* 姿势；装腔作势
position [pəˈziʃən] *n.* 位置；职位；姿势；状态；立场；*vt.* 安置；决定……的位置
positive [ˈpɔzitiv] *adj.* 确定的；积极的；肯定的；绝对的；正面的正数的；阳性的
possess [pəˈzes] *vt.* 占用；拥有(财产)持有；支配
possession [pəˈzeʃən] *n.* 占有；个人财产；控球状态
possibility [ˌpɔsəˈbiliti] *n.* 可能；可能的事；可能性；潜在的价值
possible [ˈpɔsəbl] *adj.* 可能的；可能存在的
possibly [ˈpɔsəbli] *adv.* 可能地；也许
post [pəust] *n.* 柱；桩；杆；标杆；邮件；邮政；邮寄；职位；*vt.* 贴出；邮递；发布；布置
postage [ˈpəustidʒ] *n.* 邮费；邮资
postcard [ˈpəustkɑːd] *n.* 明信片
postcode (= **zip code**) [ˈpəʊstkəʊd] *n.* 邮政编码
postman [ˈpəustmən] *n.* 邮递员
postpone [pəustˈpəun] *vt.* 延迟；推迟；延缓
pot [pɔt] *n.* 锅；壶 罐；盆
potato [pəˈteitəu] *n.* 马铃薯；土豆
potential [pəˈtenʃəl] *adj.* 潜在的；可能的；
n. 潜力；潜能
pound [paund] *n.* 磅；英镑；*vt.* 连续猛击捣碎；
vi. 跳动；大声播放
pour [pɔː] *vt.* 灌；倒；流出；倾泻；骤雨；
vi. 倾泻；蜂拥而来；倒
poverty [ˈpɔvəti] *n.* 贫穷；贫困；贫乏
powder [ˈpaudə] *n.* 粉末；药粉；火药
power [ˈpauə] *n.* 权力；能力；操纵力；职权；政权；体力；强国；实力；影响力；动力；能量；电力供应；*vt.* 供电；激励；全速前进；*adj.* 与力量有关的；与权力有关的；电力控制的
powerful [ˈpauəfəl] *adj.* 强有力的；有权威的

practical [ˈpræktikəl] *adj.* 实际的；实用的；切实可行的；明智的；实际上的
practise(-ce) [ˈpræktis] *n.* 实践；练习；业务活动；通常的做法；惯例；*vt.* & *vi.* 练习；实习；养成……的习惯；从事(医务工作、法律专业等)
praise [preiz] *n.* 赞扬；赞美；称赞；*vi.* 赞扬；*vt.* 称赞；赞美
pray [prei] *vt.* &*vi.* 请求；恳求；祈祷
prayer [prɛə] *n.* 祈祷；祈求；祷告；祷文；*v.* 祷告；祷文
preach [priːtʃ] *vt.* & *vi.* 布道，讲道；宣扬；说教；讲(道)
precious [ˈpreʃəs] *adj.* 珍贵的；宝贵的；*adv.* 极其地
precise [priˈsais] *adj.* 精确的；准确的
predict [priˈdikt] *v.* 预言；预告；预报
prefer [priˈfəː] *vt.* 宁可；宁愿；较喜欢
pregnant [ˈpregnənt] 怀孕的；饱含；充溢着
prejudice [ˈpredʒudis] *n.* 偏见；成见；伤害
preliminary [priˈliminəri] *adj.* 预备的；初步的；开始的；*n.* 初步行动；准备；初步措施
premier [ˈpremjə] *n.* 总理；首相；*adj.* 第一的；首位的；最初的
premium [ˈpriːmiəm] *n.* 额外费用；保险费；附加费；*adj.* 高昂的；优质的
prepare [priˈpɛə] *vt.* & *vi.* 准备；预备；整合
prescribe [prisˈkraib] *vt.* 命令；规定；开处(方)；*vi.* 规定；开药方
presence [ˈprezns] *n.* 出席；到场
present [ˈpreznt] *adj.* 现在的；当面的；出席的；*n.* 礼物；赠送物现在；目前
[priˈzent] *vt.* 赠送；介绍；提出；呈现
presently [ˈprezntli] *adv.* 一会儿；目前；不久；现在
preserve [priˈzəːv] *vt.* 保护；保存；保持；腌渍；*vi.* 保存；*n.* 蜜饯；保护区
president [ˈprezidənt] *n.* 总统；总裁；总经理；校长；会长；社长
press [pres] *vt.* 压；按；揿；催促；逼迫；*n.* 新闻界；压力
pressure [ˈpreʃə] *n.* 压力；气压；催促；紧张；*v.* 强迫
pretend [priˈtend] *vt.* 假托；借口；*vi.* 假装；伪称；*adj.* 假装的；赝品的；模拟的
pretty [ˈpriti] *adj.* 漂亮的；标致的；美好的；*adv.* 相当地
prevail [priˈveil] *vi.* 胜；优胜；获胜；流行；盛行；主导
prevent [priˈvent] *vt.* 预防；防止；阻止
preview [ˈpriːvjuː] *n.* 预演；预先评述；*v.* 预先观看；写预评；概述
previous [ˈpriːvjəs] *adj.* 先的；前的；在……之前；以前的；*adv.* 在前
price [prais] *n.* 价格；价钱；代价；*vt.* 定格；标价；比较价格
pride [praid] *n.* 骄傲；自豪；自尊
priest [priːst] *n.* 教士；牧师；神父
primary [ˈpraiməri] *adj.* 最初的；基本的；主要的；初等教育的
prime [praim] *adj.* 主要的；基本的；优质的；典型的，有代表性的；首选的；*n.* 鼎盛时期；*v.* 事先指点；事先准备
primitive [ˈprimitiv] *adj.* 原始的；远古的；发展水平低的
prince [prins] *n.* 王子；亲王；(某一领域的)杰出人物
princess [ˈprinˈses] *n.* 公主；王妃
principal [ˈprinsəpəl] *adj.* 主要的；首要的；*n.* 负责人；校长
principle [ˈprinsəpl] *n.* 原则；原理；主义；信念
print [print] *vt.* 印刷；出版；打印；*n.* 印刷字体，印刷行业；指纹；脚印；痕迹；*adj.* 印刷的
printer [ˈprɪntə(r)] *n.* 打印机；印刷商，印刷厂；印刷业从业人员
priority[praɪˈɒrəti] *n.* 优先，优先权；重点
prison [ˈprizn] *n.* 监狱；监禁
privacy [ˈprɪvəsi] *n.* 隐私，秘密；隐居；私事；不受公众干扰的状态
private [ˈpraivit] *adj.* 私人的；私下的；隐蔽的；*n.* 士兵；列兵
privilege [ˈprivilidʒ] *n.* 特权；优惠待遇；免责特权；荣幸；*vt.* 给予特权；特别优待
prize [praiz] *n.* 奖赏；奖金；奖品；珍品；战利品；*vt.* 珍视；重视；*adj.* 可以获奖的；优秀的
probable [ˈprɔbəbl] *adj.* 或有的；大概的；很可能的；*n.* 很可能的事
probably [ˈprɔbəbli] *adv.* 或许；大概
problem [ˈprɔbləm] *n.* 问题；习题；*adj.* 成问题的；难对付的
procedure [prəˈsiːdʒə] *n.* 程序；手续；过程；步骤
proceed [prəˈsiːd] *vi.* 进行；开始；着手；继续进行
process [ˈprɑːses] *n.* 过程；变化过程；做事方法；*v.* 加工；处理；冲印；审核(文件、请求等)
procession [prəˈseʃən] *n.* 队伍；行列；*v.* 列队

行进
proclaim [prə'kleim] *vt.* 宣告;宣布;表明;公布
produce [prə'djuːs] *v.* 引起;生产;生长;造出;出示;栽培;制作(电影等);
['prɒdjuːs] *n.* 农产品
product ['prɔdəkt] *n.* 产品;产物
production [prə'dʌkʃən] *n.* 生产;产品;总产量;作品;成果
productive [prə'dʌktiv] *adj.* 生产的;丰饶的;有生产价值的;多产的
profession [prə'feʃən] *n.* 职业;专业;声明;信仰
professional [prə'feʃənəl] *adj.* 职业的;专业的;*n.* 专业人员
professor [prə'fesə] *n.* 教授;宣称者
proficiency [prə'fɪʃnsi] *n.* 熟练,精通,娴熟
profile ['prəʊfail] *n.* 侧面轮廓;外形,轮廓;简介;传略;印象;形象 *vt.* 描……的轮廓;给……画侧面图;为(某人)写传略
profit ['prɔfit] *n.* 益处;利润;盈利比率;*vi.* 得益;利用;获利;*vt.* 有益于
program(me) ['prəugræm] *n.* 节目单;大纲;程序;计划;*vt.* 规划;拟定计划;制作节目
progress [prəu'gres] *n.* 前进;进展;进步;*vi.* 促进;进步;进行
prohibit [prə'hibit] *vt.* 禁止;阻止;妨碍
project [prə'dʒekt] *n.* 方案;工程;项目;计划;*vi.* 伸出;投射;放映;突出;外伸 *vt.* 计划;设计;表现,展现
promise ['prɔmis] *n.* 诺言;指望;约定(有)希望;预示;*vt.* 允诺约定;预示;有可能
promising ['prɔmisiŋ] *adj.* 有希望的;有前途的
promote [prə'məut] *vt.* 促进;发扬;提升;升迁;发起;促销
prompt[prɔmpt] *adj.* 及时的;迅速的;敏捷的;立刻的
pronounce [prə'nauns] *vt.* 发……的音;宣布;断言;发表意见
pronunciation [prə. nʌnsi'eiʃən] *n.* 发音
proof [pruːf] *n.* 证据;证明;校样;*adj.* 防……的;耐……的;能防护;*vt.* 检验;给……做防护措施
proper ['prɔpə] *adj.* 适合的;正当的;正确的;合乎体统的
property ['prɔpəti] *n.* 财产;资产;性质
proportion [prə'pɔːʃən] *n.* 比;比率;部分;均衡;*vt.* 使成比例使均衡;分摊
proposal [prə'pəuzəl] *n.* 提议;建议;求婚
propose [prə'pəuz] *vt.* 提议计划;打算;向……提议;*vi.* 求婚
prospect ['prɔspekt] *n.* 展望;前景;前程;景色;*v.* 探勘;寻找
prosper ['prɒspə(r)] *vi.* 繁盛,成功;*vt.* 使……成功;使……昌盛
prosperity [prɔs'periti] *n.* 繁荣;昌盛;兴旺
prosperous ['prɔspərəs] *adj.* 繁荣的;昌盛的;兴旺的
protect [prə'tekt] *vt.* 保护;保卫;警戒;投保;*vi.* 提供保护
protein ['prəutiːn] *n.* 蛋白质
protest ['prəutest, prə'test] *n.* 抗议;反对;抗议书;*vi.* 反对;抗议;断言;*vt.* 坚持地表示;对……提出异议
proud [praud] *adj.* 骄傲的;自豪的;壮观的
prove [pruːv] *vt.* 证明;查验;显示;*vi.* 结果是
provide [prə'vaid] *vt.* 提供;供给;装备;规定;准备;*vi.* 供给提供
provided [prə'vaidid] *conj.* 假如;若是;以……为条件;*adj.* 预备好的;由……供给的
province ['prɔvins] *n.* 省;范围;领域;部门
provision [prə'viʒən] *n.* 供应(品);预备;存粮;规定;条款;(*pl.*)食物;*vt.* 向……供应食物
psychology [saɪ'kɒlədʒi] *n.* 心理(学);思想
pub [pʌb] *n.* 酒馆,酒店;客栈
public ['pʌblik] *adj.* 公众的;公开的;众所周知的;*n.* 公共场合;公众
publication [ˌpʌbli'keiʃən] *n.* 公布;发表;出版;发行;出版物
publish ['pʌbliʃ] *vt.* 公布;发表;出版;发行;*vi.* 出版;发行
pull [pul] *vt.* 拉;拖;拔;拉;拉力;*vi.* 拔;拉;拖扳动;*n.* 拉;拖;拉;绳;影响
pump [pʌmp] *n.* 泵;抽水机;打气筒;心脏;抽水;*vt.* 用抽机抽;抽水;打气;用泵输送;盘问;涌出;*vi.* 用泵抽水;快速上下(或内外)运动
punctual ['pʌŋktjuəl] *adj.* 严守时刻的;准时的;正点的
punish ['pʌniʃ] *vt.* 罚;惩罚;处罚
pupil ['pjuːpl] *n.* 小学生;学徒
puppet ['pʌpit] *n.* 木偶;玩偶
purchase ['pəːtʃəs] *n.* 买;购买;购买的物品;*vt.* 买;购买
pure [pjuə] *adj.* 纯粹的,干净的;纯真的;纯正的;纯理论的;完全的;纯血的;标准的
purity ['pjuəriti] 纯洁,纯净;清洁,清白,清廉;(语言)纯正

purple [ˈpəːpl] *n.* 紫色;*adj.* 紫的
purpose [ˈpəːpəs] *n.* 目的;意图;效果;意志;决心;议题;*vt.* 打算;决意
purse [pəːs] *n.* 钱包;小钱袋;资金;
pursue [pəˈsjuː] *vt.* 追赶;追踪;追捕;追求;进行;继续从事
pursuit [pəˈsjuːt] *n.* 追赶;追求;事业;爱好
push [puʃ] *vt.* 推;逼迫;奋力;决心;*vi.* 推;挤;逼迫
put [put] *vt.* 放;摆,安置;使处于;*vi.* 提交;记下
puzzle [ˈpʌzl] *n.* 难题;迷惑;*vi.* 使迷惑;使困惑;解决;*vi.* 迷惑苦思
pyramid [ˈpɪrəmɪd] *n.* 金字塔(结构);角锥体;金字塔形物体

Q

qualify [ˈkwɔlifai] *vt.* 使具有资格;取得资格;有资格;限定;描述;*vi.* 取得资格;有资格
quantity [ˈkwɔntiti] *n.* 量;数量;分量;大量
quarrel [ˈkwɔrəl] *n.* 争吵;吵架;口角;争论;怨言;*vi.* 吵架;争论挑剔
quarter [ˈkwɔːtə] *n.* 四分之一;一刻钟;季度;25 美分;*vt.* 四等分;*vi.* 住宿;驻扎;*adj.* 四分之一的
queen [ˈkwiːn] *n.* 王后;女王;最重要的女子或事物;女冠军;女王蜂
question [ˈkwestʃən] *n.* 发问;问题;疑问;询问;争论点;*vt.* 询问怀疑;*vi.* 问问题
questionnaire [ˌkwestʃəˈneə(r)] *n.* 调查表;调查问卷
queue [kjuː] *n.* 行列;长队;*vi.* 排队等候
quick [kwik] *adj.* 快的;敏捷的;迅速的;机敏的;*adv.* 快;迅速地
quiet [ˈkwaiət] *adj.* 寂静的;安静的;静止的;宁静的;*adv.* 安静地;*v.* 使……平静;使……安心;*n.* 安静;闲适;平静
quilt [kwilt] *n.* 被(子);被状物
quit [kwit] *vt.* 离开;辞职;退出;停止
quite [kwait] *adv.* 完全;很;相当;的确
quiver [ˈkwɪvə(r)] *vt.* & *vi.* 微颤,抖动;*vt.* 使震动
quiz [kwiz] *n.* 小型考试;(随堂)测验
quote [kwəut] *vt.* 引用;引证;报价;举证;*n.* 引用

R

rabbit [ˈræbit] *n.* 兔子;野兔
race [reis] *n.* 赛跑;竞争;人种;民族;*v.* 参加比赛;使比赛;快速移动;剧烈跳动
racial [ˈreiʃəl] *adj.* 种族的;人种的
rack [ræk] *n.* 搁物架;行李架;*vt.* 折磨;使痛苦;拷问
radar [ˈreidɑː] *n.* 雷达;无线电探测器
radiate [ˈreidieit] *vi.* 发射光线;辐射;散发;辐射
radical [ˈrædɪkl] *adj.* 根本的,基本的;激进的;彻底的
radio [ˈreidiəu] *n.* 无线电;收音机;*v.* 用无线电通讯
radius [ˈreidiəs] *n.* 半径(距离);用半径度量的圆形面积;半径范围
rage [reidʒ] *n.* 愤怒;激烈,猛烈;渴望,疯狂;*vi.* 大发脾气,动怒;流行,风行
raid [reid] *n.* 袭击;突然搜查;劫掠;*v.* 劫掠;攫取;突击搜捕袭击
rail [reil] *n.* 围栏;轨道,钢轨;扶手
railroad = railway(英) [ˈreilrəud] *n.* 铁路
rain [rein] *n.* 雨;雨水;(复数)雨季;*vi.* 下雨;*vt.* 使大量落下
rainbow [ˈreinbəu] *n.* 虹;彩虹
raincoat[ˈreɪnkəʊt] *n.* 雨衣
raise [reiz] *vt.* 举起;引起;提高;升起;饲养;提出;*n.* 上升;增高
random [ˈrændəm] *adj.* 随机的;任意的
range [reindʒ] *n.* 排;行;山脉;炉灶;范围;行列;射程;*v.* 排列归类于……;延伸;漫游
rank [ræŋk] *n.* 地位,级别;军衔;普通士兵;等级;成员;队列;*v.* 分等级;排列
rapid [ˈræpid] *adj.* 快的;迅速的;急促的;*n.* 急流
rapidly [ˈræpidli] *adv.* 迅速地
rare [rɛə] *adj.* 稀薄的;稀有的;稀罕的;罕见

的；珍贵的；*adj.* 煎得嫩的
rarely [ˈrɛəli] *adv.* 很少；难得
rat [ræt] *n.* 老鼠；耗子
rate [reit] *n.* 速度，进度；比率；价格，费用；房产税；*v.* 评估，评价；看好；划分等级；配得上
rather [ˈrɑːðə] *adv.* 宁可；宁愿；相当；有些；反而
ratio [ˈreiʃiəu] *n.* 比；比率
rational [ˈræʃənəl] *adj.* 理性的；合理的
raw [rɔː] *adj.* 未煮过的；生的；未加工的；原始的；不熟练的；寒冷的
ray [rei] *n.* 光线，射线；一丝
reach [riːtʃ] *vt.* 抵达；到达；伸出；延伸；取得联系；*vi.* 达到；延伸；*n.* 延伸；范围；河段
react [riˈækt] *vi.* 起反应；起作用；有影响；*vt.* 做出反应
read [red, riːd] *vt.* 阅读；看懂；理解；识别；*vi.* 读；读起来；研究；*adj.* 博学的；*n.* 阅读
reader [ˈriːdə] *n.* 读者；读物；读本
readily [ˈredili] *adv.* 乐意地；欣然地；迅速地；轻而易举地
reading [ˈriːdiŋ] *n.* 读；阅读；读书；*adj.* 阅读的
ready [ˈredi] *adj.* 准备好的；愿意的；情愿的；现成的；*vt.* 做好……的准备
real [ˈriːəl] *adj.* 真的；现实的；实际的；真实的；*adv.* 非常
realise(-ze) [ˈriəlaiz] *vt.* 实现；认识到；了解；意识到
realistic [ˌriːəˈlɪstɪk] *adj.* 现实的；实际的；明智的；逼真的
reality [riˈæləti] *n.* 现实；真实；实际
really [ˈriəli] *adv.* 真正地；实在；事实上
reap [riːp] *vt. & vi.* 收割；收获；获得
rear [riə] *n.* 后部；后面；背面；臀部；*adj.* 后面的；背面的；后方的；*vt.* 养育；饲养；抚养；培养；栽种
reason [ˈriːzn] *n.* 理由；原因；理智；理性；*vi.* 推理；规劝；下判断；*vt.* 说服；总结
reasonable [ˈriːznəbl] *adj.* 合理的，公道的；明智的；过得去的
rebel [ˈrebl, riˈbel] *n.* 反政府的人；反叛者；造反者；叛逆者；*v.* 造反；反抗；背叛
recall [riˈkɔːl] *v.* 召回(残损货品等)；回想起，使想到；*n.* 记忆力；召回令
receipt [riˈsiːt] *n.* 收条；收据
receive [riˈsiːv] *vt.* 收到；得到；接待；接受；迎接；容纳；遭受；相信；*vi.* 接到；获得
recent [ˈriːsnt] *adj.* 新近的；最近的
reception [riˈsepʃən] *n.* 接待；接待会；接待仪式；接待处，接待区
recession [rɪˈseʃn] *n.* 经济衰退，不景气；后退，撤退
recipe [ˈresəpi] *n.* 食谱；秘诀
reckon [ˈrekən] *vt.* 测算，估计；认为；计算；评定，断定；*vi.* 计算；估计；猜想；料想
recognise(-ze) [ˈrekəgnaiz] *vt.* 认出，识别出某人[某事物]；承认……有效[属实]；认可；承认[认清](某事物)
recognition [ˌrekəgˈniʃən] *n.* 认识，识别；承认；赞赏
recommend [ˌrekəˈmend] *vt. v.* 推荐；介绍；劝告，建议；使受欢迎
record [ˈrekɔːd, riˈkɔːd] *n.* 记录；履历；唱片；*vt.* 记录(将声音等)录下；表明；*adj.* 关于
recorder [riˈkɔːdə] *n.* 记录员；录音机
recover [riˈkʌvə] *v.* 康复；复原；重新获得；恢复
recovery [riˈkʌvəri] *n.* 恢复；改善；失而复得
recreation [ˌriːkriˈeɪʃn] *n.* 娱乐；游戏
recruit [rɪˈkruːt] *n.* 新兵；(机构中的)新成员；*vt.* 招聘，征募；吸收新成员；*vi.* 征募新兵；恢复健康
recycle [ˌriːˈsaɪkl] *v.* 回收利用；重新使用
red [red] *adj.* 红色的；*n.* 红色
reduce [riˈdjuːs] *v.* 减少，缩小；使变成；节食；使不得不；使沦为(不好境地)；(使)浓缩
reduction [riˈdʌkʃən] *n.* 减少；降低；折扣；还原
refer [riˈfəː] *v.* 提及；涉及；称作；参考
referee [ˌrefəˈriː] *n.* 裁判员
reference [ˈrefrəns] *n.* 提及；查询；征求；引语；编号；参考书目；推荐信；介绍人；*v.* 给(书等)附参考资料
reflect [riˈflekt] *v.* 照出(影像)；反映；反射；沉思；表达
reflection [riˈflekʃən] *n.* 映像，倒影；体现；深思；反射；描述
reform [riˈfɔːrm] *v.* 改革，改进；*n.* 改革，改善
refresh [riˈfreʃ] *v.* 使精神抖擞；重新斟满；翻新；使记起；刷新
refrigerator(= fridge) [riˈfridʒə. reitə] *n.* 冰箱；冷藏库
refuge [ˈrefjuːdʒ] *n.* 避难(处)；庇护(所)；庇护者；*v.* 庇护，避难(所)
refuse [ˈrefjuːs, riˈfjuːz] *vt.* 拒绝
regard [riˈgɑːd] *vt.* 把……看作；和……有关；尊敬；尊重；视为；注视
region [ˈriːdʒən] *n.* 地区；地带；领域；行政区

register [ˈredʒistə] *vt.* 记录;登记;注册;挂号;*n.* (语)语域
regret [riˈgret] *vt.* 懊悔;为……感到遗憾;后悔;惋惜;抱歉;*n.* 懊悔;遗憾;后悔;抱歉
regular [ˈregjulə] *adj.* 规则的;有规律的;经常做某事的;稳定的;普通的;平凡的;整齐的
regulation [ˌregjuˈleiʃən] *n.* 规则;规章;管理;*adj.* 规定的 官方的
rehearse [rɪˈhɜːs] *vt. & vi.* 排练,排演;公开练习
reign [rein] *n.* 君主统治(时期)执政;*vi.* 当政;统治;占优势;支配;盛行
reinforce [ˌriːinˈfɔːs] *vt.* 增援;支援;加强;*vi.* 得到加强
reject [riˈdʒekt] *vt.* 拒绝;丢掉;丢弃;驳回;排斥
relate [riˈleit] *vt.* 叙述;使联系
relation [riˈleiʃən] *n.* 关系;联系;家属;亲戚
relative [ˈrelətiv] *adj.* 有关系的;相对的;比较的;涉及的;*n.* 亲属;同类事物;相关物
relax [riˈlæks] *vt.* 使松弛;放松;放宽(限制等);*vi.* 松弛;放松,松懈
relay [ˈriːleɪ] *n.* 接力比赛;*v.* 转播;转述;转送
release [riˈliːs] *vt.* 释放;放松;发表;准予发表;*n.* 释放;让渡;发行
relevant [ˈrelivənt] *adj.* 相关的;贴切的;切题的
reliable [riˈlaiəbl] *adj.* 可靠的;可信赖的
relief [riˈliːf] *n.* 减轻;救济(品);宽慰;解脱
relieve [riˈliːv] *vt.* 减轻;解除;缓和
religion [riˈlidʒən] *n.* 宗教;宗教信仰
religious [riˈlidʒəs] *adj.* 宗教的;虔诚的;细心的
reluctant [riˈlʌktənt] *adj.* 不愿的;勉强的
rely [riˈlai] *vi.* 依赖;依靠;信赖
remain [riˈmein] *vi.* 剩下;余留;逗留;保持;依然;留下;*n.* 遗迹剩余物;残骸
remainder [rɪˈmeɪndə(r)] *n.* 剩余物;其他人员
remark [riˈmɑːk] *vt. & vi.* 评论;注意;述及;谈论;*n.* 备注;评论注意
remarkable [riˈmɑːkəbl] *adj.* 异常的;非凡的;显著的;值得注意的
remedy [ˈremidi] *n.* 药物;治疗法;补救;*vt.* 治疗;补救;矫正
remember [riˈmembə] *vt.* 记得;想起;记住
remind [riˈmaind] *vt.* 提醒;使想起
remote [riˈməut] *adj.* 相隔很远的;遥远的;久远的;偏远的;远程的
remove [riˈmuːv] *vt.* 移动;搬开;脱掉;除去;取下;拿走;*vi.* 迁徙;离开;搬迁
render [ˈrendə] *vt.* 表示;给予;使得;使成为;提供;报答;*vi.* 给予补偿
renew [riˈnjuː] *vt.* 使更新;复始;使恢复;补充;*vi.* 更新;重新开始
rent [rent] *n.* 租金;租;*vi. & vt.* 出租;租用
repair [riˈpɛə] *v.* 修理,修补;补救;前去;*n.* 修理;修补
repay [rɪˈpeɪ] *vt.* 偿还;付还;报答;酬报;*vi.* 偿还,补偿
repeat [riˈpiːt] *vt.* 重说;重做;重复;复述;*vi.* 重复;*n.* 重复;反复;*adj.* 重复的;反复的
repetition [ˌrepiˈtiʃən] *n.* 重复;反复
replace [riˈpleis] *vt.* 把……放回;取代;更换
reply [riˈplai] *vi. & n.* 回答;答复
report [riˈpɔːt] *vt. & vi.* 报告;汇报;*n.* 传闻;报告;成绩单
reporter [riˈpɔːtə] *n.* 记者;通讯员
represent [ˈrepriˈzent] *vt.* 描绘;代表;象征;表现;表示;说明;阐明;*vi.* 提出异议
representative [repriˈzentətiv] *adj.* 代表性的;典型的;*n.* 代表;众议员;典型
republic [riˈpʌblik] *n.* 共和国;共和政体
reputation [ˌrepjuˈteiʃən] *n.* 名誉;名声;好名声
request [riˈkwest] *n. & vt.* 请求;要求
require [riˈkwaiə] *vt.* 需要;要求;命令
rescue [ˈreskjuː] *vt.* 援救;营救
research [riˈsəːtʃ] *n. & vi.* 调查;探究;研究
resemble [riˈzembl] *vt.* 像;类似;相似
resent [rɪˈzent] *vt.* 对……感到愤怒;怨恨;愤恨;厌恶
reserve [riˈzəːv] *vt.* 储备;保留;预定;*n.* 储备(量);自然保护区;矜持;谨慎
reservior [ˈrezəvwɑː] *n.* 水库;蓄水池;积蓄;储藏
residence [ˈrezidəns] *n.* 居住;驻扎;住处;住宅
resident [ˈrezidənt] *adj.* 居住的;*n.* 居民;住客;高级专科住院实习医生
resign [riˈzain] *vt.* 放弃;辞职;使顺从;*vi.* 辞职;顺从
resist [riˈzist] *vt. & vi.* 抵抗;抵制
resistance [riˈzistəns] *n.* 抵抗;抵制;反抗;阻力;反对
resolution [ˌrezəˈluːʃən] *n.* 决心;解决;坚决;决议;正式决定
resolve [riˈzɔlv] *vt. & vi.* 决定;决心;*vt.* 使消释;使分解,使解体;*n.* 决心;决定之事
resort [riˈzɔːt] *n.* (度假)胜地;诉诸;求助;应

急措施;*vi.* 求助;凭借诉诸
resource [riˈsɔːs] *n.* 资源;物力;资料
respect [riˈspekt] *n.* 尊敬;重视;方面;*v.* 尊重,仰慕;遵守
respective [riˈspektiv] *adj.* 各自的;各个的;分别的
respond [riˈspɔnd] *vi.* 作答;响应;回复;反应;应答
response [riˈspɔns] *n.* 作答;回答;响应;反应
responsibility [ri. spɔnsəˈbiliti] *n.* 责任;职责;义务
responsible [riˈspɔnsəbl] *adj.* 有责任的;尽责的;责任重大的;可靠的
rest [rest] *v.* 休息;支撑;中止;安息;*n.* 休息;剩余部分;停留;其他
restaurant [ˈrestərɔnt] *n.* 餐馆;饭店
restore [riˈstɔː] *vt.* 恢复;使复原;重新采用(或实施)
restrict [riˈstrikt] *vt.* 限制;限定;约束
result [riˈzʌlt] *n.* 成果;结果;成绩;答案;*vi.* (因……)发生;(随……)产生
resume [riˈzjuːm] *vt.* 恢复;重新开始;再继续;*n.* 简历,履历;摘要
retain [riˈtein] *vt.* 保持;保留;保有;记住
retire [riˈtaiə] *vi.* 退下;引退;撤退;退休;就寝;*n.* 退休;退职
retreat [riˈtriːt] *vi.* (被迫)退却;后退;撤退;向后倾;*n.* 撤退;退缩
return [riˈtəːn] *n.* 返回;归还;报答;报告;*vi.* 返回;归还;回来;*adj.* 返回的
reveal [riˈviːl] *vt.* 展现;揭示;显示;揭露;透露
revenge [riˈvendʒ] *vt.* 替……报仇;报复;*n.* 报仇;报复
revenue[ˈrevənjuː] *n.* (国家的)岁入,税收,(土地,财产等的)收入,收益,所得,(个人的)固定收入
reverse [riˈvəːs] *vt.* 颠倒;翻转;逆转;倒退;*n.* 背面;相反;失败挫折;*adj.* 反面的;相反的;颠倒的
review [riˈvjuː] *n.* 评审,检查;评论;回顾;检阅;复习课;*v.* 审核,复查;回顾,反思;评论
revise [riˈvaiz] *vt.* 修订;校订;校正;修改;*n.* 校订;修正;再校稿
revive[rɪˈvaɪv] *vt.* 使复活,重新使用;重新上演 *vi.* 复苏,恢复;振作,恢复
revolution [ˌrevəˈluːʃən] *n.* 革命
revolutionary [ˌrevəˈluːʃənəri] *adj.* 革命的;*n.* 革命者
reward [riˈwɔːd] *n.* 报答;报酬;赏金;*vt.* 报答;给……报酬;奖赏
rib [rib] *n.* 肋;肋骨
ribbon [ˈribən] *n.* 缎带;丝带
rice [rais] *n.* 稻;米饭
rich [ritʃ] *adj.* 富的;丰富的;浓厚的;贵重的;富饶的
rid [rid] *vt.* 使摆脱;使去掉;免除;清除;使……获自由
riddle [ˈridl] *n.* 谜;谜语
ride [raid] *v.* 骑(马);乘坐;翻越;*n.* 旅行,车程
ridge [ridʒ] *n.* 背脊,峰,隆起线;山脊,山脉,海脊
ridiculous [riˈdikjuləs] adj 荒谬的;可笑的
rifle [ˈraifl] *n.* 步枪;来复枪
right [rait] *adj.* 右边的;正确的;恰当的;正常的;正派的;完全的;健康的;*adv.* 向右;正好;立刻;一直,完全地;正确地;顺利地;*n.* 右边;权利;版权;正确;公正;右派;右手拳;*v.* 扶正;改正;使恢复正常;*int.* (语气词)好;对的;对吗;懂吗
rigid [ˈridʒid] *adj.* 刚硬的;僵硬的;刻板的;严格的
ring [riŋ] *n.* 环形物(如圈、环等);戒指;铃声;*vt.* 包围;挂铃铛;*vi.* 鸣响;回响;按铃
ripe [raip] *adj.* 熟的;成熟的;合适的;时机成熟的
rise [raiz] *vi.* 起立;升起;上涨;起身;*n.* 上升;增加;小山;斜坡
risk [risk] *n.* 风险;危险;冒险;*vt.* 冒……的危险
rival [ˈraivəl] *n.* 对手;同伴;竞争者;*adj.* 竞争的;*vt.* 与……相匹敌比得上;*vi.* 竞争
river [ˈrivə] *n.* 江;河;水道
road [rəud] *n.* 路;道路;公路
roar [rɔː] *vi.* 吼叫;大声说出;喧闹;呼喊;*vt.* 呼喊;使轰鸣;*n.* 吼咆哮;轰鸣;喧闹
roast [rəust] *vt.* & *vi.* 烤;炙,烘焙;*adj.* 烘烤的;烤过的;*n.* 烤肉;烘烤
rob [rɔb] *vt.* & *vi.* 抢劫;劫掠
robbery [ˈrɔbəri] *n.* 抢劫;劫掠;盗取
robot [ˈrəubɔt] *n.* 机器人;自动机
rock [rɔk] *vt.* 摇;使动摇;使震惊;使动心;*vi.* 摇;来回摇动;跳摇摆舞;*n.* 岩石;巨石;石头;摇滚乐
rocket [ˈrɔkit] *n.* 火箭;火箭发动机;烟火;*v.* 发射火箭;猛涨
rod [rɔd] *n.* 杆;竿;棒;戒鞭;测量杆
role [rəul] *n.* 角色;作用;影响程度

roll[rəul] *n.* 卷;滚动;名单;*v.* 卷,摇,转;(使)滚动;翻转;压平;启动;缓缓行进
romantic [rəˈmæntik] *adj.* 浪漫的;传奇的;*n.* 浪漫的人;浪漫主义作家/音乐家/艺术家
roof [ruːf] *n.* 屋顶;车顶;顶
room [ruːm] *n.* 房间;空间;地位;余地
root [ruːt] *n.* 根;根子;根源;祖先;*vi.* 生根;扎根;翻寻;起源于
rope [rəup] *n.* 绳;索;*v.* 捆 绑
rose [rəuz] *n.* 蔷薇花;蔷薇科植物;玫瑰;*v.* (rise 的过去式)起立上升;升起;*adj.* 玫瑰色的;玫瑰的
rot [rɔt] *vt. & vi.* (使)腐烂,(使)腐朽
rotate [rəuˈteit] *vi.* 旋转;*vt.* 使旋转;轮流
rotten [ˈrɔtn] *adj.* 腐烂的;腐朽的;发臭的
rough [rʌf] *adj.* 粗糙的,不平的;粗略的;粗暴的;危险的;汹涌的;有暴风雨的;艰难的;不适的;味道差的;*n.* (高尔夫球场的)长草区;草稿;暴徒;*v.* 过艰苦生活;*adv.* 粗鲁地;流浪地
round [raund] *adj.* 圆/球/环/弧形的;整数的;*adv.* (在)周围;围绕;到处;转过来;绕弯;依次;到某地;大概;*prep.* 围(绕);绕过;遍及;基于;克服;大概;*n.* 轮,局,回合;惯常活动;递送路线;一巡饮料;一阵;一枪;圆块;*v.* 绕过;变圆;四舍五入
rouse [rauz] *vt.* 唤醒;唤起;惊起;鼓舞;激起;*n.* 觉醒;奋起
route [ruːt] *n.* 路;(公共汽车和列车等的)常规路线;航线;渠道,途径
routine [ruːˈtiːn] *n.* 例行公事;常规;无聊;*adj.* 日常的;常规的例行的;乏味的
row [rəu,rau] *n.* (一)排(一)行;船游;*vt.* 划船 成排;*vi.* 划船
royal [ˈrɔiəl] *adj.* 王室的;皇家的;盛大的
royalty [ˈrɔɪəlti] *n.* 王族成员;版税
rub [rʌb] *vt.* 摩擦;擦;搓;涂抹上;*vi.* 摩擦;*n.* 摩擦
rubber [ˈrʌbə] *n.* 橡皮擦;橡胶;合成橡胶;*adj.* 橡胶的
rubbish [ˈrʌbiʃ] *n.* 垃圾;废物;废话
rude [ruːd] *adj.* 加工粗糙的;粗野的;无礼的
rug [rʌg] *n.* 小地毯;毯子
ruin [ˈruin] *n.* (*pl.*)废墟;毁灭;*vt.* 毁坏;毁灭;*vi.* (使)破产;毁灭
rule [ruːl] *n.* 规则,条例;行事准则;常规;统治;尺;*v.* 控制,统治,支配;裁定;画(直线)
ruler [ˈruːlə] *n.* 统治者;尺;直尺
rumo(u)r [ˈruːmə] *n.* 谣言;谣传;传闻;低语;*vt.* 传闻;谣传
run [rʌn] *vt. & vi.* 跑;移动;(使)流动;*n.* 奔跑;行程;放映期;一系列;趋向,态势;*vi.* (工作等)进行;延续;逃跑;行驶;*vt.* 使奔跑;使……快速移动;运行,经营;划
rural [ˈruːrəl] *adj.* 农村的;田园的
rush[rʌʃ] *vi.* 冲(进)奔;*vt.* 催促;匆忙;猛冲;*n.* 匆促;冲进;急流;猛冲;突击;*adj.* 紧急的

S

sack [sæk] *n.* 麻袋;洗劫;*vt.* 解雇;把……装进袋里;掠夺
sacred [ˈseikrid] *adj.* 上帝的;神圣的;受尊重的
sacrifice [ˈsækrifais] *n.* 牺牲;舍弃;祭品;*vt.* 牺牲;献出;(人或动物)作祭献
sad [sæd] *adj.* 悲哀的;令人悲痛的;伤心的
saddle [ˈsædl] *n.* 鞍子;马鞍
safe [seif] *adj.* 安全的;谨慎的;*n.* 保险箱
safeguard [ˈseɪfgɑːd] *n.* 保护,保卫;防护措施;安全设施;*vt.* 保护,保卫;防护
safety [ˈseifti] *n.* 安全;保险;*vt.* 保护
sail [seil] *v.* 航行,起航;驾驶(帆船);飘过;*n.* 帆;乘船航行
sailor [ˈseilə] *n.* 水手;海员;水兵
saint [seint] *n.* 圣人;圣徒;基督教徒
sake [seik] *n.* 缘故;理由;利益;好处
salad [ˈsæləd] *n.* 色拉;凉拌生菜
salary [ˈsæləri] *n.* 薪金;薪水;*vt.* 给……薪水
sale [seil] *n.* 卖;削价出售;拍卖;销售额(量)
salesman [ˈseilzmən] *n.* 售货员;推销员
salt [sɔːlt] *n.* 盐;盐类;*adj.* 含盐的;辛辣的;*vt.* 加盐于;用盐腌
salute [səˈluːt] *n.* 招呼;行礼;*vi.* 行礼;致意;问候
same [seim] *adj.* 同一的;相同的;*adv.* 同样地;*pron.* 同样的人或事
sample [ˈsæmpl] *n.* 样品;实例;标本;*vt.* 采样;品尝;*adj.* 样例的
sand [sænd] *n.* 沙;沙子;沙滩
sandwich [ˈsændwitʃ] *n.* 三明治;夹心面包片
sarcastic [sɑːˈkæstɪk] *adj.* 讥讽的,讽刺的,挖苦的

satellite [ˈsætəlait] *n.* 卫星，人造卫星，卫星城
satisfaction [ˌsætisˈfækʃən] *n.* 满意；快事，乐事；妥善处理
satisfactory [ˌsætisˈfæktəri] *adj.* 令人满意的；良好的
satisfy [ˈsætisfai] *vt.* 满足，使满意；使……信服；*vi.* 足够；取悦
sauce [ˈsɔːs] *n.* 调味汁；酱汁
saucer [ˈsɔːsə] *n.* 茶托；浅碟
sausage [ˈsɔːsidʒ] *n.* 香肠，腊肠
save [seiv] *vt.* 救解，救；节省；储蓄；保存；*vi.* 节省；储蓄；救球；*prep.* 除……之外；*conj.* 除……之外；只有；*n.* 救球；节省
saving [ˈseiviŋ] *n.* 节省物；节省；节约；存款；(复数) savings 储蓄金；存款；*prep.* 除……之外；*conj.* 除了，除去；save 的现在分词
saw [sɔː] *n.* 锯子；*vt.* 锯，锯开；用锯子锯；*vbl.* 看见(see 的过去式)
say [sei] *vt.* 说，说明；比如说；讲；表达；假设；*vi.* 说；*n.* 发言权
scale [skeil] *n.* 天平；磅秤；秤；刻度；衡量；数值范围；标度比例
scan [skæn] *vt.* 细看；浏览；扫描；详细调查；押韵；*n.* 扫描；细查
scarcely [ˈskɛəsli] *adv.* 仅仅；几乎不；简直没有；勉强
scare [skɛə] *vt.* 惊吓(惊恐；惊慌)；*vi.* 受惊；*n.* 惊吓(惊恐；惊慌)
scatter [ˈskætə] *vt.* 使消散；撒；散播；驱散；*vi.* 分散；消散；*n.* 散布；零星少量
scene [siːn] *n.* 发生地点；道具；场；景；情景
schedule [ˈskedʒul] *n.* 时间表；计划表；一览表；计划；*vt.* 安排计划；预定；编制目录
scheme [skiːm] *n.* 计划；规划；方案；诡计；阴谋
scholar [ˈskɔlə] *n.* 学者(尤指文学方面)；获奖学金的学生
scholarship [ˈskɔləʃip] *n.* 学业成绩；奖学金；学问；学识
school [skuːl] *n.* 学校；学院；学派；鱼群；*vt.* 教育；训练；磨炼
science [ˈsaiəns] *n.* 科学；科学研究
scientific [ˌsaiənˈtifik] *adj.* 科学(上)的
scientist [ˈsaiəntist] *n.* (自然)科学家
scissors [ˈsizəz] *n.* 剪刀；剪子
scold [skəuld] *vi.* 责骂
scope [skəup] *n.* 范围；余地；机会；能力；眼界
score [skɔː] *n.* 得分；比数；成绩；刻痕；二十；乐谱；*vt.* 记分；刻画；画线；得分；给……谱曲；*vi.* 得分；记分；得胜
scorn [skɔːn] *n.* 轻蔑；嘲笑；被叱责的人；*vt.* 轻蔑；不屑做
scout [skaut] *n.* 侦察员；侦察机；童子军；守卫；*vt.* 侦察；物色人才；*vi.* 寻找；物色
scratch [skrætʃ] *vt.* & *vi.* 搔，抓，搔痒；抹掉；*n.* 搔，抓；抓痕；抓的声音；乱写；*adj.* 使皮肤发痒的；潦草的
scream [skriːm] *vi.* 尖叫；呼啸；大笑；*n.* 尖叫声
screen [skriːn] *n.* 屏，屏幕，银幕；屏风
screw [skruː] *n.* 螺旋，螺旋状物；螺丝，螺丝钉；压迫；转动；*vt.* 拧紧，扭紧；压榨；欺骗；强迫；*vi.* 旋转
script [skrɪpt] *n.* 剧本；电影剧本；广播(或讲话等)稿
sculpture [ˈskʌlptʃə(r)] *n.* 雕像；雕塑品；雕刻品；雕刻术；雕塑术；*v.* 雕刻；雕塑；刻出，雕成
sea [siː] *n.* 海，海洋
seal [siːl] *n.* 封蜡；印记；印章；封条；海豹；*vt.* 封；盖印；封闭；猎海豹
search [səːtʃ] *vt.* 在……中搜寻，搜查；探求；调查；*n.* 搜寻；探究
seaside[ˈsiːsaɪd] *n.* (尤指人们游玩、度假的)海边，海滨；*adj.* 海边的；海滨的
season [ˈsiːzn] *n.* 季；季节；时节；旺季；上演期
seat [siːt] *n.* 座；位子；所在地；*vt.* 使坐下；可容纳
secondary [ˈsekənderi] *adj.* 第二的；次要的；中级的；中等的；*n.* 次要位置；副手
secret [ˈsiːkrit] *adj.* 秘密的；隐蔽的；机密的；*n.* 秘密诀窍
secretary [ˈsekrətri] *n.* 秘书；书记；大臣；部长
section [ˈsekʃən] *n.* 切片；一段；部门；零件；部分；章节；区域；路段
secure [siˈkjuə] *adj.* 安心的；安全的；无虑的；牢靠的；稳妥的；*vt.* 固定；获得；使……安全；
security [siˈkjuːriti] *n.* 安全，安全感；防护措施；保证(金)；抵押(品)；债券；证券
see [siː] *vt.* 看见；遇见；看出；经历；明白；确保；视为；拜访；陪同；*vi.* 注意；想象；了解；调查；*n.* 主教教区；主角权限
seed [siːd] *n.* 种(子)；籽；萌芽；*vi.* (植物)结实；*vt.* 播种
seek [siːk] *vt.* 寻找；探索；试图；*vi.* 寻找
seem [siːm] *vi.* 好像，似乎
seize [siːz] *vt.* 抓住；逮捕；夺取；攻占；理解；侵袭
seldom [ˈseldəm] *adv.* 很少；不常；难得；

adj. 很少的
select [si'lekt] *vt.* & *vi.* 选择;挑选;选拔;*adj.* 精选的;优等的
selection [si'lekʃən] *n.* 选择;挑选;精选物;挑选出来的人或事
self [self] *n.* 自我;自己;本身
selfish ['selfiʃ] *adj.* 自私的;利己的
sell [sel] *vi.* 卖;销售;促销;*vt.* 出让;背叛;出卖;出售
seminar ['seminɑː(r)] *n.* (大学教师带领学生作专题讨论的)研讨课;研讨会;培训会
senate ['senit] *n.* 参议院;上院
senator ['senətə(r)] *n.* 参议员
send [send] *vt.* 送;传;寄;派遣;发射
senior ['siːnjə] *adj.* 年长的;地位较高的;高级的;资深的;*n.* 年长者;上司;毕业班学生
sense [sens] *n.* 感官;感觉;见识;侦测;理智;意义;*vt.* 感觉;了解;检测
sensible ['sensəbl] *adj.* 感觉得到的;明智的;可察觉的;意识到的
sensitive ['sensitiv] *adj.* 敏感的;灵敏的;易受伤害的;感光的;善解人意的;*n.* 敏感的人
sentence ['sentəns] *n.* 判决;句子;意见;宣判;刑罚;命题;*vt.* 宣判,判决;使遭受
separate ['sepəreit] *adj.* 分离的;个别的;各自的,单独的;*v.* 分开;隔开;分居
series ['siəriːz] *n.* 连续;系列;系列节目;丛书
seriously ['siriəsli] *adv.* 严肃地;认真地;严重地
serious ['siəriəs] *adj.* 严肃的;认真的;庄重的;严重的;危急的
servant ['səːvənt] *n.* 仆人,佣人;雇工
serve [səːv] *vt.* 为……服务;招待;可作……用
service ['səːvis] *n.* 服务;行政部门,公务部门;服役
session ['seʃən] *n.* 会议;一段时间;开庭期;市盘;学期
set [set] *vt.* 放;安置;设定;*vi.* (太阳)落下去;*n.* 组合,集合;设定;一套;一副;一局比赛
setback ['setbæk] *n.* 挫折;阻碍
setting ['setiŋ] *n.* 安装;调整;环境;放置;周围
settle ['setl] *vt.* 安排;安放;安顿;调停;解决;决定;付清(欠款);*vi.* 定居;降落
several ['sevərəl] *adj.* 几个;数个;各自的;*pron.* 若干
severe [si'viə] *adj.* 严格的;严厉的;剧烈的;严重的;严峻的
sew [səu] *vt.* 缝制;缝合;*vi.* 缝纫
sex [seks] *n.* 性别;性;性欲;*vt.* 区别……性别;引起……性欲
shade [ʃeid] *n.* 荫;遮光物;荫凉处;*vi.* 荫蔽,遮蔽
shadow ['ʃædəu] *n.* 阴影;阴;影子;阴暗
shake [ʃeik] *vt.* 摇;使震动;挥拳;摇晃;去除;动摇;*vi.* 摇晃;颤抖;握手;发颤音;*n.* 摇动;摇晃;震动;地震;颤抖(音);奶昔
shall [ʃæl] aux. *v.* 将要;必须;应,应该
shallow ['ʃæləu] *adj.* 浅的;浅薄的;肤浅的;浅显易懂的
shame [ʃeim] *n.* 羞耻;羞愧;羞辱;遗憾的事;*vt.* 使羞愧
shampoo [ʃæm'puː] *n.* 洗头洗发剂;洗涤剂
shape [ʃeip] *n.* 形状;情况;形式;定形;身材;*vt.* 定形;使…… 成形;塑造
share [ʃɛə] *n.* 份,份额;股份;部分;分担;*vt.* 分享;共有;分配
shark [ʃɑːk] *n.* 鲨鱼;坑蒙拐骗的人;诈骗者;*vi.* 骗取;榨取;用不正当手段攫取;勒索诈骗
sharp [ʃɑːp] *adj.* 锋利的;敏锐的;刺耳的;*adv.* [时刻]正,准
shave [ʃeiv] *vt.* 剃;修面;*vi.* 修面;刮胡子;*n.* 修面;刮胡子
she [ʃiː] *pron.* (主格)她
shed [ʃed] *n.* 简易房,棚(用于贮藏物品);(工业上用于生产或存放设备的)厂房,工棚,库房 *v.* 去除;摆脱;使落下;使掉下;掉落(货物)
sheep [ʃiːp] *n.* 羊,绵羊
sheet [ʃiːt] *n.* 被单;床单;纸张;薄板;张;片
shelf [ʃelf] *n.* 搁板(状物);架子
shell [ʃel] *n.* 壳,贝壳
shelter ['ʃeltə] *n.* 隐蔽处;掩蔽;庇护;庇护所;避难所;*v.* 庇护保护;隐匿
shepherd ['ʃepəd] *n.* 牧羊人,羊倌;牧师;指导者
shield ['ʃiːld] *n.* 盾,盾状物;防护物;*vt.* 保护;遮蔽
shift [ʃift] *vt.* 替换;转移;变声;*vi.* 改变;更衣;*n.* 转换;交换;变化;移动;接班者
shine [ʃain] *vi.* 照耀;发光;表现出众;闪耀着;*vt.* 使发光;照射在……上;擦亮;*n.* 光,光泽;阳光;光辉
ship [ʃip] *n.* (大)船;海船;舰;*vt.* 以船运送;乘船;运送;*vi.* 上船;坐船;运送;在船上工作
shirt [ʃəːt] *n.* (男式)衬衫
shiver ['ʃivə] *vi.* 颤抖;哆嗦;*vt.* 颤动(碎裂)
shock [ʃɔk] *n.* 冲击;震惊;冲突;休克;*vi.* 震动;冲突;使…… 受电击

shoe [ʃuː] *n.* 鞋
shoot [ʃuːt] *vt.* 发射;射中;射击;发出;发芽
shop [ʃɔp] *n.* 商店,店铺;车间;*vt.* 购物;逛商店
shop-assistant [ʃɒpəsɪstənt] *n.* 售货员;店员
shopkeeper [ˈʃɔp. kiːpə] *n.* 店主;零售商人
shore [ʃɔː] *n.* 滨;岸
short [ʃɔːt] *adj.* 短,短期的;矮的;短暂的;*n.* 短裤
shortage [ˈʃɔːtidʒ] *n.* 不足;缺少;不足额
shortcoming [ʃɔːt. kʌmiŋ] *n.* 短处;缺点
shortly [ˈʃɔːtli] *adv.* 立刻,马上;简短地
shot [ʃɔt] *n.* 发射;弹丸;射门;炮弹;射击;射手;努力;*v.* 射击发出;发芽(shoot 的过去式和过去分词)
should [ʃud] *aux. v.* (常用于纠正别人)应该,应当;(提出或征询建议)该,可以;(表示预期)应该会,可能
shoulder [ˈʃəuldə] *n.* 肩,肩膀;挑起
shout [ʃaut] *n.* 呼喊;突发的大叫;*vt.* 高声呼喊;呼叫;*vi.* 呼叫,突然喊叫
show [ʃəu] *vt.* 给……看;表明;表示;显现;展现;指示;*n.* 显示;表现;表演;事情
shower [ˈʃauə] *n.* 阵雨;(一)阵;淋浴;*vi.* 倾盆而下;淋浴;*vt.* 淋湿;下骤雨
shrink [ʃriŋk] *vi.* 收缩;缩小;退缩;萎缩;*vt.* 使收缩;*n.* 收缩;萎缩
shut [ʃʌt] *vt.* 关上;闭上;关闭;防止进入;合上;停止或中止;*vi.* 关闭;停止或中止;*n.* 关闭;*adj.* 关闭的
shuttle [ˈʃʌtl] *n.* 来往于两地之间的航班(或班车、火车);梭;梭子;(英法之间英吉利海峡隧道的)穿梭火车;*v.* 频繁往来(于甲地和乙地之间);(在较近的两地之间定时)往返运送
shy [ʃai] *adj.* 易受惊的;害羞的;胆怯的;迟疑的
sick [sik] *adj.* 有病的;恶心的;腻烦的;晕的
side [said] *n.* 边,旁边;一方;侧;方面;*adj.* 旁的;侧的;*vt.* 支持同意
sidewalk [ˈsaɪdwɔːk] *n.* 人行道
sigh [sai] *n.* 呼吸;叹息(带有情感);*vi.* 发出叹息的声音;感叹;*vt.* 叹息
sight [sait] *n.* 视力;见;情景;景观;眼界
sightseeing [ˈsaitˌsiːiŋ] *n.* 观光;游览;动词 sightsee 的现在分词
sign [sain] *n.* 符号;招牌;*v.* 签;做手势;做标记
signal [ˈsignəl] *n.* 信号;*v.* 发信号
signature [ˈsignitʃə] *n.* 署名;签字;签名;签署
significance [sigˈnifikəns] *n.* 意义;意味;重要性
significant [sigˈnifikənt] *adj.* 有意义的;重要的;意味深长的;相当数量的;重大的
silence [ˈsailəns] *n.* 沉默;寂静;*vt.* 使沉默;使安静
silent [ˈsailənt] *adj.* 沉默的;寂静无声的;安静的;不吵闹的;无言的
silk [silk] *n.* 蚕丝;丝;绸;丝织品;*adj.* 丝的
silly [ˈsili] *adj.* 傻的;愚蠢的;淳朴的
silver [ˈsilvə] *n.* 银,银子;银器;*adj.* 银色的;银的
similar [ˈsimilə] *adj.* 相似的;类似的;同样的
similarly [ˈsimiləli] *adv.* 类似地;相似地
simple [ˈsimpl] *adj.* 简单的;朴素的
simply [ˈsimpli] *adv.* 简单地;朴素地;仅仅;完全地
sin [sin] *n.* 罪,罪孽;过失;*vi.* 犯罪;违反
since [sins] *conj.* 从……以来;因为;既然;自从;*prep.* 自从
sincere [sinˈsiə] *adj.* 真诚的;真挚的
sing [siŋ] *vt.* 唱;鸣唱;*vi.* 唱歌
single [ˈsiŋgl] *adj.* 单一的;独身的;单纯的;*n.* 单程票;单曲;单人房;单身者;*vt.* 单独挑出
singular [ˈsiŋgjulə] *adj.* 单一的;非凡的;个人的;单数的;独一的;唯一的;*n.* 单数
sink [siŋk] *vi.* 下沉;下垂;降低;*vt.* 下沉;*n.* 水槽
sir [səː] *n.* 先生;阁下;爵士
siren [ˈsaɪrən] *n.* 汽笛;警报器;塞壬(古希腊神话中半人半鸟或半人半鱼的女海妖,以美妙歌声诱使航海者驶向礁石或进入危险水域);妖冶而危险的女人;性感妖女
sister [ˈsistə] *n.* 姐妹;姐;妹
sit [sit] *vi.* 坐;就座
site [sait] *n.* 地点;地基;场所;位置;现场
situation [ˌsitjuˈeiʃən] *n.* 位置;处境;形势;局面;状况
size [saiz] *n.* 大小;体积;尺码;尺寸
skate [skeit] *vi.* 滑冰,溜冰
skeleton [ˈskelɪtn] *n.* 骨骼;骨架;骨骼标本
sketch [sketʃ] *n.* 略图;速写;素描;概略;草图;*vt.* 描绘略图;*vi.* 写生
ski [skiː] *n.* 滑橇;滑雪;滑雪板;*vi.* 滑雪
skill [ˈskil] *n.* 技能;技巧;熟练
skilled [skild] *adj.* 有技能的;熟练的
skin [skin] *n.* 皮,皮肤;兽皮;外皮;皮囊;*v.* 剥皮;削皮

skip [skɪp] *v.* 蹦蹦跳跳地走；跳绳；不做(应做的事等)；不参加
skirt [skəːt] *n.* 女裙；边缘
sky [skai] *n.* 天，天空
skyscraper[ˈskaɪskreɪpə(r)] *n.* 摩天大楼
slack [slæk] *adj.* 不紧的；松弛的；懈怠的；不用心的；敷衍了事的；吊儿郎当的；
slap [slæp] *v.* (用手掌)打，拍，掴
slave [sleiv] *n.* 奴隶；苦工；完全受控制的人
slavery [ˈsleivəri] *n.* 奴隶制度；苦役；奴役
sleep [sliːp] *n.* 睡眠；睡觉；*vi.* & *vt.* 睡
sleeve [sliːv] *n.* 袖子；袖套；套管
slender [ˈslendə] *adj.* 细长的；微薄的；苗条的；少量的
slice [slais] *n.* 薄片；切片；*vt.* 切成薄片，大幅降低
slide [slaid] *vi.* 滑；跌落；*vt.* 使滑动；*n.* 滑；幻灯片；雪崩；滑梯
slight [slait] *adj.* 细长的；轻微的；纤细的；脆弱的
slim[slɪm] *adj.* 苗条的；纤细的；单薄的；微薄的
slip [slip] *vi.* 滑跤；滑落；溜；滑行；下跌；*n.* 滑；疏漏；小错误
slipper [ˈslipə] *n.* 拖鞋；便鞋
slippery [ˈslipəri] *adj.* 滑的；使人滑跤的；狡猾的；不可靠的
slogan [ˈsləugən] *n.* 标语；口号
slope [sləup] *n.* 倾斜；斜面；斜坡；斜线
slow [sləu] *adj.* 慢的；迟钝的；*v.* 放慢；减速
small [smɔːl] *adj.* 小的；少的；小型的
smart [smɑːt] *adj.* 巧妙的；洒脱的；聪明的；时髦的；漂亮的，敏捷的
smell [smel] *n.* 嗅觉；气味；味道；*vt.* 嗅；闻；发臭；*vi.* 闻；发臭
smile [smail] *vi.* 微笑；赞许；一笑而过；
vt. 微笑；微笑地表示；*n.* 微笑；笑容
smoke [sməuk] *n.* 烟；抽烟
smooth [smuːθ] *adj.* 平滑的；平静的；平稳的；流畅的
smuggle [ˈsmʌgl] *v.* 走私；私运；偷运
snack[snæk] *n.* 点心；小吃；快餐；易办到的事
snake [sneik] *n.* 蛇
snatch [snætʃ] *v.* 一把抓起；一下夺过；夺去；抢走
snow [snəu] *n.* 雪；下雪；似雪花的东西；粉状物；*vi.* 下雪
so [səu] *adv.* 这样；这么；非常；如此；如是；同样；*conj.* 所以；因此；
soak [səuk] *vt.* 浸；泡；使……湿透；浸泡在液体中；*vi.* 浸泡；浸入液体；渗透
soap [səup] *n.* 肥皂
sob [sɔb] *vi.* 啜泣；呜咽
soccer [ˈsɔkə] *n.* 英式足球
social [ˈsəuʃəl] *adj.* 社会的；社交的；群居的；社团的
socialism [ˈsəuʃəlizəm] *n.* 社会主义
socialist [ˈsəuʃəlist] *adj.* 社会主义的；*n.* 社会主义者
society [səˈsaiəti] *n.* 社会；团体；社交界；阶层圈子
sock [sɔk] *n.* 短袜；*vt.* 给……穿短袜
soda [ˈsəudə] *n.* 碳酸钠；纯碱；汽水；苏打
soft [sɔft] *adj.* 软的；柔软的；柔和的；温和的；不强烈的；轻的
software [ˈsɒftweə(r)] *n.* 软件
softly [ˈsɔftli] *adv.* 柔软地；温柔地；柔和地；静静地
soil [sɔil] *n.* 泥土；土壤；土地
solar [ˈsəulə] *adj.* 太阳的；太阳能的；日光的
soldier [ˈsəuldʒə] *n.* (陆军)士兵；军人
sole [səul] *n.* 脚底；鞋底；袜底；*adj.* 唯一的；单独的；独占的
solemn [ˈsɔləm] *adj.* 庄严的；严肃的；隆重的
solid [ˈsɔlid] *adj.* 固体的；结实的；实心的；可靠的；*n.* 固体；立方体
solution [səˈluːʃən] *n.* 解决；解答；解决办法；溶解；溶液
solve [sɔlv] *vt.* 解答；解释；解决
some [sʌm，səm，sm] *adj.* 一些；若干；
adv. 大约；在某种程度上；*pron.* 一些(人或物)；若干
somebody [ˈsʌmbədi] *pron.* 某人；有人；*n.* 重要人物
somehow [ˈsʌmhau] *adv.* 由于某种原因；不知怎么地；以某种方式
someone [ˈsʌmwʌn] *pron.* 某人；有人
something [ˈsʌmθiŋ] *pron.* 某事；某物；有价值或重要的人或物；*adv.* 稍微；有点；非常
sometime [ˈsʌmtaim] *adv.* 在某一时候；从前；改天；来日；*adj.* 以前的；某一时间
sometimes [ˈsʌmtaimz] *adv.* 不时；有时；间或
somewhat [ˈsʌmwɔt] *pron.* 一点儿；一些；某物；*adv.* 有点；多少几分
somewhere [ˈsʌmwɛə] ad. 在某处；到某种程度；大约；差不多；*n.* 某地；某处
son [sʌn] *n.* 儿子；孩子(长者对后辈的称呼)

song [sɔŋ] *n.* 歌唱;歌曲;歌词
soon [suːn] *adv.* 不久;很快;早;快
sophisticated [səˈfistikeitid] *adj.* 老于世故的;高级的;诡辩的;精密的;老练的;尖端的
sore [sɔː] *adj.* 痛的;痛心的;恼火的
sorrow [ˈsɔrəu] *n.* 悲痛;悲哀;悲伤;伤心事
sorry [ˈsɔri] *adj.* 对不起的;抱歉的;难过的;遗憾的;*int.* 对不起
sort [sɔːt] *n.* 种类;类别;特征;方法;*vt.* 分类;整理;使明确
soul [səul] *n.* 灵魂;精神;人;心灵;精髓;鬼魂
sound [saund] *adj.* 健康的;健全的;完好的;可靠的;合理的;*n.* 声音;*v.* 听起来;发出声音
soup [suːp] *n.* 汤;羹
sour [ˈsauə] *adj.* 酸的;酸腐的;刻薄的;脾气坏的
source [sɔːs] *n.* 河的源头;根源;发源地;来源;原始资料
south [sauθ] *n.* 南;南方
southern [ˈsʌðən] *adj.* 南方的;南部的;来自南方的
southward(s) [ˈsaʊθwəd(z)] *adv.* & *adj.* 向南方(的)
souvenir[suˌːvəˈnɪə(r)] *n.* 纪念物;纪念品;(度假时买回来送人的)礼物
sow [sau] *vt.* 播(种);散布;*vi.* 播种;散布
space [speis] *n.* 空间;场地;空地;空白;太空;间隔
spaceship [ˈspeisʃip] *n.* 航天飞船
spade [speid] *n.* 铲;铁锹;在扑克牌中指黑桃;*v.* 铲;*vt.* (用铲子)铲
span [spæn] *n.* 跨距;跨度;间距;一段时间;*vt.* 横跨;贯穿;估量
Spanish [ˈspæniʃ] *adj.* 西班牙的;西班牙人的;西班牙语的;*n.* 西班牙人;西班牙语
spare [spɛə] *vt.* 节约;抽出;饶恕;赦免;*adj.* 多余的;闲置的;备用的;*n.* 剩余;备用品
spark [spɑːk] *n.* 火花;火星;*vi.* 闪烁;冒火花;*vt.* 激发;引起
sparkle [ˈspɑːkl] *vi.* 发火花;闪耀;冒火花;*vt.* 使闪耀;*n.* 闪耀火花
speak [spiːk] *vi.* 说话;发言;*vt.* 说;讲;演说
speaker [ˈspiːkə] *n.* 说话者;发言者;说某种语言者;扬声器
spear [spiə] *n.* 矛;枪;*vt.* 用矛刺
special [ˈspeʃəl] *adj.* 特殊的;特别的;专门的;*n.* 特别的东西;特价;特刊;特色菜
specialist [ˈspeʃəlist] *n.* 专家
species [ˈspiːʃiːz] *n.* 种,物种
specific [spiˈsifik] *adj.* 特有的;特殊的;明确的;具体的
specify [ˈspesifai] *vi.* 指定;详细说明;阐述
spectator [spekˈteɪtə(r)] *n.* (尤指体育比赛的)观看者,观众
speech [spiːtʃ] *n.* 言语;演说;演讲
speed [spiːd] *n.* 快;速率;速度;迅速;*vi.* 快行;加速;急行
spell [spel] *vt.* 拼写;缓慢地或吃力地读;用符咒镇住(某人)
spend [spend] *vt.* 用钱;花费;浪费;度过
sphere [sfiə] *n.* 球;圆体;范围;领域;天体
spice [spaɪs] *n.* (调味)香料;额外的趣味(或刺激等);*v.* 在……中加香料;给……增添趣味;使……变得刺激
spider [ˈspaidə] *n.* 蜘蛛
spill [spil] *vt.* 使溢出;洒;使……流出;泄漏;*vi.* 溢出;*n.* 溢出;流
spin [spin] *vt.* 使旋转;疾驰;纺织;结网;眩晕;*n.* 旋转;纺织;眩晕;疾驰
spirit [ˈspirit] *n.* 精神;气魄;情绪;心灵;幽灵;精灵
spiritual [ˈspiritjuəl] *adj.* 精神的;心灵的
spit [spit] *vi.* 吐;吐唾沫;吐出;*n.* 唾液口水
spite [spaɪt] *n.* 恶意;怨恨
splash [splæʃ] *n.* 飞溅的水;污点;*vt.* 溅湿;溅开;泼;飞溅
splendid [ˈsplendid] *adj.* 壮丽的;显著的;极好的;辉煌的;壮观的;杰出的
split [split] *vt.* 劈开;分离;分开;*vi.* 被劈开
spoil [spɔil] *vt.* 损坏;破坏;糟蹋;宠坏;溺爱
sponsor [ˈspɒnsə(r)] *n.* (广播电视节目、音乐会或运动会的)赞助者,赞助商;为慈善活动捐资的人;*v.* 赞助(活动、节目等);主办;举办;促成
spoon [spuːn] *n.* 匙;调羹;匙状物
sport [spɔːt] *n.* 运动;体育;运动会
sportsman [ˈspɔːtsmən] *n.* 运动员
spot [spɔt] *n.* 点;斑点;污点;地点;场所;职位;*adj.* 当场的;现场买卖的
spouse [spaʊs] *n.* 配偶
spray [sprei] *n.* 浪花;喷雾;水沫;喷雾器;*vt.* 喷;喷雾;扫射;喷射
spread [spred] *vt.* 伸开;伸展;展开;传播;散布;铺开 *n.* 传播;伸展;铺开
spring [spriŋ] *vi.* 跳;跃;射出;涌入(出);发芽 *vt.* 弹起;使喷涌;越过;弹出;释放;发生 *n.* 春天;春季;跳跃;弹跳;泉,泉水;弹簧

spy [spai] *n.* 间谍；特务；侦探；侦察；*vt.* 侦察；侦探；看到；找出；*vi.* 看；侦察
square [skwɛə] *n.* 正方形；广场；街区；平方
squeeze [skwiːz] *vt.* & *vi.* 榨；挤；压榨；挤压；塞进
squirrel [ˈskwirəl] *n.* 松鼠；松鼠皮毛
stability [stəˈbiliti] *n.* 稳定；稳定性
stable [ˈsteibl] *adj.* 稳定的；不变的；安定的；可靠的；*n.* 厩；马厩；马棚；牛棚
stadium [ˈsteidiəm] *n.* 露天大型运动场；竞技场
staff [stɑːf] *n.* 工作人员；参谋；全体人员；同事；*vt.* 配备员工
stage [steidʒ] *n.* 舞台；驿站；戏剧；阶段；*vt.* 上演；实行；进行
stain [stein] *vt.* 玷污；弄脏；给……着色；*n.* 污点；瑕疵；染料；着色剂
stair [stɛə] *n.* 楼梯
staircase [ˈstɛəkeis] *n.* 楼梯；楼梯间
stamp[stæmp] *n.* 邮票；印；章；戳；印记；戳记；*v.* 跺（脚）；重踩；重踏；迈着重重的步伐走；在……上盖（字样或图案等）；把（字样或图案等）盖在……上
stand [stænd] *vi.* 站；坐落；位于；停滞；忍受；*n.* 架；台；站立；货摊
standard [ˈstændəd] *n.* 标准；规格；*adj.* 标准的；规范的；普通的
star [stɑː] *n.* 星；恒星；明星；*v.* 以星状物装饰；变成演员
stare [steə(r)] *vi.* 盯 凝视；*n.* 凝视
start [stɑːt] *vi.* 跳起；出发；开始；起身；*vt.* 开始；使震惊；*n.* 起点
startle [ˈstɑːtl] *vt.* 使大吃一惊；使……惊愕；*n.* 吃惊；惊愕
starve [stɑːv] *vi.* 饿死；挨饿；受饿；*vt.* 使饿死；使挨饿
state [steit] *n.* 状态；国家；州；情形；*adj.* 国家的；州的；*vt.* 说；说明；阐明；陈述；声明；规定
statement [ˈsteitmənt] *n.* 陈述；声明
statesman [ˈsteitsmən] *n.* 政治家；国务活动家
station [ˈsteiʃən] *n.* 站；台；所；局；车站；位置；地位
statue [ˈstætjuː] *n.* 塑像；雕像；铸像
status [ˈsteitəs] *n.* 地位；身份；情形；状况
stay [stei] *vi.* 停留；逗留；住；*n.* 逗留；停留
steady [ˈstedi] *adj.* 稳固的；稳定的；坚定的
steak[steɪk] *n.* 牛排；肉排
steal [stiːl] *vt.* 偷，窃取
steam [stiːm] *n.* 蒸汽；水蒸气；*vi.* 蒸发；蒸；冒热气；*vt.* 蒸
steel [stiːl] *n.* 钢；钢铁；钢制品
steep [stiːp] *adj.* 险峻的；陡峭的；（价格）过高的；*n.* 陡坡
steer [stiə] *vt.* & *vi.* 驾驶；掌舵；引导；操纵
stem [stem] *n.* 茎；（树）干；柄；*vi.* 起源；
step [step] *n.* （脚）步；步骤；步伐；踏级；*vi.* 走；*vt.* 踏；以步测量
stern [stəːn] *adj.* 严厉的；坚定的；坚决的；苛刻的
stick [stik] *n.* 棍；棒；枝；杆；手杖；*vi.* 钉住；粘贴；坚持
stiff [stif] *adj.* 硬的；僵直的；生硬的；拘谨的；不灵活的
still [stil] *adj.* 静止的；不动的；静寂的；*adv.* 仍然；更；静止地；*conj.* 然而；但是
stimulate [ˈstimjuleit] *vt.* 刺激；激励；激发；鼓舞；*vi.* 起刺激作用
sting [stiŋ] *vt.* 刺，刺痛；使苦恼；*vi.* 刺；叮；刺痛；*n.* 刺痛，刺；讽刺
stir [stəː] *vt.* 动；拨动；激动；惹起；搅和；*vi.* 搅拌；激动；*n.* 激动；搅拌；骚乱
stock [stɔk] *n.* 原料；库存品；存货；股本；股份；储备；家畜
stocking [ˈstɔkiŋ] *n.* 长（统）袜
stomach [ˈstʌmək] *n.* 胃，胃口；肚子；食欲
stone [stəun] *n.* 石，石头，石块
stool [stuːl] *n.* 凳子；搁脚凳
stoop [stuːp] *vi.* 俯身；弯下；弯下上身；*n.* 弯腰
stop [stɔp] *vt.* 塞住；阻止；停止；停留；*n.* 停止；车站；逗留
store [stɔː] *n.* 贮藏；贮存品；商店；仓库；*vt.* 储存；贮藏；供给；保存；（在计算机里）存贮；记忆
storey [ˈstɔːri] *n.* （层）楼 = story（美）
storm [stɔːm] *n.* 风暴；暴（风）雨；*v.* 起风暴；暴怒
story [ˈstɔːri] *n.* 故事；小说；传说；叙述；新闻报道；楼层（ = storey）
stove [stəuv] *n.* 炉子；火炉；电炉
straight [streit] *adv.* 笔直地；平正地；成直线；直接 *adj.* 直的；直筒型（非紧身）的；准的；正中目标的；*n.* 异性恋者；直道部分
straightforward [ˌstreɪtˈfɔːwəd] *adj.* 简单的；易懂的；不复杂的；坦诚的；坦率的；率直的
strain [strein] *vt.* 拉紧；劳累；过分使用；*vi.* 尽力

strange [streindʒ] *adj.* 陌生的;奇怪的
stranger [ˈstreindʒə] *n.* 陌生人;新来者;外地人;新手
strategy [ˈstrætidʒi] *n.* 战略;策略
straw [strɔː] *n.* 稻草;麦秆;吸管
strawberry [ˈstrɔːbəri] *n.* 草莓
stream [striːm] *n.* 河(人、车、气)流;水流
street [striːt] *n.* 街;街道;行车道
strength [streŋθ] *n.* 力;力量;力气;长处;强度
strengthen [ˈstreŋθən] *vt.* 加强;变坚固;巩固
stress [stres] *n.* 压力;紧张;重音;负载;*vt.* 着重;强调;*vi.* 强调;着重
stretch [stretʃ] *vt.* 伸展;张开;*vi.* 伸,延伸;*n.* 伸展;张开
strict [strikt] *adj.* 严格的;严谨的;精确的;完全的
strike [straik] *vt.* & *vi.* 打;击;撞;罢工;划燃;*n.* 罢工;打击;殴打
striking [ˈstraɪkɪŋ] *adj.* 引人注目的;异乎寻常的;显著的;俊秀的
string [striŋ] *n.* 线;细绳;一串;字串;*vt.* 串起;成串;*vi.* 给……装弦;*adj.* 线的
strip [strip] *vt.* 剥夺;剥去;夺去;脱衣;*n.* 条带;长条;条状;脱衣舞
stroke [strəuk] *n.* 打;击;鸣声;中风;笔画;连续的动作;心跳;抚摩;捋
strong [strɔŋ] *adj.* 强壮的;强烈的;坚强的;浓的;擅长的
structure [ˈstrʌktʃə] *n.* 结构;构造;建筑物
struggle [ˈstrʌgl] *n.* & *vi.* 斗争;挣扎;竞争;奋斗
stubborn [ˈstʌbən] *adj.* 固执的;执拗的;顽固的;倔强的;难以去除(或对付)的
student [ˈstjuːdənt] *n.* 学生;研究生;学者
studio [ˈstjuːdiəʊ] *n.* (广播、电视的)录音室,录像室,演播室,制作室;(音乐)录音棚;电影摄影棚;电影公司;电影制片厂
study [ˈstʌdi] *n.* 学习;研究;学科;沉思;书房;*vt.* 学;读书;记忆;调查
stuff [stʌf] *n.* 材料;原料;东西;*vt.* 装;填塞;填满;塞满
stupid [ˈstjuːpid] *adj.* 愚蠢的;感觉迟钝的;笨拙的
style [stail] *n.* 风格;文体;式样;时尚;类型
subject [ˈsʌbdʒikt, səbˈdʒekt] *n.* 题目;学科;[语]主语;主题;话题;题材;主观;实验对象;*adj.* 服从的;易患的;*vt.* 使隶属;使服从;使遭遇
subjective [səbˈdʒektɪv] *adj.* 主观的(非客观的);主观的(非现实世界的);主语的;主格的
submit [səbˈmit] *vt.* 使服从;屈服;呈送;递交
subscribe [səbˈskraɪb] *v.* 定期订购(或订阅等);定期交纳(会员费);定期(向慈善机构)捐款;定期捐助;认购(股份)
subsequent [ˈsʌbsikwənt] *adj.* 随后的;后来的
substance [ˈsəbstəns] *n.* 物质;实质
substantial [səbˈstænʃəl] *adj.* 物质的;坚固的;实质的;可观的;大量的
substitute [ˈsʌbstitjuːt] *n.* 代替人;代用品;*vt.* 用……代替
subtract [səbˈtrækt] *vt.* 减,减去;去掉;扣掉;*vi.* 减少
suburb [ˈsʌbəːb] *n.* 郊区;郊外;近郊
subway [ˈsʌbwei] *n.* 地道;地下铁路
succeed [səkˈsiːd] *vt.* 继……之后;*vi.* 成功;继承;接着发生
success [səkˈses] *n.* 成功;成就;胜利;发财;成功者;成功的事物
successful [səkˈsesful] *adj.* 成功的;结果良好的;圆满的
successor [səkˈsesə(r)] *n.* 接替者;继任者;接替的事物;后继的事物
such [sʌtʃ] *pron.* (指上文)这样的,那样的,类似的;(指后文)这样的,下述一类的;(强调程度)这样,非常,如此程度
sudden [ˈsʌdn] *adj.* 突然的;意外的;快速的;出乎意料的;*n.* 突发之事
suddenly [ˈsʌdnli] *adv.* 突然地
suffer [ˈsʌfə] *vt.* 遭受;忍受;容许;允许;*vi.* 受苦;患病;受损失
sufficient [səˈfiʃənt] *adj.* 足够的;充分的
sugar [ˈʃugə] *n.* 糖
suggest [səˈdʒest] *vt.* 建议;暗示;启发;要求
suggestion [səˈdʒestʃən] *n.* 建议;意见;暗示;迹象
suit [sjuːt] *n.* 套装;*vt.* 适合;取悦;满足
suitable [ˈsjuːtəbl] *adj.* 合适的;适宜的
suitcase [ˈsuːtkeɪs] *n.* (旅行用的)手提箱
suite [swiːt] *n.* (尤指旅馆的)一套房间,套房
sum [sʌm] *n.* 总数;金额;*vi.* 共计;总计概括
summary [ˈsʌməri] *n.* 摘要;概要;一览
summer [ˈsʌmə] *n.* 夏,夏季
summit [ˈsʌmɪt] *n.* 最高点;顶点;山顶;(政府间的)首脑会议;峰会
sun [sʌn] *n.* 太阳;日;阳光
sunny [ˈsʌni] *adj.* 阳光充足的;晴朗的;明媚的;快活的
sunrise [ˈsʌnraiz] *n.* 日出(时分)

sunset [ˈsʌnset] *n.* 日落(时分);衰落时期(尤指人的晚年)
sunshine [ˈsʌnʃain] *n.* (直射)日光;阳光
super [ˈsjuːpə] *adj.* 极好的;超级的
superior [suːˈpiəriə] *adj.* 较高的;优越的;上层的;上好的;出众的;高傲的;*n.* 上级;高手
supermarket [ˈsjuːpə. mɑːkit] *n.* 超级市场
supper [ˈsʌpə] *n.* 晚饭,晚餐;晚餐会
supplement [ˈsʌplimənt, ˈsʌpliment] *n.* 补充物;补充;增刊;增补;*vt.* 补充;增补
supply [səˈplai] *n.* 补给;供给;供应;贮备;*vt.* 补给;供给;提供;提供足够以满足
support [səˈpɔːt] *vt.* 支撑;支持;供养;帮助;*n.* 支持;援助;供养
suppose [səˈpəuz] *vt.* 猜想;假定;认为;应该
supreme [sjuːˈpriːm] *adj.* 最高的;最大的;至上的;极度的
sure [ʃuə] *adj.* 确信的;确实的;肯定的;*adv.* 当然;确实地;无疑地
surf [sɜːf] *n.* 激浪;拍岸浪花;*v.* 进行冲浪运动;冲浪;(互联网上)冲浪,漫游,浏览
surface [ˈsəːfis] *n.* 地面;表面;外表;平面;*adj.* 表面的;肤浅的
surgeon [ˈsəːdʒən] *n.* 外科医师;军医
surgery [ˈsəːdʒəri] *n.* 外科;外科手术;诊所
surname [ˈsəːneim] *n.* 姓;*vt.* 冠姓
surprise [səˈpraiz] *vt.* 使惊奇;使诧异;*n.* 惊奇;诧异;惊讶
surprising [səˈpraiziŋ] *adj.* 惊人的;出人意料的令人惊讶的;动词 **surprise** 的现在分词
surrender [səˈrendə] *v.* 交出;让与;投降;屈服;*n.* 投降;屈服;放弃
surround [səˈraund] *vt.* 围,围绕;圈住;包围;环绕
survey [səːˈvei] *vt.* 检查;调查;测量;*n.* 调查;纵览;视察;测量
survive [səˈvaiv] *vt.* 幸免于;比……活得长;艰难度过;*vi.* 活下来;活着;继续存在
suspect [səsˈpekt] *vt.* 怀疑;猜想;*vi.* 疑心;猜想;*n.* 嫌疑犯;*adj.* 令人怀疑的;不可信的
suspend [səsˈpend] *vt.* 吊;推迟;悬挂;暂停;取消;*vi.* 悬挂;中止;停止偿付债务
suspicious [səˈspɪʃəs] *adj.* 怀疑的;令人怀疑的;持怀疑态度的
sustain [səsˈtein] *vt.* 支撑;支持;供养;忍受;承受;经受
swallow [ˈswɔləu] *n.* 燕子;吞咽;一次吞咽的量;*vt.* 吞下;咽下忍受;不流露感情;收回;*vi.* 咽口水;忍气吞声;吞下;咽下
sway [swei] *vt. & vi.* 摇摆;摇动;支配;影响;*n.* 摇摆;动摇;支配
swear [swɛə] *vt.* 宣(誓);发誓;*vi.* 诅咒;*n.* 宣誓;誓言
sweat [swet] *n.* 汗;水珠;*vi.* 出汗;渗出;*vt.* (使)出汗;使渗出
sweater [ˈswetə] *n.* 厚运动衫;毛线衫;毛衣
sweep [swiːp] *vt.* 扫;扫过;扫除;拂去;刮起;掠过;席卷
sweet [swiːt] *adj.* 甜的;愉快的;可爱的;*n.* 糖;甜食
swell [swel] *vi.* 膨胀;隆起;增长;*vt.* (使)膨胀;(使)鼓起;(使)增长
swift [swift] *adj.* 快的;反应快的;迅速的;*n.* 雨燕;线轴;*n.* 斯威夫特(人名)
swim [swim] *vi.* 游,游泳;*n.* 游泳
swing [swiŋ] *vi.* 摇摆;回转;旋转;动摇;*n.* 摇摆;改变
switch [switʃ] *n.* 开关;转换;*vt.* 转换;改变;交换
sword [sɔːd] *n.* 剑;刀
symbol [ˈsimbəl] *n.* 象征;符号;记号;标志
sympathetic [ˌsimpəˈθetik] *adj.* 同情的;和谐的;共鸣的
sympathy [ˈsimpəθi] *n.* 同情;同情心
symptom [ˈsɪmptəm] *n.* 症状;征候;征兆
syndrome [ˈsɪndrəʊm] *n.* 综合征;综合症状
system [ˈsɪstəm] *n.* (思想或理论)体系;方法;制度;体制;系统

T

table [ˈteibl] *n.* 桌子;台子;餐桌;表格;项目表
tablet [ˈtæblit] *n.* 碑;匾;片状物;药片
tackle [ˈtækl] *v.* 应付,处理,解决(难题或局面)
tag [tæg] *n.* 附加语;附属物;名称;*vt.* 附以签条;尾随;添饰;*vi.* 紧随;尾随
tail [teil] *n.* 尾巴;尾部;后部;辫子;跟随者;*vt.* 跟踪;盯……的梢;为……装尾巴;*vi.* 尾随;附于其后
tailor [ˈteilə] *n.* 裁缝;*vt.* 裁制衣服;剪裁;*vi.* 做裁缝

take [teik] *vt.* 拿;抓;吃;拿走;取;修(课程);花费;记录;认为;搭乘
tale [teil] *n.* 故事;传说
talent [ˈtælənt] *n.* 天才;才能;人才;天资
talk [tɔːk] *vi.* 讲话;说; *vt.* 谈论;商讨; *n.* 谈话;会谈;讲话;讨论
tall [tɔːl] *adj.* 高的;身材高的
tame [teim] *adj.* 驯服的;顺从的;柔顺的;乏味的;*vt.* 驯养;使…… 驯服;*vi.* 变得驯服
tank [tæŋk] *n.* 坦克;大容器;槽;箱;罐;贮水池
tap [tæp] *n.* 龙头;塞子;窃听;轻拍;轻敲; *vi.* 轻拍;轻击;*vt.* 装龙头;窃听
tape [teip,tep] *n.* 录音带;磁带;胶布
target [ˈtɑːgit] *n.* 靶;标的;目标;对象; *vt.* 把……作为目标;瞄准
tariff [ˈtærɪf] *n.* 关税;(旅馆、饭店或服务公司的)价目表
task [tɑːsk] *n.* 任务;工作;作业
taste [teist] *vt.* 尝,尝到;品尝;尝试;*n.* 味觉;味道;品味;尝试
tax [tæks] *n.* 税;税款;负担;重负
taxi [ˈtæksi] *n.* 出租汽车;*v.* 用出租车运送;乘计程车
tea [tiː] *n.* 茶,茶叶;茶树;茶点
teach [tiːtʃ] *vt.* 讲;教育;教,教书;教训
teacher [ˈtiːtʃə] *n.* 教师;老师
team [tiːm] *n.* 队;组;*adj.* 团队的
tear [tiə] *n.* 眼泪;泪珠;(撕破的)洞或裂缝;撕扯;*vt.* 撕掉;撕开;撕裂;扯下;*vi.* 流泪;撕破
tease[tiːz] *v.* 取笑;戏弄;揶揄;寻开心;招惹,逗弄(动物)
technical [ˈteknikəl] *adj.* 技术的;工艺的
technique [tekˈniːk] *n.* 技术;技巧;技能
technology [tekˈnɔlədʒi] *n.* 工艺学;工艺;技术
teenager [ˈtiːn. eidʒə] *n.* 青少年;13 岁到 19 岁的年轻人
telegram [ˈteligræm] *n.* 电报;*vt.* 向……发电报
telegraph [ˈteligrɑːf] *n.* 电报机;电报;*vt.* 打电报;显示
television [ˈteliviʒən] *n.* 电视;电视机;电视节目;电视行业
tell [tel] *vt.* 讲述;吩咐;辨别;告诉;*vi.* 讲述;告诉
temper [ˈtempə] *n.* 调剂;韧度;心情;情绪;脾气;性情;*vt.* 使缓和;调和
temperature [ˈtempritʃə(r)] *n.* 温度;体温;气温;发烧
temple [ˈtempl] *n.* 圣堂;神殿;庙宇;寺院
temporary [ˈtempərəri] *adj.* 暂时的;*n.* 临时工
tempt [tempt] *vt.* 引诱;诱惑;吸引;勾引
tend [tend] *vt.* 趋向;易于;走向;倾向
tendency [ˈtendənsi] *n.* 趋向;趋势;倾向
tender [ˈtendə] *adj.* 嫩的;脆弱的;温柔的;亲切的;敏感的;未成熟的
tennis [ˈtenis] *n.* 网球;网球运动
tense [tens] *n.* (动词)时态;*adj.* 拉紧的;绷紧的;紧张的;*v.* 使紧绷;拉紧
tension [ˈtenʃn] *n.* 紧张局势(或关系、状况);矛盾;对立;(情绪上的)紧张,烦躁
tent [tent] *n.* 帐篷;*v.* 住帐篷;宿营
term [təːm] *n.* 期;学期;条件;词;术语;名词;期限;条款
terminal [ˈtəːminl] *adj.* 末端的;终点的;晚期的;*n.* 末端;终端机;终点;终点站
terrible [ˈterəbl] *adj.* 可怕的;极度的;糟糕的
terrific [təˈrifik] *adj.* 极好的;非常的
territory [ˈteritəri] *n.* 领土;版图;领域;范围
terror [ˈterə] *n.* 恐怖;惊骇; <口>令人惧怕或讨厌的人或事物
test [test] *n.* 测试;试验;考验;*vt.* 测试;试验
text [tekst] *n.* 原文;本文;课文;正文; *v.* 发短信
textbook [ˈtekstbuk] *n.* 课本;教科书
than [ðæn] *conj.* (比较级)比;*prep.* 比(用于两者之间的比较)
thank [θæŋk] *vt.* 谢谢;感谢;*n.* 感谢;谢意
Thanksgiving [ˌθæŋksˈgɪvɪŋ] *n.* 感恩节(美国的公共假日,在 11 月的第四个星期四)
that [ðæt] *adj.* 如此的;上文提到的;特定的;*pron.* 那;*adv.* 那样 *conj.* 引导从句
the [ðə,ði] *art.* (定冠词)这;那;这些;那些;*adv.* (用于比较级前)更加;(用于形容词、副词比较级前)越……越……
theatre [ˈθiətə] *n.* 戏院;戏剧;教室 = theater
theft[θeft] *n.* 偷;偷窃;盗窃罪
their [ðεə] *pron.* 他(她、它)们的;*adj.* 他们的;她们的;它们的
theirs [ðεəz] *pron.* 他(她)们的东西
them [θem] *pron.* (宾格)他(她、它)们
themselves [ðəmˈselvz] *pron.* 他(她、它)们自己
then [ðen] *adv.* 当时;然后;那么;而且;*n.* 当时
theory [ˈθiəri] *n.* 理论;原理;学说;意见
therapy[ˈθerəpi] *n.* 治疗;疗法
there [ðεə(ðə)] *adv.* 在那里;在那点上;从那里;到那里;*n.* 那一点;那个地方;*pron.* 表示存在

（与 be 连用）
therefore [ˈðɛəfɔː] *adv.* 因此；所以
these [ðiːz] *adj. & pron.* 这些
they [ðei] *pron.* （主格）他（她）们
thick [θik] *adj.* 厚的；粗的；密的；浓
thief [θiːf] *n.* 窃贼；偷窃犯；小偷
thin [θin] *adj.* 薄的；淡的；稀的；*vi.* 变薄；变瘦
thing [θiŋ] *n.* 物；用品；事；情况
think [θiŋk] *vt.* 想；认为；考虑；
thinking[ˈθɪŋkɪŋ] *n.* 思想；思考；思维；想法；见解；*adj.* 思想的；有理智的；有思考力的；
think 的现在分词
thirdly [ˈθəːdli] *adv.* 第三
thirst [θəːst] *n.* 渴，口渴；渴望；*vi.* （for）渴望；渴求
thirsty [ˈθəːsti] *adj.* 口渴的；渴望的
this [ðis] *adj.* 这；*pron.* 这，这个；*adv.* 这么；这样
thorough [ˈθʌrə] *adj.* 彻底的；详尽的；完全的；精心的
those [ðəuz] *pron.* 那些；*adj.* 那些
though [ðəu] *conj.* 虽然；尽管；*adv.* 可是；然而；不过
thought [θɔːt] *n.* 思想；思维；想法；观念；意向
动词 **think** 的过去式和过去分词
thoughtful [ˈθɔːtfəl] *adj.* 沉思的；体贴的
thread [θred] *n.* 线；细丝；头绪；线索；思路
threat [θret] *n.* 威胁；恐吓；凶兆
threaten [ˈθretn] *vt. & vi.* 威胁；恐吓
thrill [θril] *n.* 一阵激动；震颤；激动；*v.* （使）震颤；兴奋；激动
thrive [θraiv] *vi.* 兴旺；繁荣；旺盛；茁壮成长
throat [θrəut] *n.* 咽喉；喉咙；嗓音
throne [θrəun] *n.* 宝座；御座；王位；君主
through [θruː] *prep.* 经过；穿过；凭借；
adv. 从头到尾；穿越；完全
throughout [θruːˈaut] *prep.* 遍及；贯穿；
adv. 到处；自始至终
throw [θrəu] *vt.* 投；掷；抛；扔；*n.* 投掷；抛
thrust [θrʌst] *vt.* 插；刺；推挤；*n.* 插；刺；力推
thumb [θʌm] *n.* （大）拇指；*v.* 翻阅；示意要求搭车
thunder [ˈθʌndə] *n.* 雷，雷声；*vi.* 打雷；轰隆地响
thus [ðʌs] *adv.* 如此；这样；因而；因此；从而
tick [tik] *n.* 滴答声；记号；勾号；*vt.* 给……标记号；*vi.* 滴答作响
ticket [ˈtikit] *n.* 票；券；标签；罚款单
tide [taid] *n.* 潮；潮汐；潮流；潮水；趋势
tidy [ˈtaidi] *adj.* 整洁的；整齐的；*vt.* 使整洁；整理
tie [tai] *n.* 领带；结；束缚；不分胜负；联系；
vt. 系；约束；捆绑；*vi.* 打结；联结
tiger [ˈtaigə] *n.* 老虎；凶残之人
tight [tait] *adj.* 紧的；紧身的；严厉的；密集的；拮据的
till [til] *prep. & conj.* 直到……为止
timber [ˈtimbə] *n.* 木材；木料
time [taim] *n.* 时间；时机；次数；回；倍；
vt. 为……安排时间；计时；定时；乘；*adj.* 根据时间的；时间上的
timetable [ˈtaimˌteibl] *n.* 时间表；时刻表；课程表
tin [tin] *n.* 锡；罐头；听头
tiny [ˈtaini] *adj.* 微小的；极小的
tip [tip] *n.* 梢；末端；尖；尖端；小费；提示；
vi. 给小费；装顶端；*vt.* 轻击
tired [ˈtaiəd] *adj.* 疲劳的；疲倦的；累的；厌倦的
[**tire** 的过去式和过去分词形式]
tissue [ˈtiʃuː] *n.* 薄绢；薄纸；（生物的）组织；织物；纸巾
title [ˈtaitl] *n.* 标题；题目；称号；头衔；称号；
vt. 予称号；加标题于
to [tuː] *prep.* （表示方向）到；向；达到；（表示间接关系）给；对于；为了；*adv.* （表示方向）去
toast [təust] *n.* 烤面包；吐司；祝酒；祝酒词；
vt. 烘烤；*vi.* （为……）祝酒
tobacco [təˈbækəu] *n.* 烟草；烟叶
today [təˈdei] *adv.* 在今天；现在；当今；
n. 今天；当今；*adj.* 现在的
toe [təu] *n.* 脚趾；足尖；*vi.* 踮着脚尖走
together [təˈgeðə] *adv.* 共同；一起
toilet [ˈtɔilit] *n.* 厕所；盥洗室；浴室
tolerate [ˈtɔləreit] *vt.* 忍受；容忍；宽恕
tomato [təˈmɑːtəu，təˈmeitəu] *n.* 番茄；西红柿
tomb [tuːm] *n.* 坟；冢；*vt.* 埋葬
tomorrow [təˈmɔrəu] *adv.* 在明天；*n.* 明天；将来
ton [tʌn] *n.* 吨；大量
tone [təun] *n.* 音；腔调；声调；音调；语气；品质；色调
tongue [tʌŋ] *n.* 舌，舌头；舌状物；语言；口才
tonight [təˈnait] *adv.* 在今夜；*n.* 今夜
too [tuː] *adv.* 也；还；太；过分；很
tool [tuːl] *n.* 工具；器具；用具；手段；被利用者；
vt. 用工具加工；*vi.* 使用工具

tooth [tuːθ] *n.* 牙齿;齿状物;嗜好;(复)teeth [tiːθ]
top [tɔp] *n.* 顶;顶部;首位;*adj.* 顶的;最高的;顶端的;*v.* 高过;加顶;高耸
topic [ˈtɔpik] *n.* 题目;论题;话题
torch [tɔːtʃ] *n.* 火炬;火把;手电筒;*v.* 用火炬点燃
torture [ˈtɔːtʃə] *n.* 拷问;折磨;痛苦;*vt.* 拷打;拷问;使痛苦;曲解
toss [tɔs] *vt.* & *vi.* 扔;抛;掷;投掷;辗转;*n.* 投掷;震荡
total [ˈtəutl] *adj.* 总的;全体的;完全的;*vi.* 合计;总共;*n.* 总数合计
touch [tʌtʃ] *vt.* 触摸;触动;触及;感动;*vi.* 接触;联系;*n.* 触;触觉;接触
tough [tʌf] *adj.* 坚韧的;健壮的;强硬的;艰苦的;棘手的;严厉的
tour [tuə] *n.* & *vi.* 旅行;游历;旅游;周游;观光
tourist [ˈtuərist] *n.* 旅游者;观光者
tow [təʊ] *v.* (用绳索)拖,拉,牵引,拽;*n.* (车、船等的)牵引,拽引
toward [təˈwɔːd] *prep.* 向;对于;接近;关于;将近;朝;= towards
towel [ˈtauəl,taul] *n.* 毛巾;手巾
tower [ˈtauə] *n.* 塔;高楼;*vi.* 屹立;高耸
town [taun] *n.* 镇;市镇;城镇;城市
toy [tɔi] *n.* 玩具;玩物
trace [treis] *n.* 痕迹;踪迹;微量;丝毫;*vt.* 跟踪;追踪;*vi.* 追踪
track [træk] *n.* 行踪;踪迹;路径;轨道
tractor [ˈtræktə] *n.* 拖拉机;牵引车
trade [treid] *n.* 贸易;交易;买卖;职业;*vi.* 交易;进行交易;做买卖;交换
trademark[ˈtreɪdmɑːk] *n.* 商标;(人的行为或衣着的)特征,标记
tradition [trəˈdiʃən] *n.* 传统;惯例
traffic [ˈtræfik] *n.* 交通;通行;(人或车等)交通流量
tragedy [ˈtrædʒidi] *n.* 悲剧;惨事;惨案;灾难
trail [treil] *n.* 痕迹;踪迹;小径;尾;*vt.* 跟踪;追踪;拖拽;*vi.* 拖尾随;追踪
train [trein] *vt.* 培养;训练;培训;*n.* 列车;火车
training [ˈtreiniŋ] *n.* 训练;锻炼;培养;动词 **train** 的现在分词和动名词形式
transfer [trænsˈfəː] *vt.* & *vi.* 转移;调动;调转;调任;*n.* 迁移;移动;换车
transform [trænsˈfɔːm] *vt.* 改变;改造;变换;转换;变形;*vi.* 改变;*n.* 变形
transit [ˈtrænzɪt] *n.* 运输;运送;搬运;载运;通过;经过;通行 *v.* 经过;穿过;经过
translate [trænsˈleit] *vt.* & *vi.* 翻译;译;解释
translation [trænsˈleiʃən] *n.* 翻译;译文;译本
transmit [trænzˈmit] *vt.* 传送,传达;发射;传输;代代相传;*vi.* (以无线电或有线电的方式)发送信号
transparent [trænsˈperənt] *adj.* 透明的;易识破的;明显的;清晰的
transport [trænsˈpɔːt] *vt.* 运输;*n.* 运输、运输工具
trap [træp] *n.* 陷阱;诡计;圈套;困境;*vt.* 诱骗,设圈套;陷入(困境)
travel [ˈtrævl] *vt.* & *vi.* & *n.* 旅行;传播;移动
travel(l)er[ˈtræv(ə)lə] *n.* 旅行者;游客
treasure [ˈtreʒə] *n.* 财富;珍宝;*vt.* 珍视
treat [triːt] *vt.* 对待;处理;治疗;请客;视为;*n.* 款待;宴飨
treatment [ˈtriːtmənt] *n.* 待遇;对待;处理;治疗;疗法
treaty [ˈtriːti] *n.* 条约;协议;协定
tree [triː] *n.* 树;树状物
tremble [ˈtrembl] *vi.* 发抖;哆嗦;摇动;战栗;*n.* 战栗;颤抖
tremendous [triˈmendəs] *adj.* 极大的;非常的;巨大的;惊人的
trend [trend] *n.* 趋势;倾向;方位
trial [ˈtraiəl] *n.* 试;试验;试用;审判;讯问;审讯;尝试
triangle [ˈtraiæŋgl] *n.* 三角(形)
tribe [traib] *n.* 部落;宗族;种族;一伙人
trick [trik] *n.* 诡计;欺诈;把戏;诀窍;*vt.* 哄骗;戏弄;欺骗
trifle [ˈtraifl] *n.* 小事;琐事;少许;少量
trim [trim] *vt.* 使整齐;使整洁;修除;削剪;*n.* 整齐;修剪下来的部分
trip [trip] *vi.* 绊,绊倒;失足;旅行;*vt.* 绊倒;使跌倒;使犯错;*n.* 旅行;摔倒;差错
triumph [ˈtraiəmf] *n.* 凯旋;胜利;欢欣;*vi.* 成功;得胜;庆功
trolley = trolly[ˈtrɒli] *n.* 手推车;手拉车;(运或送食品、饮料的)小推车
troop [truːp] *n.* 军队;一群;组;大量
tropical [ˈtrɔpikəl] *adj.* 热带的;炎热的;热带植物的
trouble [ˈtrʌbl] *n.* 烦恼;困难;烦恼;*vi.* 烦恼;麻烦;苦恼;费神
trousers [ˈtrauzəz] *n.* 裤子;长裤

truck [trʌk] *n.* 卡车;载重汽车
true [truː] *adj.* 真的;真实的;忠实的
trunk [trʌŋk] *n.* 树干;大衣箱;皮箱;躯干;干线;象鼻;(汽车后部)行李箱
trust [trʌst] *n.* 信任;信托;*vt.* 相信;委托
truth [truːθ] *n.* 真理;真实,真实性;真像;事实
try [trai] *vt.* 试,尝试;试验;审问;审判;考验;*vi.* 尝试;试验;*n.* 尝试;试验
tub [tʌb] *n.* 桶;盆;浴缸;浴盆
tube [ˈtjuːb] *n.* 管,管状物;电子管;显像管;气管
tumble [ˈtʌmbl] *vi.* 摔倒;跌倒;打滚;下跌;*vt.* 使摔倒;使混乱
tune [tjuːn] *n.* 调子;和谐;曲调;协调;调整;*vt.* 调整;为……调音;*v.* 和谐;调音
tunnel [ˈtʌnl] *n.* 隧道;坑道;地道
turkey [ˈtəːki] *n.* 火鸡;火鸡肉;Turkey:土耳其
turn [təːn] *vt.* 转,翻;*vi.* 转动;旋转;转向;轮流;翻转;*n.* 转;动;轮流
tutor [ˈtjuːtə] *n.* 家庭教师;导师;*v.* 当家庭教师;当导师;指导
twice [twais] *adv.* 两次;两倍
twin [twin] *adj.* 孪生的;*n.* 孪生儿;双胞胎之一
twist [twist] *vt. & vi.* 拧;捻;搓;扭曲;弯曲
type [taip] *n.* 型,类型;种类;典型;*vi.* 打字
typewriter [ˈtaipraitə(r)] *n.* 打字机;打字员
typical [ˈtipikəl] *adj.* 典型的;代表性的;特有的;独特的
tyre [taiə] *n.* 轮胎;车胎 = tire(美)

U

ugly [ˈʌgli] *adj.* 丑陋的;难看的;可怕的
ultimate [ˈʌltimit] *adj.* 最后的;最终的;终极的;根本的
umbrella [ʌmˈbrelə] *n.* 伞;雨伞
unable [ʌnˈeibl] *adj.* 不能的;不会的
unanimous[juˈnænɪməs] *adj.* (决定或意见)一致的,一致同意的;(团体)意见一致的,一致同意某事的
uncertain [ʌnˈsəːtn] *adj.* 无常的;不确定的
uncle [ˈʌŋkl] *n.* 伯父;叔父;舅父;姨父;姑父;伯;舅;叔
under [ˈʌndə] *prep.* 在……下面;低于;在……内;在……控制下
undergo [ˌʌndəˈgəu] *vt.* 经历;经受;忍受;遭受
underground [ˈʌndəgraund] *adj.* 地下的;秘密的;*adv.* 在地下;秘密地;*n.* 地下;地铁;地道;秘密活动
underline [ˌʌndəˈlain] *vt.* 在……下面画线
underneath [ˌʌndəˈniːθ] *adv.* 在下面;在底下;*n.* 下部;底部;*prep.* 在……下面
understand [ˌʌndəˈstænd] *vt.* 理解;认为;*vi.* 懂得;理解
understanding [ˌʌndəˈstændiŋ] *n.* 理解;理解力
undertake [ˌʌndəˈteik] *vt.* 从事;承担
undertaking [ˌʌndəˈteikiŋ] *n.* 任务;事业
undo [ʌnˈduː] *vt.* 解开;打开;松开;取消
uniform [ˈjuːnifɔːm] *adj.* 一样的;一致的;统一的;*n.* 制服;*vt.* 穿制服;使统一
union [ˈjuːnjən] *n.* 联合;团结;协会;结合;政党;工会
unique [juːˈniːk] *adj.* 唯一的;独一无二的;独特的;稀罕的
unit [ˈjuːnit] *n.* 单位;单元;部件;组件
unite [ju(ː)ˈnait] *vi.* 联合;合并;统一;团结;*vt.* 使联合
unity [ˈjuːniti] *n.* 单一;统一;团结;个体;一致;结合
universal [ˌjuːniˈvəːsəl] *adj.* 宇宙的;普遍的;通用的;全体的;全世界的
universe [ˈjuːnivəːs] *n.* 宇宙;世界;万物
university [ˌjuːniˈvəːsiti] *n.* 大学;综合性大学
unknown [ˈʌnˈnəun] *adj.* 不知道的;未知的;不出名的
unless [ənˈles] *conj.* 除非;如果不;*prep.* 除……外
unlike [ˈʌnˈlaik] *adj.* 不同的;不相似的;*prep.* 不像……;和……不同
until [ənˈtil] *prep. & conj.* 直到……为止
unusual [ʌnˈjuːʒuəl] *adj.* 不平常的;独特的;异常的
up [ʌp] *adv.* 向上;起床;起来;上升;*prep.* 向上;*adj.* 向上的;上行的;*n.* 上升
update [ˌʌpˈdeɪt, ˈʌpdeɪt] *v.* 使现代化;更新;向……提供最新信息;给……增加最新信息
upon [əˈpɔn] *prep.* 在……上;在……旁
upper [ˈʌpə] *adj.* 上面的;地位较高的;上部的;较高的
upset [ʌpˈset] *vt.* 弄翻,打翻;倾覆;推翻;扰乱;

使心烦;*adj.* 心烦的;苦恼的;不安的
upstairs [ˌʌpˈstɛəz] *adv.* 在楼上;往楼上;*adj.* 楼上的;*n.* 楼上
up-to-date [ˌʌptəˈdeit] *adj.* 直到最近的;现代的;最新的
upward [ˈʌpwəd] *adj.* 向上的;上升的;*adv.* 向上;上升; = upwards
urban [ˈɜːbən] *adj.* 城市的;都市的;城镇的
urge [əːdʒ] *vt.* 推进;催促;驱策;鼓励;*vi.* 极力主张;*n.* 冲动
urgent [ˈɜːdʒənt] *adj.* 紧急的;强求的;坚持要求的;急迫的
us [ʌs] *pron.* (we 的宾格)我们
usage [ˈjuːsidʒ] *n.* 使用;用法;对待;惯用法
use [juːz] *vt.* 用,使用,利用;[juːs] *n.* 用,运用;用法;使用权;价值
used [juːst] *vi.* 过去常常;*adj.* 使用过的;二手的;
动词 **use** 的过去式和过去分词
useful [ˈjuːsfəl] *adj.* 有用的;有益的;实用的;值的
usual [ˈjuːʒuəl] *adj.* 通常的;平常的;惯常的;惯例的
usually [ˈjuːʒuəli] *adv.* 通常
utilize(-se) [ˈjuːtəlaiz] *v.* 使用;利用;运用;应用
utility [juːˈtiliti] *n.* 效用;实用,实用品;公共设施
utter [ˈʌtə] *adj.* 完全的;彻底的;全然的;*vt.* 发出;作声;发表;说;讲

V

vacant [ˈveikənt] *adj.* 空的;空虚的;木然的;未被占用的
vacation [veiˈkeiʃən] *n.* 假期;休假;*vi.* 度假
vaccine [ˈvæksiːn] *n.* 疫苗;菌苗
vain [vein] *adj.* 徒劳的;无效的;自负的;虚荣的
valid [ˈvælid] *adj.* 有效的;有根据的;正当的;合法的
valley [ˈvæli] *n.* (山)谷;溪谷;流域
valuable [ˈvæljuəbl] *adj.* 值钱的;有价值的;*n.* (*pl.*)贵重物品
value [ˈvæljuː] *n.* 价值;重要性;价格(pl)价值观;*vt.* 评价;估价重视
van [væn] *n.* 大篷车;运货车;面包车;*vt.* (用货车)运
vanish [ˈvæniʃ] *vi.* 突然不见;消失;绝迹
variation [ˌvɛəriˈeiʃən] *n.* 变化;变动
variety [vəˈraiəti] *n.* 多样化;种类
various [ˈvɛəriəs] *adj.* 各种各样的;不同的
vary [ˈvɛəri] *v.* 改变;变化;使多样化
vase [veis] *n.* 瓶,花瓶
vast [vɑːst] *adj.* 巨大的;大量的;广阔的
vegetable [ˈvedʒitəbl] *n.* 植物;蔬菜;植物人
vegetarian [ˌvedʒəˈteəriən] *n.* 素食者;吃素的人
vehicle [ˈviːikl] *n.* 车辆;机动车;交通工具;手段;工具;传播媒介
veil [veil] *n.* 面纱;面罩;遮蔽物;掩饰物;*vt.* 给……戴面纱或面罩;*vi.* 戴面纱或面罩
venture [ˈventʃə] *n.* & *vi.* 冒险;风险;投机;*vt.* 谨慎地做;冒险一试
verb [vəːb] *n.* 动词
verge [vɜːdʒ] *n.* (路边的)小草地,绿地;边缘;接近于
verify [ˈverifai] *vt.* 证实;查证;证明;核实
version [ˈvəːʃən] *n.* 译文;说法;改写本;版本;译本
vertical [ˈvəːtikəl] *adj.* 垂直的;竖式的
very [ˈveri] *adv.* 很;完全;真正地;*adj.* 真的,真正的;同一的;仅仅的;恰好的
vessel [ˈvesl] *n.* 容器;器皿;船;飞船;管;脉管;血管
veto [ˈviːtəʊ] *n.* 否决权;拒绝认可;禁止;*v.* 行使否决权;拒绝认可;禁止;拒不接受;反对;否定
via [ˈvaiə] *prep.* 经过;通过
vice [vais] *n.* 罪恶;恶习;缺点;邪恶;*adj.* 副的;代理的
victim [ˈviktim] *n.* 牺牲者;受害者;牺牲
victory [ˈviktəri] *n.* 胜利;战胜;成功
video [ˈvidiəu] *adj.* 视频的;录像的;*n.* 视频;录像
view [vjuː] *n.* 看;视力;风景;视野;见解
village [ˈvilidʒ] *n.* 乡村;村庄
vinegar [ˈvinigə] *n.* 醋
violate [ˈvaɪəleɪt] *v.* 违反,违背(法律、协议等);侵犯(隐私等)
violence [ˈvaiələns] *n.* 猛烈;激烈;暴力;暴行
violent [ˈvaiələnt] *adj.* 猛烈的;狂暴的;暴力

的;极端的
violet [ˈvaiəlit] *n.* 紫罗兰;紫色;*adj.* 紫色的
violin [ˌvaiəˈlin] *n.* 小提琴
virtual [ˈvəːtʃuəl] *adj.* 很接近的;几乎……的;事实上的;实际上的;实质上的;(通过计算机软件,如在互联网上)模拟的,虚拟的
virtue [ˈvəːtjuː] *n.* 善;美德;优点;德行
virus[ˈvaɪrəs] *n.* 病毒
visa [ˈviːzə] *n.* (护照的)签证
visible [ˈvizəbl] *adj.* 可见的;看得见的;*n.* 可见物
vision [ˈviʒən] *n.* 视力;视觉;眼力;想象力;梦幻;幻觉
visit [ˈvizit] *vt.* & *n.* 访问;参观;拜访;探访
visitor [ˈvizitə] *n.* 访问者;游客;参观者
visual [ˈvizjuəl] *adj.* 看的;看得见的;视觉的
vital [ˈvaitl] *adj.* 生命的;有生命力的;至关重要的;生死攸关的;有活力的
vitamin [ˈvaitəmin] *n.* 维生素;维他命
vivid [ˈvivid] *adj.* 鲜艳的;生动的;栩栩如生的
vocabulary [vəˈkæbjuləri] *n.* 词汇表;词汇;语汇;词汇量
vocation [vəʊˈkeɪʃn] *n.* 工作,职业
voice [vɔis] *n.* 说话声;声音;嗓音;意见;[语]语态;*vt.* 表达;发音
volcano [vɔlˈkeinəu] *n.* 火山
volleyball [ˈvɔlibɔːl] *n.* 排球;排球运动
volume [ˈvɔljum] *n.* 卷,册;容积,体积;音量
volunteer [ˌvɒlənˈtɪə(r)] *n.* 义务工作者;志愿者;自告奋勇者;主动做某事的人;志愿兵;*v.* 自愿做;义务做;无偿做;主动建议(或告诉);自愿参军;当志愿兵
vote [vəʊt] *n.* 选举;投票;表决;投票结果;选举权;*v.* 投票;选举;表决
voyage [ˈvɔiidʒ] *n.* & *vi.* 航海;航空;航行;旅行;旅程

W

wage [weidʒ] *n.* 工资;报酬
waggon [ˈwægən] *n.* 四轮运货马车;敞篷货车 = wagon(美)
waist [weist] *n.* 腰;腰部
wait [weit] *vi.* 等,等候;*n.* 等待;等候
waiter [ˈweitə] *n.* 侍者;(男)服务员
wake [weɪk] *v.* 醒;醒来;唤醒;弄醒;唤起(记忆)
walk [wɔːk] *vi.* 步行;散步;走;*vt.* 陪……走;走过;使行走;*n.* 散步;步行;人行道
wall [wɔːl] *n.* 墙;壁;围墙;城墙;墙状物
wallet [ˈwɔlit] *n.* 钱包;皮夹子
wander [ˈwɔndə] *vi.* 漫游;迷路;离题;徘徊;漫步;闲逛;*vt.* 漫步于;*n.* 漫游;闲逛;徘徊
want [wɔnt] *vt.* 要,想要
war [wɔː] *n.* 战争;冲突;斗争;竞争;*vi.* 作战;斗争
warm [wɔːm] *adj.* 温暖的;暖和的;热烈的;热情的;*v.* 使暖和;变暖
warn [wɔːn] *vt.* 警告;告诫;预先通知;*vi.* 发生警告
wash [wɔʃ] *vt.* 洗;冲出;*vi.* 洗涤;洗清;*n.* 洗,洗濯
waste [weist] *n.* 浪费;垃圾;*v.* 浪费;滥用;消耗;*adj.* 浪费的;无用的
watch [wɔtʃ] *vt.* & *vi.* 观看;注视;看守;*n.* 手表;看管;监视
water [ˈwɔːtə] *n.* 水;雨水;*vt.* 使湿;灌溉;给……浇水;给……供水
wave [weiv] *n.* 波,波涛;波浪;波纹;*vi.* 波动;挥动;飘动
wax [wæks] *n.* 蜡,蜂蜡;(一阵)情绪;增大;*vt.* (用蜡)涂
way [wei] *n.* 路,路线,道路;方法,方式;方向;*adv.* 非常;远远地
we [wiː] *pron.* (主格)我们
weak [wiːk] *adj.* 弱的,软弱的;虚弱的,无力的;差的
weakness [ˈwiːknis] *n.* 虚弱;软弱;弱点
wealth [welθ] *n.* 财富,财产;丰富;大量
weapon [ˈwepən] *n.* 武器,兵器
wear [wɛə] *vt.* 穿着;戴;磨损;*n.* 穿着;磨损;耐久性
weary [ˈwɪəri] *adj.* 疲倦的;*vt.* 使疲乏
weather [ˈweðə] *n.* 天气
weave [wiːv] *vt.* 织;编;组合;编排;*vi.* 纺织;编织;*n.* 编法;织法;编织
web [web] *n.* 网状物;网络;错综复杂的事物;*vt.* 在……上织网;用网缠住;形成网状
website[ˈwebsaɪt] *n.* 网站
wedding [ˈwediŋ] *n.* 婚礼;结合
Wednesday [ˈwenzdei, ˈwenzdi] *n.* 星期三

weed [wiːd] *n.* 杂草,野草
week [wiːk] *n.* 星期,周
weekday [ˈwiːkdei] *n.* 周工作日(星期一至星期五的任何一天)
weekend [wiːkˈend, ˈwiːkend] *n.* 周末,周末假期
weekly [ˈwiːkli] *adj.* 每周的;一周一次的;周刊的;*adv.* 每周;一周一次;*n.* 周刊;周报
weigh [wei] *vt.* 称……的重量;掂量;衡量;重达……
weight [weit] *n.* 重,体重;砝码;重担
weird [wɪəd] *adj.* 奇异的;不寻常的;怪诞的;离奇的;诡异的
welcome [ˈwelkəm] *vt.* 欢迎;*adj.* 受欢迎的;*n.* 欢迎;*int.* 欢迎(客人来访或新成员的加入)
welfare [ˈwelfɛə] *n.* 幸福;福利;福利事业;*adj.* 福利的
well [wel] *n.* 井;源泉;楼梯井;*adj.* 健康的;良好的;适宜的;*adv.* 很好地;适当地;完全地;*int.* 好吧;啊;嘿
well-known [ˈwelˈnəun] *adj.* 众所周知的;出名的
west [west] *n.* 西,西方,西部;*adj.* 西方的;*adv.* 向(在)西方
western [ˈwestən] *adj.* 西方的;西部的;西洋的
westward [ˈwestwəd] *adj.* 向西的;西方的;*adv.* 向西
wet [wet] *adj.* 湿的;下雨的,雨天的;*n.* 潮气;雨天;*vt.* (使)弄湿
what [wɔt] *pron.* 什么;*adj.* 什么;任何;*adv.* 什么;怎么
whatever [wɔtˈevə] *pron.* 无论什么;*adj.* 不管怎样的;*adv.* 无论如何;不管怎样
wheat [wiːt] *n.* 小麦;小麦色
wheel [wiːl] *n.* 轮,车轮;方向盘;周期;旋转
when [wen] *adv.* 什么时候;当……时;*conj.* 当……时;然后;*pron.* 什么时候
whenever [wenˈevə] *conj.* 无论何时;每当;随时;*adv.* 无论何时
where [wɛə] *adv.* 在哪里;*pron.* 哪里;*conj.* 在……地方
whereas [ˌweərˈæz] *conj.* (用以比较或对比两个事实)然而,但是,尽管
wherever [wɛərˈevə] *adv.* 究竟在哪里;无论什么地方;在……的各个地方;*conj.* 无论在哪里
whether [ˈweðə] *conj.* 是否;无论;不管
which [witʃ] *pron.* 哪一个;哪些;*adj.* 哪一个;哪一些
while [wail] *conj.* 当……的时候;然而;虽然;尽管;*n.* 一会儿;一段时间
whip [wip] *vt.* 鞭笞,抽打;鞭策;*n.* 鞭子;鞭打;鞭状物
whirl [wəːl] *vt. & vi.* 使……旋转;急转;回旋;迅速移动;*n.* 回旋;旋转;繁忙
whisky [ˈwiski] *n.* 威士忌酒 = whiskey
whisper [ˈwispə] *vt.* 低声地讲;耳语;私语;*vi.* 低语;低声说;窃窃私语;*n.* 低语;窃窃私语
whistle [ˈwisl] *n.* 口哨;汽笛;命令的哨声;吹口哨;*vi.* 吹口哨;鸣汽笛
white [wait] *adj.* 白色的;白种的;纯洁的;*n.* 白色;白种人
who [huː] *pron.* 谁;……的人
whoever [huˈevə] *pron.* 无论谁;不管谁;任何人
whole [həul] *adj.* 完整的;全部的;整体的;*n.* 全部;完整;整体
whom [huːm] *pron.* (who 的宾格)谁
whose [huːz] *pron.* 谁的;哪个人的;*adj.* 谁的
why [wai] *adv.* 为什么;*conj.* 为什么;……的理由
wicked [ˈwikid] *adj.* 坏的;令人厌恶的;邪恶的;缺德的
wide [waid] *adj.* 宽阔的;广泛的
width [wɪdθ] *n.* 宽度;广度
wife [waif] *n.* 妻子,夫人
wild [waild] *adj.* 野生的;野蛮的;未开发的;*adv.* 失去控制地;胡乱地;*n.* 荒野;荒地
will [wil] *aux. v.* 将要;会;愿;必须;*n.* 意志;决心;愿望;遗嘱
willing [ˈwiliŋ] *adj.* 愿意的;心甘情愿的
win [win] *vi.* 获胜;赢;*vt.* 赢得;*n.* 胜利
wind [wind, waind] *n.* 风;气息;*v.* 使气急;吹(号角等);*vt.* 绕;缠绕;*vi.* 卷曲
window [ˈwindəu] *n.* 窗子,窗户,窗口;橱窗;视窗
wine [wain] *n.* 葡萄酒;果酒,酒
wing [wiŋ] *n.* 翼,翅膀,翅;(组织中的)派别
winter [ˈwintə] *n.* 冬天;冬季
wipe [waip] *vt.* 擦;抹;揩;消除;拭去;用力打;*n.* 擦拭;用力打
wire [ˈwaiə] *n.* 金属线;电缆;电线;*v.* 发电报;装电线;(通过电线)接通
wireless [ˈwaiəlis] *adj.* 不用电线的;无线的;*n.* 无线电;收音机
wisdom [ˈwizdəm] *n.* 智慧;才智;明智;至理名言;聪明
wise [waiz] *adj.* 有智慧的;聪明的;明智的;有

[illegible]

First, ... Second, ... Finally, ...

First of all, ... Secondly, ... The third reason is that...

To start with, ... In the second place, ... Eventually, ...

[illegible] ... the last reason is...

To start with, ... Then, ... Moreover, ... Furthermore, ... In addition, ... Finally, ...

[illegible]

[illegible]

In a word, ...

In summary, ...

[illegible]

In brief, ...

In short, ...

From what has been discussed above, we can safely come to the conclusion that...

[illegible]

It is high time that effective measures were taken to stop... For example, ... In addition, ... All these measures will certainly...

[illegible]

[illegible]

[illegible] measures that ... should be taken ...

[illegible]

见识的
wish [wiʃ] *vt.* 祝;想要;希望;*n.* 希望;渴望;愿望;(复数)祝颂
wit [wit] *n.* 智力;才智;智能;机智
with [wie] *prep.* 和……一起;具有;用;随着;包括
withdraw [wið·drɔː] *vt.* 收回;撤回;取回;撤退;*vi.* 撤退;退回;走开
withhold [wɪð·həʊld] *v.* 拒绝给;不给
within [wi·ðin] *prep.* 在……里面;*adv.* 在内
without [wið·aut] *prep.* 无;没有;不;在外面;*adv.* 在缺乏的情况下;在外面
withstand [wið·stænd] *vt.* 抵挡;反抗;对抗;经得起;承受
witness [·witnis] *n.* 证据;目击者;证人;*vt.* 目击;见证
wolf [wulf] *n.* 狼;残暴的人
woman [·wumən] *n.* 妇女;女人;女性;*adj.* 女人的
wonder [·wʌndə] *n.* 惊异;惊奇;奇迹;惊愕;*v.* 惊奇;想知道;怀疑
wonderful [·wʌndəfəl] *adj.* 惊人的;极好的;精彩的
wood [wud] *n.* 树林;森林;木头;木材
wooden [·wudn] *adj.* 木制的
wool [wul] *n.* 羊毛;毛线;绒线;毛织品
woollen [·wulən] *adj.* 羊毛制的;毛线的
word [wəːd] *n.* 词;单词;话;消息;语言;诺言
work [wəːk] *n.* 工作;作品;*vi.* 工作;创造;实现;做工作;起作用;操作;正常运转;成功;产生影响;逐渐进行;*vt.* 造成;产生;使运转;锻造;奋力达到
worker [·wəːkə] *n.* 工人;工作者;人员
workshop [·wəːkʃɔp] *n.* 车间;工场;创作室;研讨会;讲习班
world [wəːld] *n.* 世界;世间;地球;领域;*adj.* 世界的
worldwide [·wəːld·waild] *adj.* 遍及全球的;世界范围的
worm [wəːm] *n.* 虫;蠕虫;可鄙之人;[计]蠕虫病毒
worry [·wʌri] *vt.* 使烦恼;使焦虑;*vi.* 发愁;担心;*n.* 烦恼;担心;忧虑
worse [wəːs] *adj.* 更坏的;更差的;*adv.* 更坏;以更坏的方式;变得更坏
worship [·wəːʃip] *n.* 礼拜;做礼拜;崇拜;爱慕;*vt.* 崇拜;爱慕;*v.* 做礼拜
worst [wəːst] *adj.* 最坏的;最差的;最不利的;形容词 bad 或 ill 的最高级;*adv.* 最坏;最差
worth [wəːθ] *adj.* 值……的;值得的;值钱的;*n.* 价值;财富
worthy [·wəːði] *adj.* 有价值的;可尊敬的;值得的;配得上的
would [wud] *aux. v.* 将;愿,愿意;总是;总会;可能;大概;will 的过去式
wound [wuːnd] *n.* 创伤;伤口;伤;*vt.* 使受伤;使伤害
wrap [ræp] *vt.* 裹;包;捆;覆盖;包围;*n.* 披肩;围巾;包装材料
wreck [rek] *n.* 失事;残骸;*vt.* 破坏;使遇难;使失事
wrist [rist] *n.* 腕,腕关节;手腕
write [rait] *vt.* 书写,写;*vi.* 写
writer [·raitə] *n.* 作者,作家;文学家
writing [·raitiŋ] *n.* 书写,写;著作;写作;笔迹;作品;动词 write 的现在分词形式
wrong [rɔŋ] *adj.* 错误的;有毛病的;不正常的;*adv.* 错;不对;*n.* 错误;不公正;坏事;*vt.* 冤枉;委屈(某人);不公正地对待

Y

yard [jɑːd] *n.* 院子;庭院;场地;码(长度单位)
year [jiə] *n.* 年;年度;年龄;学年
yellow [·jeləu] *adj.* 黄(色)的;*n.* 黄(色);蛋黄;黄种人;*v.* (使)变黄
yes [jes] *adv.* 是,是的;*n.* 是(表示肯定)
yesterday [·jestədi] *n.* & *adv.* 昨天,昨日
yet [jet] *adv.* 还;已经;仍然;*conj.* 而;然而;但是
yield [jiːld] *vt.* & *vi.* 出产;屈服;投降;弯下去;*n.* 产量;生产量;投资收益
you [juː] *pron.* 你,你们
young [jʌŋ] *adj.* 年轻的;没有经验的;初期的;*n.* 青年人;幼崽
your [juə] *pron.* 你的,你们的
yours [jɔːz] *pron.* 你们的(东西)
yourself [jɔː·self] *pron.* 你(们)自己,你(们)亲自
youth [juːθ] *n.* 青春,青年人,青年;年轻;初期

Z

zero [ˈziərəu] *n.* 零;零点;零度;最低点;完全没有;无足轻重的人或物;*v.* 把……调零;瞄准;集中注意;迫近

zone [zəun] *n.* 地区;区域;范围;地域;地带

zoo [zuː] *n.* 动物园

zoom [zuːm] *v.* 快速移动;迅速前往;急剧增长;猛涨;*n.* (车辆等)疾驰的声音

n. Noun 名词
adj. Adjective 形容词
v. Verb 动词
adv. Adverb 副词
vt. Verb Transitive 及物动词
vi. Verb Intransitive 不及物动词
aux. v. Auxiliary Verb 助动词
abbr. Abbreviated 缩写
prep. Preposition 介系词
pron. Pronoun 代词
rel. Relative 关系词
int. Interjection 感叹词
conj. Conjunction 连词
interrog. Interrogative 疑问词
part. Participle 分词
aux. Auxiliary 助词
art. Article 冠词
def. art. Definite Article 定冠词
indef. art. Indefinite Article 不定冠词
pref. Prefix 前缀
symb. Symbol 符号
[U]不可数名词
[C]可数名词
[sing]单数名词